Culinary greetings from

HOLLAND AMERICA LINE

HOLLAND AMERICA LINE

A Taste of
CELEBRATION
COOKBOOK

VOLUME III
Culinary Signature Collection

RUDI SODAMIN

First published in the United States of America in 2010
by Rizzoli International Publications, Inc.
300 Park Avenue South
New York, NY 10010
www.rizzoliusa.com

2010 2011 2012 2013 / 10 9 8 7 6 5 4 3 2 1

ISBN-13: 978-0-8478-3315-3

Library of Congress Control Number: 2010925642

Design by Susi Oberhelman

Distributed in the U.S. trade by Random House, New York

Printed in China

Page 1: Grand Marnier Chocolate Mousse Cake (page 164)
Page 2: Baked Alaska with Cherries Jubilee (page 154)
Page 6: Baked Half Lobster Thermidor Surf 'n' Turf (pages 142–143)

DEDICATION

To my mother, Bibianna Sodamin

Fortunate is the man who can sincerely say that he has had a wonderful mother. I must say, I am, indeed, an extremely fortunate man.

This book is about celebrations, and I dedicate it to my mother in celebration of the life she has lived and the feasts she has wrought for those of us lucky enough to have ever had the privilege to sit around her table.

Growing up in Austria in my family of twelve children, I watched my mother take such great pleasure and pride in nourishing each and every one of us in heart, mind, and soul through her cooking. My mother taught her best lessons about life over a gently simmering stockpot in the kitchen, and demonstrated her profound devotion to her large family every day as she set out food before us at mealtime.

But the full spectrum of her culinary resourcefulness, her creativity, and her talent for making life special was never more apparent than during holidays and those times when we were fortunate enough to have something to celebrate. The impressions of those very special times, many now several decades old, remain indelible and are among the happiest moments in my life—and this from a man who has traveled the world over, cooked for and dined with royalty and world leaders, and received accolades beyond what I could have ever imagined for myself as a young boy tagging behind by my mother's apron strings. Yet it's true.

Indeed I have been blessed with both good fortune and a good mother who taught me that regardless of what life brings, it's easy to find much to feel happy about. So thank you, Mom, it is from you that I learned how to celebrate life through food, how to bring excitement to the table and to the party, and how to create unforgettable memories from whatever I can find in a kitchen.

Ich werde immer Dein Herz in meiner Kueche finden

CONTENTS

SIGNATURE

America Line the undisputed leader in the premium cruise market. We never put forth what's "new" simply for the sake of newness itself—our decisions and our innovative spirit take their direction from continually delivering a memorable culinary experience for our guests.

Everything we do aboard our ships during the holidays and for special celebrations that our guests choose to share with us is built on the deepest regard for entrusting us with their special occasion—whether a honeymoon, an anniversary, a birthday, a family reunion, or any other event that holds special meaning for them. It is a source of great pride when guests return year after year because the experiences we have created are so memorable, uniquely customized, and personal that Holland America Line has become a part of a cherished family memory and tradition.

Holland America Line is central in the life and holiday traditions of my family. We love cruising together, especially during the holidays. Christmas and Easter are my particular favorites because the ships are so elegantly decorated, the food is even more lavishly spectacular, and there is an unmistakable spirit of friendship and celebration unlike anything that I've experienced anywhere else in the world.

Working at Holland America Line has had a profound influence on how I entertain in my own home as well. The culinary department has so many wonderful programs and classes with opportunities to learn everything about cooking, from the basics to the finishing flourishes. Watching Master Chef Rudi Sodamin has taught me the importance of quality ingredients and proper presentation. I'm convinced that these two things are the secrets to good eating.

I've brought home the culinary concepts I've learned at work, because while traveling the world on board the magnificent ships of Holland America Line is one of the greatest privileges of my position

of ELEGANCE

here, I believe there is nothing more heartwarming than entertaining friends and family in our home. My wife Linda and I love to cook together, and even Chef Rudi—the most highly decorated chef on the seven seas—says I'm a fairly decent cook!

Rudi has been a key player in elevating everything culinary on our ships in the last few years. His enthusiasm is contagious as he strives for supreme creativity—and perfection—in everything he does. He has developed hundreds of wonderful, innovative recipes for our menus, contributing immensely to our outstanding, award-winning culinary reputation. Rudi is a teacher who works with our chefs to enhance their skills and their knowledge of cooking. He has also taught me.

One thing I've learned from Rudi over the years is to relax while I am hosting a party and to enjoy the experience. I highly recommend that you take that advice to heart as well—especially learning to relax in the kitchen. While Rudi is very serious about his cooking, he also has fun and makes sure his guests have fun, too. I always enjoy cooking at his side when I have the opportunity.

It is with great pleasure that I now invite you to bring Master Chef Rudi into your own kitchen with *Holland America Line Culinary Signature Collection Volume III: A Taste of Celebration*. Rudi is the perfect kitchen companion. His vast knowledge of world food traditions, combined with his willingness to bring innovation and excitement to the table, will no doubt inspire you as he has me, our culinary department, and our guests.

On behalf of our entire culinary team, it is our great pleasure to share these recipes. Now all may enjoy the wonderful dishes of Holland America Line, whether on board one of our five-star ships or at home. Bon appetit.

STEIN KRUSE
President and Chief Executive Officer

M E N U S   F O R

Holidays, birthdays, other special occasions, and, naturally, vacations are the exclamation points of our lives. They are the moments that help us appreciate all we have. All celebrations are good ones to me; I'll celebrate anything and everything. I think life is too short not to find as much as we can to be happy about, and to celebrate it.

Because I've traveled the world so extensively, I suspect that I've encountered most holidays. I've been so enriched—and have gotten so many good ideas—by taking part in the culinary traditions and cultural heritage I find in other countries. In fact, Thanksgiving has become my favorite holiday (I think perhaps because the food itself is the focal point of the celebration).

I grew up in Austria, so I'll never forget taking part in my first American Thanksgiving dinner. I was working at the Waldorf-Astoria hotel in New York City; I never saw such turkey in my life. Likewise, I was invited to a friend's home to celebrate Passover and was deeply moved by all the symbolism in the meal, in the reverence for the rituals, and in the ancient culinary traditions that inspired the marvelous dinner.

Our celebrations create our most cherished memories, some that will follow us throughout our lives. The Christmases of my childhood took place in the snow-covered mountains of Austria. I remember fondly the Christmas carols I sang with my many brothers and sisters while the warm, inviting aroma of Mom's holiday roast wafted tantalizingly through the house. For many years now, I've lived in the U.S. in Florida, so come Yuletide, the setting could not be more dramatically different than the Christmases of my youth in Austria. But the memory of those cozy childhood celebrations are so deeply etched in my heart that they are quickly recalled each year at Christmastime. Our holidays should always provide such treasured memories.

It has been my privilege and a particular joy in my life to help people celebrate a special occasion when they are on one of our ships. When our guests entrust us with creating their holiday

M E M O R I E S

memories, our goal is to take what is already memorable—each day of the cruise and its spectacular culinary offerings at every meal—and make it absolutely unforgettable.

We're very proud of the stellar reputation we enjoy for creating unique culinary celebrations (see Master Chef's Dinner for a sample of one of Holland America Line's signature events). The work and the creativity that go into our distinctive brand of culinary excellence never stops. We're always developing fresh, unforgettable ways to prepare foods (such as Lobster Macaroni and Cheese for Father's Day) and present them with great flair (Scallops with Spicy Garlic-Lime Dipping Sauce served on lemongrass skewers for a cocktail party).

We also take a lot of pleasure in what we do, and the most gratifying part to me is when guests at an event ask me if it would be possible to get the recipe for one of the dishes on the menu. That's when I know beyond a doubt that the culinary arts team has done it again: created a culinary moment so compelling that the guests want to be able to re-create the experience at home.

When I give cooking demonstrations and classes in the Culinary Arts Center on board whichever ship I happen to be visiting for a culinary evaluation or training, guests in the audience will invariably ask me after the class about some dish they enjoyed in the main Dining Room, at a cocktail gathering, in the Pinnacle Grill—or in one of our specialty restaurants like our fine Italian dining venue, Canaletto, or Tamarind, the Pan-Asian restaurant exclusive to the ms *Eurodam* and ms *Nieuw Amsterdam*.

In *A Taste of Celebration*, I've collected the recipes requested most often from these guests, who are interested in creating special meals for loved ones to celebrate holidays or other special occasions. Each dish scores high on the "Wow!" factor and is truly wonderful both to look at and to eat. While some of these recipes are more complicated and take more time than others, none are hard to make with planning and preparation.

I chose to present the recipes in the context of full menus because even some of the more accomplished home cooks I've met lack confidence in attempting to put together a well-rounded menu for entertaining.

In the pages that follow, you'll find sixteen different menus that will take you from one end of the year to the other, each one featuring distinctive four-star dishes from our extensive recipe collection. Each menu is tailored to a specific calendar holiday or a special event, so you'll find food for lovers in our Valentine's menu and food for thought in the suggested recipes for Hanukkah.

By all means, take these menus and create them exactly as presented here for the prescribed holiday or celebration; however, I also encourage you to mix and match menus to create your own. Each menu is appropriate to its season, so you might want to take two of the recipes from the Memorial Day menu, for example, and match them with one from the Fourth of July menu, and perhaps a fourth from the Labor Day menu. Or throw a party and make only two dishes from any menu.

There are no rules with this book. It's your event, it's your party, and you can cook what you want to—and with this repertoire of recipes, in any combination, you can't go wrong.

I tell the students in my cooking classes the following: "You're not just trying to put together a great meal, you're working to create a great memory." Crafting amazing memories for our guests is what Holland America Line does best; we hope you'll enjoy creating wonderful moments at home with these unforgettable recipes.

Enjoy!

RUDI SODAMIN
Master Chef

A quintet of cocktail party favorites (*clockwise from top left*): Peppered Beef Tenderloin Rolls, Mahi-Mahi Ceviche, Cherry Tomatoes and Mini Mozzarella, Vegetable Spring Rolls, and Dungeness Crab Salad.

The Captain's Dinner has long been a cherished tradition, harkening back to the heyday of ocean liners. Back in the day, the Captain's Dinner was a formal, black-tie affair, and nothing was served that wasn't the utmost in luxury and refinement. Guests at each table would meet the captain of the ship personally and have a formal picture taken with him standing tall in his full nautical regalia. | This dinner was a major event on a cruise—one that elicited an unmistakable once-in-a-lifetime feeling of excitement and importance. I chose to launch *A Taste of Celebration* with this Captain's Dinner menu to highlight an unforgettable kind of entertaining— one that is completely unique to the cruise line industry—and to illustrate the idea that on any given night you can create an extraordinary experience that captures the same sense of excitement and indulgence at home. | Of all the menus you'll find in *A Taste of Celebration*, the Captain's Dinner puts forth the most luxurious—and most expensive—ingredients. This is the pull-out-all-the-stops menu in terms of the ingredients used, but nothing here is hard to make. If you do all the prep work in advance, this is a menu that you can reasonably serve on a Friday night after work. I say follow the tradition all the way: Get dressed up, use your good china, light the candles, uncork a nice bottle of wine, and by all means, capture the meal and the moment with a photo. | I include this menu to suggest that we shouldn't always put off creating a happy memory while waiting for a holiday or special occasion. The Captain's Dinner concept reminds us that we can celebrate the presence of a single person in our lives, and feel deeply honored to have him or her sitting at our table.

CAPTAIN'S DINNER

M E N U

Leek and Potato Soup

• • •

*Mussels Steamed in Wine with Tri-Color Bell Peppers
and Garlic Bread*

• • •

*Filet Mignon with Vegetable Ragoût, Red Wine Sauce,
and Ravioli Crown*

• • •

Chocolate Soufflé with Chocolate Sauce

Leek and Potato Soup

YIELD: 4 TO 6 SERVINGS

2 tablespoons unsalted butter

¼ cup chopped onion

½ cup chopped leeks, white part only

1 medium garlic clove, smashed

2 cups peeled and chopped russet potatoes

2 cups low-sodium store-bought chicken broth or stock, or homemade

½ cup heavy cream or half-and-half

1 teaspoon celery salt

1 teaspoon freshly ground white pepper

½ cup crème fraîche, for garnish (see Belgian Endive Canapés with Caviar and Crème Fraîche, page 171)

½ cup finely chopped chives, for garnish

When served chilled, this soup is called vichyssoise. Its creator, the French-born Louis Diat, named it after the town of Vichy, near his birthplace. In 1910, Diat became chef of the Ritz-Carlton in New York City, a position he held for many, many years. It was during his tenure there that he created his famous soup.

1. In a medium saucepan, heat the butter over medium heat. Add the onion and cook, stirring, until softened and translucent, about 5 minutes. Add the leeks and garlic and cook, stirring, for 2 to 3 minutes. Stir in the potato and chicken broth and bring to a boil. Reduce the heat and simmer until the potato is tender, about 15 to 20 minutes.

2. Transfer half the soup to a blender, along with half the cream. Puree until smooth. (When pureeing hot soups, fill the container no more than halfway and release one corner of the lid to prevent a vacuum effect. Place a kitchen towel over the top of the machine while you pulse.) Immediately strain the soup through a fine sieve into a clean saucepan. Repeat with the remaining soup and cream.

3. Stir the celery salt and pepper into the soup. (The soup can be made up to 2 days in advance to this point; see the note below for details on how to chill and store it.) Reheat the soup on the stove just until it gently simmers. To serve, divide the soup among bowls. Add a small dollop of crème fraîche to each bowl and sprinkle with the chopped chives.

NOTE | To serve this soup cold as vichyssoise, after blending, strain the soup into a metal bowl, add the celery salt and pepper, and place the metal bowl in a bowl of ice water to chill the soup quickly. Stir every 15 minutes or so. When it is well cooled, cover and refrigerate it until it is completely cold, about 1 hour. (The soup can be kept this way for up to 2 days. If necessary, thin it with additional stock before serving.) Serve the vichyssoise at a temperature below 41°F. To serve the soup hot, bring it to a temperature of 165°F very quickly, then serve.

Mussels Steamed in Wine with Tri-Color Bell Peppers and Garlic Bread

This recipe calls for white wine, but you can substitute a light and silky red such as pinot noir instead. To use red wine, increase the quantity to 1½ cups, do not add any Pernod or cream, and swirl 2 tablespoons unsalted butter into the liquid right before returning the mussels to the pot in step 3.

GARLIC BREAD

Heat the broiler. On a cutting board, mash the garlic with the salt until a paste forms. In a small saucepan, melt the butter over medium heat and stir in the garlic paste and parsley. Remove from the heat. Halve each loaf of bread horizontally and brush the garlic butter on the cut sides. Place on a baking sheet cut-side up; set aside.

MUSSELS

1. In a large saucepan, heat the oil over medium heat. Add the minced garlic, bell peppers, onion, and dried herbs. Cook, stirring, for 1 minute.
2. Add the washed mussels and wine and bring to a boil; reduce the heat, cover, and simmer the mussels until they open, 4 to 5 minutes. Using tongs, transfer the mussels to a medium bowl (discard any that remain closed after cooking).
3. Add the Pernod and cream to the saucepan; boil until the liquid is slightly reduced, about 4 minutes. Return the mussels and any accumulated juices to the pot. Simmer until the mussels are warmed through, about 1 minute.

TO SERVE

Place the garlic bread under the broiler about 4 inches from the heat and broil until golden, 1 to 2 minutes. Divide the mussels among four bowls. Season the broth (with its vegetables) with salt and pepper and ladle the broth over the mussels. Garnish with parsley, and serve with the garlic bread on the side.

YIELD: 4 SERVINGS

GARLIC BREAD

2 teaspoons minced garlic

Pinch salt

4 tablespoons unsalted butter

2 teaspoons minced fresh flat-leaf parsley, plus extra for garnish

2 (12-inch) loaves French or Italian bread

MUSSELS

1 tablespoon extra-virgin olive oil

1 teaspoon minced garlic

½ each red, yellow, and green bell peppers, cut into thin strips

½ red onion, cut into thin strips

¼ teaspoon each dried basil, thyme, and oregano

2 pounds mussels, scrubbed and debearded

1¼ cups dry white wine (such as unoaked sauvignon blanc, pinot blanc, or dry riesling from Alsace)

3 tablespoons Pernod or other anise liqueur

½ cup heavy cream

Salt and freshly ground black pepper

Filet Mignon with Vegetable Ragoût, Red Wine Sauce, and Ravioli Crown

YIELD: 4 SERVINGS

RED WINE SAUCE

2 tablespoons unsalted butter

⅔ cup minced shallots

1 tablespoon minced garlic

1 teaspoon dried thyme

1 tablespoon all-purpose flour

2 cups beef stock or canned low-salt beef broth

1½ cups dry red wine (such as cabernet sauvignon)

Salt and freshly ground black pepper

VEGETABLE RAGOÛT

2 tablespoons extra-virgin olive oil

2 teaspoons minced garlic

2 medium zucchini, cut into chunks

2 cups cubed potatoes, steamed until almost tender

20 niçoise olives, pitted

2 cups cherry tomatoes, red and/or yellow, halved

Salt and freshly ground black pepper

LEEK GARNISH

Peanut oil, for frying

4 small leeks, white and pale green parts only, washed and cut into julienne, divided

2 tablespoons unsalted butter

Salt and freshly ground black pepper

I f you can find (and afford) filet mignon that's been dry aged, then by all means buy it. It's extremely flavorful and tender. But if you can't, this dish, with all its diversity in color and texture, will still turn any steak into a star.

RED WINE SAUCE

Heat the butter in a medium skillet over medium-high heat. Add the shallots, garlic, and thyme; sauté until tender, about 3 minutes. Add the flour and stir for 1 minute. Add the stock and wine. Bring the mixture to a boil and cook, stirring occasionally, until the sauce thickens and reduces to 1 cup, about 15 minutes. Season with salt and pepper. Strain the sauce through a fine sieve into a small saucepan and set aside.

VEGETABLE RAGOÛT

Heat the oil in a large skillet over medium heat. Add the garlic, zucchini, potatoes, and olives; cook, stirring, for 2 minutes. Add the tomatoes, stir once, and season with salt and pepper. Set aside.

LEEK GARNISH

1. In a small, heavy saucepan, heat 1 inch peanut oil over medium-high heat until a deep-frying thermometer registers 350°F (do not allow the oil to smoke). Line a wire rack with paper towels.
2. Place half of the leeks in a small bowl and set aside. Working in small batches and very carefully, fry the remaining half of the leeks until they are golden brown, about 30 seconds. With a slotted spoon, transfer the fried leeks to the paper towels to drain. (The fried leeks can be stored at room temperature in an airtight container for up to 1 day.)
3. In a small skillet, heat the butter over medium heat. Add the reserved leeks and cook, stirring, until just tender, about 2 to 3 minutes. Season with salt and pepper; set aside.

ASSEMBLY

1. Bring a medium saucepan of salted water to a boil. Add the ravioli and gently simmer until just al dente. Remove a coffee cup full of cooking liquid and drain the ravioli. Place the reserved cooking liquid and ravioli back into the saucepan, cover, and set aside.

2. Heat the oil in a 10- or 12-inch skillet until hot but not smoking. Season the steaks with salt and pepper and add them to the skillet. Cook the steaks until brown on both sides and cooked to desired doneness, about 5 minutes per side for medium-rare. Divide the steaks among four warmed plates.

3. To serve, rewarm (in their respective pans) the reserved sauce, reserved vegetable ragoût, and reserved sautéed leeks. Ladle sauce and ragoût around each fillet. Sprinkle with parsley. Top each fillet with a drained ravioli, some sautéed leeks, and some fried leeks. Serve immediately.

ASSEMBLY

4 large, fresh spinach- or mushroom-filled ravioli

2 tablespoons vegetable oil

4 (6-ounce) filet mignon steaks

Salt and freshly ground black pepper

1 tablespoon finely chopped fresh flat-leaf parsley

Chocolate Soufflé with Chocolate Sauce

CHOCOLATE SAUCE

7 ounces semisweet chocolate, finely chopped

1 cup heavy cream

CHOCOLATE SOUFFLÉ

3½ ounces bittersweet (not unsweetened) chocolate, roughly chopped

4 tablespoons unsalted butter

1 cup all-purpose flour

1½ cups whole milk

9 large eggs, separated, plus 1 large egg white

½ cup granulated sugar

¼ cup cornstarch

¼ cup natural (not Dutch-process) cocoa powder

2 tablespoons confectioners' sugar

For some soufflés you need to make a delicate French custard base or Italian meringue, both of which require specific timing, techniques, and temperatures. This recipe is easier on the cook and yields just as professional a result.

CHOCOLATE SAUCE

Place the chocolate in a bowl. In a 1-quart saucepan, bring the cream to a boil. Pour the hot cream over the chocolate and gently whisk until smooth. Keep warm over a pan of hot water (off heat) or at room temperature.

CHOCOLATE SOUFFLÉ

1. Heat the oven to 375°F. Lightly butter ten 1½-cup individual ramekins or custard cups. Dust the ramekins with sugar; tilt to coat and tap out the excess.

2. Place the chocolate in the top of a double boiler placed over 1 inch of simmering (not boiling) water. Whisk until the chocolate is smooth and no small lumps remain. Remove the pan from the heat; set aside.

3. In a heavy saucepan, melt the 4 tablespoons butter over medium heat. Add the flour and cook, stirring constantly, until the paste is pale golden (do not let it brown at all), about 2 minutes.

4. Meanwhile, in another saucepan, heat the milk gently over low heat just until little bubbles begin to form at the edges. Remove the milk from the heat and add it, a little at a time, to the flour mixture, whisking constantly until very smooth. Bring the mixture to a boil and cook, whisking constantly, until quite thick, 1 to 2 minutes more. Remove from the heat and immediately stir in the melted chocolate.

5. Scrape the chocolate batter into a large mixing bowl. With an electric mixer, beat in the egg yolks, one at a time, scraping down the sides of the bowl after each yolk is incorporated. Set the chocolate base aside.

6. Place the egg whites in the very clean bowl of an electric mixer fitted with the whisk attachment, or in a large mixing bowl. With the electric mixer or a hand mixer, beat the egg whites on medium speed just until foamy, about 30 seconds. Slowly begin sprinkling in the ½ cup sugar, and then the cornstarch, continuing to beat until the whites form stiff peaks.

7. Put the cocoa powder in a small sieve and place on a plate. Scrape the egg white meringue into the chocolate base. Using a rubber

spatula, very gently fold the egg white meringue into the chocolate base while simultaneously sprinkling the cocoa powder over the mixture as you fold. (The entire process should be done gently but should take no more than 15 seconds—if possible, ask someone to sprinkle the cocoa powder for you.)

8. Bring a large kettle of water to a boil. With a spoon, transfer the soufflé batter to a piping bag fitted with a large plain tip. Pipe the soufflé batter into the prepared ramekins. Place the ramekins into a large roasting pan. Transfer the roasting pan to the oven and add enough boiling water to the pan to reach halfway up the sides of the ramekins. Bake the soufflés for 10 to 14 minutes, or until they are puffed above the rims and crusted on top but still moist in the center. Carefully transfer the ramekins to small serving plates. Place the confectioners' sugar in a sieve and sprinkle it over the tops of the soufflés. Serve immediately with the chocolate sauce in a small pitcher on the side.

Everything on board a Holland America Line vessel is an event— and the American Super Bowl is no exception. It's not just the die-hard football fans who eagerly anticipate the game, either; even self-professed sports haters inevitably find themselves gravitating to one of the areas where the annual American ritual is being played out on flat screens in lounges and special-event rooms throughout each ship. | It is an exciting time, particularly if the word "football" kicks up a guest's appetite for game food: Frequently on board you'll hear fewer questions about who's playing and many more about what foods are being served. The Super Bowl party is by now such a cultural phenomenon it has evolved its own food rubric. Seriously, what's a Super Bowl without some super-spicy chicken wings? Finger-licking food is clearly in the rule book some-where. | A Super Bowl gathering has some other unspoken regulations: It clearly anticipates eating at the coffee table in the TV room rather than at the table in the dining room. What I love about having a get-together for Super Bowl Sunday is its intentional casualness. After all the formal entertaining of the holiday season, for which the good china is hauled out (then hand washed!), there's something to be said for hosting a party that ostensibly involves noshing Beef Nachos off paper plates and digging a wooden spoon into a crock for a helping of Vegetarian Black Bean Chili. | Classic Super Bowl fare is always about spicing up the big game. But why wait for the Super Bowl? There's football *every* Sunday and Monday for seventeen weeks. Which of your friends wouldn't want to head over to your place for some Crispy Chili Chicken Wings to catch a game on a Monday night? Any reason is reason enough to celebrate life and to be together.

SUPER BOWL SUNDAY

MENU

Hot Artichoke and Spinach Dip

. . .

Beef Nachos

. . .

Crispy Chili Chicken Wings

. . .

Vegetarian Black Bean Chili

. . .

Coconutty Blondies

. . .

Light Lemon Mousse

Hot Artichoke and Spinach Dip

YIELD: 6 SERVINGS

1 (14-ounce) can artichoke hearts, drained

1½ cups grated Italian cheese blend (such as mozzarella, Romano, and Asiago), divided

1 teaspoon minced garlic

⅛ teaspoon freshly grated nutmeg

1 (10-ounce) package frozen chopped spinach, thawed and squeezed dry

½ cup heavy cream

4 ounces cream cheese, at room temperature

1 Roma tomato, seeded and diced

5 leaves basil, minced (optional)

Serve this creamy, colorful dip with tortilla chips, if you like. And a crispy homemade bread bowl can make it even more festive looking (see Clam Chowder in a Bread Bowl, pages 128–129).

1. Heat the oven to 350°F. Butter a 6-cup casserole dish.
2. In a food processor, combine the artichoke hearts, ½ cup of the Italian cheese blend, garlic, and nutmeg. Pulse until chopped but not ground. Set aside.
3. In a bowl, combine the spinach, heavy cream, cream cheese, and remaining 1 cup Italian cheese blend; stir well. Fold in the artichoke mixture until well combined. Transfer the dip to the prepared casserole dish.
4. Bake the dip for 20 to 25 minutes, or until browned on the top and heated through. Sprinkle with the tomato and the basil (if using). Serve immediately.

Beef Nachos

Nachos are the ultimate Super Bowl snack, and this recipe is both easy and over-the-top delicious, especially when you offer your guests lots of extra garnishes on the side to add color and layers of flavor.

1. Heat the oven to 350°F. In a skillet, brown the ground beef and onion over medium heat until the beef is no longer pink and the onions are softened. Add the bell pepper, spices, refried beans, and tomato sauce. Reduce the heat to low and simmer, stirring, for 10 to 15 minutes.

2. Spread some of the beef mixture on each chip and arrange the chips in a single layer on a large baking sheet or use smaller ovenproof plates or dishes. Sprinkle the tortillas with the grated cheese and place the nachos in the oven until the cheese is melted and the beef mixture is cooked through, about 8 minutes. Serve immediately with any extra garnishes you choose on the side.

YIELD: 6 SERVINGS

4 ounces ground beef (at least 85% lean)

½ cup chopped onion

½ cup chopped green bell pepper

1 tablespoon chili powder

2 teaspoons ground cumin

1 teaspoon paprika

1 teaspoon sea salt

1 teaspoon black pepper

½ teaspoon garlic powder

½ teaspoon onion powder

¼ teaspoon crushed red pepper

¼ teaspoon dried oregano

1 (16-ounce) can refried beans

1 (8-ounce) can tomato sauce

1 large bag plain tortilla chips

1 cup shredded cheddar and Monterey Jack cheese blend

SIDE GARNISHES

Seeded and diced plum tomatoes

Thinly sliced scallions

Thinly sliced or minced jalapeño pepper

Sliced black olives

Chopped fresh cilantro

Sour cream

Guacamole

Crispy Chili Chicken Wings

T hese sticky-sweet wings are made even better with the unexpected addition of ginger slices and peanuts. They will stay crispy for up to four hours.

YIELD: 8 SERVINGS

20 whole chicken wings

2 teaspoons salt

½ teaspoon freshly ground pepper

2 large eggs, lightly beaten

½ cup all-purpose flour

½ cup cornstarch or potato starch

Vegetable oil, for frying

1 cup peeled, sliced fresh ginger

2 tablespoons soy sauce

⅔ cup packed light brown sugar

¼ cup white vinegar

1 cup light corn syrup

1 cup roasted peanuts

½ cup sesame seeds

1 teaspoon crushed red pepper

1. For each chicken wing, remove and discard the relatively meatless tips, then cut each wing between the joint to make 40 pieces. Rinse, pat dry thoroughly, and place in a large bowl. Add the salt, pepper, eggs, flour, and cornstarch. Mix the ingredients with your hands until each piece of chicken is well coated.

2. In a 10- or 12-inch heavy skillet or cast-iron pot, heat 2 inches vegetable oil over medium-high heat until a deep-frying thermometer registers 350°F (do not allow the oil to smoke). One at a time, add 10 wings to the oil. Cook for 6 minutes, then, using tongs, turn them over and cook another 6 minutes. Transfer the cooked wings to a colander to drain. Repeat with the remaining chicken wings.

3. Meanwhile, make the sauce: In a large skillet or wok, bring 1 cup water to a boil. Add the ginger and boil for 30 seconds. Add the soy sauce, brown sugar, and vinegar; allow to boil for 5 minutes. Add the corn syrup and reduce the heat to medium low; continue simmering. To check doneness, after 20 to 30 minutes, allow some sauce to drip from the side of a large spoon. If it thickens to the point where the last drops form a soft "icicle" hanging from the spoon, it's done. Turn off the heat and set aside.

4. Fry the wings a second time: With a slotted spoon, remove any particles from the oil in the skillet and reheat it to 350°F (add more oil if necessary). Add half the chicken wings and fry until deeply browned and crispy, about 2 minutes on each side. With tongs, remove the chicken pieces and place them in a colander to drain. Repeat with the remaining chicken wings.

5. Reheat the sauce to again reach the hanging-icicle stage in step 3. Add the wings to the sauce, along with the peanuts and sesame seeds. Using a spoon, very carefully toss the wings in the sauce until each piece is thoroughly coated. Sprinkle with crushed red pepper and toss again to distribute it; immediately remove from the heat.

6. Use tongs to place the chicken wings on a serving plate. Spoon any ginger slices and peanuts remaining in the bowl on top.

Vegetarian Black Bean Chili

YIELD: 6 TO 8 SERVINGS

1 pound dried black beans, soaked overnight

1 (28-ounce) can whole plum tomatoes (with juice), roughly chopped

1 large onion, chopped

2 medium carrots, chopped

2 stalks celery, chopped

1 tablespoon minced garlic

2 tablespoons chili powder

2 teaspoons ground cumin

4 vegetable bouillon cubes

1 orange, scrubbed well and quartered (with peel)

2 teaspoons Tabasco hot pepper sauce

½ cup chopped fresh cilantro or flat-leaf parsley, for garnish

The flavors of this chili improve when it is made the night before you serve it (but remember to soak the beans the night before *that*). The best vegetable bouillon cubes are generally organic and contain no MSG. They can make all the difference in a dish like this. Beef bouillon or beef stock can be used in place of water, if strict vegetarianism is not necessary.

1. Rinse the soaked beans and place in a large pot. Cover with water by 1 inch and bring to a boil. Reduce the heat and simmer, uncovered, for 1 hour.
2. Add the remaining ingredients except for the Tabasco and cilantro. Continue to simmer for 1½ hours longer, or until the beans are tender (if necessary, add more water to keep the beans from sticking).
3. Remove the orange quarters from the chili. Season with Tabasco. Divide the chili among bowls and sprinkle with cilantro.

Coconutty Blondies

YIELD: 16 BARS

1¼ cups all-purpose flour

½ teaspoon baking soda

½ teaspoon salt

8 tablespoons (1 stick) unsalted butter

⅓ cup granulated sugar

½ cup firmly packed light brown sugar

1 large egg

½ teaspoon vanilla extract

1 cup sweetened flaked coconut, divided

¾ cup (3 ounces) pecans or macadamia nuts, toasted, cooled, and coarsely chopped

A plate of these chewy, golden bar cookies alongside a batch of your favorite brownies will please everyone, no matter which team they're rooting for.

1. Heat the oven to 350°F and position a rack in the middle. Butter and flour an 8-inch-square baking pan.
2. Sift flour, baking soda, and salt into a bowl; set aside. In another bowl, combine butter, granulated sugar, and brown sugar; beat with an electric mixer at medium speed until fluffy. Add the egg and vanilla and beat well. Gradually add the flour mixture, beating on low speed until just combined.
3. With a wooden spoon, stir in ¾ cup of the coconut and all the nuts.
4. Spread the batter into the prepared pan. Sprinkle with the remaining ¼ cup coconut. Bake for 20 to 25 minutes, or until a toothpick inserted in the center comes out clean. Place the pan on a wire rack and let cool completely before cutting into bars.

Light Lemon Mousse

This light-as-a-cloud mousse is a delicious complement to the Coconutty Blondies.

1. Place ½ cup water in a small saucepan and bring to a simmer. Remove it from the heat and sprinkle with the gelatin; whisk until dissolved. Let cool slightly. Grate the zest from three of the lemons and set it aside. Squeeze ⅔ cup juice from the lemons, using the fourth one if needed; set aside.

2. In a large glass or ceramic bowl, combine the egg yolks and sugar; beat with an electric mixer at medium speed until pale in color, stopping occasionally to scrape down the sides of the bowl with a rubber spatula. Add the grated lemon zest and continue beating. Gradually beat in the lemon juice and set aside.

3. In a metal bowl, using the mixer, whip the cream until soft peaks form. With a rubber spatula, fold the cream into the lemon mixture. Add the gelatin and continue folding until the mixture begins to thicken. Set aside.

4. Place the egg whites in a clean bowl and add the cream of tartar. Using the mixer, with very clean beaters, beat the whites until stiff. Fold the whites into the reserved cream and lemon mixture.

5. Place some raspberries or strawberries in the bottom of individual goblets or bowls and divide the mousse among them. Cover and refrigerate until well chilled, at least 4 hours. Serve garnished with mint sprigs.

YIELD: 10 SERVINGS

See photograph, page 10

2 tablespoons unflavored gelatin

3 to 4 lemons

5 large eggs, separated (see note)

1⅓ cups sugar

2 cups heavy cream

Pinch cream of tartar

6 to 8 ounces raspberries or strawberries, stemmed

Mint sprigs, for garnish

NOTE You can eliminate the small risk of salmonella contamination in raw egg preparations by using pasteurized shell eggs.

I love Valentine's Day because I always equate food with love. There are no better ways to nourish the heart and spirit of a couple than by cooking together, or eating a beautiful meal designed to stimulate the senses while holding hands across the table, gazing into each other's eyes over a flickering candle. | The cruises that coincide with Valentine's Day are invariably booked far in advance—and with good reason. There are few better places to fan the flames of passion. But romance flourishes in every season at Holland America Line: We get countless honeymooners—those just starting out their lives together—and an equal number of older couples who have lived the decades together and experienced the journey of life side by side. Our Pinnacle Grill restaurant gives our onboard lovers tables for two spread with Bvlgari fine china, Reidel stemware, and Frette linens. Invariably, the couples you see in the restaurant are in a world of their own. To me, that is the whole point of Valentine's Day. | The day should celebrate a couple's unique qualities, and how they like to do things. This menu, including Tournedos Rossini (a favorite from the Pinnacle Grill menu), can be very formal, served on luscious linens in a room full of candles and on your best china—with you and the love of your life dressed to the hilt. Or, this menu works equally well if you want to have a cozy dinner on the couch while watching a favorite movie. | This is an easy menu to make and can bring you and your sweetheart together in the kitchen for slicing, dicing, dipping—and stirring things up. This menu and Valentine's Day have the same raison d'être: making something happen and letting something happen all at the same time.

VALENTINE'S DAY

MENU

"Heart" of Tuna Tartare with Curry Mayonnaise
and Pink Radish

• • •

Risotto with Butternut Squash and Arugula

• • •

Tournedos Rossini with Roasted Garlic and Turned Vegetables

• • •

Sweetheart Sugar Cookies

• • •

Chocolate-Dipped Fruit and Sugared Grapes

"Heart" of Tuna Tartare with Curry Mayonnaise and Pink Radish

TUNA TARTARE

4 ounces sushi-quality tuna

1 tablespoon finely minced radish

1 tablespoon finely minced celery

1 teaspoon finely minced scallion
or chive

Salt and freshly ground black
pepper

CURRY MAYONNAISE

2 teaspoons curry powder

2 teaspoons mango chutney
(any large mango chunks minced)

½ teaspoon ground saffron,
preferably Spanish (optional)

1 tablespoon crème fraîche,
store-bought or homemade
(see page 171)

1½ tablespoons prepared
mayonnaise

Salt and freshly ground black
pepper

ASSEMBLY

4 to 5 slices white toast

2 whole radishes, thinly sliced,
for garnish

Leaves of chervil or other herbs,
for garnish

This elegant spin-off of spicy tuna maki—a standby at Japanese sushi restaurants everywhere—substitutes curry for wasabi and arrives brimming with love from the chef.

TUNA TARTARE

With a sharp knife, dice the tuna into ¼-inch cubes and place them in a small bowl. Add the radish, celery, and scallion. Toss to combine. Season with salt and pepper. Cover and refrigerate until needed.

CURRY MAYONNAISE

In a small bowl, combine the curry powder, chutney, saffron (if using), and 1 tablespoon hot water. When the mixture has cooled, whisk in the crème fraîche and mayonnaise. Season with salt and pepper. Cover and refrigerate until needed.

ASSEMBLY

1. With a large heart-shaped mold or cutter, cut a heart from each slice of toast. (Alternatively, to make canapés, use a smaller heart cutter to cut two hearts from each toast slice.) Position the heart mold on a plate. With a spoon or small offset spatula, gently pack it with the tuna mixture all the way to the top. Remove the mold. Repeat with the remaining tuna on separate plates. (Alternatively, for canapés, on a platter position a small heart mold on top of a heart-shaped piece of toast and spoon tuna tartare onto the toast, filling the cutter to the top. Remove the mold and repeat with more toast and tartare.)

2. To serve, put the curry mayonnaise in a squeeze bottle and use it to decorate the tuna and the plate. Garnish with the radish circles and herbs and serve immediately with the heart toasts on the side.

NOTE If you don't have a heart-shaped mold or cutter, a ring mold can substitute. You can even create your own ring mold by removing the top and bottom of an emptied and washed tuna can.

Risotto with Butternut Squash and Arugula

For a rustic presentation, you can serve this in a roasted acorn squash half. Just roast a couple acorn squashes while you roast the butternut squash: Trim the top and bottom (so they'll stand up on the plate), then cut them in half on the equator. Seed, oil, and season the halves with salt and pepper. Place them cut side down on a greased baking sheet. Bake them until they're tender (this should take about one hour), then spoon the finished risotto into the cavity.

SQUASH

Heat the oven to 450°F. In a bowl, toss the squash with olive oil until thoroughly coated. Season with salt and pepper. Transfer the squash to a baking sheet and roast in the oven, turning occasionally, for 30 minutes, or until tender. Set aside.

DRESSING

Whisk the lime juice and zest in a small bowl. Slowly whisk in the extra-virgin olive oil. Season with salt and pepper. Cover and refrigerate until ready to use.

RISOTTO

1. Bring the broth to a boil in a medium saucepan. Reduce the heat and keep the broth at a low simmer.
2. In a medium enamel-lined cast-iron casserole or other heavy pot, heat 1 tablespoon of the butter over medium heat. Add the onion, ginger, and garlic; cook, stirring, until softened, about 5 minutes. Add the rice and nutmeg and stir with a wooden spoon until the rice becomes slightly toasted, about 3 minutes.
3. Add the wine and cook, stirring constantly, until the liquid is absorbed. Add one-third of the simmering broth and cook, stirring constantly, until the liquid is absorbed. Add half the remaining broth and cook, stirring constantly, until the liquid is absorbed. Add a bit more broth if necessary so that the risotto is creamy but still slightly firm in the center.
4. Add the reserved roasted squash, the remaining 1 tablespoon butter, and Parmesan. Cook, stirring gently, until the squash is heated through. Season with salt and pepper.
5. To serve, toss the baby arugula in a large bowl with the lime dressing. Divide the risotto among warmed plates. Top with arugula salad and serve immediately.

YIELD: 4 TO 6 SERVINGS

SQUASH

2 pounds butternut squash, peeled, seeded, and cut into ½-inch cubes

1 tablespoon olive oil

Salt and freshly ground black pepper

DRESSING

2 teaspoons fresh lime juice

½ teaspoon finely grated lime zest

1½ tablespoons extra-virgin olive oil

Salt and freshly ground black pepper

RISOTTO

4 cups low-sodium store-bought chicken broth or stock, or homemade

2 tablespoons unsalted butter, divided

½ cup minced onion

1½ teaspoons minced fresh ginger

1 teaspoon minced garlic

1 cup Arborio rice

¼ teaspoon freshly grated nutmeg

¼ cup dry white wine (such as sauvignon blanc, chenin blanc, or pinot blanc)

¼ cup grated Parmesan cheese

Salt and freshly ground black pepper

2 ounces (3 cups) baby arugula, washed well and spun dry

Tournedos Rossini with
Roasted Garlic and Turned Vegetables

YIELD: 4 SERVINGS

GARLIC AND VEGETABLES

12 large garlic cloves, unpeeled

¼ cup olive oil

Coarse sea salt or handcrafted salt

2 medium carrots, trimmed and cut into 1-inch-by-1½-inch pieces, then carved into ovals

1 medium zucchini, trimmed and cut into 1-inch-by-1½-inch pieces, then carved into ovals

1 medium yellow squash, trimmed and cut into 1-inch-by-1½-inch pieces, then carved into ovals

¾ cup haricots verts (thin French green beans)

8 thin asparagus, trimmed and cut into 2- to 3-inch lengths

TOURNEDOS

2 tablespoons canola oil, plus extra if needed

3 medium garlic cloves, thinly sliced

4 (6-ounce) filet mignon steaks (1½ to 2 inches thick)

Coarse sea salt

Freshly ground black pepper

6- to 8-ounce piece raw duck foie gras at room temperature, cleaned, deveined, and cut crosswise into 4 slices (see note, page 42)

1 medium shallot, finely chopped

½ cup port

½ cup Madeira

½ cup low-sodium store-bought beef stock or broth, or homemade

Continued on page 42

T he Italian opera composer Gioacchino Rossini was famous for his love of food and wine, and many chefs in Europe dedicated dishes to him, including this one. To be traditional, slice a small (2-ounce) black truffle and let it simmer very gently in the sauce for about two minutes before serving.

GARLIC AND VEGETABLES

1. For the garlic, heat the oven to 350°F. Toss the garlic cloves and olive oil in a small baking dish; cover with an ovenproof lid or seal with foil. Bake until the garlic begins to brown, about 35 minutes. Remove from the oven and drain the oil into a small dish; reserve this garlic-flavored oil for another use. Peel the garlic and set aside. (The garlic can be prepared to this point 1 day ahead and refrigerated, covered.)

2. Prepare a large bowl of ice water. Bring 6 quarts water and 1 tablespoon salt to a boil. Add the carrots; cook until the carrots are crisp-tender, about 3 minutes. With a slotted spoon or strainer, transfer the carrots to the bowl of ice water to stop the cooking. Remove them from the ice water to a large bowl; set aside. Repeat the process with the zucchini and squash (cook these together for 2 minutes) and the haricots verts and asparagus (cooked together for 1 to 2 minutes), removing each batch with a strainer and plunging it into the ice water before setting it aside in the bowl. (The vegetables can be prepared to this point up to 4 hours ahead and refrigerated, covered.)

TOURNEDOS

1. Heat the oven to 180°F and place a baking sheet in it. In a large, heavy skillet, heat the oil over medium-high heat. Add the sliced garlic and cook, stirring, just until it starts to turn brown, about 1 minute. With a slotted spoon, remove the garlic; discard.

2. Sprinkle the steaks with salt and pepper and add them to the skillet. Cook on one side until browned, about 3 minutes. Flip the steaks and cook for 3 to 4 minutes more (for medium rare), or until the doneness desired. Transfer the steaks to the baking sheet in the oven to keep warm.

3. Add more oil to the skillet if necessary and reduce the heat to medium. When the oil is hot but not smoking, season the foie gras

Continued from page 40

ASSEMBLY

5 tablespoons unsalted butter, divided

4 slices good-quality white bread, trimmed to the size of the steaks

Coarse sea salt and freshly ground black pepper

1 cup baby watercress

slices with salt and pepper and add them to the skillet (use caution because the fat may spatter). Sauté until golden, 45 to 60 seconds on each side (they will still be pink inside). Quickly transfer them to a plate lined with paper towels to drain. Transfer the drained foie gras to the baking sheet in the oven to keep warm.

4. Drain off all but 1 tablespoon fat from the skillet and add the shallot. Cook, stirring, until softened, about 2 minutes. Add the port and Madeira. Increase the heat to high and boil rapidly until the liquid is reduced by half. Stir in the beef stock and boil rapidly until the sauce is reduced slightly and the flavors are incorporated. Season with salt and pepper and remove from the heat.

ASSEMBLY

1. Make the croutons: In a large, heavy skillet, heat 2 tablespoons of the butter over medium heat until it just starts to foam. Add the bread slices and fry them until nicely browned on both sides. Transfer the bread to the baking sheet in the oven to keep warm.

2. Reheat the vegetables: In a 10-inch skillet, heat another 2 tablespoons of butter over medium heat. Add the reserved roasted garlic and vegetables and sauté, stirring gently, until heated through, about 2 to 3 minutes. Transfer to a bowl and season with salt and pepper.

3. To serve, divide the reserved bread slices among four plates. Place a steak on each bread slice and top each steak with a foie gras slice (be gentle with the foie gras because it gets soft and difficult to handle when warm). Add any steak juices from the baking sheet to the sauce in the skillet and whisk in the remaining 1 tablespoon butter. Pour sauce over each foie-gras-topped steak and top with the watercress. Spoon vegetables around the plate and serve immediately, passing the remaining sauce separately.

NOTE | Slices of goose liver pâté can be substituted for the foie gras. Do not sauté them. After you have cooked the steaks on the first side and flipped them, lay a slice of goose liver pâté on top of each as the second side is cooking.

Sweetheart Sugar Cookies

T o decorate these cookies, sprinkle them with confectioners' sugar or drizzle them with any leftover chocolate from the dipped fruit.

1. In a large mixing bowl, beat the butter and sugar with an electric mixer at medium-high speed until light and fluffy, about 3 minutes in a stand mixer or 6 minutes with a hand mixer. Beat in the egg, vanilla, and lemon juice. Reduce the mixer speed to low and sift the flour and salt together over the egg mixture, beating until just combined.

2. Form the dough into 2 balls and flatten each into a 6-inch disk. Wrap the disks in plastic wrap and chill until firm, at least 2 hours and up to 3 days.

3. Heat the oven to 350°F and position a rack in the middle. Remove 1 disk of dough from the refrigerator and use a well-floured rolling pin to roll it out ¼ inch thick on a well-floured work surface. (Alternatively, roll the dough between two sheets of wax paper, which allows you to easily rechill the dough if it becomes too soft to handle.) With a heart-shaped cookie cutter, cut out as many cookies as possible and transfer them to two ungreased baking sheets, spacing the cookies about 1 inch apart.

4. Bake the cookies, one sheet at a time, until pale golden, 10 to 12 minutes. With a metal spatula, immediately transfer them to a rack placed over a sheet of wax paper and sprinkle them with confectioners' sugar; cool completely.

5. Meanwhile, gather the dough scraps and chill until firm enough to reroll (reroll scraps only once). Be sure the baking sheets are cool before baking more batches on them.

YIELD: 2 TO 3 DOZEN COOKIES

14 tablespoons (1¾ sticks) unsalted butter, at room temperature

½ cup granulated sugar

1 large egg

2 drops vanilla extract

2 drops fresh lemon juice

2⅓ cups all-purpose flour

Pinch salt

2 tablespoons confectioners' sugar

Chocolate-Dipped Fruit and Sugared Grapes

YIELD: 4 SERVINGS

CHOCOLATE-DIPPED FRUIT

1¼ pounds chocolate, semisweet or white, chopped into ¼-inch chunks, divided

½ pound fresh pineapple slices, cut into bite-size pieces

1 pint strawberries with stems, lightly rinsed and dried

3 kiwis, peeled and sliced

2 to 3 ounces marzipan, rolled into walnut-size balls

SUGARED GRAPES

½ pound seedless grapes, still on their stems, at room temperature

2 large egg whites (or ¼ cup pasteurized liquid egg whites)

¾ cup superfine sugar

In addition to the fresh fruits suggested below for dipping, try using dried fruits such as slices of dried pineapple, peach, and pear. If you're feeling in a playful mood, warm up any leftover chocolate and feed it to your sweetheart on a spoon!

CHOCOLATE-DIPPED FRUIT

1. Line a baking sheet with parchment paper; set aside. Place ½ pound of the chocolate in the top of a double boiler and tightly cover with plastic wrap. Place the chocolate over 1 inch of water and heat over medium heat for 12 minutes.
2. Remove the chocolate from the heat and let stand for 5 minutes before removing the plastic wrap. With a rubber spatula or whisk, stir until smooth. Continue to stir until the temperature of the chocolate is reduced and a candy thermometer registers 90°F.
3. With a fork, dip the pineapple pieces, one by one, ½ inch to 1 inch into the chocolate. Allow the excess chocolate to drip back into the double boiler, then place the fruit onto the prepared baking sheet. Refrigerate for 10 to 15 minutes, until the chocolate has hardened. Transfer the pineapples to the center of a large serving platter and refrigerate.
4. Repeat steps 1, 2, and 3 with the remaining chocolate and fruit (holding the strawberries by their stems). Dip the marzipan balls into the chocolate so they are half coated. Refrigerate for 10 to 15 minutes, until the chocolate has hardened.
5. Arrange the chocolate-dipped strawberries, kiwis, and marzipan on the serving platter with the pineapple and return the platter to the refrigerator, covered, and keep chilled until 10 minutes before serving.

SUGARED GRAPES

1. Line a rimmed baking sheet with parchment paper. Place a wire rack over the pan. Use scissors to cut the bunch of grapes into clusters. Place the egg whites and 2 teaspoons water in a teacup and stir with a fork to blend. Holding a cluster by the stem, dip the grapes into the egg whites. With a small brush, paint any part of the grapes that did not get dipped into the whites.
2. Place the grape cluster on the wire rack and immediately sprinkle with sugar, turning the grapes in order to coat all sides. Pick up the

cluster and gently shake off excess sugar. Repeat with remaining grapes. (Vary the amount of sugar on some of the grapes to create the effect of the white powdery substance found on the skins of grapes.)

3. Allow the grapes to dry completely at room temperature, about 2 hours. The sugared grapes will keep at room temperature for up to 2 days; do not cover.

The eight-day holiday of Passover is one of the oldest continuously observed festivals in the history of the western world—dating back more than three thousand years. The first two nights of Passover are traditionally observed with a seder, a multicourse meal that includes symbolic foods and a retelling of the story of the Exodus from Egypt. │ I really love to be on board during Passover. We serve a traditional Passover seder presided over by a rabbi. Even though I'm not Jewish, I love the ritual of the seder meal because every single ingredient used and everything on the table has significance. On board ship during Passover, it is particularly touching to see a multigenerational celebration of this important religious observance. Passover is a holiday that looks forward even as it commemorates the past. This Passover menu does the same, incorporating a seder's symbolic elements and traditional flavors with a decidedly modern sensibility and style. │ Whether or not you celebrate Passover, this is an excellent menu for late-winter, early-spring entertaining—rich in flavor yet with a lightness that hints at the coming of spring. The Honey Glazed Chicken with Rosemary, Lemon, and Garlic is a surefire winner for an elegant dinner party that won't break the bank. The salad of tender beets, watercress, oranges, and fennel with orange/maple dressing is a gorgeous accompaniment to any menu. For many families, it simply wouldn't be Passover without macaroons, but these tasty cookies make for a truly delicious dessert for any occasion. │ From a culinary standpoint, the dishes in this menu have great simplicity, but each recipe and presentation is appropriate for this special celebratory meal of thanksgiving. No matter what the season, or what the faith, it's always appropriate to give thanks, particularly with food—and this traditional menu will help you do just that with great dignity and grace.

Passover

M E N U

Gefilte Fish Timbales with Apple-Horseradish Sauce

• • •

Roasted Beet Salad with Orange Dressing

• • •

Honey Glazed Chicken with Rosemary, Lemon, and Garlic

• • •

Charoset

• • •

Macaroons with Bittersweet Chocolate

Gefilte Fish Timbales
with Apple-Horseradish Sauce

YIELD: 6 SERVINGS

GEFILTE FISH

12 ounces whitefish fillet, skin and all bones removed

12 ounces pike fillet, skin and all bones removed

3 medium onions, quartered, divided

1½ stalks celery, trimmed and chopped into 3-inch pieces

1½ medium carrots

3 large eggs, beaten

2 teaspoons sugar

1 teaspoon salt

¼ teaspoon freshly ground white pepper

⅓ cup olive oil

½ cup matzo meal

6 cups fish stock

APPLE-HORSERADISH SAUCE

2 tart apples, peeled, cored, and cut into wedges

¾ cup water

1 tablespoon fresh lemon juice

¼ cup sugar

¼ teaspoon ground cinnamon

⅛ teaspoon ground allspice

3 tablespoons prepared horseradish

TIMBALE ASSEMBLY

6 leaves romaine lettuce

¼ cup chopped fresh flat-leaf parsley

½ tart apple, cut into 12 thin wedges, for garnish

1 tablespoon fresh lemon juice

2 hard-cooked eggs, cut into wedges, for garnish

I like to shape gefilte fish using a timbale mold, but if you prefer, you can leave them in the traditional oval-shaped quenelle form. Whitefish is traditional, and so is pike or carp, but any other white-fleshed fish can be substituted for the pike or carp.

GEFILTE FISH

1. In a food processor, combine the fish, quarters from two of the onions, two-thirds of the chopped celery, and one carrot; puree until no large pieces of fish remain. Transfer the fish to a large bowl and add the eggs, sugar, salt, pepper, and olive oil. With a wire whisk, mix everything until incorporated. Add the matzo meal and continue to stir until everything is thoroughly blended. Cover and refrigerate for least 3 hours.

2. In a large stockpot, bring the fish stock and 6 cups water to a rolling boil. Add the remaining onion pieces, the half carrot, and chopped celery. Divide the fish mixture into six equal-size portions (the texture will be loose, which is what helps give the gefilte fish its light texture). To make quenelles: Use two spoons to shape each piece of gefilte fish into an oval and gently lower it into the boiling stock. If you will be making timbales, see below, form the fish mixture into a ball. Reduce the heat and simmer for 1½ hours. Remove the gefilte fish quenelles or balls and store, covered, in the refrigerator. Discard the cooking liquid with its vegetables.

APPLE-HORSERADISH SAUCE

1. In a medium saucepan, bring the apples, water, and lemon juice to a boil over medium heat. Stir in the sugar, cinnamon, and allspice and cook, stirring constantly, until the sugar dissolves and the apples are tender. Remove the mixture from the heat, transfer to a glass or ceramic bowl, and cover. Refrigerate until cool.

2. In a food processor, combine the apple mixture and horseradish. Puree until thoroughly combined. Serve the sauce cold or at room temperature. (The sauce can be stored, covered, in the refrigerator for up to 3 days.)

TIMBALE ASSEMBLY

1. To make the timbales, line a timbale mold or custard cup with plastic wrap and add some of the cooked gefilte fish. With the back of a spoon, gently press the fish down to shape it.

2. Unmold the fish onto a lettuce-lined plate and sprinkle with the parsley. Brush the apple slices with the lemon juice. To serve, garnish the gefilte fish with a wedge of hard-cooked egg, 2 apple slices, and the Apple-Horseradish Sauce. Serve immediately.

Roasted Beet Salad with Orange Dressing

For a less hectic holiday, roast and peel the beets one day ahead. Keep them sealed in a plastic bag in the refrigerator and slice them before serving.

ORANGE DRESSING

In a small glass or ceramic bowl, whisk together the orange juice, vinegar, and maple syrup. Slowly whisk in the olive oil. Season with salt and white pepper. Cover and refrigerate until ready to use.

BEETS

1. Heat the oven to 425°F. Tightly wrap the beets in double layers of heavy-duty foil and roast on a baking sheet placed on the middle rack of the oven until they are tender and a small knife easily pierces the flesh, 30 to 45 minutes for smaller beets (1 to 1½ hours for larger beets). Cool to warm in the foil, about 20 minutes.

2. When the beets are cool enough to handle, peel them, discarding the stems and root ends. Cut them crosswise into ⅛-inch-thick slices (you can use a mandolin slicer if you have one).

3. Brush some dressing on each plate and arrange the beet slices in a single layer on the plate. Brush the beets with more dressing. In a bowl, combine the oranges and fennel and gently toss with just enough dressing to lightly coat. Arrange the oranges and fennel on the plates. In the same bowl, toss the watercress with a light amount of dressing. Top the beets, oranges, and fennel with a small pile of watercress and garnish with fennel fronds. Serve immediately.

NOTE | Raw beets will keep for a few weeks, sealed in a plastic bag in the refrigerator. If you bought beets with greens attached, remove them before storing the beets, but don't throw them out! They're packed with nutrients and are delicious, but should be cooked soon after purchase. Just rinse them, cut them in ribbons, and sauté them in butter or olive oil with salt and pepper.

YIELD: 6 TO 8 SERVINGS

ORANGE DRESSING

1 tablespoon orange juice

2 tablespoons white wine vinegar

1 tablespoon maple syrup

¼ cup extra-virgin olive oil

Salt and freshly ground white pepper

BEETS

2 pounds beets, trimmed with 1 inch of stems still attached, and scrubbed (see note)

2 oranges, cut into sections

1 bulb fennel, thinly sliced, fronds reserved for garnish

2 bunches baby watercress

Honey Glazed Chicken with Rosemary, Lemon, and Garlic

1 (7-pound) roasting chicken

1 lemon

3 tablespoons minced fresh rosemary

5 medium garlic cloves, minced

2 tablespoons extra-virgin olive oil

Salt and freshly ground black pepper

¼ cup honey

¼ cup dry white wine

2 tablespoons brandy

About 1 cup low-sodium store-bought chicken broth or stock, or homemade

1 tablespoon cornstarch

Try adding peeled and quartered red-skin potatoes and baby carrots to the roasting pan about one hour before removing the chicken from the oven. You can even skip the gravy—it will still be delicious without it!

1. Heat the oven to 450°F. Rinse the chicken and pat it dry. Place the chicken in a roasting pan, preferably on a V-rack. Grate the zest from the lemon and reserve it; cut the lemon into quarters and reserve.

2. In a small bowl, mix the rosemary, garlic, lemon zest, and olive oil. Set aside 1 tablespoon of the mixture for the sauce and rub the remainder all over the chicken, placing some under the skin. Sprinkle the chicken with salt and pepper. Place the lemon quarters in the cavity of the chicken. Tie the legs together with string.

3. Place the chicken breast side down on the rack in the roasting pan and roast for 15 minutes. Reduce the oven temperature to 375°F and continue roasting for 45 minutes. Remove from the oven. Insert a large kitchen fork into the main cavity of the chicken and turn the chicken breast side up. Brush all over with the honey. Continue roasting until a meat thermometer inserted into the thickest part of the inner thigh registers 180°F, about 55 minutes longer. Lift the chicken and tilt it slightly to empty the juices from the cavity into the pan. Transfer the chicken to a serving platter and loosely tent it with foil to keep it warm.

4. Pour the pan juices into a large glass measuring cup. Spoon the fat off the top. Add the wine to the roasting pan and place over high heat. Bring to a boil, scraping up any browned bits, and cook, stirring, for 1 minute. Add the brandy to the pan and cook for 1 minute more. With a heatproof rubber spatula, scrape the wine mixture into the measuring cup with the pan juices. Add enough chicken broth to the cup to measure 1½ cups.

5. Transfer the broth mixture to a saucepan. Combine the cornstarch thoroughly with 1 tablespoon water, then stir this mixture together with the reserved 1 tablespoon rosemary-garlic oil. Whisk into the broth mixture. Place the broth mixture over medium heat and bring to a boil; reduce the heat to low and cook, stirring, until slightly thickened, about 2 minutes. Season with salt and pepper and pour through a fine sieve into a sauceboat. Slice the chicken and serve with the gravy.

Charoset

YIELD: 2 CUPS

2 medium apples, 1 tart (such as Granny Smith) and 1 sweet (such as McIntosh or Golden Delicious)

¼ cup finely chopped almonds and/or walnuts

½ cup finely chopped dates

1½ teaspoons ground cinnamon

¼ cup dry red wine

¼ cup sweet red wine

Prepared horseradish, for serving

Matzo, for serving

This tasty fruit, nut, and wine mixture is eaten during the Passover seder. It is a symbol of the mortar used by the Jewish people to build the cities of Egypt during their enslavement.

1. Peel the apples and grate them into a glass or ceramic bowl. Add the chopped almonds and/or walnuts, dates, and cinnamon; mix well.
2. Slowly stir in the wines until the mixture forms a paste. Cover and let stand for 3 to 6 hours, until the wine is absorbed by the other ingredients. Serve with horseradish on matzo.

Macaroons with Bittersweet Chocolate

YIELD: 2 DOZEN MACAROONS

4½ cups dried, shredded unsweetened coconut

3 large eggs

5 large egg yolks

1 cup sugar

⅓ cup good-quality honey

Pinch salt

Juice of ½ lemon

12 ounces bittersweet (not unsweetened) chocolate, finely chopped

These sweet macaroons with a bittersweet chocolate base are an essential ending to an elegant Passover meal.

1. Heat the oven to 325°F. Line two large baking sheets with nonstick silicone liners (such as Silpat) or parchment paper.
2. In a large bowl, stir together all the ingredients except the chocolate until combined. Drop the batter by rounded tablespoonfuls onto the prepared sheets, spacing the mounds about 2 inches apart. Bake the macaroons one sheet at a time, until the coconut is golden brown and the centers of the macaroons are set (they should still be moist inside), 18 to 22 minutes. Cool the macaroons on the sheet for 5 to 10 minutes before transferring them to a rack to finish cooling completely.
3. Clean the silicone liners and reposition them or reline the baking sheets with fresh parchment. Place three quarters of the chocolate in the top of a double boiler over simmering water. Heat the

chocolate, stirring occasionally, until it reaches about 110°F (just barely too hot to the touch). Remove the pan from the heat and stir in the remaining chocolate until smooth.

4. Dip the bottom of each macaroon into melted chocolate to a depth of ¼ inch. Place the dipped macaroons on the prepared baking sheets, chocolate side down. Chill until the chocolate is firm, about 1 hour. (The macaroons can be made up to 1 day ahead. Transfer them to an airtight container and keep refrigerated. Let stand at room temperature for 1 hour before serving.)

Easter is a joyous occasion—and we like to go a little overboard with it. Our staff always does an incredible job making sure our youngest passengers have a great time during holidays, but at Easter, crew members outdo themselves: They arrange for visits with the Easter bunny, conduct egg-decorating parties, and organize the most inspired Easter egg hunts imaginable. Plus, they get children into the kitchen for cookie decorating. | For the adults, Holland America Line's renowned culinary ingenuity makes Easter aboard one of our ships a memorably elegant and sophisticated holiday. While Easter doesn't command the flamboyant attention or excessive trappings of the Christmas season, it is the most important religious holiday of the Christian calendar. So, whether you celebrate this special Sunday on the high seas or at home, Easter calls for an exceptional meal. | In my many years working on ships, I've always felt that there is great synergy between the Easter holiday and a cruise. To me, both are about rejuvenating the spirit. Easter's position in late winter or early spring serves to reinforce the message of the promise of good things to come. Likewise, a cruise undoubtedly creates a rebirth of energy and an enthusiasm for life. | This Easter menu captures that enthusiasm. There's a delicacy to the subtle mix of tastes and textures that embody the gentleness of emergent spring. The tender peas in the soup offer up creamy sweetness and the first hint of the pale pastels that define the pleasing color palette of early springtime. The earthy redolence and succulence of spring lamb encrusted with fresh herbs is light, yet each bite brings a luxurious layering of richly complex flavor. The menu culminates with a burst of excitement—spiked with rum. This custard tart, taking its cues from the sun itself, shines with bright color and the tangy zest for life delivered by the beautiful blooming of spring.

EASTER DINNER

MENU

Chilled Pea Soup with Chives

• • •

Tomato Stack with Frisée, Bell Peppers, and Lemon Dressing

• • •

Herb-Crusted Roast Leg of Lamb with
Sautéed Potato Wedges, Green Beans, and Carrots

• • •

Rum Custard Tart with Mango and Kiwi

Chilled Pea Soup with Chives

YIELD: 4 TO 6 SERVINGS

1 tablespoon unsalted butter

1 small onion, chopped

1 tablespoon all-purpose flour

2 (14½-ounce) cans store-bought vegetable broth or low-sodium chicken broth or stock, or 3½ cups homemade

1 (10-ounce) package frozen peas or 1½ pounds fresh peas, shelled

1 tablespoon chopped fresh chives, plus extra for garnish

Salt and freshly ground white pepper

Sugar (optional)

¼ teaspoon Tabasco hot pepper sauce or lemon juice, plus extra if necessary

½ cup whole-milk yogurt or sour cream

Mint sprigs, for garnish

ou can substitute fresh mint or dill for the chives in this refreshing springtime soup.

1. In a heavy, medium saucepan, heat the butter over medium-low heat. Add the onion and cook, stirring, until translucent and softened, about 8 minutes. Add the flour and stir for 2 minutes.
2. Gradually stir in the broth. Add the peas and chopped chives. Cook, stirring, until the peas are very tender, about 15 minutes. Pour the soup through a sieve into a bowl, reserving the peas and liquid separately.
3. Prepare a large bowl of ice water; set aside. Transfer the peas to a blender, along with ½ cup of the cooking liquid. Puree until smooth. (When pureeing hot soups, fill the container no more than halfway and release one corner of the lid to prevent a vacuum effect. Place a kitchen towel over the top of the machine while you pulse.) Gradually blend in the remaining cooking liquid.
4. Immediately strain the soup through a fine sieve into a metal bowl. Taste and season with salt, pepper, sugar (if necessary for sweetness), and hot sauce or lemon juice to your taste (see note). Place the metal bowl in the bowl of ice water to chill the soup quickly, stirring every 15 minutes or so. When it is chilled, cover and refrigerate until it is completely cold, about 2 hours. (The soup can be stored this way for up to 2 days. If necessary, thin it with additional stock and adjust seasoning before serving.)
5. To serve, divide the soup among chilled bowls. Top each bowl with a dollop of yogurt, chopped chives, and mint sprigs; serve immediately.

NOTE The sweetnes and starch content of the peas may vary. Taste and adjust the seasoning as needed, including adding sugar for sweetness. The starch content will affect the thickness of the soup. If necessary, add more broth to attain the right consistency.

Tomato Stack with Frisée, Bell Peppers, and Lemon Dressing

S implicity and elegance should define springtime entertaining. This simple salad—with its dramatic vertical presentation—is another way to present tomatoes and lettuce.

YIELD: 4 SERVINGS

SALAD

SALAD

4 red and/or yellow globe tomatoes, peeled but not seeded (see Peeling Tomatoes, page 152)

¼ cup extra-virgin olive oil

1 tablespoon fresh lemon juice

Salt and freshly ground black pepper

¼ pound mixed baby greens (such as arugula, frisée, and red oak)

1. Slice each peeled, whole tomato crosswise into four slices. Keep the slices stacked on each other and set aside.
2. In a small glass or ceramic bowl, slowly whisk the oil into the lemon juice. Season with salt and pepper.
3. Place the greens in a large bowl and drizzle them with just enough of the dressing to lightly coat; toss gently.

BASIL LEAF GARNISH

BASIL LEAF GARNISH

8 large fresh basil leaves

2 cups vegetable oil, for deep-frying

1. Gently rinse and thoroughly dry the basil leaves. (Placing them on a kitchen towel in front of a fan will get them drier than a salad spinner.) Have a splatter screen ready. Line a baking sheet with paper towels.
2. In a 10- or 12-inch frying pan or cast-iron skillet, heat the vegetable oil over medium-high heat until a deep-frying thermometer registers 350°F (do not allow the oil to smoke).
3. When the oil is ready, add the basil leaves. Quickly cover the pan with the splatter screen and fry for 2 to 3 seconds, until the leaves turn a brilliant green and become crisp. With a slotted spoon, transfer the basil leaves to the prepared baking sheet. (Fried basil leaves should be used immediately, or else they lose their crispness.)

ASSEMBLY

ASSEMBLY

½ each red, yellow, and green bell peppers, diced

Thin toast, trimmed of crust and cut into triangles

Use tongs to place a portion of the dressed salad greens between each layer of tomato. Place each salad tomato on a plate and surround it with diced bell peppers. Place 2 fried basil leaves on the top of each tomato stack; serve with toast points.

Herb-Crusted Roast Leg of Lamb with Sautéed Potato Wedges, Green Beans, and Carrots

In honor of the spring season, try to buy genuine young baby carrots rather than the cut, tumbled pieces of adult carrots that are available year-round.

YIELD: 4 SERVINGS

LAMB

1 (5- to 6-pound) leg of lamb, trimmed of fat

12 small garlic cloves

⅓ cup Dijon mustard

2 tablespoons extra-virgin olive oil

1 tablespoon minced fresh rosemary

1 tablespoon minced fresh thyme

1 tablespoon minced fresh oregano

Salt and freshly ground black pepper

¾ cup chopped onion

½ cup chopped celery

⅓ cup chopped carrot

4 cups homemade dark chicken stock (see note)

POTATOES

1¼ pounds small potatoes, cut into quarters

1½ tablespoons unsalted butter

Salt and freshly ground black pepper

1 tablespoon minced fresh flat-leaf parsley

GREEN BEANS AND CARROTS

1 pound green beans, trimmed

12 ounces slender baby carrots, trimmed, leaving ½ inch of stems intact

2 tablespoons unsalted butter

½ teaspoon ground cumin

Salt and freshly ground black pepper

LAMB

1. Heat the oven to 350°F. Cut 12 slits into the lamb, about ½ inch in length. Push the garlic cloves into the slits. In a small bowl, combine the mustard, oil, rosemary, thyme, and oregano and rub the mixture all over the lamb. Season with salt and pepper.

2. Roast the lamb in a large flameproof roasting pan for 1 hour and 45 minutes, or until medium rare, basting occasionally with the pan juices. (An instant-read thermometer should register 150°F.) Transfer to a warmed serving platter and tent with foil to keep warm.

3. Spoon off most of the fat from the roasting pan and leave the meat juices behind. Place the pan over medium heat. Add the onion, celery, and carrot and cook, stirring, until browned. The meat juices should have caramelized on the bottom of the pan and separated from the fat. Spoon off any fat left in the pan.

4. Add the chicken stock and any juices from the resting lamb. Scrape up the browned bits from the bottom of the roasting pan and stir to dissolve them. Bring to a simmer and cook, stirring, until the liquid is reduced by one-third. Adjust the seasonings and keep warm.

POTATOES

1. In a steamer placed over boiling water, steam the potatoes, covered, for 10 minutes, or until they are almost tender. Remove from the steamer and let cool. (The potatoes can be prepared to this point 1 day ahead; cover and refrigerate them, then proceed to the next step just before serving.)

2. Just before serving, in a large nonstick skillet, melt the butter over medium-high heat. Add the potatoes and season with salt and pepper. Sauté the potatoes until crisp and golden, about 7 minutes. Sprinkle with the parsley.

GREEN BEANS AND CARROTS

1. Bring a large pot of salted water to a boil and prepare a bowl of ice water. Add the green beans to the boiling water and cook until crisp-

tender, about 3 minutes (taste one to check tenderness). With a slotted spoon or strainer, remove the green beans and immediately place them in the bowl of ice water to stop the cooking. Transfer them from the ice water to a bowl; set aside. Repeat the process with the baby carrots, cooking them for 2 minutes; store the carrots separately. (The vegetables can be prepared to this point up to 4 hours ahead and refrigerated, covered.)

2. Just before serving, divide the butter between two skillets and heat it over medium heat. Add the reserved green beans to one skillet and the carrots to the other. Sauté the vegetables, stirring gently, until they are heated through, about 2 to 3 minutes. Toss the carrots with the cumin. Transfer the vegetables to separate bowls and season with salt and pepper.

ASSEMBLY

Strain the juices from the reserved jus through a fine sieve into a warmed sauceboat. Serve the lamb with the gravy, potatoes, and vegetables alongside.

NOTE Dark chicken stock is a very rich stock made from roasted chicken bones. It adds great depth to this dish.

Rum Custard Tart with Mango and Kiwi

YIELD: 12 SERVINGS

CUSTARD

6 large egg yolks

½ cup sugar

¼ cup cornstarch

1½ cups whole milk

½ cup heavy cream

1 vanilla bean, split lengthwise

1 tablespoon dark rum

CRUST

1½ cups all-purpose flour

2 tablespoons sugar

Pinch salt

10 tablespoons (1¼ sticks) chilled unsalted butter, cut into ½-inch pieces

2 tablespoons (or more) ice water

1 large egg yolk

ASSEMBLY

3 mangoes, peeled, halved, and cut crosswise into ¼-inch-thick slices

1 to 2 strawberries, hulled and very thinly sliced (optional)

2 kiwis, trimmed, peeled, and thinly sliced

¼ cup apricot preserves, melted and strained through a sieve

I f you make the filling the day before and the crust in the morning, this tart will come together very easily when you need to serve it.

CUSTARD

1. In a large bowl, combine the egg yolks, sugar, and cornstarch; whisk until light in color and well blended; set aside.
2. In a heavy, medium saucepan, bring the milk and cream to a simmer over medium heat. As it heats, use a blunt-ended knife to scrape the seeds from the vanilla bean into the pan and then add the whole bean, too.
3. As soon as the milk mixture simmers, remove the vanilla bean. Gradually whisk 1 cup of the milk mixture into the yolk mixture in a slow stream, then add the remaining milk, whisking constantly. With a spatula, scrape the custard back into the saucepan and cook it over medium heat, whisking constantly, until it becomes thick and starts to bubble, about 8 minutes. Quickly transfer it to a medium bowl. Allow the custard to cool slightly and whisk in the rum. Cover the surface directly with plastic wrap (to keep a skin from forming) and refrigerate it until cold, at least 6 hours. (The custard can keep, covered, in the refrigerator for up to 24 hours.)

CRUST

1. In a food processor with the knife blade attached, combine the flour, sugar, and salt; pulse until blended.
2. Add the butter and pulse until the mixture resembles coarse meal. In a small bowl, whisk 2 tablespoons ice water with the egg yolk. Add the yolk mixture 1 tablespoon at a time to the flour mixture, pulsing with minimal short pulses until moist clumps form. If the dough is dry at that point, add more water by teaspoonfuls, but do not overmix.
3. Gather the dough into a ball; flatten it into a disk. Wrap the disk in plastic wrap and refrigerate until it is firm enough to roll, about 1 hour. (If the dough is chilled overnight, let it stand 30 minutes at room temperature before rolling.)
4. Heat the oven to 400°F. On a lightly floured surface, with a floured rolling pin, roll the disk into a 13- to 14-inch round. Transfer the dough round to an 11-inch tart pan with a removable bottom. Press the dough onto the bottom and up the side of the pan folding in the

overhang to form double thick sides. Pierce the crust all over with a
fork and freeze it for 30 minutes.

5. Line the tart shell with foil and fill it with pie weights or dry beans.
Bake for 20 minutes. Remove the foil and weights and bake about
15 minutes longer or until golden. (Cover the rim of the tart with
foil if it browns too quickly.) If the center of the crust puffs up
during baking, gently press it down with the back of a spoon. Cool
the crust in the pan on a wire rack for about 30 minutes.

ASSEMBLY

1. Spoon the custard into the baked tart shell and spread evenly. Blot
the mango slices with a paper towel to remove excess moisture and
arrange them in overlapping slices on top of the tart, inserting slices
of strawberry (if using) for added color. Arrange the kiwi slices in
the center.

2. Brush the apricot preserves over the fruit. Remove the tart from the
side of the pan and place it, still on its base, on a serving platter. (If
you don't need to serve it right away, cover and refrigerate it for up
to 2 hours.)

On any of our cruises, every mom gets to enjoy the ultimate indulgence: a chance to pamper herself and focus on her own well-being. You can always tell which guests have just paid a visit to the ship's Greenhouse Spa and Salon—they absolutely glow. Being able to spend some time rejuvenating mind and body is undoubtedly uplifting, and certainly the most oft-purchased gifts for Mother's Day during a cruise are certificates for manicures, pedicures, facials, wraps, and other spa treatments. | This menu for Mother's Day is designed around the idea of total beauty. Naturally, I think all menus should be as pleasing to the eye as to the palate, but I selected recipes and presentations for this menu that are particularly lovely to behold, because the special women in our lives invariably notice and appreciate the little beautiful extras: a single rose on the tray upon which breakfast is being delivered; the hand-drawn "World's Best Mom" sign lovingly made as a placemat; the tangle of flowers—and some weeds—picked by little hands with the greatest of care. | This menu should not only make Mom feel good because it's a celebration in her honor, but also because it honors what's good for her. Taking its cues from spa cuisine, each dish is designed to be fresh and refreshing yet thoroughly satisfying. Frequently, brunch spreads—while delicious and indulgent—can be filled with choices that are dense with calories and fat. Such typical brunch buffet feasts of sausage, strata, pasta, potatoes, doughnuts, Danish, and other similar fare are often topped off with a heaping helping of guilt. | What we have here is anything but a run-back-to-the-treadmill–type brunch. There's no remorse on this menu for mothers. Instead, this sophisticated feast serves up foods that are healthy and light and that will make any mom—and everyone else at the brunch table—feel as vibrant and pampered as they would if they just stepped out of the most wonderfully luxuriant visit to the spa.

MOTHER'S DAY BRUNCH

M E N U

Mimosa

• • •

*Berry Salad with Greens, Radicchio,
and Balsamic Vinaigrette*

• • •

*Poached Sole and Salmon Braid with
Leek and Carrot Compote*

• • •

Strawberries Romanoff

Mimosa

YIELD: 8 SERVINGS

See photograph, page 11

C hildren will love drinking theirs with sparkling grape juice. If you'd like, drop a berry or grape into each glass for added color.

Combine the orange juice and pineapple juice in a half-gallon pitcher and chill. When ready to serve, pour in the chilled Champagne or sparkling grape juice or ginger ale. To serve, pour the mimosa into wine glasses. Garnish each glass with an orange slice.

12 ounces (1½ cups) orange juice

24 ounces (3 cups) canned unsweetened pineapple juice

1 (750 milliliter) bottle extra-dry Champagne or sparkling wine, or 1 (1-liter) bottle sparkling grape juice or ginger ale, chilled

8 orange slices, for garnish

Berry Salad with Greens, Radicchio, and Balsamic Vinaigrette

YIELD: 4 TO 6 SERVINGS

B erries and balsamic vinegar make perfect sense in a salad, since it's a classic dessert combination, too. For the best results, try to use a good-quality balsamic.

1. Chop the strawberries finely in a food processor or mini chopper. Push them through a medium sieve until you have 3 tablespoons strawberry puree.
2. In a small bowl, combine the strawberry puree, vinegar, mustard, and shallot. Slowly whisk in the olive oil. Season with salt and pepper.
3. To serve, divide the greens and mixed berries among salad plates. Drizzle with the berry vinaigrette. Sprinkle with the almond slices and serve.

5 medium strawberries, hulled

1 tablespoon balsamic vinegar

1 teaspoon Dijon mustard

1 tablespoon minced shallot

¼ cup extra-virgin olive oil

Sea salt and freshly ground black pepper

4 cups baby spinach leaves

1 bunch arugula

⅓ head radicchio, leaves separated

2 cups mixed fresh berries (such as strawberries, raspberries, blueberries, blackberries, and pitted cherries)

½ cup sliced almonds, toasted

Poached Sole and Salmon Braid with Leek and Carrot Compote

YIELD: 4 SERVINGS

½ pound carrots, trimmed, divided

3 medium leeks, white and pale green parts only, washed, divided

1 tablespoon olive oil

Salt and freshly ground white pepper

12 ounces sole, cut into 8 (4-inch-by-1-inch) strips

12 ounces salmon fillet, cut into 8 (4-inch-by-1-inch) strips

2 tablespoons fresh lemon juice

½ cup fresh orange juice

½ cup dry white wine

1 tablespoon white wine vinegar

1 shallot, finely chopped

3 strips orange zest, removed with a vegetable peeler

1 teaspoon minced garlic

½ teaspoon dried thyme

¼ cup light cream

For a pretty presentation, press a portion of saffron rice or brown rice into a ramekin and unmold it off center onto the plate. Place the fish alongside and surround it with steamed asparagus or haricots verts.

1. Set aside 1 carrot and 1 leek. Cut the remaining carrots and 2 leeks into 1-inch pieces.

2. In a large pot with water just to cover, boil the cut carrots and leeks until the carrots are tender and easily pierced with the tip of a knife, 10 to 12 minutes. Drain (reserving the cooking water) and transfer the leeks and carrots to a food processor fitted with a steel blade; puree. Transfer to a saucepan and stir in some of the reserved cooking water for a looser consistency; set aside. (The carrot and leek puree can be stored, covered, in the refrigerator for up to 2 days.)

3. Cut the reserved carrot and leek into thin strips about 2½ inches long. In a nonstick skillet, heat the oil over medium heat. Add the carrot and leek and sauté until the leeks are tender, about 5 minutes; season with salt and white pepper. Remove from the heat and set aside.

4. In a glass or ceramic bowl, gently toss the sole and salmon with the lemon juice (the lemon juice will help firm up the flesh of the fish slightly so it will be easier to weave). Set aside for 5 minutes.

5. Cut four 5-inch squares of parchment. Place a square on your work surface and on top of it weave 2 sole strips and 2 salmon strips into a simple lattice. Season with salt and white pepper and set aside. Repeat with the remaining parchment and fish strips.

6. In a skillet large enough to hold two portions of fish, bring the orange juice, wine, vinegar, shallot, orange zest, garlic, and thyme to a boil over medium-high heat. Continue to boil, shaking the skillet, until most of the liquid is evaporated. Add 1 cup water, return the mixture to a boil, and carefully add two portions of fish right on their parchment paper base (keeping them on the parchment will make handling easier). Immediately reduce the heat to low and poach the fish, partially covered, at a bare simmer until just opaque inside, 6 to 8 minutes.

7. With a large slotted spatula, transfer each portion of fish (discard the parchment) to a separate plate; cover and keep warm. Repeat the poaching process with the remaining two portions of fish.

8. Boil the poaching liquid until reduced by half; strain it through a
   fine sieve into a glass measuring cup. Meanwhile, separately reheat
   the reserved carrot and leek puree and the reserved carrot and leek
   strips. Stir the cream into the carrot and leek puree and just enough
   poaching liquid to thin the mixture to a sauce consistency. Return
   to a simmer and season with salt and white pepper.

9. To serve, spoon the sauce over the fish and top it with the sautéed
   leek and carrot strips.

Strawberries Romanoff

Antonin Carême, the most important chef in post-Revolution France, created this dish when he traveled to Russia to work for Tsar Alexander.

1. In a glass or ceramic bowl, combine the strawberries, 2 tablespoons Grand Marnier, and sugar. Cover and allow to marinate in the refrigerator for 2 hours.
2. In a chilled mixing bowl, whip the heavy cream until it forms stiff peaks. In another chilled bowl, beat the vanilla ice cream with a wooden spoon. With a rubber spatula, fold the whipped cream, lemon juice, and remaining Grand Marnier into the ice cream; blend until the mixture is smooth.
3. Arrange some of the strawberries on the bottom of four parfait glasses, followed by some of the whipped ice cream. Top with more strawberries and more whipped ice cream and garnish each with a mint sprig. Serve at once.

NOTE | If you don't have parfait glasses, iced-tea glasses or even cereal bowls will make a fine substitute.

YIELD: 4 SERVINGS

3 pints fresh strawberries, rinsed, hulled, and halved

½ cup Grand Marnier, divided

1 tablespoon sugar

1 cup heavy cream

1 pint vanilla ice cream, softened

¼ cup fresh lemon juice

4 mint sprigs, for garnish

No matter where our ships are in the world, or how hot—or not—the climate is through which we are traveling, when Memorial Day comes, Americans know that it's the official kickoff of summer. When putting together this menu for Memorial Day, I did so with the thought that every dish on it should be one that you can entertain with all summerlong. | The centerpiece of this menu is what I think of as a quintessentially American dish, a burger. To me, hamburgers never taste quite as good as they do during those first few cookouts of summer. The recipe here is for a burger topped with mozzarella (a favorite grill item onboard our ships year-round), but the important thing to note in this recipe is the burger itself: It's not just beef, but has ground pork mixed in; this gives grilled burgers more succulence and flavor. If you do the same at home, you will make the best burgers around, and unless you tell them, none of your guests will know quite what magic you've worked to make a better burger. | The pesto is another recipe that can be a staple in your weeknight dinners: make it, store it, and pull it out for an easy summer supper. The grilled vegetable salad here is simple to make when you've got the grill fired up; the flavors and textures are terrific and the presentation is easy to replicate yet looks impressive. Keep an eye on what's best at the farmer's market and take advantage of the opportunity to make this salad with the freshest of fresh summer vegetables—it's sensational. | Summer always seems to go by faster than we want it to—so this menu will help you celebrate summer's unique bounty while it lasts.

MEMORIAL DAY

M E N U

Sangria

. . .

Margarita

. . .

Char-Grilled Vegetable Salad with Balsamic Marinade

. . .

Beef and Pork Burgers with Pesto, Mozzarella,
Tomatoes, and Steak Fries

. . .

Summer Pudding with Berries

Sangria

YIELD: 4 TO 6 SERVINGS

2 large oranges, well washed

1 large lemon, well washed and sliced

¼ cup superfine sugar

2 red apples, well washed, cored, and chopped

¼ cup triple sec

¼ cup brandy, or a mixture of half brandy and half Grand Marnier

1 (750 milliliter) bottle inexpensive dry red wine (such as rioja), chilled

½ cup sparkling water, chilled (optional)

6 ice cubes

I've suggested that you add a touch of Grand Marnier if you've got it on hand; it will impart a subtle citrusy flavor and aroma. The option of adding sparkling water is there because it will also help lift the aromas to the nose, though it can be omitted completely if you'd prefer. In addition to citrus fruits, almost any fresh fruit except bananas can be added to sangria. Try pitted cherries, sliced peaches, or diced pears or plums. Stir in softer fruits right before serving so they remain intact.

1. Slice one orange and juice the other; set them aside separately.
2. In a large pitcher, combine the orange slices, lemon slices, and sugar. With a wooden spoon, mash the fruit gently until some juice is released and the sugar dissolves but the fruit isn't totally crushed. Stir in the apples, the reserved fresh orange juice, triple sec, brandy, and wine. Refrigerate for at least 2 hours or overnight.
3. Right before serving, stir in the sparkling water (if using) and the ice cubes, making sure to reach the fruit that has settled on the bottom. Divide the sangria among glasses—let a few pieces of fruit pour into each one—and serve immediately.

Margarita

W hat better way to kick off the summer than a drink that for many people means "party"? Margaritas served straight up (rather than blended with ice) are gaining in popularity.

1. Salt the rim of your glass (if using): Rub a lime wedge around the rim of a pint glass and then dip the rim (or just half the rim) in a pile of coarse salt on a plate; set aside.
2. Make the drink: In a second pint glass, press the lime wedges with a muddler. Fill the glass with ice. Add the tequila, triple sec, and sour mix. Cap with a Boston-style shaker can (or pour into a cocktail shaker) and shake vigorously. Pour the margarita into the prepared pint glass. Top with the soda water and stir. Serve with a straw.

HOMEMADE SOUR MIX

Although you can store it, refrigerated, for a week or two, the fresher the sour mix, the fresher tasting your drink will be. It is ideal if you can combine the simple syrup and citrus juice in the quantity you need right before you start to make your drinks. Whether you make it with lime or lemon juice depends on the overall flavor desired for the drink you're making; for example, in margarita mix, you use lime juice; for a whiskey sour you'd use lemon.

YIELD: 2 CUPS

2 cups sugar

2 cups water

1 cup fresh Key lime or Persian lime juice, or lemon juice

1. Begin by making simple syrup: In a large, heavy pan, combine the sugar and water. Bring to a boil, stirring to dissolve the sugar. Boil for 2 minutes. Remove the pan from the heat and let the syrup cool. Transfer it to a clean bottle or container and chill, covered, until needed. (This quantity of simple syrup will yield a bit more than you need for the sour mix; see note.)
2. For the sour mix: In a jar with a lid, combine 1 cup simple syrup (save the remainder for another use) and lime or lemon juice. (The sour mix will keep, chilled, for up to 2 weeks; see headnote.)

YIELD: 1 COCKTAIL

Coarse salt, for the rim (optional)

2 lime wedges

1½ ounces tequila

1½ ounces triple sec

2 ounces Homemade Sour Mix made with Key limes (below)

1 ounce soda water

NOTE | Simple syrup, an ingredient useful for making cocktails and fresh lemonade, or for sweetening beverages such as coffee and iced tea, can be made in any quantity you need by combining equal parts sugar and water and following the instructions in step 1 left. It may be made two weeks ahead and stored, covered, in the refrigerator. Prepared simple syrup is also available at the grocery store.

Char-Grilled Vegetable Salad with Balsamic Marinade

Add or substitute other vegetables if you like, such as baby eggplant halved vertically, carrots cut on a deep diagonal into ¼-inch-thick slices, even portobello mushroom caps (slice the mushrooms after grilling them whole).

1. Heat a charcoal, gas, or electric grill to medium hot (when you can hold your hand 5 inches above the rack for 3 to 4 seconds).

2. Make the lemon garnish and marinade: With a sharp knife, trim the top and bottom off 1 lemon. Stand it upright and cut downward to remove the rind and pith in thick strips. Working over a bowl, cut between the membranes to release the segments. If possible, transfer 1 tablespoon lemon juice from the segments to a glass measuring cup; if not, squeeze the needed juice from the second lemon. Cover the lemon segments with plastic wrap and reserve them for the garnish. Stir the balsamic vinegar and garlic into the lemon juice. Slowly whisk in the olive oil. Season the vinaigrette with salt and pepper, reserve.

3. Place the asparagus, zucchini, yellow squash, bell peppers, red onion slices, and tomato slices on a baking sheet. Brush with vinaigrette and season with salt and pepper. Grill everything except for the tomatoes until nicely browned and just cooked through: Place the onions on the grill (they will take 6 minutes per side); a few minutes later, add the zucchini, yellow squash, and peppers and grill them 4 minutes per side. When you turn the squash to cook the second side, add the asparagus to the grill and cook it 2 minutes on each side.

4. To serve, place a tomato slice on each plate and top it with assorted grilled vegetables. Garnish with the basil sprigs and reserved lemon segments and serve.

YIELD: 4 SERVINGS

1 to 2 large lemons

1 tablespoon balsamic vinegar

1 teaspoon minced garlic

6 tablespoons olive oil

Salt and freshly ground black pepper

12 medium asparagus spears, base trimmed and pared down if thick

1 zucchini, no more than 8 inches long, trimmed and sliced lengthwise into ¼-inch-thick slices

1 yellow squash, trimmed and sliced lengthwise into ¼-inch-thick slices

2 red bell peppers, stemmed, seeded, and quartered

1 large red onion, cut into ¾-inch-thick rounds

2 large yellow tomatoes, sliced

4 sprigs basil, for garnish

Beef and Pork Burgers with Pesto, Mozzarella, Tomatoes, and Steak Fries

YIELD: 4 BURGERS

STEAK FRIES

3 large Idaho potatoes, washed and scrubbed clean

1 cup vegetable oil, for deep-frying

Salt and freshly ground black pepper

BURGERS

1 tablespoon olive oil

2 tablespoons minced yellow onion

1 pound ground beef chuck

8 ounces ground pork

Salt and freshly ground black pepper

4 sturdy hamburger buns or kaiser rolls

4 slices Bibb or butter lettuce

1 large red tomato, cut into ¼-inch-thick slices

1 large yellow tomato, cut into ¼-inch-thick slices

4 (⅓-inch-thick) slices fresh mozzarella cheese

1 medium red onion, thinly sliced

½ cup pesto, store-bought or homemade

4 basil sprigs, for garnish

You can cook these burgers on a well-seasoned flat griddle, too, or in a large nonstick sauté pan over medium-high heat. The timing will be about the same.

STEAK FRIES

1. Heat the oven to 250°F. With a sharp knife, cut the potatoes into ¾-inch-thick slices. Cut the slices into ¼-inch-thick strips. (At this stage, the strips can be stored, covered with cold water, in the refrigerator for up to 3 hours.)
2. In a large, heavy-duty skillet or large sauté pan, heat the oil over high heat until a deep-frying thermometer registers 375°F (do not allow the oil to smoke). While the oil is heating, drain and thoroughly dry the potatoes on paper towels.
3. Add half the potatoes to the oil and cook until crispy and brown, 6 to 7 minutes. With a slotted spatula, transfer the cooked fries to a plate lined with paper towels. Season with salt and pepper, transfer to a baking sheet, and place in the oven to keep warm. Repeat with the remaining potatoes. The fries will hold for up to 30 minutes in the oven while you grill the burgers.

BURGERS

1. In a small sauté pan, heat the olive oil over medium heat. When it is hot but not smoking, add the onion and sauté lightly until translucent, about 3 minutes. Transfer the onion to a small plate and place it, uncovered, in the refrigerator for a few minutes to cool.
2. In a stainless steel bowl, gently but thoroughly combine the cooled onions, beef, and pork, mixing with a fork until just incorporated. Form the meat mixture into four 1-inch-thick patties. Place the burgers on a platter and cover them with plastic wrap. (They can be stored this way for up to 6 hours in the refrigerator.)
3. Heat a charcoal, gas, or electric grill to medium hot (when you can hold your hand 5 inches above the rack for 3 to 4 seconds). Season the patties with salt and pepper and grill them for 7 to 8 minutes on each side, or until an instant-read meat thermometer inserted through the side of the patty into the thickest part registers at least 160°F.
4. Toast the buns, cut side down, on the grill until golden brown, about 1 minute. Serve the burgers in the buns with lettuce, tomatoes, mozzarella, red onion slices, and pesto. Place a serving of fries beside each burger and garnish the plate with a basil sprig.

Summer Pudding with Berries

T his British-style "pudding" isn't steamed like its wintertime counterpart. Instead it depends solely on the oozing juice of fresh, ripe fruit for its moisture. Quick and easy, it is the perfect dessert to toss together after a morning of berry picking.

YIELD: 4 TO 6 SERVINGS

4 pints mixed ripe summer berries (such as strawberries, raspberries, blueberries, blackberries, black or red currants), gently rinsed and dried, and strawberries hulled and sliced

⅔ cup sugar

1 tablespoon fresh lemon juice

12 (½-inch-thick) slices good-quality white bread, challah, or brioche, left out overnight to stale

Whipped cream, for serving

Mint sprigs, for garnish

1. In a large saucepan over medium heat, combine the berries, sugar, and 1 tablespoon water. Gently cook, stirring, until the berries have released their juice and the sugar has dissolved, about 5 minutes. Remove from the heat and stir in the lemon juice. Let cool to room temperature.

2. Lightly grease cereal bowls with butter and line them with plastic wrap, making sure the plastic wrap lies flat against the surface of the bowl, leaving no air space (the butter helps the wrap stay in place). Remove the crusts from the bread and line each bowl with the bread slices, trimming them to fit and ensuring there are no gaps. Spoon some fruit and juices into each bowl, add a layer of bread, add more fruit, and finish with a slice of bread trimmed to completely cover the top.

3. Loosely cover each bowl with plastic wrap and place a saucer and a weight (like a can of beans) on top. Refrigerate for at least 8 hours and up to 24 hours. To serve, remove the weight, saucer, and plastic wrap and unmold onto individual plates. Serve with whipped cream and garnish with mint sprigs.

Among the great pleasures of my career working aboard cruise ships is the unique perspective of being around families while they are on vacation. Time spent with loved ones away from day-to-day cares is so precious, and seeing family members enjoy themselves and one another, laughing, eating, and having new experiences, is heart-warming. | The Father's Day menu celebrates the joyful dynamics of that coming together in a different context. The meal pairs some sophisticated ingredients, like lobster, with a homey presentation—in a macaroni-and-cheese bake. You'll also find the caramelized goodness of grilled pineapple paired up with the tropical flavors of mango whipped cream and a lime-butter sauce. | Because I was putting this menu together in honor of fathers, I also had some fun playing with the clichéd notions of "guy food." I incorporated ingredients that would probably be at the top of the list of ingredients that are popular among dads of all ages. Tabasco and Worcestershire sauce flavor the soup and give it some extra kick. The onion sauce in the Lobster Macaroni and Cheese gives a no-fuss, familiar feel to this upscale take on a favorite dish. This is a fun menu that is packed with delicious flavor. | Togetherness and fun should never be underrated. Personally, my ideal Father's Day doesn't feature fancy gifts or surprises; it is just about being together with my three children, Magnus, Kenneth, and Kristina. And if at the end of the day, one of my children tells me, "I had a good time, Dad. It was fun," I've received the best gift of all.

Father's Day

M E N U

Chilled Red Pepper Soup with Roasted Red Bell Peppers

· · ·

Salade Niçoise

· · ·

Lobster Macaroni and Cheese

· · ·

Grilled Pineapple with Mango Whipped Cream
and Lime-Butter Sauce

Chilled Red Pepper Soup with Roasted Red Bell Peppers

9 large red bell peppers, divided

2 tablespoons extra-virgin olive oil

1 large onion, chopped

6 medium garlic cloves, minced

1 cup dry white wine

4 cups low-sodium store-bought chicken broth or stock, or homemade

1 (28-ounce) can whole tomatoes, drained, seeded, and chopped

2 teaspoons Worcestershire sauce

2 teaspoons Tabasco hot pepper sauce

1 tablespoon rice wine vinegar

Salt and freshly ground black pepper

Fresh thyme sprigs, for garnish

This soup is just as delicious served hot as it is chilled. In either case, be sure to season it well to bring out all its flavors.

1. Roast two of the red bell peppers (see sidebar). Seed the peppers and cut them into strips; reserve them, covered, in the refrigerator.
2. Core, seed, and chop the remaining 7 bell peppers. In a large soup pot, heat the oil over medium heat. Add the chopped bell peppers, onion, and garlic. Cook, stirring, until the vegetables soften, 8 to 10 minutes. Add the wine and simmer until the liquid is reduced by half. Add the chicken broth and tomatoes and bring to a boil. Reduce the heat and simmer, stirring occasionally, for 30 minutes.
3. Prepare a large bowl of ice water. Transfer the soup in batches to a blender and puree until smooth. (When pureeing hot soups, fill the container no more than halfway and release one corner of the lid to prevent a vacuum effect. Place a kitchen towel over the top of the machine while you pulse.) Immediately strain the soup through a fine sieve into a clean saucepan. Bring it to a simmer over medium-low heat. Cook, stirring, for 5 minutes. Add the Worcestershire sauce, Tabasco, and vinegar. Season with salt and pepper.
4. Transfer the soup to a large glass or ceramic bowl. Place the bowl in the ice water to chill the soup quickly. When it is chilled, cover and refrigerate until it is completely cold. To serve, divide the soup among chilled soup bowls and garnish with the reserved roasted red pepper strips and thyme sprigs.

ROASTING PEPPERS

Working with two peppers at a time, place the peppers directly on the burner grate of a gas stove and char, turning them often with long tongs, until they are blackened on all sides. (Alternatively, roast them in a 500°F oven, stem-end down, on a baking sheet until uniformly charred, 8 to 10 minutes.) When the peppers are charred, immediately remove them from the heat and place them in a heavy-duty brown-paper bag, close it tightly, and secure it with a clip or rubber band. Let the peppers steam in the bag for 10 minutes. When the peppers are cool enough to handle, peel off the charred skin and discard it; use a blunt knife to remove any bits of skin that adhere.

Salade Niçoise

Traditionally, this salad also includes slices of steamed potato, which makes it filling enough for a luncheon. I've left them out here so it can be enjoyed as a light salad appetizer.

LEMON PARSLEY DRESSING

In a glass or ceramic bowl, combine the lemon zest and salt, mashing them together with the back of a spoon. Add 1 tablespoon fresh lemon juice and the mustard, stirring well to combine. Slowly whisk in the oil. Season with pepper and more lemon juice, if desired. Stir in the minced parsley, cover, and refrigerate until ready to serve.

SALAD

1. Bring a large pot of salted water to a boil and prepare a bowl of ice water. Add the green beans to the boiling water and cook until crisp-tender, 3 to 4 minutes (taste one to check tenderness). Drain and transfer the beans to the ice water to cool. Drain and pat dry.

2. In a large glass or ceramic bowl, combine the beans, onion, tuna, and capers. Add half the dressing and toss gently, leaving the tuna in large chunks if possible. Let marinate, covered, in the refrigerator for 1 hour. Drain and reserve the excess dressing.

3. To serve, arrange the greens on plates and sprinkle with some dressing. Top with the tuna mixture. Toss the tomato wedges with some dressing and place them on the plates. Garnish with the egg wedges, anchovies, and olives and serve immediately.

YIELD: 8 SERVINGS

LEMON PARSLEY DRESSING

Grated zest and juice of 1 large lemon

¼ teaspoon salt

2 teaspoons Dijon mustard

⅔ cup grapeseed or sunflower oil

Freshly ground black pepper

2 teaspoons minced fresh flat-leaf parsley

SALAD

½ pound green beans

1 whole red onion, halved and thinly sliced

1 (12-ounce) can oil-packed tuna, drained well

2 tablespoons drained capers in brine (chopped if large)

¾ pound mixed spring greens (such as arugula, mizuna, tatsoi, oakleaf, red chard, radicchio, or baby mustard greens)

2 Roma tomatoes, cored and quartered

4 hard-cooked eggs, peeled and quartered

10 anchovy fillets

1 cup niçoise olives

Lobster Macaroni and Cheese

CREAM SAUCE

12 tablespoons (1½ sticks) salted butter

¼ pound white or sweet onion, very finely minced

5 cups heavy cream

¼ teaspoon kosher salt

⅛ teaspoon freshly ground white pepper

LOBSTER AND MACARONI

12 tablespoons sea salt

4 live (1-pound) chicken lobsters, or 14 ounces cooked lobster meat

3 ounces sharp cheddar cheese, shredded

3 ounces Asiago cheese, grated

1 cup prepared garlic-seasoned croutons, crushed finely

1 pound dried large elbow macaroni

6 ounces grated Italian fontina cheese

1 tablespoon plus 1 teaspoon minced fresh tarragon leaves

6 ounces Délice de Bourgogne, sliced (optional, see note)

Some supermarkets have large steamers behind the fish counter and will steam your lobsters for you while you wait. Be sure to tell them you'd like the lobsters par-cooked, because the lobster meat will cook for another minute or so in the sauce before serving.

CREAM SAUCE

1. In a large saucepan, heat the butter over medium heat. Reduce the heat to low and add the onion. Cook, stirring, until the onion softens, 5 to 8 minutes. (Do not let the onion brown.)

2. Add the cream and bring the sauce to a simmer. Continue to simmer for 45 minutes, stirring often to avoid scorching, until the cream is slowly reduced by about 20 percent.

3. Meanwhile, prepare a large bowl of ice water. Remove the cream sauce from the heat and add the salt and pepper. Transfer the sauce to a metal bowl. Place the bowl in the ice water to chill the sauce quickly. Stir the sauce often to ensure that the butter doesn't separate from the sauce. When cooled, cover and refrigerate until ready to use.

LOBSTER AND MACARONI

1. Cook the lobster: Bring 6 quarts water to a boil in a large pot filled no more than three-quarters full and add 6 tablespoons of the sea salt. When the water is at a rolling boil, add 2 lobsters, heads first. Cook for 3½ minutes, loosely covering the pot with a lid, then drain and cool at room temperature. Allow the water to return to a boil and repeat the process with the remaining 2 lobsters.

2. When the lobster is still slightly warm, remove the claws with the knuckles attached. Remove the meat from the knuckles and claws and the cartilage from the claw meat. Using a large knife, split the lobster in half lengthwise, beginning at the tail end. Remove the tail meat. Remove the intestine from the tail meat and cut all the lobster meat into 1-inch chunks. Squeeze the meat out of the legs with a rolling pin. Cover the lobster meat with plastic wrap and refrigerate. (The recipe can be prepared up to this point 1 day in advance.)

3. Heat the broiler. In a bowl, combine the cheddar, Asiago, and croutons. Cover and refrigerate until ready to use.

4. Cook the macaroni in a stockpot of boiling salted water until tender but firm, 6 to 8 minutes. Meanwhile, in a saucepan, bring the

reserved cream sauce to a boil and reduce by about 10 percent. Stir in the fontina until melted, then add the reserved lobster and tarragon and cook, stirring gently, until the lobster is heated through, about 1 minute.

5. When the macaroni is cooked, drain it and transfer it to a large bowl. Pour the lobster sauce over the macaroni and toss gently to coat. Pour the mixture into a large ovenproof casserole dish or divide it among individual ovenproof dishes. Sprinkle with the reserved cheese and crouton mixture. Broil the lobster macaroni and cheese about 3 inches from the heat until the top starts to slightly brown and becomes crisp, about 1½ minutes (watch carefully so the topping doesn't burn). Immediately top the casserole with slices of Délice de Bourgogne (if using). Serve at once.

NOTE Délice de Bourgogne is a triple-cream cow's-milk cheese with a subtle complexity in flavor and melt-in-your-mouth texture.

Grilled Pineapple with Mango Whipped Cream and Lime-Butter Sauce

This light and refreshing dessert is the perfect balance of sweet and tart. Instead of firing up the grill, you can cook the pineapple in an oiled grill pan over medium-high heat.

YIELD: 6 SERVINGS

GRILLED PINEAPPLE

1. In a small saucepan, combine the honey, brown sugar, butter, and rum. Bring the mixture to a low simmer, whisking often, until the sugar has melted and the glaze is slightly thickened, about 5 minutes.
2. Heat the grill to medium-high. Grill the pineapple slices, brushing frequently with the honey glaze, until browned, 2 to 3 minutes per side. Set aside.

LIME-BUTTER SAUCE

In a small saucepan, whisk the sugar and cornstarch to blend. Add 1 cup water and stir over medium heat until the mixture boils and thickens Remove from the heat and stir in the butter. Whisk in the lime juice. (The sauce will keep, covered, in the refrigerator for up to 2 days.)

MANGO WHIPPED CREAM

In a food processor or blender, puree the mango chunks until smooth (see note); set aside. With a whisk or electric mixer, beat the cream and sugar until stiff peaks form. With a rubber spatula, fold the mango into the whipped cream. Use immediately.

ASSEMBLY

Transfer the pineapple slices to plates and drizzle with the lime-butter sauce. Top with a dollop of the mango whipped cream and garnish with the toasted pistachios.

GRILLED PINEAPPLE

2 tablespoons honey

2 tablespoons light brown sugar

2 tablespoons unsalted butter

1 tablespoon light rum

1 ripe pineapple, peeled and sliced into ¼-inch-thick rounds

LIME-BUTTER SAUCE

⅓ cup sugar

1 tablespoon cornstarch

1 tablespoon unsalted butter

7 tablespoons fresh lime juice

MANGO WHIPPED CREAM

⅔ cup mango chunks (from about 1 large mango)

1 cup heavy cream, well chilled

⅓ cup sugar

ASSEMBLY

½ cup shelled unsalted natural pistachios, toasted and coarsely chopped

> **NOTE** | For the smoothest texture, push the pureed mango through a fine sieve before folding it into the whipped cream.

I have found myself in all corners of the globe on Independence Day, and no matter which port of call I've been in on the Fourth of July, I feel the excitement of this American holiday as profoundly as if I were at home in Florida. | It's such a great holiday—basically, an entire day devoted to fun and spectacle. Everyone gets into the spirit. On board, passengers of all nationalities can be found wearing Old Glory's red, white, and blue. Crew members, many hailing from Indonesia and the Philippines, have an Independence Day celebration that includes traditional Fourth of July picnic events, such as sack races, tug-of-war, and a water balloon toss. The musical talents of our crews take the spotlight as members sing "God Bless America" in the talent show. | On the Fourth of July, everyone is American and celebrates the very notion of freedom as a fundamental human need and right. To me, Independence Day represents and celebrates fun itself. Adults and children alike enjoy with equal enthusiasm simple pleasures like parades and picnics as well as the star-spangled spectacular of a midsummer night's fireworks display—in fact, I often find it hard to tell who is enjoying the festivities more, the adults or the children. | Like Independence Day itself, this menu offers something for everyone. The more sophisticated patriots will take pleasure in the cheeky spiced up presentation for the Seared Scallops and the architectural build of the delicious and summery Romaine Salad. And it will be hard to tell who has enjoyed with the most gusto the finger-licking Baby Back Ribs, Herb-Buttered Corn, and Peach and Blueberry Cobbler—those with the napkins on their laps or those with the sauce on their faces.

FOURTH OF JULY

M E N U

Seared Scallops Tossed with Herbs, Lemon, and Olive Oil

• • •

Romaine Salad with Oregano Dressing

• • •

Apple-Glazed Baby Back Ribs with
Herb-Buttered Corn and Fruity Coleslaw

• • •

Peach and Blueberry Cobbler

Seared Scallops Tossed with Herbs, Lemon, and Olive Oil

YIELD: 8 SERVINGS

DRESSING

6 tablespoons chopped fresh basil, plus extra for garnish

2 tablespoons chopped fresh rosemary, plus extra for garnish

1 tablespoon chopped fresh thyme, plus extra for garnish

3 medium garlic cloves, minced

5 tablespoons fresh lemon juice

1 cup extra-virgin olive oil

Salt and freshly ground black pepper

SCALLOPS

2 pounds sea scallops (20 to 25 per pound), rinsed and muscle removed

Salt and freshly ground black pepper

3 tablespoons olive oil

1 small red bell pepper, cored, seeded, and minced

1 small yellow bell pepper, cored, seeded, and minced

Searing scallops lends them extra flavor, but the key is not overcrowding the pan, which lowers the cooking temperature. If you see juice exuding from the scallops as they cook, the pan's temperature is too low and they are steaming, not searing (they will likely overcook before they can take on any flavorful color). Cook the scallops in batches, and remove them from the pan before the second side has had a chance to completely brown—you don't want to overcook them.

DRESSING

In a glass or ceramic bowl, combine the herbs, garlic, and lemon juice. Slowly whisk in the olive oil. Season with salt and pepper. Set aside.

SCALLOPS

1. Pat the scallops dry and season them with salt and pepper. In a heavy, large skillet, heat 1 tablespoon of the oil over medium-high heat. Add a third of the scallops and cook, without moving them, until they are golden brown on the bottom, about 1 minute. Turn and cook the other side until the scallop is just opaque in the center (the other side may not be browned before the scallop is cooked). Transfer the scallops to a large glass or ceramic bowl. Cook the remaining scallops in the same way in two more batches, using 1 tablespoon oil for each batch; transfer them to the bowl as they are cooked.

2. Add the diced bell peppers to the scallops. Toss with just enough herb dressing to lightly coat. Serve immediately in scallop shells or in small martini glasses, garnished with fresh herbs.

Romaine Salad with Oregano Dressing

his salad, with its simple, subtly delicious dressing, is an enduring favorite.

YIELD: 4 TO 6 SERVINGS

DRESSING

2 tablespoons red wine vinegar

2 teaspoons fresh lemon juice

1 small garlic clove, minced

1 teaspoon dried oregano or 1 tablespoon minced fresh oregano

¼ teaspoon salt

¼ teaspoon freshly ground black pepper

3 tablespoons extra-virgin olive oil

SALAD

1 head romaine lettuce, trimmed of outer leaves, and washed and torn into 3-inch pieces (about 5 cups)

2 large tomatoes, cored and sliced into wedges

1 medium cucumber, peeled, halved lengthwise, and sliced

1 medium red onion, thinly sliced

½ cup kalamata olives, pitted if desired

6- to 8-ounce block feta cheese, sliced

DRESSING

In a small glass or ceramic bowl, whisk together the vinegar, lemon juice, garlic, oregano, salt, and pepper. Slowly whisk in the olive oil. Cover and refrigerate until ready to use.

SALAD

In a large shallow bowl, combine the lettuce, tomatoes, cucumber, onion, and olives. Pour the dressing over the salad and use tongs or a large fork and spoon to toss the salad so the dressing mixes in. Divide the salad among plates. Top each salad with a slice of feta cheese and serve immediately.

Apple-Glazed Baby Back Ribs with Herb-Buttered Corn and Fruity Coleslaw

T hese ribs can also be finished under the broiler instead of the grill, making them a year-round treat!

YIELD: 4 SERVINGS

1. Combine 2 tablespoons of the sugar, the salt, and spices in a small bowl. With a small, sharp knife, loosen the membrane from the underside of each rib rack. Use your fingers or a pair of pliers to pull off the membrane from the rack. (Alternatively, leave the membrane on the rack but carefully score it with a knife.)

2. Rub 1 tablespoon of seasoning mix into each side of each rack. Place the ribs in a large roasting pan, cover with plastic wrap, and let marinate in the refrigerator for at least 6 hours. (The ribs can be stored this way for up to 1 day.)

3. Heat the oven to 325°F. In a glass or ceramic bowl, whisk together ¼ cup of the cider, the remaining ¼ cup sugar, the apple butter, brandy, vinegar, and mustard. Cover and refrigerate until ready to use.

4. Remove the ribs from the refrigerator and lift them up so you can scatter the onion slices under them. Pour the remaining 1 cup apple cider in the pan and arrange the ribs meat side down on the onions. Cover the pan with foil and roast the ribs until the meat is tender and begins to pull away from the bones, about 2 hours. Uncover; allow to cool at least 30 minutes and up to 2 hours.

5. Heat a grill to medium-high. Grill the ribs until heated through and slightly charred, about 5 minutes per side. Brush the ribs on all sides with the basting sauce, then grill the ribs about 3 minutes longer per side. Transfer the racks to a cutting board and cut between the bones to separate the ribs. Arrange on a platter and present any remaining sauce on the side. Serve Herb-Buttered Corn and Fruity Coleslaw as side dishes.

6 tablespoons packed light brown sugar, divided

1 tablespoon kosher salt

2 tablespoons paprika

1 tablespoon freshly ground black pepper, or to taste

1 tablespoon ground cumin

1 tablespoon chili powder

2 (2- to 2¼-pound) racks baby back pork ribs

1¼ cups apple cider or unfiltered apple juice, divided

½ cup apple butter

¼ cup apple brandy, brandy, or dark rum

¼ cup apple cider vinegar

2 tablespoons Dijon mustard

1 large onion, sliced

Herb-Buttered Corn (see page 100)

Fruity Coleslaw (see page 100)

HERB-BUTTERED CORN

YIELD: 6 TO 8 SIDE-DISH
SERVINGS

4 tablespoons unsalted butter, at room temperature

1 tablespoon chopped fresh flat-leaf parsley

1 tablespoon chopped fresh basil leaves

Sea salt and freshly ground black pepper

4 large ears of corn, shucked

1. In a small bowl, combine the butter, parsley, and basil. Use a rubber spatula to press and fold the ingredients together. Season with sea salt and pepper. Scrape the mixture onto a sheet of wax paper and form into a log about 1½ inches in diameter. Roll in plastic wrap and chill in the refrigerator until firm, at least 2 hours and up to 2 days. (The herb butter can be frozen for up to 2 months.)
2. Cook the corn in a large pot of boiling water until crisp-tender, about 3 minutes. Serve with slices of herb butter.

FRUITY COLESLAW

YIELD: 6 TO 8 SIDE-DISH
SERVINGS

1 pineapple

1 large egg yolk (see note)

1½ tablespoons beaten whole egg

1½ teaspoons Dijon mustard

1½ tablespoons fresh lemon juice, divided

1 cup olive oil

½ teaspoon honey

1½ tablespoons pineapple juice

Salt and freshly ground white pepper

¾ pound finely shredded green cabbage

⅓ cup chopped dried apricots

⅓ cup almond slices, toasted

1½ Golden Delicious apples, cored and chopped

Pineapple leaves, for garnish

1. Trim, peel, and chop enough fresh pineapple to make ¾ cup; set aside in a large glass or ceramic bowl. Finely chop ½ cup more fresh pineapple and place it in a medium sieve over a bowl; press down on it with a ladle until you produce 1½ tablespoons fresh pineapple juice; set aside the juice in a small bowl. Reserve the pineapple top; you will use the leaves for garnish.
2. Make the dressing: In a food processor, combine the egg yolk, beaten whole egg, mustard, and 1 tablespoon of the lemon juice. Process for 1 minute. With the motor running, add the oil very slowly through the feed tube, stopping once or twice to scrape down the sides. Add the honey and process for 1 minute. With the motor running, slowly add the reserved 1½ tablespoons pineapple juice. Season with salt and white pepper. Transfer the dressing to a container. Cover and refrigerate it until ready to use.
3. Assemble the coleslaw: Add the cabbage, apricots, and almond slices to the bowl with the chopped pineapple. Toss the apples with the remaining ½ tablespoon lemon juice and add to the cabbage mixture. Add enough dressing to lightly coat all the ingredients and transfer the slaw to a serving dish. Garnish with pineapple leaves and serve immediately.

> **NOTE** You can eliminate the small risk of exposure to salmonella contamination in raw egg preparations by using pasteurized shell eggs.

Peach and Blueberry Cobbler

W e serve these in individual ramekins on board, but for casual celebrations using a single baking dish makes for an even more inviting presentation. Don't forget the vanilla ice cream!

1. Heat the oven to 350°F. Spread the melted butter into the bottom of a 9-inch-square baking dish or divide it among six ramekins placed on a baking sheet. Add the peaches and blueberries to the butter and toss gently. Bake for 20 minutes, until the fruit begins to bubble. Maintain the oven temperature.

2. In a mixing bowl, whisk the flour, sugar, baking powder, cinnamon, and salt. Stir in the milk just until combined. (Do not overmix.) Spoon the batter over the fruit.

3. Return the cobbler to the oven and bake for 25 more minutes (20 minutes for the ramekins) or until the top is brown and the fruit is bubbling. Serve warm, with vanilla ice cream.

YIELD: 6 SERVINGS

8 tablespoons (1 stick) unsalted butter, melted

5 to 6 medium peaches, peeled, halved, pitted, and sliced

1 cup fresh blueberries

1 cup all-purpose flour

1 cup sugar

1 teaspoon baking powder

1 teaspoon ground cinnamon

¼ teaspoon salt

½ cup whole milk

Vanilla ice cream, for serving

Even though I was born and raised in Austria, Thanksgiving in America is my favorite holiday. After all, what could be better than a day completely orchestrated around cooking all day and eating all evening? | I've never met anyone who celebrates Thanksgiving who doesn't look forward to it and enjoy it heartily. Certainly, on board our ships, no matter where we are or where we are bound, come Thanksgiving, our guests are looking for turkey and all the trimmings—and we give it to them in abundance! | The recipes in this Thanksgiving menu are beloved traditions for guests of ours who return year after year to celebrate the holiday with us. The menu starts with a dish I designed to delight. To me, there's no stronger icon of fall than a pumpkin. I adore pumpkin because of its distinctive texture and flavor; the color is so remarkable as well. The pumpkin shells themselves make beautiful serving bowls for the soup, and these never fail to delight and surprise when they are brought out and set on the table. | Often, salad is not a part of the menu for Thanksgiving at home, but I think that a good salad is a perfect and elegant refresher course between the rich fall soup and the main event of turkey, replete with its giblet gravy and cornbread and sausage stuffing. | While these dishes make perfect Thanksgiving fare, any one or combination of these recipes would be terrific anytime. The Chocolate Pecan Pie certainly would warm up some blah gray day in February . . . and those sugared cranberries might be just the thing to serve alongside a piece of grilled pork in July.

Thanksgiving

MENU

Mini Pumpkin Soup Bowls

• • •

*Bibb Lettuce Salad with Oranges, Fennel,
and Green Goddess Dressing*

• • •

*Roast Turkey with Cornbread and Sausage Stuffing,
Giblet Gravy, and Glazed Cranberries*

• • •

Chocolate Pecan Pie

Mini Pumpkin Soup Bowls

Here's a delightful way to kick off the Thanksgiving meal. The pumpkin "bowls" can roast while the turkey is resting. Though the traditional jack-o'-lantern variety of pumpkin is fine for the bowls, use any other variety, even butternut squash, for the soup.

YIELD: 12 SERVINGS

1. Heat the oven to 350°F. Brush a shallow baking pan with 1 tablespoon of the oil and arrange the pumpkin or squash in the pan cut sides up. Cover the pan with foil and bake for 45 minutes, or until soft. Spoon out the pulp (there should be 6 to 8 cups) and transfer it to a bowl with any pan juices. (The pulp can be stored, covered and refrigerated, for up to 1 day. Bring to room temperature before using.)

2. Increase the oven heat to 375°F. Cut the tops off the small pumpkins and reserve them, then scoop out and discard the seeds. Cut the butter into bits and divide it among the pumpkins. Replace the pumpkin tops and place the pumpkins in the shallow baking pan. Roast them for 30 to 40 minutes, or until they are tender when pierced with a knife but still intact.

3. Meanwhile, make the soup. In a large soup pot, heat the remaining 5 tablespoons oil over medium-high heat. Add the onion, leeks, carrot, celery, ginger, allspice, nutmeg, cumin, and salt. Cook, stirring, until the vegetables soften, about 8 minutes.

4. Add the wine and cider and scrape up any browned bits from the bottom of the pot, stirring to dissolve them. Add the reserved pumpkin pulp, chicken stock, and bouquet garni. Bring to a boil. Reduce the heat to low and simmer, stirring occasionally, until the vegetables are very tender, about 30 minutes. Remove the pot from the heat and let the soup cool for at least 5 minutes.

5. Discard the bouquet garni. Transfer the soup in batches to a blender and puree until smooth. (When pureeing hot soups, fill the container no more than halfway and release one corner of the lid to prevent a vacuum effect. Place a kitchen towel over the top of the machine while you pulse.) Strain the soup through a fine sieve into a saucepan. Return the soup to the stove and bring it to a simmer. Adjust the consistency with additional cider or stock. Season with salt and pepper.

6. The roasted pumpkins and soup should be done at about the same time. To serve, lift the tops from the pumpkins and carefully ladle the soup into each one, filling it about two-thirds full. Replace the pumpkin tops and serve immediately.

---

6 tablespoons vegetable oil, divided

4 pounds pumpkin or other winter squash (such as butternut, halved, with strings and seeds discarded)

12 small (6 to 7 inches in diameter) unblemished pumpkins

2 tablespoons unsalted butter

2¼ cups chopped onion

4 cups chopped leeks, white and light green parts only

1 cup chopped carrot

1½ cups chopped celery

1 teaspoon ground ginger

¼ teaspoon ground allspice

½ teaspoon freshly grated nutmeg

½ teaspoon ground cumin

1 teaspoon salt

¾ cup dry white wine (such as sauvignon blanc, chenin blanc, or pinot blanc)

3 cups apple cider, plus extra as needed

8 cups low-sodium store-bought chicken broth or stock, or homemade, plus extra as needed

1 bouquet garni (1 bay leaf, 2 sprigs fresh thyme, 5 fresh parsley stems, 4 star anise, and 10 black peppercorns bundled in a piece of cheesecloth and tied with string)

Salt and freshly ground black pepper

Bibb Lettuce Salad with Oranges, Fennel, and Green Goddess Dressing

YIELD: 6 SERVINGS

GREEN GODDESS DRESSING

1 cup prepared or homemade mayonnaise

2 anchovy fillets, drained and finely chopped

3 small scallions, finely chopped

1 tablespoon finely chopped fresh flat-leaf parsley

1 tablespoon tarragon vinegar

1 tablespoon fresh lemon juice

1 teaspoon minced garlic

3 tablespoons sour cream

Salt and freshly ground black pepper

SALAD

5 oranges

3 heads Bibb lettuce, leaves separated, rinsed, and dried

2 large fennel bulbs, trimmed, halved lengthwise, and sliced crosswise very thinly

Salt and freshly ground black pepper

1 tablespoon chopped fresh flat-leaf parsley, for garnish

This salad contrasts sweet and salty with creamy and tangy. And the tarragon in the dressing boosts the wonderful, subtle flavor of the fennel.

GREEN GODDESS DRESSING

In a blender or food processor, puree the mayonnaise, anchovies, scallions, parsley, vinegar, lemon juice, garlic, and sour cream until smooth. Season with salt and pepper. Transfer the dressing to a container. Cover and refrigerate until ready to use.

SALAD

1. With a sharp knife, trim the top and bottom from each orange. Stand them upright and cut downward to remove the rind and pith in thick strips. Working over a bowl, cut between the membranes to release the segments. Cover the orange segments with plastic wrap and reserve.
2. Divide the lettuce leaves among six chilled plates. In a large bowl, combine the orange segments and fennel; save the accumulated orange juice for another use. Season with salt and pepper. Place a portion of orange and fennel on each plate of lettuce and top with Green Goddess dressing. Sprinkle the salad with parsley and serve immediately.

Roast Turkey with Cornbread and Sausage Stuffing, Giblet Gravy, and Glazed Cranberries

T hanksgiving menus can be simple or special, but special ones like this one often require advance preparation. For this menu, be sure to make the glazed cranberries the night before and soak the raisins at least two hours in advance. This turkey also entails an aromatic stuffing cooked inside the bird, made with fruits and vegetables; it's not meant to be eaten but just to flavor the drippings and infuse the meat. The cornbread stuffing is cooked in a separate pan, for convenience and to ensure a safe and fully cooked temperature. If you don't like cornbread stuffing, this one will taste just as terrific made with cubes of dense white bread. Allow the bread to sit out overnight to go stale, or dry out the cubes in a 250°F oven for forty minutes.

YIELD: 12 SERVINGS

GLAZED CRANBERRIES

1 cup sugar

1 cup cranberry juice

1 cup cranberries

TURKEY

1 (9-pound) fresh turkey (be sure it comes with the giblets and neck)

2 tablespoons chopped fresh sage or 1 tablespoon dried sage

2 tablespoons chopped fresh thyme or 1 tablespoon dried thyme

2 tablespoons chopped fresh rosemary or 1 tablespoon dried rosemary

Salt and freshly ground black pepper

2 Granny Smith apples, cored and chopped

2 yellow onions, chopped

2 large oranges, peeled, sectioned, and chopped

1 stalk celery, chopped

GLAZED CRANBERRIES

In a medium saucepan over low heat, whisk the sugar and juice until the sugar dissolves. Bring the syrup to a simmer and immediately add the cranberries. Cook, stirring, until the moment the cranberries begin to pop. Immediately remove them from the heat. Cover and refrigerate for at least 8 hours or overnight.

TURKEY

1. Heat the oven to 350°F. Remove the giblets and neck and refrigerate them, covered, until you are ready to make the gravy. Rinse the turkey inside and out with cold water and pat it dry with paper towels. In a small bowl, combine the sage, thyme, rosemary, salt, and pepper. Season the turkey inside and out with the herb mixture.
2. In a medium bowl, combine the remaining ingredients. Spoon the apple mixture into the cavity of the turkey and truss the bird with twine. Transfer it to a large flameproof roasting pan and roast, uncovered, for 3 hours, or until an instant-read thermometer inserted into the thickest part of the thigh registers 180°F. The juices that drain from the leg joints should run clear.
3. Transfer the turkey to a warmed serving platter and tent it with foil to keep warm. Let rest for 30 minutes. Set the roasting pan, with the turkey juices in it, aside.

CORNBREAD AND SAUSAGE STUFFING

1 cup raisins

½ cup port

¼ cup B&B liqueur or brandy

1 pound sweet Italian sausage, casings removed

2 cups finely diced yellow onion

2 cups finely diced celery

2 tablespoons chopped fresh thyme or 1 tablespoon dried thyme

1 tablespoon chopped fresh sage or 1½ teaspoons dried sage

1 tablespoon chopped fresh rosemary or 1½ teaspoons dried rosemary

6 cups cornbread crumbs

1½ cups canned or roasted (and peeled) chestnuts

1 cup finely diced Granny Smith apple

1 cup chopped fresh flat-leaf parsley

Salt and freshly ground black pepper

2 cups low-sodium store-bought chicken broth or stock, or homemade

GIBLET GRAVY

Reserved turkey giblets and neck

1 small onion, sliced

1 small or ½ large garlic clove

1 small bay leaf

⅛ teaspoon dried basil, crumbled

⅛ teaspoon dried rosemary, crumbled

⅛ teaspoon dried thyme, crushed

Salt and freshly ground black pepper

¼ cup flour

CORNBREAD AND SAUSAGE STUFFING

1. At least 2 hours before you make the stuffing, combine the raisins, port, and B&B in a small bowl and let them soak. (You can leave the raisins soaking overnight, if you like.)

2. Heat the oven to 350°F, or plan to put the stuffing in the oven with the turkey about 2 hours into the turkey's baking time. Lightly coat a baking dish with butter or vegetable oil.

3. In a large sauté pan, brown the sausage over medium-high heat. Drain off any excess fat. Add the onion and cook, stirring, until softened and translucent, about 2 minutes. Add the celery and cook for 2 to 3 minutes. Stir in the thyme, sage, and rosemary and transfer the mixture to a large bowl.

4. Add the remaining ingredients to the bowl and stir until well combined. Pour the stuffing into the prepared baking dish and cover it with foil. Bake for 45 minutes. Remove the foil and bake for 15 minutes more, or until the top is golden brown.

GIBLET GRAVY

1. About halfway through the turkey's roasting time, combine the giblets, neck, and 3 cups water in a large saucepan. Add the onion, garlic, bay leaf, basil, rosemary, thyme, and ⅛ teaspoon salt. Bring to a boil over high heat. Reduce the heat to low and simmer, stirring occasionally, for 15 minutes, or until the liver is tender. Remove the liver and reserve.

2. Continue to simmer the mixture for 1 hour, or until the giblets are tender. Strain, reserving both solids and liquid. Discard the neck, vegetables, and bay leaf and chop the giblets and reserved liver. Set aside.

3. When the turkey is done, pour the roasting pan juices into a large glass measuring cup. After the juices separate, remove ¼ cup fat from the top and return it to the roasting pan. Spoon off and discard any remaining fat in the measuring cup, leaving only the turkey juices behind.

4. Sprinkle the flour over the fat in the roasting pan and place the pan over low heat. Cook, stirring, for 2 to 3 minutes. Add 1 cup water, 2 cups reserved giblet stock, and the degreased juices from the measuring cup. Scrape up any browned bits from the bottom of the pan and cook, stirring constantly, until the browned bits dissolve and the liquid begins to bubble.

5. Strain the gravy into a saucepan. Add the giblets and liver and bring the mixture to a boil over high heat. Reduce the heat and simmer, stirring, until the gravy is thick enough to lightly coat a spoon. Serve.

6. To serve, remove and discard the aromatic stuffing from the turkey's cavity and carve the meat. Serve slices of the turkey on plates with some stuffing and glazed cranberries alongside. Transfer the giblet gravy to a sauceboat and pass it separately.

Chocolate Pecan Pie

YIELD: 12 SERVINGS

PIECRUST

1½ cups all-purpose flour

1 teaspoon sugar

½ teaspoon salt

6 tablespoons unsalted butter, chilled and cut into pieces

3 tablespoons vegetable shortening, chilled and cut into pieces

FILLING

2 cups pecan halves

7 ounces bittersweet (not unsweetened) chocolate, chopped into ½-inch pieces

3 tablespoons all-purpose flour

12 tablespoons (1½ sticks) unsalted butter, softened

1 cup packed dark brown sugar

6 large eggs, at room temperature

¾ cup light corn syrup

¼ cup molasses

1½ tablespoons Cointreau

2¼ teaspoons vanilla extract

½ teaspoon salt

Lightly sweetened whipped cream, for serving

 ere's a terrific variation on one of the most popular holiday pies. Be sure to cut small slices—it's rich.

PIECRUST

1. In a large bowl, whisk together the flour, sugar, and salt. Using your fingertips, a pastry blender, or two knives, work the butter and shortening into the flour until the mixture resembles coarse meal. (Alternatively, combine the ingredients in a food processor, using short pulses.)

2. In a small bowl, combine ¼ cup water with a few cubes of ice. Using a fork, stir the water into the flour mixture 1 tablespoon at a time, using only as much as needed to gather the mixture into a soft ball. Pat the dough into a disk, cover it with plastic wrap, and refrigerate for at least 1 hour or up to 3 days.

3. Heat the oven to 400°F. On a lightly floured surface, roll out the dough into a round about ⅛ inch thick. Drape the dough over a rolling pin and fit it into a 10-inch pie pan. Fold the edge under and crimp. Place the pie shell in the freezer for 20 minutes.

4. Prick the dough all over with the tines of a fork to prevent bubbling during baking. Place a piece of foil over it and fill it with pie weights or dried beans. Place the pie shell in the oven and bake for 10 to 12 minutes. Remove the foil and weights and continue baking for an additional 8 to 10 minutes. Place it on a wire rack and let it cool completely.

FILLING

1. Reduce the oven to 350°F. Spread the pecans on a baking sheet and bake for 7 to 10 minutes, until fragrant. Let cool, roughly chop, and place them in a medium mixing bowl. Add the chopped chocolate and flour, and stir to mix. Set aside.

2. In a large mixing bowl, beat the butter and brown sugar with an electric mixer until light and fluffy. Gradually beat in the eggs, one at a time, stopping two or three times to scrape down the sides of the bowl. Beat in the corn syrup, molasses, Cointreau, vanilla, and salt until fully incorporated.

3. Add the chocolate mixture to the egg mixture and stir until well combined. Pour the filling into the prepared pie shell and bake for 1 hour, or until lightly set in the center. Transfer the pie to a wire rack and let cool completely before serving (see note).

NOTE This pie can be kept in the refrigerator, covered in plastic wrap, for up to one day. Serve it at room temperature, topped with lightly sweetened whipped cream.

Hanukkah, the festival of lights that takes place during the darkening days of late fall/early winter, is the celebration of a thousands-year-old miracle: There was only enough oil to keep the sacred eternal light lit for one night, but the small amount of oil kept the Temple lights burning for eight nights. | To me, Hanukkah represents the miracle of abundance in our lives. Certainly guests who happen to be on board one of our fifteen vessels during the eight days and nights of Hanukkah are blessed with the great bounty of everything their hearts could desire, from food to entertainment, the beauty of the ocean, and the excitement of the ships' destinations. | I always hope that guests will bring this sense of abundance home with them, and manifest some of the specialness that goes into every detail of their cruise into their daily lives. Hanukkah, however, celebrates the idea that we can make little go a long way. As a chef—and as someone who was raised in a family with twelve children—this idea has great resonance. Making more out of less coaxes us into greater culinary creativity and teaches us how to turn what we have into what we need. | Featured are some humble, inexpensive, easy-to-find ingredients like potatoes, carrots, brisket, apples, and even ketchup, which are transformed into deliciously elegant dishes that are right at home on the luxurious main dining room menu. | Because Hanukkah is an eight-day celebration, there's plenty of opportunity to have friends or family in for a special meal during the holiday. In fact, once your guests try the brisket recipe, which is best made ahead of time anyway, you might find yourself entertaining every night for longer than the holiday lasts. Such is the miracle of a memorable meal.

HANUKKAH

MENU

Smoked Salmon Tartlets with Caramelized Onions,
Capers, and Tahini

• • •

Latkes with Sweet Carrot Puree

• • •

Red-Wine Braised Brisket with Onions and Paprika

• • •

Honey Roasted Apples and Candied Dates with Marzipan

Smoked Salmon Tartlets with Caramelized Onions, Capers, and Tahini

YIELD: 12 SERVINGS

4 (17-by-12-inch) phyllo sheets, thawed if frozen, stacked between 2 sheets wax paper and covered with a towel

⅓ cup extra-virgin olive oil, divided

4 large sweet onions (such as Walla Walla or Vidalia)

Sea salt and freshly ground black pepper

½ cup well-stirred tahini (see note)

¼ cup fresh lemon juice

½ teaspoon minced garlic

½ pound thinly sliced smoked salmon

¼ cup drained capers in brine

12 small sprigs fresh dill, for garnish

1 tablespoon chopped fresh flat-leaf parsley, for garnish

When making the tartlet shells, be sure to work quickly to prevent the phyllo from drying out.

1. Heat the oven to 325°F. Lightly spray a standard 12-cup muffin pan with nonstick spray.

2. Make the phyllo shells: On a work surface, arrange a phyllo sheet with a long side facing you and brush it lightly with some olive oil. Top with a second and third phyllo sheet, brushing lightly with olive oil after adding each one (you will use about 3 tablespoons of the olive oil). Place the fourth phyllo sheet on top.

3. With a 3½-inch-round cutter, cut 12 circles from the phyllo stack. (Alternatively, use a sharp knife to cut the stack into 12 squares.) Gently push a phyllo circle into each cup of the prepared pan, pressing it against the bottom and sides.

4. Bake the empty shells in the middle of the oven for 8 to 10 minutes, or until they are golden brown. Transfer the pan to a rack and let cool for 5 minutes. Carefully remove the phyllo shells from the pan. (The shells may be made ahead and kept in the pan, wrapped in plastic wrap, for up to 1 week at room temperature or up to 1 month in the freezer.)

5. Make the caramelized onions: Halve the onions lengthwise and cut them crosswise into ¼-inch-thick slices. In a large skillet, heat the remaining olive oil over moderately high heat until hot but not smoking. Add the onions and cook, stirring occasionally, until softened, about 5 minutes. Reduce the heat to moderate and continue to cook, stirring occasionally, until golden, about 15 minutes longer. Season with salt and pepper. Transfer the onions to a bowl and let cool. (The caramelized onions may be kept, covered, in the refrigerator for up to 1 day. Let them sit at room temperature for 30 minutes before proceeding.)

6. Make the tahini sauce: In a food processor or blender, combine the tahini, ¾ cup water, lemon juice, and garlic and pulse or blend until smooth. Season with salt and set aside.

7. To assemble the tartlets, spoon some caramelized onions into each phyllo shell. Arrange smoked salmon on top of the onions. Sprinkle with capers. With a warm fork, spoon tahini sauce into the tartlets. Garnish them with dill and parsley and serve.

NOTE | Tahini is sesame seed paste. It's available at some super-
markets and natural foods stores, and at Middle Eastern markets.

Latkes with Sweet Carrot Puree

C arrot puree is a colorful alternative to traditional applesauce. If you use a food processor to make the latkes, grate the onion and potato in alternation, which helps keep the potato from turning gray.

YIELD: 8 SERVINGS

SWEET CARROT PUREE

1 pound carrots, cut into 1-inch pieces

Salt

Juice of 1 orange

Juice of 1 lemon

¼ cup sugar

½ teaspoon ground cinnamon

¼ teaspoon ground cumin

LATKES

2½ pounds russet potatoes (about 4 large), peeled

1 yellow onion

1¼ teaspoons sea salt

⅛ teaspoon freshly ground black pepper

1 egg, lightly beaten

¼ cup matzo meal

Canola oil or light olive oil, for frying

SWEET CARROT PUREE

In a large pot, cook the carrots in enough boiling salted water to cover them by 1 inch until tender, about 30 minutes. With a slotted spoon, transfer the carrots to a food processor or blender and puree with the orange juice, lemon juice, sugar, cinnamon, and cumin. Transfer to a bowl. (The carrot puree can keep, covered, for up to one day in the refrigerator. Rewarm before serving.)

LATKES

1. Heat the oven to 180°F and line a baking sheet with a paper towel. On the large holes of a box grater, shred the potatoes and onion (or use the shredding disk of a food processor, quartering the onions and cutting the potatoes lengthwise so they fit down the feed tube).

2. With your hands or a clean kitchen towel, squeeze as much excess liquid as possible from the potatoes and onion, reserving the liquid in a large bowl. Let the starch in the liquid settle to the bottom of the bowl (it will only take a couple of minutes) and pour off the watery top. Add the drained potatoes and onion to the bowl along with the salt, pepper, egg, and matzo meal. Toss to mix evenly.

3. Pour ⅓ inch oil into a 10- or 12-inch frying pan or cast-iron skillet and heat the oil over medium-high heat. When a deep-frying thermometer registers 360°F and the oil is very hot but not smoking (a shred of potato should sizzle upon contact when it's ready), stir the potato mixture again, form 2 tablespoons of it into a pancake with your hands, and carefully slip it into the pan. Quickly form and slip in just enough additional pancakes to fit comfortably in the pan. Cook, turning them once, until they are golden brown, 2 to 3 minutes on each side. With a slotted spatula, transfer each finished batch to the baking sheet and keep it warm in the oven while making more latkes. Serve the warm latkes with the carrot puree alongside.

Red-Wine Braised Brisket with Onions and Paprika

YIELD: 10 SERVINGS

1 (6- to 7-pound) piece of beef brisket, preferably second-cut (see sidebar)

1 teaspoon salt

1 teaspoon freshly ground black pepper

3 tablespoons olive oil

8 onions, sliced

1 teaspoon paprika, preferably Hungarian

¾ cup kosher red wine

¾ cup ketchup (preferably kosher if you don't eat corn products during Passover)

I f you have a broiler, this recipe is even easier (see note). The brisket tastes best if it's made at least one day—and up to three days—ahead. When it's cooled, cover and refrigerate it overnight, then remove the congealed fat from the surface before slicing and reheating the meat.

1. Heat the oven to 350°F and position the rack in the lower third. In a roasting pan, lay out a sheet of heavy-duty foil large enough to wrap loosely around the meat. Set the pan and foil aside.

2. Season the brisket with the salt and pepper. In a heavy-bottomed, extra-large, wide skillet, heat the oil over medium-high heat until it shimmers. Add the brisket (in half sections if necessary) and sear until it is deep brown, 5 to 8 minutes per side. Place the brisket, fat side up, on the center of the sheet of foil in the roasting pan.

3. Pour off all but 1 tablespoon fat from the skillet and add as many onions as will fit in the pan. Place any onions that don't fit on top of the brisket. Sprinkle the onions in the skillet with the paprika and cook, stirring, until golden brown, 12 to 15 minutes. Add the wine and deglaze the pan, scraping up all the browned bits from the bottom with a wooden spoon. Stir in the ketchup and transfer the contents of the skillet onto the top of the brisket on the foil.

4. Bring the foil around the meat loosely but make a tight seal at all the edges to enclose the brisket. Roast the foil-wrapped meat for 2 to 2½ hours, or until tender. (After 2 hours, carefully open the package and test the meat with a fork; if it's not tender, reseal it and roast for an additional ½ hour.)

5. If you are making the brisket ahead, remove it from the oven and allow it to cool. Refrigerate it overnight (or up to 2 days). Transfer the cold meat from the foil to a board and cut across the grain into

NOTE | If you want, you can broil the brisket instead of browning it. Place it under the broiler for about five minutes per side (don't allow it to burn or the sauce will be bitter). Then place the browned brisket on the sheet of foil and top it with the raw onions, paprika, wine, and ketchup. Seal the edges of the foil and roast.

¼-inch-thick slices; place the slices directly into the roasting pan. Remove and discard as much of the fat as possible from the pan and meat. Spoon the liquid and onions onto the brisket. Cover the top of the roasting pan with foil and reheat it at 350°F for 40 minutes, or until hot. Serve immediately.

BRISKET: THE SECOND CUT

The second cut is the more marbled piece of beef brisket. It's from the thicker end (also called the point half) of the brisket and is also known as the front, thick, or nose cut. The thinner, leaner end of the brisket is the flat half, and is sometimes labeled the first or thin cut. Either the first or second cut will work with this recipe, though the second cut is more tender.

Honey Roasted Apples and Candied Dates with Marzipan

YIELD: 8 SERVINGS

CANDIED DATES

1 pound whole dates

½ (7-ounce) package marzipan or almond paste

1 cup honey

1 teaspoon vanilla extract

APPLES

8 medium baking apples (such as Golden Delicious, Braeburn, or Rome Beauty)

1 cup honey (use leftover honey from Candied Dates, above)

½ cup fresh orange juice

2 tablespoons fresh lemon juice

2 teaspoons grated orange zest

2 tablespoons minced candied ginger

The marzipan stuffing in the dates adds an elegant twist, but inserting a whole natural almond in each is easier, and quite delicious in its own way. Alternatively, you can candy the dates without stuffing them and roll them in ground, toasted almonds before serving.

CANDIED DATES

1. Line a cookie sheet with wax paper and lightly coat the wax paper with cooking spray. Set aside.

2. For each date, use a paring knife to make an incision on one of the long sides. Gently open the date and remove the pit. (If some of the inner skin comes out as well, that's fine.) Inspect each pitted date and discard any whose inner skin doesn't appear smooth and clean.

3. Pinch off a bit of marzipan and roll it between your hands to form an almond shape. Insert it into a pitted date and close up the date. Continue making and inserting marzipan "almonds" until all the dates are stuffed; set aside.

4. Bring the honey to a boil in a small saucepan over medium heat, stirring frequently. As soon as the honey boils up and begins to foam, scrape off any particles from the top of the foam and reduce the heat. Simmer, stirring, for 5 minutes. Stir in the vanilla extract, then remove the honey from the heat.

5. With a slotted spoon, place 3 to 4 of the dates into the honey mixture. Swirl the dates gently in the honey to coat all sides. Again with the slotted spoon, remove the dates one at a time, allowing the excess honey to drip back into the saucepan, and place the dates on the prepared cookie sheet. Repeat until all the dates have been coated with honey. (Leftover honey can be used for making the Honey Roasted Apples.)

6. Place the cookie sheet in the refrigerator for at least 2 hours so the honey can set; the dates will remain extremely sticky. (The candied dates will keep at room temperature for up to 2 days and refrigerated, covered, for up to 1 week.) Serve the dates with the Honey Roasted Apples.

APPLES

1. Heat the oven to 350°F. Pare the top quarter of the apples and remove the core, leaving ½ inch of core on the bottom. Place the

apples in a buttered 9-by-13-inch baking dish. Combine the honey, orange juice, lemon juice, orange zest, and ginger in a small bowl; mix well. Spoon the syrup over the apples, allowing it to fill the centers and coat the entire surface. Pour ⅔ cup hot water into the baking dish.

2. Bake the apples, covered with foil, for 15 minutes. Remove the cover and bake, basting them with the cooking liquid every 15 minutes, for 30 minutes longer, or until the apples are glazed and tender.

3. To serve, divide the roasted apples among plates and spoon the cooking liquid over. Place a few candied dates on each plate.

They say there's no place like home for the holidays, but we have passengers who return year after year to spend their holidays with us. Still, people tend to carry their cherished holiday customs with them: Some guests even have miniature pine Christmas trees set up in their staterooms. | On this menu you'll find many holiday favorites, which I encourage you to adapt to suit your family's traditions. For many of my friends, Christmas Day is very busy with presents to open, people to visit, church services to attend. Many of these family friends will serve up a veritable banquet on Christmas Eve and then have a lighter supper on Christmas Day. Other families I know do the opposite, taking in a simple meal before evening church services on Christmas Eve and saving the feast for the holiday itself. | This menu can be made in its entirety for either Christmas Eve or Christmas Day, or you might consider creating two separate meals by dividing up the menu into parts depending on your own traditions. For a light Christmas Eve supper, the creamy New England Clam Chowder served in its own sourdough bowl is a perfect option—it's rich, satisfying, and can easily be considered a meal in and of itself. | Likewise, a glazed ham is extremely popular for both Christmas Eve and Christmas Day supper. The apricot glaze and Madeira sauce give a lovely tang to the ham, and it is an easy dish to prepare. You might even make it for guests who visit during the week between Christmas and New Year's or for an open house. With this menu, good taste and joy are ready whenever you want to serve them up during the entire holiday season.

Christmas

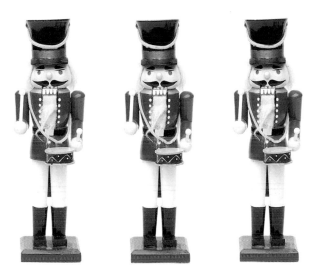

MENU

Clam Chowder in a Bread Bowl

• • •

*Salad of Greens and Radicchio with Pear, Orange,
and Cranberries in an Orange Dressing*

• • •

*Apricot-Glazed Ham with Madeira Sauce
and Roasted Potatoes*

• • •

Pumpkin Pie with Crunchy Pecan and Walnut Topping

Clam Chowder in a Bread Bowl

YIELD: 6 SERVINGS

6 round sourdough loaves (about 8 ounces each)

4 tablespoons unsalted butter, melted

5 pounds soft-shell clams (steamers) or littleneck clams (see note)

2 slices bacon, minced

1¾ cups chopped onion

1½ cups chopped celery

1 bay leaf

¾ teaspoon dried thyme or 1 tablespoon minced fresh thyme

1¼ pounds red potatoes, cut into ½-inch cubes

2 cups half-and-half

½ cup heavy cream

Salt

Cayenne pepper or Tabasco hot pepper sauce

Fresh thyme sprigs, for garnish

If you're making this at summer's end instead of year's end, scrape the kernels from a couple of cooked ears of corn and add them to the soup.

1. Heat the oven to 350°F. Cut ½ to ¾ inch off the top of each bread loaf. Scoop out the bread, leaving a ½-inch-thick shell. (Reserve the bread pieces for another use.) Brush the inside of the bread bowls and lids with melted butter; place them buttered-side up directly on the oven rack. Bake the bowls until crisp, about 20 minutes, then set them aside on a rack.

2. Scrub the clams well with a brush, discarding any that are dead or have broken shells. Soak the clams in a pot of cold water for a few minutes, drain, then repeat with fresh water 2 or 3 more times until the soaking water stays clear.

3. In an 8-quart pot, bring 2 cups water to a boil. Gently add the drained clams and cover. Let the clams steam for 4 minutes. To help the clams cook evenly, remove the lid and gently stir, taking care not to crack any of the delicate shells. Cover and continue to steam for another 4 or 5 minutes (steam a minute or so longer if all the shells aren't open).

4. With tongs, remove the clams from the pot; discard any that aren't open. Strain the liquid through a fine sieve lined with cheesecloth into a measuring cup. If you have more than 3 cups liquid, pour it into a saucepan and reduce it to that amount; set aside. When the clams are cool, remove them from their shells and cut off the siphons and the skin of each siphon and discard. Cover the clams and refrigerate until needed.

5. In a large, heavy pot, cook the bacon over medium heat until lightly crisp, about 8 minutes. Add the onion, celery, and bay leaf; sauté until the vegetables are lightly golden, about 10 minutes. Add the dried thyme and stir for 30 seconds (if using fresh thyme, add it with the cream in step 6). Add the reserved clam liquid and potatoes to the pot; bring the mixture to a boil. Reduce the heat to low, partially cover the pot, and simmer until the potatoes are almost tender, about 15 minutes.

6. Add the clams and simmer until the clams are hot and the potatoes are tender, about 5 minutes longer. (If desired, thicken the chowder by smashing a few potatoes against the side of the pan with a spoon.) Add the half-and-half, cream, and fresh thyme (if using); heat until

steaming (do not boil). Season the chowder with salt and cayenne pepper. Remove the bay leaf.

7. To serve, place the bread bowls on plates and fill them with the soup. Garnish with thyme sprigs. Place the bread lids alongside the bowls and serve immediately.

NOTE | This quantity of clams yields about 1 pound of clam meat. To save time, you can use a 1-pound container of frozen minced clams (thawed) or three 6½-ounce cans minced clams. For the clam liquid, substitute bottled clam juice (3 cups if using thawed frozen clam meat and 2½ cups if using canned clams).

Salad of Greens and Radicchio with Pear, Orange, and Cranberries in an Orange Dressing

The gourmet greens, fresh fruits, dried cranberries, and candied walnuts in this salad make it simultaneously bitter, sweet, chewy, and crunchy. It's the perfect follow-up act for the creamy, salty chowder.

CANDIED WALNUTS

In a nonstick skillet, combine the walnuts, 2 tablespoons water, sugar, and kosher salt. Cook, stirring, over medium heat until the water evaporates and the nuts are dry and golden, about 4 minutes. Remove from the heat; cool. (If covered, the walnuts will remain crunchy for up to 1 day.)

ROASTED PEARS

1. Heat the oven to 425°F and place the rack in the middle position.
2. In a large bowl, toss the pears with the oil and season with salt and pepper. Arrange them in one layer in a large, shallow roasting pan. Place the pears in the oven and roast, stirring and turning them twice, until they are tender and beginning to brown, 20 to 30 minutes. Let cool about 15 minutes. (The pears can be roasted, cooled, covered, and stored in the refrigerator for up to 4 hours.)

ORANGES AND SALAD DRESSING

With a sharp knife, trim the tops and bottoms off 2 of the oranges. One at a time, stand an orange upright and cut downward to remove the rind and pith in thick strips. Working over a bowl, cut between the membranes to release the segments. Pour any juice from the oranges into a 2-cup measuring cup, then cover the orange segments with plastic wrap and reserve. If necessary, add enough juice from the third orange to equal ⅓ cup juice; stir the vinegar and shallot into the juice. Slowly whisk in the olive oil and vegetable oil. Stir in the chives. Season with salt and pepper.

ASSEMBLY

Place the greens, roasted pears, orange segments, and dried cranberries in a large bowl. Toss with just enough dressing to lightly coat. Divide the salad among plates and sprinkle it with the candied walnuts. Serve immediately.

YIELD: 10 SERVINGS

CANDIED WALNUTS

1 cup coarsely chopped walnuts

1 tablespoon sugar

Large pinch kosher salt

ROASTED PEARS

8 ripe but firm Bosc pears (4 pounds), peeled, cored, and cut lengthwise into 8 wedges each

1½ tablespoons extra-virgin olive oil

Salt and freshly ground black pepper

ORANGES AND SALAD DRESSING

2 to 3 oranges

1 tablespoon balsamic vinegar

2 teaspoons finely minced or grated shallot

¼ cup extra-virgin olive oil

¼ cup vegetable oil

1 tablespoon minced chives

Salt and freshly ground black pepper

ASSEMBLY

10 ounces mixed gourmet greens, including some bitter greens (such as red Belgian endive, radicchio, frisée, and chicory)

½ cup dried cranberries

Apricot-Glazed Ham with Madeira Sauce and Roasted Potatoes

YIELD: 10 SERVINGS

HAM

3 tablespoons grated fresh ginger

3 tablespoons minced garlic

2 tablespoons apricot preserves or orange marmalade

Freshly ground black pepper

1 (9- to 10-pound) fully cooked bone-in ham (spiral sliced, if preferred)

About 30 whole cloves

2½ cups Madeira

1 cup fresh orange juice

Salt

ROASTED POTATOES

8 slices bacon

4 pounds small boiling potatoes (such as white, Yukon Gold, or Red Bliss), peeled

Salt and freshly ground black pepper

For the ham sauce, instead of using Madeira and orange juice, try using sherry and apple juice. To make the parts of this dish come together smoothly, increase the oven heat and add the potatoes as soon as you remove the ham. While the potatoes roast you can make the sauce and the ham will rest for twenty-five minutes before you slice it.

HAM

1. Heat the oven to 350°F. Line a large roasting pan with a double layer of foil. In a medium bowl, combine the ginger, garlic, apricot preserves, and 1 teaspoon pepper; set aside.

2. With a sharp knife, cut off any tough rind and excess fat from the top of the ham, leaving a ¼-inch-thick layer of fat. Score the fat in a 1-inch diamond pattern and place a clove in the center of each diamond. Place the ham, fat side up, in the prepared pan. Pour the Madeira and orange juice into the bottom of the pan. Bake for 1 hour and 30 minutes.

3. Remove the pan from the oven and spread the reserved apricot mixture generously over the top and sides of the ham. Continue to bake until the ham is beautifully browned, about 1 hour longer.

4. Transfer the ham to a warmed platter, loosely tent it with foil, and allow it to rest for 20 to 30 minutes. Skim and discard the fat from the pan juices. Pour the pan juices through a sieve into a medium saucepan and bring to a boil; reduce to a simmer and let thicken slightly. Season with salt and pepper.

5. To serve, slice the ham (if not pre-sliced) into ½-inch-thick slices. Serve with the sauce in a warmed sauceboat.

ROASTED POTATOES

1. In a 12-inch heavy skillet over moderate heat, cook the bacon, turning it occasionally, until browned and crisp and has rendered nearly all its fat, 6 to 8 minutes. Transfer the bacon to paper towels to drain and reserve for another use. Carefully transfer the drippings from the skillet to a small heatproof bowl; set aside.

2. Heat the oven to 450°F. Combine the potatoes with enough salted cold water to cover them by 1 inch in a 6-quart pot. Bring to a simmer and cook, uncovered, until almost tender but not yet finished cooking, 12 to 20 minutes.

3. Drain the potatoes in a colander and return them to the empty pot. Place a lid on the pot and shake it a few times to rough up the potatoes' outside edges. Remove the lid, drizzle the potatoes with the reserved bacon fat, then spread them in a single layer in a large roasting pan. Bake until golden, turning them once, about 30 minutes. Season with salt and pepper and serve immediately.

Pumpkin Pie with Crunchy Pecan and Walnut Topping

No need to choose between pumpkin and pecan this Christmas—here's a pie to please everyone who craves traditional desserts.

PIECRUST

1. In a cup, mix 6 tablespoons water with ice and set aside. In a large bowl, whisk the flour and salt together. Using your fingertips, a pastry blender, or two knives, work the shortening into the flour until the mixture resembles coarse meal. (Alternatively, combine the ingredients in a food processor, using short pulses.)
2. With a fork, stir in the water, 1 tablespoon at a time, using only as much as needed to gather the mixture into a soft ball. Pat the dough into a disk, cover with plastic wrap, and refrigerate for at least 1 hour or up to 3 days.
3. On a lightly floured surface, roll out the dough into a round about ⅛ inch thick. Drape the dough over a rolling pin and fit it into a 9-inch pie pan. Fold the edge under and crimp. Place the pie shell in the freezer for 20 minutes.

FILLING

1. Heat the oven to 425°F. In a large mixing bowl, whisk together the pumpkin, sugar, spices, and salt. With an electric mixer, beat in the eggs and evaporated milk until thoroughly combined.
2. Pour the pumpkin filling into the prepared pie shell and jiggle the pan gently to level out the top. Bake for 15 minutes. Reduce the oven temperature to 350°F and bake for another 45 minutes, or until a knife inserted halfway between the center and edges comes out clean. Transfer the pie to a wire rack and let cool completely.

CRUNCHY PECAN AND WALNUT TOPPING

Heat the broiler. In a small bowl, combine all the topping ingredients. Mix with a fork until crumbly. Sprinkle the topping over the pie and place it under the broiler about 5 inches from the heat source until the mixture begins to bubble, about 1 minute. Let the pie cool to room temperature before serving.

YIELD: 6 SERVINGS

PIECRUST

1 cup all-purpose flour

½ teaspoon salt

⅓ cup chilled vegetable shortening

FILLING

2 cups pureed pumpkin, canned or fresh made

¾ cup granulated sugar

1 teaspoon ground cinnamon

½ teaspoon ground ginger

¼ teaspoon ground cloves

½ teaspoon salt

2 large eggs

1 (13-ounce) can evaporated milk

CRUNCHY PECAN AND WALNUT TOPPING

3 tablespoons unsalted butter or margarine, at room temperature

⅔ cup packed light brown sugar

⅓ cup coarsely chopped pecans

¼ cup coarsely chopped walnuts

New Year's Eve should dazzle. No matter how intimate the setting, or how big the blast, New Year's Eve should live up to the luxurious promise of its classic Champagne toast. │ When a Champagne cork is popped you know there's something to celebrate. New Year's Eve is always a double celebration worthy of a glass of bubbly, a time to reflect on the blessings of the year coming to a close and to toast the unknown adventure that begins January 1 of a brand-new year. │ Every dish on this menu for a spectacular New Year's Eve combines old-world luxury and new-world sophistication. The starter sets the tone of opulence for the entire meal by incorporating that icon of indulgence, caviar. │ Bisque is a classic soup to serve on New Year's Eve or New Year's Day. Here, though, I chose this beautifully hued, richly textured Butternut Squash Bisque drizzled with Basil Oil, because the soup is refined and elegant and allowed me to shine the spotlight on lobster as the star of the main event. │ Since I always think of New Year's Eve as a double celebration, it's only fitting that the entrée course be double the pleasure: Lobster paired with filet mignon. Lobster Thermidor is a classic and recalls the days of highly formal dining. My updated version makes this lobster dish a true delicacy, with cremini mushrooms, paprika, sherry, and lobster all folded into a delicious custard and served on the half shell. │ No less marvelous is the filet mignon, but it couldn't be easier. All you need is a great cut from the butcher to brush with a little oil, season, and broil. That's it. The beef has virtually no prep time and a very short cooking time. For the grand finale, this Flourless Chocolate Cake brings a deeply satisfying richness and sweetness. This entire meal celebrates a moment—right at the stroke of midnight—when we can have the very best of everything, past and future.

NEW YEAR'S EVE

M E N U

Potatoes with Asparagus,
Smoked Salmon, and Caviar

. . .

Butternut Squash Bisque Drizzled with Basil Oil

. . .

Baked Half Lobster Thermidor Surf 'n' Turf

. . .

Individual Flourless Chocolate Cakes

Potatoes with Asparagus, Smoked Salmon, and Caviar

T angy, lime-scented sour cream bridges the ethereal and earthy elements of this stunning appetizer.

1. Place the potatoes in a pot and cover them by 1 inch with salted cold water. Bring to a simmer and cook until just tender, about 10 minutes. (The potatoes will continue to cook after draining; do not overcook them at this point or they will break apart.) Immediately drain the potatoes and rinse them under cold water until they are slightly cooled.

2. While the potatoes cook, blend the sour cream, lime juice, and lime zest in a small bowl; set aside.

3 Place the asparagus in a wide skillet with enough salted water to come halfway up the asparagus. Bring it to a simmer and cook for 4 minutes, until the asparagus is crisp-tender and still bright green. When they have cooled, sliver them on the diagonal.

4. To serve, cut each potato in half. Place the halves on a platter, cut side up. Top each half with some asparagus, salmon, egg white, onion, sour cream, and finally, a dollop of caviar. Serve immediately.

> **NOTE** | Fingerling potatoes are long and thin, with a smooth texture and a nutty flavor. They raise the level of any dish they're in and are worth seeking out at farmers' markets, specialty foods stores, and better supermarkets.

YIELD: 4 SERVINGS

1½ pounds small boiling potatoes or fingerling potatoes, with peel on (see note)

Salt

½ cup sour cream

2 tablespoons fresh lime juice

1 teaspoon finely grated lime zest

1 pound fresh asparagus, trimmed

¾ pound sliced smoked salmon, cut into 2- to 3-inch strips

1 hard-cooked egg white, finely minced

2 tablespoons finely minced red onion

2 ounces Russian caviar

Butternut Squash Bisque
Drizzled with Basil Oil

YIELD: 8 SERVINGS

BASIL OIL

1 pound fresh basil leaves, stems discarded

1 medium garlic clove, peeled and smashed

1 cup extra-virgin olive oil

½ teaspoon kosher salt

BISQUE

4 tablespoons unsalted butter or olive oil

1 large onion, diced

3 pounds butternut squash, peeled, seeded, and cut into 1-inch cubes

3 Golden Delicious apples, peeled, cored, and chopped

8 cups low-sodium store-bought chicken broth or stock, or homemade chicken or vegetable stock

1 bay leaf

1 sprig fresh thyme

2 tablespoons maple syrup or honey

1 teaspoon freshly grated nutmeg

Salt and freshly ground white pepper

1 cup heavy cream (optional)

½ cup shredded cheddar, Asiago, or fontina cheese (optional)

Butternut squash bisque is like a blank canvas—there are so many terrific versions. Here we've provided two in one: a nondairy version and a version with cream and cheese added. We've served both at different times on board. The basil oil is what adds a celebratory touch. Store any remaining basil oil covered, in the refrigerator, for up to one week (let it come to room temperature before using). We also drizzle basil oil on pasta or over grilled or roasted vegetables right before serving or swirl it onto plates to add flavor, color, and pizzazz.

BASIL OIL

1. Bring a pot of water to a boil and prepare a bowl of ice water. Plunge the basil leaves into the boiling water for 10 seconds. Immediately remove the leaves and plunge them into the ice water; this will set the color of the basil. Squeeze out as much water as possible from the leaves and put them in a blender.

2. Add the garlic and oil to the basil leaves and puree until fully blended. Transfer the mixture to a coffee-filter-lined sieve placed over a bowl and allow it to drip. The resulting basil oil should be a clear green color.

3. Store the basil oil, covered, in a container in the refrigerator until ready to serve the soup. (Do not discard the puree remaining in the coffee filter. It may be stored frozen in ice cube trays or in a well-covered plastic container and used to make compound butter, to flavor soups or hummus, in lasagna or other pasta fillings, or brushed on pizza.)

BISQUE

1. In a large saucepan, melt the butter over medium heat. Add the onion and cook, stirring, until translucent, about 5 minutes. Add the squash and apples and cook, stirring, for 2 minutes longer. Increase the heat to medium high and add the stock, bay leaf, thyme, maple syrup, and nutmeg. Bring the mixture to a boil. Immediately reduce the heat to low and simmer, uncovered, until the squash is very soft, about 25 minutes.

2. Remove and discard the bay leaf and thyme; let the soup cool for 10 minutes.

3. Transfer the soup in batches to a blender and puree until smooth.
   (When pureeing hot soups, release one corner of the lid to prevent a
   vacuum effect and place a kitchen towel over the top of the machine
   while you pulse.) Season with salt and pepper. Return the soup to
   the saucepan and (if using) add the heavy cream and cheese. Heat
   over low heat, gently stirring, until the cheese is melted and the
   soup is warm.

4. To serve, divide the soup among warmed soup bowls and drizzle
   with basil oil.

Baked Half Lobster Thermidor Surf 'n' Turf

See photograph, page 6

**LOBSTER THERMIDOR
AND FILET MIGNON**

Sea salt

1 (1-pound) live chicken lobster (see note)

1 cup heavy cream

4 tablespoons unsalted butter

2 shallots, finely minced

¼ pound cremini and/or oyster mushrooms, trimmed and diced

¾ teaspoon paprika

2½ tablespoons medium-dry sherry, divided

1 tablespoon minced fresh flat-leaf parsley

Freshly ground black pepper

2 large egg yolks

Small pinch cayenne pepper

2 (5-ounce) filet mignon steaks (each about ¾ inch thick)

1 tablespoon olive oil

1 tablespoon grated Parmigiano-Reggiano cheese

BABY VEGETABLES

3 ounces slender baby carrots, trimmed, leaving ½ inch of green tops attached

3 ounces baby zucchini or haricots verts (if using zucchini, cut lengthwise in half)

1 tablespoon unsalted butter

Coarse sea salt

If you cook the lobster the day before, this luscious dish comes together surprisingly quickly. Serve any colorful vegetables you like as an accompaniment.

LOBSTER THERMIDOR AND FILET MIGNON

1. Cook the lobster: Bring 3 quarts water to a boil in a large pot filled no more than three-quarters full and add 3 tablespoons sea salt. When the water is at a rolling boil, add the lobster head first. Cook for 3½ minutes, loosely covered with a lid, then drain and cool at room temperature. Meanwhile, scald the cream in a small saucepan by heating it just until you see bubbles forming at the edges, then remove it from the heat.

2. When the lobster is still slightly warm, remove the claws with the knuckles attached. Remove the meat from the knuckles and claws and the cartilage from the claw meat. Using a large knife, split the lobster in half lengthwise, beginning at the tail end. Leaving the halves intact, remove the tail meat. Remove the intestine from the tail meat and cut all the lobster meat into ½-inch chunks. Squeeze the meat out of the legs with a rolling pin. Cover both the lobster meat and empty lobster shell halves with plastic wrap and refrigerate. (The recipe can be prepared up to this point 1 day in advance.)

3. Make the mushroom mixture: In a heavy 2-quart saucepan, heat the butter over medium heat. Add the shallots and cook, stirring, until softened, about 2 minutes. Add the mushrooms and cook, stirring, until they begin to brown and the liquid they release has evaporated, about 5 minutes.

4. Add the reserved lobster meat and paprika to the mushrooms. Reduce the heat to low and cook, shaking the pan gently, for about 1 minute. Add 1½ tablespoons of the sherry and ½ cup of the hot cream to the lobster mixture and simmer for 4 minutes. Add the parsley and season with salt and pepper. Remove the mixture from the heat. In a shallow baking pan, arrange the reserved lobster shells cut sides up and divide the lobster mixture between them; reserve.

5. Make the custard sauce: In a saucepan, bring about 1 inch of water to a simmer. Adjust the heat so that the water is at a bare simmer. Combine the egg yolks and the remaining 1 tablespoon sherry in a heatproof mixing bowl that can sit comfortably on the pan. Whisk until incorporated. Slowly whisk in the remaining ½ cup hot cream,

then place the bowl over the pan of simmering water. Whisking constantly, cook the mixture until it thickens and registers 160°F on an instant-read thermometer. Adjust the seasonings and add the cayenne. Spoon the custard sauce over the lobster mixture in the shells; reserve.

6. Broil the steaks: Place an ovenproof skillet on an oven rack 6 inches from the broiler's heating element and heat the broiler to high. Brush the filet mignon steaks with the olive oil and season with salt and pepper. Pull out the rack with the skillet and place the steaks in the skillet (be very careful, the pan is extremely hot and the oil on the meat may spatter). Broil the steaks for 3 minutes on each side for medium rare (they should register about 135°F on an instant-read thermometer inserted into the thickest part). Transfer the steaks to plates and tent them loosely with foil to keep warm. Leave the broiler on high.

7. Broil the Lobster Thermidor: Sprinkle the top of the lobster mixture with the Parmigiano-Reggiano. Broil the lobster mixture in the shells until the surface is golden brown, 4 to 5 minutes.

BABY VEGETABLES

1. Prepare a large bowl of ice water. Bring 6 quarts water to a boil. Add the carrots and baby zucchini (or haricots verts). Add 1 tablespoon salt and cook the vegetables until al dente, about 3 minutes. Drain in a colander and immediately place in the bowl of ice water to stop the cooking. Drain again and place in a bowl; set aside. (The vegetables can be prepared at this point up to 1 day ahead. Cover and refrigerate until ready to use.)

2. To serve, heat the butter in a skillet over medium heat. Add the reserved baby vegetables and cook, stirring gently, until heated through, about 2 to 3 minutes. Season with salt and pepper. Serve to accompany the filet mignon and Lobster Thermidor, with the remaining custard sauce on the side.

NOTE If you're doubling the recipe, you need to double the water and salt, too, or else cook the lobsters one at a time, making sure the water returns to a boil before adding the second lobster.

Individual Flourless Chocolate Cakes

With a touch of a fork, these cakes burst open to reveal their own molten sauce. The best part is they can be put together in advance and baked while you're clearing the dishes from the main course.

1. Heat the oven to 425°F. Lightly butter four 6-ounce individual ramekins or custard cups. Dust the ramekins with flour (or rice flour, to avoid wheat flour completely); tilt to coat and tap out the excess. Separate the eggs and reserve 2 of the egg whites for another use. Set aside the yolks and 2 remaining egg whites.

2. Place the chocolate, butter, and salt in the top of a double boiler over 1 inch of simmering (not boiling) water. Whisk until the chocolate is smooth and no small lumps remain. Remove the pan from the heat; let cool 10 minutes.

3. In a large bowl, combine the egg yolks and 3 tablespoons of the sugar. Beat until the mixture is thick and light, about 2 minutes. With a rubber spatula, scrape the chocolate mixture into the egg mixture and gently fold the two together.

4. Place the 2 egg whites in a clean, grease-free mixing bowl. With clean beaters, beat on low speed until frothy. Increase speed to medium and gradually add the remaining 1 tablespoon sugar. When the sugar is incorporated, increase the speed to medium-high and beat until the whites hold stiff, but not dry, peaks. With a rubber spatula, gently fold the egg whites into the chocolate mixture until well combined.

5. Divide about one-quarter of the batter among each ramekin. Add a chocolate truffle to the center of each and cover with the remaining batter. (The recipe can be prepared to this point up to 4 hours ahead. Cover the ramekins with plastic wrap and refrigerate them until 15 minutes before you plan to bake them.)

6. Bake the cakes for 11 minutes, or until they are puffed but still soft in the center. Transfer the baking sheet to a wire rack and let the cakes cool for 5 minutes. Run a small knife around the sides of the cakes to loosen them. Place plates on top of the ramekins and invert the cakes onto the plates. Serve warm, with berries and whipped cream (if using).

YIELD: 4 CAKES

4 large eggs

6½ ounces bittersweet (not unsweetened) or semisweet chocolate, chopped

3 tablespoons unsalted butter

Pinch salt

4 tablespoons sugar, divided

4 chocolate truffles (such as Lindt's Lindor truffles), in your favorite flavor

Fresh berries, for serving (optional)

Whipped cream, for serving (optional)

Holland America Line has the most extensive menus of any cruise line. We are known worldwide for our culinary excellence and our commitment to providing the best dining experiences possible for our guests. Over the years I've been with the company, many people have asked me, "How do you do it? How do you always keep everything so fresh and exciting?" The answer is easy: We thrive on the challenge of outdoing ourselves. | Creating something new, doing something that's never been done, challenging oneself to go all out, is a lot of fun. Several years ago, I floated the idea of holding a special event that would be part musical, part spectacle, and all about dinner. The culinary and entertainment executives loved the concept and worked with me to develop what has become an unrivaled culinary experience at sea: dinner as theater. | During a Signature Master Chef's Dinner, hundreds of guests in the main dining room are all decked in chefs' whites and crowned with tall toques, creating a dramatic visual backdrop against which the drama of dinner—a truly magnificent meal—is played out. White-apron-clad waitstaff swoop around the dining room serving, while performers conduct a show of song and dance numbers about what happens behind the galley doors, on the stove, and at the table. | My idea for the Master Chef's Dinner was just that, an idea. But it was one that has become a dazzling signature Holland America Line tradition. I now challenge you to create your own Master Chef's Dinner. Pick up some inexpensive white aprons and have your "Guest Chefs" work in your kitchen to help you create this high-drama meal. Put away any kitchen performance anxiety you may harbor, pull out your creativity, and get cooking. | The whole idea here is to embrace your inner master chef and create a theatrical culinary experience that you and your guests will not soon forget—and that might just become a "signature" party tradition in your home.

MASTER CHEF'S DINNER

MENU

Brie in Crispy Phyllo with Apple Cranberry Chutney

. . .

Cold Carrot Bisque with Lobster

. . .

Shrimp Provençal with Seasoned Yellow Rice

. . .

Individual Baked Alaska with Cherries Jubilee

Brie in Crispy Phyllo with Apple Cranberry Chutney

YIELD: 6 SERVINGS

APPLE CRANBERRY CHUTNEY

1½ pounds tart green apples (such as Granny Smith), peeled, cored, and chopped into ½-inch pieces

1 large red onion, chopped

⅔ cup cider vinegar

1 cup packed light brown sugar

3 ounces (¾ cup) dried cranberries

½ tablespoon chopped fresh rosemary

1 medium garlic clove, minced

2 teaspoons grated orange zest

½ teaspoon salt

⅛ teaspoon cayenne pepper

Pinch ground allspice

½ cup blanched slivered almonds, toasted and chopped

BRIE IN PHYLLO

6 scallions, green parts only

3 (17-by-12-inch) sheets of phyllo dough, thawed according to package instructions, stacked between 2 sheets wax paper, and covered with a towel

8 tablespoons (1 stick) unsalted butter, melted

3 ounces brie cheese, cut into 6 equal pieces and frozen for 30 minutes

The chutney inside these little pouches is delicious with game birds and ham, too. If you like, you can use your favorite prepared chutney instead.

APPLE CRANBERRY CHUTNEY

In a medium saucepan, combine all the ingredients except for the almonds. Add 1 cup water to the pan and bring the mixture to a boil over medium-high heat, stirring until the sugar dissolves. Reduce the heat to medium-low; simmer until most of the liquid has evaporated and the chutney is thick, stirring occasionally, about 20 minutes. Mix in the almonds. Transfer the chutney to a bowl, cover, and refrigerate until cold, about 3 hours. (The chutney will keep in the refrigerator, covered, for up to 1 week.)

BRIE IN PHYLLO

1. Heat the oven to 350°F and prepare a bowl of ice water. Bring a saucepan of water to a boil and blanch the scallions for 1 minute. Immediately transfer them to the ice water to stop the cooking. When cool, drain and pat them dry. Keep them wrapped in a damp paper towel until ready to use.

2. On a work surface, arrange a phyllo sheet with a long side facing you and brush it lightly with butter. Repeat with the remaining sheets, brushing each with butter. Cut the stacked phyllo lengthwise into 3 strips and crosswise into 2 strips to make 6 squares that are 6 inches by roughly 5½ inches each. Using a small knife and a cereal bowl or lid as a template, cut 5½-inch circles out of the squares.

3. Place a piece of frozen brie onto the center of each phyllo circle. Top it with 1 teaspoon chutney. Brush water onto the circle all around the edge of the brie filling and gather the phyllo around the filling to make a pouch. Brush the entire pouch with butter.

4. Place the pouches on a baking sheet and bake for 8 to 10 minutes, or until golden brown. Cool the pouches on the baking sheet until still slightly warm. When cooled, tie a scallion green around each brie purse. Serve immediately.

Cold Carrot Bisque with Lobster

Lobster brings a touch of elegance wherever it's added, but this creamy and flavorful carrot soup can certainly stand alone without it.

1. In a large saucepan, heat the butter over medium heat. Add the onion and cook, stirring, until translucent but not browned, about 5 minutes. Add the carrots and garlic and cook, stirring, for 3 minutes. Add the cumin, smoked paprika (if using), and chicken broth and bring to a boil. Reduce the heat to low and simmer, covered, until the carrots are tender, 15 to 20 minutes. Remove the pan from the heat and allow the soup to cool for 10 minutes.

2. Prepare a large bowl of ice water; set aside. Transfer the soup in two batches to a blender and puree until smooth, adding half the cream to each batch. (When pureeing hot soups, fill the container no more than halfway and release one corner of the lid to prevent a vacuum effect. Place a kitchen towel over the top of the machine while you pulse.) Immediately strain each batch through a fine sieve into a metal bowl. Season with salt and white pepper. Place the metal bowl into the bowl of ice water to chill the soup quickly, stirring every 15 minutes or so. When it is chilled, cover and refrigerate until it is completely cold, about 1 hour. (The soup can be kept this way for up to 2 days. If necessary, thin it with additional stock before serving.)

3. To serve, divide the cold soup among chilled soup bowls and top with the diced lobster meat. Garnish with parsley and serve. The soup can also be served hot (see note).

YIELD: 4 TO 6 SERVINGS

1 tablespoon unsalted butter

1 cup chopped onion

2 cups diced carrots

1 teaspoon finely minced garlic

Pinch ground cumin

Pinch smoked paprika (optional)

4 cups low-sodium store-bought chicken broth or stock, or homemade

½ cup light cream

Salt and freshly ground white pepper

4 ounces fully cooked lobster meat, cut into ½ inch dice

4 sprigs fresh flat-leaf parsley or cilantro, for garnish

NOTE When reheating, be sure to bring the soup up to a temperature of 165°F very quickly and then serve immediately. If serving cold, keep the temperature below 41°F.

Shrimp Provençal with Seasoned Yellow Rice

YIELD: 4 SERVINGS

SHRIMP PROVENÇAL

1½ pounds large shrimp, peeled and deveined

2 tablespoons extra-virgin olive oil

1 teaspoon finely minced garlic

Coarse sea salt

Freshly ground black pepper

¼ cup sliced scallions

2 tablespoons prepared horseradish

1 teaspoon grated orange zest

½ teaspoon fennel seeds

¼ cup dry white wine (such as sauvignon blanc, chenin blanc, or pinot blanc), or homemade shrimp stock (see sidebar)

1¼ pounds tomatoes, peeled, seeded (see sidebar), and chopped

2 teaspoons chopped fresh thyme

1 tablespoon chopped fresh flat-leaf parsley

SEASONED YELLOW RICE

3 tablespoons unsalted butter

1 medium red onion, chopped

1 medium green bell pepper, cored, seeded, and chopped

1 stalk celery, chopped

1¼ cups long-grain white rice

1 teaspoon Creole seasoning

½ teaspoon turmeric

2½ cups low-sodium store-bought chicken broth and/or homemade shrimp stock (see sidebar)

Coarse sea salt

Freshly ground black pepper

f locally grown sun-ripened tomatoes aren't available, by all means use good-quality canned Italian plum tomatoes for this dish. Drain, seed, and chop them before adding.

SHRIMP PROVENÇAL (PREPARATION)

In a medium bowl, combine the shrimp, oil, and garlic. Toss well. Cover and let marinate for up to 2 hours.

SEASONED YELLOW RICE

1. Melt the butter in a medium pot over medium heat. Add the onion, bell pepper, and celery. Sauté until the vegetables are tender, about 12 minutes. Add the rice, Creole seasoning, and turmeric; stir for 1 minute. Add the broth or stock and bring to a boil.
2. Cover the pot and reduce the heat to low. Simmer, without stirring, until the rice is tender and all the liquid is absorbed, about 25 minutes. Season with salt and pepper.

SHRIMP PROVENÇAL (FINISH)

1. While the rice is cooking, heat a large skillet over medium-high heat until hot. Add the shrimp with its marinade and season with sea salt and pepper. Cook, stirring occasionally, until the shrimp turn pink but are not yet cooked through, about 3 minutes. With a slotted spoon, remove the shrimp to a plate and set aside.
2. Immediately reduce the heat to medium and add the scallions, horseradish, orange zest, and fennel seeds to the skillet. Cook, stirring, for 1 minute. Add the wine and bring to a boil. Reduce the liquid, scraping up any browned bits, for about 1 minute. Add the

PEELING TOMATOES

To peel and seed tomatoes, use a paring knife to cut out the stems from the tomatoes and make a small X in the opposite ends. Plunge the tomatoes in boiling water and leave them in just until the skins are loosened, 10 to 20 seconds. With a slotted spoon, transfer the tomatoes to a bowl of cold water to cool. Slip off the skins. To seed: Cut the tomatoes in half along the equator. Gently but firmly squeeze the seeds from the halves. Now you're ready to chop or dice.

tomatoes, thyme, parsley, and reserved shrimp. Cook, stirring, until heated through. Season with salt and pepper and serve immediately with the seasoned rice.

SHRIMP STOCK

Reserve the shells from the 1½ pounds shrimp and roast them in a small roasting pan at 400°F for about 10 minutes. Put them in a medium saucepan and fill with water to cover by an inch. Place over medium-high heat and when little bubbles rise to the surface, reduce the heat to medium. Never let the liquid boil, and do not stir. Skim off any foam and add a small amount of any vegetables—such as sliced onion, carrots, and celery—and herbs that you wish. Cook very gently for about 30 minutes, strain, then return to the saucepan. Over medium-high heat, reduce to the quantity you need for the recipe.

Individual Baked Alaska with Cherries Jubilee

YIELD: 6 SERVINGS

See photograph, page 2

CAKE AND ICE CREAM

6 tablespoons unsalted butter

1⅓ cups all-purpose flour

½ teaspoon salt

6 large eggs

1 cup sugar

2 teaspoons pure vanilla extract

1½ pints cherry ice cream, softened

MERINGUE AND CHERRIES JUBILEE SAUCE

2½ cups sugar, divided

8 egg whites

2 tablespoons cornstarch

¼ cup cherry juice (available in health food stores)

¼ cup orange juice

1 pound Bing or other dark, sweet cherries, rinsed and pitted (or use frozen pitted cherries)

½ teaspoon finely grated orange zest

¼ teaspoon almond extract

¼ cup brandy or kirsch (clear cherry brandy)

 kitchen torch makes Baked Alaska much easier to prepare than it was in the past. And individual portions lend them a current cachet.

CAKE AND ICE CREAM

1. Heat the oven to 350°F. Butter a 12-by-17-inch baking sheet and line with parchment paper. Butter and flour the paper and the sides of the pan and set aside.

2. In a small saucepan, melt the 6 tablespoons butter and set it aside to cool. In a large bowl, whisk the 1⅓ cups flour with the salt; set aside.

3. Bring about 1 inch of water to a bare simmer in a wide saucepan. In a large heatproof mixing bowl that can sit on the saucepan or in the metal bowl of a stand mixer, combine the eggs and sugar; whisk until pale in color.

4. Set the bowl over the simmering water and whisk constantly until the egg mixture is warm. Remove bowl from over water. Using a hand mixer or the whisk attachment of the stand mixer, beat the warm egg mixture until it is lemony looking, tripled in volume, and very thick, stopping two or three times to scrape down the sides of the bowl. Continue beating until the bottom of the bowl is cool.

5. Remove the bowl from the mixer (if using) and, with a sieve, sprinkle a third of the flour mixture over the egg mixture. With a rubber spatula, fold them together. Repeat with the next third of the flour, then fold in the melted butter. Finally, fold in the remaining third of the flour.

6. Spread the batter evenly into the prepared baking sheet. Bake for 20 minutes, or until the cake springs back when touched. Place the baking sheet on a wire rack to cool completely. Invert the cake onto the rack and peel away the parchment paper.

7. Cut the cake into six 4-inch squares, reserving the remainder for another use (it can be frozen, well wrapped, for up to 2 months). Place the squares on a parchment-lined baking sheet and top each with ¾ cup ice cream, spreading it out smoothly as best as you can before it melts. Cover with plastic wrap and freeze until ready to use.

MERINGUE AND CHERRIES JUBILEE SAUCE

1. For the meringue: In a small saucepan, stir 2 cups of the sugar and 1 cup water over medium heat until the sugar is dissolved. Bring to a

boil without stirring and continue to boil until a candy thermometer registers 248°F.

2. A few minutes before the sugar syrup reaches temperature, beat the egg whites in an electric mixer fitted with the whisk attachment until stiff peaks form. With the mixer on low, slowly pour in the hot sugar syrup, taking care not to pour it directly on the beaters (which could make it splatter). Gradually increase the speed to high and continue whisking until the meringue is stiff and cool, about 7 minutes. Reserve.

3. For the cherries: In a wide saucepan, whisk together the remaining ½ cup sugar and the cornstarch. Stir in the cherry juice and orange juice; bring to a boil over medium high heat, whisking constantly, until thickened.

4. Stir in the cherries and orange zest and return to a boil. Immediately reduce the heat and simmer, stirring occasionally, for 10 minutes.

5. While the cherries are cooking, remove the cake and ice cream and place the squares on individual plates. Check the meringue; if it has firmed up, rewhisk it briefly. Working quickly, cover each ice-cream cake with a generous amount of meringue, using a spreader or spoon to form little peaks all over the surface. Using a kitchen torch (see note), heat the meringue until the edges of the peaks are nicely browned.

6. To assemble: Turn off the heat under the cherries and make sure there's plenty of clear air space above the saucepan. Stir in the almond extract and pour in, without stirring, the brandy. Standing well back from the stove, tilt the saucepan away from you and carefully ignite the alcohol with a long match held at the edge of the saucepan. After it's lit, move the saucepan gently back and forth until the flames die out. Spoon the sauce around each baked Alaska and serve immediately.

NOTE If you don't have a kitchen torch, you will need to use the oven and to plan ahead a little more. An hour before you need to serve the desserts, place the ice-cream cakes on ovenproof plates and cover them with the meringue. Return the desserts to the freezer, uncovered. Heat the oven to 425°F. After an hour, remove the desserts from the freezer, sprinkle them with granulated sugar, and bake for 3 to 6 minutes, until the meringue is browned. Surround the Baked Alaskas with the Cherries Jubilee sauce and serve immediately.

Birthdays are an opportunity to spoil loved ones. On someone's birthday, you are allowed to fuss, to surprise, and to invest some time in making that person feel special. When the birthdays of my friends, colleagues, and children roll around, it's truly my honor to make lovely meals for them. | The luxurious menu on the next few pages is perfect for birthdays, or anniversaries, no matter where on the calendar they happen to fall. The Tomato and Olive Confit on crostini make an elegant and deeply flavorful appetizer that won't fill your guests up before they get to the dinner table. The Italian Fish Soup is a favorite dish from Canaletto, the Italian fine-dining restaurant aboard a number of our ships. Although the ingredients can be a bit expensive, it's well worth the splurge for an important occasion. | Veal is another ingredient that most people love; because it can be on the pricey side, most of us tend to reserve it as an occasional break from the ordinary. Taking my cues from the Dutch tradition, I look for tender milk-fed veal chops that are thick so that the center remains moist and juicy through the cooking process. Of course, no birthday celebration would be complete without a grand finale of a cake! And this one—flavored with Grand Marnier chocolate mousse—is a chocolate lover's birthday wish come true. | I like to think of birthdays as each person's own New Year—a personal new beginning. I can't think of a more positive and tasteful way to help someone begin the next chapter of his or her life.

BIRTHDAY
OR ANNIVERSARY
CELEBRATION

MENU

Tomato and Olive Confit

• • •

Italian Fish Soup

• • •

*Veal Chops with Creamy Porcini Sauce
and Baby Vegetables*

• • •

Grand Marnier Chocolate Mousse Cake

Tomato and Olive Confit

YIELD: 2 CUPS

5 tablespoons olive oil

2 large onions, finely chopped

1 medium red bell pepper, peeled (see note) and finely chopped

1 tablespoon minced garlic

3 tomatoes, peeled and seeded (see Peeling Tomatoes, page 152), chopped

6 sun-dried tomatoes, chopped

12 niçoise olives, pitted and chopped

2 tablespoons drained capers in brine (chopped if large)

2 cups basil leaves, chopped, plus extra basil sprigs, for garnish

Sea salt and freshly ground black pepper

Splash balsamic vinegar

Here's a terrific spoon food for crackers or bread, or use it to perk up a grilled fish dish. If niçoise olives are hard to find, feel free to substitute any other rich-flavored black olive.

1. In a large, heavy skillet, heat the oil over medium heat. Add the onions, bell pepper, and garlic; sauté until the vegetables begin to soften, about 5 minutes. Add the fresh and sun-dried tomatoes, olives, and capers; sauté gently until the tomatoes are soft, about 3 minutes. Transfer the mixture to a glass or ceramic bowl, and let cool completely.
2. Stir the chopped basil into the confit and season with salt, pepper, and vinegar. Garnish with basil sprigs and serve at room temperature.

NOTE During cooking, the skins of bell peppers and tomatoes separate from the vegetable and don't break down, which is why many chefs prefer to remove the skins before cooking. For a single pepper you can use a sharp vegetable peeler to remove the skin. For multiple peppers, it is easiest to use the charring method (see Roasting Peppers, page 86).

Italian Fish Soup

We serve this soup at our Canaletto restaurant on board the ms *Eurodam*, where it's called Zuppa di Pesci. Its fresh seafood flavors and aromatic broth have made it one of the most popular dishes on that menu.

1. In a heavy 6- or 8-quart soup pot or enamel-lined casserole, heat 3 tablespoons of the oil over medium heat. Add the carrot and leek strips and cook, stirring, until the vegetables are just beginning to soften, about 2 minutes. With tongs, transfer about half of the carrots and leeks to a bowl and set aside for the garnish. Add the onions and garlic to the remaining vegetables in the pan and cook, stirring, until the onions are softened, about 5 minutes (reduce the heat if the vegetables begin to take on color).

2. Add the saffron and crushed red pepper; cook, stirring, for 2 minutes. Add the tomatoes and tomato paste and cook, stirring, for 4 minutes. Add the wine and simmer, uncovered, until the liquid is reduced by about half.

3. Stir in the fish stock and bring to a boil. Reduce the heat to low and simmer, uncovered, for 30 minutes. Carefully pour the soup through a fine sieve into another soup pot; discard the solids in the sieve.

4. Season the strained soup with salt. Add the striped bass, salmon, shrimp, scallops, and squid; bring the soup to a simmer (by the time it simmers, the fish should be cooked through). Adjust the seasoning.

5. Meanwhile, in a sauté pan, reheat the reserved carrot and leeks strips in the remaining 1 tablespoon oil until the carrots are cooked through but still slightly firm to the bite. Season with salt. To serve, divide the snapper pieces and soup among warmed bowls. Top with the carrot and leek strips. Garnish with the sprigs of fennel and serve immediately, passing a pepper mill (if using).

YIELD: 6 SERVINGS

4 tablespoons olive oil, divided

½ pound carrots (about 3 medium), peeled and cut into thin strips

½ pound leeks (about 2 medium), white and light green parts only, washed and cut into thin strips

2 medium onions, minced

1½ tablespoons minced garlic

¼ teaspoon saffron threads

⅛ teaspoon crushed red pepper

1 pound tomatoes, cored, peeled (see Peeling Tomatoes, page 152), and finely diced

3 tablespoons tomato paste

½ cup dry white wine (such as unoaked sauvignon blanc or pinot blanc)

8 cups white fish stock

Sea salt

1 pound (16 ounces) striped bass, Alaskan rockfish, or red snapper with skin on, cut into 6 pieces

4 ounces salmon, cut into ½-inch pieces

4 ounces medium shrimp, shelled and deveined

4 ounces bay scallops

4 ounces squid, cut into rings

6 sprigs fresh fennel or flat-leaf parsley, for garnish

Freshly ground black pepper (optional)

Veal Chops with Creamy Porcini Sauce and Baby Vegetables

YIELD: 4 SERVINGS

BABY VEGETABLES

¼ pound slender baby carrots, trimmed, leaving ½ inch of green tops still attached

¼ pound baby zucchini or haricots verts (if using zucchini, cut lengthwise in half)

¼ pound baby yellow pattypan squash, trimmed and cut in half

1 tablespoon coarse sea salt

VEAL CHOPS AND PORCINI SAUCE

1 ounce dried porcini mushrooms

1 tablespoon olive oil

4 (1¼-inch-thick) veal rib chops (12 to 14 ounces each), frenched, if desired

2 tablespoons unsalted butter

½ cup finely chopped shallots

1 teaspoon minced garlic

2 teaspoons minced fresh thyme

½ cup heavy cream

Salt and freshly ground black pepper

ASSEMBLY

2 tablespoons unsalted butter

2 small red onions, sliced into rings, for garnish

Salt and freshly ground black pepper

4 sprigs fresh thyme, for garnish

Veal chops are the ultimate special-occasion food. Unlike steak and lobster, which can be dressed up or down depending on the occasion (and where you live in the country), veal chops are generally reserved for celebrating. Baby vegetables are available in gourmet stores and even in grocery stores during the end-of-year holidays. If you can't find them, substitute ¼ pound each of regular carrots, zucchini, and yellow squash cut into two- or three-inch-long matchsticks or batons.

BABY VEGETABLES

Bring 6 quarts water to a boil. Add the carrots, zucchini or haricots verts, and pattypans. Add the salt and cook the vegetables until al dente, about 3 minutes. While the vegetables cook, prepare a large bowl of ice water. Drain the vegetables in a colander and immediately place them in the bowl of ice water to stop the cooking. Drain again and place in a bowl; set aside. (The vegetables can be prepared at this point up to 1 day ahead. Cover and refrigerate them until ready to use.)

VEAL CHOPS AND PORCINI SAUCE

1. Place the mushrooms in a 2-cup glass measuring cup; add enough hot water to equal 2 cups. Let the mushrooms soak until soft, about 20 minutes. Remove the mushrooms from the soaking liquid, reserving the liquid. Lightly rinse the mushrooms to remove any grit and coarsely chop them; set aside. Strain the reserved mushroom liquid through a fine sieve lined with cheesecloth or a damp paper towel and reserve the liquid separately.

2. Heat the oven to 375°F. In a heavy 12-inch skillet, heat the oil over medium-high heat (do not allow the oil to smoke). Sear the veal chops in batches until golden brown, about 3 minutes on each side. Transfer the chops to a shallow baking pan (do not wash the skillet). Roast the chops in the oven until an instant-read thermometer inserted horizontally into the chops registers 160°F for medium, about 20 to 25 minutes.

3. Meanwhile, pour out the excess oil from the veal skillet and add the butter; heat over medium heat. Add the shallots and garlic and cook, stirring to release any browned bits, until golden and tender, about 4 minutes. Add the reserved mushrooms and the thyme; sauté for 2 minutes. Stir in 1 cup of mushroom-soaking liquid and

the cream; bring to a boil and reduce the heat. Cook, stirring, until the sauce is thick enough to lightly coat the back of a spoon, about 3 minutes. Season with salt and pepper.

ASSEMBLY

1. In a 10-inch skillet, heat the butter over medium heat. Add the red onion and sauté until slightly softened, 1 to 2 minutes; transfer to a bowl. Add the reserved baby vegetables to the skillet and cook, stirring gently, until heated through, 2 to 3 minutes. Transfer to a bowl and season with salt and pepper.

2. When the veal chops are cooked, pour any meat juices from the baking pan into the porcini sauce and bring to a boil. Adjust the seasoning. Divide the veal chops among warmed plates and garnish with red onion rings. Spoon the baby vegetables and porcini sauce on the plates and garnish with thyme sprigs. Serve immediately.

Grand Marnier Chocolate Mousse Cake

CHOCOLATE GÉNOISE

4 tablespoons unsalted butter

1 teaspoon vanilla extract

4 large eggs

⅔ cup superfine sugar

⅓ cup sifted all-purpose flour

⅓ cup sifted unsweetened Dutch-process cocoa powder

MOUSSE

1 pound semisweet chocolate, finely chopped

1 cup sugar

10 large eggs, separated (see note)

2 tablespoons Grand Marnier

Sweetened whipped cream, for garnish

6 to 8 strawberries, hulled and cut into 3 or 4 wedges each, for garnish

Semisweet or bittersweet chocolate shavings, for garnish

Here's a birthday cake strictly for adults, a luxurious liqueur-flavored mousse on a foundation of chocolate génoise—no candles necessary!

CHOCOLATE GÉNOISE

1. Clarify and brown the butter: In a small, heavy saucepan, melt the butter over medium heat. When the butter starts to look clear, watch carefully until the solids drop and begin to brown. When they become deep brown, pour the butter immediately through a fine strainer, or a strainer lined with cheesecloth, into a small bowl. Transfer 3 tablespoons of the butter to a medium bowl. Add the vanilla and set aside.

2. Heat the oven to 350°F. Butter a 9-inch round cake or springform pan, line the bottom with parchment or wax paper, and butter and flour the bottom and sides.

3. In a wide saucepan, bring about 1 inch of water to a bare simmer, adjusting the heat as needed to maintain it. Combine the eggs and sugar in a large heatproof mixing bowl big enough to sit on the pan. With an electric mixer, beat until the mixture is pale in color, stopping 2 or 3 times to scrape down the sides of the bowl, until the eggs are lukewarm (105°F).

4. Turn the heat off and remove the bowl from the pan, but leave the pan on the stove. Continue to beat the egg mixture at high speed until it is cooled (touch the outside of the bowl to tell) and tripled in volume. The egg foam will be thick and will form a slowly dissolving ribbon falling back onto the whipped eggs when the mixer blades are lifted.

5. Place a sheet of wax or parchment paper on your work surface and sift the flour and cocoa powder together three times over it. Put the flour mixture back into the sifter or sieve and sift about a third of it over the egg mixture. With a rubber spatula, fold the flour mixture into the eggs gently but quickly, until combined. Fold in half of the remaining flour mixture in the same way, then the remaining flour mixture.

6. If the reserved butter mixture has cooled, briefly set it over the pan of water on the stove to remelt it. Place the bowl of butter on your work surface and add about a cup of the egg batter to it. With a rubber spatula, fold them together, then scrape this mixture back into the remaining egg batter and fold. Scrape the batter into the prepared cake pan and level the surface.

7. Bake the génoise for 30 to 35 minutes, or until the cake begins to shrink slightly around the edges and the top springs back when pressed. Allow the cake to cool completely in the pan on a rack. To unmold it, run a small knife around the edges and invert it onto a rack. Remove the parchment and turn the cake right side up.

MOUSSE

1. Lightly butter the sides of a 9-inch springform cake pan and line the sides with a strip of parchment cut exactly to fit. Cut a ½-inch-tall layer of the chocolate génoise and place it in the bottom of the prepared springform pan. Set aside.
2. Place the chocolate in a large bowl; set aside. In a small saucepan, combine the sugar and 1 cup water and place the pan over medium heat. As soon as the sugar has dissolved and the syrup begins to boil, remove it from the heat and pour it over the chocolate. Let the mixture rest briefly, to melt the chocolate, then whisk until completely combined. Beat in the egg yolks, one at a time, stopping occasionally to scrape down the sides of the bowl, until they are fully incorporated. Beat in the Grand Marnier.
3. Place the egg whites in the very clean bowl of a stand mixer fitted with the clean whisk attachment, or in a large, clean mixing bowl. With the stand mixer or a hand mixer, beat the egg whites on medium speed until soft peaks form. Use a large rubber spatula to transfer about a third of the whites to the bowl with the chocolate and fold them together, to lighten the mixture. Very gently fold the remaining whites into the chocolate, taking care not to deflate them too much.
4. Pour the mousse mixture into the prepared springform pan and smooth the top. Place the pan, uncovered, in the refrigerator until it is fully chilled. Cover it with plastic wrap and keep it refrigerated until ready to serve.
5. To serve, remove the side from the springform pan and gently remove the parchment paper. Put the whipped cream into a pastry bag and pipe rosettes on top of the cake. Garnish with the strawberries and shaved chocolate.

NOTE | You can eliminate the small risk of exposure to salmonella contamination in raw egg preparations by using pasteurized shell eggs.

There's something so special, so unique about a cocktail party. While there can be other types of events at which people might find themselves eating while standing or perching a plate on a lap, when you say "Cocktail Party," it's as if the fun is presumed. | There's a lightheartedness about this kind of entertaining. Inviting someone over to a "dinner party" seems like a much more serious affair. The other thing I love about throwing a cocktail party is that it's scalable. On board, the galley might whip up a menu for an intimate gathering of four people as a prelude to their evening's entertainment or, for certain types of special events like the inauguration of a ship, we might play host to eight thousand guests sipping and grazing their way through the evening. | Cocktail parties know no season, nor do they need to be held for any particular reason. Because I travel so frequently, I've often been at sea for many of the traditional calendar holidays. When I am home, though, I make it a point to entertain regularly so that too much time doesn't pass between visits with friends. | I'll invite some people over and plan a menu of appetizers, and the evening always starts with everyone in the kitchen, some standing and sipping, others rolling up their sleeves and helping me assemble a dish or two. Conversation over the ingredients or the recipes breaks the ice and gets the convivial atmosphere going; by the time we move to the living room, the party is in full swing. | I culled the recipes in this section from the most popular and praised dishes in our extensive collection of cocktail appetizers. You can choose to make all of the items or just a few—either way, your party is sure to be a success.

COCKTAIL PARTY

MENU

Classic Martini | Vodka Mojito | Grapefruit "Martini"

. . .

Belgian Endive Canapés with Caviar and Crème Fraîche

. . .

Peppered Beef Tenderloin Rolls with Horseradish-Mustard Sauce

. . .

Lemongrass Skewered Scallops with Spicy Garlic-Lime
Dipping Sauce

. . .

Vegetable Spring Rolls with Spicy-Sweet Peanut Dipping Sauce

. . .

Dungeness Crab Salad with Apples and Red Radishes

. . .

Mahi-Mahi Ceviche

. . .

Cherry Tomatoes and Mini Mozzarella with Basil

. . .

Fruit "Brochettes" Marinated with Citrus and Mint

. . .

Sweet and Spicy Chicken Drumettes

Classic Martini

YIELD: 1 COCKTAIL

1⅛ ounces dry vermouth

3 ounces gin or vodka

1 or 3 green olives on a toothpick
(see note)

NOTE | It is traditional to only use an odd number of olives in a martini.

Traditional martinis are made with gin, but many people prefer vodka, so be sure to have both on hand. For all the cocktails in this chapter, remember to chill the serving glasses, which will keep the drinks cold for longer. You can chill them in the freezer or simply fill them with ice and water before you make the drink, then dump out the ice water and wipe out the glasses before pouring in the drinks.

Fill a pint glass with ice. Add the vermouth, then immediately strain it out and discard it (this coats the ice and glass with the right amount of vermouth for the drink). Add the gin or vodka and stir about 30 times with a long spoon to ensure the drink is well chilled. Strain the drink into a chilled martini glass, add the olive skewer, and serve.

Vodka Mojito

YIELD: 1 COCKTAIL

1½ ounces fresh lemon juice

1 ounce fresh lime juice

2 tablespoons sugar

3 sprigs fresh mint, divided

2½ ounces vodka

Splash of Sprite

On board, we serve our own spin on a traditional Cuban mojito, made with light rum, fresh mint, fresh juices, and soda. The recipe for that cocktail appears in our first cookbook, *A Taste of Excellence*. Here's a version for anyone who prefers vodka to rum.

1. In a pint glass, stir the lemon juice, lime juice, and sugar with a long spoon until the sugar is almost dissolved. Add enough crushed ice to come halfway up the glass. Snip the leaves off 2 mint sprigs, stack them between your fingers, and rub them along the rim of the glass. Tear the leaves in half and drop them into the glass.
2. Stir the drink again to further dissolve the sugar and flavor the juices with the mint. Add the vodka and enough crushed ice to fill the glass. Add the Sprite and stir briefly (just once or twice). Top with the remaining mint sprig and serve with a straw.

Grapefruit "Martini"

T his isn't a true martini by any means, but it makes terrific use of the delicious grapefruit vodkas that are currently on the market. For a nonalcoholic version, replace the vodka with a grapefruit soda (such as Squirt) or your favorite lemon-lime soda (but stir in the soda after straining, to preserve its effervescence).

Fill a pint glass (or a cocktail shaker) with ice. Add the vodka and juices. Cap with a Boston-style shaker can (or cap the cocktail shaker) and shake vigorously. Strain the drink into a chilled martini glass, garnish with the grapefruit zest, and serve.

YIELD: 1 COCKTAIL

1½ to 2 ounces grapefruit vodka

3 ounces fresh pink grapefruit juice

½ ounce pineapple juice

1 long zest of fresh grapefruit

Belgian Endive Canapés with Caviar and Crème Fraîche

This recipe includes easy instructions for making homemade crème fraîche, but it does require you start a full day ahead. You can substitute store-bought crème fraîche, if you are in a hurry.

1. Make the crème fraîche: Heat the heavy cream over low heat in a small saucepan, stirring continuously, for approximately 6 minutes, until just lukewarm. Do not boil. Remove from the heat.

2. In a medium mixing bowl, thoroughly whisk the sour cream until smooth, approximately 2 minutes. Add the lukewarm heavy cream to the sour cream and whisk until well combined. Cover the mixture with a clean kitchen towel and let stand at room temperature for 15 hours, or until thick.

3. Transfer the mixture to a container; cover and refrigerate overnight. (The crème fraîche will keep this way for up to 10 days.)

4. Make the canapés: Place a small dollop of crème fraîche at the root end of each endive leaf or in the center of a cucumber slice. Scoop a little caviar on top. Garnish with the minced red onion and chive and serve immediately

YIELD: 12 CANAPÉS

1 cup heavy cream

¾ cup sour cream

12 Belgian endive leaves or ⅛-inch-thick slices of cucumber

6 ounces Russian caviar

2 tablespoons finely minced red onion, for garnish

12 chives, for garnish

Peppered Beef Tenderloin Rolls with Horseradish-Mustard Sauce

2 teaspoons vegetable oil

2 (8-ounce) beef tenderloin steaks, each about 1 inch thick

Salt and freshly ground black pepper

⅓ cup sour cream

2 tablespoons Dijon mustard

1 tablespoon olive oil

1 tablespoon prepared white horseradish, or more to taste

2 tablespoons extra-virgin olive oil

1 large bunch watercress, coarse stems discarded, for garnish

48 cocktail-size bamboo skewers

Coarsely cracked black pepper (see note)

D on't skimp on the beef tenderloin for these little rolls. Buy the best quality you can afford to get the right melt-in-your-mouth texture.

1. Heat the vegetable oil in a large, heavy skillet over medium-high heat. Season the steaks with salt and pepper. Add them to the skillet and cook to the desired doneness, about 5 minutes per side for medium-rare. Transfer them to a plate to cool.

2. Meanwhile, in a small glass or ceramic bowl, whisk together the sour cream, mustard, olive oil, and 1 tablespoon horseradish until blended. Taste and season with salt and pepper and a bit more horseradish if desired. (This sauce will keep, covered, in the refrigerator for up to 1 day.)

3. Cut each cooled steak across the grain into 24 thin strips. With a small offset spatula or the back of a spoon, spread about ½ teaspoon mustard-horseradish sauce down the center of each strip. Starting at a short end, roll up each beef strip. Brush the roll with a little extra-virgin olive oil and top with a sprig of watercress. Secure each roll with a bamboo skewer and sprinkle it with cracked pepper. Serve immediately at room temperature.

NOTE Freshly cracked peppercorns look terrific sprinkled on these rolls. To prepare them, place about 30 whole peppercorns in a mortar and pestle or wrap them in a kitchen towel. Crush them with the pestle or the bottom of a heavy skillet into coarse pieces.

Lemongrass Skewered Scallops with Spicy Garlic-Lime Dipping Sauce

Y ou can just as easily broil or pan-sear these skewered scallops, or substitute extra-large shrimp instead (if you do, increase the marinating time to 10 minutes and grill for 3 minutes). Serve it with this take on a Vietnamese *nuoc cham* dipping sauce. You will need nam pla fish sauce, which can be found in the international aisle of many grocery stores, or at any Asian market.

SPICY GARLIC-LIME DIPPING SAUCE

In a small, heatproof serving bowl, use a spoon to mash the garlic, sugar, and crushed red pepper into a grainy paste. Pour ¼ cup hot water over the mixture to dissolve the sugar. Let cool slightly, then stir in the lime juice, nam pla, and vinegar. Set aside.

SKEWERED SCALLOPS

1. Trim off and discard the tough root end of each lemongrass stalk. Peel away the outermost layer of each stalk. Finely mince the trimmed end of 1 or 2 stalks until you have 3 tablespoons minced lemongrass; set aside. To make lemongrass skewers, cut the remaining lemongrass stalks into 2- to 3-inch lengths (if they're fat, you can also cut these segments in half lengthwise), discarding any top portions that are too grassy. Whittle one end of each segment to a point. Soak the skewers, whether lemongrass or bamboo, in water for 30 minutes.

2. Heat the grill to medium high. In a large freezer bag, combine the finely minced lemongrass with the shallot, garlic, soy sauce, oil, nam pla, sugar, and pepper; shake for 1 minute. Add the scallops and let marinate for 5 minutes.

3. Lightly oil the grill grate. Thread the scallops onto the lemongrass skewers and grill them, turning them just once, until they are nicely browned and just cooked through, about 2 minutes per side. Serve immediately with the dipping sauce.

YIELD: 24 HORS D'OEUVRES

SPICY GARLIC-LIME DIPPING SAUCE

1 teaspoon minced garlic

2 tablespoons sugar

½ teaspoon crushed red pepper

3 tablespoons fresh lime juice

1 tablespoon nam pla fish sauce

1 teaspoon unseasoned rice vinegar

SKEWERED SCALLOPS

8 long, plump stalks fresh lemongrass (or 2 stalks lemongrass plus 24 cocktail-size bamboo skewers)

1 large shallot, finely minced

1 tablespoon finely minced garlic

2 tablespoons reduced-sodium soy sauce

2 tablespoons canola oil

1 tablespoon nam pla fish sauce

1 teaspoon sugar

¼ teaspoon freshly ground black pepper

24 sea scallops (1½ pounds), patted dry and side muscles removed

Vegetable Spring Rolls with Spicy-Sweet Peanut Dipping Sauce

SPICY-SWEET PEANUT DIPPING SAUCE

¼ cup peanut oil

1 cup finely chopped onion

¼ cup minced fresh ginger

3 tablespoons minced garlic

3 small red hot chili peppers, seeded and finely chopped

¼ cup sugar

⅓ cup soy sauce

3 tablespoons fresh lime juice

1 cup chunky peanut butter

½ cup unsweetened canned coconut milk, plus extra if needed

¼ cup chopped fresh cilantro

SPRING ROLLS

1 ounce dried shiitake mushrooms (about 16)

Peanut oil, for sautéing and frying

2 teaspoons minced garlic

4 scallions, chopped

½ cup chopped red bell pepper

4 cups shredded Chinese cabbage

¼ cup chicken stock, store-bought or homemade, or vegetable stock

1 tablespoon soy sauce

1 tablespoon cornstarch

½ cup sugar

40 small thin Vietnamese rice paper rounds (*banh trang*), 6½ inches in diameter (available in Asian grocery stores, see note)

1 large egg white, lightly beaten

Unlike fresh summer rolls, which have their own charms, fried spring rolls are tantalizingly crunchy and hold together so well they can easily be dipped and eaten with one hand. You can make these ahead of time: After frying the rolls, let them cool and freeze them, well wrapped in plastic freezer bags, for up to 5 days. Reheat the rolls, unthawed, on a rack set in a shallow baking pan in a preheated 450°F oven for 10 minutes.

SPICY-SWEET PEANUT DIPPING SAUCE

1. In a skillet, heat the oil over medium heat. Add the onion, ginger, garlic, and chili peppers. Cook, stirring, until the vegetables are softened and the onion is barely browned, 8 to 10 minutes.
2. Meanwhile, in a small bowl, combine the sugar, soy sauce, and lime juice and stir to dissolve the sugar. When the onion is browned, add the sugar mixture, peanut butter, and ½ cup coconut milk to the pan. Cook, stirring constantly, for 5 minutes. Add more coconut milk to thin the sauce, if necessary. Remove the pan from the heat and let cool. Stir in the cilantro and reserve.

SPRING ROLLS

1. Soak the shiitakes in 1 cup hot water for 20 minutes, then drain them and pat dry. Cut off and discard the stems from the mushrooms and mince the caps; set aside. In a skillet, heat 1½ tablespoons of the oil over medium heat. Add the garlic and cook for 30 seconds. Add the shiitakes and cook, stirring, for 2 minutes. Stir in the scallions, bell pepper, and cabbage. Cook, partially covered, until the cabbage is wilted, about 10 minutes.
2. Meanwhile, whisk together the chicken stock, soy sauce, and cornstarch. When the cabbage is wilted, add the cornstarch mixture and cook, stirring, for 2 minutes. Remove the pan from the heat.
3. Assemble the rolls: In a large bowl, combine 4 cups warm water with the sugar. Have several kitchen towels ready. Immerse the rice paper, one sheet at a time, in the warm water. Quickly remove it and lay it flat on a dry kitchen towel (this will help the rice paper quickly become pliable). Do this with four sheets one after the other, without letting them touch each other, and keep them covered with a barely damp cloth until right before filling.

4. Working with one moistened rice paper round at a time, place a heaping teaspoon of filling on the bottom third of the sheet. Brush the outer edge of the round with the egg white (this will help hold the spring roll closed). Fold the sides of the rice paper in and roll it up like a cylinder. Repeat with the remaining rounds and filling. Don't stack the finished rolls or allow them to touch each other—they'll be very sticky.

5. Heat the oven to 200°F and place a baking sheet in it. In a 12-inch cast-iron skillet or wok, heat 2 inches of peanut oil over medium-high heat until a deep-frying thermometer registers 325°F (a small piece of bread dropped into the oil should float to the surface almost immediately and brown within 1 minute). Line a wire rack with paper towels.

6. When the oil is ready, add a small batch of rolls to the skillet without letting them touch. Fry the rolls, turning them often with tongs, until they are golden brown and crispy, 10 to 12 minutes. Drain the finished rolls on the paper towels, then transfer them to the baking sheet in the oven. Repeat with the remaining rolls, checking the oil temperature in between batches and adjusting the heat accordingly. Serve with the Peanut Dipping Sauce.

NOTE Ideally, the rice paper rounds should be the thin kind, which are mostly found in Asian grocery stores. The rice paper rounds found in gourmet food markets are thick and, while fine for raw summer rolls, don't fry well. As an alternative, use square spring roll pastry wrappers (not wonton wrappers) made with wheat flour. They come in a larger size, so add more filling, cook them in more batches, and cut in half on the diagonal right before serving.

Dungeness Crab Salad with Apples and Red Radishes

YIELD: 20 HORS D'OEUVRES

8 ounces Dungeness crabmeat, picked over

½ cup finely diced apple (preferably a sweet and slightly tart variety such as Braeburn)

¼ cup finely diced red radish

2 tablespoons prepared mayonnaise

1½ teaspoons fresh lemon juice, plus extra if needed

1 teaspoon chopped chives

Salt and freshly ground black pepper

1 seedless (English) cucumber, cut into ½-inch to ¾-inch slices

20 sprigs fresh dill, for garnish

For an alternative presentation, cut the cucumber slices ¼ inch thick, use a small cutter to cut out the inner seeds and create cucumber rings, then place the rings on party-size slices of pumpernickel bread and mound crab salad on top.

1. In a glass or ceramic bowl, combine the crabmeat, apple, radish, mayonnaise, 1½ teaspoons lemon juice, and chives. With a rubber spatula, gently fold the mixture together. Season with salt and pepper and additional lemon juice to taste (if desired).

2. With a melon baller, scoop out the centers of the cucumber slices, leaving the bottom shell intact. Fill the centers, then slightly mound the crab mixture atop the cucumber. Garnish each with a dill sprig, transfer to a platter, and serve.

Mahi-Mahi Ceviche

n ceviches, citrus juice gives a cooked texture and look to the fish. This recipe requires the freshest fish you can find, but please also choose based on sustainability. Alternatives to the shot-glass presentation include serving the ceviche in a big bowl with fried tortillas for dipping, or spooning it into soft corn tortillas with avocado, shredded cabbage, and black beans to create a variation on fish tacos.

In a glass bowl, combine all the ingredients and stir gently, making sure the juice makes contact with all surfaces of the diced fish. Cover with plastic wrap and marinate, in the refrigerator, for at least 1 hour and up to 3 hours. To serve, drain off most of the citrus juice and divide the fish and vegetables among shot glasses. Provide small spoons for eating the ceviche.

YIELD: 12 TO 15 HORS D'OEUVRE SERVINGS

1 pound fresh mahi-mahi (or other firm, white-fleshed fish), cut into ¼-inch dice

1 cup fresh lime juice (about 12 limes), or a mixture of lime and lemon juices equaling 1 cup

1 medium tomato (or 3 Roma tomatoes), cored, seeded, and diced

½ medium red bell pepper, finely diced

⅓ cup finely diced red onion

3 tablespoons minced fresh cilantro leaves

½ jalapeño pepper, seeded and finely diced (or to taste)

Cherry Tomatoes and Mini Mozzarella with Basil

YIELD: 30 HORS D'OEUVRES

15 mini mozzarella balls, halved

15 cherry tomatoes, halved

Salt and freshly ground black pepper

½ cup basil oil (see Butternut Squash Bisque Drizzled with Basil Oil, page 140)

1 bunch basil

30 cocktail-size bamboo skewers

Send these little bites around and watch people smile—they're familiar, and they're fun. If your time is limited, top the hors d'oeuvres off with prepared pesto instead of tossing the mozzarella balls in homemade basil oil.

1. Put the mozzarella and tomatoes in two different bowls. Season each with salt and pepper and toss gently with basil oil.
2. For each hors d'oeuvre, sandwich a small basil leaf between a tomato half and a mozzarella half. Secure it with a small bamboo skewer and drizzle with more basil oil.

Fruit "Brochettes" Marinated with Citrus and Mint

N o grilling necessary—this is just fruit salad made easy to eat. You can substitute chunks of other kinds of fruit. Balls of watermelon or cantaloupe are also attractive.

In a large glass bowl, whisk together the lime zest, lime juice, honey, mint, and Grand Marnier (if using). Add the fruit and gently stir. Cover and let marinate in the refrigerator for 15 minutes, stirring occasionally. Thread 3 to 4 pieces fruit on each skewer and serve.

YIELD: 16 TO 20 SERVINGS

1 teaspoon grated lime zest

¼ cup fresh lime juice

¼ cup mild honey

¼ cup chopped fresh mint

1 tablespoon Grand Marnier or Cointreau (optional)

2 cups medium strawberries, hulled

3 cups kiwi chunks

2 cups fresh pineapple chunks

20 cocktail-size bamboo skewers

Sweet and Spicy Chicken Drumettes

T he drumette is the upper bone of the chicken wing, the meaty part that resembles a mini drumstick.

1. Heat the oven to 400°F. Line a rimmed baking sheet with foil and place a greased rack on the foil; set aside.
2. With a small, sharp knife, cut around the thin tip of each drumette to loosen the flesh. Using the back of the knife, push the flesh to the bottom of the drumette, scraping the bone clean. Remove any flesh left on the exposed bone with a paper towel. (The drumettes can be prepared to this stage, then covered and refrigerated, up to 24 hours in advance.)
3. Sprinkle the chicken with salt. Stand the drumettes, bone end up, on the prepared rack. Bake until the juices run clear when the chicken is pierced, about 40 minutes. Remove the chicken from the oven and turn the oven to broil.
4. Put the sweet chili sauce in a bowl and use tongs to dip the meaty portion of each wing into the sauce; use a brush to remove the excess. Return the drumettes to the rack and broil them about 6 inches from the heat, watching carefully, turning, and rearranging them as necessary, until they are crisp and browned, about 2 minutes. Serve hot.

YIELD: 24 DRUMETTES

24 chicken wing drumettes (about 3 pounds)

¼ teaspoon salt

2 (10-ounce) bottles Thai-style sweet chili sauce (see note)

NOTE | If you can't find Thai-style sweet chili sauce, you can make another style of sweet and spicy sauce by mixing 1 cup prepared hot pepper sauce (such as Frank's Red Hot Sauce) with 1 cup honey.

ACKNOWLEDGMENTS

Celebrations take many forms, as all the varied menus in this book attest. Celebrations also mark some special happening: Sometimes we celebrate a calendar or religious holiday; sometimes we celebrate a significant anniversary or milestone reached; and at other times, a special event is designed to pay particular tribute to an accomplishment—a job well done.

I wish to pay tribute here to the talented group of individuals who helped create this stunning book. While I get the singular honor of having my name emblazoned on the cover and title page alongside the prestigious name of Holland America Line, the fact is that there's not enough room on the cover to reflect the fine work of the many people who had a hand in producing it.

This book in and of itself is a celebration of artistry and collaboration. Many of the people I acknowledge herein have worked with me for many years, producing the series of beautiful Holland America Line cookbooks that have been so well received and praised by home cooks worldwide. I feel honored to work with each of you and include no small measure of gratitude for the personal friendships forged through our professional collaborations. I am so proud of what we are able to accomplish and how much we enjoy doing it together.

As always, I am extremely grateful to Johan Groothuizen, Vice President, Marine Hotel Operations, Holland America Line, for his commitment to making this popular series of cookbooks a reality. I celebrate and salute Johan for supporting the publication of the first-ever Holland America Line cookbook *A Taste of Excellence* (2006) and for ensuring that this popular series continued with *A Taste of Elegance* (2008). It is thanks to Johan's leadership that I have the great pleasure of bringing you *A Taste of Celebration*.

Likewise, I raise a glass to all the members of the Holland America Line culinary team on board the ships, to each of our thousands of cooks, the culinary shore staff, and the marine hotel department. This book is a tribute to you for the great pride you take in the work you do. A special thanks to Steve Kirsch, Director, Culinary Operations; John Mulvany, Traveling Corporate Executive Chef; and Senior Executive chefs Eberhard Schmidt and Andreas Summerfeld, whose culinary feedback is always insightful and whose company always delightful. Many thanks as well go to Jan Willem Kuipers, Manager, Marine Hotel; John Peijs, Manager, Marine Hotel Operations Procurement; and Oliver Hammerer, Director, Beverage and Signature Services.

A warm appreciation goes to my tireless recipe editor, Monica Velgos, who ensures that each recipe is picture-perfect for print for the home cook. Your dedication to every reader is apparent, and you ensure that he or she may *always* succeed in the kitchen.

The dynamic duo of photography, Herb Schmitz and Pat Doyle, shot this beautiful feast for the eyes entirely on location—that is to say, aboard the ms *Eurodam*—as it sailed to the Caribbean. As always, your work provides beautiful inspiration for the home chef. Many thanks.

My friend and longtime writer Marcelle Langan has, over our many years of collaboration, never failed to help me find the right words—lots of them. There's no one out there better than you.

I feel so lucky to have Tricia Levi as my editor, and I am very pleased to be working once again with Rizzoli Publications, Inc., which produces the most gloriously gorgeous books in the world. A very special thanks to Susi Oberhelman for designing another Holland America Line cookbook that makes me want to stand up and cheer, to Rizzoli's terrific production department, and to Chris Steighner, who helped to shepherd the project through. And, as always, I thank my publisher at Rizzoli, Charles Miers—ours is a collaboration worthy of fêting.

I believe that nothing important ever happened and nothing brilliant was ever produced that wasn't the direct result of great leadership. With that thought, I offer my inestimable admiration to the formidable leaders at Holland America Line: Stein Kruse, President and Chief Executive Officer; Richard Meadows, Executive Vice President, Marketing, Sales, & Guest Programs; Dan Grausz, Senior Vice President, Fleet Operations; Paul Goodwin, Senior Vice President, Onboard Revenue Services/Tour Operations; Judy Palmer, Vice President, Marketing Communications; and Sally Andrews, Vice President, Public Relations. Every day these individuals make the world a more interesting, vital place through innovation and a relentless quest for excellence in all things.

In celebration of long-term friendships that have meant the world to me, I acknowledge the fellow revelers in this life who have truly made a difference: Zane Tankel, Sigrid and Klaus Reisch, Sirio Maccioni, and Mike Smith.

I offer a very special message to my innermost and most important circle, my children: Magnus, Kenneth, and Kristina. You three are my center—the heart of every celebration, the driving force behind my every achievement and the principal architects of the most important and memorable moments of my life.

And, finally, to all of you readers who will choose a recipe or a menu to serve friends and family: Thank you. On behalf of myself and Holland America Line, we are very honored that you have brought our distinctive *A Taste of Celebration* into your home. Thanks so much for bringing us to your party.

Cheers!

RUDI SODAMIN

Master Chef, Holland America Line

CONVERSION TABLES

WEIGHTS

AMERICAN	METRIC
⅛ ounce	3.5 grams
¼ ounce	7.5–8 grams
½ ounce	15 grams
¾ ounce	20 grams
1 ounce	30 grams
2 ounces	55 grams
3 ounces	85 grams
4 ounces (¼ pound)	110 grams
5 ounces	140 grams
6 ounces	170 grams
7 ounces	200 grams
8 ounces (½ pound)	225 grams
9 ounces	255 grams
10 ounces	285 grams
11 ounces	310 grams
12 ounces (¾ pound)	340 grams
13 ounces	370 grams
14 ounces	400 grams
15 ounces	425 grams
16 ounces (1 pound)	450 grams
1¼ pounds	560 grams
1½ pounds	675 grams
2 pounds	900 grams
3 pounds	1.35 kilos
4 pounds	1.8 kilos
5 pounds	2.3 kilos
6 pounds	2.7 kilos
7 pounds	3.2 kilos
8 pounds	3.4 kilos
9 pounds	4.0 kilos
10 pounds	4.5 kilos

TEMPERATURES

FAHRENHEIT	CELSIUS	GAS MARK
40	4.45	
50	10	
65	18.3	
105	40.5	
115	46	
120	49	
125	51.65	
130	54.4	
135	57.25	
150	70	
175	80	
200	100	0
225	110	¼
250	130	½
275	140	1
300	150	2
325	170	3
350	180	4
375	190	5
400	200	6
425	220	7
450	230	8
475	240	9
500	250	
525	270	
550	290	

LIQUID MEASURES

	FLUID OUNCES	MILLILITER
¼ cup	3	60
⅓ cup	4	80
½ cup	6¼	120
1 cup	12.5	240
1 pint (2 cups)	20	570
¾ pint	15	425
½ pint	10	290
⅓ pint	6.6	190
¼ pint	5	150
1 quart	50	960
1 gallon	200	3.84 liters
2 scant tablespoons	1	28
1 tablespoon	½	15
1 teaspoon	–	5
½ teaspoon	–	2.5
¼ teaspoon	–	1.25

LENGTHS

AMERICAN	METRIC
¼ inch	6 millimeters
½ inch	12 millimeters
1 inch	2½ centimeters
2 inches	5 centimeters
4 inches	10 centimeters
6 inches	15 centimeters
8 inches	20 centimeters
10 inches	25 centimeters
12 inches	30 centimeters
14 inches	35 centimeters
16 inches	40 centimeters
18 inches	45 centimeters

APPROXIMATE AMERICAN/METRIC CONVERSIONS

ITEM	AMERICAN	METRIC
Flour	1 cup / 4¼ ounces	115 grams
Granulated sugar	1 cup / 7 ounces	200 grams
Brown sugar (packed)	1 cup / 8 ounces	225 grams
Brown sugar (packed)	1 tablespoon / ½ ounce	15 grams
Butter	1 cup / 8 ounces	225 grams
Raisins (loose)	1 cup / 5¼ ounces	145 grams
Uncooked rice	1 cup / 7 ounces	200 grams
Cocoa powder	¼ cup / ¾ ounce	20 grams

INDEX

FIFTH
EDITION

Measurement and Evaluation in Psychology and Education

ROBERT M. THORNDIKE
Western Washington University

GEORGE K. CUNNINGHAM
University of Louisville

ROBERT L. THORNDIKE
Columbia University

ELIZABETH P. HAGEN
Columbia University

Macmillan Publishing Company
New York

Collier Macmillan Canada, Inc.
Toronto

Maxwell Macmillan International Publishing Group
New York   Oxford   Singapore   Sydney

Editor: Robert Miller
Production Editor: Mary M. Irvin
Art Coordinator: Raydelle M. Clement
Text Designer: Debra A. Fargo
Cover Designer: Brian Deep

This book was set in Garamond.

Macmillan Publishing Company
866 Third Avenue, New York, New York 10022

Collier Macmillan Canada, Inc.

Library of Congress Cataloguing-in-Publication Data
Measurement and evaluation in psychology and education/Robert M. Thorndike . . .
[et al.].—5th ed.
    p. cm.
    Rev. ed. of: Measurement and evaluation in psychology and education/Robert L.
Thorndike, Elizabeth P. Hagen.
    Includes bibliographical references and index.
    ISBN 0−02−420775−6
    1. Educational tests and measurements.   I. Thorndike, Robert M. II. Thorndike,
Robert Ladd, 1910−   Measurement and evaluation in psychology and education.
LB1131.M433   1991
371.2'6—dc20   90-40130
                                                                                CIP

Printing: 1   2   3   4   5   6   7   8   9   Year: 1   2   3   4

PREFACE

It has been 36 years since two of us (R. L. Thorndike and E. P. Hagen) prepared the first edition of this book. During those years there have been major changes in educational theory and practice. Concern for the rights of all individuals without regard to color, gender, handicapping condition, or any number of other characteristics has become a central issue that has led to attempts to provide optimal educational experiences for all children. Society at large has been pressured to assure that everyone is given equal opportunity for access to higher education and to desirable employment. But even with these changes (and perhaps because of them), the need for objective, dependable information as the basis for making decisions remains. Tests provided much of that information in 1955, when the first edition was published, and they still remain an important source of information. The first four editions of this book have helped almost two generations of educators and psychologists develop the skills to use test information; this fifth edition is intended to continue providing that service.

When Macmillan Publishing Company acquired the rights to publish this book and requested a new edition, the two original authors found it desirable to bring in some new blood. First, R. M. Thorndike was added to the team, then G. K. Cunningham. Together, we have revised the book to make it responsive to the needs of the 1990s.

This fifth edition continues our tradition of treating tests as sources of information that aid in decision making. We emphasize that tests exist to help people make decisions and that the quality of those decisions depends on a knowledgeable use of test information. Many of the problems that have been attributed to tests are as much a consequence of improper test use as of poorly constructed tests. Our purpose is to provide users with the information and skills needed to avoid making mistakes in using and interpreting test information.

Changes in the Fifth Edition

Reorganization

We have reorganized the book into four parts. The first part, Chapters 1 through 5, provides a general overview of the issues in testing with which any user of test information should be familiar. It includes a chapter setting out our basic theme, followed by a chapter on necessary quantitative concepts, one on frames of reference (norm and criterion), and concludes with chapters on reliability and validity of measurement procedures.

Once these matters are mastered, the reader can proceed to material related to locally constructed measurement for use in classroom settings (the second part) or to standardized tests and inventories (the third part). The chapters in the second part, Chapters 6 through 9, discuss test and scale construction for local use and how to analyze the results of a test to evaluate the test items. The third part, Chapters 10 through 13, reviews selected instruments to appraise achievement, aptitudes, and interests and personality. We conclude with the fourth part, Chapters 14 through 16, which focuses on special issues and topics in testing and some speculations on the future of testing. While our treatment is in some senses sequential, only the material in the first part is prerequisite to any later section.

Pedagogical Aids

Each chapter begins with a listing of topics to be covered and ends with a summary statement. The topic listings help students by giving them a brief overview of the material they will encounter; the summaries allow them to review and remember key points. Most chapters are also followed by suggested readings, which can provide alternate perspectives on the issues covered in the chapter or present the material in greater depth, and by study questions, which allow students to test their understanding of concepts. A complete reference list appears at the end of the book.

Updated Sources for Tests

We have continued our practice of including a chapter that gives detailed information on where to get information about tests. We have revised Chapter 10 to include references to the major electronic data bases as well as the more traditional sources. We have also continued to include extensive appendices providing annotated lists of various kinds of tests, a list of major test publishers, and computational details for certain statistics.

Supplementary Materials

An **Instructor's Manual,** available free to professors who adopt the text, provides over 500 test items. These test items are available in **computerized form** for use with IBM-PC's and compatibles and Macintosh. Students can purchase the **Study Guide,** which contains detailed chapter outlines, review exercises and activities, and applied activities that address the underlying issues of each chapter.

Acknowledgments

Preparation of this manuscript has been a transcontinental matter, with the authors spread from New York to the state of Washington. Our work was greatly aided by the assistance of many editors and staff at Macmillan and by the following colleagues who reviewed early drafts: Betty M. Davenport, Campbell University; Dale G. Shaw, University of Northern Colorado; James S. Taylor, Pittsburg State University; James L. Wardrop, University of Illinois—Urbana-Champaign; Richard M. Wolf, Teachers College Columbia University.

We would like to express our appreciation to all of them, as well as to our families, who, in each case, are being put through the process of authorship for at least the second time, and who continue to offer support and understanding.

Robert M. Thorndike
George K. Cunningham
Robert L. Thorndike
Elizabeth P. Hagen

CONTENTS

CHAPTER 7
Locally Constructed Tests 191

CHAPTER 14
Testing in Special Situations   422

CHAPTER 15
Social and Political Issues in Testing   450

CHAPTER 1

Fundamental Issues
in Measurement

Introduction

Societies and individuals have always had to make decisions. Making decisions is a requirement of daily life for everyone. We all decide when to get up in the morning, what to have for breakfast, and what to wear; we make so many personal decisions with such regularity that we hardly think about the process.

Some decisions that must be made less frequently require careful thought and analysis: Shall I go to college? What should I major in? Should I accept a job with XYZ Enterprises? Decisions of this kind are best made based on information about the alternative choices and their consequences: Am I interested in a college education? What job prospects will it open for me? What are the chances that I will succeed?

Other decisions are made by individuals acting for the larger society. Daily, every classroom teacher must make decisions about the best educational experiences to provide for his or her students based on an assessment of their current knowledge and abilities. A school counselor may have to decide whether to recommend a special educational experience for a child who is having difficulty in reading or mathematics. School, district, and state educational administrators must make decisions about educational policy and may have to produce evidence for state and local school boards on the achievement of students. Employers must decide which job applicants to hire and which positions they should fill. A college counselor must decide what action to take with a student who is having difficulty adjusting to the personal freedom that a college environment provides. The list of decisions that people must make is as long as the list of human interactions.

We generally assume that the more people know about the factors involved in their decisions the better their decisions are likely to be. That is, more and better information is likely to lead to better decisions. Of course, merely having information is no guarantee that it will be used to the best advantage. The decision maker must also know how to use the information and what inferences it does and does not support. Our purpose in this book is to present some of the basic concepts, practices, and methods that have been developed in education and psychology to aid in the decision-making process. With these methods, the potential decision maker will be prepared to obtain and use the information needed to make sound decisions.

A Little History

Although educational measurement has gained considerable prominence in recent decades, the formal evaluation of educational achievement and the use of this information to make decisions has been going on for centuries. As far back as the dawn of the Christian era, the Chinese used competitive examinations to select mandarins for civil service (DuBois, 1970; R. M. Thorndike, 1990a). Over the centuries, they developed an elaborate system of checks and controls to eliminate possible bias in their testing—procedures that in many ways resembled the best of modern practice. For example, examinees were isolated to prevent possible cheating, compositions were copied by trained scribes to eliminate differences in penmanship, and each examination was scored by a pair of graders, differences being resolved by a third judge. In a number of ways, Chinese practice served as a model for developing civil service examinations in western Europe and America during the 1800s.

Formal measurement procedures began to appear in Western educational practice during the 19th century. For several centuries, secondary schools and universities had been using essay and oral examinations to evaluate student achievement, but in 1897, William Rice used some of the first uniform written examinations to test spelling achievement of students in the public schools of Boston. Rice wanted the schools to make room in the curriculum for teaching science and argued that some of the time spent on spelling drills could be used for that purpose. He demonstrated that the amount of time in spelling drills was not related to achievement in spelling and concluded that this time could be reduced, thus making time to teach science. His study represents one of the first times tests were used to evaluate curriculum and to make a curriculum decision.

Throughout the latter half of the 19th century, the pioneering work in the infant science of psychology involved developing new ways to measure human behavior and experience. Many of the measurement advances of the time came from laboratory studies such as those of Hermann Ebbinghaus, who in 1896 introduced the completion test (fill in the blanks) as a way to measure mental fatigue in students. Other important advances, such as the development of the correlation coefficient by Sir Francis Galton and Karl Pearson, were made in the service of research on the distribution and causes of human differences. The late 1800s have been characterized by DuBois (1970) as the *laboratory period* in the history of psychological measurement.

Interest in human differences in the second half of the 19th century can be traced to the need to make decisions in three contexts. First, there was the growing demand for objectivity and accountability in assessing student performance in the public schools, which resulted from the enactment of mandatory school attendance laws. These laws brought into the schools for the first time a large number of students who were of lower socioeconomic background and unfamiliar with formal education. Many of these children performed poorly and were considered by many educators of the time to be "feebleminded" and unable to learn. The development of accurate measurement methods and instruments was seen as a way to differentiate those children with true mental handicaps from those who suffered from disadvantaged backgrounds. Second, the medical community was in the process of refining its ideas about abnormal behavior. Behavioral measurements were seen as a way to classify and diagnose patients. Third, all sorts of government agencies began to replace patronage systems of employment with examinations of the prospective employees' abilities. Tests began to be used as the basis of employee selection.

Not until the first years of the 20th century did well-developed prototypes of modern educational and psychological measurements begin to appear. Although it is difficult to identify a single event that started it all, the 1905 publication of the Binet-Simon scales of mental ability is often taken as the beginning of the modern era in behavioral measurement. These scales, originally published in French but soon translated into English, represented the first successful attempt to measure complex mental processes with a standard set of tasks of graded complexity. Binet's first scales were designed to aid educators in identifying students whose mental ability was insufficient for them to benefit from standard public education. On the basis of the mental measurement, the decision was then made whether to place these students in special classes. Subsequent editions of the scales, published in 1908 and 1911, contained tasks that spanned the full range of abilities for school-age children and could be used to identify students at either extreme of the ability continuum.

At the same time that Binet was developing the first measures of intelligence, E. L. Thorndike and his students at Teachers College of Columbia University were tackling problems related to measuring school abilities. Their work ranged from theoretical developments on the nature of the measurement process to the creation of scales to assess classroom learning of reading and arithmetic and level of skill development in tasks such as handwriting.

It is convenient to divide the history of mental testing in the 20th century into five periods: the early period, the boom period, the first period of criticism, the battery period, and the second period of criticism.

The Early Period

The *early period,* which comprises the years before American entry into World War I, was a period of tentative exploration and theory development. The Binet-Simon scales were revised twice by Binet and were brought to the United States by several pioneers in measurement. The most influential of these was Lewis Terman of Stanford University. In 1916, Terman published the first English version of a test that in its fourth edition is still one of the standards by which measures of intelligence are judged: the Stanford-Binet Intelligence Scale. Working with Terman at this time, Arthur Otis began to explore the possibility of testing the mental ability of children and adults in groups. In Australia, S. D. Porteus prepared a maze test of intelligence for use with people with hearing or language handicaps.

During the time Binet was developing the first modern test of intelligence, Charles Spearman published two important theories relating to the measurement of human abilities. The first was a statistical theory that proposed to describe and account for the inconsistency of human behavior. The second theory claimed to account for the fact that different measures of intelligence showed substantial consistency in the ways that they ranked people. The statistical theory to describe inconsistency has developed into the concept of reliability that we will discuss in Chapter 4. Spearman's second theory, that there is a single dimension of ability underlying most human performance, played a major role in determining the direction that measures of ability took for many years. Spearman proposed that the consistency of people's performance on different ability measures was the result of the level of general intelligence that they possessed.

The Boom Period

American involvement in World War I brought a need to expand the army very quickly. For the first time, the new science of psychology was called on to play a part in a military situation. This event started a 15-year *boom period* during which there were many advances and innovations in the field of testing and measurement. As part of the war effort, a group of psychologists expanded Otis' work to develop and implement the first large-scale group testing of ability with the Army Alpha (a verbal test) and the Army Beta (a test using mazes and puzzles similar to Porteus' that required no spoken or written language). The Army Alpha was the first widely distributed test to use the multiple-choice item form. The first objective measure of personality, the Woodworth Personal Data Sheet, was also developed for the army to help identify those emotionally unfit for military service. The Alpha and Beta were used to select officer trainees and to remove the intellectually handicapped from military service.

In the 12 years following the war, the variety of behaviors that were subjected to measurement continued to expand rapidly. E. K. Strong and his students began to measure vocational interests to help college students choose majors and careers consistent with their interests. Measurements of personality and ability were developed and refined, and the use of standardized tests for educational decisions became more widespread. In 1929, L. L. Thurstone proposed ways to scale and measure attitudes and values. Many people considered it only a matter of time before accurate measurement and prediction of all types of human behavior would be achieved.

The First Period of Criticism

The 1930s saw a crash not only in the stock market but also in the expectations for mental measurement. This time covered the *period of criticism* and *consolidation*. To be sure, new tests were published, most notably the original Kuder scales of vocational interests and the Minnesota Multiphasic Personality Inventory. Major advances were also made in the mathematical theory underlying tests, particularly L. L. Thurstone's refinements of a statistical procedure known as factor analysis. However, it was becoming clear that the problems of measuring human behavior had not all been solved and were much more difficult than they had appeared to be in the heady years of the 1920s.

The Battery Period

In the 1940s, psychological measurement was once again called on for use in the military service. As part of the war effort, batteries of tests were developed that measured several different abilities. Based on the theory developed by Thurstone and others that there were several distinct types or dimensions of abilities, these test batteries were used to place military recruits in the positions for which they were best suited. The success that this approach achieved in reducing failure rates in various military training programs led the measurement field into a period of emphasis on test batteries and factor analysis. Until about 1965, efforts were directed toward analyzing the dimensions of human behavior by developing an increasing variety of tests of ability and personality. Taxonomies of ability, such as those of Bloom (1956) and Guilford (1959, 1985), were offered to describe the range of mental functioning.

During the 1950s, educational and psychological testing grew to become big business. The use of nationally normed, commercially prepared tests to assess student progress became a common feature of school life. Business, industry, and the civil service system made increasing use of measurements of attitudes and personality, as well as ability, in hiring and promotion decisions. Patients in mental institutions were routinely assessed through a variety of measures of personality and adjustment. The widespread use and misuse of tests brought about a wave of protests.

The Second Period of Criticism

The beginning of this *second period of criticism* was signaled in 1965 by a series of congressional hearings on testing as an invasion of privacy. Since that time, there has been a continuing debate over the use of ability and personality testing in public education and employment. A major concern has been the possible use, intentional or otherwise, of tests to discriminate against women and/or members of minority groups in education and employment. As a result of this concern, certain types of testing practices have been changed, and much more attention is given to the rights of individuals. We will take a closer look at the controversies surrounding educational and psychological uses of tests in Chapter 13.

Types of Decisions

Educational and psychological evaluation and measurement have evolved to help people make decisions related to people, individually or in groups. Teachers, counselors, school administrators, and psychologists in business and industry, for example, are continuously involved in making decisions about people or in helping people to make decisions for and about themselves. The role of measurement procedures is to provide information that will permit these decisions to be informed and appropriate.

Some decisions are *instructional;* many decisions made by teachers are of this sort. The decisions may relate to the class as a whole: For example, should class time be spent reviewing "carrying" in addition? Or does most of the class have adequate competency in this skill? Others relate to specific students: For example, what reading materials are likely to be suitable for Mary, in view of her interests and level of reading skill? If such decisions are to be made wisely, it is important to know, in the first case, the level of skill of the class in "carrying" and, in the second, how competent a reader Mary is.

Some decisions are *curricular.* A school may be considering a curricular change such as introducing computer-assisted instruction to teach the principles of multiplying fractions. Should the change be made? A wise decision hinges on finding out how well children are found to progress in learning to multiply fractions using this approach rather than the conventional one. The evidence of progress can only be as good as the measures of mathematics competence we use to assess the outcomes of the two alternative instructional programs.

Some decisions are *selection* ones made by an employer or a decision maker in an educational institution. A popular college must decide which applicants to admit to its freshman class. Criteria for admission are likely to be complex, but one criterion will usually be that the admitted student is likely to be able to complete successfully the academic work that the college requires. Selection decisions also arise in employment. The employer, seeking to identify the potentially more effective employees, may find that performance in a controlled testing situation provides information that can improve the accuracy and objectivity of hiring decisions, resulting in improved productivity and greater employee satisfaction.

Sometimes decisions are *placement,* or *classification,* decisions. A high school may have to decide whether a senior should be put in the advanced placement section in mathematics or in the regular section. An army personnel technician may have to decide whether a recruit should be assigned to the school for electronic technicians or the school for cooks and bakers. A family doctor makes a classification decision when he or she diagnoses a backache to be the result of muscle strain or a pinched nerve. For placement decisions, the decision maker needs information to help predict how much the individual will learn from or how successful the candidate will be in each of the alternative programs. Information helps the person making a classification, or placement, decision to identify the group to which the individual most likely belongs.

Finally, many decisions can best be called *personal* decisions They are choices that each individual makes at the many crossroads of life. Should I plan to go to college or to some other type of post-high school training? Or should I seek a job at the end of high school? If a job, what kind of job? In light of this decision, what sort of program should I take in high school? The more information people have about their own interests and abilities, the more informed decisions they can make on questions like these.

Measurement and Decisions

Educational and psychological measurement techniques can help people make better decisions by providing more and better information. Throughout this book, we will identify and describe properties that measurement devices must have if they are to help people to make sound decisions. We will show the form in which test results should be presented if they are to be most helpful to the decision maker. As we look at each type of evaluation technique, we will ask for what types of decisions the particular technique can contribute valuable information. We will be concerned with the variety of factors, including poor motivation, emotional upset, inadequate schooling, or atypical cultural background, all of which can distort the information provided by a test, questionnaire, or other assessment procedure. We will also consider precautions that need to be observed in using the information in decision making.

The Role of Values in Decision Making

Measurement procedures do not make decisions; *people* make decisions. At most, measurement procedures can provide information on some of the factors that are relevant to the decision. A scholastic aptitude test can provide an indication of how well Grace is likely to do in college-level work. Combined with information about how academically demanding the engineering program is at Siwash University, the test score can be used to make a specific estimate of how well Grace is likely to do in the engineering program at Siwash. However, only Grace can decide whether she should go to Siwash and study engineering. Is she interested in engineering? Does she have a personal reason for wanting to go to Siwash rather than to some other university? Are there economic factors? What role does Grace aspire to serve? Maybe she has no interest in further education and would rather be a beachcomber.

This example should make it clear that decisions about courses of action to take involve values as well as facts. A scholastic aptitude test produces a score that is a *fact,* and that fact may lead to a prediction that Grace has five chances in six of being admitted to Siwash and only one chance in six of being admitted to Harvard. But, if she considers Harvard 10 times more desirable than Siwash, it still might be a sensible decision for her to apply to Harvard despite her radically lower chance of being admitted. The test provides no information about the domain of values. This information must be supplied from other sources before Grace can make a sensible decision.

The issue of values affects institutional decision makers as well as individuals. An aptitude test may permit an estimate of the probability of success for a black or a Hispanic student, in comparison with the probability of success for a white student, in some types of professional training. However, an admission decision would have to include, explicitly or implicitly, some judgment on the relative value to society of adding more white people to the profession in comparison with the value of having increased black or Hispanic representation.

Such issues of value are always complex and often controversial, but issues of value are frequently deeply involved in decision making. It is important that this fact be recognized, and it is also important that assessment procedures that can supply better information not be blamed for the ambiguities or conflicts that may be found in our value system. We should not kill the messenger who brings us news we do not want to hear. Rather, we should consider policies and procedures that might change the unwelcome facts.

As we suggested at the beginning of this chapter, all aspects of human behavior involve decisions. We *must* make decisions. Even taking no action in a situation is a decision. In most cases, people weigh the evidence on the likelihood of various outcomes and the positive and negative consequences of each possible outcome. The role of educational and psychological assessment procedures can be no more than to provide some of the information on which certain kinds of decisions may be based. The evidence suggests that, when properly used, these procedures can provide useful information that is more accurate than that provided by alternate approaches. The study of educational and psychological assessment should yield an understanding of the tools and techniques available for obtaining the kinds of information about people that these measures can yield. Beyond that, such study should provide criteria for evaluating the information that these tools offer, for judging the degree of confidence that can be placed in the information, and for sensing the limitations inherent in that information.

So far, we have considered practical decisions leading to action. Measurement is also important in providing information to guide theoretical decisions. In these cases, the desired result is not action but instead understanding. Do girls read better than boys do? A reading test is needed to obtain the information on which to base a decision. Do students who are anxious about tests do worse on them than students who are not anxious? A questionnaire on "test anxiety" and a test of academic achievement could be used to obtain information helpful in reaching a decision on this issue. Measurement is fundamental to answering nearly all the questions that science asks, not only in the physical sciences but also in the behavioral and biological sciences.

Steps in the Measurement Process

In this book, we discuss the measurement of human abilities, interests, and personality traits. We need to pause for a moment and to look at what is implied by measurement and what requirements must be met if we are legitimately to discuss measurement. We also need to ask how well the techniques for measuring the human characteristics of interest do in fact meet these requirements.

Measurement in any field involves three common steps: (1) identifying and defining the quality or the attribute that is to be measured, (2) determining the set of operations by which the attribute may be isolated and displayed, and (3) establishing a set of procedures or definitions for translating observations into quantitative statements of degree or amount. An understanding of these steps and of the difficulties that each presents provides a sound foundation for understanding the procedures and problems of measurement in psychology and education.

Identifying and Defining the Attribute

We never measure a thing or a person. We always measure a *quality* or an *attribute* of the thing or person. We measure, for example, the *length* of a table, the *temperature* of a blast furnace, the *durability* of an automobile tire, the *flavor* of a soft drink, the *intelligence* of a school child, or the *emotional maturity* of an adolescent. Educators and psychologists frequently use the term *construct* to refer to the more abstract and difficult-to-observe properties of people, such as their intelligence or personality.

When we deal with simple physical attributes, such as length, it rarely occurs to us to wonder about the meaning or definition of the attribute. A clear meaning for length was established long ago in the history of both the species and the individual. The units for expressing length and the operations for making the property manifest have changed over the years; however, the underlying concepts have not. Although mastery of the concepts of "long" and "short" may represent significant accomplishments in the life of a preschool child, the concepts are automatic in adult society. We all know what we mean by "length." The construct of length is one about which there is little disagreement, and the operations by which length can be determined are well known.

However, this level of agreement and clarity of definition do not exist for all physical attributes. What do we mean by durability in an automobile tire? Do we mean resistance to wear and abrasion from contact with the road? Do we mean resistance to puncture by pointed objects? Do we mean resistance to deterioration and decay with the passage of time and exposure to the elements? Or do we mean some combination of these three and possibly other factors? Until we can reach some agreement on what we mean by durability, we can make no progress toward measuring it. To the extent that we disagree on what durability means (i.e., on a definition of the construct), we will disagree on what procedures are appropriate for measuring it. If we use different procedures, we are likely to get different results from our measurements, and we will disagree on the value that we obtain to represent the durability of a particular brand of tire.

The problem of agreeing on what a given construct means is even more acute when we start to consider those attributes of concern to the psychologist or educator. What do we mean by intelligence? What kinds of behavior shall we characterize as intelligent? Shall we define the construct primarily in terms of dealing with ideas and abstract concepts? Or will it include dealing with things —with concrete objects? Will it refer primarily to behavior in novel situations? Or will it include responses in familiar and habitual settings? Will it refer to speed and fluency of response or to level of complexity of reaction without regard to time? Will it include skill in social interactions? What kinds of products result from the exercise of intelligence: a theory about atomic structures, a ballet, or a snowman? We all have a general idea of what we mean when we characterize behavior as intelligent, but there are many specific points on which we may disagree as we try to make our definition precise. This problem of precisely defining the attribute is true for almost all psychological constructs— more for some than for others. And the first problem that psychologists or educators face as they try to measure the attributes is arriving at clear, precise, and generally accepted definitions of those attributes.

Of course, there is another question that we must answer before we face the problem of defining the attribute. We must decide which attributes are relevant and important to measure if our description is to be useful. A description may fail to be useful for the need at hand because we choose irrelevant features to describe. In describing a painting, we might report its height, breadth, and weight. We might report these attributes with great precision and reach high agreement about the amount of each property the painting possesses. If our concern were to crate the picture for shipment, these might be just the items of information that we would need. However, if our purpose were to characterize the painting as a work of art, our description would be useless; the attributes of the painting we just described would essentially be irrelevant to its quality as a work of art.

Similarly, a description of a person may be of little value for our purpose if we choose the wrong things to describe. A company selecting employees to become truck drivers might test their verbal comprehension and ability to solve quantitative problems, getting very accurate measures of these functions. It is likely, however, that information on these factors would be of little help in identifying people who have low accident records and would be steady and dependable on the job. Other factors, such as eye-hand coordination, depth perception, and freedom from uncontrolled aggressive impulses might prove much more relevant to the tasks and pressures that a truck driver faces.

Consider a high school music teacher who thoroughly tested the pupils' knowledge of such facts as who wrote the "Emperor Concerto" and whether andante is faster than allegro. The teacher would obtain a dependable appraisal of their knowledge about music and musicians without presenting them with a single note of actual music, a single theme or melody, a single interpretation or appraisal of living music. As an appraisal of musical appreciation, such a test seems almost worthless because it uses bits of factual knowledge *about* music and composers in place of information that would indicate progress in appreciation of the music itself. It is important to measure traits that are relevant to the decisions to be made rather than merely to measure traits that are easy to assess. We will discuss the issue of relevance again when we cover validity in Chapter 5.

Determining Operations to Isolate and Display the Attribute

The second aspect of measurement is finding or inventing a set of operations that will isolate the attribute of interest and display it. The operations for measuring the length of an object such as a table have been essentially unchanged for many years. We convey them to the child early in elementary school. The ruler, the meterstick, and the tape measure are uniformly accepted as appropriate instruments, and laying one of them along an object is an appropriate procedure for displaying to the eye the length of the table, desk, or other object. But the operations for measuring length, or distance, are not always so simple. By what operations do we measure the distance from New York to Chicago? From the earth to the sun? From our solar system to the giant spiral galaxy in Andromeda? How shall we measure the length of a tuberculosis bacillus or the diameter of a neutron? Physical science has progressed by developing instruments that extend the capabilities of our senses and indirect procedures that make accessible to us amounts too great or too small for the simple direct approach of laying a measuring stick along the object. The operations for measuring length, or distance, have become indirect, elaborate, and increasingly precise. These less intuitive methods (such as the shift of certain wavelengths of light toward the red end of the spectrum) are accepted because they give results that are consistent, verifiable, and useful.

Turning to the example of the durability of the automobile tire, we can see that the operations for eliciting or displaying that attribute will depend on and interact with the definition that we have accepted for it. If our definition is in terms of resistance to abrasion, we need to develop some standard and uniform procedure for applying an abrasive force to a specimen and gauging the rate at which the rubber wears away, that is, a standardized simulated road test. If we have indicated puncture resistance as the central concept, we need a way of applying graduated puncturing forces. If our definition is in terms of resistance to deterioration from sun, oil, and other destructive agents, our procedure must expose the samples to these agents and provide some index of the resulting loss of strength or resilience. A definition that incorporates more than one aspect will require an assessment of each, with appropriate weight, and combine the aspects in an appropriate way. That is, if our definition of durability, for example, includes resistance to abrasion, punctures, and deterioration, then a measure of durability must assess all of these properties and combine them in some way to give a single index of durability.

The definition of an attribute and the operations for eliciting it interact. On the one hand, the definition we have set up determines what we will accept as relevant and reasonable operations. Conversely, the operations that we can devise to elicit or display the attribute constitute in a very practical sense the definition of that attribute. An attribute defined in this way is said to have an *operational definition*. The set of procedures we are willing (or forced by our lack of ingenuity) to accept as showing the durability of an automobile tire become the operational definition of durability for us.

The history of psychological and educational measurement during the 20th century has largely been the history of the invention of instruments and procedures for eliciting, in a standard way and under uniform conditions, the behaviors that serve as indicators of the relevant attributes of people. The series of tasks devised by Binet and his successors constitute operations for eliciting behavior that is indicative of intelligence, and the Stanford-Binet and other tests have come to provide operational definitions of intelligence. The fact that there is no single universally accepted test and that different tests vary somewhat in the tasks they include and the order in which they rank people are evidence that we do not have complete consensus on what intelligence is or on what the appropriate procedures are for eliciting it. This lack of consensus is generally characteristic of the state of the art of psychological and educational measurement. There is enough ambiguity in our definitions and enough variety in the instruments we have devised to elicit the relevant behaviors that different measures of what is alleged to be the same trait may rank people quite differently. This fact requires that we be very careful not to overgeneralize the results of our measurements.

The problem of developing an operational definition for the attribute, or characteristic, of interest is also present in the classroom. Almost daily, teachers face the problem of assessing student performance, but what we will call performance is closely linked with the way we assess it. Only to the extent that teachers agree on their operational definitions of student achievement will their assessments have comparable meaning. If one teacher emphasizes quick recall of facts in his assessments and another looks for application of principles in hers, they are, to some undetermined extent, evaluating different behaviors, and the grades they give their students will mean different things. Here, we do not suggest that this difference in emphasis is inappropriate, only that it is a fact of which educators should be aware. This variability in definitions also provides a major impetus for standardized achievement tests because such tests are seen as providing a common definition of the attribute to be measured and the method of measurement. The common definition provided by the test may not exactly represent what either teacher means by achievement in Subject X, but such definitions are usually developed to provide an adequate fit to the definitions most teachers espouse. Procedures for defining the behaviors of interest as the outcome of instruction are described in Part II, as are methods for making those behaviors manifest.

Quantifying the Attribute

The third step in the measurement process, once we have accepted a set of operations for eliciting an attribute, is to express the result of those operations in quantitative terms. Measurement involves assigning numbers to objects or people; the numbers represent how much of the attribute is present in the person or thing. Using numbers has several advantages, two of which concern us. First, quantification makes communication more efficient and precise. We know much more from the statement that Ralph is 6 ft tall and weighs 175 lbs than we could learn from an attempt to describe Ralph's size in nonquantitative terms. We will see in Chapter 3 that much of the meaning that numbers have comes from the context in which the measurements are made, but, given that context, information in quantitative form is more compact and more easily understood than is the same information in other forms, such as verbal descriptions or photographs. In fact, we are so accustomed to communicating some types of information, such as temperature or age, in quantitative terms that we would have difficulty using another framework.

A second major advantage of quantification is that we can apply the power of mathematics to our observations to make them more meaningful. Consider, for example, trying to describe the performance of a class on a reading test or the accomplishments of a batter in baseball. In both cases, we are accustomed to using the average as a summary of several individual performances. For many purposes, it is useful to be able to add, subtract, multiply, or divide to bring out the full meaning that a set of information may have. Some of the mathematical operations that are useful to educators and psychologists in summarizing their quantitative information are described in Chapter 2.

The critical initial step in quantification is to use a set of rules for assigning numbers so that we may answer the question, "How many or how much?" In the case of the length of a table the question becomes "How many inches?" The inch, or the meter, represents the basic unit, and the set of rules includes the measuring instrument itself and the act of laying the instrument along the object to be measured. We can demonstrate that any inch equals any other inch by laying two inch-long objects side by side and seeing their equality. Such a demonstration is direct and straightforward proof of equality that is sufficient for some of the simplest physical measures. For measuring devices such as the thermometer, equality of units rests on a *definition*. Thus, we define equal increases in temperature to correspond to equal amounts of expansion of a volume of mercury. Long experience with this definition has shown it to be useful because it gives results that relate in an orderly and meaningful way to many other physical measures. (Beyond a certain point, the boiling point of mercury, this particular definition breaks down. However, other procedures can be shown to yield results equal to those of the mercury thermometer that can be used outside this range. The same principle allows educators to use a graded series of tests to assess student progress over several years.)

None of our psychological attributes have units whose equality can be demonstrated by direct comparison in the way that the equality of inches or pounds can, at least not by any currently available definition or measurement procedure. How will we demonstrate that arithmetic problem X is equal, in amount of arithmetic ability that it represents, to arithmetic problem Y? How can we show that one symptom of anxiety is equal to another anxiety indicator? For the qualities of concern to the psychologist or educator, we always have to fall back on some definition to provide units and quantification. Most frequently, we call one task successfully completed—a word defined, an arithmetic problem solved, an analogy completed, or an endorsement of an attitude statement— equal to any other task in the series and count the total number of successes for an individual. This count of tasks successfully completed or of choices of a certain type provides a plausible and manageable definition of amount, but we have no adequate evidence of the equivalence of different test tasks or different questionnaire responses. By what right or evidence do we treat a number series item such as "1, 3, 6, 10, 15, __?__, __?__" as showing the same amount of intellectual ability as, for example, a verbal analogies item like "Hot is to cold as wet is to __?__"?

The definition of equivalent tasks and, consequently, of units for psychological tests is shaky at best. When we have to deal with a teacher's rating of a student's cooperativeness or a supervisor's evaluation of an employee's initiative, for example, where a set of categories such as "superior," "very good," "good," "satisfactory," and "unsatisfactory" is used, the meaningfulness of the units in which these ratings are expressed is even more suspect.

Problems Relating to the Measurement Process

In psychological and educational measurement, we encounter problems in relation to each of the three steps just described.

First, we have problems in selecting the attributes of concern and in defining them clearly, unequivocally, and in mutually agreeable terms. Even for something as straightforward as reading ability, we can get a range of interpretations. To what extent should a definition include each of the following abilities?

1. Read quickly
2. Convert visual symbols to sounds
3. Obtain direct literal meanings from the text
4. Draw inferences that go beyond what is directly stated
5. Be aware of the author's bias or point of view

As we deal with more complex and intangible concepts, such as cooperativeness, anxiety, adjustment, or rigidity, we may expect even more diversity in definition.

Second, we encounter problems in devising procedures to elicit the relevant attributes. For some psychological attributes, we have been fairly successful in setting up operations that call on the individual to display the attribute and permit us to observe it under uniform and standardized conditions. We have had this success primarily in the domain of abilities, where standardized tests have been assembled in which the examinee is called on, for instance, to read with understanding, to perceive quantitative relationships, or to identify correct forms of English expression. However, there are many attributes with which we clearly have been less successful. By what standard operations can we elicit, in a form in which we can assess it, a potential employee's initiative, a school pupil's anxiety, or a soldier's suitability for combat duty? With continued research and with more ingenuity, we may hope to devise improved operations for making certain of these attributes or qualities manifest, but identifying suitable measurement operations for many psychological attributes will remain a problem.

Finally, even our best psychological units of measure leave much to be desired. Units are set equal by definition; the definition may have a certain plausibility, but the equality of units cannot be established in any fundamental sense. For this reason, the addition, subtraction, and comparison of scores will always be somewhat suspect. Furthermore, the precision with which the attribute is assessed—the consistency from one occasion to another or from one appraiser to another—is often discouragingly low.

In spite of the problems involved in developing educational and psychological measuring devices, the task has proved to be worthwhile. The procedures now available have developed a record of usefulness in helping individuals make decisions in a wide variety of human contexts. The efficiency of education and the equality of opportunity are enhanced by the proper use and interpretation of tests. Interest and personality inventories have led to greater self-understanding and reduced psychological discomfort. Measures of human abilities have been used to provide access to educational and occupational positions without regard to ethnic or racial background. Critics of testing are quick to point out that inequalities in test performance still exist, but, in the last 25 years, the users of tests have become much more cautious in their interpretations and much more sensitive to the rights of the test taker. Generally, the information provided by tests is more accurate than that available from other sources.

Some Current Issues in Measurement

Educational and psychological assessments are far from perfect. Since the earliest attempts were made to develop measurement techniques in a systematic way, the procedures have been a target for a wide spectrum of critics. Much of this criticism has been a justified response to some of the naive enthusiasm of measurement proponents and some of their ill-conceived applications and interpretations of measurement results. In our discussion of test interpretation and use in subsequent chapters, we will try to be sensitive to earlier criticisms and to the more technical questions that arise concerning the reliability and validity of test results. At this point, we will identify and comment briefly on some of the issues that recently have been of special concern.

Testing Minority Individuals

In recent years, the use and interpretation of tests within minority and other groups whose experiences and cultures differ from that typical of the general population have received a great deal of attention. There are, of course, all sorts of subgroups in our society, differing from one another in a variety of ways. The ethnic and linguistic minorities are probably the most clear-cut of these; they are the ones for whom the appropriateness of tests and questionnaires designed to reflect the values and experiences of the typical middle-class white American are most open to question. Additionally, feminist groups complain that test material is often male oriented. Major test publishers are now going to considerable lengths to ensure that their test items do not present an unfair challenge to females or to members of ethnic or linguistic minority groups.

Some questions arise concerning achievement tests that attempt to assess what a student *has learned* to do. In part, these questions center on the degree to which the same educational objectives hold for groups from minority cultures. Is the ability to read standard English with understanding an important goal for black, Hispanic, or Native American children? Is knowledge about the U.S. Constitution as relevant for these groups as for the middle-class white eighth grader? One senses that as far as the basic skills of dealing with language and numbers are concerned, many of the same objectives would apply but that as one moves into the content areas of history and literature there might be more divergence.

In part, the questions focus on the specific materials through which basic skills are exhibited. Is the same reading passage about the life of the Eskimo appropriate in a reading test for a black or Native American youngster? Or should test materials be specifically tailored to the life and experiences of each? We know too little about the importance of factors of specific content on performance in areas such as reading comprehension and need to do further research to make informed decisions.

The motivation of minority groups to do well on tests in school is also an issue. Some minority groups, such as recent immigrants from Southeast Asia, place great emphasis on academic achievement in their culture. But for others, we must ask whether unfortunate experiences with testing in school have soured them on the whole enterprise, so that they withdraw from the task and do not try. It is perhaps a challenge to the whole pattern of education, not just to the choice of testing instruments, to provide a reasonable mixture of satisfying and success-enhancing experiences in school with all types of school tasks. Tasks and tests must be adapted to the present capabilities and concerns of the individual student.

Many more questions—perhaps more serious ones—are raised when tests are used as a basis for deciding what an individual *can learn to do,* that is, as aptitude measures. An inference from a test score obtained at Time 1 concerning what a person can learn to do by Time 2 is clearly a more questionable inference than an inference that merely states what that person can do at Time 1. There are many intervening events that can throw the prediction off. And there are correspondingly more possibilities of biasing factors coming in to distort systematically the prediction for minority group members. Present facts that imply one prediction for the majority group may imply a different prediction for a minority group member whose experiences before testing were far from typical.

The problem is to learn what types of inferences *can* appropriately be made for individuals with differing backgrounds and what types of adjustments or modifications of inferences need to be built into the system to permit the most accurate and equitable inferences and decisions for all people.

Invasion of Privacy

A second concern frequently expressed in recent years involves invasion of privacy. What kind of information is it reasonable to require individuals to give about themselves and under what circumstances? This issue arises not only in relation to testing, but also in relation to all types of information from and about a person. What types of records should appropriately be kept? And to whom should they be made available? At one end of the spectrum are tests of job knowledge or skill, such as typing tests, to which no one is likely to object when the skill is clearly and directly relevant to the position for which the person is applying. At the other end of the spectrum are self-descriptive instruments that lead to inferences about emotional stability or a scattering of tests that try to assess honesty under temptation to lie or steal; in these latter tests, individuals are led to give information about themselves without being aware of what information they are giving or how it will be used. The use of these instruments seems most open to question. In-between are instruments that involve varying degrees of self-revelation and that appear to have varying degrees of immediate relevance to a decision.

The issue is not only what information is being obtained, but also the purpose for which it is being obtained. Is the information being obtained at the individual's request to provide help with personal or vocational problems or for use in a counseling relationship? The fact that the person has come for help implies a willingness on his or her part to provide the information that is needed for help to be given; here, invasion of privacy becomes a matter of relatively minor concern. However, when the information is obtained to further institutional objectives—that is, those of an employer, of an educational institution, or of "science,"—then concern for the individual's right to privacy mounts, and some equitable balance must be struck between individual values and rights and social ones. For example, more students were willing to allow the use of a questionnaire to verify the emotional stability of an airline pilot, who is responsible for many lives, than to verify that of a bank clerk (75% vs. 34%). The rights of the individual are not absolute, but the feeling is often expressed that these rights have received too little consideration in the past.

To an increasing extent, the courts are taking a role in deciding what information is allowable. Several recent cases have required a demonstration of the validity or relevance of test scores or personality profiles to job performance before such instruments could be used for employee selection. These court decisions have affected the type of information that may be collected by limiting invasion of privacy and by attempting to advance the causes of affirmative action and antidiscrimination.

The Use of Normative Comparisons

A somewhat different type of issue has been raised concerning the emphasis, in test interpretation, on comparing the performance of one student with norms representing the typical performance of a national, or sometimes a local, sample of students. The point that has been made with increasing fervor is that many of the decisions for which tests are used, especially instructional ones, do not call for and are only confused by comparisons with other people. The essential information is whether the student can perform a specified task; this information should guide decisions on what should be taught or what tasks should be undertaken next. Of course, there are settings in which comparison with others is essential to sound judgment and decision. Is the latest applicant at the personnel office a good typist? How do we define "good typist" except in terms of the performance of other job applicants? A rate of 40 words per minute with two errors per minute is meaningless unless we know that the average graduate from a commercial school can type about 50 words per minute with perhaps one error per minute. The employer wants an employee who comes up to a standard of typical performance, and that standard is set by the performance of others. In the same way, a school system trying to evaluate the reading achievement of its sixth graders as "good," "satisfactory," or "needing improvement" needs some benchmark against which to compare its own performance. No absolute standard of reading performance exists. Whether it is reasonable to expect the sixth graders in Centerville to read and understand a particular article in *Reader's Digest* can only be judged by knowing whether representative groups of sixth graders nationwide are able to read and understand the same article.

In the past, normative comparisons with an outside reference group have often been used to guide decisions for which they had little or no relevance.

Currently, a reaction has set in against such misuses of normative data. Great emphasis is being given to content-referenced, criterion-referenced, and mastery tests. These tests have an important place in making some sorts of decisions, but not all. We need to know which type of comparison is useful for which situation. When should we ask if a student can satisfactorily perform a specific task? And when should we ask how that student compares in relation to other students? This issue is discussed in more detail in Chapter 3.

Other Factors that Influence Scores

An issue that has concerned measurement professionals and consumers for many years is the effect of extraneous factors on performance. One such factor that has received considerable study is the effect of anxiety. Does anxiety raise or lower performance on achievement tests? If it does have a systematic effect, what can or should the teacher or examiner do to minimize the effect?

Other factors such as the nutritional status of students or their ability to concentrate on the tasks at hand may also affect scores. Two particular factors that have received considerable theoretical attention are (1) the racial, ethnic, and gender relationship between examiner and examinee and (2) the effect of coaching on test performance. Although the effects of these extraneous factors are not clear, public concern over their possible effects has prompted increasing attention to them among educators and measurement professionals.

Professional Standards in Testing

To promote the responsible and ethical use of tests in education and psychology, the American Psychological Association, the American Educational Research Association, and the National Council on Measurement in Education (1985) have published a series of standards for the development and use of tests. The most recent edition of the *Standards for Educational and Psychological Testing* was published in 1985. From time to time, we will refer to specific sections of these standards as they apply to the topic being discussed. All regular users of tests should be familiar with these standards.

Summary

The objective of this book is to improve the knowledge and understanding of decision makers by giving them a better basis for evaluating different measurement procedures and for knowing what each signifies and how much confidence can be placed in each. To this end, we will describe the process of preparing test exercises, develop the general criteria of validity and reliability by which all types of measures are evaluated, provide a familiarity with the different ways of reporting test scores, and describe and evaluate a number of the techniques and instruments commonly used for appraising human characteristics. Our success will be measured by the extent to which our readers use measurement results with wisdom and restraint in their decision making.

Questions and Exercises

1. List some instances, preferably recent, of decisions you made about yourself or others made about you in which results from some kind of educational or psychological measurement played a part. Classify each decision as (1) instructional, (2) selection, (3) placement or classification, or (4) personal.

2. Describe one or more instances from your personal experience of a decision for which an educational or psychological measurement could have been helpful but was unavailable. On what basis was the decision actually made?

3. What are some alternatives to educational or psychological measurements as guides for each of the following decisions?
   (a) How much time should be spent on phonics in the first-grade reading program?
   (b) Which 5 of 15 applicants should be hired as computer programmers?
   (c) Should Charles Turner be encouraged to realize his desire to go to college and law school and to become a lawyer?

4. What are the advantages of the alternatives you proposed in Question 3, in comparison with some type of test or questionnaire? What are the disadvantages?

5. To what extent and in what way might *values* be involved in each of the decisions stated in Question 3?

6. Give an example of each of the following types of tests.
   (a) A criterion-referenced achievement test
   (b) A norm-referenced achievement test
   (c) An aptitude test
   (d) A measure of likes and preferences
   (e) A measure of personality or adjustment
   (f) A measure of a trait or construct

7. For one of the attributes listed here, describe how you might (1) define the attribute, (2) set up procedures to make that attribute observable, and (3) quantify the attribute.
   (a) Critical thinking
   (b) Friendliness
   (c) "Good citizenship" in an elementary school pupil
   (d) Competence as an automobile driver

8. The usefulness of tests for decisions involving minority group members depends on the type of decision involved. For what sorts of decisions would a standardized test be most defensible? For what sorts would one be most questionable?

9. Which of the following practices would you consider acceptable? Which would you consider to be an invasion of privacy? What factors influenced your opinion?
   (a) Requiring medical school applicants (1) to take an achievement test in chemistry, (2) to fill out a questionnaire designed to assess emotional stability, or (3) to take a scale of attitudes toward socialized medicine.
   (b) Requiring applicants for a secretarial job (1) to take a test of general intelligence, (2) to take a test of typing speed and accuracy, or (3) to fill out a questionnaire designed to appraise dependability.
   (c) Giving a 10-year-old boy whose reading achievement is at the 8-year-old level (1) a nonverbal test of intellectual ability, (2) an interview focused on the conditions in his home, or (3) a series of diagnostic tests of specific reading skills.

10. Why is it important for test users to know and adhere to professional recommendations for appropriate test use?

Suggested Readings

Aiken, L. R. (1985). *Psychological testing and assessment* (5th ed.). Boston: Allyn and Bacon.

Alexander, L., & James, H. T. (1987). *The nation's report card: Improving the assessment of student achievement.* Washington, DC: National Academy of Education.

American Psychological Association, American Educational Research Association, & National Council on Measurement in Education. (1985). *Standards for educational and psychological testing.* Washington, DC: American Psychological Association.

Anastasi, A. (1988). *Psychological testing* (6th ed.). New York: Macmillan.

Cronbach, L. J. (1975). Five decades of public controversy over mental testing. *American Psychologist, 30,* 1–14.

DuBois, P. H. (1970). *A history of psychological testing.* Boston: Allyn and Bacon.

Gottfredson, L. S., & Scharf, J. C. (1988). *Fairness in employment testing: A special issue of the Journal of Vocational Behavior, 33(3).* Duluth, MN: Academic Press.

Gronlund, N. E., & Linn, R. L. (1990). *Measurement and evaluation in teaching* (6th ed.). New York: Macmillan.

Haney, W. (1981). Validity, vaudeville, and values: A short history of social concerns over standardized testing. *American Psychologist, 36,* 1021–1034.

Hopkins, K. D., & Stanley, J. C. (1981). *Educational and psychological measurement and evaluation* (6th ed.). Englewood Cliffs, NJ: Prentice-Hall.

Howard, G. S. (1985). The role of values in the science of psychology. *American Psychologist, 40,* 255–265.

Jones, L. V. (1971). The nature of measurement. In R. L. Thorndike (Ed.), *Educational measurement* (2nd ed.) (pp. 335–355). Washington, DC: American Council on Education.

Linn, R. L. (1989). Current perspectives and future directions. In R. L. Linn (Ed.), *Educational measurement* (3rd ed., pp. 1–12). New York: Macmillan.

Page, E. B. Struggles and possibilities: The use of tests in decision making. In B. S. Plake (Ed.), *Social and technical issues in testing* (pp. 11–38). Hillsdale, NJ: Erlbaum.

Thorndike, R. M. (1990). *A century of ability testing.* Chicago: Riverside Publishing.

Vold, D. J. (1985). The roots of teacher testing in America. *Educational Measurement: Issues and Practice, 4*(3), 5–8.

Wigdor, A. K., & Garner, W. R. (Eds.). (1982). *Ability testing: Uses, consequences, and controversies: Pt. 1. Report of the committee.* Washington, DC: National Academy Press.

CHAPTER 2
Measurement and Numbers

Questions to Ask About Test Scores

Catherine Johnson and Peter Cordero wanted to gather information about achievement levels in their two sixth grade classes. They gave their students a reading test provided in their current reading series, a review test from the mathematics book, and a dictation spelling test based on the words their classes had been studying over the past 6 weeks. They marked the papers, counted the number of correct answers on each, and recorded the scores. Then they made up a joint class list that showed the three scores for each student. With three scores for each of 44 students, they wondered what they should do with all those numbers.

Tests *do* produce scores, and scores *are* numbers. So, if we are to think about and use test scores, we must be prepared to think with and work with numbers. The numbers that represent test scores can be organized to provide the answers to a range of questions, but first we must know what kinds of questions to ask. Once we have the questions in mind, we can begin to ask how the numbers can be arranged to provide the answers.

Look at the numbers (scores) shown in Table 2.1 for the sixth graders in the two classes. What kinds of questions might the two teachers ask about this set of numbers? What questions can *you* ask? Before reading further, study the sets of scores and jot down the questions that come to your mind in connection with these scores. See how many of the question types identified you can anticipate.

A first, rather general type of question that you might ask is, what is the general pattern of the set of scores? How do they "run"? What do they "look like"? How can we get a picture of the set of reading scores, for example, so that we can get an impression of the group as a whole? To answer this type of question, we will need to consider simple ways of tabulating and graphing a set of scores.

A second type of question that will almost certainly arise is, what is this group like, on the average? In general, have they done as well on the test as some other sixth-grade group? What is the typical level of performance in the group? All these questions call for some single number to represent the group as a whole, some measure of where the middle of the group lies. To answer this type of question, we will need to become acquainted with statistics developed to represent the average, or typical, score.

Third, to describe the group you might feel a need to describe the extent to which the scores spread out away from the average value. Have all the children in the group made about the same progress, or do they show a wide range of achievement? How does this group compare with other classes with respect to the *spread* of scores? This type of question calls for a study of measures of variability.

Fourth, you might ask how a particular individual stands on one of the tests. You might want to know whether James A. did well or poorly on the mathematics test. And if you decide that his score is a good one, you might want some way of saying just how good it is. You might ask whether James A. did better in

TABLE 2.1
Scores for Two Sixth Grade Classes at School X

Name	TEST SCORES		
	Reading	Mathematics	Spelling
Carol A.	32	3	27
James A.	36	29	33
Mary B.	27	27	26
Albert B.	21	16	13
Ruby C.	31	9	23
Donald C.	27	7	24
Alice D.	36	18	32
Peter D.	37	29	31
Theresa E.	47	21	38
Samuel E.	46	36	37
Ida F.	42	34	38
George F.	33	10	31
Vivian G.	22	4	13
Roger G.	17	14	14
Grace H.	50	42	46
Newton H.	35	18	30
Opal I.	20	18	12
Karl I.	30	12	25
Ursula J.	37	2	36
Isidore J.	22	30	17
Beatrice K.	25	10	21
John K.	43	9	37
Karen L.	37	13	30
Benjamin L.	31	15	29
Susan M.	28	20	18
Theodore M.	50	38	48
Jane N.	34	15	32
Michael N.	34	20	27
Dorothy O.	31	19	28
Herman O.	30	15	29
Frances P.	21	2	17
Charles P.	52	39	47
Elizabeth Q.	35	48	30
Patrick Q.	40	33	33
Pearl R.	59	41	54
William R.	42	6	33
Joan S.	44	41	39
Martin S.	17	26	17
Nancy T.	32	40	28
Frank T.	32	20	23
Judith U.	56	24	54
Ralph U.	38	20	30
Edith V.	38	24	37
Thomas V.	29	29	33

Note: Maximum score = 60. Number of correct answers are given.

reading or in mathematics. To answer this question, you will need a common yardstick on which to express performance in two quite different areas. One need, then, is for some uniform way of expressing and interpreting the performance of an individual that is independent of the particular test. How does this person stand relative to the group?

A fifth query is of the following type: To what extent do those who excel in reading also excel in mathematics? To what extent do these two abilities go together in the same individuals? Is the individual who is superior in one likely to be superior in the other? To express this association between two measurements, we will need to become acquainted with indices of correlation.

Many other questions may arise with respect to a set of scores. The most important ones concern the drawing of general conclusions from data on a limited group. For example, the 22 girls in this group have an average reading score of 35.6, and the 22 boys have an average score of 33.7. These are *descriptive* facts of this testing of these particular girls and boys. But these children might be considered to represent a larger population, such as all students in this school district. From the results in these two classes, we might want to make an estimate or best guess of the average level of reading achievement in the larger group. We also might want to know whether we can safely conclude that the total population of girls from which this sample is drawn would surpass the total population of boys on this same test. These problems are of *inference*. Problems of statistical inference make up the bulk of advanced statistical work, but, in this book, we are only concerned with them in a few specialized situations. They do not enter into the basic interpretation of test scores for an individual or a group.

The routines developed for organizing numbers to answer these and other questions constitute the field called *statistics*. This name and, in fact, the very prospect of working with numbers seem a bit scary to some people. Fortunately, much of the mechanics of working with numbers can now be performed on a pocket calculator; so we can concentrate on the questions to ask and on the ways in which the numbers are arranged to answer them rather than worry about computational details.

Although we present the answers to the above questions as though we had only a pencil and paper, in practice, almost all statistical work is now done on electronic calculators and computers. For analyses of any size, hand calculation is rarely used, and the skill of calculating the basic statistics described here is becoming somewhat obsolete, just as mathematics in the home is. In a time when most people have pocket calculators on hand to check their income tax returns or the per pound price of groceries in the supermarket and many schools and individuals have their own microcomputers that easily compute statistical indices, it may seem unnecessary to learn hand procedures for calculating basic statistics. However, experience has shown that the best way to come to understand a statistical procedure and what the results of a statistical analysis mean is to "get your hands dirty" by doing some of the calculations by hand. After you have mastered the ideas, you can leave the daily calculations to a machine; however, there may even be situations in which no computer or calculator is available. For these reasons, we continue to display some of the long-established computational routines.

In Table 2.1, we showed a record sheet on which test scores for 44 sixth graders were recorded. Let us look at the scores in the column headed Reading and consider how they can be rearranged to give a clearer picture of how the pupils have performed on the reading test.

The simplest rearrangement is merely to list the scores in order from highest to lowest as follows:

59	40	34	28
56	38	33	27
52	38	32	27
50	37	32	25
50	37	32	22
47	37	31	22
46	36	31	21
44	36	31	21
43	35	30	20
42	35	30	17
42	34	29	17

This arrangement gives a somewhat better picture of the way the scores fall than does Table 2.1. We can see the highest (59) and lowest (17) scores at a glance. It is also easy to see that the middle person in the group falls somewhere in the mid-30s. We can see by inspection that roughly half of the scores fall between 30 and 40. But this simple rearrangement of scores still has too much detail for us to see the general pattern clearly. We need to condense the data into a more compact form.

Preparation of a Frequency Distribution

A step in organizing scores for presentation is to prepare a display called a *frequency distribution,* a table that shows how often each score has occurred. Each score value is listed, and the number of times it occurs is shown. A portion of the frequency distribution for the reading test is shown in Table 2.2. However, Table 2.2 is still not a very good form for reporting the facts. The table is too long and spread out. We have shown only part of it: the whole table would take 43 lines, almost as many as the original listing of scores. It would have a number of zero entries, and there would be marked variations in the Frequency column from one score to the next.

To improve the form of presentation further, scores are often *grouped* into broader categories. We discard some detail in the data to make it easier to grasp the picture presented by the entire set of scores. In our example, we have grouped three adjacent scores, so that each grouping *interval* includes three points of score. When this is done, the set of scores is represented as shown in Table 2.3, a fairly compact table illustrating how many people there are in each *score interval.* Thus, for example, we have six people in interval 34–36. We do not know how many of them got 34s, 35s, or 36s; we have lost this information in the grouping. We assume that they are evenly spread throughout the interval.

TABLE 2.2
Frequency Distribution of Reading Scores (Ungrouped Data)

Test Score	Frequency
59	1
58	0
57	0
56	1
55	0
54	0
53	0
52	1
51	0
50	2
.	.
.	.
.	.
20	1
19	0
18	0
17	2

In most cases, there is no reason to believe that one score will occur more often than any other, and this assumption is a sound one, so the gains in compactness and convenience of presentation more than make up for any slight inaccuracy introduced by the groupings. (In some special applications, such as reports of family income, certain values are more likely than others, for example, $10,000, $18,000, $25,000, etc. Special precautions are required when grouping material of this type. An effort should be made to get the most popular values near the middle of an interval to reduce distortion.)

In practical situations, we always face the problem of deciding how broad the groupings should be, that is, whether to group by 3, 5, 10, or some other number of points of score. The decision is a compromise between (1) losing detail from our data and (2) obtaining a convenient, compact, and smooth representation of the results. A broader interval loses more detail but condenses the data into a more compact picture. A practical rule of thumb is to choose an interval that will divide the total score range into roughly 15 groups. In our example, the highest score is 59, and the lowest is 17. The range of scores is 59 to 17, giving a range of 42 points. Dividing 42 by 15, we get 2.8. The nearest whole number is 3; so we group the data by 3s. In addition to the "rule of 15," we also find that intervals of 5, 10, and multiples of 10 make convenient groupings. Because the purpose of grouping scores is to make a convenient and clear representation, factors of convenience enter as a major consideration.

In cases where graphs are going to be prepared using the scores in their grouped form, it is also convenient to use an interval that includes an odd number of score points, for example, 3, 5, or 7, because it is sometimes neces-

TABLE 2.3
Frequency Distribution of Reading Scores (Grouped Data)

Score Interval	Tallies	Frequency
58–60	/	1
55–57	/	1
52–54	/	1
49–51	//	2
46–48	//	2
43–45	//	2
40–42	///	3
37–39	////	5
34–36	//// /	6
31–33	//// //	7
28–30	////	4
25–27	///	3
22–24	//	2
19–21	///	3
16–18	//	2

sary to use the midpoint of the score interval. If there is an even number of scores in the interval, this point will be half way between two actual scores, although if an odd number is used for the interval width, the midpoint will be a whole score value.

It also should be noted that sometimes there is no need to group the data into broader categories. If the original scores cover a range of no more than, say, 20 points, grouping may not be required. Also, with modern calculators, it is usually easier to compute the statistical indices described later in the chapter from the original set of scores unless a large number of scores are being analyzed. In this latter case, it is highly likely that a computer will be available, further easing the burden.

In practice, when we tabulate a set of data, deciding on the size of the score interval is the first step. Next, we set up the score intervals, as shown in the left-hand column of Table 2.3. Each individual is then represented by a tally mark, as shown in the middle column. (It is easier to keep track of the tallies if every fifth tally is a diagonal line across the preceding four.) The column headed Frequency is obtained by counting the number of tallies in each score interval.

Graphic Representation

It is often helpful to translate the facts of a table like Table 2.3 into a pictorial representation. A common type of graphic representation, called a *histogram,* is shown in Figure 2.1. This type of graph can be thought of, somewhat grimly, as "piling up the bodies." The score intervals for the reading test scores are shown along the base line (the *abscissa*), and the vertical height of the pile (the *ordinate*) represents the number of people whose scores fall in that interval. The diagram shows that there are two "bodies" piled up in interval 16–18, three in interval 19–21, and so forth. This figure gives a clear picture of how the scores pile up, with most of them in the 30s and a long low "tail" running up to the high scores.

Another way of picturing the same data is by preparing a *frequency polygon,* such as that shown in Figure 2.2. Here, we have plotted a point at the midpoint of each of the score intervals. (Note that because we used an interval width of 3, these midpoints are whole numbers.) The height at which we have plotted the point corresponds to the number of cases, or frequency, *(f),* in the interval. These points have been connected, and the jagged line provides a slightly different picture of the same set of data illustrated in Figure 2.1. The frequency polygon permits you to see the data more clearly when two different groups are included in the same chart. Otherwise, the choice between the two is a matter of personal preference because they are interchangeable ways of showing the same facts. Many computer programs that can prepare frequency distributions can also plot graphs of those distributions using any interval width you select.

FIGURE 2.1
Histogram of 44 reading scores.

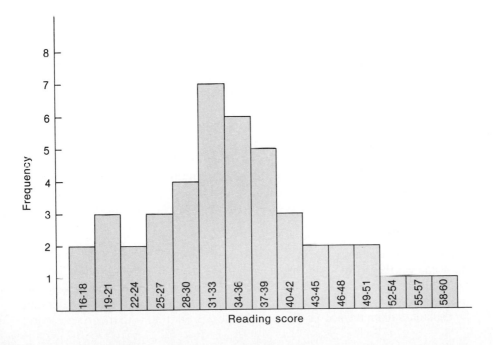

Reading score

FIGURE 2.2
Frequency polygon of 44 reading scores.

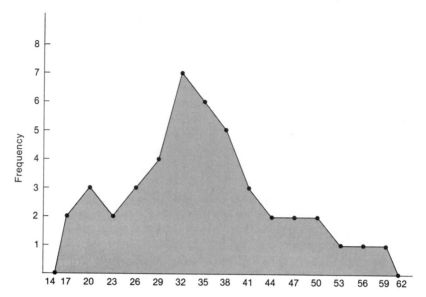

Measures of Central Tendency

We often need a statistic to represent the typical, or average, or middle score of a group of scores. A very simple way of identifying the typical score is to pick the one that occurs most frequently. This score is called the *mode* and corresponds to the highest point in the frequency polygon. If you examine the array of scores in the tabulation that follows Table 2.1, you will find that the scores 37, 32, and 31 each occur three times. A unique value for the mode does not exist with these data. If one of the students who scored 38 had instead scored 37, the mode would be 37. If one of the 30s had been a 31, then 31 would have been the mode. The mode is sensitive to such minor changes in the data and is therefore a crude and not very useful indicator of the typical score. In Table 2.3, where we have the grouped frequency distribution, the *modal interval* is 31–33. When the scores are grouped in this way, we can call the midpoint of the modal interval, 32, the *mode*.

The Median

A much more useful way of representing the typical, or average, score is to find the value on the score scale that separates the top half of the group from the bottom half. This value is called the *median*. In our example, with 44 cases, this means separating the top 22 from the bottom 22 pupils. The required value can be estimated from the scores shown in Table 2.3. Starting with the lowest score, we "count up" until we have the necessary 22 cases. The counting up is best done in a systematic way, as shown in Table 2.4, which presents the *cumulative frequency* as well as the frequency in each interval. Each entry in the column labeled Cumulative Frequency shows the total number of individuals having a score equal to or less than the highest score in that interval; that is, there are $(2 + 3) = 5$ cases scoring at or below 21, $(2 + 3 + 2) = (5 + 2) = 7$ scoring at or below 24, 10 scoring at or below 27, and so forth. As was indicated, we want to identify the point below which 50% of the cases fall. Because 50% of 44 is 22, we must identify the point below which 22 pupils fall.

Table 2.4 shows that 21 individuals have scores of 33 or below. We need to include 1 more case to obtain the required 22 cases. Note that in the next score interval (34–36), there are six individuals. We require only one sixth of these individuals. Now how shall we think of these cases being spread out over the score interval 34–36? As noted earlier in this chapter, a reasonable assumption is that they are spread out evenly over the interval. Then to include one sixth of the scores, we would have to go one sixth of the way from the bottom of the interval toward the top.

At this point, we must define what we mean by a score of 34. First, let us note that although test scores go by jumps (or discrete increments) of one unit (34, 35, and 36), we consider the underlying ability that the test measures to have a continuous distribution that takes in all the intermediate values between two scores. We might liken the situation to a digital clock. Although time is continuous, the recording instrument runs by jumps, with one jump every time the basic unit of 1 minute is passed.

TABLE 2.4
Frequency Distribution and Cumulative Frequencies for Reading Scores

Score Interval	Frequency	Cumulative Frequency
58–60	1	44
55–57	1	43
52–54	1	42
49–51	2	41
46–48	2	39
43–45	2	37
40–42	3	35
37–39	5	32
34–36	6	27
31–33	7	21
28–30	4	14
25–27	3	10
22–24	2	7
19–21	3	5
16–18	2	2

Figure 2.3 illustrates this point. The heavy line represents the continuum of ability. We define "34" as the interval on the continuum that is closer to the point 34 than to either 33 or 35. Thus, in Figure 2.3, 34 is represented as a slice extending from 33.5 to 34.5. Although somewhat arbitrary, this definition of a score is a reasonable one and is accepted by most authorities. The score interval 34–36 is really to be thought of as extending from 33.5 to 36.5, as is shown in the figure. We do not get scores lying *between* 33 and 34—not because those levels of ability do not exist, but just because our measuring instrument does not register any values between 33 and 34.

Because we require one sixth of the cases in interval 34–36, we must go one sixth of the way from 33.5 to 36.5; that is, we have

$$(1/6)(36.5 - 33.5) = (1/6) \times 3 = 3/6 = 0.5$$

We must add 0.5 to the value 33.5, which is the lower limit of the score interval that contains the median. The median for this set of scores is 33.5 + 0.5 = 34.0. Note that the median need not be a whole score value. Had there been 45 students, we would have needed 22.5 people to make up half of the group. We would then have taken 1.5/6 = 1/4 of the interval and obtained a median of 34.25.

Steps in Computing the Median.   Following are the steps used to compute the median:

1. Calculate the number of cases that represents 50% of the total group (0.5 × *N*, where *N* is the number in the total sample).
2. Starting with the lowest score interval, add the scores up through each interval to get the cumulative frequencies.
3. Find the interval for which the cumulative frequency is just less than the required number of cases. The next interval contains the median.
4. Find the score distance to be added to the top of this interval to include the required number of cases, by the following operation:

$$\frac{\text{No. of added cases needed}}{\text{No. of cases in next interval}} \times \text{No. of points in interval}$$

FIGURE 2.3
Relation between scores and ability continuum.

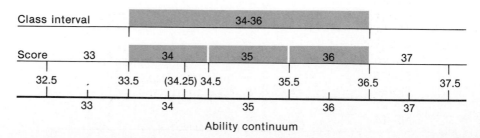

Ability continuum

5. Add this amount to the upper limit of the interval identified in Step 3 to give the median.

In our example, we compute the median as follows using the listed steps:

1. $0.5 \times 44 = 22$.
2. The cumulative frequencies, as shown in Table 2.4, are 2, 5, 7, 10, 14, etc.
3. The cumulative frequency through interval $31-33$ is 21.
4. $(1/6)(3) = 0.5$.
5. $33.5 + 0.5 = 34.0$.

Some computer programs are taking a slightly different approach to defining the median. In these programs, the median is defined as the score obtained by the middle person. Such programs work on the original set of scores as shown in Table 2.1 rather than on the frequency distribution. In this case, the two middle people have identical scores of 34, so the program would report a median equal to the one we found using the traditional procedure, but this will not usually be the case. Because the differences found in computing the median by these two approaches are usually small, the differences are not likely to be important to test users.

Percentiles

The same steps used to compute the median may be used to find the score below which any other percentage of the group falls. These values are called *percentiles*. The median is the 50th percentile, that is, the score below which 50% of the individuals fall. If we want to find the 25th percentile, we must find the score below which 25% of the cases fall. Twenty-five percent of 44 is 11. Eleven cases take us through interval $25-27$, and include one of the four cases in interval $28-30$. So, the 25th percentile is computed to be $27.5 + (1/4)3 = 27.5 + 0.75 = 28.25$.

As another illustration, consider the 85th percentile. We have $(0.85)(44) = 37.4$. Because 37 cases carry us to the top of interval $43-45$, and there are 2 cases in the next interval, for the 85th percentile, we have $45.5 + [(37.4 - 3/)/2](3) = 46.1$. Other percentiles can be found in the same way. Percentiles have many uses, especially in connection with test norms and the interpretation of scores.

Arithmetic Mean

Another frequently used statistic for representing the middle of a group is the familiar average of everyday experience. Because statisticians speak of all measures of central tendency as averages, they identify this one as the *arithmetic mean (M)*. It is computed as the sum of a series of scores divided by the total number of scores. Thus, the arithmetic mean of 4, 6, and 7 is

$$\frac{4 + 6 + 7}{3} = 5.67$$

In our example, we can add the scores of all 44 individuals in the group, giving us 1,526. Dividing by 44, we get 34.68 for the average or arithmetic mean for this group.

Steps in Computing the Arithmetic Mean. Following are the steps used to compute the arithmetic mean:

1. Add all of the scores.
2. Divide this total by the total number of scores.

Like the median, the mean can be computed from data in the form of a grouped frequency distribution. Procedures for computing the mean and standard deviation *(SD)* from a grouped frequency distribution are illustrated in Appendix 1, as are the procedures for computing the correlation coefficient *(r)*.

The arithmetic mean and the median seldom correspond exactly, but usually they do not differ greatly. In our example, the values are 34.68 and 34.0, respectively. The mean and the median will differ substantially only when the set of scores is *skewed* greatly, that is, when there is a piling up of scores at one end and a long thin tail at the other. Figure 2.4 shows three distributions that differ

FIGURE 2.4
Frequency distributions differing in skewness. *(a)* Positively skewed; *(b)* negatively skewed; *(c)* symmetrical.

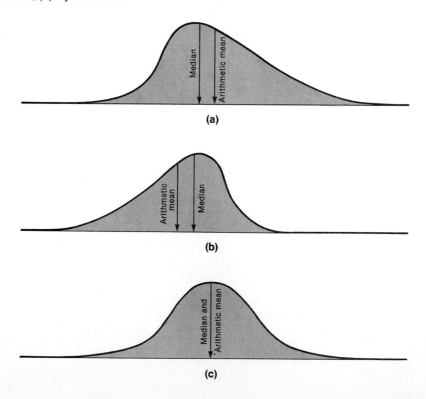

in the amount and direction of skewness. The top figure is positively skewed; that is, it has a tail running up to the high scores. We might get a distribution like this for income in the United States because there are many people with small and moderate incomes and only a few with very large incomes. The center figure is negatively skewed. A distribution like this would result if a class were given a very easy test that resulted in a piling up of perfect and near-perfect scores. The bottom figure is symmetrical and is not skewed in either direction. Many psychological and educational variables give such a symmetrical distribution. In the distributions that are approximately symmetrical, either the mean or the median will represent the average of the group equally well, but with skewed distributions, the median generally seems preferable because it is affected less by a few cases out in the long tail. The mean is used more often when the distribution is symmetrical for reasons that will become clear later in this chapter, when we discuss the normal distribution.

Measures of Variability

When describing a set of scores, it is often significant to report how *variable* the scores are—that is, how much they spread out from high to low scores. For example, two groups of children, each with a median age of 10 years, would represent quite different educational situations if one group had a spread of ages from 9 to 11 and the other ranged from 6 to 14. A measure of this spread is an important statistic for describing a group.

A simple measure of variability is the *range* of scores in the group, which is simply the difference between the highest and the lowest scores. In our reading test example, the range of scores is 59 to 17, giving a range of 42 points. However, the range depends only on the two extreme cases in the total group. This fact makes the range quite undependable because it can be changed quite a bit by the addition or omission of a single extreme case.

Semi-Interquartile Range

A better measure of variability is the range of scores that includes a specified part of the total group—usually the middle 50%. The middle 50% of the cases in the group are the cases lying between the 25th and the 75th percentiles. We can compute these two percentiles, following the procedures outlined earlier. For our example, the 25th percentile was computed to be 28.25. If you calculate the 75th percentile, you will find that it is 40.5. The distance between the 25th and 75th percentiles is thus 12.25 points of score.

The 25th and 75th percentiles are called the *quartiles,* because they cut off the bottom quarter and the top quarter of the group, respectively. The score distance between them is called the *interquartile range.* A statistic that is often reported as a measure of variability is the *semi-interquartile range (Q),* which is half of the interquartile range. It is the average distance from the median to the two quartiles; that is, it tells how far the quartile points lie from the median on the average. In our example, the semi-interquartile range is

$$Q = \frac{40.5 - 28.25}{2} = 6.125$$

If the scores spread out twice as far, Q would be twice as large; if they spread out only half as far, Q would be half as large. Two distributions that have the same mean, the same total number of cases, and the same general form and that differ only in that one has a variability twice as large as the other are shown in Figure 2.5.

Standard Deviation

The semi-interquartile range belongs to the same family of statistics as the median. Its computation is based on percentiles. There are also measures of variability that belong to the family of the arithmetic mean and are based on score deviations from the mean. Suppose we had four scores: 4, 5, 6, and 7. Adding these scores and dividing by the total number of scores, we find the arithmetic mean to be

$$\frac{4 + 5 + 6 + 7}{4} = \frac{22}{4} = 5.5$$

But now we ask how widely these scores spread out around that mean value. Suppose we find the difference between each score and the mean; that is, we subtract 5.5 from each score. We then have -1.5, -0.5, 0.5, and 1.5. These represent *deviations* of the scores from the mean. The bigger the deviations, the

FIGURE 2.5
Two distributions differing only in variability. *(a)* Large variability; *(b)* small variability.

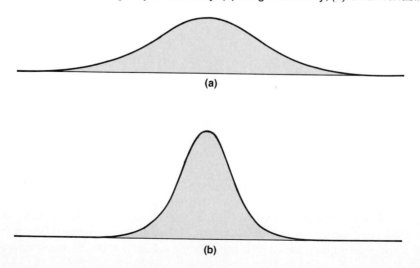

(a)

(b)

more widely the set of scores spreads out around the mean. What we require is some type of average of these deviations to give us an overall measure of the variability, or spread, present in the data.

If we simply add the four deviation values in the preceding paragraph, we find that they add up to zero. The positive deviations exactly balance the negative ones. This outcome will always be true because one of the definitions of the arithmetic mean is that it is the point around which the sum of deviations is zero. We will have to do something else to get an index of the amount spread. The procedure that statisticians have devised for handling the plus (positive) and the minus (negative) signs is to square all the deviations, thus getting only plus values. (A minus times a minus is a plus.) An average of these squared deviations is obtained by adding them and dividing by the total number of cases. This value is called the *variance* and is widely used in more advanced statistical proce-dures.

To compensate for squaring the individual deviations, the square root of this average value is computed. The resulting statistic is called the *standard devia-tion*. It is the square root of the average of the squared deviations from the mean or variance. (With most calculators, you need only press the designated key to get the square root of a number.) For the example used in the preceding equation, calculations are as follows:

$$SD = \sqrt{\frac{(-1.5)^2 + (-0.5)^2 + (0.5)^2 + (1.5)^2}{4}}$$

$$= \sqrt{\frac{2.25 + 0.25 + 0.25 + 2.25}{4}} = \sqrt{\frac{5.00}{4}}$$

$$= \sqrt{1.25} = 1.12$$

The variance is 1.25; the standard deviation is 1.12.

Computing the Standard Deviation. Most calculators include a program that will calculate the standard deviation for a set of data. Because the exact proce-dures vary from one brand of calculator to another, here we outline the general steps in the process. Your calculator will probably carry out these steps auto-matically, but it is useful to know what the calculator is "thinking," that is, how it computes the standard deviation.

The first step in the process is to square each person's score. Carol A.'s reading score of 32 becomes 1,024 when squared, Mary B.'s 27 yields 729, and so forth. The second step is to add all of the squared scores. A statistician would express the first two steps in the process with the symbols ΣX^2. The symbol Σ means to "take the sum of," and X^2 stands for the square of each person's raw, or original, score. Next, we divide the quantity X^2 by N, the number of people in the group. From this quantity, we subtract the *square of the group's mean,* and, finally, we take the square root of the result.

Although this procedure may sound more complicated than the first method used to compute the standard deviation, it is really much easier because we do not have to find a deviation, which is usually a decimal number, for each person. For the set of four scores (4, 5, 6, and 7) we find the standard deviation with the following steps:

$$\Sigma X^2 = 4^2 + 5^2 + 6^2 + 7^2 = 126$$

and

$$SD = \sqrt{\frac{\Sigma X^2}{N} - M^2}$$

$$= \sqrt{\frac{126}{4} - (5.5)^2} = \sqrt{31.5 - 30.25}$$

$$= \sqrt{1.25} = 1.12$$

The two procedures yield the same answer. (Procedures for computing the standard deviation from a grouped frequency distribution are given in Appendix 1.) To compute the standard deviation for the set of reading scores in Table 2.1, we first find $\Sigma X^2 = 57{,}288$. The mean for all 44 students was 34.68, and

$$SD = \sqrt{\frac{57{,}288}{44} - (34.68)^2} = \sqrt{1302 - 1{,}202.7}$$

$$= \sqrt{99.3} = 9.96$$

There is one factor in computing the standard deviation that may cause your calculator to give results that are different from the ones presented here or that are obtained by a classmate when you are both working with the same set of data. Earlier in the chapter, we mentioned that statistical inference was the term applied when using the data from a sample to estimate a characteristic of a larger group (called a population). This distinction does not affect the mean (the same value serves as a description of the sample and as an estimate for the population), but it does affect the standard deviation. In the standard deviation that is used to describe the variability of the sample, the sum of the squared deviations from the mean is divided by the number of members of the sample. The best estimate (from the sample data) of the standard deviation of the population is found by dividing the sum of squared deviations from the sample mean by $N - 1$. Using $N - 1$ in the denominator has the effect of making the population estimate slightly larger than the sample value. The difference is not of practical importance for most measurement applications, but it can cause some confusion when people compare their answers to a problem.

Interpreting the Standard Deviation.   It is almost impossible to say in simple terms what the standard deviation is or what it corresponds to in pictorial or geometric terms. Primarily, it is a statistic that characterizes the spread of a distribution of scores. It increases in direct proportion to the scores spreading out more widely. The larger the standard deviation, the greater the variability among the individuals. A student sometimes asks, but what is a small standard deviation? What is a large one? There is really no answer to either question. Suppose that for some group the standard deviation of weights is 10. Is this value large or small? It depends on whether we are talking about ounces, pounds, or kilograms and on whether we are dealing with the weights of mice, men, or mammoths.

The standard deviation gets its most clear-cut meaning for one type of distribution of scores, the *normal distribution* or *normal curve*. This distribution is defined by a particular mathematical equation, but to the everyday user, it is defined approximately by its pictorial qualities. The normal curve is a symmetrical curve having a bell-like shape. That is, most of the cases pile up in the middle score values; as one goes away from the middle in either direction, the pile drops off, first slowly and then more rapidly and then slowly again as the cases trail out into relatively long tails at each end. An illustration of a typical normal curve is shown in Figure 2.6. This curve is the normal curve that best fits the reading test data taken from Table 2.1. It has the same mean, standard deviation, and total area (number of cases) as the reading test data. The histogram of reading test scores (Figure 2.1) appears in the dotted lines, so one can see how closely the curve fits the actual test scores.

For the normal curve, there is an exact mathematical relationship between the standard deviation and the proportion of cases. The same proportion of cases will always be found within the same standard deviation limits. This relationship is shown in Table 2.5. From this table, we can see that in any normal curve about two thirds (68.2%) of the cases fall in the range between +1.0 and −1.0 SD from the mean. Thus, if the mean is 50 and the standard deviation is 10, about 68% of the cases will fall in the range from a score of 40 to a score of 60 (34% between 40 and 50 and 34% between 50 and 60). Approximately 95% will fall between +2.0 and −2.0 SD from the mean, and nearly all the cases will fall between +3.0 and −3.0 SD from the mean. Because of this constant relationship between the standard deviation and the proportion of cases, we know that in a

FIGURE 2.6
Normal curve fitted to reading test scores.

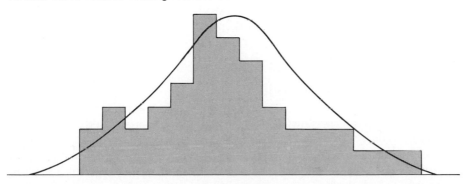

TABLE 2.5
Proportion of Cases Falling Within Certain Specified Standard Deviation *(SD)*
Limits for a Normal Distribution

Limits Within Which Cases Lie	% of Cases
Between the mean and *either* +1.0 *SD* or −1.0 *SD*	34.1
Between the mean and *either* +2.0 *SD* or −2.0 *SD*	47.7
Between the mean and *either* +3.0 *SD* or −3.0 *SD*	49.9
Between +1.0 *SD* and −1.0 *SD*	68.2
Between +2.0 *SD* and −2.0 *SD*	95.4
Between +3.0 *SD* and −3.0 *SD*	99.8

normal distribution, an individual who gets a score 1 *SD* above the mean will surpass 84% of the group—the 50% who fall below the mean and the 34% who fall between the mean and +1.0 standard deviation.

This unvarying relationship of the standard deviation unit to the arrangement of scores in the normal distribution gives the standard deviation a type of *standard* meaning as a unit of score. It becomes a yardstick in terms of which groups may be compared or the status of a given individual on different traits. For example, if John's score in reading is one *SD* above the mean and his score in mathematics is two *SD*s above the mean, then his performance in mathematics is better than his performance in reading. (The use of the standard deviation and the normal distribution for expressing relative performance is discussed in Chapter 3.) Although the relationship of the standard deviation unit to the score distribution does not hold *exactly* in distributions other than the theoretical normal distribution, frequently the distributions of test scores and other measures approach the normal distribution closely enough for the standard deviation to continue to have nearly the same meaning.

In summary, the statistics most used to describe the variability of a set of scores are the semi-interquartile range and the standard deviation. The semi-interquartile range is based on percentiles—specifically, the 25th and 75th percentiles—and is commonly used when the median is being used as a measure of the middle of the group. The standard deviation is a measure of variability that goes with the arithmetic mean. It is useful in the field of testing primarily because it provides a standard unit of measure having comparable meaning from one test to another.

Interpretation of the Score of an Individual

The problems of interpreting the score of an individual are treated more fully in Chapter 3, where we turn to test norms and units of measure. It will suffice now to indicate that the two sorts of measures we have just been considering—percentiles and standard deviation units—give a framework in which we can view the performance of a specific person. Both provide a way to view the person's performance relative to a specific reference group. Percentile informa-tion tells us what point in the score distribution just exceeds a specified fraction of the scores for the group; the standard deviation provides a common unit of distance from the mean of the group. The individual's score can then be ex-pressed as a distance above or below the mean in these common units.

Measures of Relationship

We look now for a statistic to express the relationship between two sets of scores. For example, in Table 2.1, we have a reading score and a mathematics score, as well as a spelling score, for each pupil. To what extent did those pupils who scored well in mathematics also score well on the reading test? In this case, we have two scores for each individual. We can picture these scores by a plot in two dimensions, one for each test. Such a plot is shown in Figure 2.7. The first person listed in Table 2.1, Carol A., had a score on the reading test of 32 and a score on the mathematics test of 3. Her scores are represented by the X in Figure 2.7, plotted at 32 on the vertical or reading scale and at 3 on the horizontal or mathematics scale. A dot represents each of the other 43 children's scores.

FIGURE 2.7
Scatter plot of reading and mathematics scores.

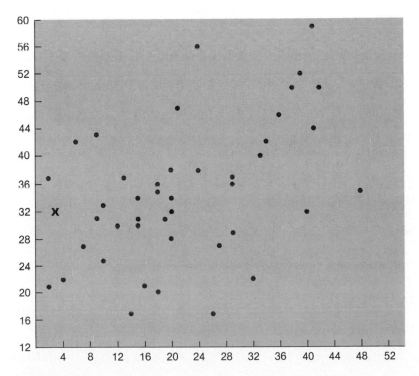

When a child who does well in reading also does well in mathematics, the dot representing those two scores falls in the upper right-hand part of the figure. The dot for a child who does poorly on both tests falls in the lower left. Where a good score on one test is paired with a poor score on the other, we find the points falling in the other corners, that is, the upper left and the lower right. Children who score in the middle on both tests are represented by points in the center of the plot. Inspection of Figure 2.7 reveals some tendency for the scores to scatter in the lower left to the upper right direction, from low reading and low mathematics to high reading and high mathematics, but there are many exceptions. The relationship is far from perfect; it is a matter of degree. We need some index to express this degree of relationship.

As an index of degree of relationship, a statistic known as the correlation coefficient can be computed. (The symbol r is used to designate this coefficient.) This coefficient can take values ranging from +1.0 through zero to −1.0. A correlation of +1.0 signifies a perfect positive relationship between the two variables. It means that the person with the highest score on one test also had the highest score on the other, the next highest on one was the second highest on the other, and so forth, exactly parallel through the whole group. A correlation of −1.0 means that the scores on one test go in exactly the reverse direction from the scores on the other. The person highest on one test is the lowest on the other, the second highest on one is the second lowest on the other, and so forth. A zero correlation represents a complete lack of relationship; that is, there is no tendency for people who score high on one test to be either above or below average on the other. The pattern is essentially random. In-between values of the correlation coefficient represent tendencies for a relationship to exist, but with discrepancies.

Every correlation coefficient contains two pieces of information. One is the *sign* of the correlation, which tells whether the two variables tend to rank people in the same order (plus) or in the reverse order (minus). The second piece of information is the *magnitude* of the correlation, which tells how strong the relationship is. The correlations +0.50 and −0.50 indicate the same strength of relationship, but the first reveals that there is some tendency for people to be in the same rank order on both variables; the second shows some tendency for people with the highest scores on one variable to have the lowest scores on the other.

Figure 2.8 illustrates four different levels of relationships. In Figure 2.8*a,* the correlation is zero, and the points scatter in a pattern that is almost circular. All combinations are found—high-high, low-low, high-low, and low-high. Figure 2.8*b* corresponds to a correlation of +0.30. You can see a slight trend for the points to group in the low-low and high-high direction. This tendency is more marked in Figure 2.8*c,* which represents a correlation of +0.60. In Figure 2.8*d,* which portrays a correlation of +0.90, the trend is much more pronounced. Note that when the correlation is −0.60 (Figure 2.8*e*) or −0.90 (Figure 2.8*f*), the scattering of the points is the same, but the swarm of dots falls along the opposite diagonal from that of Figures 2.8*c* and 2.8*d*—from the upper left-hand corner to the lower right-hand corner. But even with as high a correlation as

FIGURE 2.8

Distribution of scores for representative values of correlation coefficient. *(a)* Correlation of 0.00; *(b)* correlation of +0.30; *(c)* correlation of +0.60; *(d)* correlation of +0.90; *(e)* correlation of −0.60; *(f)* correlation of −0.90.

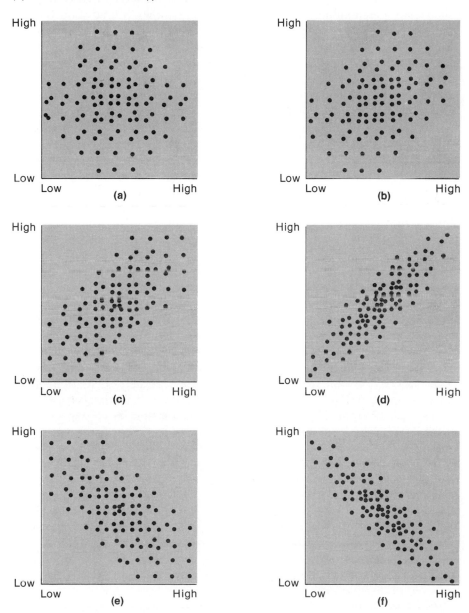

+0.90, the scores spread out quite a bit and do not all lie directly on the line from low-low to high-high. The scores plotted in Figure 2.7 correspond to a correlation coefficient of +0.47. Procedures for computing the correlation coefficient are outlined in Appendix 1 for readers who wish to carry out the calculations with a numerical example. In this appendix, we also show how to compute the mean and standard deviation for data from a frequency distribution rather than for data in their raw form. As is the case for the standard deviation, many modern pocket calculators include a program to compute the correlation coefficient.

Correlation coefficients will be encountered in connection with testing and measurement in three important settings. The first situation is one in which we are trying to determine how precise and consistent a measurement procedure is. Thus, if we want to know how consistent a measure of speed we can expect to get from a 50-yd dash, we can have each person run the distance twice, perhaps on successive days. Correlating the two sets of scores will give information on the stability, or *reliability,* of this measure of running speed. The second situation is one in which we are studying the relationship between two different measures to evaluate one as a *predictor* of the other. Thus, we might want to study a scholastic aptitude test as a predictor of college grades. The correlation of the test with grades would give an indication of the test's usefulness as a predictor. These two uses of the correlation coefficient are described more fully in Chapters 4 and 5.

The third situation in which we encounter correlation coefficients is more purely descriptive. We often are interested in the relationships between variables, simply to understand better how behavior is organized. What correlations do we find between measures of verbal and quantitative abilities? How close is the relationship between interest in mechanical jobs and comprehension of mechanical devices? Is rate of physical development related to rate of intellectual development? Many research problems in human behavior can only, or perhaps best, be studied by observing relationships as they develop in a natural setting.

We face the problem, in each case, of evaluating the correlation we obtain. Suppose the two sets of 50-yd dash scores yield a correlation of 0.80. Is this satisfactory? Suppose the aptitude test correlates 0.60 with college grades. Should we be pleased or discouraged? (The wording of this question implies that we want correlations to be high. When a correlation expresses the reliability, or consistency, of a test, or its accuracy in predicting an outcome of interest to us, it is certainly true that the higher the correlation, the more pleased we are. In other contexts, however, "bigness" does not necessarily correspond to "goodness," and we may not have a preference on the size of a correlation or may even prefer a low one.)

The answer to the last question lies in part in the plots in Figure 2.8. Clearly, the higher the correlation, the more closely one variable goes with the other. If we think of discrepancies away from the diagonal line from low-low to high-high as "errors," the errors become smaller as the correlation becomes larger. But these discrepancies are still discouragingly large for even rather substantial

TABLE 2.6
Correlations Between Selected Variables

Variable	Correlation Coefficient
Heights of identical twins	.95
Intelligence test scores of identical twins	.88
Reading test scores in Grade 3 versus Grade 6	.80
Rank in high school class versus teacher's rating of work habits	.73
Height versus weight in 10-year-olds	.60
Arithmetic computation test score versus nonverbal intelligence test (Grade 8)	.54
Height of brothers (adjusted for age)	.50
Intelligence test score versus parents' occupational level	.30
Stength of grip versus running speed	.16
Height versus intelligence test score	.06
Ratio of head length to width versus intelligence test score	.01
Armed Forces Qualification Test scores of recruits versus number of school grades repeated	−.27
Artist interest score versus banker interest score	−.64

correlation coefficients, for example, Figure 2.8c. We must always be aware of these discrepancies and realize that with a correlation such as +0.60 between an aptitude test and school grades (which is about as high as correlations between these measures usually get), there will be a number of children whose school performance differs a good deal from what we have predicted from the tests.

However, everything is relative, and any given correlation coefficient must be interpreted in comparison with values that are commonly obtained. Table 2.6 contains a number of correlations that have been reported for different types of variables. The nature of the scores being correlated is described, and the coefficient is reported. An examination of this table will provide some initial background for interpreting correlation coefficients. The coefficient will gradually take on added meaning as you encounter coefficients of different sizes in your reading and as you work with tests.

Summary

All measurements produce numbers. It is usually desirable to summarize the numbers that result from measurements so that we can answer specific questions about the people we have measured and draw general conclusions. We focused on five basic types of questions.

1. *What does the general array of numbers "look like"? Or how do they arrange themselves?* The answer to this question involved sorting the scores into a frequency distribution (Table 2.2) or a grouped frequency distribution (Table 2.3). We also found that plotting histograms (Figure 2.1) or frequency polygons (Figure 2.2) could give a picture of the data.

2. *What does the typical individual look like? Or where is the middle of the group?* The mode, median (or 50th percentile), and mean are indices of where the middle of the group falls. The mean, or arithmetic average, is the most commonly used measure of the center of the group.

3. *How widely do the scores spread out around their center? Or what is their spread?* The spread of scores can be represented by the range, the semi-interquartile range (half the distance between the 25th and the 75th percentiles), and the standard deviation, which is a measure of how far scores deviate, on the average, from the mean.

4. *How should we interpret the score of any individual?* We will discuss this topic in Chapter 3.

5. *To what extent do the scores from two measurements "go together"? Or what is the degree of relationship between the two sets of scores?* Generally, the most useful measurement of relationships is the correlation coefficient. This index runs from +1.00, indicating a perfect positive relationship or exact agreement, through 0.00, indicating no association between the sets of scores, to −1.00, indicating a perfect negative relationship or exact disagreement on the order of individuals on the two traits. The correlation coefficient is important as an index of stability of measurement and as a measure of how well one trait can be predicted from another.

Questions and Exercises

1. For each of the following sets of scores, select the most suitable score interval and set up a form for tallying the scores:

Test	Number of cases	Range of scores
Mathematics	103	15–65
Reading Comprehension	60	60–140
Interest Inventory	582	65–248

2. In each of the following distributions, indicate the size of the score interval, the midpoints of the intervals shown, and the real limits of the intervals (i.e., the dividing points between them):

(a)	(b)	(c)
4–7	17–19	70–69
8–11	20–22	70–79
12–15	23–25	80–89
.	.	.
.	.	.
.	.	.

3. Using the spelling scores given in Table 2.1, make a frequency distribution and a histogram. Compute the median and the upper and lower quartiles. Also, compute the arithmetic mean and the standard deviation from the original scores and from the frequency distribution.

4. The Bureau of Census uses the median in reporting average income. Why is this index used rather than the mean?

5. A 50-item mathematics test was given to the 150 students in five classes at Sunnyside School. Scores ranged from 16 to 50, with 93 of the students getting scores above 40. What would this score distribution look like? What could you say about the suitability of this test for this group? What measures of central tendency and variability would be most suitable? Why?

6. A high school teacher gave two sections of a biology class the same test. The results were as follows:

	Section A	Section B
Median	74.6	74.3
Mean	75.0	73.2
75th percentile	79.0	80.0
25th percentile	71.0	64.4
Standard deviation	6.0	10.5

From these data, what can you say about these two classes? What implications do the test results have for teaching the two groups?

7. A test in history given to 2,500 10th-grade students had a mean of 52 and a standard deviation of 10.5. How many standard deviations above or below the mean would the following students fall?

Heather	48	Rob	60	Marc	31
Krista	56	Tina	36	Bill	84

8. If the distribution in Question 7 was approximately normal, what percentage of the group would Heather, Krista, Rob, Tina, Marc, and Bill each surpass?

9. Assuming that a set of scores is normally distributed with a mean of 82 and a standard deviation of 12, what would be the percentile rank of each of the following scores?
   (a) 74
   (b) 85
   (c) 99

10. Explain the meaning of each of the following correlation coefficients:
   (a) The correlation between scores on a reading test and scores on a group test of general intellectual ability is +0.78.
   (b) Ratings of students on good citizenship and on aggressiveness show a correlation of −0.56.
   (c) The correlation between weight and sociability is +0.02.

Suggested Readings

Comrey, A. L., Bott, P. A., & Lee, H. B. (1989). *Elementary statistics: A problem-solving approach* (2nd ed.). Dubuque, IA: Brown.

Ferguson, G. A., & Takane, Y. (1989). *Statistical analysis in psychology and education* (6th ed.). New York: McGraw-Hill.

Kirk, R. E. (1990). *Statistics: An introduction* (3rd ed.). Fort Worth, TX: Holt, Rinehart, and Winston.

Spence, J. T., Cotton, J. W., Underwood, B. J., & Duncan, C. P. (1990). *Elementary statistics* (5th ed.). Englewood Cliffs, NJ: Prentice-Hall.

Wike, E. L. (1985). *Numbers: A primer of data analysis.* Columbus, OH: Merrill.

CHAPTER 3
Giving Meaning to Scores

The Nature of a Score

Johnny got a score of 15 on his spelling test. What does this score mean and how should we interpret it?

Standing alone, the number has no meaning at all and is completely uninterpretable. At the most superficial level, we do not even know whether this number represents a perfect score of 15 out of 15 or a very low percentage of the possible score, such as 15 out of 50. Even if we do know that the score is 15 out of 20, or 75%, what then?

Look at the two 20-word spelling tests in Table 3.1. A score of 15 on Test A would have a vastly different meaning from the same score on Test B. A person who gets only 15 correct on Test A would not be outstanding in a second- or third-grade class. Have a few friends or classmates take Test B. You will probably find that not many of them can spell 15 of these words correctly. When this test was given to a class of graduate students, only 22% spelled 15 or more of the words correctly. A score of 15 on Test B is a good score among graduate students of education.

TABLE 3.1
Two 20-word Spelling Tests

Test A	Test B
bar	baroque
cat	catarrh
form	formaldehyde
jar	jardiniere
nap	naphtha
dish	discernible
fat	fatiguing
sack	sacrilegious
rich	ricochet
sit	citrus
feet	feasible
act	accommodation
rate	inaugurate
inch	insignia
rent	deterrent
lip	eucalyptus
air	questionnaire
rim	rhythm
must	ignoramus
red	accrued

As it stands, then, a score of 15 words correct, or even of 75%, has no direct meaning or significance. The score has meaning only when we have some standard with which to compare it.

Frames of Reference

The way that we derive meaning from a test score depends on the context or frame of reference in which we wish to interpret it. This frame of reference may be described using three basic dimensions. First, there is what we might call a temporal dimension: Is the focus of our concern what pupils can do now or what they are likely to do in the future? Are we interested in describing the current state or in forecasting the future? A second dimension involves the contrast between what people *can* do and what they would *like* to do or would normally do. When we assess a person's capacity, we determine their maximum performance, and when we ask about their preferences or habits, we assess typical performance. A third dimension is the nature of the standard against which we compare a person's behavior. In some cases, the test itself may provide the standard; in some cases, it is the person's own behavior in other situations or on other tests that provides the standard; and in others, it is the person's behavior in comparison with that of other people. Thus, a given measurement is interpreted as being either oriented in the present or oriented in the future; as measuring either maximum or typical performance; and as relating the person's performance to a standard defined by the test itself, to the person's own scores on this or other measures, or to the performance of other people.

Many instructional decisions in schools call for information about what a student or group of students can do now. Walter is making a good many mistakes in his oral reading. To develop an instructional strategy that will help him overcome this difficulty, we need to determine the cause of his problem. One question we might ask is whether he can match words with their initial consonant sounds. A brief test focused on this specific skill, perhaps presented individually by the teacher while the other students work on other tasks, can help to determine whether a deficiency in this particular skill is part of Walter's problem. How many children in Walter's class have mastery of the rule on capitalizing proper nouns? A focused test such as the one in Table 3.2 can provide evidence to guide a decision on whether further teaching of this skill is needed. Is the current program in mathematics in Centerville producing satisfactory achievement? A survey mathematics test with national or regional norms can permit a comparison of Centerville's students with students in the rest of the country, and this comparison can be combined with other information about Centerville's pupils and its schools to make a decision on whether progress is satisfactory.

Whenever we ask questions about how much a person can do, there is also the issue of the purpose of our evaluation. There are two fundamental purposes for evaluating capacity in an educational context. One is to reach a summary statement of the person's accomplishments to date, such as teachers do at the end of each marking period. Evaluation for this purpose is called *summative*

TABLE 3.2
A Focused Test

Test on Capitalizing Proper Nouns

Directions: Read the paragraph. The punctuation is correct, and the words that begin a sentence have been capitalized. No other words have been capitalized. Some need to be. Draw a line under *each word* that should begin with a capital.

We saw mary yesterday. She said she had gone to chicago, illinois, to see her

aunt helen. Her aunt took her for a drive along the shore of lake michigan. On the

way they passed the conrad hilton hotel, where mary's uncle joseph works. Mary

said she had enjoyed the trip, but she was glad to be back home with her own

friends.

evaluation. By contrast, teachers are often interested in using tests to determine their students' strengths and weaknesses, the areas where they are doing well and those where they are doing poorly. Testing for this purpose, to guide future instruction, is called *formative evaluation.*

The type of maximum performance test that describes what a person *has learned to do* is called an *achievement test.* The oral reading test given to Walter, the capitalization test in Table 3.2, and the mathematics test given to the students in Centerville are illustrations of sharply contrasting types of achievement tests. The test on initial consonant sounds is concerned with mastery of one specific skill by one student, and no question is raised on whether Walter's skill in this area is better or worse than that of any other student. The only question is, can he perform this task well enough to read adequately?

Similarly, Walter's teacher is concerned with the level of mastery, *within* this class, of a specific skill in English usage. Tests concerned with level of mastery of such defined skills are often called *domain-referenced* or *criterion-referenced* tests because the focus is solely on reaching a standard of performance on a specific skill called for by the test exercises. The test itself and the domain of content it represents provide the standard. Many, perhaps most, assessments needed for instructional decisions are of this sort.

We may contrast these with the mathematics survey test given to appraise mathematics achievement in Centerville. Here, the concern is whether Centerville's students are showing satisfactory achievement *when compared with the students in other towns like Centerville.* Performance is evaluated not in relation to the set of tasks per se, but in relation to the performance of some more general reference group. A test used in this way is spoken of as a *norm-referenced* test because the quality of the performance is defined by comparison with the behavior of others. A norm-referenced test may appropriately be used in many situations calling for curricular, guidance, or research decisions. Occasionally throughout this book, we will compare and contrast criterion-referenced and norm-referenced achievement tests with respect to their construction, desired characteristics, and use.

Some decisions that we need to make require information on what a person *can learn to do*. Will Helen be able to master the techniques of computer programming? How readily will Richard assimilate calculus? Selection and placement decisions typically involve predictions about future learning or performance, based on present characteristics of the individual. A test that is used in this way as a predictor of future performance is called an *aptitude test*. Aptitude tests are usually norm-referenced.

Note that some of the effective predictors of future learning are measures of past learning. Thus, for both computer programming and calculus, an effective predictor might be a test measuring competence in high school algebra. Such a test would measure previously learned knowledge and skill, but we would be using that measure to predict future learning. Any test, whatever it is called, assesses a person's present characteristics. We cannot directly measure a person's hypothetical "native" or "inborn" qualities. All we can measure is what that person is able and willing to do in the here and now. That information may then be used to evaluate past learning, as when an algebra test is used to decide whether Roxanne should get an A in her algebra course, or to predict future learning, as when a counselor must decide whether Roxanne has a reasonable probability of successfully completing calculus. The distinction between an aptitude and an achievement test often lies more in the purpose for which the test results are used than in the nature or content of the test itself.

Domains in Criterion- and Norm-Referenced Tests

It is important to realize that all achievement tests relate to a specified domain of content. The mathematics survey test covers a fairly broad array of topics, while the test on the rules for capitalization is restricted to a narrowly defined set of behaviors. Thus, it is not really appropriate to differentiate between criterion-referenced and norm-referenced tests by saying that the former derive their meaning from a precisely specified domain while the latter do not. A well-constructed norm-referenced test will represent a very carefully defined domain, but the domain is generally more diverse than that of a criterion-referenced test, and has only a small number of items covering a given objective. The criterion-referenced test will represent a narrowly defined domain and will therefore cover its referent content more thoroughly than will a norm-referenced test of the same length.

There is a second dimension to using information from an achievement test in addition to the traditional distinction between criterion-referenced and norm-referenced tests on the breadth of the domain they cover. This dimension relates to the way that the level, or altitude, of performance is represented or used in reaching decisions. A test score from either type of test gets its content meaning from the domain of content that the test represents, but the kind of inference that the teacher draws from the score can be either absolute or relative. The teacher makes a judgment on the basis of the test score. If the judgment is that when a student or group of students have gained a particular level of proficiency with respect to that content they have mastered the material, then the judgment is an absolute, *mastery/nonmastery* one. The decision reached is either that the students have mastered the material or that they have not; degree of mastery is not an issue. Decisions of this type are called *mastery* decisions. The usual definition of a criterion-referenced test is a test that covers a narrow domain and is used for mastery decisions.

By contrast, teachers can also use tests to judge relative achievement of objectives. Relative mastery involves estimating the percentage of the domain that students have mastered. For example, the teacher may decide that students have mastered an objective relating to spelling when they can spell correctly 19 out of 20 words from the domain. But the same teacher might use the information that the average student got a score of 14 on the spelling test to indicate that the students had achieved about 70% mastery of the domain. We refer to decisions of this kind as relative achievement decisions, but the frame of reference is still the domain of content without regard to the performance of anyone other than the current examinees.

The typical norm-referenced test uses neither of these ways to represent the level of performance. Rather, level is referenced to a larger group. A normative interpretation of a score could lead to the conclusion that the individual was performing at a very high level compared with an appropriate reference group, but the same performance might fall far below mastery from the criterion-referenced perspective. Conversely, a ninth grader who has achieved mastery of multiplication facts at the level of 95% accuracy ordinarily would not show a high level of performance when compared with other ninth graders.

Criterion-Referenced Evaluation

We can approach the problem of a frame of reference for interpreting test results from the two rather different points of view mentioned earlier. One, criterion-referenced evaluation discussed here, focuses on the tasks themselves, and the other, norm-referenced testing, on the performance of typical people. Consider the 20 spelling words in Test A of Table 3.1. If we knew that these had been chosen from the words taught in a third-grade spelling program and if we had agreed on some grounds (at this point unspecified) that 80% correct represented an acceptable standard for performance in spelling when words are presented by dictation with illustrative sentences, then we could interpret Ellen's score of 18 correct on the test as indicating that she had reached the criterion of mastery of the words taught in third-grade spelling and Peter's score of 12 correct as indicating that he had not. Here, we have test content selected from a defined domain and a mastery test interpretation. The test is criterion referenced in that (1) the tasks are drawn from and related to a specific instructional domain, (2) the form of presentation of the tasks and the response to them is set in accordance with the defined objective, and (3) a level of performance acceptable for mastery, with which the performance of each student is compared, is defined in advance. That is, criterion-referenced tests relate to a carefully defined domain of content, and they focus on achievement of behavioral objectives; the results are often (but not necessarily) used for mastery judgments.

The "mastery" frame of reference is an appropriate one for some types of educational decisions. For example, decisions on what materials and methods should be used for additional instruction in spelling with Ellen and Peter might revolve around the question of whether they had reached the specified criterion of mastery of the third-grade spelling words. More crucially, in a sequential subject such as mathematics, the decision on whether to begin a unit involving "borrowing" in subtraction might depend on whether the student had reached a criterion of mastery on a test of two-place subtraction that did not require borrowing.

By contrast, teachers also often use tests to judge the relative achievement of objectives. Relative mastery may involve estimating the percentage of a domain that the students have mastered. We refer to decisions of this type as relative achievement decisions.

Although historically the two topics of domain referencing of test content and a mastery/nonmastery decision about achievement have been linked, it is important to realize that they are quite different and independent ideas that have recently come to be treated together. It is also important to realize that both exist in a sociopolitical context that invests them with normative meaning. What, for example, should a third grader be expected to know about multiplication? The answer to this question depends on what is expected of second and fourth graders insofar as these expectations put norm-referenced boundaries on what is taught in the third grade. Professional judgment and many years of experience combine to define the reasonable domain of content. A test may then be constructed, using procedures we discuss in Chapter 7, that represents this content.

Given a test that is designed to represent a particular domain of content, the scores from that test may be interpreted strictly with respect to that content or they may be interpreted in a normative framework by comparing one person's performance with that of others. Domain-referenced interpretation means that the degree of achievement is assessed relative to the test itself and the instructional objectives that gave rise to the test. The evaluation may result in a dichotomous judgment that the person has mastered the material and is ready for further instruction, for certification or licensure, or for whatever decision is the object of the measurement. Or, the evaluation may result in a judgment of degree of mastery. The latter approximates what teachers do when they assign grades, while the former is similar to a pass/fail decision or a decision to begin new material.

For the group of tests that are typically called criterion referenced, the standard, then, is provided by the definition of the specific objectives that the test is designed to measure. When the type of decision to be made is a mastery decision, this description of the content together with the level of performance that the teacher, school, or school system has agreed on as representing an acceptable level of mastery of that objective provide an absolute standard. Thus, the illustrative content-referenced test of capitalization of proper nouns in Table 3.2 is presumed to provide a representative sample of tasks calling for this specific competence. If we accept the sample of tasks as representative and if we agree that 80% accuracy in performing this task is the minimum acceptable performance, then a score of 10 out of 13 words correctly underlined defines the standard in an absolute sense.

Even the dichotomous or mastery judgment is made in a sociopolitical, hence normative, context. The teacher or school has to decide what constitutes mastery, and there are some not-so-subtle social pressures that affect such decisions. Most teachers define the level of achievement necessary for mastery in such a way that an "appropriate" number of students are identified as masters. In practice, this means that over a period of time the teacher develops a fairly accurate idea of how typical students will perform on his or her tests covering a course of instruction. The tests, grading practices, or passing standards are adjusted so that, in the long run, the right number of students pass, which makes the setting of passing standards basically a normative decision! (See Shepard [1984] for a discussion of setting standards in criterion-referenced testing.)

In the usual classroom test for summative evaluation such a standard operates indirectly and imperfectly, partly through the teacher's choice of tasks to make up the test and partly through his or her standards for evaluating the responses. Thus, to make up their tests, teachers pick tasks that they consider appropriate to represent the learnings of their students. No conscientious teacher would give spelling Test A to an ordinary high school group or Test B to third graders. When the responses vary in quality, as in essay examinations, teachers set standards for grading that correspond to what they consider is reasonable to expect from students like theirs. Quite different answers to the question "What were the causes of the War of 1812?" would be expected from a ninth grader and from a college history major.

However, the inner standard of the individual teacher tends to be subjective and unstable. Furthermore, it provides no basis for comparing different classes or different areas of ability. Such a yardstick can give no answers to such questions as, are the children in School A better in reading than those in School B? Is Mary better in reading than in mathematics? Is Johnny doing as well in algebra as most ninth graders? We need some broader, more uniform, objective, and stable standard of reference if we are to be able to interpret those psychological and educational measurements that undertake to appraise some trait or to survey competence in some broad area of the school curriculum. Most of this chapter is devoted to describing and evaluating several normative reference frames that have been used to give a standard meaning to test scores.

Norm-Referenced Evaluation

The other frame of reference for interpreting test performance is based not on a somewhat arbitrary standard defined by a particular selection of content and interpreted as representing mastery of that content domain but rather on the typical performance of typical people. This represents a norm-referenced interpretation. Thus, the scores of Ellen and Peter can be viewed in relation to the performance of a large reference group of typical third graders or of students in different school grades. Their performance is viewed not in terms of mastery versus nonmastery or in terms of relative mastery of the subject matter, but instead as above average, average, or below average; ways are sought to refine that scale of relative performance so that all degrees of excellence can be expressed in quantitative terms.

In seeking a scale to represent degrees of excellence, we would like to report results in units that have the following properties:

1. Uniform meaning from test to test, so that a basis of comparison is provided through which we may compare different tests—for example, different reading tests, a reading test with an arithmetic test, or an achievement test with a scholastic aptitude test
2. Units of uniform size, so that a gain of 10 points on one part of the scale signifies the same thing as a gain of 10 points on any other part of the scale
3. A true-zero point of "just none of" the quality in question, so that we can legitimately think of scores as representing "twice as much as" or "two-thirds as much as"

The different types of norm-referenced scales that have been developed for tests represent marked progress toward the first two of these objectives. The third can probably never be reached for the traits with which we are concerned in psychological and educational measurement. We can put five 1-lb loaves of bread on one side of a pair of scales, and they will balance the contents of one 5-lb bag of flour placed on the other side. "No weight" is *truly* "no weight," and units of weight can be added so that 2 lb is twice 1 lb. But we do not have that type of zero point or that type of adding in the case of educational and psychological measurement. If you put together two below average students, you will not get a genius, and a pair of bad spellers cannot jointly win a spelling bee. In some cases, this deficit is the result of the particular way we have chosen to measure the trait, but for many psychological and educational traits, the deficit is a result of how we conceptualize the trait itself.

Basically, a raw point score on a test is given normative meaning only by referring it to some type of group or groups. A score on the typical test is not high or low or good or bad in any absolute sense; it is higher or lower or better or worse than other scores. There are two general ways that we may relate one person's score to a more general framework. One way is to compare the person with a graded series of groups and see which one he or she matches. Each group in the series usually represents a particular school grade or a particular chronological age. The other way is to find where in a particular group the person falls in terms of the percentage of the group surpassed or in terms of position relative to the group's mean and standard deviation. Thus, we find four main

TABLE 3.3
Main Types of Norms for Educational and Psychological Tests

Type of Norm	Type of Comparison	Type of Group
Grade norms	Individual matched to group whose performance he or she equals	Successive grade groups
Age norms	Same as above	Successive age groups
Percentile norms	Percentage of group surpassed by individual	Single age or grade group to which individual belongs
Standard score norms	Number of standard deviations individual falls above or below average of group	Same as above

patterns for interpreting the score of an individual. These are shown schematically in Table 3.3. We shall consider each in turn, evaluating its advantages and disadvantages.

Grade Norms

For any trait that shows a progressive and relatively uniform increase from one school grade to the next, we can prepare a set of grade norms. The norm for any grade, in this sense, is the average score obtained by individuals in that grade. In simplest outline, the process of establishing grade norms involves giving the test to a representative sample of pupils in each of a number of consecutive grades, calculating the average score at each level, and then establishing *grade equivalents* for the in-between scores. Thus, a reading comprehension test, such as that from the Iowa Tests of Basic Skills (ITBS)—Form J, Level 9, might be given in November to pupils in grades 2, 3, 4, and 5, with the following results.

Grade Level	Average Raw Score
2.3	13
3.3	22
4.3	31
5.3	37

The testing establishes grade equivalents for raw scores of 13, 22, 31, and 37. However, grade equivalents are also needed for the in-between scores. These are usually determined arithmetically by interpolation, although sometimes intermediate points may be established by actually testing at other times during the school year. After interpolation, we have the following table.

Raw Score	Grade Equivalent	Raw Score	Grade Equivalent
10	1.9	24	3.5
11	2.0	25	3.6
12	2.2	26	3.7
13	2.3	27	3.8
14	2.5	28	3.9
15	2.6	29	4.0
16	2.8	30	4.1
17	2.9	31	4.3
18	3.0	32	4.4
19	3.1	33	4.5
20	3.2	34	4.7
21	3.2	35	4.9
22	3.3	36	5.1
23	3.4	37	5.3

Because raw scores on this particular test can range from 0 to 49, some way is needed to establish grade equivalents for the more extreme scores. Establishing such grade equivalents is often done by equating scores on the level of the test on which we are working with scores from lower and higher levels of the same test series, forms that have been given to earlier and later grades. In this way, grade equivalents are extended down as low as the first month of kindergarten (denoted K.1) and up as high as the end of the first year in college (denoted 13.9), and a complete table to translate raw scores to grade equivalents is prepared. (The reading test of the ITBS actually is a multilevel test that uses six overlapping sets of passages and items in a single booklet. In this way, some of the same items are used for three different levels of the test, and the projection of grade equivalents is simplified and made more accurate.)

If Jennifer got a raw score of 28 on this test, it would give her a grade equivalent of 3.9, and this score could be translated as "performing as well as the average child who has completed 9 months of third grade." This is a seductively simple interpretation of a child's performance, but it has a number of drawbacks, as we will see presently.

A first major question about grade norms is whether we can think of them as providing precisely or even approximately equal units. In what sense is the growth in ability in paragraph reading from grade 3.2 to 4.2 equal to the growth from grade 6.2 to 7.2? Grounds for assuming equality are clearly tenuous. When the skill is one that has been taught throughout the school years, there may be some reason to expect a year's learning at one level to be about equal to a year's learning at some other. And there is evidence that during the elementary school (and possibly the junior high) grade-score units are near enough to equal to be quite serviceable. However, even in this range and for areas where instruction has been continuous, the equality is only approximate. If, on the other hand, we are concerned with a subject like Spanish, in which instruction typically does not begin until secondary school, or in something like biology, for which instruction is concentrated in a single grade, grade equivalents become almost completely meaningless. In addition, instruction in many skills, such as the basic skills in reading and in arithmetic computation, tapers off and largely stops by high school, so grade units have little or no meaning at this level. For this reason many achievement batteries show a grade equivalent of 10.0+ or 11.0+ as representing the whole upper range of scores. When grade equivalents such as 12.5 are reported, these do not really represent the average performance of students tested in the middle of the 12th grade, but rather, they are an artificial and fictitious extrapolation of the score scale to provide some converted score to be reported for the most capable 8th and 9th graders.

A further note of caution must be introduced with respect to the interpretation of grade norms. Consider a bright and educationally advanced child in the third grade. Suppose we find that on a standardized mathematics test this child gets a score with the grade equivalent of 5.9. This score does *not* mean that this child has a mastery of the mathematics taught in the fifth grade. The *score* is as high as that earned by the average child at the end of fifth grade, but this higher score almost certainly has been obtained in part by superior mastery of third grade work. The average child falls well short of a perfect score on the topics that have been taught at his or her own grade level. The able child can get a number of additional points (and consequently a higher grade equivalent) merely by complete mastery of this "at-grade" material. This warning is worth remembering. The fact that a child has a grade equivalent of 5.9 need not mean that the child is ready to move ahead into sixth-grade work. The grade equivalent is only the reflection of a score and does not tell in what way that score was obtained. Reference to the content of the questions that the child answered correctly would be needed to reach a judgment that the child had sufficient mastery of fifth grade material to be able to move into the sixth grade.

Finally, there is reason to question the comparability of grade equivalents from one school subject to another. Does being a year ahead (or behind) one's grade level in language usage represent the same amount of advancement (or retardation) as the same deviation in arithmetic concepts? A good deal of evidence exists, which we consider later in this chapter, that it does not. Growth in different school subjects proceeds at different rates, depending on in-school emphasis and out-of-school learning. For this reason, the glib comparison of a pupil's grade equivalent in different school subjects can result in quite misleading conclusions.

To summarize, grade norms, which relate the performance of an individual to that of the average child at each grade level, are useful primarily in providing a framework for interpreting the academic accomplishment of children in the elementary school. For this purpose, they are relatively convenient and meaningful, even though we cannot place great confidence in the equality of grade units or their exact equivalence from one subject to another.

Grade norms are relatively easy to determine because they are based on the administrative groups already established in the school organization. In the directly academic areas of achievement, the concept of grade level is perhaps more meaningful than age level. It is in relation to his or her grade placement that a child's performance is likely to be interpreted and acted on. Outside the school setting, grade norms have little meaning.

Age Norms

If a trait is one that may be expected to show continuous and relatively uniform growth with age, it may be appropriate to convert the score into an *age score,* or *age equivalent,* as a type of common score scale. During childhood we can observe continuous growth in height and weight, in various indices of anatomical maturity, and in a wide range of perceptual, motor, and cognitive performances. It makes a crude type of sense to describe an 8-year-old as being as tall as a 10-year-old and having the strength of grip of a 9-year-old as well as the speaking vocabulary of a 6-year-old. In the early development of intelligence and aptitude tests, raw scores were typically converted into age equivalents, and the term "mental age" was added to the vocabulary of the mental tester and the general public alike, with occasionally unfortunate results.

An age equivalent is, of course, the average score of individuals of a given age and is obtained by testing representative samples of 8-year-olds, 9-year-olds, 10-year-olds, and so forth. In this respect, it parallels the grade equivalent described in the previous section. And, as in the case of grade equivalents, a major issue is whether we can reasonably think of a year's growth as representing a standard and uniform unit. Is growth from age 5 to age 6 equal to growth from age 10 to age 11? And is growth in any 1 year equivalent to growth in any other year on our scale? As we move up the age scale, we soon reach a point where we see that the year's growth unit is clearly not appropriate. There comes a point, some time in the teens or early 20s, when growth in almost any trait that we can measure slows down and finally stops. In Figure 3.1, which illustrates the normal growth of height for girls, the slowdown takes place quite abruptly after age 14. A year's growth after 14 seems clearly to be much less than a year's growth earlier on the scale. At about age 14 or 15, the concept of height-age ceases to have any meaning. The same problem of a flattening growth curve is found, varying only in the age at which it occurs and in abruptness, for any trait that we can measure.

The problem introduced by the flattening growth curve is most apparent when we consider the individual who falls far above average. What age equivalent shall we assign to a girl who is 5 ft 10 in. (70 in.) tall? The average woman *never* gets that tall at any age. If we are to assign any age value, we must invent some hypothetical extension of our growth curve such as the dashed line in Figure 3.1. This line assumes that growth after 14 continues at about the same rate that was typical up to age 14. On this extrapolated curve, the height of 5 ft 10 in. is assigned a height-age of about 16 years and 6 months. But this is a completely artificial and arbitrary age equivalent. It does *not* correspond to the

FIGURE 3.1

Girls' age norms for height. (Adapted from Boynton, 1936.)

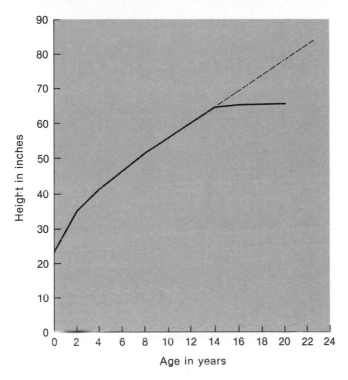

average height of $16\frac{1}{2}$-year-olds. It does not correspond to the average height at *any* age. It merely signifies "taller than average." Unfortunately, there is no cue to be gotten from these extrapolated age equivalents that suggests their arbitrary nature.

Age norms, which are based on the characteristics of the average person at each age level, provide a readily comprehended framework for interpreting the status of a particular individual. However, the equality of age units is open to serious question, and as one goes up to adolescence and adulthood age ceases to have any meaning as a unit in which to express level of performance. Age norms are most appropriate for the elementary school years and for character-istics that grow as a part of the general development of the individual, such as height, weight, or dentition. General mental development, such as the cognitive characteristics embodied in the concept of mental age, show a sufficiently uni-versal pattern to be useful normative indicators of status, but, in general, age norms should not be used for cognitive characteristics beyond the elementary school years because the patterns of growth of these functions depend too heavily on formal school experiences or have not been found to show the pattern of growth necessary for age norms to be appropriate.

Percentile Norms

We have just seen that in the case of age and grade norms, meaning is given to the individual's score by determining the age or grade group in which he or she would be exactly average. But, often such a comparison group is inappropriate or some other group would be more useful. For example, we are frequently concerned with the performance of people who are no longer in the elementary grades where grade norms have meaning. Or, we may be interested in person-ality or attitude characteristics for which age or grade norms are wholly unus-able. Or, the type of information that we seek may require that we specify the group of interest more narrowly than is practical for age or grade norms. For example, we may be interested in people who are all the same age or are all in the same grade.

Each individual belongs to many different groups. An individual who is 18 years old belongs to some of the following groups, but not to others: all 18-year-olds, 18-year-olds in the 12th grade, 18-year-olds applying to college, 18-year-olds not applying to college, 18-year-olds applying to Ivy League colleges, 18-year-olds attending public (or parochial) schools, and 18-year-olds attending school in California. For some purposes it is desirable or necessary to define the comparison group more narrowly than is possible with grade or age norms. One system of norms that is universally applicable is the percentile norm system.

The typical percentile norm, or *percentile rank,* uses the same information that we used to compute percentiles in Chapter 2, but the procedure is slightly different. Percentile ranks are calculated to correspond to obtainable score values. If a test has 10 items, it can yield 11 different raw scores, the whole scores from 0 to 10. There are only 11 possible values that percentile ranks could assume for this test, one for each obtainable score, but it would still be possible to calculate any number of percentiles. For example, one could compute, using the procedures described in Chapter 2, the 67.4th percentile as well as the 67th and 68th. But only the 11 obtainable scores would have corresponding percen-tile ranks. The normative interpretation of test scores more often uses percentile ranks than percentiles.

The procedure for determining percentile ranks starts with a frequency dis-tribution such as the one shown in Table 3.4. We assume, as we did for per-centiles, that the underlying trait that the test measures is continuous, that each observable score falls at the midpoint of an interval on this continuum, and that the people who obtained a given raw score are spread throughout the interval. Because each raw score falls at the middle of an interval, half of the people in the interval are considered to be below the midpoint and half above. Even if only one person falls in a particular interval, we assume that half of the person falls above the midpoint of the interval and half falls below.

To find the percentile rank of a raw score, we count the number of people who are below the score and divide by the total number of people. The number of people below a raw score value includes all of the people who obtained lower scores plus half of the people who received the score in question (the latter group because they are assumed to be in the bottom half of the interval

TABLE 3.4
Determining Percentile Ranks for a 10-Item Test

Raw Score	Frequency	Cumulative Frequency	Percentile Rank
10	1	60	99
9	3	59	96
8	5	56	89
7	12	51	75
6	15	39	52
5	9	24	32
4	7	15	19
3	4	8	10
2	2	4	5
1	1	2	2
0	1	1	1

and therefore below the raw score). For example, to calculate the percentile rank of a raw score of 4 in Table 3.4, we would take the eight people who got scores below 4 and half of the seven people at 4. The result is $(8 + 3.5)/60 = 11.5/60 = 0.1917$. In reporting percentile ranks it is conventional to round the answer to two places and multiply by 100 to remove the decimal point. The percentile rank that corresponds to a raw score of 4 is 19.

The major procedural difference between calculating percentiles such as the median and percentile ranks such as those in Table 3.4 is where one starts. To calculate percentiles a percent of interest, such as the 25th or 60th, is specified and the answer, a point on the score scale, is determined. The values that correspond to these percentages need not be, and seldom are, whole points of score. When calculating percentile ranks, we start with the obtainable score values and find as the answer the percentage of the group that falls below the chosen point of score.

Percentile norms are very widely adaptable and applicable. They can be used wherever an appropriate normative group can be obtained to serve as a yardstick. They are appropriate for young and old and for educational and industrial situations. To surpass 90% of a reference comparison group signifies a comparable degree of excellence whether the function being measured is how rapidly one can solve simultaneous equations or how far one can spit. Percentile norms are widely used and their meaning is readily understood. Were it not for the two points we must now consider, they would provide a framework very nearly ideal for interpreting test scores.

The first issue that faces us in the case of percentile norms is specifying the norming group. On what type of group should the norms be based? Clearly, we will need different norm groups for different ages and grades in the population. A 9-year-old must be evaluated in terms of 9-year-old norms; a sixth grader, in terms of sixth-grade norms; an applicant for a job as real estate agent, in terms of norms for real estate agent applicants. The appropriate norm group is in every case the group to which the individual belongs and in terms of which his or her status is to be evaluated. It makes no sense, for example, to evaluate the performance of medical school applicants on a biology test by comparing their scores with norms based on high school seniors. If the test is to be used by a medical school, the user must find or develop norms for medical school applicants.

If percentile norms are to be used, multiple sets of norms are usually needed. There must be norms appropriate for each distinct type of group or situation in which the test is to be used. This requirement is recognized by the better test publishers, and they provide norms not only for age and grade groups but also for special types of educational or occupational populations. However, there are limits to the number of distinct populations for which a test publisher can produce norms, so published percentile norms will often need to be supplemented by the test user, who can build up norm groups particularly suited to local needs. Thus, a given school system will often find it valuable to develop local percentile norms for its own pupils. Such norms will permit scores for individual pupils to be interpreted in relation to the local group, a comparison that may be more significant for local decisions than is comparison with national, regional, or state norms. Likewise, an employer who uses a test with a particular category of job applicants may well find it useful to accumulate results over a period of time and prepare norms for this particular group of people. These strictly local norms will greatly facilitate evaluating a new applicant. Thus, the possibility of specifying many different norm groups for different uses of a test constitutes both a problem, in the sense of greater complexity, and a strength, in that more accurate comparisons can be made.

The second issue in relation to percentile norms relates to the question of equality of units. Can we think of 5 percentile points as representing the same amount throughout the percentile scale? Is the difference between the 50th and 55th percentile equivalent to the difference between the 90th and 95th? To answer this question of equality of units, we must notice the way in which the test scores for a group of people usually pile up. We saw one histogram of scores in Figure 2.1 of Chapter 2. This picture is fairly representative of the way the scores fall in many situations. Cases pile up around the middle score values and tail off at either end. The ideal model of this type of score distribution, the normal curve, was also considered in connection with the standard deviation in Chapter 2 (see Table 2.5 and Figure 2.6) and is shown in Figure 3.2. The exact normal curve is an idealized mathematical model, but many types of test results distribute themselves in a manner that approximates a normal curve. You will notice the piling up of most cases in the middle, the tailing off at both ends, and the generally symmetrical pattern.

In Figure 3.2, four score points have been marked: the 50th, 55th, 90th, and 95th percentiles. The baseline represents a trait that has been measured in a scale with equal units The units could be items correct on a test. Note that near the median 5% of the cases (the 5% lying between the 50th and 55th percentiles) fall in a tall narrow pile. Toward the tail of the distribution, 5% of cases (the 5%

FIGURE 3.2
Normal curve, showing selected percentile points.

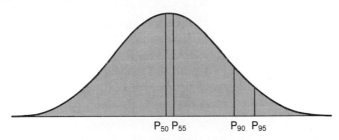

P_{50} P_{55} P_{90} P_{95}

between the 90th and 95th percentiles) make a relatively broad low bar. Five percent of the cases spread out over a considerably wider range of the trait in the second case than in the first. The same number of percentile points corresponds to about three times as much of the trait when we are around the 90th–95th percentiles as when we are near the median. The farther out in the tail we go, the more extreme the situation becomes.

Thus, percentile units are typically and systematically unequal relative to the raw score units. The difference between being first or second in a group of 100 is many times as great as the difference between being 50th and 51st. Equal percentile differences do not, in general, represent equal differences in amount of the trait in question. Any interpretation of percentile ranks must take into account the fact that such a scale has been pulled out at both ends and squeezed in the middle. Mary, who falls at the 50th percentile in arithmetic and at the 55th in reading, shows a trivial difference in these two abilities, whereas Alice, with respective percentiles of 90 and 95, shows a larger difference, one that may be important for decision making.

One of the consequences of this inequality of units in the percentile scale is that percentiles cannot be treated with many of the procedures of mathematics. For example, we cannot add two percentile ranks together and get a meaningful result. The sum or average of the percentiles of two raw scores will not yield the same result as determining the percentile rank of the sum or average of the two raw scores directly. A separate table of percentile equivalents would be needed for every combination of raw scores that we wish to use.

Standard Scores

Because the units of a score system based on percentiles are so clearly unequal, we are led to look for some other unit that does have the same meaning throughout its whole range of values. *Standard-score scales* have been developed to serve this purpose.

In Chapter 2 we became acquainted with the standard deviation *(SD)* as a measure of the spread, or scatter, of a group of scores. The standard deviation was a function of the deviations of individual scores away from the mean. Any score may be expressed in terms of the number of standard deviations it is away from the mean. The mean *mathematics* score for ninth graders on the Tests of

Achievement and Proficiency is 24.1 and the standard deviation is 9.8, so a person who got a score of 30 falls

$$\frac{30 - 24.1}{9.8} = 0.60$$

SD units above the mean. A score of 15 would be 0.93 SD units *below* the mean. In standard deviation units, we would call these scores +0.60 and −0.93, respectively.

Scores that are reported as deviations away from the group mean in standard deviation units are called *standard scores,* or *z* scores. A *z* score can be found in any score distribution by first subtracting the group mean (*M*) from the raw score (*X*) of interest and then dividing this deviation by the standard deviation:

$$z = \frac{X - M}{SD}$$

If this is done for every score in the original distribution, the new distribution of *z* scores will have a mean of zero, and the standard deviation of the new distribution will be 1.0. About half of the *z* scores will be negative, indicating that the people with these scores fell below the mean. Most of the *z* scores (about 99%) will fall between −3.0 and +3.0.

Suppose we have given the Tests of Achievement and Proficiency—Form G during the fall to the pupils in a ninth-grade class, and two pupils have the following scores on mathematics and reading comprehension.

Pupil	Mathematics	Reading Comprehension
Henry	30	48
Joe	37	42

Let us see how we can use standard scores to compare performance of an individual on two tests or the performance of the two individuals on a single test.

The mean and standard deviation for mathematics and reading comprehension are as follows:

	Mathematics	Comprehension
Mean	22.7	33.8
SD	9.4	11.1

On mathematics, Henry is 7.3 points above the mean. His *z* score is 7.3/9.4 = +0.78. On reading comprehension, he is 14.2 points above the mean, or *z* = 14.2/11.1 = +1.28. Henry is about one-half of a standard deviation better in reading comprehension than in mathematics. For Joe, the corresponding calculations for mathematics give

$$\frac{37 - 22.7}{9.4} = +1.52$$

and for reading comprehension give

$$\frac{42 - 33.8}{11.1} = +0.74$$

Thus, Henry has done about as well on mathematics as Joe has done on reading comprehension while Joe's mathematics score is about one-quarter of a standard deviation better than Henry's score on reading comprehension.

Each pupil's level of excellence is expressed as a number of standard deviation units above or below the mean of the comparison group. z scores provide a standard unit of measure having essentially the same meaning from one test to another. For aid in interpreting the degree of excellence represented by a standard score, see Table 2.5.

Converted Standard Scores

z scores are quite satisfactory except for two matters of convenience: (1) They require use of plus and minus signs, which may be miscopied or overlooked, and (2) they get us involved with decimal points, which may be misplaced. Also, people do not generally like to think of themselves as negative or fractional quantities. We can get rid of the need to use decimal points by multiplying every z score by some constant, such as 10. We can get rid of minus signs by adding a convenient constant amount, such as 50. Then, for Henry's scores on mathematics and reading comprehension we would have

	Mathematics	Reading Comprehension
Mean of distribution of scores	22.7	33.8
SD of distribution	9.4	11.1
Henry's raw score	30	48
Henry's z score	+0.78	+1.28
z score $\times$ 10	8	13
Plus a constant amount (50)	58	63

(It is conventional to round such converted scores to the nearest whole number, consistent with the objective of making them easy to use.)

Converted standard scores are based on a simple equation that changes the size of the units and the location of the mean. In symbolic form, the equation for the above transformation is

$$C = 10(z) + 50$$

where z is the standard score defined earlier and C is the converted standard score.

The use of 50 and 10 for the mean and standard deviation, respectively, of a linear transformation is an arbitrary decision. We could have used values other than 50 and 10 in setting up the conversion into convenient standard scores. The army has used a standard score scale with a mean of 100 and a standard deviation of 20 for reporting its test results. The College Entrance Examination Board has long used a scale with a mean of 500 and a standard deviation of 100 for reporting scores on the Scholastic Aptitude Test, the Graduate Record Examination, and other tests produced under its auspices. The navy has used the 50 and 10 system; many intelligence tests use a mean of 100 and a standard deviation of 15 or 16.

The scale of scores following a conversion such as this one is stretched out or squeezed together (depending on whether the original standard deviation is smaller or larger than the new one), but the stretching is uniform all along the scale. The *size* of the units is changed, but it is changed uniformly throughout the score scale. If the raw score scale represented equal units to begin with, the new scale still does, but nothing has been done to make unequal units more nearly equal. Because the above equation is an equation for a straight line, this type of transformation of scores is called a *linear conversion,* or a *linear transformation.* (It is necessary here to add a note on terminology. We use the symbol z to stand for standard scores in their original form and C to stand for *any* linear transformation of a z score. Some authors use the symbol T for the special case of a linear transformation using a mean of 50 and a standard deviation of 10. While details of notation are a matter of personal preference, this use of the symbol T is historically incorrect. The symbol T was first used by William McCall in 1922 to stand for the special kind of *nonlinear transformation* described in the next section. Only relatively recently has the distinction been lost, and it seems useful to reinstate the traditional notation to make the important distinction between scores that have been normalized and those that have not.)

Normalizing Transformations

Frequently, standard score scales are developed by combining the percentile ranks corresponding to the raw scores with a linear transformation of the z scores that are associated with those percentile ranks in the normal distribution, making the assumption that the trait that is being measured has a normal distribution. (This is called an *area conversion* of scores. Because the complete transformation cannot be expressed by a straight line, or linear equation, it is also called a nonlinear transformation.) Thus, in the mathematics test, we might find that 35% of ninth-grade boys fall below a score of 17. In the table of the normal distribution (provided as Appendix 2), the z score below which 35% of the cases fall is -0.39. Consequently, we would *assign* to a raw score of 17 a standard score of -0.39. Expressing this result on a scale in which the standard deviation is to be 10 and the mean 50, we have

$$T = 10\ (-0.39) + 50 = -4 + 50 = 46$$

As we discussed earlier, the designation of T score and the symbol T have often been used to identify this particular type of normalized standard score scale.

The complete process of preparing a normalized standard score scale by the area conversion method involves finding the percentile rank for each obtainable raw score. The z score below which the specified percentage of the normal distribution falls is then substituted for the raw score, resulting in a set of z scores that yield a normal distribution for the group on which we have obtained our data. These z scores are then subjected to a linear transformation using whatever mean and standard deviation are desired (50 and 10, respectively, for T scores).

A second type of normalized standard score that is gaining popularity in education is the scale of normal curve equivalents, or NCE scale. This scale is developed using the same procedures and mean as the T scale uses, but the standard deviation is set at 21.06 rather than at 10. The reason for choosing this particular standard deviation is that it gives a scale in which a score of 1 corresponds to a percentile rank of 1 and a score of 99 corresponds to a percentile rank of 99. Most major publishers of educational achievement tests provide tables of NCE scores. This practice enables one to compare relative performance on different tests. As these publishers note, however, the tests differ in content, so a common score scale does not imply that one test could be substituted for another.

We have now identified two ways to develop standard score scales based on an arbitrary mean and standard deviation. In one, the linear transformation method, z scores are *computed* from the observed mean and standard deviation and the resulting z scores are further transformed by first being multiplied by an arbitrary new standard deviation and then added to an arbitrary new mean. This method does not change the relative distances between scores and leaves the shape of the score distribution unchanged. In the other method, the area or normalizing transformation, percentile ranks are used to *assign* z scores to raw scores based on the percentage of the normal distribution that falls below the z score. These assigned z scores are then transformed with an arbitrary standard deviation and mean to a desired scale. The resulting scores will form a normal distribution regardless of the shape of the distribution of the raw scores.

Normalized standard scores make sense whenever it seems likely that the group is a complete one that has not been curtailed by systematic selection at the upper or lower ends. Furthermore, they make sense whenever it seems likely that the original raw score scale does not represent a scale of equal units but the underlying trait could reasonably be assumed to have a normal distribution. Many test makers systematically plan to include in their tests many items of medium difficulty and few easy or hard items. The effect of this practice is to produce tests that spread out and make fine discriminations among the middle 80% or 90% of pupils, while making coarser discriminations at the extremes. That is, the raw score units in the middle of the distribution correspond to smaller true increments in the ability being measured than do raw score units at the extremes. The "true" distribution of ability is pulled out into a flat-topped distribution of scores. The operation of normalizing the distribution reverses this process.

A type of normalized standard score that has become quite popular for educational tests in recent years is the *stanine* (condensation of the phrase "standard nine-point scale") score. Stanine units each represent half of a standard deviation on the basic trait dimension. Stanines tend to play down small

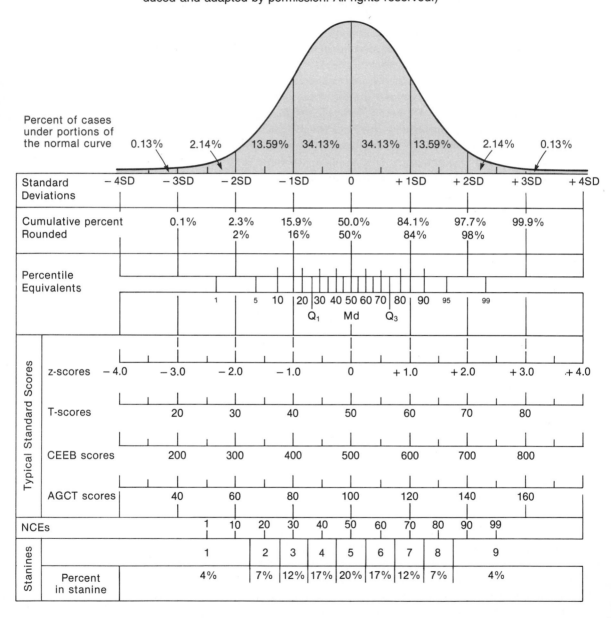

FIGURE 3.3

Various types of standard score scales in relation to percentiles and the normal curve. (Differential Aptitude Test © 1982, 1972, by The Psychological Corporation. Reproduced and adapted by permission. All rights reserved.)

differences in score and to express performance in broader categories, so that attention tends to be focused on differences that are large enough to make a difference.

The relationships among a number of the different standard score scales (after normalization) and the relationship of each to percentiles and to the normal distribution are shown in Figure 3.3. This figure presents the model of the normal curve, and beneath the normal curve are a scale of percentiles and several of the common standard score scales. This figure illustrates the equivalence of scores in the different systems. Thus, a College Board standard score of 600 would represent the same level of excellence (in relation to some common reference group) as an army standard score of 120, a Navy standard score (or *T* score) of 60, a stanine score of 7, a percentile rank of 84, or an NCE of 71. The particular choice of score scale is arbitrary and a matter of convenience. It is unfortunate that all testing agencies have not been able to agree on a common score unit. However, the important thing is that the same score scale and comparable norming groups be used for all tests in a given organization, so that results from different tests may be directly comparable.

Earlier, we discussed the importance of identifying an appropriate norm group to allow interpretation of a raw score using percentile norms. The same requirement applies with equal force when we wish to express a person's characteristics within a standard score framework. The standard score must be based on a relevant group of which the individual with whom we are concerned can be considered a member. It makes no more sense to determine an engineering graduate student's standard score on norm data obtained from high school physics students than it does to express the same comparison in percentiles.

In summary, standard scores, like percentile ranks, base the interpretation of the individual's score on his or her performance in relation to a particular reference group. They differ from percentiles in that they are expressed in units that are presumed to be equal. The basic unit is the standard deviation of the reference group, and the individual's score is expressed as a number of standard deviation units above or below the mean of the group. Standard score scales may be based on either a linear or an area (normalizing) conversion of the original scores. Different numerical standard score scales have been used by different testing agencies. Standard score scales share with percentile ranks the problem of defining an appropriate reference group.

Interchangeability of Different Types of Norms

Whichever type of normative scale is used, a table of norms will be prepared by the test publisher. This table will show the different possible raw scores on the test, together with the corresponding score equivalents in the system of norms being used. Many publishers provide tables giving more than one type of score equivalent. Table 3.5 gives an example, which shows the norms for the vocabulary test of the ITBS—Form J, Level 9. Four types of norms are shown. The

TABLE 3.5
Vocabulary Norms for the Iowa Tests of Basic Skills—
Form J, Level 9

Raw Score	Grade Equivalent	Percentile Rank	Normal Curve Equivalent	Stanine
1	K.3	1	1	1
2	K.5	1	1	1
3	K.8	1	1	1
4	1.1	2	7	1
5	1.3	4	13	1
6	1.6	8	20	2
7	1.8	11	24	2
8	2.0	15	28	3
9	2.3	21	33	3
10	2.5	26	36	4
11	2.7	31	40	4
12	2.8	35	42	4
13	2.9	39	44	4
14	3.0	43	46	5
15	3.1	47	48	5
16	3.2	51	51	5
17	3.3	55	53	5
18	3.4	58	54	5
19	3.6	65	58	6
20	3.8	72	62	6
21	3.9	74	64	6
22	4.0	77	66	7
23	4.2	82	69	7
24	4.4	86	73	7
25	4.6	89	76	8
26	4.8	92	80	8
27	5.1	95	85	8
28	5.5	98	93	9
29	6.0	98	93	9
30	6.8	99	99	9

percentiles are based on a group tested early in the third grade. The NCE score scale assigns a mean of 50 and a standard deviation of 20.06 to an early third-grade group. Thus, a boy with a raw score of 21 can be characterized as follows:

1. Having a grade equivalent of 3.9

2. Falling at the 74th percentile in the third-grade group

3. Receiving an NCE of 64

4. Receiving a stanine of 6

From Table 3.5, it is easy to see that the different systems of norms are different ways of expressing the same thing. We can translate from one to another, moving back and forth. Thus, a child who falls at the 66th percentile in the third-grade group tested in October has a grade equivalent of 4.0. A grade equivalent of 4.0 corresponds to a percentile rank of 77 and a stanine of 7. The different systems of interpretation support one another for different purposes.

However, the different norm systems are not entirely consistent as we shift from one school subject or trait to another. This inconsistency occurs because some functions mature or change more rapidly from one year to the next, relative to the spread of scores at a given age or grade level.

This can be seen most dramatically by comparing reading comprehension and mathematics. The phenomenon is illustrated by the pairs of scores shown in Table 3.6, based on the ITBS. It is assumed that the three boys were tested at the end of 2 months in the fifth grade. John received scores on both tests that were just average. His grade equivalent was 5.2, and he was close to the 50th percentile for pupils tested after 2 months in the fifth grade. Henry shows superior performance, but how does he compare in the two subjects? From one point of view, he does equally well in both; he is just 1 full year ahead in grade placement. But in terms of percentiles he is better in mathematics than in reading, that is, the 84th percentile compared with the 74th percentile. Will, on the other hand, falls at just the same percentile in both reading and mathematics. However, in his case the grade equivalent for reading is 7.2, and for mathematics, it is 6.6.

The discrepancies that appear in the above example result from the differences in the variability of performance and rate of growth in reading and mathematics. Reading shows a *wide* spread within a single grade group, relative to the mean change from grade to grade. Some fifth graders read better than the average eighth or ninth grader, so a reading grade equivalent of 8.0 or even 9.0 is not unheard of for fifth graders. In fact, a grade equivalent of 8.0 corresponds to the 95th percentile for pupils at grade 5.2 in this particular test series. By contrast, a fifth grader almost never does as well in mathematics as an eighth or ninth grader—in part because the fifth grader has not encountered or been taught many of the topics that will be presented in the sixth, seventh, and eighth grades and included in a test for those grade levels. All the basic skills that are involved in reading have usually been developed by fifth grade, so changes in

TABLE 3.6
Comparison of Grade Equivalents and Percentiles

Type of Score	READING COMPOSITE			MATHEMATICS COMPOSITE		
	John	Henry	Will	John	Henry	Will
Raw score	27	36	44	156	186	198
Grade equivalent	5.2	6.2	7.2	5.2	6.2	6.6
Grade 5.2 percentile rank	50	74	90	53	84	90

performance result largely from greater mastery of those processes. With mathematics the case is quite different. Eighth graders are not doing better the same things fifth graders do; eighth graders are doing different things. For example, fifth graders are likely to be working with whole numbers and relatively simple fractions, while eighth graders will be studying decimals, complex fractions, and geometry. A fifth grader might well be able to read an eighth-grade history book, but very few could do eighth-grade mathematics. Thus, fifth graders are more homogeneous with respect to mathematics than to reading skills.

The preceding point must always be kept in mind, particularly when comparing grade equivalents for different subjects. A bright child will often appear most advanced in reading and language and least so in mathematics and spelling, when the results are reported in grade equivalents. This difference may result, in whole or in part, simply from the differences in the growth functions for the subjects and need not imply a genuinely uneven pattern of progress for the child. For this reason most testing specialists are quite critical of grade equivalents and express a strong preference for percentile ranks or some type of standard score. However, because they appear to have a simple and direct meaning in the school context, grade equivalents continue to be popular with school personnel and are provided by many test publishers.

Quotients

In the early days of mental testing, after age norms had been used for a few years, it became apparent that there was a need to convert the age score into an index that would express rate of progress. The 8-year-old who had an age equivalent of $10\frac{1}{2}$ years was obviously better than average, but how much better? Some index was needed to take account of chronological age (actual time lived) as well as the age equivalent on the test (score level reached).

One response to the need was the expedient of dividing the test age by the chronological age to yield a quotient. This procedure was applied most extensively with tests of intelligence, where the age equivalent on the test was called a *mental age* and the corresponding quotient was an *intelligence quotient* (IQ). In the 1920s it became common practice to multiply this fraction by 100 (to eliminate decimals), thus giving rise to the general form of the scale that is now so well known in education and psychology.

The notion of the IQ is deeply imbedded in the history of the testing movement and, in fact, in 20th-century American language and culture. The expression "IQ test" has become part of our common speech. We are probably stuck with the term. But the way that the IQ is defined has changed. IQs have become, in almost every case, standard scores with a mean of 100 and a standard deviation of about 15; we should think of them and use them in this way.

In a number of recent tests of intelligence, the scores that are reported are, in fact, normalized standard scores, based on the type of normalizing area transformation discussed earlier in this chapter. These are sometimes referred to as deviation intelligence quotients, or deviation IQs because they are basically standard scores expressed as a deviation above or below a mean of 100. The latest revision of the Stanford-Binet Intelligence Scale has substituted the term *standard age score* for IQ to reflect more accurately the true nature of the scores.

Unfortunately, the score scale for reporting IQs does not have *exactly* the same meaning from test to test. The Wechsler test series is based on a mean of 100 and a standard deviation of 15, while the Stanford-Binet and most group tests are based on a mean of 100 and a standard deviation of 16. Furthermore, tests are normed at different points in time and use different sampling procedures. These differences in procedure also lead to some variation in the norms and, consequently, in the distribution of IQs they yield for any given school or community. A study by Flynn (1984) also suggests that there has been a long-term rise in IQs in the United States, dating at least to the mid-1930s, which would mean that norms that are 20 to 30 years old are probably not appropriate for use today. Such a change in mean performance makes it difficult to compare results over time or between successive test forms.

Profiles

The various types of normative frames of reference we have been considering provide a way of expressing scores from quite different tests in common units, so that the scores can be meaningfully compared. No direct way of comparing a score of 30 words correctly spelled with a score of 20 arithmetic problems solved exists. But, if both are expressed in terms of the grade level to which they correspond or in terms of the percentage of some defined common group that gets scores below that point, then a meaningful comparison is possible. A set of different test scores for an individual, expressed in a common unit of measure, is called a *score profile*. The separate scores may be presented for comparison in tabular form by listing the converted score values. A record showing such converted scores for several pupils is given in Figure 3.4. The comparison of different subareas of performance is made pictorially clearer by a graphic presentation of the profile. Two ways of plotting profiles are shown in Figures 3.5 and 3.6.

Figures 3.4 and 3.5 show a class record form and an individual profile chart for the ITBS, respectively. The class record illustrates the form in which the data are reported back to the schools by the test publisher's computerized test scoring service. (The precise form that the report of results takes differs from one scoring service to another.) There are two norm-referenced scores reported for each pupil on each test (see Figure 3.4). The upper right-hand scores are grade equivalents, and because the tests were given after the pupils had spent 2 months in the fifth grade, the norm for the country as a whole would be 52. (The decimal point is omitted in the printout, so the 65 in vocabulary for Trent Birch should be read as 6.5.) The scores in the lower left of each box are percentile ranks for a fall testing in the fifth grade.

Figure 3.5 shows data for four testings of a girl in grades 2.2, 3.3, 4.2, and 5.2.

FIGURE 3.4

List report of pupil scores. (Copyright © 1990 by THE UNIVERSITY OF IOWA. Reprinted with permission of the Publisher, THE RIVERSIDE PUBLISHING COMPANY, 8420 W. Bryn Mawr Avenue, Chicago, IL 60631.

FIGURE 3.5

Pupil profile chart. (Copyright © 1990 by THE UNIVERSITY OF IOWA. Reprinted with permission of the Publisher, THE RIVERSIDE PUBLISHING COMPANY, 8420 W. Bryn Mawr Avenue, Chicago, IL 60631.)

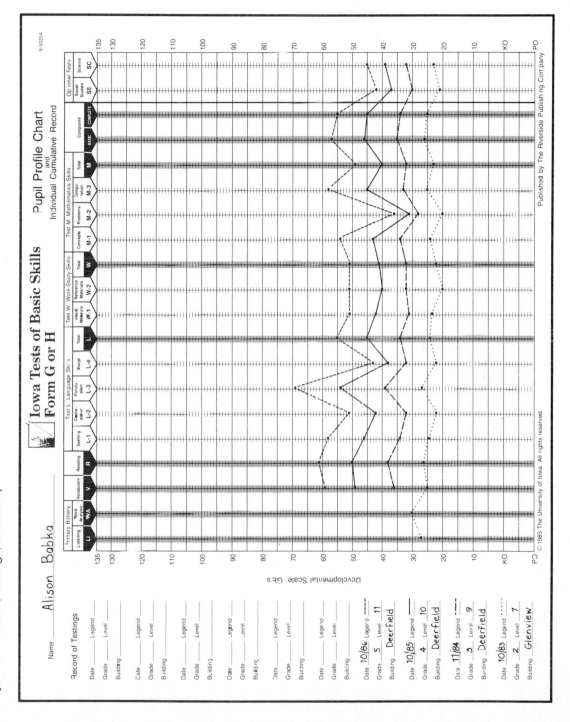

FIGURE 3.6

Profile narrative report. (Copyright © 1990 by THE UNIVERSITY OF IOWA. Re-printed with permission of the Publisher, THE RIVERSIDE PUBLISHING COMPANY, 8420 W. Bryn Mawr Avenue, Chicago, IL 60631.)

PROFILE NARRATIVE REPORT

Iowa Tests of Basic Skills

Published by THE RIVERSIDE PUBLISHING COMPANY

Pupil: TRENT BIRCH
I.D. No.:
Grade: 5
Sex: M
Birth Date: 5/76
Age: 10 YRS   5 MOS
Order No.: 000-010192-001

Class/Group: MRS NEWTON
Building: DEERFIELD
System: CRYSTAL FALLS
Norms: FALL
Test date: 10/86
Level/Form: 11/G

Tests	Scores		National Percentile Rank
	GE	NPR	
VOCABULARY	65	83	
READING	58	64	
SPELLING	54	55	
CAPITALIZATION	86	98	
PUNCTUATION	79	93	
USAGE/EXPRESSION	61	67	
LANGUAGE TOTAL	70	87	
VISUAL MATERIALS	74	93	
REFERENCE MATERIALS	55	58	
WORK-STUDY TOTAL	64	80	
MATH CONCEPTS	67	87	
MATH PROBLEMS	69	91	
MATH COMPUTATION	58	75	
MATH TOTAL	65	89	
COMPOSITE	64	82	
SOCIAL STUDIES	78	86	
SCIENCE	67	72	

GE: Grade Equivalent. NPR: National Percentile Rank

COPY FOR THE TEACHER OF TRENT BIRCH

TRENT WAS GIVEN THE IOWA TESTS OF BASIC SKILLS (FORM G, LEVEL 11), IN OCTOBER, 1986. TRENT IS IN THE FIFTH GRADE AT DEERFIELD IN CRYSTAL FALLS. THIS REPORT WILL HELP EXPLAIN THE DETAILS OF THE TEST RESULTS.

TRENT'S COMPOSITE SCORE IS THE BEST INDICATOR OF HIS OVERALL ACHIEVEMENT ON THE TESTS. TRENT EARNED A COMPOSITE GRADE EQUIVALENT OF 64, WHICH MEANS THAT HIS TEST PERFORMANCE WAS APPROXIMATELY THE SAME AS THAT MADE BY A TYPICAL PUPIL IN THE SIXTH GRADE AT THE END OF THE FOURTH MONTH. TRENT'S PERFORMANCE WAS MEASURED WITH THE LEVEL 11 TEST. TRENT'S STANDING IN OVERALL ACHIEVEMENT AMONG FIFTH GRADE PUPILS NATIONALLY IS SHOWN BY HIS COMPOSITE PERCENTILE RANK OF 82. THIS MEANS THAT TRENT SCORED BETTER THAN 82 PERCENT OF FIFTH GRADE PUPILS NATIONALLY AND THAT 18 PERCENT SCORED AS WELL OR BETTER. TRENT'S OVERALL ACHIEVEMENT APPEARS TO BE ABOVE AVERAGE FOR HIS GRADE.

THE SCORES OF ONE PUPIL ARE OFTEN COMPARED WITH OTHER PUPIL'S SCORES. GENERALLY, TRENT'S SCORES ARE ABOVE AVERAGE WHEN DESCRIBED IN THIS WAY. HOWEVER, SKILLS CAN ALSO BE COMPARED WITH EACH OTHER TO DETERMINE AN INDIVIDUAL'S STRENGTHS AND WEAKNESSES. IN TRENT'S CASE, THE HIGHEST SCORES ARE IN CAPITALIZATION AND VISUAL MATERIALS. THESE ARE STRONG POINTS WHICH CAN BE USED TO IMPROVE OTHER SKILLS. TRENT'S LOWEST SCORES ARE IN SPELLING AND REFERENCE MATERIALS. THESE ARE AREAS IN WHICH TRENT APPEARS TO NEED THE MOST WORK.

A PUPIL'S COMMAND OF READING SKILLS IS RELATED TO SUCCESS IN MANY AREAS OF SCHOOL WORK, SINCE MOST SUBJECTS REQUIRE SOME READING. TRENT'S READING SCORE IS SOMEWHAT ABOVE AVERAGE WHEN COMPARED WITH THOSE OF OTHER FIFTH GRADE PUPILS NATIONALLY. TRENT'S READING SCORE IS ABOUT AVERAGE WHEN COMPARED WITH HIS OWN TEST PERFORMANCE IN OTHER AREAS.

The so-called "developmental scale" referred to toward the left is actually a scale of grade equivalents. Thus, this pupil had a vocabulary grade equivalent of 2.5 when she was tested in second grade. By fourth grade her grade equivalent on this test was 4.9, and in fifth grade it was 6.0.

The results show her vocabulary score to have been generally above the national average. Again, an examination of her profile for the fifth grade test indicates that she was strongest in punctuation skills and weakest in mathematics problems. Some of the hazards of paying a great deal of attention to small ups and downs in a profile can be seen in a comparison of her performance on successive testings. Although the profile shows a relatively consistent pattern of highs and lows over the years, relative superiority changes substantially from year to year.

Figure 3.6 shows a second type of profile chart for the ITBS. Here, the scores for one of the students in the class list (see Figure 3.4) are shown for each of the separate subtests of the battery. Note that in this case the different tests are represented by separate bars rather than by points connected by a line. The scale used in this case is a percentile scale, but in plotting percentile values, appropriate adjustments in the scale have been made to compensate for the inequality of percentile units. That is, the percentile points have been spaced in the same way that they are in a normal curve, being more widely spaced at the upper and lower extremes than in the middle range. This percentile scale corresponds to the scale called percentile equivalents that is shown in Figure 3.3. By this adjustment, the percentile values for an individual are plotted on an equal unit scale. A given linear distance can reasonably be thought to represent the same difference in amount of ability whether it lies high in the scale, low in the scale, or near the middle of the scale. By the same token, the same distance can be considered equivalent from one test to another.

In the profile in Figure 3.6, the middle 50% is shaded to indicate a band of average performance for the norm group. The scores of this student have been plotted as bars that extend from the left side of the chart. For this type of norm, the average of the group constitutes the anchor point of the scale, and the individual scores can be referred to this base level. This type of figure brings out the individual's strengths and weaknesses quite clearly. Note also that the numerical values for this student's percentile ranks are given, together with grade equivalents, to the left of the profile. In addition, this particular test publisher's scoring service provides a narrative interpretation of the profile. Such an interpretation can also help draw the attention of teachers and parents to noteworthy features of the student's performance.

The profile chart is a very effective way of representing an individual's scores, but profiles must be interpreted with caution. First, procedures for plotting profiles assume that the norms for the tests are comparable. For this to be true, age, grade, or percentile scores must be based on equivalent groups for all the tests. We usually find this to be the case for the subtests of a test battery. Norms for all the subtests are established at the same time on the basis of testing the same group. This guarantee of comparability of norms for the different component tests is one of the most attractive features of an integrated test battery. If separately developed tests are plotted in a profile, we can usually only hope that the groups on which the norms were established were comparable and that the profile is an unbiased picture of relative achievement in different fields. When it is necessary to use tests from several different sources, one way to be sure of having equivalent norm groups is to develop local norms on a common population and to plot individual profiles in terms of those local norms.

A second problem in interpreting profiles is that of deciding how much attention to pay to the ups and downs in the profile. Not all the differences that appear in a profile are meaningful, either in a statistical or in a practical sense. We must decide which of the differences deserve some attention on our part and which do not. This problem arises because no test score is completely exact. No magic size exists at which a score difference suddenly becomes worthy of attention, and any rule of thumb is at best a rough guide. But, differences must be big enough so that we can be reasonably sure (1) that they would still be there if the person were tested again and (2) that they make a practical difference, before we start to interpret them and base action on them. We will return to this topic during our discussion of reliability in Chapter 4.

Criterion-Referenced Reports

Interest in criterion-referenced interpretations of test scores has led test publishers to produce a profile of student performance based on specific item content. A well-designed test will include items that tap various aspects of skill or knowledge development. Modern test scoring and computer technology have made it possible to report a student's performance on subsets of items that are homogeneous with respect to a particular kind of content. An example of such a report for the ITBS is shown in Figure 3.7.

The report presented in Figure 3.7 lists each subtopic for each test of the ITBS along with the number of items assessing that skill. The number of items the student attempted, the number and percentage of items correct for the student, and the percentages correct for the class and nation are also given. This report allows the teacher to identify specific strengths and weaknesses at a more fine-grained level than is possible with the ordinary norm-referenced report. For example, this student seems to have particular problems with vowel omissions or additions in spelling, although her overall spelling performance is average, and she shows relative strength in consonant substitutions or reversals. Although each subskill is measured by too few items to yield a very reliable assessment, the information can be valuable to the classroom teacher in designing the instructional program for the individual student.

An even more detailed description of this student's performance can be provided in an individual item analysis such as that shown in Figure 3.8. The item numbers are given, organized by the skill they measure, and the student's score on the item is indicated. Because this is a multilevel test (levels 9–14 are in one book) and Trent Birch took Level 11, he began the vocabulary test with Item 25 and ended it with Item 63.

Figure 3.7 illustrates quite clearly the way content-based and norm-based

FIGURE 3.7

Student criterion-referenced skills analysis. (Copyright © 1990 by THE UNIVERSITY OF IOWA. Reprinted with permission of the Publisher, THE RIVERSIDE PUBLISHING COMPANY, 8420 W. Bryn Mawr Avenue, Chicago, IL 60631.)

Iowa Tests of Basic Skills

The Riverside Publishing Company

Student: BABKA, ALISON Page: 2
I.D. No.:
Class/Group: MRS NEWTON
Building: DEERFIELD
System: CRYSTAL FALLS
Level: 11 Form: G Grade: 5
Norms: FALL Test Date: 10/86
Order No.: 000-010192-001

SERVICE 1:
STUDENT CRITERION-REFERENCED SKILLS ANALYSIS

Copyright © 1986 by The Riverside Publishing Company. All Rights Reserved. Printed in U.S.A.

FIGURE 3.8

Individual item analysis. (Copyright © 1990 by THE UNIVERSITY OF IOWA. Reprinted with permission of the Publisher, THE RIVERSIDE PUBLISHING COMPANY, 8420 W. Bryn Mawr Avenue, Chicago, IL 60631.)

frames of reference can coexist in the same test and can supplement each other. The report shows this student's performance, by content area, with reference to the number of items covering that content, the average performance of her class, and the average performance of the grade-equivalent national norm group. Additional reports are available that show the performance of the class on each item relative to national, system, and building norms (school performance). However, it is important to keep in mind that criterion-referenced interpretations of standardized tests are based on very small numbers of items for each content area or objective. Therefore, any conclusions based on such information should be tentative and should be confirmed using other information.

Norms for School Averages

Up to this point, we have asked how we can interpret an individual's standing on a test. Sometimes a question arises about the relative performance of a class, a school, a school district, or even the schools of a whole state. The recent emphasis on accountability in education provides ample reason for educators to be concerned about evaluating the performance of students taken as groups. When evaluating the achievement of a school in relation to other schools, it is necessary to have norms for school averages.

It should be clear that the variation from school to school in average ability or achievement is much less than the variation from pupil to pupil. No school average comes even close to reaching the level of its ablest student, and no average drops anywhere near the performance of the least able. Thus, a single pupil at the beginning of fifth grade who gets a reading grade equivalent of 6.2 might fall at the 75th percentile, whereas a school whose *average* reading grade equivalent of beginning fifth graders is 6.2 might fall at about the 94th percentile of schools. The relationship between norms for individuals and groups is illustrated more fully in Table 3.7.

The two distributions center at about the same point, but the greater variation among individuals quickly becomes apparent. On this test, an individual grade equivalent of 6.0 ranks at the 60th percentile, but a school in which the average performance is a grade equivalent of 6.0 is at the 85th percentile. The same effect is found for performances that are below average.

When a school principal or an administrator in a central office is concerned with interpreting the average performance in a school, norms for school averages are the appropriate ones to use, and it is reasonable to expect the test publisher to provide them. Most of the better test publishers will also provide item analyses and criterion-referenced reports at the level of the class, building, district, and state.

Cautions in Using Norms

For a test that assesses standing on some trait or competence in some area of knowledge, norms provide a basis for interpreting the scores of an individual or

TABLE 3.7
Individual and School Average Norms for the Iowa
Tests of Basic Skills Vocabulary Test (Grade 5)

Grade Equivalent	Individual Percentile Rank	Percentile Rank for School Averages
8.6	99	99
7.0	87	99
6.7	83	98
6.5	79	96
6.0	60	85
5.5	57	65
5.2	50	52
5.0	46	43
4.5	34	23
4.0	24	9
3.5	16	2
3.4	14	1
2.5	5	1
1.7	1	1

a group. Converting the score for any test taken singly into an age or grade equivalent, percentile rank, or standard score permits an interpretation of the level at which the individual is functioning on that particular test. Bringing together the set of scores for an individual in a common unit of measure, and perhaps expressing these scores in a profile, brings out the relative level of performance of the individual in different areas.

The average performance for a class, a grade group in a school, or the children in the same grade throughout a school system may be reported similarly. We can then see the average level of performance within the group on some single function or the relative performance of the group in each of several areas. Norms provide a frame of reference within which the picture may be viewed and bring all parts of the picture into a common frame. Now, what does the picture mean and what should we do about it?

Obviously, it is not possible, in a few pages, to provide a ready-made interpretation for each set of scores that may be obtained in a practical testing situation. However, we can lay out a few general guidelines and principles that may help to forestall some unwise interpretations of test results.

The most general point to keep in mind is that test results, presented in any normative scale, are a *description of what is,* not a *prescription of what should be.* The results make it possible to compare an individual or a class with other individuals and classes with respect to one or more aspects of accomplishment or personality, but they do not in any absolute sense tell us whether the individual is doing "well" or "poorly." They do not provide this information for several reasons.

Normative Scores Give Relative Rather Than Absolute Information.   They
tell whether an individual pupil's achievement is as high as that of other pupils
or whether a class scores as high as other classes. But they do not tell us whether
the basic concepts of numbers are being mastered or whether the pupils read
well enough to comprehend the instructions for filling out an income tax return.
Furthermore, they give us little guidance on how much improvement we might
expect from *all* pupils if our educational system operated throughout at higher
efficiency.

Remember that, by the very nature of relative scores, there will be as many
people below average as above. When "the norm" means the average of a
reference group, it is a statistical necessity that about half of the group be, to a
greater or lesser degree, below average. There has been an enormous amount
of foolishness—both in single schools and in statewide legislation—about
bringing all pupils "up to the grade norm." Conceivably, this might be done
temporarily if we had a sudden and enormous improvement in educational
effectiveness; however, the next time new norms were established for the test it
would take a higher absolute level of performance to, say, "read at the sixth-
grade level." So we would be back again with half of the pupils falling at or
below average. And if the effectiveness of the schools were to return to the
former level, we would be faced with the unhappy prospect of more than half
of the students testing "below grade level."

The relative nature of norms has been recognized in the criterion-referenced
test movement. When a teacher or a school is concerned with appraising mastery of some *specific* instructional objective, it may be more useful to develop
test exercises that appraise that objective, to agree on some standard as representing an acceptable level of mastery, and to determine which students do and
which do not have mastery of that specific objective than to know how the
students from this school perform relative to those from other schools.

Output Must Be Evaluated Relative to Input.   Test results typically give a
picture of output—of the individual or of the group as it exists at the present
time, after a period of exposure to educational effort. But what of the input?
Where did the group start?

The notion of input is a complex and rather subtle one. Our conception of
input should include not only earlier status on the particular ability being measured and individual potential for learning, as far as we are able to appraise this,
but also the familial circumstances and environmental supports that make it
easier for some children to learn than for others. Parental aspirations for the
child, parental skills at tuition and guidance of learning, parental discipline and
control, linguistic patterns, and cultural resources in the home are part of the
input just as truly as are the biological characteristics of the young organism.
Furthermore, peer group and community attitudes are an additional real,
though possibly modifiable, part of the input as far as the prospects for learning
for a given child are concerned. We must recognize that the adequate appraisal
of input is no simple matter, and that, correspondingly, the appraisal of output
as "satisfactory" or "unsatisfactory" is something we can do with only modest
confidence.

Output Must Be Evaluated Relative to Objectives.   The design, content, and norms for published standardized tests are based on the authors' perception of common national curricular objectives. The topics included, their relative emphasis, and the levels at which they are introduced reflect that perceived general national pattern. To the extent, then, that a given school system deviates in its objectives and curricular emphases from the national pattern, as interpreted by the test maker, its output at a given grade level can be expected to deviate from the national norms. If computational skills receive little emphasis, it is reasonable to find that computational facility will be underdeveloped. If map reading has been delayed beyond the grade level at which it is introduced into the test, it is reasonable to find that relative standing on that part of the test will suffer. Unevenness of the local profile, in relation to national norms, should always lead one to inquire whether the low spots represent failures of the local program to achieve its objectives or a planned deviation of emphasis from what is more typical of schools nationally. Low performance that results from conscious curricular decisions would be much less cause for alarm than a similar level of performance would be in area of curricular emphasis. Which of these conditions obtains will no doubt influence what is done with the finding.

If these considerations and some of the caveats discussed in the next two chapters are borne in mind, test results, as they are reported to the teacher, principal, superintendent, or school board, will be interpreted with increased wisdom and restraint.

Summary

A raw score, taken by itself, rarely has meaning. A score may be given meaning by a consideration of the domain of instructional content that the test items represent. The performance of individuals or groups may then be assessed either in terms of the percentage of the domain that they have mastered or relative to a standard of performance set before the test is administered. These methods of giving meaning to a raw score are called criterion-referenced interpretations. They are appropriate for tests that focus on one or a small number of carefully defined objectives and for which standards of performance can be either empirically or logically derived.

Because many tests are designed to appraise several objectives, and because meaningful absolute standards of performance are not available for most tests, a raw score is generally given meaning by comparison with some reference group or groups. This method of giving a raw score meaning is called norm-referenced interpretation. The comparison may be with

1. A series of grade groups (grade norms)
2. A series of age groups (age norms)
3. A single group, in which performance is indicated by what percentage of that group the score surpassed (percentile norms)
4. A single group, in which performance is indicated by the number of standard deviations the score is above or below the group mean (standard score norms). (Norms of this type may be subjected to a linear conversion to eliminate decimal

points and negative values or to nonlinear transformations to normalize the score distribution.)

Each alternative has certain advantages and certain limitations.

To get a single index to express the degree to which individuals deviated from their age group, quotients such as the IQ were developed. Because of their various limitations, quotients have been replaced by standard scores, and the term IQ is no longer technically appropriate.

If the norms available for a number of different tests are of the same kind and are based on comparable groups, all the tests can be expressed in comparable terms. The results can then be shown pictorially in the form of a profile. Profiles emphasize score differences within the individual. When profiles are used, care must be taken not to overinterpret their minor ups and downs.

Norms represent a descriptive framework for interpreting the score of an individual, a class group, or some larger aggregation. However, before a judgment can be made on whether an individual or group is doing well or poorly, allowance must be made for ability level, cultural background, and curricular emphases. The norm is merely an average and not a straitjacket into which everyone can be forced to fit. It describes the person's current performance relative to some specified comparison group.

Questions and Exercises

1. Why does the frame of reference used to interpret a test score make a difference?
2. Can the same test be interpreted in both a criterion-referenced and a norm-referenced manner? If so, how would the two interpretations differ?
3. A pupil in the sixth grade received a raw score of 25 on the Level 12 Reading Test (Form J) of the Iowa Tests of Basic Skills. What additional information would be needed to interpret this score?
4. Why do standardized tests designed for use with high school students almost never use age or grade norms?
5. What limitations would national norms have for use by a county school system in rural West Virginia? What might the local school system do about the limitations?
6. What assumptions lie behind developing and using age norms? Grade norms? Normalized standard scores?
7. In Figure 3.3, why are the standard scores evenly spaced while the percentile scores are unevenly spaced?
8. State A gives a battery of achievement tests each May in the 4th, 8th, and 11th grades. The median grade level in each subject in each district in the state is reported to the State Board of Education. Should these results be reported? If so, what else should be included in the report? In what ways might the Board use the results to promote better education? What uses should the Board avoid?
9. Ms. P takes pride in the fact that each year she has gotten at least 85% of her fourth-grade class "up to the norm" in each subject. How desirable is this as an educational objective? What limitations or dangers do you see in it.?
10. School F has a policy of assigning transfer students to a grade on the basis of their average grade equivalent on an achievement battery. Thus, a boy with an average grade equivalent of 5.3 would be assigned to the fifth grade, no matter what his age

or his grade in his previous school. What are the values and limitations of such a practice?

11. The superintendent of schools in Riverview, Iowa, noted that Springdale Elementary School fell consistently about a half grade below national norms on an achievement battery. He was distressed because this performance was the lowest of any school in the city. How justified is his dissatisfaction? Do you need other information to answer this question? If so, what?

12. The Board of Education in East Centerville noted that the fourth and fifth grades in their community fell substantially below national norms in mathematics, although they scored at or above average in all other subjects. They propose to study this situation further. What additional information do they need?

13. The third grade teachers in Bigcity school district have prepared a 30-item test to assess mastery of the basic multiplication facts. What score should they accept as demonstrating "mastery" of these facts? How should such a score be determined?

14. What are the advantages of reporting test performance in terms of stanines? In terms of normal curve equivalents? What problems arise from using each of these forms of normative report?

15. Obtain the manual for some test, and study the information that is given about norms.
    (a) How adequate is the norming population? Is sufficient information given for you to make a judgment?
    (b) Calculate the chance score (i.e., the score to be expected from blind guessing) for the test and note its grade equivalent. What limitations does this suggest for using the test?
    (c) What limitations are there on the usefulness of the test at the upper end of its range?
    (d) How many raw score points correspond to 1 full year on the grade equivalent scale? Is this number of points of score the same throughout the range of the test?

Suggested Readings

Angoff, W. H. (1971) Scales, norms, and equivalent scores. In R. L. Thorndike (Ed.), *Educational measurement* (2nd ed., pp. 508–600). Washington, DC: American Council on Education.

Holland, P. W., & Rubin, D. B. (Eds.). (1982). *Test equating.* New York: Academic Press.

Hoover, H. D. (1984). The most appropriate scores for measuring educational development in the elementary schools: GE's. *Educational Measurement: Issues and Practices, 3,* 8–14.

Kolen, M. J. (1988). Defining score scales in relation to measurement error. *Journal of Educational Measurement, 25,* 97–110.

Livingston, S. A., & Zieky, M. J. (1982). *Passing scores: A manual for setting standards of performance on educational and occupational tests.* Princeton, NJ: Educational Testing Service.

Michell, J. (1986). Measurement scales and statistics: A clash of paradigms. *Psychological Bulletin, 3,* 398–407.

Nitko, A. J. (1984). Defining "criterion-referenced test." In R. A. Berk (Ed.), *A guide to criterion-referenced test construction* (pp. 8–28). Baltimore: Johns Hopkins University Press.

Petersen, N. S., Kolen, M. J., & Hoover, H. D. (1989). Scaling, norming, and equating. In R. L. Linn (Ed.), *Educational measurement* (3rd ed., pp. 221–262). New York: Macmillan.

Shepard, L. A. (1984). Setting performance standards. In R. A. Berk (Ed.), *A guide to criterion-referenced construction (pp. 169–198).* Baltimore: Johns Hopkins University Press.

Thorndike, R. L. (1982). *Applied psychometrics.* Boston: Houghton Mifflin.

Yen, W. M. (1986). The choice of scale for educational measurement: An IRT perspective. *Journal of Educational Measurement, 23,* 299–325.

CHAPTER 4
Qualities Desired in Any Measurement Procedure: Reliability

Introduction

Whenever we would like to use a test to provide information to help in some decision, we face the problem of which test to use or whether there is any test that will really help in the decision. There are usually several tests that have been designed to help or that seem at least to have the possibility of helping with the decision. We would like to know whether any tests will indeed provide useful information And if any will, which is the best one to use?

Many specific considerations enter into the evaluation of a test, but we will consider them under three main headings: reliability, validity, and practicality. *Reliability* refers to the accuracy and precision of a measurement procedure. Indices of reliability give an indication of the extent to which the scores produced by a particular measurement procedure are consistent and reproducible. *Validity* has to do with the degree to which the test scores provide information that is relevant to the inferences that are to be made from them. Thus, a judgment of validity is always in relation to a specific decision or use, and evidence that test scores are appropriate for one purpose does not necessarily mean that the scores are appropriate for another. *Practicality* is concerned with a wide range of factors of economy, convenience, and interpretability that determine whether a test is realistically employable for our purpose.

Reliability and validity are both required of any test that we would choose, regardless of how practical it is to use. Validity is the absolutely essential quality for a test to have, but in a sense, reliability is a necessary precondition for validity. Test scores must be at least moderately reliable before they can have any validity, but a reliable test may be devoid of validity for the application we have in mind. Although the true bottom line in selecting a test is the test's validity for our proposed use, we discuss reliability first as a necessary condition for validity to exist. Validity and practicality are discussed in Chapter 5.

Reliability as Consistency

When we ask about a test's reliability, we are asking not what it measures, but instead how accurately it measures whatever it does measure. What is the precision of the resulting score? How accurately will the score be reproduced if we measure the individual again?

Some degree of inconsistency is present in all measurement procedures. Consider the experience of one of your authors (RMT) who bought a new digital electronic bathroom scale because he did not trust the old spring-operated one he had been using for 20 years. When he brought the new scale home and tried it out, the first reading seemed reasonable. Then, just to show himself that the new scale was an improvement, he tried it again. The reading was 7 lbs lower! Not believing that a diet could work that fast, he took a third reading and then a fourth. After 10 minutes of testing the scale, he decided to return it because the readings had spread over a range of 15 lbs.

This little experience illustrates the central issue in reliability. RMT's actual weight was, for all practical purposes, constant throughout the series of measurements, but his scores differed from one testing to the next. If we call his real, constant weight his *true score (T)*; then each observation or *measurement (X)* includes his true score plus some *error of measurement (e)*. That is,

$$X = T + e$$

On the bathroom scale, and indeed in all measurements, many errors of measurement appear to be random; sometimes they are positive, making the score too high, and sometimes they are negative, making the score too low. Most of them are fairly small, but some are quite large. Their distribution often looks like the normal distribution that we discussed in Chapter 2.

There are other errors of measurement that remain constant from one measurement to another. The scale could have read 10 lbs too high on every repetition. Errors of this kind cannot be detected just by repeating the measurement; the instrument must be compared to another one in which the error is not present. However, constant errors do not lead to inconsistency, so they do not affect the reliability of the measuring instrument.

The bathroom scale offers a unique opportunity to observe random errors of measurement in action, but that situation is far removed from the environment in which educational or psychological measurements are made. Measurements of human behavior are particularly susceptible to inconsistency.

Let us consider a second example that is also somewhat artificial but more nearly approximates a testing context. Suppose we were to test all the girls in a class one day and again the next day to see how far each can throw a football. We mark a starting line on the field, give each girl one of the old footballs that the physical education department has for team practice, send an assistant out to mark where the ball hits, and tell each girl to throw the ball as far as she can. With a steel tape, we measure the distance from the starting line to where the assistant marked the fall of the ball. On each occasion, we have each girl make one throw.

When we compare the two scores for an individual, we will find that they are seldom the same. Most of the differences will be fairly small, but some will be moderately large. The differences show that one throw is not perfectly reliable as a measure of a person's throwing ability. Results are, to some degree, inconsistent from one day's throw to the next.

Sources of Inconsistency

We can identify three classes of reasons for inconsistency between a throw one day and a throw the next day.

1. The person may actually have changed from one testing to the next. On one day, a girl may have been more rested than she was on the other. On one day, she may have been motivated to try harder on the task. She may even have gotten some special coaching from a parent between the two tests. If the interval between the two tests is months rather than days, there may have been real physical growth that differed from girl to girl between the two testings. This example has involved changes affecting physical performance, but it is easy to think of similar categories of change that would apply to a test of mental ability or to a self-report inventory dealing with mood or with interests.

2. The task may have been different for the two measurements. For example, the ball Betty used one day may have been tightly inflated, whereas the one she had on the next day may have been a squashy one that permitted a somewhat different grip. Or, one day the examiner may have permitted the girls to take a run up to the release line, whereas the examiner on the second day may have allowed only one or two steps. Environmental factors such as the presence of a head wind may also have been present on one day and not on another. These variations may have helped some girls more than others. In paper-and-pencil tests we often use one form of the test on one occasion and a second, parallel form on the second occasion. The specific items are different, and some pupils may happen to be better able to handle one sampling of tasks, while others are better at the other sampling.

3. The limited sample of behavior may have resulted in an unstable and undependable score. Even if we had each girl make two throws with the same ball and the same instructions, with only a 5-minute rest in between, the two distances would rarely come out to be the same. A single throw, like a single test item, is a meager sample of behavior. That sample and the evaluation of it are subject to all sorts of chance influences. Maybe Betty's finger slipped. Maybe she got mixed up in the coordination of her legs and her arm. Maybe the ball was held a little too far forward or a little too far back. Maybe the scorer was looking the other way when the ball landed. Maybe there was a gust of wind just as she threw. Maybe any of a hundred things occurred—some favorable, some unfavorable. The effect of such unknown random influences on an observed performance is that a small sample of behavior does not provide a stable and dependable characterization of an individual—whether the sample be of footballs thrown for distance or of sentences read for understanding. The average of 100 throws of the football would provide a much more stable index of this ability than would the result of a single throw.

Two Ways to Express Reliability

There are two ways in which we can express the reliability, or precision, of a set of measurements or, from the reverse point of view, the variation within the set. One approach addresses directly the amount of variation to be expected within a set of repeated measurements of a single individual. If we were to take 200 readings of the bathroom scale or if it were possible to have Betty throw the football 200 times (assuming for the present that this could be done without introducing effects of practice or fatigue), we could produce a frequency distribution of weights or of distances thrown. This frequency distribution has an average value, which we can think of as approximating a person's "true" weight or the "true" distance that Betty can throw a football. It also has a standard deviation, describing the spread or scatter of the measurements. Because the scatter results from errors of measurement, we will call this variation the *standard error of measurement*. It is the standard deviation of the "errors" of measuring the distance of throw or the weight of a person.

With psychological or educational data, we usually cannot make a whole series of measurements on each individual. There *are* practice and fatigue effects; besides, time does not permit giving 200 reading tests or 200 interest inventories. Often, we are fortunate if we can get *two* scores for each individual. But, if we have a pair of measurements for each individual, we can make an estimate (see Interpretation of Reliability Data later in this chapter) of what the scattering of scores would have been for the average person if we had made the measurements again and again.

Reliable measurement also implies that the individual stays in about the same place in the group. The girl who scores highest on the football throwing test the first time should also be one of the highest the next time, and each person in the group should stay in about the same position. The correlation coefficient provides a statistical index of the extent to which two things go together, high with high and low with low. If the two things we are correlating happen to be two applications of the same measure, the resulting correlation provides an indicator of reliability. We can designate it a *reliability coefficient*. The characteristics of the correlation coefficient are those that we have already seen in Chapter 2. But the relationship now before us is that of two measurements with the same or an equivalent measuring instrument. The more nearly individuals are ranked in the same order the second time, the higher the correlation and the more reliable the test.

Ways to Assess Reliability

A measure is reliable, then, to the extent that an individual remains nearly the same on repeated measurements—nearly the same as represented by a low standard error of measurement (low variation in the person's performance over repeated measurements) or by a high reliability coefficient (consistent ranking of individuals within the group from one measurement to another). But what exact type of data do we need to get an appropriate estimate of this degree of stability or precision of measurement? We will consider three distinct possibilities, noting their similarities and differences and evaluating the advantages and disadvantages of each:

1. Repeating the same test or measure (retest)
2. Administering a second "equivalent" form of the test (parallel test forms)
3. Subdividing the test into two or more equivalent fractions from a single administration (single-administration method)

Retest with the Same Test

If we wish to find out how reliably we can evaluate an individual's football throw, we can test the person twice. It may be a reasonable precaution to have the two measures taken independently by two testers. We do not want the examiner's recollection of the first score to affect perception of the second. It may be desirable to have the two testings done on different days, depending on what we are interested in. If we want to know how accurately a single throw (or possibly a single set of throws) characterizes a person at a specific point in time, the two measurements should be carried out one immediately after the other. Then, we know that the *person* has stayed the same and that the only source of variation or "error" is in the measuring operation. If we want to know how precisely a given measurement characterizes a person from day to day—how closely we can predict an individual's score next week from what he or she does today—it would be appropriate to measure the person on two separate occasions. Now, we are interested in *variation of the individual from time to time* as well as *variation due to the operation of measurement*.

Sometimes we are interested in variation in the individual from day to day; sometimes we are not. We may ask, how accurately does our measurement characterize Sam at this moment in time? Or we may ask, how accurately does our measurement of Sam describe him as he will be tomorrow, or next week, or next month? Each is a sensible question. But the questions are not the same. The data we must collect to answer one are different from the data we need to answer the other.

To study the reliability of measurement of such a physical characteristic of a person as weight or height, repetition of the measurement is a straightforward and satisfactory operation. The bathroom scale's reading on one occasion is not affected by the reading it gave on a previous weighing. Simple repetition of the measurement appears satisfactory and applicable also with some simple aspects of behavior, such as speed of reaction or the type of motor skill that is exemplified by the football throw. But suppose now that we are interested in the reliability of a measure of reading comprehension. Let us assume that the test is made up of six reading passages with five questions on each. We administer the test once and then immediately administer it again. What happens? Certainly the children are not going to have to reread all of the material that they have just read. They may do so in part, but to a considerable extent, their answers the second time will involve merely remembering what answers they had chosen the first time and marking them again. Those who had not been able to finish the first time will now be able to work ahead and spend most of their time on new material. These same effects hold true to some degree even over longer periods of time. Clearly, a test like this one given a second time does not present the same task that it did the first time.

A second consideration enters into the repetition of a test such as a reading comprehension test. Suppose that one of the six passages in the test was about baseball and that a particular girl was an expert on baseball. The passage would then be especially easy for her, and she would in effect get a bonus of several points. This portion of the test would overestimate her general level of reading ability. But note that it would do so consistently on both testings if the material remained the same. The error for this individual would be a *constant error* in the two testings. Because the error would affect both her scores in the same way, it would make the test look reliable rather than unreliable.

In an area of ability such as reading, we must recognize the possibility that an individual does not perform uniformly well throughout the whole area. Specific interests, experiences, and backgrounds give individuals different strengths and weaknesses. A particular test is *one sample* from the whole domain of behavior. How well an individual does on the test, relative to other people, is likely to depend to some degree on the particular sample of tasks chosen to represent the particular domain of ability or personality we are trying to appraise. If the sample remains the same for both measurements, the person's behavior will stay more nearly the same than if the sample of tasks is varied.

Note that so far we have identified three main sources of variation in performance that will tend to reduce the consistency, or stability, of a particular score as a description of an individual:

1. Variation from trial to trial in responding to the task at a particular moment in time
2. Variation in the individual from one time to another
3. Variation arising out of the particular sample of tasks chosen to represent a domain of behavior

Retesting the individual with an identical test can be arranged to reflect the first two sources of "error," but this procedure cannot evaluate the effects of the third type. In addition, there may be memory or practice effects such as those to which we referred above.

Parallel Test Forms

Concern about variation resulting from the particular sample of tasks chosen to represent a domain of behavior leads us to another set of procedures for evaluating reliability. If the sampling of items may be a significant source of "error" and if, as is usually the case, we want to know with what accuracy we can generalize from the specific score based on one sample of tasks to the broader domain that the sample is supposed to represent, we must develop some procedures that take into account variation resulting from the sample of tasks. We may do this by correlating scores from two alternate, or parallel, forms of a test.

Alternate forms of a test should be thought of as forms built according to the same specifications but composed of separate samples from the defined behavior domain. Thus, two parallel reading tests should contain reading passages and questions of the same difficulty. The same sorts of questions should be asked; for example, there should be a balance of specific fact and general idea questions. The same types of passages should be represented, such as expository, argumentative, and aesthetic. But the specific passage topics and questions should be different.

If we have two forms of a test, we may give each pupil first one form and then the other. The tests may follow each other immediately if we are not interested in stability over time, or they may be separated by an interval if we are interested in stability. The correlation between the two forms will provide an appropriate reliability coefficient. If a time interval has been allowed between the testings, all three sources of variation will have a chance to get in their effects—variation arising from the measurement itself, variation in the individual over time, and variation from the sample of tasks.

To ask that a test yield consistent results under the conditions of parallel tests separated by a time interval is the most rigorous standard we can set for it. And, if we want to use test results to generalize about what Johnny will do on other tasks of this general sort next week or next month, then this standard is the appropriate one by which to evaluate a test. For most educational situations, this procedure *is* the way we want to use test results, and so evidence based on equivalent test forms with a time interval between administrations should usually be given the most weight in evaluating the reliability of a test.

The use of two parallel test forms provides a sound basis for estimating the precision of a psychological or educational test. This procedure does, however, raise some practical problems. It demands that two parallel forms of the test be available and that time be allowed for testing each person twice. Often, no second form of the test exists or could reasonably be constructed, or no time can be found for a second testing. To administer a second test is often likely to represent a somewhat burdensome demand on available resources. These practical considerations of convenience and expediency have made test makers receptive to procedures that extract an estimate of reliability from one administration of one form of a test. However, such procedures are a compromise at best. The correlation between two parallel forms, usually administered after a lapse of several days or weeks, represents the preferred procedure for estimating reliability in most applications.

Single-Administration Methods

Internal Consistency Reliability.   Practical considerations often dictate that a reliability estimate be obtained from a single administration of the test. Although several procedures for obtaining such estimates have been developed, the ones that are now most widely used are based on the idea that each item in a test can be considered to be a one-item test. The total test of n items is then seen as a set of n parallel but very short tests. (Here, n is the number of test items.) An estimate of the reliability of the total test is developed from an analysis of the statistics of the individual items.

The procedure for estimating the reliability of a test from a single administration of a single form depends on the consistency of the individual's performance from item to item and is based on the standard deviation of the test and the standard deviations of the separate items. In its most general form, this procedure is called *coefficient alpha* and is given by the following equation:

$$\alpha = \left(\frac{n}{n-1}\right)\left(\frac{SD_t^2 - \Sigma SD_i^2}{SD_t^2}\right) \tag{4.1}$$

where α is the estimate of reliability,

n is the number of items in the test,

SD_t is the standard deviation of the test scores,

Σ means "take the sum of" and covers the n items, and

SD_i is the standard deviation of the scores from a group of individuals on an item.

When each item is scored as either 1 or 0, that is, as either passed or failed,

$$SD_i^2 = p_i q_i$$

where p_i is the proportion passing the item and

q_i is the proportion failing the item.

Equation 4.1 then becomes

$$r_{11} = \left(\frac{n}{n-1}\right)\left(\frac{SD_t^2 - \Sigma p_i q_i}{SD_t^2}\right) \tag{4.2}$$

where r_{11} is the estimated reliability of the full-length test. This equation, called Kuder-Richardson Formula 20 (KR-20) after its originators and the numbering in their original article, is a special form of coefficient alpha that applies when the items are scored right-or-wrong. Both coefficient alpha and KR-20 provide an estimate of what is called the *internal consistency* of a test, that is, the degree to which all of the items measure a common characteristic of the person. When the test is homogeneous, in the sense that every item measures the same general factors of ability or personality as every other item, coefficient alpha and KR-20 estimates can reasonably be interpreted as reflecting the reliability of the test.

A formula involving simpler calculations and based on an assumption that all items are of the same difficulty is called Kuder-Richardson Formula 21 (KR-21). This formula substitutes $M_t(1 - M_t/n)$, where M_t is the mean score on the test, for $\Sigma p_i q_i$ in Equation 4.2 and yields a close but conservative approximation to KR-20. KR-21 can be particularly useful for teachers who would like to estimate the reliability of the tests they use in their classes because it can be easily calculated from the mean and standard deviation of the distribution of test scores.

The appealing convenience of the internal consistency procedures has led to their wide use. Many test manuals will be found to report this type of reliability coefficient and no other. Unfortunately, KR-20, KR-21, and coefficient alpha have several types of limitations.

First, because all of the item responses have occurred during a single testing, they all necessarily represent the individual as he or she is at a single moment in time. Even events lasting only a few minutes will affect many items about equally. In other words, variation in the individual from day to day cannot be reflected in this type of reliability coefficient. It can only give evidence on the precision with which we can appraise the person at a specific moment.

A second factor will sometimes make item sets more alike than would be true of separate parallel forms. If the test includes groups of items based on common reference material, such as reading items based on a single passage or science items all referring to a single described experiment, performance on all of these items will depend to some extent on the common act of comprehending the reference materials. Thus, the examinee who succeeds on one item of the set is more likely to succeed on the others than would be the case for truly independent items.

Finally, an internal consistency reliability coefficient becomes meaningless when a test is highly speeded. Suppose we had a test of simple arithmetic made up of 100 problems like $3 + 5 = $ ___?___, and that the test was being used with adults with a 2-minute time limit. People would differ widely in scores on such a test, but the differences would be primarily differences in speed. Computation errors would be a minor factor. The person who got a score of 50 would very probably have attempted just 50 items. The position of an item in the test then determines almost completely whether an individual attempts the item. Because almost everyone who attempts an item gets the item correct, the values of p and q for the item are determined by its placement in the test, and this fact will greatly inflate the apparent consistency of performance.

Few tests depend as completely on speed as does the one chosen to illustrate the point; however, many tests involve some degree of speeding. This speed factor tends to inflate estimates of reliability based on internal consistency procedures. The amount of overestimation depends on the degree to which the test is speeded, being greater for those tests in which speed plays a greater role. But speed enters in sufficiently general a manner so that internal consistency estimates of reliability should usually be discounted somewhat.

Subdivided Tests. A procedure that has been widely used in the past for obtaining a reliability estimate from a single administration of a test divides the test into two presumably equivalent halves. The half-tests may be assembled on the basis of a careful examination of the content and difficulty of each item, making a systematic effort to balance out the content and difficulty level of the two halves. A simpler procedure, often relied on to give equivalent halves, is to put alternate items into the two half-tests, that is, to put the odd-numbered items into one half-test and the even-numbered items in the other half. This procedure is usually a sensible one because items of similar form, content, or difficulty are likely to be grouped together in the test. For a reasonably long test, 60 items or more, splitting the test in this way will tend to balance out factors of item form, content covered, and difficulty level. The two half-tests will have a good probability of being "equivalent" tests.

The procedures we are now discussing divide the test in half only for scoring, not for administration. That is, a single test is given with a single time limit at a single sitting. However, two separate scores are derived—one by scoring the odd-numbered items and one by scoring the even-numbered items. The correlation between these two scores, called an odd-even reliability coefficient or, more generally, a split-half reliability, provides a measure of the accuracy with which the test is measuring the individual at this point in time. Split-half reliability coefficients provide an estimate of what the correlation would be between two equivalent tests.

However, it must be noted that the computed correlation is between two half-length tests. This value is not directly applicable to the full-length test, which is the actual instrument prepared for use. In general, the larger a sample of a person's behavior we have, the more reliable the measure will be. That is, the more behavior we record, the less our measure will depend on chance elements in the behavior of the individual or in the particular sampling of tasks. Single lucky answers or momentary lapses in attention will be more nearly evened out.

Where the halves of the test, which gave the scores actually correlated, are equivalent, we can get an unbiased estimate of the total-test reliability from the correlation between the two half-tests. The estimate is given by the following equation:

$$r_{11} = \frac{2r_{1/2\,1/2}}{1 + r_{1/2\,1/2}} \tag{4.3}$$

where r_{11} is the estimated reliability of the full-length test and $r_{1/2\,1/2}$ is the actual correlation between the two half-tests.

Thus, if the correlation between the halves of a test is 0.60, Equation 4.3 would give

$$r_{11} = \frac{2(0.60)}{1 + 0.60} = \frac{1.20}{1.60} = 0.75$$

as our best estimate of the reliability of the total test. This equation, referred to generally as the Spearman-Brown Prophecy Formula from its function and the names of its originators, makes it possible to compute an estimate of reliability from a single administration of a single test. It has the advantage over the internal consistency methods that it does not assume homogeneous content across all items, only between the two halves, but it is still a single-administration method. Also, the split-half method is sensitive to the equivalence of the two halves.

Internal consistency methods were developed in part to overcome this problem. The value given by coefficient alpha is the average of all possible Spearman-Brown–corrected half-test correlations, so it evens out the possible effects of an inappropriate split.

Comparison of Methods

A summary comparison of the different procedures for estimating reliability is given in Table 4.1. The table shows the four factors (sources of variation) we have discussed that may make a single test score an inaccurate picture of the individual's usual performance and which sources of error are reflected in score variation in each of the procedures for estimating reliability. In general, the more Xs there are in a column, the more conservative (i.e., lower) an estimate of a test's reliability we will get. It can be seen that the different procedures are not equivalent. Only administration of parallel test forms with a time interval between testings permits all sources of instability to have their effects. Each of the other methods masks some source of variation that may be significant in the actual use of the test. Retesting with an identical test neglects variation arising out of the sampling of items. Whenever all testing is done at one point in time, variation in the individual from day to day is omitted. When the testing is done as a single unit with a single time limit, variation in speed of responding is neglected. The facts brought out in this table should be borne in mind in evaluating reliability data found in a test manual or in the report of a research study. Test users should demand that commercial publishers provide estimates based on parallel forms of the test and on retesting after a delay whenever possible so that a reasonable estimate of the effects of the sources of unreliability can be assessed.

TABLE 4.1

Sources of Variation Represented in Different Procedures for Estimating Reliability

Sources of Variation	EXPERIMENTAL PROCEDURE FOR ESTIMATING RELIABILITY				
	Immediate Retest, Same Test	Retest After Interval, Same Test	Parallel Test Form Without Interval	Parallel Test Form With Interval	Single-Administration Methods[a]
Variation arising within the measurement procedure itself	X	X	X	X	X
Changes in the person from day to day		X		X	
Changes in the specific sample of tasks			X	X	X
Changes in the individual's speed of work	X	X	X	X	

Note: X indicates that this source of variation can affect reliability from this method of testing.
[a]The single-administration methods are Kuder-Richardson Formulas 20 and 21, coefficient alpha, and split-half.

Interpretation of Reliability Data

Suppose that analysis of data obtained from an elementary school test of academic aptitude has yielded a reliability coefficient of 0.90. How should we interpret this result? What does it mean concerning the precision of an individual's score? Should we be pleased or dissatisfied to get a coefficient of this size?

One interpretation of test reliability is found in the relationship between the reliability coefficient and the standard error of measurement. The standard error of measurement is the standard deviation that would be obtained for a series of measurements of the same individual. (It is assumed that the individual is not changed by being measured.) The standard error of measurement can be estimated from the reliability coefficient by the following equation:

$$SD_m = SD_t\sqrt{(1 - r_{tt})} \tag{4.4}$$

where SD_m is the standard error of measurement and

r_{tt} is the reliability of the test determined by one of the methods presented earlier.

Suppose that the test with a reliability of 0.90 has a standard deviation of 15 points. Then, we have

$$SD_m = 15\sqrt{(1 - 0.90)} = 15\sqrt{0.10} = 15(0.316) = 4.7$$

In this instance, a set of repeated measures of some one person (such as that obtained for RMT's weight) would be expected to have a standard deviation (i.e., a standard error of measurement) of 4.7 points. Remember that in a normal distribution a fairly uniform proportion of observations falls within any given number of standard deviation units of the mean; about 32% of cases, or about one in three, differ from the mean by more than 1 standard deviation; 4.6% by more than 2 standard deviations. This situation is illustrated for the present example in Figure 4.1.

Applying this to a case in which the standard deviation is 4.7 points, one could say that there is about 1 chance in 3 that an individual's observed score differs from his or her "true" score (falls outside the 68% band in Figure 4.1) by as much as 4.7 points in either direction. There is about 1 chance in 20 that it differs by as much as 9.4 points (2 standard errors of measurement). A little less than one-third of the scores from such a measurement are likely to be in error by 5 points or more, while about 1 in 25 will be in error by 10 or more points.

Another way to view the standard error of measurement is as an indication of how much a person's score might change on retesting. Each person's score on the first testing includes some amount of error. Most of the errors will be fairly small, but some will be quite large. About half of the errors will be positive (make the observed score too high) and about half will be negative (make the observed score too low). But we see only the observed score and have no way of knowing how large the error of measurement is for any individual or in what direction.

The numerical values of 0.90 for the reliability and 15 for the standard devi-

FIGURE 4.1

The standard error of measurement (SD_m) can be used to determine a range for estimating an individual's true score.

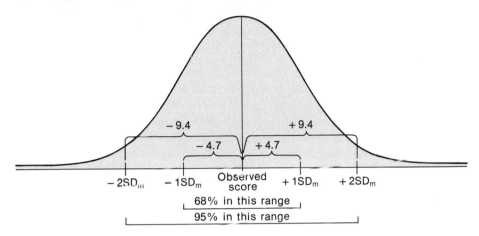

ation are fairly representative of what might be found for standard scores from one of the commercially distributed academic aptitude tests for children in the upper elementary grades. Note that even with this relatively high reliability coefficient, appreciable errors of measurement are possible in at least a minority of cases. With a standard deviation of 15 or 16, shifts of 5 or 10 points from one testing to another can be expected fairly frequently just because of errors of measurement. Anyone who is impressed by and tries to interpret a score difference of five points between two people or two testings of the same person on a test such as this has been fooled into thinking that the test has a precision that it simply does not possess. Further testing could reverse the result. Any interpretation of test scores must be made with acute awareness of the standard error of measurement.

The manner in which the standard error of measurement is related to the reliability coefficient is shown in Table 4.2. Column 1 contains selected values for the reliability, column 2 gives the value of the expression $\sqrt{1 - r_{tt}}\,(SD_t)$, and column 3 gives the value of SD_m when SD_t is 15. Note that the magnitude of errors decreases as the reliability coefficient increases, but also that errors of appreciable size can still be found with reliability coefficients of 0.90 or 0.95. In interpreting the score of an individual, it is the standard error of measurement that must be kept in mind. A range extending from 2 standard errors of measurement above the obtained score to 2 below will produce a band within which we can be reasonably sure (19 chances in 20) that the individual's true score lies. Thus, in the case of the aptitude test described in this section, we can think of a test standard score of 90 as meaning rather surely a score lying between about

TABLE 4.2
Standard Error of Measurement for Different Values of Reliability Coefficient

	STANDARD ERROR OF MEASUREMENT	
Reliability Coefficient	General Expression[a]	When $SD_t = 15$
.50	$.71SD_t$	10.6
.60	$.63SD_t$	9.5
.70	$.55SD_t$	8.2
.80	$.45SD_t$	6.7
.85	$.39SD_t$	5.8
.90	$.32SD_t$	4.7
.95	$.22SD_t$	3.4
.98	$.14SD_t$	2.1

Note: SD_t signifies the standard deviation of the test.
[a]$\sqrt{1 - r_{tt}}(SD_t)$.

80 and 100. If we think in these terms, we will be much more discreet in interpreting and using test results.

When interpreting the test score of an individual, it is desirable to think in terms of the standard error of measurement and a band of uncertainty, and to be somewhat humble and tentative in drawing conclusions from that test score. But for making comparisons between tests and for a number of types of test analyses, the reliability coefficient will be more useful. Where measures are expressed in different units, as height in inches and weight in pounds, the reliability coefficient provides the only possible basis for comparing precision of measurement. Because the competing tests in a given field, such as primary reading, are likely to use types of scores that are not directly comparable, the reliability coefficient will usually represent the only satisfactory basis for test comparison. *Other things being equal,* the test with the higher reliability coefficient, that is, the test that provides a more consistent ranking of the individuals within their group, should be preferred.

The other things that may not be equal are primarily considerations of validity and practicality. Validity, insofar as we can appraise it, is the crucial requirement for a measurement procedure. Reliability is important only as a necessary condition for a measure to have validity. The ceiling for the possible validity of a test is set by its reliability. A test must measure *something* before it can measure what we want to measure. A measuring device with a reliability of 0.00 is reflecting nothing but chance factors. It does not correlate with itself and cannot correlate with anything else.

The theoretical ceiling for the correlation between any two measures is the square root of the product of their reliabilities:

$$r_{12} \leqq \sqrt{r_{11}r_{22}}$$

Thus, if a selection test has a reliability of 0.80 and a set of supervisory ratings has a reliability of 0.50, the theoretical maximum for the correlation between the two is $\sqrt{(0.80)(0.50)} = \sqrt{0.40} = 0.63$. Often there is not too much we can do about the reliability of the criterion variable, except to get information about it, but we can take steps to assure reasonable reliability in our predictor tests.

The converse of the relationship we have just presented does not follow. A test may measure with the greatest precision and still have no validity for our purposes. For example, we can measure head size with a good deal of accuracy, but this measure is still useless as an indicator of intelligence. Validity is something beyond mere accuracy of measurement, and we consider it in Chapter 5.

Considerations of cost, convenience, and so on may also sometimes lead to a decision to use a less reliable test. We may accept a less reliable 40-minute test in preference to a more reliable 3-hour one because 3 hours of testing time is too much of a burden in view of the purpose that the test is designed to serve.

Factors Affecting Reliability

Within the limitations discussed in the preceding paragraphs, we prefer the more reliable test. There are several factors that must be taken into account, however, before we can fairly compare the reliability coefficients of two or more different tests:

1. Range of the group
2. Level of ability in the group
3. Length of the test
4. Operations used for estimating the reliability

Range of the Group

The reliability coefficient indicates how consistently a test places each individual relative to others in the group. When there is little shifting from test to retest or from Form A to Form B, the reliability coefficient is high and vice versa. But the extent to which individuals will switch places depends on how similar they are. It does not take very accurate testing to differentiate the reading ability of second graders from that of seventh graders. But to place each second grader accurately within a second-grade class is much more demanding.

If children from several different grades are pooled together, we may expect a much higher reliability coefficient. For example, the manual for the Otis Quick-Scoring Mental Ability Test—Beta once reported alternate-form reliabilities for single grade groups that ranged from 0.65 to 0.87, with an average value of 0.78. But for a pooling of the complete range of grades (4–9), the reliability coefficient was reported as 0.96. These data are all for the same test. They are the same set of scores, just grouped differently. They reflect the same precision. Yet the coefficient for the combined groups is strikingly higher simply as a function of the greater range of individual differences in the combined group.

In evaluating the reported reliability coefficient, the range of ability of the group tested must be taken into account. If the reliability coefficient is based on a combination of age or grade groups, it must usually be discounted. But, even in less extreme cases, we must take into account the variability of talent. Reliability coefficients for age groups will tend to be somewhat higher than for grade groups because a group of children of the same age will usually contain a greater spread of talent than will the students in a single grade. A sample made up of children from a wide range of socioeconomic levels will tend to yield higher reliability coefficients than a very homogeneous sample. In comparing different tests, we must take account of the type of sample on which the reliability data were based, insofar as this can be determined from the reported facts, and judge more severely the test whose estimated reliability is based on data from a more heterogeneous group.

Level of Ability in the Group

Precision of measurement by a test may be related to the ability level of the people being measured; however, no simple rule can be formulated for stating the nature of this relationship. The nature of the relationship depends on the way the test was built. For those people for whom the test is very hard, such that they are doing a large amount of guessing, accuracy is likely to be low. At the other extreme, if the test is very easy for the group, such that all of them can do most of the items very easily, that test may be expected to be ineffective in discriminating among the group members. When most of the items are easy for the group being tested, it is as if one had shortened the test because all differentiation is based on just those harder items that some can do and some cannot. This factor of most of the pupils getting extreme scores is a particular concern in mastery testing, which is given special consideration in this chapter under Reliability of Criterion-Referenced Tests.

Also, the test may vary in accuracy at different intermediate difficulty levels. The meticulous test constructor will report the standard error of measurement for the test at different score levels. When separate values of the standard error of measurement are reported in the manual, they provide a basis for evaluating the precision of the test for different types of groups and permit a more appropriate estimate of the accuracy of a particular individual's score. Each individual's score can be interpreted in relation to the standard error of measurement for scores of that level. For example, the Iowa Tests of Basic Skills—Form G/H, which reports scores in grade equivalents, reported the standard error of measurement at different score intervals for the vocabulary test as shown in Table 4.3.

This test measures somewhat more accurately those pupils who score near the center of the distribution than those who succeed with only a few items or with almost all. The test authors produced this result intentionally by including many items of moderate difficulty that discriminate degrees of ability in the middle range and relatively few very hard or very easy items. In effect, a longer test is operating for pupils in the middle range rather than at the extremes, and the result is a more accurate measurement of this large middle group.

TABLE 4.3
Iowa Tests of Basic Skills Standard Error of Measurement for the Vocabulary Test

Grade Equivalent Interval	STANDARD ERROR OF MEASUREMENT IN GRADE EQUIVALENT UNITS		
	Grade 4	Grade 6	Grade 8
20–29	5.4		
30–39	3.8		
40–49	3.1	9.0	
50–59	3.6	6.3	10.1
60–69	4.0	4.5	8.1
70–79	4.9	3.8	6.8
80–89		5.3	5.9
90–99		7.6	5.5
100–109			5.3
110–119			5.7
120–129			6.1
Total distribution	4.5	5.5	6.6

Length of the Test

As we saw earlier in discussing the split-half reliability coefficient, test reliability depends on the length of the test. If we can assume that the quality of the test items, the traits measured by those items, and the nature of the examinees remain the same, then the relationship of reliability to length can be expressed by the following equation:

$$r_{kk} = \frac{kr_{tt}}{1 + (k - 1)\, r_{tt}} \tag{4.5}$$

where r_{kk} is the reliability of the test k times as long as the original test,
r_{tt} is the reliability of the original test, and
k is the factor by which the length of the test is changed.

This is a more general form of Equation 4.3.

Suppose we have a spelling test made up of 20 items that has a reliability of 0.50. We want to know how reliable the test will be if it is lengthened to contain 100 items comparable to the original 20. The answer is

$$r_{nn} = \frac{5(0.50)}{1 + 4(0.50)} = \frac{2.50}{3.00} = 0.83$$

As the length of the test is increased, the chance errors of measurement more or less cancel out, the score comes to depend more and more completely on the characteristics of the person being measured, and a more accurate appraisal of the individual is obtained.

Of course, how much we can lengthen a test is limited by a number of practical considerations. It is limited by the amount of time available for testing. It is limited by factors of fatigue and boredom on the part of examinees. It is sometimes limited by our inability to construct more equally good test items. But within these limits, reliability can be increased as needed by lengthening the test, subject only to the constraint that each item measures with some reliability other than zero.

We should note, however, that there is a point of diminishing returns in lengthening a test. When the reliability is already moderately high it takes a considerable increase in test length to accomplish a modest increase in reliability. Quintupling the length of our 20-item spelling test yielded a substantial increase in its reliability (from 0.50 to 0.83). But, doubling the length again to 200 items would produce only a modest increase from 0.83 to 0.91. Adding 200 more items would bring the reliability to 0.95, a rise that is hardly worth the increase in testing time.

One special type of lengthening is represented by increasing the number of raters who rate a person or a product the person has produced. To the extent that the unreliability of an assessment results from the inconsistency with which a sample of behavior is judged, this source of unreliability can usually be reduced by increasing the number of judges, or raters. If several raters are available who have equal competence with the materials to be rated or equal familiarity with the ratee if the ratings are of a person, then a pooling of their ratings will produce a composite that is more reliable; the increase to be expected is described approximately by Equation 4.5. For example, if a typical pair of judges evaluating samples of writing show a correlation of 0.40, then the pooled ratings of three judges could be expected to correlate with three others as follows:

$$\frac{3(0.40)}{1 + 2(0.40)} = \frac{1.20}{1.80} = 0.67$$

It is also possible to estimate the loss in reliability that would occur if a measurement procedure is shortened. Suppose we have a 100-item spelling test that has a reliability of 0.90, and we wish to estimate the reliability of a 40-item test made up of a sample of items from the longer test. The length of the new test is $40/100 = 0.40$ times the length of the original one, so our estimate of the reliability of the shorter test is

$$r_{kk} = \frac{0.40(0.90)}{1 + (0.40 - 1.00)(0.90)} = \frac{0.36}{1 + (-0.60)(0.90)} = \frac{0.36}{0.46} = 0.78$$

This procedure is quite useful for judging whether the shortened test would have sufficient reliability for our purposes.

Operations Used for Estimating the Reliability

How high a value will be obtained for the reliability coefficient depends also on which of the several sets of experimental operations is used to estimate the reliability. We saw in Table 4.1 that the different procedures treat different sources of variation in different ways and that it is only the use of parallel forms

TABLE 4.4
Comparison of Reliability Coefficients Obtained from Test-Retest and Kuder-Richardson Formula 20 (KR-20) and Equivalent Forms

Test	TEST-RETEST (MONTHS)			KR-20	Equivalent Forms[b]
	8	24[a]	48[a]		
Cognitive Abilities Test, Level C					
Verbal	.91	.85	.83	.93	
Quantitative	.87	.82	.79	.91	
Nonverbal	.86	.75	.73	.93	
Iowa Tests of Basic Skills, Grade 5					
Mathematics composite	.85	.84	.64	.94	.88
Language composite	.88	.89	.75	.96	.91
Gates-MacGinitie Reading Test, Survey D					
Vocabulary, Grade 4	.87			.91	.89
Comprehension, Grade 4	.82			.91	.82

[a]24- and 48-month retests were not available for the Gates-MacGinitie Reading Test.
[b]Equivalent forms correlations were not available for the Cognitive Abilities Test.

of a test with a period intervening that includes all four possible sources of instability as "error." That is, this procedure of estimating reliability represents a more exacting definition of the test's ability to reproduce the same score. The individual must then show consistency both from one sample of tasks to another and from one day to another. In Table 4.4, we have gathered a few examples that show reliability coefficients for the same test when the coefficients have been computed by different procedures and with different time intervals.

The procedures compared in Table 4.4 are test-retest correlations with an interval of 8, 24, or 48 months, correlations between equivalent forms with a very short interval, and KR-20 internal consistency reliabilities. Note that the test-retest correlation is as low as or lower than the other coefficients in every case and is lower for longer intervals than for shorter ones. The differences between the procedures vary, but in every case, it is necessary to discount the internal consistency estimate. Had the alternate forms of these tests been administered with an interval of 8 months, we would expect the correlations between different forms of the test on different occasions to be lower than the test-retest coefficients.

Minimum Level of Reliability

Obviously, other things being equal, the more reliable a measuring procedure, the better satisfied we are with it. A question that is often raised is, what is the *minimum* reliability that is acceptable? If we *must* make some decision or take some course of action with respect to an individual, we will do so in terms of the best information we have—however unreliable it may be—provided only that the reliability is better than zero, in which case we have *no* information. (Of course, here as always the crucial consideration is the validity of the measure.) The appraisal of any new procedure must always be in terms of other procedures with which it is in competition. Thus, a high school mathematics test with a reliability coefficient of 0.80 would look relatively unattractive if tests with reliabilities of 0.85 or 0.90 were readily available at similar cost. On the other hand, a procedure for judging "leadership" that had a reliability of no more than 0.60 might look very attractive if the alternative was a set of ratings having a reliability of 0.45 or 0.50.

Although we cannot set an absolute minimum for the reliability of a measurement procedure, we can indicate the level of reliability that is required to enable us to achieve specified levels of accuracy in describing an individual or a group. Suppose that we have given a test to two individuals and that Individual A fell at the 75th percentile of the group while Individual B fell at the 50th percentile. What is the probability that Individual A would still surpass Individual B if they were tested again? In Table 4.5, the probability of a reversal is shown for different values of the reliability of the test. Thus, where the reliability is 0.00, there is exactly a 50-50 chance that the order of the two individuals will be reversed because both measurements represent completely random error. When the reliability is 0.50, the probability of a reversal is more than 1 in 3. For a correlation of 0.90, there is still 1 chance in 12 that we will get a reversal on repetition of the testing. To have 4 chances in 5 that our difference will stay in the same direction, we require a reliability of 0.80.

Table 4.5 also shows the percentage of expected reversals of two groups— groups of 25 and of 100. For example, if in Class A, of 25 pupils, the average fell at the 75th percentile of some larger reference group and in Class B, also of 25

TABLE 4.5
Percentage of Times Direction of Difference Will Be Reversed in Subsequent Testing for Scores Falling at 75th and 50th Percentiles

	PERCENTAGE OF REVERSALS WITH REPEATED TESTINGS		
Reliability Coefficient	Scores of Single Individuals	Means of Groups of 25	Means of Groups of 100
.00	50.0	50.0	50.0
.40	40.3	10.9	.7
.50	36.8	4.6	.04
.60	32.5	1.2	
.70	27.1	.1	
.80	19.7		
.90	8.7		
.95	2.2		
.98	.05		

pupils, the average fell at the 50th percentile, what is the probability that we would get a reversal if the testing were repeated? Here, we still have a 50–50 chance in the extreme case in which the reliability coefficient is 0.00. However, the security of our conclusion increases much more rapidly with groups than with individuals as the reliability of the test becomes greater. With a reliability of 0.50, the probability of a reversal is already down to 1 in 20 for groups of 25, to 1 in 2,500 for groups of 100. With a correlation of 0.70, the probability of a reversal is only 1 in 1,000 for groups of 25 and is vanishingly small for groups of 100. Thus, a test with relatively low reliability will permit us to make useful studies of and draw dependable conclusions about groups, especially groups of substantial size, but quite high reliability is required if we are to speak with confidence about individuals.

Reliability of Difference Scores

Sometimes we are less interested in single scores than we are in the relationship between scores taken in pairs. We may be concerned with the differences between scholastic aptitude and reading achievement in a group of pupils, or we may wish to study gains in reading from an initial test given in October to a later test given the following May. In these illustrations, the significant fact for each individual is the difference between two scores. We must inquire how reliable our estimates of these differences are, knowing the characteristics of the two component tests.

It is unfortunately true that the appraisal of the difference between two test scores usually has substantially lower reliability than the reliabilities of the two tests taken separately. This lower reliability is due to two factors: (1) the errors of measurement in both separate tests accumulate in the difference score, and (2) whatever is common to the two tests is canceled out in the difference score. We can illustrate the situation by a diagram such as that in Figure 4.2.

Each bar in Figure 4.2 represents performance (more precisely, variance in performance) on a test, broken up into a number of parts to represent the factors producing this performance. The first bar represents a scholastic aptitude test, and the second a reading test. Notice that we have divided reading performance into three parts. One part, labeled "common factors," is a complex of general intellectual abilities that operate in both the reading and the scholastic aptitude tests. Another part, labeled "specific reading factors," includes abilities that appear only in the reading test. The third part, labeled "error," is the chance error of measurement that is reflected in the standard error of measurement for the test. Three similar parts are indicated for the aptitude test.

Now examine the third bar (and the fourth, which shows the third with blank space removed). The third and fourth bars represent the difference score—that is, the reading score expressed in some type of standard score units minus the aptitude test score expressed in those same units. In this bar, the common factors have disappeared. They appeared with a positive sign in the reading test and a negative sign (due to the subtraction) in the aptitude test and thus can-

FIGURE 4.2
Nature of a difference score.

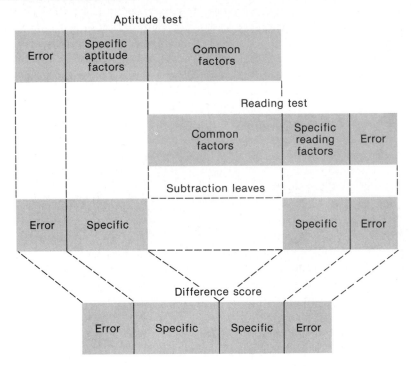

celed out. Only the specific factors and errors of measurement remain. The specific factors are the factors that determine the difference score. The errors of measurement make up a much larger proportion of this third bar, showing that the reliability of the difference scores will be lower than that of either of the original tests. For example, if error made up 25% of each test, and specific factors made up another 25% of each test, the difference score would contain 50% error and 50% specific factor. Thus, the difference score would be much less reliable than either of the original tests. If the two tests measured exactly the same abilities so that there were only common and error factors, only the errors of measurement would remain in the difference scores, and these scores would have exactly zero reliability. This problem is particularly acute when you attempt to assess educational gains by retesting with the same or a parallel test, because in such a case the common factors are at a maximum.

The reliability of the difference between two measures expressed in standard scores can be obtained by the following fairly simple equation:

$$r_{\text{diff}} = \frac{\frac{1}{2}(r_{AA} + r_{BB}) - r_{AB}}{1 - r_{AB}} \tag{4.6}$$

where r_{diff} is the reliability of the difference score,

r_{AA} is the reliability of Test A,

r_{BB} is the reliability of Test B, and

r_{AB} is the correlation between the two tests.

Thus, if the reliability of Test A is 0.80, the reliability of Test B is 0.90, and the correlation between Tests A and B is 0.60, for the reliability of the difference score, we get

$$r_{diff} = \frac{\frac{1}{2}(0.80 + 0.90) - 0.60}{1 - 0.60} = \frac{0.25}{0.40} = 0.62$$

In Table 4.6, the value of r_{diff} is shown for various combinations of values of $\frac{1}{2}(r_{AA} + r_{BB})$ and r_{AB}. If the average of the two reliabilities is 0.80, the reliability of the difference score is 0.80 when the two tests are exactly uncorrelated and is 0.00 when the correlation is 0.80. It is clear that as soon as the correlation between the two tests begins to approach the average of their separate reliabilities, the reliability of the difference score drops very rapidly.

The low reliability that tends to characterize difference scores is something to which the psychologist and educator must always be sensitive. Lower reliability becomes a problem whenever we wish to use test patterns for diagnosis. Thus, the judgment that Herbert's reading lags behind his scholastic aptitude is a judgment that must be made a good deal more tentatively than a judgment about either his scholastic aptitude or his reading taken separately. The conclusion that Mary has improved in reading more than Jane must be a more tentative judgment than that Mary is now a better (or poorer) reader than Jane. Any difference needs to be interpreted in the light of the standard error of measurement of that difference, which will be about 1.4 times as large as the average of the two standard errors of measurement. This caveat applies with particular force to the

TABLE 4.6
Reliability of a Difference Score

Correlation Between Two Tests (r_{AB})	AVERAGE OF RELIABILITY OF TWO TESTS $(1/2(r_{AA} + r_{BB}))$					
	.50	.60	.70	.80	.90	.95
.00	.50	.60	.70	.80	.90	.95
.40	.17	.33	.50	.67	.83	.92
.50	.00	.20	.40	.60	.80	.90
.60		.00	.25	.50	.75	.88
.70			.00	.33	.67	.83
.80				.00	.50	.75
.90					.00	.50
.95						.00

practice of assigning grades to students based on an assessment of their improvement or growth, a subject discussed more fully later.

Many differences will be found to be quite small relative to their standard error and, consequently, quite undependable. This caution especially applies for the interpretation of profiles and of gain scores. (Recent work on patterns of growth suggests that some of the problems with measures of change may be overcome by using measurements at more than two points in time. However, the problems with interpreting differences between scores in a profile remain. See Willett (1988) for a review.)

Effects of Unreliability on Correlation Between Variables

There is one further effect of unreliability that merits brief attention here because it affects our interpretation of the correlations between different measures. Let us think of a measure of reading comprehension and one of mathematical reasoning. In each of these tests, the individual differences in score result in part from "true" differences in ability and in part from chance "errors of measurement." But, if the errors of measurement are really chance matters, the reading test errors and the mathematical reasoning test errors are uncorrelated. These uncorrelated errors are part of the total or observed score for each individual, which means that they must dilute any correlation that exists between the true scores on reading and the true scores on mathematical reasoning. That is, because the observed scores are a combination of true scores and errors of measurement, the correlation between observed scores is a compromise between the correlation that exists between the underlying true scores and the 0.00 correlation between the errors of measurement on the two tests.

We would often like to extract an estimate of the correlation between the underlying true scores from our obtained data to understand better how much the functions involved have in common. Fortunately, we can do this quite simply. The process is called correcting for attenuation due to unreliability. The estimate is provided by the following equation:

$$r_{1\infty2\infty} = \frac{r_{12}}{r_{11}r_{22}} \qquad (4.7)$$

where $r_{1\infty2\infty}$ is the correlation of the underlying true scores,
$\quad r_{12}$ is the correlation of the observed scores, and
$\quad r_{11}$ and r_{22} are the reliabilities of the two measures.

If, for example, the correlation between the reading test and the mathematical reasoning test were found to be 0.56 and the reliabilities of the two tests were 0.71 and 0.90, respectively, we would have

$$r_{1\infty2\infty} = \frac{0.56}{(0.71)(0.90)} = 0.70$$

Our estimate of the correlation between error-free measures of mathematics and reading would be 0.70. In thinking of these two *functions,* it would be appropriate to think in terms of the correlation as 0.70 rather than 0.56, though the *tests* correlate only 0.56.

Reliability of Criterion-Referenced Tests

Our discussion of reliability up to this point has assumed that our tests are continuous variables that have no upper limit or "ceiling," which is usually the case for tests that are developed for use within a normative frame of reference. We have excluded the idea that a large number of examinees would achieve perfect or near-perfect scores. However, criterion-referenced tests are generally designed to be sharply focused on a limited range of behavior that is being taught in a program of instruction. For tests of this type, it is reasonable to expect that a substantial proportion of the examinees may get perfect or near-perfect scores on the test. Traditional measures of reliability do not work well for tests of this type because there is little variability in the set of scores and, as we saw earlier, this lack of variability tends to yield a low reliability coefficient.

Criterion-referenced test scores are interpreted in three basic ways. The first of these is mastery/nonmastery of the particular skill or body of knowledge that is being tested. Individuals are classified as masters (as having achieved the requisite level of performance with this material) if their test scores surpass a preset cutoff and as nonmasters if their scores fail to reach this level. There is no middle ground and all masters are considered equal.

The second way in which criterion-referenced test scores are interpreted is as reflecting the degree of mastery. In this approach, each person's score is again compared to a preset standard, but people whose scores greatly exceed the cutoff are considered to be more complete masters than are those who just barely surpass the cutoff. Likewise, people whose scores fall far short of the cutoff are considered farther from mastery than are those who just missed the cutoff.

The third interpretation of criterion-referenced tests is based on the idea that the test items sample a domain of content. The examinee's score on the test is seen as an estimate of his or her *domain score,* the score he or she would have gotten on a test that included every item in the domain. The question becomes one of how accurately the domain score is estimated.

There has been considerable progress in the estimation of reliability for criterion-referenced tests. Although somewhat different approaches are required for each interpretation of a criterion-referenced test, all approaches share the notion of consistency of information. We will examine in detail the issue of consistency as this applies to mastery/nonmastery decisions and then mention briefly some of the issues for the other interpretations. Systematic reviews of all of the available methods for all three interpretations are provided by Berk (1984), Brennan (1984), and Subkoviak (1984).

The mastery/nonmastery approach requires that examinees be classified into one of two categories. Reliability for this interpretation is assessed by evaluating the consistency with which classifications are made either by the same test administered on two occasions or by alternate forms of the test (there are also single-test methods analogous to KR-20). As an example, consider a test that was designed for use with foreign students studying English to assess their mastery of certain specific English constructions. In one such test, Blatchford (1970) assessed mastery of each of 10 English constructions, using four items for each construction. Two forms of the test were developed and administered to groups of students with an interval of about 1 week between testings. Multiple-choice items illustrating two of the constructions are shown in Figure 4.3. The student

FIGURE 4.3
Two samples from a mastery test of English constructions. Asterisk indicates the correct answer.

Set 6. *The use of "but" after an "although" clause.*
(1) Because he was late, he still attended the meeting.
*(2) Although he was late, he still attended the meeting.
(3) Although he was late, but he still attended the meeting.
(4) Because he was late, but he still attended the meeting.

Number Correct—Form B	Number Correct—Form A (%)					Total
	0	1	2	3	4	
4	2	1	2	6	36	47
3	1	1	1	4	7	14
2	1	1	1	1	1	5
1	3	1	1	1	1	7
0	21	3	1	1	1	27
Total	28	7	6	13	46	

Set 10. *The use of "most" with plural nouns.*
(1) The most of the students must study three hours every night.
*(2) Most students must study three hours every night.
(3) Most student must study three hours every night.
(4) Most of student must study three hours every night.

Number Correct—Form B	Number Correct—Form A (%)					Total
	0	1	2	3	4	
4	1	3	4	12	18	38
3	1	2	3	5	5	16
2	2	2	1	3	2	10
1	4	4	1	1	1	11
0	15	5	1	3	1	25
Total	23	16	10	24	27	

was required to choose the construction that was correct English usage. Each item is followed by a table showing the percentage of students getting zero, one, two, three, or four items correct on each of the testings. For example, the entry in the top row and first column for set 6 shows that 2% of the group got zero correct on Form A and four correct on Form B.

Let us look first at Set 6 in Figure 4.3. Note that 36% of the students got perfect scores of four on *both* testings and 21% got zero scores on *both* testings. For this 57% of the group, the little four-item test gave perfectly consistent and unequivocal information. One group appeared to have completely mastered the correct usage, and the other group appeared to be completely in the dark or to possess misinformation. The other 43% showed some inconsistency within a test or between the two tests. How shall we express this degree of inconsistency or unreliability?

The important thing to remember is that a test such as this is being used to decide whether each student has mastery of a specific skill. We might set a severe standard and accept only a perfect performance—four correct out of four—as indicating mastery. Or we might be willing to accept a more relaxed standard of three out of four as satisfactory performance, recognizing that lowered vigilance or some extraneous factor might have been responsible for a single error. Whichever standard is adopted, the question we ask is, how often would the decision have been reversed on the other testing? Or how often would we have switched from "pass" to "fail" or the reverse?

The results from Set 6 are shown here for the two standards.

SEVERE STANDARD (ALL FOUR CORRECT) FORM A			LENIENT STANDARD (THREE OUT OF FOUR CORRECT) FORM A		
Form B	Fail	Pass	Form B	Fail	Pass
Pass	11	36	Pass	8	53
Fail	43	10	Fail	33	6

Using the severe standard, we would reach the same decision for both forms for 79% of students and opposite decisions for 21%. With the more relaxed standard, the corresponding percentages are 86% and 14%.

The decisions for Set 10 can be expressed in the same way.

SEVERE STANDARD (ALL FOUR CORRECT) FORM A			LENIENT STANDARD (THREE OUT OF FOUR CORRECT) FORM A		
Form B	Fail	Pass	Form B	Fail	Pass
Pass	20	18	Pass	14	40
Fail	53	9	Fail	35	11

Clearly, the percentage of reversals is greater for Set 10 than for Set 6. There are 29% and 25% reversals by the severe and lenient standards, respectively. This set provides a less reliable basis for the central decision: Has the student mastered the skill?

For a test that is being used for the single "go-no go" decision of "mastery" versus "nonmastery," the percentage of consistent decisions seems to be the best index of reliability. Unfortunately, this index is a function of the characteristics of the group as well as of the test. If many students are close to the threshold of mastery—having learned a certain skill, but just barely having learned it—there are likely to be numerous reversals from one testing to another. If, on the other hand, there are many who have considerably overlearned the skill or many who have never learned it at all, reversals will be relatively infrequent. Also, if the consistency of the decisions is assessed during a period of active instruction in the skill, students may be changing from nonmasters to masters in the interval between administrations. It will be important, therefore, to evaluate the reliability of a test that is to be used for mastery decisions with groups of students who have reached just about the same degree of assurance in their mastery of the skill as those with whom the test will eventually be used. It is also important to conduct the reliability study when active instruction is not taking place.

We now need some way to decide what percentage of consistent decisions represents a satisfactory test. At one extreme, with two choices (i.e., master or nonmaster), pure chance would produce agreement 50% of the time. If the test yields no more consistent results than flipping a coin, it is obviously worthless. At the other extreme, if there were 100% agreement between the two forms in the decision to which they led, the reliability of that decision is clearly perfect. It is the intermediate percentages, which almost always occur, that require evaluation. Are the agreements of 79%, 86%, 71%, and 75% that were found for the two four-item tests by two standards of mastery good, just tolerable, or unsatisfactory?

It is hard to give a general answer to the above question. The answer depends on the length of the test on the one hand, and on the seriousness and irreversibility of the decision on the other. The shorter the test, the more reversals we can expect. The less crucial the decision, the more reversals we can tolerate. Considering that the tests that we have analyzed were composed of only four items, consistencies ranging from 70% to 85% are probably as good as can be expected. If the test results were to be used merely to guide review and remedial instruction, this level of consistency might be quite tolerable because errors in the initial decision would usually be corrected in later testing.

The illustration that we have discussed used data from alternate test forms given about 1 week apart. Of course, it would be possible to subdivide a test and get two scores from a single testing. These scores could be tabulated to determine the frequency of reversals of the decision of mastery. However, it seems likely that with students who are just on the threshold of mastery, changes from one testing to another will be much more common than those from one subscore to another at a single point in time. Blatchford (1970) found median reliability coefficients for a four-item test at a single moment in time to be 0.80, while the median correlation between forms given 1 week apart was only 0.61. Such a result suggests that two very short tests given on different days may provide a good deal more conservative and probably a sounder basis for a decision on mastery than a longer test at one specific point in time if the students are still in a period of instruction on the skill.

Methods for estimating the reliability of degree of mastery measurements as well as methods for assessing the accuracy of estimates of domain scores require a more complex statistical methodology than we can cover in detail in this book. Detailed reviews of available methods are given by Berk (1984) and Brennan (1984). We will, however, describe the logical processes that underlie these methods.

The basic feature of methods for estimating reliability in these cases is the use of *variance components*. As we noted in Chapter 2, variances are squares of standard deviations. (More accurately, they are what you have before you take the square root to get the standard deviation.) The size of the variance of any set of scores depends on how many sources of variability go into the scores. For example, the scores of a group of white, middle-class, 10-year-old girls from a farming community in Kansas on a test measuring knowledge of the geography of the American Great Plains could be expected to show a much smaller variance than would the scores from a group of the same size drawn at random from the general American population on a test of general American geography. The reason for the difference is that the scores on the test in the latter case might be affected by variation in racial or ethnic background (race, socioeconomic status, and geographic factors), gender, age, and the greater diversity of the test items themselves.

It is possible to estimate the effect of each of these factors (and many others that might be of interest) on the variance in a set of test scores by systematically controlling the other sources of variability. For example, the difference in reliability using the test-retest procedure and that obtained from a procedure with parallel forms provides a simple estimate of the variance that can be attributed to the sampling of items because in the first case the items remain constant, and in the second they vary. The impact of gender, age, and many other variables can be estimated by comparing the variances of scores when these characteristics are held constant with the variances from groups where they vary.

The procedures for assessing the reliability of estimates of domain scores and of degree of mastery measures require variance components that reflect the variability among all examinees across all items in the test and the inconsistency of each person's performance from item to item across the test. Different variance components are used, depending on which type of consistency is being assessed. The resulting ratios indicate the proportion of variance in test scores that can be attributed to different sources, some of which represent reliable aspects of performance. A detailed discussion of this issue and other advanced issues in reliability estimation is provided by Feldt and Brennan (1989).

Summary

Reliability, or consistency, is a necessary property for any measurement procedure to have. The differences between individuals that are revealed by the measuring instrument should represent, to the greatest extent possible, real differences on the characteristic of interest. Because any measurement is made with some error, reliability may be viewed as the instrument's relative freedom from error.

There is not a single value that is the correct reliability for any instrument. The observed reliability is a function of the properties of the underlying trait, the test itself, the group being tested, and the situation in which the information about reliability is obtained. All of these factors must be considered when evaluating the reliability of a test.

How reliable a test must be depends on the purpose of the testing. If the decisions to be made from the test scores are relatively unmodifiable, we would want to be quite certain of the accuracy of our information and would require the highest possible reliability. If, on the other hand, the instrument is being used for short-range decisions that are easily changed, we may be satisfied with a considerably lower level of reliability. Also, the use we will make of the scores affects the type of reliability we will want. If we are concerned with assessing current levels of performance, a reliability coefficient that reflects the internal consistency of the test or its short-term stability will yield the information we need. By contrast, if the use we have for the scores involves forecasting future levels of achievement, a reliability index that shows the stability of those scores over an equivalent time span is needed. In either case, when we are concerned with describing the performance of individuals the standard error of measurement derived from the appropriate design is the best index of the consistency we can expect for individual scores. The better test publishers provide several types of reliability information for their products so the user can make an informed decision.

Questions and Exercises

1. Look at the evidence presented on reliability in the manuals of two or three tests. How adequate is the evidence? What are its shortcomings? For what types of test use is it appropriate? What sources of variability does each type of evidence permit?
2. List two situations in which the standard error of measurement would be needed as an index of stability of performance.
3. The publishers of Test X suggest that it can be used to assess current levels of achievement in reading and to predict reading achievement after an additional year of instruction. What evidence of reliability should you expect the publisher to provide to support each test use?
4. The manual for Test T presents reliability data based on (1) retesting with the same test form 2 weeks later, (2) alpha coefficients, and (3) correlating Form A with Form B, the two forms having been taken 2 weeks apart. Which procedure would you expect to yield the lowest coefficient? Why? Which one should yield the most useful estimate of reliability? What additional information do you need to give an answer?
5. For each of the following situations, indicate whether the change would raise or lower the reliability:
   (a) Reliability is determined for scores from all elementary grades combined, rather than within each grade.

(b) A test with 25 items is used in place of a 100 item test.

(c) The ratings of four judges are averaged, instead of using a single judge.

(d) Reliability is determined using Kuder-Richardson Formula 20 rather than correlating scores on equivalent forms.

6. A student has been given a Wechsler Intelligence Scale for Children four times during her school career, and her cumulative record shows the following global intelligence quotients: 98, 107, 101, and 95. What significance should be attached to these fluctuations in scores?

7. A school plans to give Form R of a reading test in September and Form S in May to study individual differences in improvement during the year. The reliability of each form of the test is known to be about 0.85 for a grade group. The correlation between the two forms on the two occasions turned out to be 0.80. How much confidence can be placed in individual differences in amount gained? What factors other than real differences in learning can account for individual differences in gain?

Suggested Readings

American Psychological Association, American Educational Research Association, & National Council on Measurement in Education. (1985). *Standards for educational and psychological testing.* Washington, DC: American Psychological Association.

Blixt, S. L., & Shama, D. B. (1986). An empirical investigation of the standard error of measurement at different ability levels. *Educational and Psychological Measurement, 45,* 545–550.

Brennan, R. L. (1984). Estimating the dependability of the scores. In R. A. Berk (Ed.), *A guide to criterion referenced test construction* (pp. 292–334). Baltimore: Johns Hopkins University Press.

Feldt, L. S., & Brennan, R. L. (1989). Reliability. In R. L. Linn (Ed.), *Educational measurement* (3rd ed., pp. 105–146). New York: Macmillan.

Jarjoura, D. (1985). Tolerance intervals for true scores. *Journal of Educational Measurement, 10,* 1–17.

Kane, M. T., & Wilson, J. (1984). Errors of measurement and standard setting in mastery testing. *Applied Psychological Measurement, 4,* 107–115.

Lord, F. M. (1984). Standard errors of measurement at different score levels. *Journal of Educational Measurement, 21,* 239–243.

Lord, F. M., & Novick, M. R. (1968). *Statistical theories of mental test scores.* Reading, MA: Addison-Wesley.

Rogosa, D. R., & Willett, J. B. (1983). Demonstrating the reliability of the difference score in the measurement of change. *Journal of Educational Measurement, 20,* 335–343.

Thorndike, R. L. (1982). *Applied psychometrics.* Boston: Houghton Mifflin.

Thorndike, R. M. (1987). Reliability. In B. Bolton (Ed.), *Handbook of measurement and evaluation in rehabilitation* (2nd ed., pp. 21–36). Baltimore: Paul Brookes.

CHAPTER 5
Qualities Desired in Any Measurement Procedure: Validity

Introduction

Although reliability is a necessary feature that a test must have to be useful for decision making, it is not the most important characteristic. A test may be highly reliable and still bear no relationship to the property we wish to assess. Who, for example, would suggest that head circumference, which can be measured quite reliably, provides a measure of reading achievement? In education and psychology, as elsewhere, the foremost question to be asked with respect to any testing procedure is; how valid is it? When we ask this question, we are inquiring whether the test measures what we want to measure, all of what we want to measure, and nothing but what we want to measure. In words from the *Standards for Educational and Psychological Testing,* "the concept [of validity] refers to the appropriateness, meaningfulness, and usefulness of the specific inferences made from test scores. Test validation is the process of accumulating evidence to support such inferences" (American Psychological Association, American Educational Research Association, & National Council on Measurement in Education, 1985, p. 9). Thus, a test does not have "validity" in any absolute sense. Rather, the test scores are valid for some uses and not valid for others.

When we place a steel tape measure on the top of a desk to determine its length, we have no doubt that the tape does in fact measure the length of the desk and that it will give information directly related to our decision, which may be to decide whether we can put the desk between two windows in our room. Long-time experience with this type of measuring instrument has confirmed beyond a shadow of a doubt its validity as a tool for measuring length.

Now suppose we give a test of reading achievement to a group of children. This test requires the children to select certain answers to a series of questions based on reading passages and to make pencil marks on an answer sheet to indicate their choices. We count the number of pencil marks made in the predetermined correct places and give the children as scores the number of correct answers each one marked. We call these scores measures of their reading comprehension. But a score by itself is not the comprehension. It is the *record* of a *sample* of behavior taken at a particular point in time. Any judgment regarding comprehension is an inference from this number of allegedly correct answers. The validity of the score interpretation is not self-evident but is something we must establish on the basis of adequate evidence.

Consider also the typical personality inventory that endeavors to provide an appraisal of "emotional adjustment." In this type of inventory, the respondents mark a series of statements about feelings or behaviors as being characteristic of or not characteristic of themselves. On the basis of this type of procedure, certain responses are keyed as indicative of emotional maladjustment. A score is obtained by seeing how many of these responses an individual selects. But making certain marks on a piece of paper is a good many steps removed from actually exhibiting emotional disturbance. We must find some way of establishing the extent to which the performance on the test actually corresponds to the quality of the behavior in which we are directly interested. Our problem is to determine the validity of such a measurement procedure.

Types of Evidence of Validity

A test may be thought of as corresponding to some aspect of human behavior in any one of three senses. The terms that have been adopted to designate these senses are (1) content-related validity, (2) criterion-related validity, and (3) construct-related validity. We will examine each of these senses so that we may understand clearly what is involved in each case and for what kinds of tests and testing situations each is relevant.

Content-Related Evidence of Validity

Consider a test that has been designed to measure competence in using the English language. How can we tell whether the test does in fact measure that achievement? First, we must reach some agreement as to the skills and knowledge that comprise correct and effective use of English. If the test is to be used to appraise the effects of classroom instruction, we must specify the subset of skills and knowledge that have been the objectives of that instruction. (In Chapter 7 we discuss instructional objectives in detail. Then we must examine the test to see what skills, knowledge, and understanding it calls for. Finally, we must match the analysis of *test content* with the analysis of *course content* and instructional objectives to see how well the former represents the latter. To the extent that our objectives, which we have accepted as goals for our course, are represented in the test, the test appears valid for use in our school.

Because the analysis is essentially a rational and judgmental one, this process has sometimes been spoken of as *rational* or *logical validity.* The term *content validity* has also been used widely because the analysis is largely in terms of test content. However, we should not think of content too narrowly because we may be interested in *process* as much as in simple content. In the field of English expression, for example, we might be concerned on the one hand with such "content" elements as the rules and principles for capitalization, use of commas, or spelling words with "ei" and "ie" combinations. But we might also be interested in such "process" skills as arranging ideas in a logical order, writing sentences that present a single unified thought, or picking the most appropriate word to convey the desired meaning. In a sense, *content* is what the pupil works with; *process* is what the pupil does with the content. The term content-related validity refers to an assessment of whether a test contains appropriate content *and* requires the appropriate processes to be applied to that content.

The problem of appraising content-related validity is closely parallel to the problem of preparing the blueprint for a test (Chapter 7) and then building a test to match the blueprint. A teacher's own test has content validity to the extent that a wise and thoughtful analysis of course objectives has been made in the blueprint and that care, skill, and ingenuity have been exercised in building test items to match the blueprint. A standardized test may be shown to have validity for a particular school or a particular curriculum insofar as the content of that test corresponds to and represents the objectives accepted in that school or that curriculum.

It should be clear that rational or content validity evidence is of primary importance for measures of achievement. In particular, validity of a formative test concerned with mastery of one or more specific educational objectives, the type of test that has been called content- or criterion-referenced, will be judged on how well the test tasks represent the defined objectives. But for the summative, norm-referenced achievement test (such as a standardized end-of-course test), as well, we will be primarily concerned with how well the test represents what the best and most expert judgment would consider to be important knowledge and skill for our academic environment. If the correspondence is good, the test will be judged to have high validity for this application; if poor, the validity must be deemed to be low.

Responsible makers of tests for publication and widespread use go to considerable pains to determine the widely accepted goals of instruction in the fields in which their tests are to be developed and used. Test constructors may, and often do, resort to many sources, including the following:

1. The more widely used textbooks in the field
2. Recent courses of study for the large school units such as state, county, and city school systems
3. Reports of special study groups that often appear in yearbooks of one or another of the educational societies
4. Groups of teachers who give instruction on the topic
5. Specialists in university, city, and state departments concerned with the training or supervision of teachers in the field

Gathering information from these sources, the test maker develops the blueprint for the test, and the test items are prepared in terms of this blueprint. Because of variations from community to community, no test published for national distribution can be made to fit exactly the content or objectives of every local course of study. In this sense, a test developed on a national basis is always less valid than an equally well-developed test tailored specifically to the local objectives. However, the well-made commercial test can take the common components that appear repeatedly in different textbooks and courses of study and build a test around these components. Such a test represents the common core that is central to the different specific local patterns. In addition, commercial tests are prepared by people who are testing specialists. The items are written by experienced and well-trained item writers and the tests are subjected to a thorough review both for style and for possible bias in either phrasing or content. Thus, the items are likely to be of higher quality, which may be a reasonable trade-off for the poorer fit to local instructional objectives.

It should be clear from the previous paragraphs that the relationship between teaching and testing is typically intimate. Test content is drawn from what has been taught or what is proposed to be taught. An instructional program is the original source of achievement test materials. Sometimes the specification of test content may precede the curricular objectives underlying a local course of study, as when specialists have been brought together to design a test corresponding to some emerging trend in education. Sometimes the test may lag behind, as when the test is based on the relatively conventional objectives emphasized in established textbooks. But usually, test content and classroom instruction are closely related to one another, and the test may be appraised by how faithfully it corresponds to the significant goals of instruction.

To appraise the validity of test scores as representing the degree of achievement of curricular objectives, there is no substitute for a careful and detailed examination of the actual test tasks. A test may be labeled "mathematical concepts," but call for nothing except knowledge of definitions of terms. A test of "reading comprehension" may only call for answers to questions concerning specific details that appear in the passages. It is the tasks presented by the items that really define what the test is measuring, and one who would judge the validity of its content for a specific curriculum must take a hard look at the individual items.

Criterion-Related Evidence of Validity

Frequently, we are interested in using a test in connection with a decision that implies predicting some specific future outcome. We give a scholastic aptitude test to predict how likely the high school student is to be successful in College X, where success is represented at least approximately by grade-point average. We give an employment test to select machine operators who are likely to be successful employees, as represented by some such criterion as high production with low spoilage and low personnel turnover. For this purpose, we care very little what a test looks like. We are interested almost entirely in the degree to which it correlates with some chosen criterion measure of job or academic success. Some other measure (often, but not necessarily, one that becomes available later) is taken as the criterion of "success," and we judge a test in terms of its relationship to that criterion measure. The higher the correlation, the better the test. (This statement that we do not care what a test looks like is not entirely true. What a test "looks like" may be of importance in determining its acceptability and reasonableness to those who will be tested. A group of would-be pilots may be more ready to accept a mathematics test dealing with wind drift and fuel consumption than they would be to accept a test with the same essential problems phrased in terms of costs of crops or recipes for baking cakes. This appearance of reasonableness is sometimes called *face validity*.)

Evaluation of a test as a predictor is primarily an empirical and statistical evaluation, and the collection of evidence bearing on this aspect of validity has sometimes been spoken of as *empirical* or *statistical validity*. The basic procedure is to give the test to a group that is entering some job or training program, to follow them up later, to get for each one a specified criterion measure of success on the job or in the training program, and then to compute the correlation between the test scores and the criterion measures of success. The higher the correlation, the more effective the test is as a predictor and the higher is its criterion-related validity.

We can picture this relationship in various ways. For example, the bar chart in Figure 5.1 shows the percentage of candidates passing air force pilot training at each of nine score levels on a test battery designed to assess aptitude for flight training. The chart shows a steady increase in the percentage passing as we go from low to high scores, so successful completion of training is related to aptitude level. The relationship pictured in the chart corresponds to a correlation coefficient of 0.49.

The Problem of the Criterion. We said that empirical validity can be estimated by determining the correlation between test scores and a suitable measure of success on the job or in the classroom. The joker here is the phrase "suitable criterion measure." One of the most difficult problems that the investigator of selection tests faces is that of locating or creating a satisfactory measure of success to be used as a criterion measure for test validation. This problem is

FIGURE 5.1
Percent of cadets completing pilot training at each aptitude level. The correlation coefficient is 0.49.

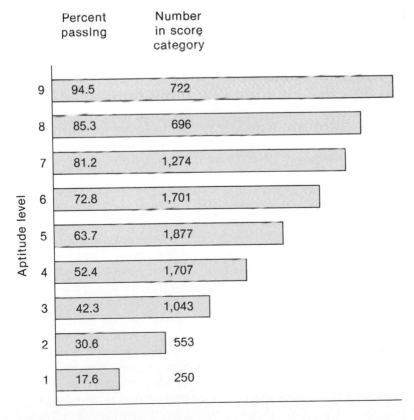

most serious in employment settings, but is also quite troublesome in the academic environment. It might appear that it should be a simple matter to decide on some measure of rate of production or some type of rating by superiors to serve as a criterion measure. It might also seem that this measure, once decided on, should be obtainable in a simple and straightforward fashion. Unfortunately, identifying a satisfactory criterion measure is not so easy. Finding or developing acceptable criterion measures usually involves the research worker in the field of tests and measurements in a host of problems.

Each possible type of criterion measure presents its own problems. A record of actual performance has a good deal of appeal—number of widgets made, freedom from errors as a cashier, or amount of insurance sold, for example. But there are many jobs or positions, such as physician, teacher, secretary, or receptionist, that yield no objective record of performance or production. And, when such records do exist, the production is often influenced by an array of factors that are outside the worker's control. The production record of a weaver may depend not only on personal skill in threading and adjusting the loom, but also on the condition of the equipment, adequacy of the lighting in the work environment, or the color of thread being woven. The sales of an insurance agent are a function not only of individual effectiveness as a seller, but also of the territory to be covered and the supervision and assistance the agent receives.

Because of the absence or the shortcomings of performance records, the personnel psychologist has often depended on some type of rating by a supervisor as a criterion measure. Such ratings may exist as a routine part of the personnel procedures in a company, as when each employee receives a semiannual efficiency report, or the ratings may have to be gathered especially for the selection study. In either event, they will typically be found to depend as much on the person giving the rating as on the person being rated. Ratings tend to be erratic and influenced by many factors other than performance. The problems in using rating procedures to describe and evaluate people are discussed in Chapter 8.

There are always many criterion measures that might be obtained and used for validating a selection test. In addition to quantitative performance records and subjective ratings, we might use later tests of proficiency. This type of procedure is involved when a college entrance mathematics test is validated in terms of its ability to predict later performance on a comprehensive examination on college mathematics. Here, the comprehensive examination serves as the criterion measure. Another common type of criterion measure is the average of grades in some type of educational or training program. Tests for the selection of engineers, for example, may be validated against course grades in engineering school.

All criterion measures are partial in the sense that they measure only a part of success on the job or only the preliminaries to actual job performance. This last point is true of the engineering school grades just mentioned, which represent a relatively immediate but partial criterion of success as an engineer. The ultimate criterion would be some appraisal of lifetime success in the profession. In the very nature of things, such an ultimate criterion is inaccessible, and the investigator must be satisfied with substitutes for it. These substitutes are never completely satisfactory. The problem is always to choose the most satisfactory measure or combination of measures from among those that it appears feasible to obtain. The investigator is faced, then, with the problem of deciding which of the criterion measures is most satisfactory. How shall one decide?

Qualities Desired in a Criterion Measure.   There are four qualities desired in a criterion measure. In order of their importance, they are:

1. relevance
2. freedom from bias
3. reliability
4. availability

We judge a criterion measure to be relevant to the extent that standing on the criterion measure corresponds to or exemplifies success on the job. In appraising the relevance of a criterion, we must revert to rational considerations. There is no empirical evidence that will tell how relevant freshman grade-point average is, for example, as an indicator of having achieved the objectives of Supercolossal University. For achievement tests, we have found it necessary to rely on the best available professional judgment to determine whether the content of a test accurately represented our educational objectives. In the same way, with respect to a criterion measure, it is necessary to rely on professional judgment to provide an appraisal of the degree to which some available criterion measure can serve as an indicator of what we would really like to predict. We could even say that relevance corresponds to the content validity of the criterion measure.

The second most important factor in the criterion measure is freedom from bias. By this, we mean that the measure should be one on which each person has the same opportunity to make a good score or, more specifically, one on which each equally capable person obtains the same score (except for errors of measurement), regardless of the group to which he or she belongs. Examples of biasing factors are such things as variation in wealth from one district to another for our previous example of the insurance agent, variation in the quality of equipment and conditions of work for a factory worker, variation in "generosity" of the bosses who are rating private secretaries, or variation in the quality of teaching received by students in different classes. To the extent that the criterion score depends on factors in the conditions of work, in the evaluation of work, or in the personal characteristics of the individual, rather than on competence in the job, there is no real meaning to the correlation between test results and a criterion score. A criterion measure that contains substantial bias cannot at the same time reveal relevant differences among people on the trait of interest.

The third factor is reliability. As it applies to criterion scores, the problem is merely that a measure of success on the job must be stable or reproducible if it is to be predicted by any type of test device. If the criterion score is one that jumps around in an unpredictable way from day to day, so that the person who shows high job performance one week may show low job performance the next, or the person who receives a high rating from one supervisor gets a low rating from another, there is no possibility of finding a test that will predict that score. A measure that is completely unstable itself cannot be predicted by anything else.

Finally, in choosing a criterion measure, we always encounter practical problems of convenience and availability. How long will we have to wait to get a criterion score for each individual? How much is it going to cost—in dollars or in disruption of normal activities? Though a personnel research program can often afford to spend a substantial part of its effort getting good criterion data, there is always a practical limit. Any choice of a criterion measure must take this practical limit into account.

Interpretation of Validity Coefficients.   Suppose that we have gathered test and criterion scores for a group of individuals and computed the correlation between them. Perhaps the predictor is a scholastic aptitude test, and the criterion is an average of college freshman grades. How will we decide whether the test is a good predictor?

Obviously, other things being equal, the higher the correlation, the better. In one sense, our basis for evaluating any one predictor is in relation to other possible prediction procedures. Does Peter's Perfect Personnel Predictor yield a higher or lower validity coefficient than other tests that are available? Does it yield a higher or lower validity coefficient than other types of information, such as high school grades or ratings by the school principal? We will look with favor on any measure whose validity for a particular criterion is higher than that of measures previously available, even though the measure may fall far short of perfection.

A few representative validity coefficients are exhibited in Table 5.1. These give some picture of the size of correlation that has been obtained in previous work of different kinds. The investigator concerned with a particular course of study or a particular job will, of course, need to become familiar with the validities that the tests being considered have been found to have for the criterion measure that will be used.

The usefulness of a test as a predictor depends not only on how well it correlates with a criterion measure but also on how much *new* information it gives. For example, the social studies subtest of the Tests of Achievement and Proficiency (TAP) was found to correlate on the average 0.51 with ninth-grade social studies grades, and the reading comprehension subtest to correlate 0.51 with the same grades. But, the two tests have an intercorrelation of 0.77. They overlap and, in part at least, the information either test provides is the same as that provided by the other test. The net result is that pooling information from the two tests can give a validity coefficient of no more than 0.53. If the two tests had been uncorrelated, each giving evidence completely independent of the other, the combination of the two would have provided a validity coefficient of 0.70. Statistical procedures have been developed that enable us to determine the best weighting to give to two or more predictors and to calculate the correlation that will result from this combination. (The procedures for computing the weights for the predictor tests [*regression weights*] and the correlation [*multiple*

TABLE 5.1
Validity of Selected Tests as Predictors of Certain Educational and Vocational Criteria

Predictor Test[a]	Criterion Variable[b]	Validity Coefficient
CogAT	TAP reading (Grade 12)	.79
Verbal	TAP social studies (Grade 12)	.78
Quantitative	TAP mathematics (Grade 12)	.79
ITED composite (Grade 9)	Cumulative high school GPA	.49
	College freshman GPA	.41
	SAT total	.84
ITBS composite (Grade 6)	Final college GPA	.44
Seashore Tonal Memory Test	Performance test on stringed instrument	.28
Short Employment Test		
Word knowledge score	Production index—bookkeeping machine operators	.10
	Job grade—stenographers	.53
Arithmetic score	Production index—Bookkeeping machine operators	.26
	Job grade—stenographers	.60

[a]CogAT = Cognitive Abilities Test; ITED = Iowa Tests of Educational Development; ITBS = Iowa Tests of Basic Skills
[b]TAP = Tests of Achievement and Proficiency; GPA = grade point average; SAT = Scholastic Aptitude Test.

correlation] resulting from the combination are beyond the scope of this discussion. Presentation of these methods will be found in intermediate statistics texts such as those of Pedhazur [1982] and Cohen and Cohen [1983].)

Clearly, the higher the correlation between a test or other predictor and a criterion measure, the better. But, in addition to this relative standard, we should like some absolute one. How high must the validity coefficient be for the test to be useful? What is a "satisfactory" validity? This last question is a little like asking, "How high is up?" However, we can try to give some sort of answer.

To an organization using a test as a basis for deciding whether to hire a particular job applicant or to admit a particular student, the significant question is, how much more often will we make the right decision on whom to hire or to admit if we use this test than if we operate on a purely chance basis or on the basis of some already available but less valid measure? The answer to this question depends in considerable measure on the proportion of individuals who must be accepted, called the *selection ratio*. A selection procedure can do much more for us if we need to accept only the individual who appears to be the best 1 in every 10 applicants than if we must accept 9 out of 10. However, to provide a specific example, let us assume that we will accept half of the applicants. Let us examine Table 5.2.

The model is set up to show 200 people in all, 100 in the top half on the test and 100 in the top half on the job. If there were absolutely no relationship

TABLE 5.2
Two-by-Two Table of Test and Job Success

		PERFORMANCE ON THE JOB		
		Bottom Half— "Failures"	Top Half— "Successes"	Total
Score on Selection Test	Top half (accepted)			100
	Bottom half (rejected)			100
	Total	100	100	200

between the test and job performance, there would be 50 people in each of the four cells of the table. Defining "success" as being in the top half on the job, the success rate would be 50 in 100 for those accepted and also for those rejected. There would be no difference between the two, and the correlation between the selection test and job performance would be zero.

Table 5.3 shows, for correlations of different sizes, the percentage of correct choices (i.e., "successes") among the 50% we accept. A similar percentage of correct rejections occurs in the 50% who are not accepted. The improvement in our "batting average" as the correlation goes up is shown in the table. Thus, for a correlation of 0.40, we will select correctly 63.1% of the time and be in error 36.9% of the time; with a correlation of 0.80 the percentage of correct decisions will be 79.5, and so forth.

The table shows not only the accuracy for any given correlation but also the gain in accuracy if we improve the validity of the predictor. If we were able to replace a predictor with a validity of 0.40 by one with a validity of 0.60, we would increase the percentage of correct decisions from 63.1 to 70.5. The percentages

TABLE 5.3
Percentage of Correct Assignments when 50% of Group Must be Selected

Validity Coefficient	Percentage of Correct Choices
.00	50.0
.20	56.4
.40	63.1
.50	66.7
.60	70.5
.70	74.7
.80	79.5
.90	85.6

in Table 5.3 refer, of course, to the ground rules set above, that is, that we are selecting the top 50% of the group on the prediction test and that 50% of the complete group of 200 candidates would be successful. However, Table 5.3 gives a fairly representative basis for understanding the effects of a selection program from the point of view of the employing or certifying agency.

In many selection situations, the gain from greater validity can be crudely translated into a dollars-and-cents saving. If it costs a company $500 to employ and train a new employee to the point of useful productivity, a selection procedure that raises the percentage of successes from 56.4 to 63.1 would yield a saving in wasted training expenses alone of $3,350 per 100 new employees. This computation of benefits takes no account of the possibility that the test-selected workers might also be *better* workers after they had completed their training. The dollar saving would be balanced, of course, against any increase in cost in applying the new selection procedure. A selection procedure which cost $5,000 per candidate to administer would hardly be worthwhile for such modest savings.

Another way of appraising the practical significance of a correlation coefficient—one that is perhaps more meaningful from the point of view of the person being tested—is shown in Table 5.4. The rows in the tabulations represent the fourths of a group of applicants, potential students, or employees, with respect to a predictor test. The columns indicate the number of cases falling in each quarter on the criterion measure. Look at the tabulation in Table 5.4 corresponding to a validity coefficient of 0.50. Note that of those who fall in the lowest quarter on the predictor, 480 out of 1,000 (48.0%) fall in the lowest quarter in terms of the criterion score, 27.9% in the next lowest quarter, 16.8% in the next to highest quarter, and 7.3% in the highest quarter. Another way to view this relationship is in terms of our previous example which defined successful performance as being in the top half on the criterion, only about one person in four who scored in the lowest quarter on the predictor test (168 + 73 = 241 out of 1,000) would prove to be a "successful" employee. The diagonal entries in boldface print represent cases that fall in the same fourth on both the predictor and the criterion. The farther we get from the diagonal, the greater the discrepancy between prediction and performance. Cases on or near the diagonal represent cases where the predictor has been right; cases falling far from the diagonal represent cases in which the predictor has been decidedly wrong.

As an empirical example of the spread of criterion performance that one may find for people with the same predictor score, consider Table 5.5. This table shows the distribution of scores on the Scholastic Aptitude Test (SAT) earned by 260 11th-grade students with different levels of performance on the reading comprehension test of the TAP. It is clear from the table that as TAP scores go up, SAT scores also tend to go up, but it is equally clear that some students with TAP scores of 200 earn higher SAT scores than do some of the students with TAP scores of 250.

Tables 5.4 and 5.5 emphasize not so much the gain from using the predictor as they do the variation in criterion performance still remaining for those who

TABLE 5.4
Accuracy of Prediction for Different Values of the Correlation Coefficient (r).

r = .00

Quarter on Predictor	QUARTER ON CRITERION			
	4th	3rd	2nd	1st
1st	250	250	250	**250**
2nd	250	250	**250**	250
3rd	250	**250**	250	250
4th	**250**	250	250	250

r = .40

Quarter on Predictor	QUARTER ON CRITERION			
	4th	3rd	2nd	1st
1st	104	191	277	**428**
2nd	191	255	**277**	277
3rd	277	**277**	255	191
4th	**428**	277	191	104

r = .50

Quarter on Predictor	QUARTER ON CRITERION			
	4th	3rd	2nd	1st
1st	73	168	279	**480**
2nd	168	258	**295**	279
3rd	279	**295**	258	168
4th	**480**	279	168	73

r = .60

Quarter on Predictor	QUARTER ON CRITERION			
	4th	3rd	2nd	1st
1st	45	141	277	**537**
2nd	141	264	**318**	277
3rd	277	**318**	264	141
4th	**537**	277	141	45

r = .70

Quarter on Predictor	QUARTER ON CRITERION			
	4th	3rd	2nd	1st
1st	22	107	270	**601**
2nd	107	270	**353**	270
3rd	270	**353**	270	107
4th	**601**	270	107	22

r = .80

Quarter on Predictor	QUARTER ON CRITERION			
	4th	3rd	2nd	1st
1st	6	66	253	**675**
2nd	66	271	**410**	253
3rd	253	**410**	271	66
4th	**675**	253	66	6

Note. There are 1,000 cases in each row and column.

TABLE 5.5
Probabilities of Scoring Within Specified Ranges on the Verbal Test of the Scholastic Aptitude Test (SAT), Given Scores on the Reading Comprehension Test of the Tests of Achievement and Proficiency (TAP)

TAP Standard Score Range	SAT VERBAL SCORE RANGE					
	200–250	251–350	351–450	451–550	551–650	651+
251+			10	40	40	10
241–250		6	19	44	25	6
231–240		4	11	53	28	4
221–230			20	44	28	8
211–220			31	48	21	
201–210		11	36	40	3	
191–200	3	14	43	40		
181–190	3	20	56	21		
171–180	11	22	61	3	3	
Below 171	23	54	19		4	

Note. The data in this table represent a correlation of 0.61 between the reading comprehension test of TAP and the verbal test of the SAT.

are similar in predictor scores. From the point of view of schools or employers, the important thing is to improve the percentage of correct decisions as is illustrated in Table 5.3. Dealing with large numbers, they can count on gaining from any predictor that is more valid than the procedure currently in use. From the point of view of the single individual, the marked discrepancies between predicted and actual success shown in Tables 5.4 and 5.5 may seem at least as important. Applicants who have done poorly on the test may be less impressed by the fact that the *probability* is that they will be below average on the job or in the training program than by the fact that they *may* still do very well. Each individual may be the exception.

Base Rates and Prediction.   We noted in introducing Table 5.2 that a selection procedure will be most helpful if we need to accept only a small number of candidates. Although this principle is true, the facts in Tables 5.4 and 5.5 reveal that we would miss many potentially successful candidates if we take only those in the top 10%–20% on the predictor. The overall value of a selection procedure depends on several factors, including (1) how we define success, (2) the selection rule that we use, (3) the "value" of a correctly identified success, (4) the "cost" of accepting someone who subsequently fails, and (5) the "cost" of missing a candidate who would have succeeded.

The proportion of a group of applicants who would have succeeded if all were admitted is called the *base rate* for success. The selection rule that we impose is known as the *cutting score*. If we consider being in the top half on the criterion as being a success, then the base rate is 50%.

When using any particular cutting score, some of our decisions will be correct and some will not. At one extreme, if we admit all candidates, we will correctly identify all potentially successful individuals, but at the cost of admitting the 50% who will be failures. At the other extreme, if we reject all candidates, we will admit no failures, but at the cost of missing all of the potentially successful candidates. The proportion of correct decisions that result from our selection strategy—the proportion of correctly identified successes plus the proportion of correctly rejected failures—is known as the *hit rate* for the cutting score. Each cutting score has a hit rate that depends on the base rate of success in the population and the correlation between the predictor and the criterion. The values in Table 5.3 show the hit rates for a base rate of 50% and a cutting score that admits the top half of the applicants on the predictor variable.

As the base rate departs from 50% (either higher or lower), the hit rate for the selection procedure diminishes. If we define success as being in the top 25% on the criterion (i.e., the base rate is 0.25) and consider the results of using a predictor that has a correlation of 0.60 with this criterion, the results from using four cutting scores are as follows:

Cutting Score	Hit Rate
Admit all	.25
Admit top 75%	.37
Admit top 50%	.66
Admit top 25%	.77

The hit rate of 0.66 for a cutting score that admits the top 50% is slightly lower than the value in Table 5.3, and the drop results from the change in base rate. The decrease in overall gain from using the predictor becomes much more marked in situations with more extreme base rates. The greatest total gains from using a selection procedure occur in those situations where the rate of successful criterion performance in the population is close to 50%.

Standard Error of Estimate.   We have seen that when the relationship between a predictor and a criterion is less than perfect, there will be some variability in criterion performance for people who all have the same predictor score. Not all people who fall in a given quarter of the predictor test distribution will fall in the same quarter of the criterion distribution. There will be an average criterion performance for people with a particular predictor score, and there will be variation around that average. Regression procedures, which were mentioned earlier, are used to find the mean criterion performance for all people who scored at the same level on the predictor. The spread of actual criterion performances around that mean is reflected by the *standard error of estimate*. The standard error of estimate is the standard deviation of the distribution of actual criterion performances around predicted performance. Another way to say the same thing is to say that the standard error of estimate is the standard deviation of criterion scores for people who all got the same score on the predictor variable.

This principle is illustrated schematically in Figure 5.2 for the data in Table 5.5. The large normal distribution on the left in the figure is the distribution of

FIGURE 5.2
Predicted score on the criterion variable (Scholastic Aptitude Test [SAT]) is the mean
of criterion scores earned by those at chosen level of predictor (Tests of Achievement
and Proficiency [TAP]). Standard error of estimate is the standard deviation of observed scores around that mean.

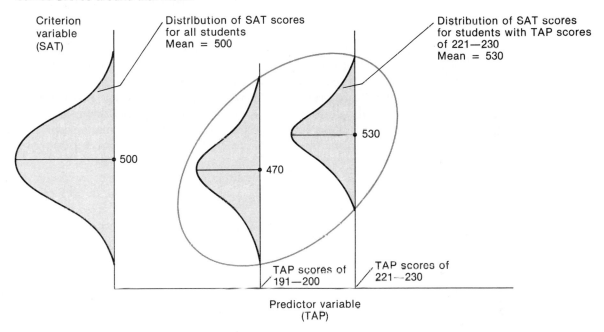

all SAT scores. It has a mean of 500 and a standard deviation of 100. The ellipse
is the scatter plot of SAT and TAP scores, and the two smaller normal distributions to the right are the distributions of SAT scores for those individuals who
earned TAP scores between 191–200 and 221–230, respectively. The mean of
the first distribution is 470, and this mean is the SAT score that we would predict
for this group of individuals. The mean of the second distribution, 530, is the
SAT score we would predict for individuals with TAP scores of 221–230. The
standard deviations of these distributions are the standard errors of estimate for
predicting SAT scores from TAP scores.

Two things are important to note in the figure. First, because there is a
moderate positive correlation ($r = 0.61$) between the two variables, the predicted score is higher in the right-hand group than in the one to the left. People
with higher TAP scores are predicted to earn higher SAT scores. Second, the
predictions are in error by some small amount for most people and by a considerable amount for some. The standard deviation of observed scores around
the predicted score is the standard error of estimate.

An overall value for the standard error of estimate can be obtained from the
following equation:

$$SD_e = SD_{crit}\sqrt{(1 - r_{xy}^2)} \tag{5.1}$$

where SD_e is the standard error of estimate,
SD_{crit} is the standard deviation of the *entire*
distribution of criterion scores, and
r_{xy}^2 is the squared validity coefficient of the
predictor test for predicting this criterion.

Notice that this formula looks quite similar to Equation 4.2 (Chapter 4) for the standard error of measurement. The standard error of measurement is an index of instability of performances on a test. It uses the test reliability to provide a way of estimating how much an individual's score might change from one testing to another. The standard error of estimate is an index of the error that may be made in forecasting performance on one measure from performance on another. It uses the correlation between the test and some criterion to provide an estimate of how much a predicted score might be in error as an estimate of a person's actual performance on the criterion. Both the standard error of measurement and the standard error of estimate are important, but for criterion-related validity, the standard error of measurement is a property that can be determined by the test publisher as characterizing the predictor test, while the standard error of estimate is unique to each criterion measure and must therefore be determined locally.

Let us look again at predicting SAT performance from scores on the TAP. We found (in Table 5.5) a correlation of 0.61 between the test and the criterion measure, and the standard deviation of SAT scores is 100. Using Equation 5.1, we find

$$SD_e = 100\sqrt{(1 - 0.61^2)} = 100\sqrt{0.63} = 79$$

The standard error of estimate is 79.

We may use standard error of estimate to place a band of uncertainty around our prediction in the same way that we used standard error of measurement to produce a band of uncertainty for test scores. If we assume that the errors of prediction have a normal distribution, about two out of three students will earn SAT scores within 1 standard of error of estimate of the score that was predicted for them. In the example shown in Figure 5.3, 68% of the students for whom a prediction of 530 was made will actually earn SAT scores between 450 and 610 (SAT scores are reported only in multiples of 10), while about 95% will have criterion performances between 370 and 690.

The standard error of estimate is a sobering index because it illustrates clearly the limitations in predicting human behavior. *Even with the best measures available, predictions in psychology and education are approximate.* The regression techniques that are used to make predictions yield point estimates such as the predicted SAT score of 530 in Figure 5.3. By considering the standard error of estimate, teachers, counselors, and personnel workers get an appropriately pessimistic view of our present ability to predict human performance. This is not to say that we should stop trying to predict or that tests are often seriously wrong. On the contrary, predictions made from test scores are, *on the*

FIGURE 5.3

Two people out of three will have criterion scores within 1 standard error of estimate (SD_e) of their predicted scores on the Scholastic Aptitude Test (SAT). Nineteen in 20 will be within 2 SD_e.

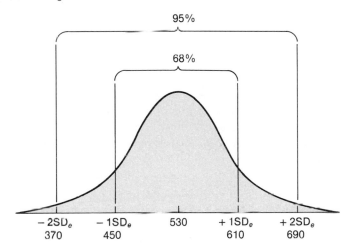

average, correct. But, healthy skepticism is required to keep from overinterpreting test scores, particularly when, as is usually the case, we are making predictions about individuals.

Two other factors tend to distort validity coefficients and complicate their interpretation. The first is unreliability of the predictor and of the criterion that is being predicted. This attenuation effect was discussed earlier. The second is restriction of the range of ability in the group by some type of preselection. Low reliability on the one hand or preselection on the other will tend to lower the values that are obtained for validity coefficients, so that "true validities" are typically higher than the values obtained in validation studies.

An example of the effect that restricting the range in the predictor can have on the apparent validity of a predictor comes from a recent experience at a public university where there was dramatic growth in its pool of applicants. With over three times as many applicants as could be accommodated, the school changed from what had been a first-come, first-served admissions policy to one in which students were admitted on the basis of a combination of high school grades and aptitude test scores. The correlation of college grades with high school grades in the last class admitted under the old rules was 0.61. When the new admissions criteria were applied and only those students who would have been admitted under the new rules were included, the correlation dropped to 0.47. This change in the apparent validity of high school grades as a predictor of college grades occurred solely as a result of the smaller range of talent among the selected students.

Let us emphasize one additional point. Validity is fairly specific to a particular curriculum or a particular job. Although the concept of validity generalization, discussed in Chapter 15, indicates that certain tests may be valid across a range of jobs, when an author or publisher claims that a test is valid, it is always appropriate to ask, valid for what? For example, an achievement test in social studies that accurately represents the content and objectives of one program of instruction may be quite inappropriate for the program in a different community. An achievement test must always be evaluated against the objectives of a specific program of instruction. An aptitude test battery that is quite valid for picking department store sales clerks who will be pleasant to customers, informed about their stock, and accurate in financial transactions may be entirely useless in identifying insurance agents who will be effective in going out and finding or creating new business. Validity must always be evaluated in relation to a situation as similar as possible to the one in which the measure is to be used.

Criterion-related validity is most important for a test that is to be used to predict outcomes that are represented by clear-cut criterion measures. The more readily we can identify a performance criterion that unquestionably represents the results that we are interested in, the more we will be prepared to rely on the evidence from correlations between a test and measures of that criterion to guide our decision on whether to use the test. There are two elements in this statement—prediction and clear-cut criterion measures. The main limitation to using criterion-related validity within the prediction context lies in the limited adequacy of the available criterion measures.

Construct Validity

Sometimes we ask, with respect to an educational or psychological test, neither "How well does this test predict future performance?" nor "How well does this test represent our curriculum?" but instead "What do scores on this test *mean* or *signify?*" What does the score tell us about an individual? Does it correspond to some meaningful trait or construct that will help us to understand the person? For this last question, the term *construct validity* has been used. (The term *construct* is used in psychology to refer to something that is not observable but is literally *constructed* by the investigator to summarize or account for the regularities or relationships in observed behavior. Thus, most names of traits refer to constructs. We speak of a person's "sociability" as a way of summarizing observed consistency in past behavior in relation to people and of organizing a prediction of how the individual will act on future occasions. The construct is derived from observations, but constructs may actually predict what we would observe in new situations. Such is the case in the research program described next.)

Let us examine a classic case of one specific testing procedure and see how its validity as a measure of a useful psychological quality or construct was studied. McClelland, Atkinson, Clark, and Lowell (1953) developed a testing procedure to appraise the individual's need or motivation to achieve—to succeed and do well. The test used pictures of people in various ambiguous situations. The individual was called on to make up a story about each picture, telling what was happening and how it turned out. A scoring system was developed for these stories, based on counting the frequency with which themes of accomplishment, mastery, success, and achievement appeared in the story material. In this way, each individual received a score representing the strength of his motivation to achieve. The question posed by construct validity is whether this measure has validity in the sense of truthfully describing a meaningful aspect of the individual's makeup. McClelland and his co-workers proceeded as described here.

In essence, the investigators began by asking, to what should a measure of achievement motivation, as we have conceived of it, be related? They made a series of predictions, some of which follow:

1. Those students scoring high on achievement motivation should do well in college in relation to their scholastic aptitude.

2. Achievement motivation should be higher for students just after they have taken tests described to them as measuring their intelligence.

3. Those students scoring high on achievement motivation should complete more items on a speeded test where the students are motivated to perform well.

4. Achievement motivation should be higher for children of families emphasizing early independence.

Each of these predictions was based on a sort of "theory of human behavior." For example, academic achievement is seen as a combination of ability and effort. Presumably, those with higher motivation to achieve will exert more effort and will, ability being equal, achieve higher grades. A similar chain of reasoning lies behind each prediction.

In general, McClelland et al. (1953) found that most of their predictions were supported by the experimental results. The fact that the test scores were related to a number of other events in the way that had been predicted from a rational analysis of the trait that the test was presumably measuring lent support to the validity of the test procedure as measuring a meaningful trait or construct. The essential characteristics of the trait are fairly well summarized by the label "achievement motivation." When a series of studies supports the construct validity of a measure, the validity of the theory that gave rise to the construct is also supported.

A great many psychological tests and, to a lesser extent, some educational tests are intended to measure general traits or qualities of the individual. General intelligence, verbal reasoning, spatial visualization, sociability, introversion, and mechanical interest are all designations of traits or constructs. Tests of these functions have construct validity insofar as they behave in the way that such a trait should reasonably be expected to behave.

A theory about a trait will lead to predictions of the following types, all of which can be tested to see if they hold up.

Predictions About Correlations. The nature of the trait, and therefore of valid measures of it, will indicate that it should be positively related to certain other measures and, perhaps, unrelated or negatively related to still others. These other measures might be already accepted measures of the function in question. Many subsequent group intelligence tests, for example, have been validated in part by their correlations with earlier tests, especially the Stanford-Binet. Also, the other measures may be ones with which the trait should logically be related. Thus, intelligence tests have been validated, in part, through their correlation with success in school and measures of mechanical aptitude by their correlation with rated proficiency in mechanical jobs.

One way of studying the constructs or traits that a test measures is to study jointly the intercorrelations of this test and a number of others. The patterning of these correlations makes it possible to see which tests are measuring some common dimension or factor. An examination of the tests clustering in a single factor may clarify the nature and meaning of the factor and of the tests that measure it. However, this internal or "factorial" validity still needs evidence of a relationship to life events outside the tests themselves if the factor is to have much substance, vitality, and scientific or educational utility.

It may also be appropriate to predict that the measure of Construct X will show low or zero correlations with measures of certain other attributes, that is, that the construct is different from what the other tests measure. A test designed to measure mechanical comprehension should show only a modest correlation with a test of verbal ability. A measure of sociability should not show too high a correlation with a measure of assertiveness, if the two assess genuinely different constructs. High correlations between measures of supposedly unrelated constructs are evidence against either the validity of the instruments as measures of the constructs, the validity of the constructs as separate dimensions of human functioning, or both.

Predictions About Group Differences.   A theory will often suggest that certain kinds of groups should possess an especially high or low amount of a trait and consequently score exceptionally high or low on a test of that trait. It seems reasonable that a group of salespeople should be high on a measure of ascendance, or assertiveness, and that a group of librarians should be low. We would probably predict that children of professional and business parents would be more ascendant than those whose parents were in clerical or semiskilled occupations. For any given trait, our general knowledge of our society and the groups within it will suggest an array of group differences that seem to make sense. Applying a test to these groups, the investigator finds out how consistently the predictions are borne out. Of course, the predictions could fail because, on the one hand, the test is not a valid measure of the characteristic or, on the other, because the world is not consistent with the theory that gave rise to the predictions. Failure of our predictions does not tell us which of these conditions obtains (or is correct).

Predictions About Response to Experimental Treatments or Interventions.   A theory may imply that the expression of a human characteristic will be modified as a result of certain experimental conditions or treatments. For example, one could reasonably predict that anxiety would increase just before a person was to undergo a minor operation. Rate of flicker fusion has been proposed as an indicator of anxiety level. (The *rate of flicker fusion* is the rate at which alternation of black and white stimulation fuses into a steady gray.) In one study (Buhler, 1953), it was found that, as predicted, the flicker fusion threshold was lower before the operation than after it when anxiety had presumably relaxed. Other studies using anxiety-arousing stimuli such as dental chairs have found similar results, lending credence to the construct of anxiety and to certain measures of it.

For any test that presumes to measure a trait or quality, we can formulate a network of theory, leading to definite predictions. These predictions can be tested. Insofar as they are borne out, the validity of the test as a measure of the trait or construct is supported. Insofar as the predictions fail to be verified, we are led to doubt the validity of the test, our theorizing, or both.

Construct validity, as Messick (1989) has pointed out, is really the central concept underlying test validation because the validity of a test concerns what the test scores mean—that is, what kinds of inferences they support. The meaning may be couched in terms of relationships either with a defined body of subject matter (which we have called rational or content validity) or with other observations of human variation (criteria). Both of these sources are used to build the meaning of the test's scores as indicators of traits in the network of a theory about behavior.

Messick (1989) also points out that what is validated is not the test itself but interpretations of the test scores for particular purposes or uses. If we collect some test scores and lock them away in a vault, validation is not an issue. But, once we take the scores from the vault and use them for a purpose—any purpose—we must ask about the appropriateness of the scores for that use. The evidence to justify the use is, as we have seen, partly rational and partly empirical. Rational consideration of what is measured takes center stage when we are considering an end-product—either a test that describes an individual's past learning or some indicator that we are accepting as a criterion measure. Such is the case when we use scores on an achievement test to represent the amount of material a student has learned from a course of instruction. It is also the case when we use grade point average (which may well result from an averaging of scores on several such tests) as an overall measure of learning or supervisor ratings as an indicator of job performance. The elaboration of a theory by which we decide how to test the validity of a measure of a psychological construct is also a rational exercise. By contrast, when we use a test as a selection device to predict some accepted criterion measure, validation becomes primarily statistical. Checking the theory that we have developed for a measure of some construct is also an empirical undertaking. Judgment and evidence join in the validation enterprise.

Overlap of Reliability and Validity

One way of thinking about the usefulness of a test is to ask to what extent one might safely generalize from a test score. If two forms of the test are given on the same day, the correlation between them tells us with what degree of confidence we can generalize from one set of test tasks to another set built to the same specifications and, by implication, with what degree of confidence we can generalize from the score to the whole domain of tasks sampled by the test. If the testing is conducted on different days, we gather evidence over a domain of occasions. And, if the testing on different days is also with different test forms, we gather evidence on the degree of generalizability over both tasks and occasions. If two different but similar tests are given, each intended by its author to measure the same trait or construct, we get evidence of generalizability from test to test. We are now considering a still broader domain that includes not merely samples of tasks chosen according to a common blueprint or design but also a range of blueprints or designs prepared by different authors. We are moving beyond what is ordinarily thought of as reliability into the realm of validity. And, of course, it is possible to consider generalizability from a test to other indicators of the same attribute, such as self-description or ratings by peers, supervisors, or teachers. Do the test scores allow us to draw inferences about what those ratings would be?

The notion of generalizability encompasses both reliability and validity, indicating that the two concepts differ only in the breadth of the domain to which generalization is undertaken. The concept of generalizability may eventually come to replace the several types of reliability and validity that we have discussed in this and the preceding chapter. Figure 5.4 provides an illustration of the notion of generalizability. We can view the situation as resembling the layers of an onion and can ask concerning any test how well it enables us to generalize our conclusions to situations at successive levels of remoteness from the central core.

FIGURE 5.4
Layers of generalization from a test score.

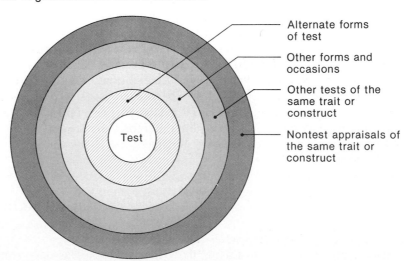

Validity for Criterion-Referenced Tests

Criterion-referenced tests are concerned with the measurement of particular, narrowly defined instructional objectives. For this reason, the critical concern in assessing the validity of criterion-referenced tests is *content validity*. As is discussed in more detail in Chapter 7, an instructional objective includes two elements, the information content of the domain and what the student should be able to do with that content. Both of these elements must be present in the item in the form called for by the objective if the item is to be considered a valid indicator of achievement of that objective.

An often overlooked part of the content of a test is the conditions under which the examinees exhibit their performance. If the time allowed for testing is too short to enable most of the examinees to attempt all of the items, then speed of performance becomes a part of the content of the test. If the administration conditions are poor, these conditions become part of the test content *for these examinees*. To the extent that factors such as these vary from one group of examinees to another, the content of the test also varies. Content validity relates to the test score and all of the factors, including clarity of directions and adequacy of scoring procedures, that affect it. When the content is critical to the use of the test, careful attention must be paid to all factors that make up the test's content.

Content validity, as we have seen, is primarily a matter of professional judgment on the part of teachers and subject-matter experts. There is, however, a useful type of empirical or statistical evidence that can be used to appraise the validity of criterion-referenced tests. This type of procedure is based on the point, made by Berk (1980), that a criterion-referenced test should maximize differences between groups that have achieved mastery of the objectives and those that have not achieved mastery, while it should minimize differences within the groups. That is, the ideal mastery-oriented test should divide the examinees into two homogeneous groups of individuals: those who have achieved mastery and those who have not.

The problem, of course, is how to define mastery. One commonly used approach is to have teachers identify those pupils who they are certain have mastered the objective and those who they are certain have not mastered it. This method can yield two widely separated groups, but the middle pupils must be omitted. A second approach is to compare those who have received instruction on the objective with those who have not yet had such instruction. A third approach is to compare the performance of students before instruction with their performance following a period of instruction. Each of these approaches has certain limitations, and all are affected by the problem of the unreliability of difference or change scores. But any one of them provides some evidence of the joint validity of the instructional activities aimed at the objectives and the test as a measure of mastery of those objectives.

The validation procedure is similar to the item analysis methods discussed in Chapter 7. The examinees are divided into two groups—masters versus non-masters or instructed versus uninstructed—and the proportion in each group who answered each item correctly is determined. The valid items are those for which the success rate in the master or instructed group is substantially higher than the success rate in the nonmaster or uninstructed group. In the extreme case, the success rate on each item for masters should be 100%, while the nonmasters should experience a chance rate of success. The total test should divide the examinees into masters, all of whom achieve perfect or near-perfect scores, and nonmasters, all of whom score at about the chance level. In the ideal test, there should be no misclassifications.

Mastery of an instructional objective is seldom an all-or-none thing. In any class, there will be varying degrees of mastery. In fact, one problem with the mastery concept in testing is deciding on an acceptable definition of mastery. The advantage of the criterion-referenced mastery philosophy of evaluation is that we know, in theory, what the students who have gained mastery can do— that is, what classes of problems or tasks they can solve. This type of knowledge is an essential part of formative evaluation. But, there are many situations, both in the school setting and elsewhere, where the question that is asked is one of relative position. Summative evaluations often call for norm-referenced tests that focus explicitly on relative performance.

Factors Making for Practicality in Routine Use

Although validity and reliability may be all-important in measures that are to be used for special purposes, when a test is to be used in classrooms throughout a school or school system a number of down-to-earth practical considerations must also be taken into account. It is easy for the administrator to pay too much attention to small financial savings or to economies of time that make it possible to fit a test into a standard class period with no shifting of schedules; nevertheless, these factors of economy and convenience are real considerations. Furthermore, other factors relating to the readiness with which the tests may be given, scored, and interpreted bear importantly on the use that will be made of the tests and the soundness of the conclusions that will be drawn from them.

Economy

The practical significance of dollar savings does not need to be emphasized in the current environment of tight educational budgets. Dollars are of real significance for any educational or industrial enterprise. Economy in the case of tests depends in part on the cost of test materials and scoring services per examinee, and it depends in part on the possibility of reusing the test materials. For example, in the upper elementary grades and beyond, it is feasible to administer a test using separate answer sheets and to use the test booklets for a number of testings. If a test will be used in successive years or if testing can be scheduled so that different classes or schools can be tested on different days, an important economy can be effected by using the same booklet a number of times.

A second aspect of economy is savings in time of test administration; however, this economy is often a false one. We saw in an earlier section that the reliability of a test depends largely on its length. As far as testing time is concerned, we get about what we give. Some tests may be a little more efficiently designed, so that they give a little more reliable measure per minute of testing time, but, by and large, any reduction in testing time will be accomplished at the price of loss in the precision or breadth of our appraisal.

A third, and quite significant aspect of economy is the ease of scoring. The clerical work of scoring a battery of tests by hand can become either burdensome if it is done by the already busy teacher or expensive if it is carried out by clerical help hired especially for the purpose. As a result, test users rely heavily on mechanized scoring, and test publishers are producing tests that can be processed by the increasingly sophisticated equipment that is being developed. A number of commercially published tests, such as the SAT and the Strong-Campbell Interest Inventory, can be scored only by the publisher or at special centers licensed by the publisher. Other tests, such as the individually administered Stanford-Binet, are scored only by hand. But, for many published tests, test users have the option of hand scoring their own tests, of setting up their own mechanized scoring units, or of sending tests to one of the test scoring services that specialize in test processing.

Several test-scoring services provide efficient test scoring and reporting, often giving 24 hour turnaround; that is, they will score the tests and put the results in return mail within 24 hours of the time that they receive the completed answer sheets. Also, test scoring equipment is becoming so inexpensive and available that many schools or districts maintain their own scoring services. The basic equipment consists of a photoelectric document reader combined with a computer. The document reader responds to marks on an answer sheet or in the test booklet (At least three companies sell the scanning part of a test scoring system for under $5,000, a cost that is within the means of many school districts and modest-sized companies. There are now even optical scanners, called optical character readers, that will read printed text, but these scanners are considerably more expensive than the equipment just mentioned.)

Using a separate answer sheet is familiar to most American college students, but separate answer sheets are not satisfactory for young children. The complications of finding an answer in the test booklet, keeping the code letter of the chosen answer in mind while locating the proper place on the answer sheet, and then marking the proper spot on the answer sheet are too much for children in the primary grades. However, current equipment makes it possible to use a booklet at the primary level and either to slice the bound edge off the test booklet and run the separate pages through the scanner or to print the test in a fanfold booklet that can be unfolded and run through the scanner as a unit. Modern scanning equipment can handle 50 or more different answer sheet patterns in a single run.

The information from the optical scanner is fed into the computer where it is compared with a key that has been recorded in the computer's memory. One or more scores are determined and printed out on a record form. The computer can also produce various statistics such as means and standard deviations for classes, schools, or school systems and also local percentiles. Thus, the scoring service, whether it is a commercial agency or a district office, can generally provide not only test scores for individuals but also the complete range of statistical information about the test results that are of interest to the local school system. Some of the scoring services will also accumulate results over a period of years, providing a longitudinal picture of the local test results. One advantage to the local school system of having its own scoring and computing equipment is that it is then much easier to carry out item analyses (see Chapter 7) on locally constructed tests as well as to accumulate local norms and longitudinal results.

A test that is to be economical for use in large-scale testing programs will be available in a format for scoring by different types of scanning and scoring equipment. Almost any type of answer sheet can be hand-scored relatively efficiently by using an overlay stencil. Some test publishers supply plastic overlay stencils for this purpose. Others use a special type of answer sheet made up of two sheets fastened together, the back of one carbon covered or pressure sensitive. The key is printed on the back of the first sheet, and as the examinee marks the front, the carbon-covered or pressure-sensitive material transfers the marks to the back of the sheet, where the number of marks falling in the printed key spaces can be counted.

Potential test purchasers will want to determine what types of answer forms and what scoring services are available for any test that they are considering using. If scoring is to be done locally, any restrictions imposed by the available scanner should be known. Test publishers who allow local scoring of their tests will generally have answer sheets that can be scored by the common types of scanners.

Features Facilitating Test Administration

In evaluating the practical usability of a test, one factor to be taken into account is the ease of administration. A test that can be handled adequately by the regular classroom teacher with no more than a session or so of special briefing is much more readily fitted into a testing program than a test requiring specially trained administrators. Several factors contribute to the ease of giving and taking a test.

1. A test is easy to give if it has clear, full instructions. The instructions for the administrator should be written out completely, so that all the examiner must do is read and follow them. Instructions for the examinee should also be complete and should provide appropriate practice exercises. The amount of practice that should be provided depends on how novel the test task is likely to be for those being tested. When it is a familiar type of task or a simple and straightforward instruction, no more than a single example will be needed; however, for an unusual item format or test task more practice will be desirable.

Familiarity with the types of tasks the test requires is also a possible source of irrelevant differences between examinees. Thus, many underprivileged children are not as familiar with testing situations as are children from more advantaged homes. A plentiful supply of practice items can help reduce the negative effect of task unfamiliarity and yield a more accurate picture of the abilities of disadvantaged children. With the prevalence of tests in society, instruction in how to take tests, by administering a number of practice tests, may even be a reasonable educational activity in the earlier grades because it would reduce "testwiseness" as one irrelevant source of individual differences in scores.

2. A test is easy to give if there are few separately timed units and if close timing is not crucial. Timing a number of brief subtests to a fraction of a minute is a bothersome undertaking, and the timing is likely to be inaccurate unless a stopwatch is available for each tester. Some tests have as many as 8 or 10 parts, each taking only 2 or 3 minutes. A test made up of 3 or 4 parts, with time limits of 5, 10, or more minutes for each, will be easier to use. Errors in timing are also less likely with fewer parts.

3. The layout of the test items on the page has a good deal to do with the ease of taking the test. Items in which the response options all run together on the same line, items with small or illegible pictures or diagrams, items that are crowded together, and items that run over from one page to the next all create difficulty for the examinee. Item difficulty should come from the content and the thought processes required to determine the right answer, not from the test format. Print and pictures should be large and clear. Response options should be well separated from one another. All parts of an item and all items referring to a single figure, problem, or reading passage should appear on the same page or a double-page spread. Also, to the extent that the physical layout of the test is difficult for examinees to follow, scores may be lower than they should be, a fact that would adversely affect the validity of the test and be particularly detrimental for a criterion-referenced test.

Features Facilitating Interpretation and Use of Scores

Although the point is sometimes overlooked, it seems axiomatic that a test is given so that the results can be used. If the score is to be used, it must be interpreted and given meaning. The author and publisher of the test have the responsibility of providing users with information that permits them to make sound appraisals of the test in relation to their needs and to give appropriate meaning to the score of each individual. The authors and publishers do this primarily through the *test manual* and other collateral materials prepared to accompany the test. What may the test user reasonably expect to find in the manual for a test, together with its supporting materials? We have outlined below the aids that the user should expect.

1. A statement of the functions the test was designed to measure and of the general procedures by which it was developed. In this statement, the author tells what he or she considers the test to be valid for and provides the evidence that proper steps have been taken to achieve that validity. Particularly for achievement tests, in which we are concerned primarily that the test measures a particular content and cognitive process, the manual should describe the procedures by which the choice of content was made or how the analysis of the functions being measured was carried out. If the author is unwilling to expose his or her thinking to our critical scrutiny, we may perhaps be skeptical of the thoroughness or profundity of that thinking.

Procedures to be reported include not only the rational procedures by which the range of content or types of objectives were selected but also the empirical procedures by which the items were reviewed, tried out, and screened for final inclusion in the test. The validity of the test—the interpretations it supports and the uses to which it may properly be put—is its most important property. The author's plan and procedures for construction are vital steps in achieving validity and should be explicitly stated so that potential users can judge the quality of these activities.

2. Detailed instructions for administering the test. Earlier in this section we discussed the need for this aid to uniform and easy administration by teachers or others who will have to use the test. Of course, proper administration is also vital to achieving scores that are valid for the user's purpose.

3. Scoring keys and specific instructions for scoring the test. The problems of scoring have also been discussed. If the test can be scored locally, the manual and supporting materials should provide detailed instructions on how the score is to be computed, how errors are to be treated, and how part scores are to be combined into a total score. Scoring keys and stencils should be planned to facilitate as much as possible the onerous task of hand scoring, when scoring is to be done by the local user, and instructions should be given for electronic scoring.

4. Norms for appropriate reference groups. These norms together with information on how the norms were obtained and instructions for their use should be included in the test manual. A full consideration of types of test norms and their uses was presented in Chapter 3. It is therefore sufficient at this time to point out the responsibility of the test producer to develop suitable norms for the groups with which the test is to be used. General norms are a necessity, and norms suitable for special types of communities, special occupational groups, and other more limited subgroups will add to the usefulness of the test in many cases.

5. Evidence of the reliability of the test. This evidence should indicate not only the simple reliability statistics but also the operations used to obtain the reliability estimates and the descriptive and statistical characteristics of each group on which reliability data are based. If a test is available in more than one form, it is highly desirable for the producers to report the correlation between the two forms, in addition to any data that were derived from a single testing. If the test yields part scores, and particularly if it is proposed that any use be made of these part scores, reliability data should be reported for the separate part scores. It is good procedure for the author to report standard errors of measurement as well as reliability coefficients. An author who indicates what the standard error of measurement is at each of a number of score levels should particularly be commended because this information shows the range of scores over which the test retains its accuracy.

6. *Evidence on the intercorrelations of subscores.* If the test provides several subscores, the manual should provide information on the intercorrelations of the subscores This information is important in guiding the interpretation of the subscores and particularly in judging how much confidence to place in the *differences* between the subscores. If the correlations among the subscores approach their reliabilities, indicating that they measure much the same things, the differences between them will be largely meaningless and uninterpretable. Information on the reliability of the subscores, coupled with knowledge of their correlations, permits an accurate evaluation of the degree to which difference scores add information to the original scores.

7. *Evidence on the relationship of the test to other variables.* Insofar as the test is to be used as a predictive device, correlations with criterion measures constitute the essential evidence on how well it does in fact predict. Full information should be provided on the nature of the criterion variables, the groups for which data are available, and the conditions under which the data were obtained. Only then can the reader judge the validity of the test fairly as a predictor.

It will often be desirable to report correlations with other measures of the same function as collateral evidence bearing on the construct validity of the test. For example, correlations with an individual intelligence test are relevant in the case of a group measure of intelligence.

Finally, indications of the relationship of test scores to age, sex, type of community, socioeconomic level, and similar facts about the individual or group are often helpful. They provide a basis for judging how sensitive the measure is to the background of the group members and to the circumstances of their life and of their education. Evidence of this kind is also useful for judging whether the norm groups used by the publisher are appropriate for the local population.

8. *Guides for using the test and for interpreting results obtained with it.* The developers of a test presumably know how it is reasonable for the test to be used and how the results from it should be evaluated. They are specialists in that test. For the test to be most useful to others, especially the teacher with limited specialized training, suggestions should be given of ways in which the test results may be used for diagnosing individual and group weaknesses, forming class groupings, organizing remedial instruction, counseling the individual, or whatever other activities may appropriately be based on results from that particular type of instrument.

A Final Word on Quality. A final point to keep in mind is that the care that has gone into preparing the test manual is often itself a good indicator of the care that has been exercised in constructing the test. Test authors who do a careful, thorough job of describing how the test was constructed and how evidence of its reliability and validity was obtained are likely to have carried out those steps in a thoughtful, professional manner as well. We can assume that they probably care enough to give their very best.

Guide for Evaluating a Test

As an aid to the potential user, we end this chapter with a guide for evaluating a test. This guide consists of a series of questions, based in large part on the *Standards for Educational and Psychological Testing.* Careful study of the complete *Standards* will repay the person who would become a more sophisticated test user. (The most recent edition of the *Standards* differs from its predecessors in that it places more emphasis on the proper interpretation and use of test results. The validity of test scores depends heavily, some would say entirely, on the context of their use, and it is the responsibility of the test user to guarantee that inferences and decisions based on test scores are supported by appropriate evidence.)

You will note that many of the questions in this guide relate to the availability and adequacy of information reported about the test. There is an implied, although not explicitly stated, second question as a sequel to many of the sections of the guide, especially those relating to reliability and validity. That question is, given that the information is provided, how satisfactory does the test appear to be, in comparison with others that are available, as well as by absolute standards, for the use I want to make of it? A significant portion of the responsibility for valid testing rests with the test user. You must evaluate the evidence provided by the publisher, as well as what you know about the examinees and the intended uses of the test scores. In light of this information, you must decide whether the evidence justifies using the test.

A number of questions in this guide refer to the adequacy of norms and converted scores. You may wish to review Chapter 3 as you study this portion of the guide.

General Identifying Information

1. What is the name of the test?
2. Who are its authors—by name and position if that information is available? (It should be.)
3. Who publishes the test? And when was it published?
4. Is more than one form of the test available? If so, how many?
5. How much does the test cost?
6. How long does it take to administer the test?

Information About the Test

1. Is there a manual for the test (or some other similar source of information, such as an article in a journal) that is designed to provide the information that a potential user needs?
2. How recently has the test been revised? How recently has the manual been revised? (For major commercial tests it is reasonable to expect that both the test and its manual will be revised at least every 10 years.)

Aids to Interpreting Test Results

1. Does the manual provide a clear statement of the purposes and applications for which the test is intended?

2. Does the manual provide a clear statement of the qualifications needed to administer the test and interpret its results properly?

3. Do the test, manual, record forms, and accompanying materials guide users toward sound and correct interpretation of the test results?

4. Are the statements in the manual that express relationships presented in quantitative terms so that the reader can tell how much confidence to attach to them? (For example, it is much more informative to say that the correlation with Variable X was 0.55 than to say that the test correlates substantially with Variable X.)

Validity

1. Does the manual report evidence on the validity of the test for each type of inference for which the test is recommended?

2. Does the manual *avoid* referring to correlations between items and total test score as evidence of validity?

3. If the test is designed to be a sample of a specified domain of behaviors (e.g., an achievement test), does the manual define the domain clearly and indicate the procedures used for sampling from that domain?

4. When criterion-related validity is involved, does the manual describe the criterion variables clearly, comment on their adequacy, and indicate what aspects of the criterion performance are *not* adequately reflected in these criterion measures?

5. Are the samples used for estimating criterion-related validity adequately described? And are they appropriate to the purpose? One way spuriously to inflate apparent validity is to use samples that are much more heterogeneous than those that can be expected in actual use. Are such tricks avoided?

6. Are statistical analyses for criterion-related validity presented in a form that permits the reader to judge the degree of confidence that can be placed in inferences about individuals?

7. If the test is designed to measure a theoretical construct (e.g., trait of ability, temperament, or attitude), is the proposed interpretation clearly stated and differentiated from alternate theoretical interpretations? Is the evidence to support this interpretation clearly stated and fully presented?

In summary, to what extent does the available evidence with respect to validity justify the uses of the test suggested in the manual or the use that you would want to make of the test results? Remember that if you intend to use the test for some purpose other than that contemplated by the test developer, the responsibility for demonstrating the validity of the test for that use rests with you.

Reliability

1. Does the manual present data adequate to permit the reader to judge whether scores are sufficiently dependable for the recommended uses (or for your contemplated uses, if these are different from the recommended ones)?

2. Are the samples on which reliability data were obtained sufficiently well described that the user can judge whether the data apply to his or her situation?

3. Are the reliability data presented in the conventional statistical form of product-moment correlation coefficients and standard errors of measurement? Are standard errors presented for different levels of performance?

4. If more than one form of the test was produced, are data provided to establish comparability of the forms?

5. If the test purports to measure a generalized homogeneous trait, is evidence reported on the internal consistency (interitem or interpart correlations) of the parts that make up the test?

6. Does the test manual provide data on the stability of test performance over time?

In summary, to what extent do the reliability data provided in the manual justify the uses for the test results suggested by the authors or the uses that you would want to make of the test results?

Administration and Scoring

1. Are the directions for administration sufficiently clear and fully stated so that the administrator will be able to duplicate the conditions under which the norms were established and the reliability and validity data were obtained?

2. If the test can be scored locally, are the procedures for scoring set forth clearly and in detail, in a way that will maximize scoring efficiency and minimize the likelihood of scoring error? Are the directions for determining subscores clear and unambiguous?

3. If the test is to be scored by the publisher or a commercial scoring service, does the test scoring service provide for the accumulation of results over time to aid in preparing local norms and local validity evidence?

Scales and Norms

1. Are the scales used for reporting performance clearly and carefully described so that the test interpreter will fully understand them and be able to communicate the interpretation to an examinee?

2. Are norms reported in the manual that are in appropriate form, usually standard scores or percentile ranks in appropriate reference groups?

3. Are the populations to which the norms refer clearly defined and described? And are they populations with which you can appropriately compare your examinees?

4. If more than one form of the test is available, including revised forms, are tables provided showing equivalent scores on the different forms?

5. Does the manual discuss the possible value of local norms? Does it provide any help in preparing local norms?

Summary

The most important characteristic for a test to have is validity. But, validity is the responsibility of both the test constructor and the test user because validity refers to the use or interpretation that is made of a test score. In one context, one interpretation of a test score may be appropriate, but in a different context or for a different purpose, the same interpretation might well be invalid.

Three general types of evidence bear on the question of whether a particular test use is a valid use. First, content-related evidence reveals the relationship between the test content and the proposed interpretation. If the correspondence, which is largely a matter of expert judgment, is good, the proposed use is supported. Second, empirical or criterion-related evidence is obtained from the relationships of test scores with other variables of interest, particularly occupational and educational outcomes. Substantial correlations between test scores and measures of performance in the outcome task support the use of the test for prediction, selection, or placement decisions. Finally, construct-related evidence comes from the correspondence of the test scores to deductions from theory. Content- and criterion-related evidence help to determine fit to predictions from theory, but response to experimental interventions and agreement with predicted patterns of relationship with other variables are also important.

In addition to yielding information that is valid for the proposed use, the test must be practical to use. Practicality relates matters of expense, ease of administration and scoring, and ease with which appropriate inferences can be derived from the test scores, including the adequacy and availability of norm- or criterion-referenced interpretations.

Questions and Exercises

1. If the American College Testing Program were to develop a general survey test in science for high school seniors, what steps might the developers take to establish evidence of the validity of the test?

2. What type of validity evidence is indicated by each of the following statements that might have appeared in a test manual?
   a. Scores on the Attitudes Toward School Inventory correlated +0.43 with teachers' ratings of adjustment.
   b. The objectives to be assessed by XYZ Reading Test were rated for importance by 150 classroom teachers.
   c. Scores on the Wunderkind Programming Aptitude Test correlated +0.57 with supervisors' ratings after 6 months on the job.
   d. The Factors of Brilliance Intelligence Test yields scores that correlate +0.69 with scores on the Wechsler Adult Intelligence Scale.
   e. The Accurate Achievement Battery is based on an analysis of 50 widely used texts and 100 courses of study from all parts of the country.

3. Comment on the following statement: The classroom teacher is the only person who can judge the validity of a standardized achievement test for his or her class.

4. Examine the manuals for two or three tests of different types. What evidence for validity is presented in each? How adequate is the evidence for each test?

5. Using Table 5.4, determine what percentage of those selected would be above average on the job if a selection procedure with a validity of 0.50 were used and only the top quarter of applicants were accepted for the job. What percentage would be above average if the top three-quarters were selected? What would the two percentages be if the validity were only 0.40? What does a comparison of the four percentages indicate?

6. If personnel psychologists for the navy were doing research on tests for the selection of helicopter maintenance trainees, what might they use as a criterion of success in such a specialty? What are the advantages and disadvantages of each possible measure?

7. What are the advantages of freshman grade point average as a criterion measure for validating a college admissions test? What are the disadvantages?

8. A test manual contains the following statement: The validity of Test Q is shown by the fact that it correlates 0.80 with the Stanford-Binet. What additional evidence is needed to evaluate this assertion?

9. You are considering three reading tests for use in your school. As far as you can judge, all three are equally valid, and each reports a reliability of 0.90. What else would you need to know to make a choice among the tests?

10. Examine several tests of aptitude or of achievement that would be appropriate for a class you might teach. Write up an evaluation of one of these tests using the guidelines given in the last section of this chapter.

Suggested Readings

American Psychological Association, American Educational Research Association, & National Council on Measurement in Education. (1985). *Standards for educational and psychological testing.* Washington, DC: American Psychological Association.

Anastasi, A. (1986). Evolving concepts of test validation. *Annual Review of Psychology, 37,* 1–15.

Anghoff, W. H. (1988). Validity: An evolving concept. In H. Wainer & H. Braun (Eds.), *Test validity* (pp. 19–32). Hillsdale, NJ: Erlbaum.

Cook, T. D., & Campbell, D. T. (1979). *Quasi-experimentation: Design and analysis issues for field settings.* Chicago: Rand McNally.

Cronbach, L. J. (1988). Five perspectives on validation argument. In H. Wainer & H. Braun (Eds.), *Test Validity* (pp. 3–17). Hillsdale, NJ: Erlbaum.

Ebel, R. L. (1983). The practical validation of tests of ability. *Educational Measurement: Issues and Practices, 2*(2), 7–10.

Embretson (Whitely), S. (1983). Construct validity: Construct representation versus nomothetic span. *Psychological Bulletin, 93,* 179–197.

Fredericksen, N. (1986). Construct validity and construct similarity: Methods for use in test development and test validation. *Multivariate Behavioral Research, 21,* 3–28.

Gardner, E. F. (1983). Intrinsic rational validity: Necessary but not sufficient. *Educational Measurement: Issues and Practices, 2*(2), 13.

Haertel, E. (1985). Construct validity and criterion-referenced testing. *Review of Educational Research, 55,* 23–46.

Hambleton, R. K. (1984). Validating the test scores. In R. A. Berk (Ed.), *A guide to criterion-referenced test construction* (pp. 199–230). Baltimore: Johns Hopkins University Press.

Messick, S. (1989). Validity. In R. L. Linn (Ed.), *Educational measurement* (3rd ed., pp. 13–103). New York: Macmillan.

Schmidt, F. L. (1988). Validity generalization and the future of criterion-related validity. In H. Wainer & H. Braun (Eds.), *Test validity* (pp. 173–189). Hillsdale, NJ: Erlbaum.

Schmidt, F. L., Hunter, J. E., Pearlman, K., & Hirsh, H. R. (1985). Forty questions about validity generalization and meta-analysis. *Personnel Psychology, 32,* 697–798.

CHAPTER 6
Achievement Tests and Educational Decisions

Introduction

You are probably aware by now that a major theme of this book is the relationship between measurement and decision making. The need to make decisions is one of the most important characteristics of our increasingly complex world. Teachers certainly are not exempt from decision making, being required to make a dizzying number of decisions during the course of each school day. Other educators and parents likewise are faced with this requirement. Students, as they achieve higher levels of education, need to make decisions about their own futures. Outside of school, employers must make decisions about whom to employ or promote. Nearly everyone, at some point, has to decide where to apply for employment or whether to accept a particular job offer.

Everyone who makes a decision needs information. More specifically, each person must know what information is needed, where to obtain it, how to weigh it, and how use it effectively to arrive at a course of action.

Values and Decisions

Decision making involves values, both personal and societal, and these are difficult to quantify. Although it may be possible to measure the degree to which an individual holds a certain value, there is no available assessment procedure that can tell us what values an individual, school, or agency should have or consider in making decisions. Values may differ markedly across subgroups within a community, and there may be considerable variations among individuals and agencies regarding which values should take precedence. Many of the controversies surrounding the use of tests and evaluation procedures in decision making, particularly selection and placement decisions, stem from differences and conflicts among value systems. In some instances, these conflicts in value systems have been resolved by the state and federal courts, which have mandated actions designed to promote societal goals in making decisions. In other instances, local school boards or school faculties have reached a consensus on what values should be considered in making decisions. In most cases, unfortunately, conflicts about values remain.

Classroom Instructional Decisions

One of the most important tasks for classroom teachers is to ensure that students achieve instructional objectives. Teachers have to monitor the progress of the class and of the individual students to make good decisions about where to begin teaching, when to move on to the next unit of instruction, whether to reteach the present unit, or whether a particular student or subgroup of students needs special help to master the learning task. The quality of these decisions can strongly influence the effectiveness of the classroom instructional program.

Effective teaching requires that student progress be monitored through a process of formal and informal assessments. Informal assessments include such techniques as questioning, observing students while they work on tasks, and asking students to read aloud or to verbalize the working through of a mathematics problem. These assessments are useful in helping teachers know whether students understand the material presented and thus in helping them make better decisions about what should be taught next. Teachers specifically need to know whether there is a need for further review, or if the students are ready to have new material introduced. It also gives the teacher immediate feedback about the effectiveness of the teaching methods being employed. If students are not learning as they should, the teacher must decide whether to alter the instructional methods. These techniques are referred to as *formative evaluation.*

"High stakes" decisions about students such as grades and changes in placement are usually based on a more formal assessment called *summative evaluation.* This category includes both the tests that teachers construct and administer during a term to make decisions about grades and standardized achievement tests used to evaluate instruction and identify low performing students. These tests may influence the teacher to perform a more in-depth diagnosis of students to identify areas in which they are having difficulty in learning a specific task and the possible reasons for the learning difficulty. Ability tests are generally used as part of the information base for making decisions about placements. These decisions could include placement in special education or gifted classes.

Surveys of teacher behavior (Stiggins, Conklin, & Bridgeford, 1986) have shown that teachers prefer informal methods of assessment and use them more often than they use formal approaches. This pattern of use probably occurs because the informal assessments require less preparation and skill to construct. However, when informal assessments are used to make decisions about individual students, teachers need to record the results carefully, or the teachers may have an insufficient amount of information about the performance of their students. Classroom teachers may be reluctant to keep such records because of the time and work involved, and if this is the case, they probably should place more reliance on formal techniques, which lend themselves more easily to systematic recordkeeping.

The Use of Objectives

Typically, classroom teachers employ a wide range of instructional objectives for a particular class. Some of these may be cognitive and require building a knowledge base. Other objectives may relate to the development of cognitive skills, such as reading or writing. Others may be affective objectives that involve the development of attitudes, values, interests, and personal or social attributes. In some areas of instruction, the objectives may focus on products or performances. (See Chapter 7 for a discussion of the different types of objectives and how they are formulated and organized.)

Each type of objective requires a different method of assessment to determine whether it has been achieved by students, but, in all cases, the information collected must be accurate. If the techniques used to collect information about the achievement of an objective do not yield high-quality information, decisions or actions based on those data are likely to be faulty.

Types of Assessment Instruments

Standardized Achievement Tests.   At the beginning of the school year, when a teacher is facing a new class, the scores on standardized achievement tests might help the teacher to select reading materials that are suitable for students in the class or to decide where to start instruction in mathematics or language. However, once instruction has actually begun, the teacher needs information on the achievement of specific instructional objectives, and this information is needed promptly. Standardized achievement tests must focus on objectives that are common to schools throughout the United States, and for this reason, the tests emphasize general skills. Such tests are unlikely to assess objectives related to the specific content emphasized in a particular classroom. Furthermore, they measure only cognitive objectives that can be appraised by paper-and-pencil tests. Affective, procedural, and other objectives requiring skill in oral communication or motor performance are not usually measured by these tests. Standardized tests also require several hours for administration, which makes them impractical for frequent use. In addition, there is usually a long wait before teachers receive results, which means that the results will not be available when instructional decisions need to be made.

Assessment Material Packaged with Curricular Materials.   Some classroom teachers, particularly in the lower grades, use tests designed to accompany published curricular materials instead of constructing assessments of their own. Most basal reading series and many textbooks include such tests. These instructional materials usually match the test items with instructional objectives and may also suggest a passing score to be used to classify students as masters or nonmasters of the objective. Although such materials can reduce the burden of test construction, they should be examined carefully before they are used. In many instances, they are poorly constructed. In addition, the number of items appraising each objective is usually too small to permit judgments about mastery. Despite being labeled as criterion-referenced tests, the domain assessed is seldom defined adequately and the items may not be sufficiently representative for the tests to be classified as criterion referenced. It is also important to point out that these packaged tests are not standardized tests.

Teacher-Made Assessment Instruments.   To obtain information for making day-to-day instructional decisions, classroom teachers usually must devise their own tests or assessment procedures. There are seven general methods for collecting data on the achievement of instructional objectives:

1. paper-and-pencil tests
2. oral tests
3. product evaluations

4. performance tests

5. affective measures

Each of these methods has advantages and disadvantages, and each is appropriate for appraising the achievement of only certain types of objectives.

1. Pencil-and-Paper Tests. Objectives that call for knowledge about a particular subject area, the capacity to use that knowledge to solve problems, or a general educational skill such as reading can be most reliably and validly appraised by teacher-made paper-and-pencil tests. Unfortunately, most teacher-made tests are poor measuring instruments. There are two problems with these kinds of tests. First, the items on the tests often do not match the stated goals of the class, and second, the tests tend to have poor psychometric qualities because the items are not well written. Surveys of teachers suggest that they seldom use even minimal data analysis procedures such as determining the central tendency or variability on their test results. As a result of these weaknesses, the information obtained from such tests may be of questionable value in making instructional decisions. The methods used in constructing and evaluating these types of tests will be discussed in more detail in Chapter 7.

2. Oral Tests. Although oral tests are more time consuming for the teacher, they can be used to assess many of the same types of objectives assessed by pencil-and-paper tests. They have the advantage of providing an opportunity to assess the integration of ideas while removing the effect of level of skill in written expression. The major disadvantage to the use of this method is that the evaluation of performance is subjective.

Another use for individually administered oral tests is the diagnosis of learning problems. For example, a teacher could give a student a series of two-digit addition problems and ask him or her to solve them aloud, that is, to talk through the procedures that were used to arrive at an answer. These verbalizations can provide clues about the misconceptions that underlie not only errors but also sometimes even correct responses. In reading, oral tests provide fewer clues about a student's underlying difficulty, although the tests might help a teacher identify missing subskills required in the complex process of reading. For students with sensory or motor impairments, oral assessment may provide more accurate information than can be obtained by other methods.

3. Product Evaluations. Some instructional objectives, such as those related to penmanship, to constructing a birdhouse in wood shop class, or to typing a business letter, require a student to produce a product that meets certain standards of acceptability. These kinds of objectives cannot be assessed directly by paper-and-pencil tests; it is better to evaluate the product itself. This type of assessment is called product evaluation. The major problems with this kind of evaluation stem from the task of identifying the aspects of the product that are relevant to its quality and establishing standards to measure the aspects that will define different degrees of adequacy or excellence in the product. Product evaluation is discussed in more detail in Chapter 8.

4. Performance Tests. Some instructional objectives require a student to carry out a procedure such as giving an oral report, playing a musical instrument, or using a spreadsheet on a computer. As a rule, these kinds of performances do not leave a tangible product that can be judged, or if they do, the actual procedures used by the student to produce the product are as important as the final product. These kinds of objectives can be appraised only by assigning an appropriate task to the student, such as giving an oral report to the class, and then observing and rating the performance as it occurs. This type of evaluation is called *performance testing*. The major problems with this type of evaluation are (1) identifying the critical, or salient, aspects of the performance that should be observed and (2) identifying and applying the criteria for discriminating different degrees of competency in the performance. (Methods for improving performance assessments are also presented in Chapter 8.)

5. *Affective Measures.* Almost all instructional programs, particularly at the elementary and secondary school levels, have affective as well as cognitive objectives. Affective objectives deal with personal and social attributes that educators want students to develop such as values, interests, self-concept, and cooperation with others. Assessing objectives such as these can be quite difficult because they are based on the inner feelings or motivations of students, which cannot be measured directly. Currently, the best that we can do is to observe behavior, and from this observation, try to infer what lies behind the behavior, have peers or teachers rate students, or ask students to provide self-reports on their own feelings or motivation. These methods are discussed in Chapters 8 and 9. None of these affective measures is entirely satisfactory. However, if teachers and schools are serious about achieving their goal of accurately measuring these kinds of objectives, then they need to monitor students' achievement of the objectives so that adjustments in instruction, or in classroom or school organization can be made if the level of achievement is not satisfactory.

Summary of Evaluation Techniques

In summary, teachers use a variety of evaluation techniques to make instructional decisions. All of these techniques must be focused on the objectives and content of the classroom instruction and carefully constructed or selected to yield valid and reliable information about the achievement of students. To abstract and analyze the information so that it can be used effectively, teachers must make simple analyses of the results such as score distributions and item analyses.

Evaluation that focuses on adapting instruction to make it more effective for students is called formative evaluation. It requires frequent use of teacher-made tests or other evaluation techniques so that the needed information is available when an instructional decision has to be made.

Placement Decisions

Classroom teachers, particularly at the elementary school level, frequently divide a class into smaller, within-class groups for instruction. The primary purpose is to form small clusters of students who have similar instructional needs on which the teacher can focus and to make instruction more effective. A decision about assigning a student to a within-class group is an example of a placement decision that is made solely by the teacher and will usually be based on information about each student's progress in mastering the instructional objectives.

Sometimes placement decisions must be made for students in a class whose instructional needs differ so markedly from those of other students in the class that the teacher is not able to make the necessary adjustments within the classroom to meet these needs. Typically, these students are of two kinds. At one extreme are gifted students whose level of achievement and speed of learning greatly exceed those of other students in the class, and at the other are students who are having great difficulty learning the basic educational skills such as reading, are unable to adapt to classroom demands, or are so disruptive in a classroom that they interfere with the learning of other students. The teacher may decide to refer these kinds of students to a school psychologist or counselor for assessment and possible alternative placement.

Despite the controversies that surround placement decisions in educational settings, such decisions still need to be made because there are individual differences in achievement among students, and these differences become larger, not smaller, as students progress through school. Students differ markedly in how much they have learned from previous instruction, their motivation to learn, the instructional conditions under which they learn best, their rate of learning, and their ability to apply previous experience to new learning situations. An instructional program that facilitates learning and growth for one student may hinder it for others. Classroom teachers and other educators have long recognized the need to adapt teaching methods, learning materials and curricula to meet individual differences among students and to place students in the kind of learning environment that will optimize their educational opportunities.

The primary focus of a placement decision is or should be on the individual being placed and the benefits that would accrue to him or her from a particular placement. However, you should also recognize that some placement decisions benefit the classroom teacher or other students in the class as well. For example, the decision to remove a particularly disruptive student from the regular classroom and to place him or her in a small class with a teacher trained to handle such students can benefit not only the disruptive student but also others in the regular classroom.

How Placement Decisions Are Made

Let us return to the specific student about whom a placement decision is being made. Assignment to Treatment A (a particular course, section of the class, or entry point for instruction) rather than to Treatment B might seem advantageous either because the two treatments differ, in whole or in part, in the goals toward which they are directed or because they differ in the means used (or route taken) to reach common goals. Thus, the prime goal of a remedial college

English section might be to teach correctness and clarity in writing a simple essay, while the prime goal of the creative writing class might be to encourage originality and dramatic effectiveness in writing narrative prose or poetry. Different goals are seen as appropriate for the two groups. On the other hand, the goals of both a regular and an advanced placement mathematics section in a high school might be to progress toward and master a domain that we designate "mathematical analysis," but with the expectation that the advanced placement group would pursue topics in greater depth and at a faster rate. In the latter case, a common assessment procedure would indicate how far the members of each group had progressed toward their common goals.

Over the years, it has seemed reasonable to use some test of initial achievement as the basis or a part of the basis for placing students in different treatments to facilitate their learning. However, research evidence on the gains from such placement is mixed, with some studies finding improved learning from group-focused instruction and others failing to find such an effect. One reason for this discrepancy is the difference in how the groupings were determined. Grouping is usually based on general level of academic performance rather than on entry status in specific subject-oriented skills. It is often not clear how much or in what ways instruction in the classes has varied for different groups. If there is no noticeable adaptation in instruction, there is no good reason to expect differences in outcomes. Furthermore, we are not sure to what extent common objectives characterize the different treatments or to what extent the treatments really have different goals so that no common instrument to appraise learning would be appropriate. Tests are most likely to permit constructive placement decisions when (1) they assess specific entry knowledge and skills for a particular subject area and (2) when the alternative instructional treatments differ substantially in method, content, and tempo. Published tests must be carefully examined to determine whether their content focuses on the desired entry skills. Failing that, it may be necessary to develop a locally made test that has the desired focus.

Day-by-Day Instructional Decisions

One important role of assessments of achievement is to help the classroom teacher make decisions about what is to be taught, studied, and/or practiced by students in the class. The weekly spelling test is a venerable classroom tradition, and quizzes in grammar and mathematics have been prepared and used by teachers for many years to help make decisions about the next day's lesson or to evaluate a child's progress.

Interest in tests used for guiding instructional decisions is on the increase, as is interest in the development of procedures that can provide information about whether a student has mastered a topic or skill. The knowledge provided by such assessments can help the teacher or the student decide whether there is a need for further instruction before the student moves to the next unit. This kind of information is especially relevant for subjects that have a hierarchical structure—that is, when progress on Topic B depends on an adequate understanding of Topic A. Of course, mathematics is the prime example of such a subject; therefore, many illustrations of instructional tests of this type are drawn from that field. But, many other subjects show a similar structure. For example, children must know the alphabet and recognize letters before they can learn to spell.

A test used to measure competence in a particular skill will usually be concrete and specific. In using such tests, teachers often set some criterion—usually an arbitrary one—to represent an adequate degree of competence. The use of a criterion has occasionally caused the tests to be incorrectly labeled as criterion-referenced tests. (The qualities that a test must have to be criterion referenced are listed in Chapter 7.) What these tests do have in common with criterion-referenced tests is the presentation of a representative sample of tasks from a narrowly defined domain. Because the domain is relatively narrow, all test items tend to require the same skill, and it is reasonable to expect that a person will either correctly answer all or almost all of the items or perform not much better than at a chance level.

By way of illustration, Figure 6.1 presents two teacher-made tests. The first assesses the students in a fifth-grade class on their knowledge of prime numbers. (For those who have forgotten or may never have known, a prime number is one that cannot be divided evenly by any number other than itself or 1 [unity]. Examples are 11, 13, or 17.) The second test (which also appeared in Chapter 3) assesses skill in capitalization of proper names, and is designed to identify students who are having trouble with this skill.

You can see that each little test is quite short; there are 15 numbers from which to choose 6 prime numbers in the first, and 13 words that should be underlined in the second. Setting a criterion level of 90% correct on each test as constituting adequate competence permits the examinee to miss one item on each test but assumes that more frequent mistakes imply inadequate mastery of the concept or skill. These tests illustrate one extreme in specificity and are clearly related to judgments about what a pupil has learned. They sample from narrowly and explicitly defined domains, and ones that are relatively easy to define.

In much of education, the domain that is represented by a unit of instruction is much fuzzier, and, consequently, the stock of appropriate problems or items is much less clearly defined. Consider, for example, a unit of instruction on the Bill of Rights. We could test an individual's ability to identify or to recall each of the first 10 amendments to the Constitution. But, if we were concerned with the meaning, the significance, and the application of these same 10 amendments in contemporary America, how could we meaningfully define and sample from that domain? In this instance, the notion of "mastery" slips through our fingers.

When we can not define the boundaries of a domain, it becomes impossible to determine what constitutes a representative sample of exercises to assess degree of mastery of that domain. Different test makers may produce dissimilar sorts of test exercises to measure the same domain. Specifying a criterion level of performance that represents a defined level of "mastery" becomes almost impossible with subject matter that cannot be concretely defined. A teacher-

FIGURE 6.1
Teacher-made criterion-referenced tests.

Test of Prime Numbers

Directions: Do you know what a prime number is? Look at the numbers shown below. Six of them are prime numbers. For each one, see if it is a prime number. If it is, draw a circle around it. If it is not, leave it unmarked.

31	47	143
33	49	293
35	51	415
38	59	763
41	97	942

Test of Capitalization

Read the paragraph. The punctuation is correct, and the words that begin a sentence have been capitalized. No other words have been capitalized. Some need to be. Draw a line under each word that should begin with a capital letter.

We saw mary yesterday. She said she had gone to chicago, illinois, to see

her aunt helen. Her aunt took her for a drive along the shore of lake

michigan. On the way they passed the conrad hilton hotel where mary's

uncle joseph works. Mary said that she had enjoyed the trip, but she was

glad to be back home with her own friends.

---

made test of knowledge about abstract material may still provide some useful information to guide decisions about further teaching, but the information will not be as concrete as that provided by tests such as those in Figure 6.1.

Reporting Academic Progress

It is important to ensure that the student, the parents, and the school know whether a particular student is making satisfactory progress in schoolwork. To the student, evidence of progress and accomplishment is a substantial motivating force, and evidence of specific difficulties provides a signal indicating a need to seek help to overcome the difficulties. Focused tests of the sort found in Figure 6.1 provide an important form of feedback to guide students as well as teachers identifying gaps in knowledge or skill that call for further study or practice.

Parents are vitally concerned with the progress of their children in school. Of course, families differ in the depth of this concern and differ even more in the resources that they provide for coaching in school skills and for supporting their child's efforts to learn. But all parents must be considered partners with the school, and, if they are to be effective partners, they must know how their child is progressing. Parents specifically need to know the level at which their child is functioning in each school subject and be warned promptly of any potential difficulties. All kinds of test results provide a concrete basis for communication from school to parent and for interpretation of the child's progress and difficulties.

As described in Chapter 3, the teacher or school may provide a criterion-referenced interpretation of student progress, which would include a list of competencies that the child has recently developed to a satisfactory level of mastery or the specific skills with which he or she is currently having difficulty. More conventionally, a norm-referenced interpretation will be provided that compares the child's general level of performance in a subject area with that of his or her class, other students in the school, or a broader regional or national reference group.

In reporting a child's academic progress to parents, it is necessary to compare performance to something. Three approaches to defining the merit of a child's performance are to define

1. performance in relation to perfection
2. performance in relation to par
3. performance in relation to potential

Performance in Relation to Perfection

When judging performance in relation to perfection we ask, how close did the student come to exhibiting a perfect score on the quiz? We are likely to interpret a perfect score as "complete mastery," but this interpretation is dangerous even in the case of a narrowly focused test and is completely inappropriate for a test that covers a broad domain. In the latter case, there are always more difficult tasks that could have been set for the examinee, and we never can say that he or she knows everything there is to know about a subject. Even with tasks as specific as identifying prime numbers, some numbers turn out to be a good deal more difficult than others. So "perfection" is displayed only on the specific sample of tasks that is used to represent the domain. Interpreting "80% correct" on the usual teacher-made test as "knows 80% of the subject" is completely absurd, and at most, the interpretation might be "knows 80% of the answers that the teacher thinks a student should be expected to know." On the other hand, this standard of "what the teacher expects" is a very real one and can be important to both pupil and parent.

Performance in Relation to Par

By performance in relation to par, we have in mind the typical norm-referenced interpretation of a test score. In this case, adequacy of performance is defined by the performance of others. For a teacher-made test, it may be the student's standing in the class. For the published test, it is a student's standing in relation to a broader reference group, such as all children at this same age or grade level.

In Chapter 3, we discussed various sorts of converted scores, using different scales and reference frames for reporting the score of an individual. We expressed a preference for percentile ranks or standard scores to represent a student's performance in relation to other members of a group in which he or she logically belongs. Of these two types of converted scores, the one that probably conveys the most immediate meaning to a parent or other person not particularly sophisticated about measurement issues is the score reported in terms of relative position—at the 15th percentile, in the second tenth, or in the bottom quarter.

Two aspects of such a report are troubling. One aspect is that it is possible (although perhaps not likely) within a specific class that the differences in performance are so small that the distinction between the top quarter and the bottom quarter is of no practical importance. That is, one may be forcing distinctions where no real differences exist. The other troubling aspect is that using the group as a standard means that there must always be 50% of the total group "below the average" and 25% "in the bottom quarter," with the implication that they have somehow "failed." We face a basic problem in our use of language: to the statistician, "average" means "middle of the group," but to most people, it has come to mean "minimally acceptable," so that anything below the average carries the connotation of "unacceptable." Somehow, the two interpretations of "average" must be separated in our thinking, so that the student who falls at the 20th or 30th percentile of his group on some measure is not viewed as a failure.

With a standardized test, the normative data supplied by the publisher permit "par" to refer to some national or regional group, or the school system may develop systemwide norms. The use of national norms may ease the pressure on some fortunately situated schools that draw primarily from an advantaged community in which most children approach or exceed the national average. However, if this par is used, it accentuates the sense of failure in schools from districts or communities that are at the low end of the scale in economic and cultural resources, where a very large proportion of the students will not reach the national or regional average. A blind application of national norms, whether to schools or individuals, is likely to lead to a sense of unreality and frustration.

Performance in Relation to Potential

Recognition of the inequity of assessing performance in relation to a uniform and unvarying set of standards has led test users and educational evaluators, in general, to try to express performance in relation to potential. This orientation rejects the notion that all people are identical and interchangeable and that the same par is applicable to each person. When reporting academic progress in terms of potential, a standard for each child must be established which asks, in light of all we know about this child, what level of performance should we reasonably expect?

This question is easy to phrase. When we start to explore it, however, we find that it becomes a tricky one to answer, with a wide range of technical and even ethical overtones. How do we determine the expected level of achievement for an individual?

The need to temper our expectation by what we know about an individual is readily demonstrated by considering age. We know that it is unreasonable to expect an 8-year-old to jump as far, run as fast, read as well, or do as wide a range of arithmetic problems as a 12-year-old can do. Eight-year-old children also differ in size. Perhaps it is unreasonable to expect an undersized child of this age to jump as far as an oversized one. By the same token, children also differ in their performance on tests designed to measure general intellectual development. Perhaps it is unreasonable to expect the same level of reading or arithmetic performance from the child who obtains a low score on a scholastic aptitude test that we do from the child who obtains a high score.

Statistical analyses of the relationship between aptitude and achievement tests do yield high correlations. Children with low scores on general measures of intellectual functioning tend to get poor scores on measures of reading and math achievement. In one sense, therefore, it might be correct to conclude that they have a lower potential for academic achievement. Because this relationship exists, we are tempted to modify our interpretations of test scores. Unfortunately, what at first seems to be a reasonable course of action turns out to be unworkable in practice. This approach does not work because the difference between the two types of tests is more a function of the way they are used and interpreted than of the underlying capacities assessed. The similarities between the two tests mean that students can be expected to perform the same on both. In the event that scores on the two tests are discrepant, we must first consider measurement error as the most likely explanation for the difference. In addition, there are social consequences that may result from an application of different expectations and standards for different individuals. Individuals tend to adjust their performance to the level of expectation that is set for them. Thus, low expectations may become a partial cause for low achievement.

This subject will be discussed more extensively in terms of assigning grades later in this chapter and in terms of special education decisions in Chapter 12.

Planning Educational Futures

As children progress through the school system, they move closer and closer to and finally reach decisions concerning future educational plans. Past achievement is one type of information that should influence such decisions. Present measured achievement is the best predictor we have of future achievement. General level of achievement may likewise affect future educational decisions, and performance in a particular course may influence decisions about educational specialization.

Grades obtained in school provide one indicator of achievement, but the variability of standards from teacher to teacher within a school and from school to school limits their value as guides to planning academic futures. Grades are personal and local in their significance. For this reason, standardized tests, with broadly representative norms that are comparable from one content area to another, provide a more uniform and universal basis for appraising overall level of achievement as well as specific strengths and weaknesses.

Two mistakes must be avoided in using test results for planning purposes. One mistake is premature decision making. Individuals change, and present performance predicts the future imperfectly. Counselors should avoid closing out options—such as going to college—prematurely. The other mistake is a predominately negative use of test results. Test scores are more constructive if they are used to open doors rather than to close them. It is as important for test results to identify talent and encourage its further development as it is for them to redirect individuals for whom the typical college education seems an unrealistic goal.

Selection Decisions

Selection decisions represent attempts to choose the individuals who will have the greatest use to an organization. This type of decision can be contrasted with placement decisions, which are intended to benefit the individual who is being placed in a particular educational setting. Thus, value for an employer hiring a typist might be expressed (crudely) as number of error-free lines of text typed in an average working day, whereas value for a college might be expressed (perhaps even more crudely and incompletely) as freshman grade point average (GPA). In the simplest terms, the purpose of a system for selection decisions is to hire or admit those individuals who will maximize the total value to the institution.

The notion of value is both fuzzy and complex. Any simple indicator, such as lines typed or GPA is at best a rough, pragmatic approximation of a person's true value to an organization, be it an employer or an educational institution.

Both past achievements and present performance often have a good deal of validity as predictors of future value. Thus, high school grades consistently have been found to be among the best predictors of future college grades, and job skills at the time of hiring provide a good indication of what those same skills will be on the job.

The rationale for using an objective test of achievement in one or more academic subjects to replace or supplement high school grades as a predictor of college success is that such a test would provide a uniform set of tasks for all applicants and thus a way of compensating for the different grading standards of secondary schools.

This calibration can be done equally well by scholastic aptitude tests. Furthermore, the scores from such tests tend to depend less on what has been taught in each school. For this reason, the widely used college admission tests, the Scholastic Aptitude Test (SAT) and the American College Testing Program (ACT), have been based on rather general reading, verbal, and quantitative skills.

In the world of work, academic achievement tests appear to be an inappropriate selection device for most jobs. Mental ability tests might work in situations where the focus is on potential for learning new skills, but in most situations, proficiency tests that measure specific job skills seem to be the best option. Examples of occupations for which such tests might be appropriate are carpenters, machinists, and electricians as well as office jobs such as typists, bookkeepers, or computer programmers. Such tests need to be employed with caution. Although we might be able to measure the most obvious skills related to each job with some degree of accuracy, in most cases the most important characteristics are personal, such as getting along with others and not using drugs, and are quite difficult to measure.

Curricular Decisions

One function for which measures of achievement are needed is the evaluation of alternative curricular materials or instructional designs. In education, there is a steady flow of proposals for change—change in curricular emphasis, change in instructional materials, and change in instructional procedures. If innovations are to be introduced rationally rather than capriciously and if education is to show any cumulative progress in effectiveness rather than an oscillation from one fad to another, systematic evaluation of the outcomes from any change is imperative. Carrying out adequate studies to evaluate any proposed change is admittedly difficult. But without evaluative research studies, decisions to change are made blindly, supported only by the eloquence of their proponents.

A first requirement for any evaluative research is clear specification of what a proposed innovation is designed to achieve. That is, we need a statement of the objectives of the program. The statement must be comprehensive, covering the full range of outcomes sought by the proposed new program as well as those sought by the program that it is designed to replace. If a revised mathematics program is designed to produce improved understanding of the number system, and the program it is replacing is one that has emphasized computational skills, it is important in evaluating the outcomes that the two programs be compared both in terms of understanding the number system and in terms of computational skills. The identification of the better of the two systems can only be made on a rational basis if we know how well each program achieves not only its own objectives but also other relevant objectives. This information puts us in a position to judge the importance of different aspects of achievement in terms of a specified system of values and comes up with a composite decision about which set of outcomes is to be preferred.

Once the objectives of an instructional program have been stated with enough detail and explicitness to guide instruction and evaluation, we may ask whether some or all of the objectives can be assessed appropriately using existing published tests. There are, of course, economies of time and effort associated with existing tests, as well as some gain in the availability of normative data. The design of a published test involves a thorough analysis of the content and objectives of the field that it is to cover. This analysis may have been made some years before publication, and it will have been made in terms of a curriculum that contains elements common to all school districts. In the case of basic skills such as those encompassed in reading and mathematics curricula, no problem exists because there is considerable agreement among school districts regarding what should be taught. This agreement will not always be found in other curricular areas. Most of the content of education changes slowly, and much is common in the objectives of educational programs that differ in form and in specific content. For this reason, there is some advantage to examining existing tests before attempting to invest the resources of time, skill, and money to produce a new test specifically for the local evaluation project.

One feature of curricular evaluations, or any analysis that leads to a decision applied to a whole class, school, or school system, is that it is not necessary that every pupil be assessed with every test exercise. Suppose, for example, there are so many items needed to assess a set of objectives adequately that it would take 4 hours for a pupil to complete a test made up of these items. If only 30 minutes of testing time were available, it might be possible to divide the material into eight test forms to correspond to the eight 30-minute testing segments needed to accommodate 4 hours of testing material and to have each pupil take one of the test forms. If a school has, for example, 120 sixth-grade pupils, each of the eight forms will be taken by approximately 15 pupils. For the school as a whole, it will be possible to determine average level of performance on the complete test because all of the items will have been used and all of the pupils will have served as examinees. This procedure, which is called *item sampling,* provides a practical way to assess a wide range of curricular objectives, using a large number of examinees, with each spending only a relatively short time being tested. One drawback of item sampling is that it requires the assembly of tests specifically for the current occasion, either through local efforts or from the item files of commercial publishers. Note that with item sampling, we do not get a meaningful or useful score for any single pupil.

Public and Political Decisions

Every community is interested in and concerned about its school system. Expenditures for education represent a major item in the budget of every community and every state, and citizens want to know whether they are getting good value for those expenditures. Citizens are also interested in how their schools compare with other schools in the state and throughout the country, and how well the children in their community are learning the things that they as parents and citizens think are important. Citizens do not frequently make decisions about schools, but when they do, the decisions are likely to be negative. They may vote down a school budget, school bond issue, or school board member, or they may organize a protest against a person, program, or policy. Conversely, of course, they may decide to support the school with money, time, or approbation. The action that they select will depend on how they feel about their schools, and this feeling in turn will depend in part on what they know about their schools.

Knowing about schools is in part a matter of knowing what is going on in them—available activities, resources for learning, and new ideas. Of greatest importance is information about how much the children are learning. Thus, in its relationship with the public, each school system faces the problem of presenting to that public some picture of student progress.

One approach to reporting school progress is to report in terms of very specific competencies. Thus, the school might report, "78% of pupils at the end of Grade 3 were able to identify the number of thousands, hundreds, tens, and units in a number such as 7,562." But such a report conveys little meaning to even an informed citizen. The likely response is, "So is that good or bad? What percentage should be expected to do this? How does this compare with last year? How does this compare with Hohokus next door?" If specific accomplishments are reported, there must be so many of them that teachers and citizens alike get drowned in a mass of detail. Thus, in reporting to the public, some type of summary seems necessary. By its nature, the summary will involve comparison—comparison with last year's performance, national norms, or some group of similar schools or communities. It is possible for a school system to develop its own set of assessment instruments, to use these in successive years, and to make limited types of comparison, but locally constructed tests with local norms might not satisfy the public. In most cases, there is a need for a means to make comparisons with other communities, states, and the nation as a whole. These comparisons can only be supplied by a test for which normative data are available. Besides, the development of good tests is difficult, expensive, and time consuming. One significant role for standardized tests is to provide the basis for making comparisons with other communities.

The test that forms the most appropriate basis for presenting a school's results to the public is the test that best represents the school's educational objectives. Thus, there are no new or different criteria for selecting a test that is to provide public information; it will be the same test that is most useful for appraising the achievement level of individual pupils.

Once the test has been administered and scored, it is necessary to assemble the data and present them in a form that will fairly and clearly communicate the results to the public. "Fairly" relates to the proper comparison group; "clearly" relates to the form of presentation.

Assigning Grades

One of the most unpleasant activities required of teachers is assigning grades. It takes up a large amount of time, causes anxieties, and tends to leave a sour taste in their mouths. Few students enjoy being assigned grades, and for teachers, assigning grades is an activity that requires a great deal of time and effort. The payoff to teachers is too often a sizable number of dissatisfied students.

The evaluation of student performance is typically summarized in some condensed and highly abstract symbol. A survey (National Education Association, 1967), supported by another study by Pinchak and Breland (1974), found that a system of numerical or letter grades was used in about 80% of American school systems, except in the first grade, where the percentage was 73, and in the kindergarten, where it was 17. Unfortunately, the study of grading has not received much attention in recent literature (Stiggins, Frisbie, & Griswold, 1989).

The use of highly condensed symbols to convey the teacher's evaluation has frequently been criticized for reasons that we shall consider now. The alternatives that have been offered to replace the conventional A, B, C, D, or F system have problems of their own, and no fully satisfactory replacement for this type of grade seems to be at hand.

Importance of Grades

Grades are deeply embedded in the educational culture. They have become the basis, in whole or in part, for a wide range of actions and decisions within educational institutions and between these institutions and the outside world. Eligibility for admission to certain programs or departments, for scholarship aid, for membership on athletic teams, and for continuing in school is often determined by academic standing. Admission to college or graduate school is usually based, at least in part, on grades received at the previous academic level. Thus, there are many points within the educational system where grades interact with the administrative and instructional process to affect the student's progress.

The Need for Grades

Most learning theorists, from behaviorists to cognitive psychologists, have emphasized the need for feedback in the facilitation of learning. We know that it is difficult for someone to improve unless they know how well they are doing. The process of growing and developing requires the testing of limits, and children need to know how they stand in relation to peers or to some goal. This process is halted when the feedback is inaccurate. The natural inclination of teachers is to be helpful and supportive, and they tend to dislike giving feedback that is not positive. But, if students receive unjustified positive feedback, progress can be stunted. If students are to improve, they need to know where improvement is needed.

Parents also need to know how their children are progressing in school. There are a number of possible means of fulfilling this need, including anecdotal records, teacher conferences, and/or lists of objectives mastered or not mastered. Experience has shown that parents know, understand, and respond best to the traditional methods of assigning grades. To institute an alternate system of providing feedback to parents and students, a tremendous amount of parent education would be necessary. To date, attempts to substitute alternate methods of reporting student progress have met with strong parental objections.

Furthermore, parents have a right to the accurate reporting of their children's progress in school, in terms that they understand. Avoiding the anguish of assigning grades by only giving high grades is a dereliction of duty. Nothing is more damaging to parent-school rapport than to have parents erroneously believe that their child has no academic problems. The school does no one a favor by shielding a child in this manner. In fact, there have recently been successful lawsuits filed against schools for awarding students high school diplomas when they could not do sixth-grade work.

The school also has a responsibility to certify that students have mastered the assigned curriculum, at least at some minimal level, in the courses they have taken. If a student receives a satisfactory grade in a course, it is reasonable for a prospective employer or school to assume that the grade represents a meaningful mastery of subject matter. Clearly, certification is not a school's only responsibility, or even its first responsibility, but it is a responsibility nevertheless.

The traditional grading system has been durable and resistant to change for the reasons discussed and because no better alternative system has been found.

A Perspective for Examining Grades

Like any other deeply ingrained aspect of a culture, grading procedures are often taken for granted, with a minimum of rational analysis of their nature and their functions. As we examine them, our approach should be, in part, that of the cultural anthropologist who looks at a set of odd but presumably meaningful behavior patterns and tries to understand the functions they serve and the manner in which they relate to the total culture of which they are a part. We should try to put aside our personal involvement, look at the phenomenon with the cold eye of the social scientist, and endeavor to identify the forces that shape and sustain present grading practices. We also need to try to understand the pressures within the educational culture that make the practices resistant to change and sometimes irrational.

Technical Issues Surrounding Grading Procedures

Now that we have explored, in general terms, the role of grades in the educational culture, let us turn to some of the technical problems associated with assigning grades to students. The discussion will be organized around five main questions.

1. On what should a grade be based?
2. In relation to what should grades be assigned?
3. How should component data be weighted in arriving at a grade?
4. In how many categories, or subdivisions, should grades be reported?
5. What fraction of students should receive each grade?

Note that many of these questions are phrased in terms of a "should" and that issues of value as well as fact arise in connection with each of them. As we consider these questions in turn, we will have to address ourselves first to the underlying issues of value and then to the problems of technique and implementation. It furthermore should be remembered that a student's grade is not an inherent, fixed characteristic like blood type, and the goal of student evaluation should not be the establishment of this "true" grade. It is necessary to accept that grades are global estimates of student functioning, which to some degree are subjective and relative to the setting in which they are assigned.

On What Should a Grade Be Based?   Perhaps the most basic issue to consider is whether a grade should represent as pure and accurate an appraisal of achievement in a segment of the curriculum as can be devised on whether it should be modified by other factors. Some of the potential modifiers are extra credit work completed, neatness, legibility, correctness in the mechanics of written or oral expression, attitude, motivation, effort, interest, and personality.

We believe that the purposes for reporting student evaluations are best served by grades that are as nearly pure measures of achievement as possible. The use of extra credit is discouraged because it involves assignments completed by only some students. Such a process makes it difficult to make comparisons between students who complete extra credit work and those who do not. Likewise, neatness, legibility and correctness in the mechanics of written or oral expression should not be factors in determining grades except when the skills have been identified as legitimate objectives for a course.

Other factors that should not be considered in determining grades are attitude, motivation, effort, and personality. Their inclusion is not recommended because these characteristics are so difficult to measure. Furthermore, such a practice could lead to confusion in the interpretation of the meaning of grades. It would not be clear whether a student who received a B got the grade as a result of the achievement of the course objectives or some combination of other factors such as neatness, attitude, or personality. Even though it is not recommended, teachers tend to take these factors into account (Stiggins, Frisbie, & Griswold, 1989) They find it difficult to ignore the potential of the highly able students, requiring more of them than of other students, and they may assign lower grades to students perceived not to be functioning up to their potential. At the same time, teachers tend to give the benefit of the doubt to hard-working students with low levels of aptitude.

In Relation to What Should Grades Be Assigned?   All grading methods are based on comparisons, or references, to some standard. These comparisons are necessary because raw scores from tests are not meaningful by themselves. Raw scores can either be in the form of the number of questions correct, as is the case with an objective test, or in the form of the number of points obtained, which are often used on more subjective tests. Although these scores may have some intrinsic meaning, they do not tell us much about absolute performance, and they require further interpretation before they can be used for assigning grades. There are five approaches, or frames of reference, that can be used:

1. intuitive
2. ipsative
3. reference to perfection
4. criterion-referenced
5. norm referenced

These terms are often used to distinguish between different types of tests, but it is more accurate to think of them as representing different methods of interpreting the results of tests. The tests and the items on which they are based may all look the same; it is the way the results are expressed and the interpretation of their meaning that may differ.

1. The Intuitive Approach. The use of the intuitive approach does not require a careful delineation of course requirements and grading policies because the teacher is expected to know intuitively how a student should perform to receive a certain grade. This approach is similar to norm-referenced testing because the teacher generally makes a subconscious comparison with all of the other students with whom he or she has had experience.

The intuitive approach is most often used at the elementary school level. This approach can be justified under some circumstances, but it requires experience and permits extraneous factors to play an important role in decisions about grades. It may be possible to be successful with such an approach if you have the experience and the nerve to pull it off, but the odds are against you. It is particularly difficult to justify this approach when the resulting grades are to be used for making high stakes decisions.

2. Ipsative Approaches. There are two ways that a student's performance can be compared to his or her own characteristics: in terms of ability and in terms of effort. It is not recommended that either of these be used by teachers as the basis for assigning grades. It is instead recommended that a student's grade, as much as possible, be a pure measure of achievement. The process of basing grades on the relationship between ability and achievement is beset by measurement questions. We generally estimate potential through inferences made from measurements of achievement, and separating potential and achievement has proved to be elusive. Quantifying effort may be even more difficult. The teacher can make this judgment subjectively, but generally, like potential, it is assessed by comparing a student's performance at the beginning of a grading period with his or her performance at the conclusion. The student who starts the year behind but shows improvement might get a higher grade than the one who is far ahead at the beginning of the year, shows no improvement, but is still ahead at the year's end. The usefulness of such an approach depends on how accurately the initial level of performance is measured; therefore, this approach should not be used with sophisticated students who might fake a low-entry skill level to show large gains.

When final performance in a class depends heavily on incoming level of ability, teachers find grading difficult. The importance of incoming level of ability is particularly noticeable in courses like art, music, and foreign languages. On the first day of class, there will be some students who can perform at a level that far exceeds that which other students with less ability may ever achieve. With minimal effort, they can remain ahead of other students who work much harder. There is an understandable reluctance to ignore the degree of improvement or effort that students with less ability may exhibit over the year. The student gifted in art who does nothing for a semester may not deserve an A, despite the fact that at the end of the course he or she can produce the best project. Conversely, it seems only fair to give credit to the student who starts with little ability but who, by expending great effort, shows considerable improvement. Most teachers have no problem with such a grading policy for these or similar courses, but there is much less willingness to use a system of grading based on effort and potential in what are considered "academic" subjects. Reluctance to consider effort and potential occurs even though one is likely to encounter a similarly wide range of entry ability in an English or algebra class.

3. Reference to Perfection Approach. When a teacher walks into a classroom and places the following scale or some permutation on the chalkboard, he or she is evaluating students using the reference-to-perfection approach.

A	95–100
B	88–94
C	80–87
D	70–79
F	Below 70

This method is most often used for communicating the meaning of a student's score on a teacher-made test. Textbooks on teaching in general, as well as textbooks on measurement in particular, are highly critical of this approach. It is nevertheless a popular approach to assigning grades because it is easy to implement and has a long tradition. It even has been institutionalized by entire school systems. They tend to embrace this approach because it creates the illusion that grades mean the same thing across courses. Because a lot of high-stakes decisions are made on the basis of grades, a need exists to believe that grades have meaning beyond the individual classroom. A systemwide grading system can help maintain this illusion.

The primary assumption underlying the reference-to-perfection approach to grading is the requirement that a score of 100% represents a meaningful entity. We must know what 100% means when applied to a specific test. Consider a test administered to third graders that consists of all possible single-digit multiplication problems. Such a test (albeit a prohibitively long one) would consist of all 100 facts. In this case, a test made up of a random sample of these facts would permit meaningful statements about percentages of knowledge because the meaning of the entire domain is known. A perfect score would mean that the student knew all such facts. A score of 80% would indicate that the student knew

80% of the facts. In this case, the score has a meaningful relationship with complete mastery.

There may be some limited segments of curricular material for which it is possible to make a complete catalog of what needs to be learned. Common examples would be (1) the 100 multiplication "facts," (2) the symbols representing the chemical elements, and (3) the names of all the bones in the body. When the number of items is finite and definable, it is possible to assess the examinee with all or a representative sample of the items, and to report his or her performance as a percentage of perfect performance.

As indicated already, the subject matter for which 100% is meaningful represents only a fairly small fraction of school learning. Even for these limited segments, precision in the description of performance in terms of percentages may be somewhat illusory because we may have to specify the task so completely that it becomes trivial. Thus, a child who can answer the question "What does 4×5 equal?" may fail on the question "What will four 5-cent candy bars cost?" Does the child "know" the multiplication facts if he or she cannot apply them in a problem context? Whether the multiplication facts are known would depend on how the domain of single-digit multiplication problems was defined. It could include just the simple multiplications facts or all possible word problems whose solution requires the correct application of the "$4 \times 5 = 20$" fact. At any rate, even the most basic computational facts are not easily defined. The difficulties associated with more complex subject matter are obvious. For these reasons, basing grades on percentage correct is of limited use.

In most cases, a score of 100% correct means only that the student answered all of the questions correctly. There is a big difference between answering all of the questions correctly and knowing everything in the domain. To use the reference-to-perfection approach, we need to know how the items on a test are related to the domain of all possible questions that could be asked on a given test. We also need to know what it means when a student gets no answers correct. In other words, we need to be able to define absolute zero.

For the reference-to-perfection approach to work, we must also assume that all tests are equally and appropriately difficult. This assumption is almost always so absurd that it needs no refutation. Because various tests differ in terms of difficulty, we are not measuring a student in any absolute sense; the grade a student gets is more a function of the chance factors that go into determining the difficulty of a test than a function of anything else.

Despite its obvious limitations, this is the most often used method of assigning grades. Teachers who use this approach quickly learn that, as a result of variability in test difficulty, they are likely to obtain grade distributions contrary to their expectations. These unanticipated grade distributions lead to adjustments in the grading system. Teachers start out with a grading scale that specifies the raw score necessary for different grades, they construct and administer the test, and finally they examine the resulting grade distribution. If the test proves to be too difficult and an unacceptable number of low grades seems imminent, some sort of adjustments must be made. The usual method of adjusting the scale is either to award extra credit in some way or to make the next test easier. Similarly, if the test is too easy, the teacher will have to grade harder or make the next test more difficult. The goal is to bring the distribution within the limits of the expected range of acceptable grades. In this way, the best students still get the highest grades, the poor students get the lowest grades, and the distribution of grades is kept within acceptable limits, but it bears little relationship to the percentage of the domain that has been mastered.

Your first reaction to this might be that such adjustments are dishonest and that students should get the grade they deserve. The reference-to-perfection approach, however, does not tell us the grade a student deserves, which is its big promise and major failing. There is simply nothing innately revealing about the ratio of the number of questions a student answers correctly to the total number of items on a test.

Students are usually satisfied with explanations of grading policies based on the reference-to-perfection approach because they are familiar with them. In the event that they begin to think about this approach in any depth, they are likely to be less satisfied. Because the reference-to-perfection approach is so indirect and misleading, it cannot easily be explained to students or peers. The forced adjustments to obtain acceptable distributions of grades are not easily justified either.

The use of this method of student evaluation continues unabated, largely as a result of ignorance. Students demand an explanation of grading policies, and they get one. The use of this approach to determine grades continues as a result of the gap between what is known about the best ways to conduct educational evaluation and what teachers believe can reasonably be applied in the classroom.

4. Criterion-Referenced Approaches.   Although teacher-made tests are most often evaluated by means of reference to perfection, criterion-referenced testing has also enjoyed some popularity. One of the problems with using this method is the lack of agreement about the definition of criterion-referenced tests. (See Chapters 3 and 7 for definitions of criterion-referenced tests.)

Using criterion-referenced methods of assigning grades is awkward. Strictly speaking, using this method, a student has either mastered or not mastered an objective. The forcing of students into one of two categories makes it difficult to decide whether the student who masters should get an A, a B, or a C. Of course, it is possible to devise a system based on partial mastery or the mastery of a given proportion of objectives. The major problem encountered with such systems, however, is devising a rational basis for its accomplishment. What generally happens is that such decisions become subjective, and you are left with a system quite similar to the reference-to-perfection approach. A set of arbitrary standards must be set up to designate the number of items that must be correct before it can be said that a student has mastered an objective. Likewise, the proportion of objectives necessary for each grade must be designated. Unless the items measuring an objective were randomly selected from the domain of all possible items, the grades a student gets are determined by item difficulty and the cutoff scores that have been set by the teacher.

A pass/fail system is probably the only acceptable form of grading with this method. However, the all too common practice of assigning an A to students who master certain skills results in rampant grade inflation and a general denigration of the grading process.

5. *Norm-Referenced Approach.*   This frame of reference endeavors to express individual performance in relation to a comparison group. It is used with standardized test to establish norms, as described in Chapter 3. The reference group for grades assigned in school is generally much more limited. It may be the total student body of the school or some unit of it, the total group taking some course, the total group in a particular teacher's section, or the ill-defined total group of previous students that shape a teacher's impressions of what is good, average, or poor performance.

The simplest frame of reference is one that does not go beyond the single teacher. Grades are assigned either in relation to a specific class group or in relation to the more general but vague inner standard held by the teacher. If the specific class is used to provide the reference frame, there is always the possibility that the students in one class may in some way be unrepresentative and that each student may receive either an unfair penalty or an unwarranted bonus because of the nature of that reference group. If the "inner standard" is used, there is the problem of its subjectivity and variability from teacher to teacher or even from time to time by the same teacher.

The term "grading on the curve" is often used in connection with this type of system. Grading on the curve is difficult to define because it is used in the vernacular and it does not have the same meaning for everyone who employs it. It can refer to the same process described here in which a student's performance is interpreted in relation to that of others. Sometimes, it also refers to the discredited practice of assigning grades according to a rough approximation of the normal curve. With such a system, most students get a C. A somewhat lower but equal number of students get Bs and Ds, and a few but equal number of students get Fs or As. The irrationality of this approach seems obvious, so this approach is seldom employed. When grading on a curve, or "curving" a test, is discussed, it is a good idea to find out exactly what grading practices are being described.

How Should Component Data Be Weighted in Arriving at a Grade?   As stated earlier, a student's grade, as much as possible, should be a pure measure of a student's performance in a class. There are, however, many ways to assess performance, and teachers generally will use several. A teacher might include, for example, components of a grade, test scores, grades on papers, performance on homework assignments and projects, class participation, or other indications of student performance that a teacher might decide to include. Once the components of a grade are determined, the teacher must decide how much each is to be weighted. Typically, a teacher will want to give more weight to components of a grade that are deemed more important or more reliable indicators of student performance. The weighting of components is generally expressed in percentages. For example, a teacher might decide that weekly quizzes will constitute 20% of a student's grade, a project 30%, the final examination 40%, and class participation 10%.

Once a teacher has decided what weight to allocate to each kind of data, it is necessary to be sure that each component of a grade does, in fact, receive that weight. The usual method for combining scores is to add the raw score or points allocated to an assignment. It is often incorrectly assumed that if two tests yield the same number of points, the tests are weighted the same. This assumption is only true if the distribution of scores for each test is on the same scale, which means that they have the same standard deviation.

Suppose a teacher wishes to have a midterm examination count 30%, a final examination count 40%, a term paper count 20%, and class participation count 10%. A common but incorrect way of accomplishing this would be to include 60 items on the midterm examination and have each correct answer count a half point, for a total of 30 points; to include 80 items on the final examination for a total of 40 points; and to award 20 and 10 points for the term paper and class participation, respectively. This process of assigning points to components of grades would yield a total of 100 points and create the illusion that the various components were weighted appropriately. An example of the use of this point system with 10 students is illustrated in Table 6.1.

Notice that Jean and Betty ended up with the most points and therefore could be expected to get the highest grades. The problem is that with this approach, differences in variability among the components of the grade are ignored.

As long as tests that are to be combined are of about the same length and difficulty, the variability will probably be similar enough for the teacher to be on fairly safe ground. However, when inputs such as scores from tests of different lengths and formats and term papers that are not based on a common scoring system are combined, or when the teacher wants to weight components of the grade differently, raw scores should not be totaled. Before they can be combined in a meaningful way, they must be placed on the same scale. The best way of doing this is to compute converted scores (C scores), as was explained in Chapter 3, under "Standard Scores." These C scores can be multiplied by a weighting factor and treated mathematically with confidence that the intended weighting is the weighting that actually occurs.

Table 6.2 lists the same students as used in the previous example along with their raw scores and weighted C scores. The following formula was used to obtain the weighted C scores. It is presented in the same linear format that would be used with a computer or programmable calculator:

$$\text{Weighted } C \text{ score} = (\{[(\text{Raw Score} - \text{Mean}) \div \text{Standard Deviation}] \times 10\} + 50) \times \text{Weighting}$$

Consider Bob's score on the midterm, for example. To obtain his weighted C score, you subtract 54.4 (the mean for the midterm) from 58 (Bob's raw score on the midterm), which leaves a value of 3.6. This value (3.6) would be divided by 2.15 (the standard deviation for the midterm), giving you a value of 1.6. This

TABLE 6.1
Computation of Grades by Summing Raw Scores

| Student | Midterm | | Final | | Paper | | Class Participation | | Total | Rank |
	Raw Score	Points	Raw Score	Points	Raw Score	Points	Raw Score	Points		
Bob	58	29	70	35	3	3	1	1	68	10
Alice	56	28	64	32	12	12	6	6	78	4
June	54	27	60	30	13	13	7	7	77	5
Joe	54	27	68	34	9	9	5	5	75	6
Al	56	28	70	35	4	4	2	2	69	9
Betty	50	25	60	30	19	19	10	10	84	2
Jean	52	26	60	30	20	20	9	9	85	1
Jerry	54	27	66	33	10	10	4	4	74	7
Bill	56	28	68	34	6	6	3	3	71	8
Mary	54	27	62	31	15	15	7	7	80	3

TABLE 6.2
Computation of Grades Using Weighted C-scores

Student	Midterm		Final		Paper		Class Participation		Total	Rank
	Raw Score	C Score	Raw Score	C Score	Raw Score	C Score	Raw Score	C Score		
Bob	58	20.0	70	25.3	3	7.1	1	3.4	55.8	1
Alice	56	17.2	64	19.2	12	10.3	6	5.2	51.9	5
June	54	14.4	60	15.1	13	10.7	7	5.6	45.8	9
Joe	54	14.4	68	23.1	9	9.2	5	4.9	53.8	2
Al	56	17.2	70	25.3	4	7.4	2	3.8	53.8	2
Betty	50	8.9	60	15.1	19	12.9	10	6.6	43.4	10
Jean	52	11.6	60	15.1	20	13.2	9	6.3	46.2	8
Jerry	54	14.4	66	21.2	10	9.6	4	4.5	49.8	6
Bill	56	17.2	68	23.3	6	8.2	3	4.1	52.8	4
Mary	54	14.4	62	17.1	15	11.4	7	5.6	48.5	7
Mean	54.4		64.8		11.1		5.4			
Standard deviation	2.15		3.91		5.55		2.8			

value (1.6) would be divided by 10 and added to 50 to yield a *C* score of 66.7. Multiplying this value (66.7) by the weighting for the midterm of 0.30 results in a score of 20.02 rounded off to 20. This process would be repeated for each raw score, and the weighted *C* scores would be totaled.

An examination Tables 6.1 and 6.2 reveals a sharp contrast in the obtained ranking. They are nearly opposites. The students who seem most deserving of a high grade when points are totaled, Jean and Betty fare much worse when *C* scores are used. The above example is rather extreme. It may be unusual for those who do well on the tests to do so poorly on the term paper and class participation and vice versa. This juxtaposition of scores was selected to dramatize the differences between the results obtained by the two methods. However, this example does illustrate the crucial importance of differences in variability when scores are combined.

In How Many Categories, or Subdivisions, Should Grades Be Reported?
Evaluations may be reported very crudely in only two categories such as "pass" and "fail," in the widely used five-letter system (A, B, C, D, or F), in a 13-category system where pluses and minuses are attached to all grades except F, or in a percentage system that nominally can take any one of 100 values. How can we decide which is preferable? As usual, the issues are partly those of value and partly those of fact.

Arguments concerning the values involved tend to center on the belief that less emphasis should be given to the competitive pressures and the presumably irrelevant goals represented by grades. Those who believe that grades should be deemphasized advocate a coarse grading system that, in effect, makes only a few discriminations. This gain is bought, of course, at the expense of most of the information that the grading system might possibly supply about the individual.

When the number of categories is small, there are relatively few students who fall close to dividing lines between categories, and for these few students who do, it makes a big difference whether they are placed in the higher or the lower category. As the number of categories increases, the number of borderline decisions increases correspondingly, but each decision becomes less important because the categories differ so little. With a pass/fail system, for example, most students belong unambiguously in the pass or the fail category, but for those on the borderline, any error in categorization would be of considerable importance. At the other extreme, with a system in which performance is reported as a percentage from 1 to 100, everyone is on the border of a category, but whether a student gets an 87 or an 88 would be of little importance. With few categories, there is a decreased frequency of potential error in categorization balanced by a increase in the importance of that error. With many categories the opposite occurs; there are many more errors of categorization, which are of less significance.

What Fraction of Students Should Receive Each Grade?   Determining how many of each grade to assign is a difficult process because we are forced to rely on subjective decisions that themselves depend more on the cultural milieu in which we are operating than on any other factor. Regardless of the setting in which grades are assigned, there will be rules governing the number of each grade a teacher can assign. These rules may be written down explicitly or involve an implicit understanding. No one may ever tell the teacher the rules, but he or she will know and follow them anyway. Rules are in the form of acceptable ranges of grades. These differ from institution to institution; some will be liberal and allow many high grades, while others are more conservative and mandate that teachers give some low grades. Some teachers might choose to be at the high end of the range, give many As and be labeled an easy grader, and others might choose to function at the low end of the range, give out more low grades and be labeled with terminology unprintable here. If the teacher violates the limits, he or she will most likely hear from the principal, dean, or boss and feel peer pressure. The enforcement of the rules varies depending on the setting. The important point is that there are rules, teachers will know what the rules are, and most likely teachers will stay within the limits of the rules.

The cutoff points that determine the number of each grade assigned should be determined by three factors: (1) the limits imposed by the teaching setting; (2) whether the teacher chooses to be an easy, hard, or middle-of-the-road grader; and (3) the teacher's perception of the general level of functioning of the class. If a class seems particularly bright, the teacher will be inclined to give more As and Bs and fewer low grades. If it is the teacher's perception that the class as a whole is performing poorly, he or she is likely to assign more low grades.

In most educational institutions, an uneasy equilibrium is reached between the grading symbol system and the social consequences of particular grades. The percentage of academic failures remains fairly stable from year to year; average grades within a department maintain themselves at a fairly stable level, varying from department to department; and new faculty members are informally initiated into the culture and maintain its general character, while superimposing their individual idiosyncrasies on it. The equilibrium, however, is maintained by an intuitive, unexamined process.

GPA has been found to be unresponsive to real changes in the characteristics of the student population (e.g., see Baird & Feister, 1972) but seems to be subject to the same sort of inflationary pressures that plague national economies. The rationale for teacher, course, and department differences in distribution of grades is, to say the least, obscure. The cultural norms governing how grading symbols are used throughout a school or college deserve conscious scrutiny to make sure that the categories are, in fact, being used in ways that serve the purposes of the institution and the larger educational system of which it is a part.

Conclusions About Grades and Grading

Grading systems are deeply embedded in the educational culture and serve a number of legitimate educational ends. For this reason, they are likely to survive for some time to come. Among the purposes served with at least a minimal level of success are (1) informing parents about how their child is perceived by the school, (2) helping to form the individual's picture of himself or herself as a learner and to set goals for further levels of learning, (3) regulating the flow into specific programs and activities within an educational institution, and (4) monitoring admission to more advanced educational institutions and the world of work.

Like any deeply ingrained aspect of a culture, grading and grading practices involve motivations that are only partly accessible to inspection at the conscious level and are correspondingly resistant to change. Before grading practices can be made more sound psychometrically, their rationales must be subjected to careful scrutiny. Because many, perhaps most, of the issues relating to the assignment of grades are issues of value, an examination of grading practices must address itself first to a clarification of these values.

Summary

A major theme of this book is the examination of the relationship between measurement and decision making. The type of decisions that are emphasized occur in the classroom, but there are other types of decisions that require information about student performance obtained from other sources that are also important. The difference between formative and summative assessment is emphasized. Whether one chooses achievement tests, the assessment material packaged with instructional materials, oral tests, product evaluations, performance tests, or affective measures is determined by the nature of the decisions to be made. In this chapter, we also discuss the use of tests to make placement decisions and day-by-day instructional decisions as well as to report academic progress to parents. Additionally, we discuss assessment techniques used for making selection and curricular decisions.

One of the most important types of educational decisions is the assignment of grades. Grades are always comparative. The comparisons can be made on the basis of intuition; they can be ipsative, referenced to perfection, or criterion or norm referenced. Individuals involved in evaluating the information used to make decisions about grades need to consider what data should be taken into account in determining grades, the selection of the appropriate reference, the weighting of component data, the number of categories required, and the proportion of students that should get each grade.

Questions and Exercises

1. Prepare a brief criterion-referenced test to measure a specific skill in arithmetic, language usage, or some other field.
2. What sort of decisions might be made on the basis of performance on this test?
3. What values are implied by the use of such a test?
4. For a fifth-grade class, give an example of the type of objective that would be assessed by each of the following methods: a pencil-and-paper test, an oral test, a product evaluation, a performance test, and assessment of affective characteristics.
5. Why might a test that is suitable as a measure of past achievement have limited value for a placement decision?

6. What procedures might a community college use to place entering freshmen into sections for a required English course? What would be the objectives of such sectioning? What gains might be expected? What losses?

7. In April of the sixth grade, Helen has a reading grade equivalent on the Iowa Tests of Basic Skills of 6.2 (second month of sixth grade). How should this be interpreted if her nonverbal standard age score on the Cognitive Abilities Test is 85? If it is 115? If it is 135?

8. How does your answer to the above question change as you shift from "performance in relation to potential" to "performance in relation to par"?

9. What would be involved in preparing a proficiency test for television repairmen? What form might the test take?

10. In what ways might a testing program to evaluate a proposed modified mathematics curriculum differ from a program designed to place students in the appropriate mathematics section?

11. It has been proposed that while the A, B, C, D, F system of grading is relative, a percentage system represents an absolute appraisal. What are the arguments for and against this point of view? Are there any systems of appraisal that are based on an absolute standard? Identify one, and give the evidence to support your position.

12. In what way(s) is the grading system in a school similar to a rating procedure? In what way(s) does it differ? What factors that limit the effectiveness of ratings also limit the effectiveness of a grading system?

13. How is the general level of ability of a student's class likely to affect the grades that a student will get? How should it affect them?

14. What should be the role of student self-appraisal in evaluating educational progress? What are the limits of such an appraisal?

15. Try to get copies of the report cards used in one or more school systems. Examine them, and compare them with the cards obtained by other class members. What similarities and differences do you note? What shortcomings do you feel they have?

16. Talk to a school principal or superintendent, and find out what changes have been made in reporting practices while he or she has been in the school system. Why were the changes made? How satisfied is he or she with the result? What provisions are made for parent-teacher conferences? How satisfactorily have these worked out? What problems have arisen?

17. What problems arise when you try to have grades on a report card reflect aptitude and effort?

18. Comment on the following proposition: A course grade is most useful when it measures as accurately as possible the pupil's mastery of the direct objectives of the course and is not influenced by any other factors.

19. For a course that you might teach or plan to teach, list the types of evidence you plan to consider in arriving at course grades. Indicate the weight to be given to each. Why have you allocated the weights in this way?

20. A teacher has decided to give equal weight in a biology course to (1) a series of quizzes, (2) a final examination, and (3) laboratory grades. A study of the score distributions shows that the standard deviation of the quiz is 10—what weight should be given to the raw scores to give the desired weight to the three components of the final grade?

21. What is meant by the phrase "to grade on a curve"? When should this approach be used? How does a teacher determine the proportion of students that should receive each grade?

22. What is the difference between norm-referenced grading and grading on the curve?
23. What steps would you propose to take to reduce differences between the grading standards of teachers?
24. In College Y, there are 10 sections of freshman English. What steps could be taken to ensure uniform grading standards, so that a student is not penalized by being in a particular section?
25. It has been proposed that "schools should abandon grades and report only 'pass' or 'fail' for students." What would be the gains from such a procedure? What would be the losses? How would the functions now served (admittedly imperfectly) by grades be discharged? How adequate would these alternative procedures be?
26. A school principal remarked to his board of education: "We have higher standards than Mason High. Our passing grade is 70, and theirs is only 65." What assumptions is he making in this statement? How defensible are these assumptions?
27. It has been suggested that grades must be approached as a cultural rather than a psychometric phenomenon. What merit is there in this point of view? What are some of its implications?

Suggested Readings

Bloom, B. S., Hastings, J. T., & Madaus, C. F. (1971). *Handbook on formative and summative evaluation of student learning.* New York: McGraw-Hill.

Cunningham, G. K. (1986). *Educational and psychological measurement.* New York: Macmillan.

Gronlund, N. E., & Linn, R. L. (1990). *Measurement and evaluation in teaching.* New York: Macmillan.

Gullickson, A. R., & Hopkins, K. D. (1987). The context of educational measurement instruction for preservice teachers: Professor perspectives. *Issues and Practices, 6*(3), 12–16.

Popham, W. James. (1990). *Modern educational measurement: A practitioner's perspective.* Englewood Cliffs, NJ: Prentice-Hall.

Slavin, R. E. (1987). Mastery learning reconsidered. *Review of Educational Research, 57*(2), 175–213.

Slavin, R. E. (1988). *Educational psychology: Theory into Practice.* Englewood Cliffs, NJ: Prentice-Hall.

Stiggins, R. J., & Bridgeford, N.J. (1985). The ecology of classroom assessment. *Journal of Educational Measurement, 22*(4), 271–286.

Stiggins, R. J., Frisbie, D. A., & Griswold, P. A. (1989). Inside high school grading practices: Building a research agenda. *Educational Measurement: Issues and Practices, 8*(2), 5–14.

Terwilliger, J. S. (1989). Classroom standard setting and grading practices. *Educational Measurement: Issues and Practices, 8*(2), 15–19.

CHAPTER 7

Locally Constructed Tests

Introduction

In Chapter 6 we discussed the types of educational decisions for which measures of academic achievement might be useful. We concluded that the use of standardized achievement tests is appropriate in some cases, but in others a locally constructed test is more suitable. As a general rule, when there is a need to assess the degree of mastery of a unit of instruction or to appraise progress toward locally defined curricular goals, a test that is constructed to fit the local purpose will be more appropriate than any that could be found in test publishers' catalogs. To measure cognitive skills, paper-and-pencil tests are generally used. This chapter will focus on this type of test. The evaluation of other types of learning outcomes will be discussed in Chapters 8 and 9.

Testing Practices of Teachers

Although it is not always easy to evaluate the validity of the informal assessments made by teachers, the methods teachers use in conducting more formal assessments can be compared with what experts consider to be appropriate. Such a comparison reveals a gap between the practices that professionals in the field of test construction believe are most effective and the actual practices employed by teachers. That this situation is an aspect of measurement about which the experts agree makes the problem worse. There are procedures for constructing test items and for performing analyses of test results that can be expected to result in a good test. In contrast with other aspects of education, there is remarkable agreement regarding what these procedures should be.

Reasons for Poor Testing Procedures

There are three main reasons why test construction procedures that teachers use are less than optimum. (1) Considering its importance and the amount of time that teachers must devote to this activity, they are seldom well trained in techniques for test construction and there is a lamentably small amount of course-work on this topic required in most teacher-preparation programs. Furthermore, follow-up studies have tended to show that teachers have not retained or been willing to apply what they *have* learned. (2) The agreed-upon methodology for constructing and the methodology for conducting analyses of test results are not easy to understand, and even when they are well understood, they are time consuming. (3) Analyses of item properties and test reliability require the teacher to understand and be capable of performing difficult computations. Teachers too often conclude, considering all that they are required to do in the course of a day, that it is not worthwhile for them to devote so much time to this effort.

Given the amount of time and effort required, it is understandable that a teacher might not follow all the rules for test construction and conduct all of the necessary analyses, but there is no excuse for a teacher not using some of these techniques, particularly those that can be performed fairly easily. Furthermore, adherence to good testing procedures will increase the efficiency of testing, make the test scores more meaningful, and ultimately save time.

Requirements for Good Test Construction

To construct a good test, a teacher must devote an adequate amount of time, plan the test, and analyze the test results in some way. At a minimum, once the test has been constructed and administered, a teacher should know how the typical or average student performed on the test. The computations needed to obtain this information can be accomplished quickly and easily with a calculator. When Gullickson and Ellwein (1985) surveyed elementary and secondary teachers in a state that required a course in measurement for certification, only 13% of the teachers reported computing the mean and 12% the median. Neither of these computations require much time or statistical sophistication. With the increased availability of personal computers in schools, classrooms, and teacher's homes and better, more easily used and appropriate software, it may be possible to make even some of the more sophisticated procedures accessible. Computer availability, however, will not take the place of good teacher-training programs and appropriate in-service activities.

Some important aspects of the test construction process, for example, good planning abilities, do not require statistical skills and should be in any good teacher's repertoire of skills. Motivation may be more of a problem than is lack of knowledge. Teachers and prospective teachers need to understand that there are techniques that lead to better student assessment and to accept the idea that it is worth the effort to learn and to apply these techniques.

Time Commitment

Constructing a good classroom test takes time, and there is no way this fact can be avoided. When test construction is delayed to the point that it has to be rushed, the main objective becomes having something ready at the designated time. It is unlikely that the test that is prepared under these conditions will be able to assess student performance accurately. It is important for teachers to devote the time and effort necessary for effective planning, item writing, and follow-up evaluations of the items so that they will have an effective assessment device when the task is completed.

Planning the Test

Many locally made tests suffer from a weakness in, or even an absence of, planning carried out before work is begun on writing the test exercises. Before a single question or problem is written, planning must take place. One way to structure this planning is to provide the best answer to the following questions:

1. What is the purpose of the test? And who is it intended to serve? Will it guide immediate instructional decisions about what is to be taught or retaught? Is

it intended to assess the general level of competence or to evaluate the effectiveness of some segment of the school's program?

2. What objectives is the school or the teacher trying to achieve?

3. What content has been covered in the course? How much emphasis has been given to each topic?

4. What types of test exercises will be both practical and effective in providing evidence about how thoroughly students have achieved the course objectives?

Purpose of the Test

To do a good job of assessing student performance, a teacher must fully understand the purpose of the test and how it functions in the overall assessment program. If the test is intended to determine a student's overall ability, for the purpose of making a placement decision, then a standardized achievement test might be appropriate. If the purpose is to assess degree of mastery of some specific skill to permit a decision about what to teach or to study next, a sharply focused minitest of the type illustrated by the prime numbers test and the capitalization test (both in Figure 6.1) is called for. If the need is for diagnostic information, either a published diagnostic test or a teacher-made diagnostic test would be appropriate. Summative testing of course objectives can generally be best implemented by teacher-made surveys of course content, product evaluations, or performance tests.

Using Instructional Objectives

There is little disagreement about the need for statements of objectives. Nearly all curriculum guides used in public schools, individual education plans required for special education students, and syllabi mandated by the National Council for Accreditation in Teacher Education are required to have the objectives of their educational programs explicitly stated. In general, curriculum is described in terms of the objectives to be achieved. Differences of opinion about instructional objectives are most likely to emerge regarding the degree of specificity with which the objectives must be written, the necessity that they be stated behaviorally, the need for domain specifications, and the relative merits of norm- and criterion-referenced tests.

Defining Criterion-Referenced Tests

As defined in Chapter 3, criterion-referenced testing is a form of evaluation that reports results in terms of what a student can do rather than how the student compares to others. The purpose of this approach is to describe as accurately as possible what test results mean in terms of specific student behaviors.

Criterion- and Norm-Referenced Tests

While norm-referenced tests are used to make inferences about how much a student has learned in comparison with others, criterion-referenced tests are used to make absolute, not relative, decisions about whether a student has learned specific course content. For this reason, the author of a criterion-referenced test must carefully choose the difficulty of items and ensure that each objective refers to a well-defined domain. That is, the items associated with an objective must be samples from the domain of all possible items that could measure the objective. Of course, items for norm-referenced tests also need to be thought of as being derived from a well-defined domain. But the domain will be broader and less well defined, and direct inferences are not made about which objectives have been mastered.

The Diversity in Definitions of Criterion-Referenced Tests

Unfortunately, the term *criterion-referenced* carries with it a diversity of meaning. Its meaning to one person might be quite different from its meaning to another. The critical aspect of a criterion referenced test is its capacity to provide information about what a student has learned in terms of mastery of objectives. If the results of a test do not convey this information, the test is not criterion referenced. You are likely to see three types of tests labeled criterion-referenced, but only the last one, domain-referenced tests, should be so labeled (Nitko, 1983; Popham, 1980).

Tests with Cutoff Scores.   Tests that have a cutoff score are sometimes mislabeled as criterion-referenced tests presumably because the cutoff score is viewed as a criterion. The minimum competency tests administered by states and local school systems are good examples of how the two types of tests are confused. However, the existence of a cutoff score does not make a test criterion-referenced.

Objective-Referenced Tests.   The assessment procedure most commonly employed in educational settings and labeled criterion-referenced testing begins with the specification of the objectives to be covered in a curriculum and is followed by a set of items associated with each objective. If the student correctly answers a preset number or percentage of items, the objective is judged to have been mastered. Using this procedure, item difficulty becomes the most important factor in determining who has and who has not mastered a particular objective. This type of test is not considered to be a "real" criterion-referenced test because using this approach, whether a student masters an objective or not, depends too much on the items selected to assess the objective. If the difficulty of items is not carefully controlled, the capacity of such a test to specify whether an objective has been mastered is lost.

Prior to the introduction of behaviorally stated objectives, instructional objectives tended to be vague. By specifying the overt behavior that has to be emitted before it can be concluded that an objective has been mastered, behaviorally stated objectives make the process of deciding instructional goals much more concrete. Such objectives can easily be written when the content is concrete, such as with mathematics skills, where it is possible to specify the overt behaviors necessary for a conclusion of mastery. Most subject matter taught in school is abstract, and objectives are likely to involve cognitive activities that cannot easily be thought of on an either-or basis. For example, a student does not just understand or not understand the motivations of Hamlet. There are degrees of understanding. The overt behavior specified in instructional objectives with this sort of subject matter generally includes the requirement that the student correctly answer a predetermined proportion of items derived from the content associated with an objective but does not describe the items or their difficulty. Using behaviorally stated objectives does not enhance the precision of objectives under these circumstances.

Although the practice of haphazardly associating items with objectives is commonly referred to as criterion-referenced testing, some testing experts such as James Popham (1980) believe that the procedure does not deserve this appellation because the results of such a test do not convey much information about *what* a student has learned. Experts prefer to call this practice "objective-referenced testing" to distance it from criterion-referenced testing.

Domain-Referenced Tests.   Popham (1980) has suggested a method of writing objectives that addresses the issue of how the items that define an objective are selected. He calls the procedure domain-referenced testing. It involves a lengthy and complex description of educational goals that presents an unambiguous view of the targeted behavior and leaves no room for uncertainty concerning what was mastered. Included here is a process for generating a set of items that is representative of the entire domain of possible items associated with the construct under consideration.

Popham does not view domain-referenced testing as a procedure separate from criterion-referenced testing; he states that "a criterion-referenced test is used to ascertain an individual's status within a well defined domain" (Popham, 1980, p. 16). He does not, however, suggest the next logical step, which would be to replace the term *criterion-referenced* with *domain-referenced*.

According to Popham, instructional objectives should focus on the item rather than on the objective, whether it is behaviorally stated or not. When using the domain-referenced approach, the items must be homogeneous and measure a single skill, a characteristic described as *unidimensionality*. Furthermore, the procedure for selecting items must be specified and the items described clearly enough that the reader will understand what is being measured. The purpose of this procedure is to have the items used to assess an objective be representative of the entire domain. Because of the length and complexity of each specification, a smaller number of instructional objectives (domain specifications) is used. Instructional objectives based on the domain-referenced model have the following components:

° general description

° sample items

○ stimulus attributes

○ response attributes

○ optional specification supplement

General Description.   This section includes one or two sentences describing what the test is intended to measure. Its purpose is to give those who choose not to read the details provided in the remainder of the specifications an idea of what is being measured.

Sample Items.   Sample items provide examples similar to those that will appear on the test. They give the reader, who may neither need nor want to delve into the complexities of stimulus and response attributes, a quick description of how the construct is being measured.

Stimulus Attributes.   Because tests generally consist of stimulus materials to which the subject responds, it is important to describe just what sort of content is appropriate and what is not. This stimulus material is the question part of a multiple-choice test. The writer of such specifications must steer a careful course between being overly detailed and being so general that the specifications lack meaning.

Response Attributes.   If an objective test format in which the student selects his or her answer is used, the characteristics of the correct and incorrect answers must be specified. It is not sufficient to identify the correct answer and to state that all others will be wrong. Because the characteristics of the distractors in a multiple-choice test determine the character of an item and control its difficulty, their precise nature must be defined. When multiple-choice items are not used and students must construct their answers in an essay or short-answer format, the identification of response attributes is more difficult, because it is necessary to delineate the characteristics of all responses that are correct and make it clear how these responses differ from those that are incorrect.

Optional Specification Supplement.   The specification supplement is an optional section to be used in those cases where it is more efficient to list the specific content eligible for testing than to include that information in the stimulus and response attribute sections, each of which can then be reserved for general rules. For example, on a spelling test, the specification supplement might include the source for a list of acceptable words to be included.

Problems with Criterion-Referenced Tests

The development of educational technology has taken place over a long period of time and is based on the application of widely accepted theories of learning and instruction. Criterion-referenced tests, on the other hand, have existed for a much shorter time, and the methodologies surrounding their use are less well developed and proven.

Clerical Problems.   While norm-referenced tests are supposed to tell us how much a student has learned in relation to others, a criterion-referenced test is intended to tell us specifically what a student has learned. If the test fails to provide this sort of specificity, it is something other than a criterion-referenced one. The most obvious way to accomplish this goal of telling what a student has learned is to evaluate his or her performance in terms of objectives mastered. Achieving specificity by reporting how many objectives have been mastered becomes quite awkward when we are talking about aggregates of students such as are found in classes, schools, and school districts. Such an approach requires the listing of each student along with an enumeration of the objectives that he or she has mastered. If there are 100 objectives to be mastered in a grade (which is a conservative number), a teacher with 35 students has 3,500 objectives with which to be concerned. Of course, for each objective there must be items. It is recommended that there be at least 10 items per objective; therefore, one teacher might have to score as many as 35,000 items each year. A secondary teacher with six classes would have six times as many.

The practice of reporting objectives mastered separately for each student presents a massive clerical problem, and too much data are gathered for any sort of assimilation. Programs for use in personal computers are becoming available that can assist in these recordkeeping chores, but before personal computers can be of much help, they must be coupled with optical scanners to simplify test scoring.

When the clerical problems associated with reporting performance on individual objectives become overwhelming, teachers are likely to be tempted to use summary statistics to describe students and to make comparisons. Once summary statistics are used to report performance on objectives, the essence of criterion-referenced testing is lost, and all that is left is a hybrid approach to evaluation that lacks the advantages of either criterion- or norm-referenced testing. The psychometric and mathematical characteristics of the average number of objectives mastered is poor, and knowledge of *what* has been learned, the most useful aspect of criterion-referenced tests, is lost.

Another problem with this approach is the categorizing of students as either having mastered or not having mastered an objective. This categorization is a problem because we cannot walk into a classroom and divide the class into those who are able to read at a third-grade level and those who cannot. There will always be a range of achievement levels. To draw an arbitrary line and say that those above a certain point have reached mastery while those below have not is nonsensical. This problem is exacerbated by the fact that the performance of a group of students in a class can be expected to be approximately normally distributed. When this is the case, most students score in the middle, where we probably want to distinguish mastery from nonmastery, meaning that under these conditions the number of decision errors is maximized.

Setting Cutoff Scores.   The usual method of setting up a criterion-referenced testing program is to begin with instructional objectives and generate a set of items to measure the student's ability in relation to the objective. A cutoff score is established to determine the number of items that must be correctly answered before the item is considered mastered. Determining this criterion is one of the most important aspects of this testing technology.

The rationale for setting a cutoff score is the acknowledgment of the imperfectness of classroom assessment. We cannot realistically expect that students who have mastered an objective will correctly answer all of the items used to assess that objective. For this reason, to take measurement error into account, the cutoff score is reluctantly set below perfection. Exactly where to set it is determined intuitively, but 70% or 80% correct is typical.

Several statistical techniques are available that use the judgments of experts to obtain a cutoff score. Even though these techniques appear to be objective psychometric procedures, they depend on subjective decisions.

With the Nedelsky method (1954), judges decide for each item how many distractors the lowest passing student should be able to eliminate. The minimum passing level (MPL) is the reciprocal of the remaining choices. On a multiple-choice test with four choices, for an item on which the minimum-level student could be expected to eliminate one distractor, the MPL would be one-third, or 0.33 (the number of remaining choices is three and its reciprocal is one third or 0.33). The MPLs are then averaged across judges and summed across items to obtain a cutoff score for each objective.

Robert Ebel's method (1972) requires the construction of a 3×4 matrix based on three levels of difficulty (easy, medium, and hard) and four levels of relevance (essential, important, acceptable, and questionable). Judges place each item in the appropriate cell and also decide the minimum percentages of items, in each cell, that a student should answer correctly. The number of items is then multiplied by the percentage in each cell. This value is summed and divided by the total number of items to yield the minimum passing score.

A simpler approach and one that has become increasingly popular was proposed by William Angoff (1971). With his method, judges estimate the probability that a minimum-level student would pass each item. The estimates of each judge are summed, and the average across judges becomes the cutoff score.

Unfortunately, each method yields a different cutoff score. These differences are the result of varying standards among judges and a lack of uniformity in instructions. These methods are also time consuming and difficult to implement with teacher-made tests. In fact, it is likely to be impossible for a classroom teacher to implement such a program.

The lack of a satisfactory method for setting cutoff scores poses a major impediment to the use of criterion-referenced tests. The criterion-referenced approach places so much emphasis on separating mastery from nonmastery that, in the absence of an appropriate method for setting cutoff scores, the theoretical rationale for using criterion-referenced tests is severely undermined.

Impact on Instruction

Instruction and testing are generally thought of as separate activities, but with criterion-referenced tests they are closely related. Instead of having two distinct processes, the first of which is to provide instruction and the second to assess students, the two are intertwined. Once a decision has been made regarding what students should learn, only that material is taught. As a result, everything a student needs to learn must be described in the objectives. Although item sampling takes place within the domain of each objective, every objective is assessed. For this reason, the content to be covered must be carefully described because in all likelihood, students will learn only the objectives specified. With norm-referenced tests, content is described in general and the student does not know what will be included on a test and therefore is more likely to try to learn all material.

When a state or school district specifies a set of instructional objectives for which all students are responsible and then constructs a test to measure these objectives, the risk of ignoring a lot of other important course content exists. This problem occurs for two reasons: (1) Only content that can be easily assessed by the test format employed is likely to be included on the test, and (2) it is simply not possible to specify everything that should be included in such a test with objectives.

Writing Objectives for Norm-Referenced Tests

The previous sections describe the importance of objectives in criterion-referenced tests, why the objectives need to be precisely written, and why the items used to assess the objectives must be clearly defined. These requirements are not unique to this type of test. For any type of assessment, what students are expected to be able to do at the conclusion of instruction needs to be specified ahead of time. The difference is that with criterion-referenced tests, a student's performance on each objective must be assessed at a level of reliability that will permit conclusions about whether it has been mastered. A norm-referenced test is usually intended to yield only an overall score. The test is likely to be much broader in content. With such a test, the main priorities involve ensuring an adequate sampling of the objectives and maintaining a clear understanding of what students are expected to be able to do at the conclusion of instruction. A good indication of the clarity of objectives used to describe what is taught in a course is the degree to which others are able to understand the descriptions.

In almost all educational settings, you find statements of the aims and goals of the institution. These goals are usually general, global statements intended to provide an overall frame of reference for developing curricula, organizing learning experiences, and selecting teaching methods. They include such broad goals as "effective citizenship," "worthwhile use of leisure time," and "ability to use the scientific method." Within this framework, the teacher is responsible for developing the instructional objectives that define what is actually being taught. Teachers can turn to curriculum guides, yearbooks of national associations, taxonomies of educational objectives such as those developed by Bloom (1956) and Krathwohl, Bloom, and Masia (1964), and many other sources for help in identifying appropriate objectives. Despite the availability of these materials, the ultimate responsibility for selecting suitable objectives such that they can guide both instruction and evaluation rests with the classroom teacher.

Most statements of objectives written by teachers are too vague and global to be useful as guides to evaluation or teaching. Effective objectives will have the following characteristics.

1. Objectives should be stated in terms of student behavior rather than learning activities or teacher purposes. For example, "Observes bacteria through a microscope" is not a satisfactory statement of an objective because it merely describes a learning activity. *Why* does a teacher want the students to observe bacteria? An analysis of the activities and content of the course of study in which the objective appears might indicate that the teacher wants the student to know the characteristics of organisms that cause diseases and that observation of bacteria is incidental to this objective. It might be better to state the objective as follows: "Recalls characteristics of organisms that cause diseases."

2. Objectives should begin with an active verb that indicates the behavior that a student should exhibit at the conclusion of instruction. This format tends to guarantee a focus on the student and what he or she does. The objective should not consist of a list of content. For example, "Scurvy, beriberi, rickets, and pellagra are caused by a lack of vitamins in the body" is a statement of content not an objective. The objective should be stated in terms of the student's observable behavior, such as "Identifies certain disease conditions that are caused by lack of vitamins."

3. Objectives should be stated in terms of behavior that is observable in the classroom or school. For example, an objective such as "Always practices good health habits to prevent the spread of disease" is not stated in observable terms. The inclusion of the word "always" makes it impossible to determine whether a student has mastered the objective because it is not possible to observe a student at all times. Another example of an inappropriate objective is the following statement: "Does his share to create good emotional atmosphere during meals at home." The behavior specified in this statement occurs in a situation outside of school, one in which the teacher would be unable to observe the student. It is unlikely that the teacher will be able to get relevant evidence on the achievement of the objective. Another such example is the statement "Feels secure in making wise choices of food." In this statement "feels secure" is unobservable; it is a covert characteristic of a student. You cannot observe a feeling of security. You can only observe behavior and perhaps make inferences about the security of the student. Terms like "knows" and "understands" do not represent observable behaviors. A proper objective should specify what the student must do to lead the teacher to conclude that the student knows the fact or understands the process being assessed.

4. Objectives should be stated precisely. Use terms that have uniform meaning. For example, in the objective "Understands the responsibility of the community in controlling communicable disease," the word "understands" means different things to different people. To one teacher, it may mean that the student can name the agencies in the community that have responsibility for controlling communicable disease. To another, it may mean that the student, given a novel

TABLE 7.1
Samples of Poor and Good Openings for
Statement of an Objective

Do Not Use in Stating Objectives	Use in Stating Objectives
Understands . . .	Defines . . .
Appreciates . . .	Gives examples of . . .
Thinks critically about . . .	Compares . . .
Is aware of . . .	Describes . . .
Feels the need for . . .	Classifies . . .
Is growing in ability to . . .	Summarizes . . .
Becomes familiar with . . .	Applies in a new situation . . .
Grasps the significance of . . .	Solves a problem in which . . .
Is interested in . . .	Expresses interest in . . .
Feels the need for . . .	States what he would do if . . .

problem concerning a communicable disease, can identify the appropriate community agency or agencies responsible and indicate the services or actions to be expected from these agencies.

Teachers use a number of terms that can lead to ambiguity in formulating objectives. Some of these terms are listed in the left-hand column of Table 7.1. To provide a contrast, some active verbs that focus attention on student behavior are listed in the right-hand column. In general, you should use the words in the right-hand column and others like them and avoid using the sort of ambiguous terms and references to unobservable behavior that appear in the left-hand column.

Of course, objectives can be written at a wide range of levels of specificity. For example,

> The student will be able to understand the health risks associated with smoking.

This objective is obviously fairly general. Contrast it with the one that follows:

> Given a list of illnesses, the student will be able to identify correctly those illnesses associated with smoking.

It should be obvious that both of these examples have important limitations. The first is so general that it is difficult to know exactly what is expected. It is easy to imagine a set of test items assessing this objective that would range from extremely easy to very difficult. The second narrows the range of possible items, but it does so by requiring a type of information that might easily be thought of as trivial, particularly if such items constituted the entire test. At the same time, the level of difficulty of the item would vary depending on the item format. The objective could be measured with a series of true-false items, or it could be measured with a multiple-choice item that requires the student to select an illness caused by smoking from among several others that were not. The more plausible the distractors are to the student, the more difficult the item.

5. *Objectives should be unitary.* Each statement should refer to only one process. For example, the objective "Knows elementary principles of immunization and accepts immunization willingly" contains two processes, a cognitive process of recall of information and an affective process of acceptance of an action. The two processes are different, and one objective should not be used to define both of them because a student can master either one without the other. If each is important, each should be stated as a separate objective.

6. *Objectives should be stated at an appropriate level of generality.* The writer of instructional objectives needs to strike a balance in the level of generality. The statement of an objective should not be so general and global that it is meaningless, but, at the same time, it should not be so narrow and specific that the educational process seems to be made up of isolated bits and pieces. Under these circumstances, the list of objectives is likely to become too long and unwieldy to use effectively. For example, the objective "Knows nutrition" is too vague to serve any useful purpose. On the other hand, a series of statements such as "Identifies the function of proteins in the body," "Identifies the function of fats in the body," "Identifies the function of carbohydrates in the body,'" and "Identifies the function of vitamins in the body" is unnecessarily specific. At an appropriate level of generality, all these specific statements could be combined into one statement such as "Identifies the functions of the four classes of nutrients in the body."

7. *Objectives should represent intended direct outcomes of instruction.* It should be obvious that you would never write an educational objective for eighth graders such as "Increases in height." This statement would be inappropriate because health instruction is not directed toward making eighth graders taller. However, it is common to find statements of objectives that refer to changes in attitudes when no instructional effort is given to their development.

In such a case, either the objective concerned with attitudes should be omitted or the instruction should be redesigned so that some attention is devoted to attitude change. This example illustrates how the clarification of an objective may influence more than the evaluation procedures; the clarification of an objective also may alter the form and content of instruction.

8. *Objectives should be realistic.* The writer of instructional objectives must consider the time available for teaching and the characteristics of the students. An example of an unrealistic objective for fourth graders would be, "Understands the causes for violence in human societies." This objective would provide a daunting task for college-level students, and it may be beyond the capacity of children at this stage of cognitive development.

Another example of an objective that would be unrealistic for eighth graders reads, "Understands the principles of immunization." The principles of immunization are extremely complex and understanding the nature of immunization is probably beyond the experience level of the students in the eighth grade. The objective should be rewritten to require that the student know what the different kinds of immunizations are or be able to demonstrate a knowledge of the methods that have been developed for immunization against disease.

A second problem with this objective is that it does not involve an observable behavior. What does "understands" mean? And how can we tell that the student does understand at the level of sophistication that we intend? Again, objectives must be stated in terms of observable behavior so that we can tell from the student's behavior that he or she has mastered the objective. Understanding immunization could imply anything from listing a set of properties to designing and carrying out original research leading to a new drug or medical procedure.

Sample Set of Objectives

Table 7.2 provides an actual example of a set of objectives that were prepared for a 6-week unit on nutrition for an eighth-grade class. Column 1 lists the

TABLE 7.2
Objectives for Unit on Nutrition for an Eighth Grade Class

Objective as Originally Written in Curriculum Guide	Comment	Suggested Revision
1. Knows terms and vocabulary used in nutrition.	1. "Knows" is vague. At what level is the student supposed to know these?	1. Recalls or recognizes definitions of terms and vocabulary
2. Has a rudimentary knowledge of food nutrients and their functions.	2. What is a "rudimentary knowledge"? What kind of behavior does a student show who has a "rudimentary knowledge"?	2. Recalls or recognizes names of essential food nutrients and their functions in the body.
3. Values the health protection provided by good dietary habits.	3. "Value" is vague. How does this objective differ from 7, 9, 11, and 13?	3. (a) Identifies good sources of various food nutrients. (b) Identifies effects of poor diets.
4. Understands the digestive process.	4. "Understands" is vague. How does a student show he or she understands?	4. (a) Identifies parts of digestive system and functions of each. (b) Identifies process of digestion for each nutrient. (c) Recognizes factors that interefere with digestion.

TABLE 7.2
continued

Objective as Originally Written in Curriculum Guide	Comment	Suggested Revision
5. Plans meals and snacks using principles of good nutrition.	5. Well-stated objective. Desired student behavior is clear. Stated at an appropriate level of generality.	5. No revisions.
6. Realizes that food patterns differ in various parts of the United States and the world.	6. "Realizes" is vague. Objective is too specific.	6. Identifies factors that influence kinds and amounts of food that people eat.
7. Is willing to choose an adequate diet.	7. Willingness to do something is covert. One can observe whether a student does something, but not his or her willingness to do it.	7. Chooses adequate lunch in school cafeteria.
8. Understands that the daily food guide is based on scientific research.	8. The last part of the objective is a specific fact. What is there to "understand"? Essential part of objective is included in 12.	8. Eliminate objective.
9. Uses information about nutrition every day.	9. More of a fond hope than an objective. See comment on 3	9. Eliminate objective.
10. Persuades other members of his or her family to develop good nutritional habits.	10. Is this reasonable? How would one obtain evidence on the achievement of the objective? Is this a direct outcome of teaching?	10. Eliminate objective.
11 Recognizes flaws in his or her diet and desires to eliminate them.	11. Double objective. Contains two different behaviors. First part of objective is restatement of 2 and 5. Second part is stated in 7.	11. Eliminate objectives.
12. Is aware that advertisements and statements concerning food are not always based on facts.	12. "Is aware of" is vague. What behaviors should the student exhibit?	12. (a) Distinguishes statements about foods and diets that are based on good scientific evidence from those that are not. (b) Identifies authoritative sources of information about foods and diets.
13. Appreciates being healthy.	13. "Appreciates" is vague. What behavior is a student to show when he or she appreciates being healthy? How do you teach a student to appreciate being healthy?	13. Eliminate objective.

objectives as they appeared in the teacher's course outline. Column 2 lists the weakness, if any, of each objective, and Column 3 suggests revisions for the objectives where they are needed.

As you can see, the objectives as originally written have many faults. The revised list of objectives provides a better guide both for teaching and evaluation. The revisions in the objectives were made after studying the detailed curriculum guide. Objectives were eliminated if there were no specific learning experiences provided in the curriculum guide.

Specifying Content to Be Covered

When the purpose of a test is to appraise what each student has learned from part of a course or a curriculum, it is important to specify the content to be covered. The content is important because it is the vehicle through which the objectives are mastered. The specifications of content are often in the form of a teacher's detailed outline or set of lesson plans for a course. Otherwise, an outline of content should be prepared based on the appropriate sections of the textbook or curriculum guide.

Preparing the Test Blueprint

The basic components of a test blueprint are the specifications of instructional objectives and the description of content. These two dimensions need to be matched to show which objective relates to each segment of content and to provide a framework for the development of the test. In planning the evaluation of a unit, it is useful for the teacher to make a test blueprint that includes not only the objectives and the content but also the method or methods to be used in evaluating student progress toward achieving each objective.

An objective that requires only cognitive processes can be appraised by a paper-and-pencil test. Included in this category are objectives that specify such processes as recalling, recognizing, identifying, defining, applying, analyzing, synthesizing, generalizing, predicting, or evaluating. In the list of revised objectives in Table 7.2, all of the objectives except Objective 7 can be evaluated with a paper-and-pencil test. Objective 7 cannot be measured in this way because it involves the actual act of choosing food. The extent to which Objective 7 has been achieved can be determined only by systematic observation of students in the school cafeteria or, more practically, albeit less accurately, from student reports of what they do. Examples of other types of objectives that cannot be assessed by paper-and-pencil tests are those that involve affective behaviors, such as interests, attitudes, or positive or negative feelings toward an object, group, or institution. This type of objective would need to be evaluated through self-reports or observation. In most cases, a single test or evaluation device cannot measure all the objectives you are trying to assess.

A blueprint for a final examination in health for an eighth-grade class is provided in Table 7.3. The test will use a short-answer or objective format and contain 60 items. This test is the type for which a formal blueprint is most useful, but even if you are constructing an essay test with five or six items, the kind of thinking that goes into formulating a blueprint can be useful. The issues that are involved in the decision about the type of test exercise to use are considered later.

The objectives for the unit on nutrition as well as for the other units have been listed in the left-hand column of Table 7.3. The titles of each of the three units have been entered as column headings. Each box, or cell, under the unit headings contains content entries that relate to the objective on the same line with the cell. The complete blueprint specifies the content deemed important and how it will be measured.

In some states, test blueprints for most subject matter and courses are prepared centrally. But, when this material is not provided, preparing such a two-dimensional outline is an exacting and time-consuming task. The busy classroom teacher often falls short of achieving such a complete analysis. There is no question, however, that attempting the analysis will go far toward clarifying the objectives of a particular unit and toward guiding not only the preparation of a sound test but also the teaching of the unit itself. It is also true that once such a complete blueprint has been prepared, it can be used until the curriculum or teaching emphasis is changed.

An examination of the blueprint should make it clear to you that tests are just samples of student behavior—for four reasons

1. Only those objectives suitable for appraisal with a paper-and-pencil test are included in the blueprint.

2. The entries in the cells under each area of content are examples that illustrate but do not exhaust the total content.

3. There is an unlimited number of items that could be written for the material that is included in the blueprint.

4. The time available for testing is limited, and you can include only a small sample from the domain of all possible items.

If the test is to reflect your teaching goals, you must carefully choose the items to include on your tests. The following four issues should guide the construction of the test.

1. What emphasis should each of the content areas and objectives receive on the tests? In other words, what proportion of all the items on the test should be written for each content area and for each objective within each content area?

2. What type or types of items should be included on the test?

3. How long should the test be? How many questions or items should the total test contain? How many items should be written for each cell of the blueprint?

4. How difficult should the items be?

Relative Emphasis of Content Areas and Process Objectives. The proportion of test items allocated to each content area and to each objective should correspond to the instructional emphasis and importance of the topic. The decision-

TABLE 7.3
Blueprint for Final Examination in Health in Eighth Grade

Process Objectives	Content Areas
	A. Nutrition, 40%
1. Recognizes terms and vocabulary 20%	Nutrients Incomplete protein Vitamins Complete protein Enzymes Amino acids Metabolism Glycogen Oxidation Carbohydrate 4 or 5 items
2. Identifies specific facts 30%	Nutrients essential to health Good sources of food nutrients Parts of digestive system Process of digestion of each nutrient Sources of information about foods and nutrition 7 or 8 items
3. Identifies principles, concepts, and generalizations 30%	Bases of well-balanced diet Enzyme reactions Transfer of materials between cells Cell metabolism Functions of nutrients in body 7 or 8 items
4. Evaluates health information and advertisements 10%	Analyzes food and diet advertisements Interprets labels on foods Identifies good sources of information about foods and diets 2 or 3 items
5. Applies principles and generalizations to novel situations 10%	Identifies well-balanced diet Computes calories needed for weight-gaining or weight-losing diet Predicts consequences of changes in enzymes on digestive system Identifies services and protection provided by the Federal Food and Drug Act 2 or 3 items
No. of items	24
Total time for test—90 minutes	

making process involved is subjective, but the teacher should ensure that the test has maintained the same balance in emphasis for both content and mental processes that the teacher has tried to achieve through instruction. Allocating a different number of items to each topic and process objective is the most obvious way of weighting topics and objectives on the test.

The initial weighting of the content areas and process objectives requires the assignment of percentages to each content area and process objective such that the total for both is 100%. In the blueprint shown in Table 7.3, the test maker

Content Areas		No. of Items
B. Communicable Diseases, 40%	**C. Noncommunicable Diseases, 20%**	
Immunity Epidemic Virus Pathogenic Carrier Endemic Antibodies Protozoa Incubation period <div align="center">4 or 5 items</div>	Goiter Deficiency diseases Diabetes Cardiovascular diseases Caries <div align="center">2 or 3 items</div>	12
Common communicable diseases Incidence of various diseases Methods of spreading disease Types of immunization Symptoms of common communicable diseases <div align="center">7 or 8 items</div>	Specific diseases caused by lack of vitamins Specific disorders resulting from imbalance in hormones Incidence of noncommunicable diseases Common noncommunicable diseases of adolescents and young adults <div align="center">3 or 4 items</div>	18
Basic principles underlying control of disease Actions of antibiotics Body defenses against disease Immune reactions in body <div align="center">7 or 8 items</div>	Pressure within cardiovascular system Control of diabetes Inheritance of abnormal conditions Abnormal growth of cells <div align="center">3 or 4 items</div>	18
Distinguishes between adequate and inadequate evidence for medicines Identifies misleading advertisements for medications <div align="center">2 or 3 items</div>	Identifies errors or misleading information in health material Identifies appropriate source of information for health problems <div align="center">1 or 2 items</div>	6
Recognizes conditions that are likely to result in increase of communicable disease Identifies appropriate methods for sterilizing objects Gives appropriate reasons for regulations, processes, or treatments <div align="center">2 or 3 items</div>	Predicts consequences of changes in secretion of certain hormones Predicts probability of inheriting abnormal conditions <div align="center">1 or 2 items</div>	6
<div align="center">24</div>	<div align="center">12</div>	60

Total number of items—60

decided that Topic A, nutrition, should receive a weight of 40%; Topic B, communicable diseases, should also receive a weight of 40%; and Topic C, noncommunicable diseases, should receive a weight of 20%. Five weeks of instructional time were spent on Topic A and also on Topic B, and only 2 weeks were spent on Topic C, so the allocation of weights corresponds roughly to teaching time.

For the process objectives in Table 7.3, the test maker decided that 20% of all the items should be allocated to Objective 1, 30% each to Objectives 2 and 3, and 10% each to Objectives 4 and 5. These allocations imply that the teacher has emphasized those objectives that require remembering or recalling terms, specific facts, principles, concepts, and generalizations. In other words, the course was primarily focused on increasing the students' fund of knowledge, with less attention given to assessing their ability to use the information in novel situations. If the allocation of items to the process objectives truly reflects the teacher's emphasis in teaching, then the allocation is appropriate. We might take issue with the teacher's emphasis in teaching, but, given that emphasis, we cannot say that the allocation of test items is inappropriate.

Types of Items To Be Used.   The types of items that can be used on a teacher-made test can be classified into two categories: (1) those for which students produce their own answers, which are sometimes labeled *supply, or constructed, response items,* and (2) those for which students select their own answers from several choices, which are labeled *selection response items.* Examples of supply response items are the essay item requiring an extended answer from the student, the short-answer item requiring no more than one or two sentences for an answer, and the completion item requiring only a word or a phrase for an answer. Examples of selection type items are true-false, multiple-choice, and matching ones.

The decision about which type of item to use will depend on the process objective to be measured, the strengths and weaknesses of each item type, personal preferences, and skill in writing items. The advantages and disadvantages of each item type will be discussed in detail in a later section of this chapter.

Total Number of Items for the Test.   If the teacher decides to use an essay type of test, there will be time for only a few questions. The more elaborate the answer required, the fewer the number of questions that it is possible to include. For example, a 40-minute test in high school might have three or four questions requiring extended answers of a page each. Objective tests can involve a much larger number of items.

The total number of items included in a test should be large enough to provide an adequate sample of student performance across content areas and across process objectives. The greater the number of content areas and process objectives to be measured by a test, the longer the test needs to be. A weekly quiz can be short because the number of objectives is limited, whereas a 6-week test or final examination needs to have a larger number of items because there is more content and therefore there are more objectives to be covered on the test.

The time available for testing is a factor that limits the number of items on a test. Most teacher-made tests should be power tests, not speed tests, meaning that there should be enough time for at least 80% of the students to attempt to answer every item. There are few subject areas in which speed of answering is a relevant aspect of achievement. The number of test items that can be asked in a given amount of time depends on the following factors:

1. The type of item used on the test. A short-answer item for which a student has to write his or her answer is likely to require more time than a true-false or multiple-choice item for which a student is only required to choose an answer from among several choices. Of course, items that call for more extended written responses will take even more time.

2. The age and educational level of the student. Students in the primary grades whose reading and writing skills are just beginning to develop require more time per test item than older students do. Young children cannot attend to the same task for a long period of time. Testing time for them must be shorter, further reducing the number of items.

3. The ability level of students. Compared to lower ability students, high-ability students have better developed reading and writing skills. They also have a better command of the subject matter and better problem-solving skills. As a rule, high-ability students can answer more questions per unit of testing time than low-ability students of the same age and grade can. Thus, a test for an advanced class could be longer, and a test for a slower learning class could be shorter than a test for students of average ability.

4. The length and complexity of the items. If test items are based on a reading passages, tabular materials, maps, or graphs, time must be provided for reading and examining the stimulus material. The more stimulus material of this type that is used on a test, the fewer the number of items that can be included on it.

5. The type of process objective being tested. Items that require only the recall of knowledge can be answered more quickly than those that require the application of knowledge to a new situation.

6. The amount of computation or quantitative thinking required by the item. Most individuals work more slowly when dealing with quantitative materials than when dealing with verbal materials; therefore, if the items require mathematical computations, the time allotted per item must be longer than that for purely verbal items.

Conclusions on Total Number of Test Items.   It is impossible to give hard and fast rules about the number of items to be included in a test for a given amount of testing time. A teacher who becomes familiar with the kinds of students usually in a class will be able to judge the number of items that can be included in a given amount of time. As a rule, the typical student will require from 30 to 45 seconds to read and answer a simple factual type multiple-choice or true-false item and from 75 to 100 seconds to read and answer a fairly complex multiple-choice item requiring problem solving.

Keep in mind that there is a great deal of variation among students regarding the number of items that each student can complete in a given amount of time and that this variation is not always related to reading ability or knowledge of the content being assessed. This characteristic is also related individual learning styles. The total amount of time required for a number of items sufficient to provide adequate coverage of the blueprint may, in some cases, be more than is available in a single class period. The most satisfactory solution to this problem is to divide the test into two or more separate subtests that can be given on successive days.

For the final examination in eighth-grade health (see Table 7.3), the teacher decided to have 60 items. The blueprint is used to determine how many items to write for each cell. The first step is to determine the total number of items for each content area and process objective. The blueprint in Table 7.3 specifies that 40% of the items, or 24 items (0.40 × 60), should be on Topic A; 24 items (0.04 × 60) on topic B, and 12 items (0.20 × 60) on Topic C. These numbers are entered in the row labeled "No. of Items." The percentage assigned to each process objective is likewise multiplied by the total number of items to determine the number of items that should be written to measure each process. When this is done, we get the numbers entered in the extreme right-hand column of the blueprint.

To determine the number of items in each cell of the blueprint, we multiply the total number of items in a content area by the percentage assigned to the objective in each row. For example, to determine the number of items for the first cell under Topic A, nutrition, we multiply 24 by 0.2 (20%), which gives 4.8 items. Because the number 4.8 is between 4 and 5, we can note that we should have either 4 or 5 items covering this content and this objective. The other cells in the blueprint are filled in by the same process. It must be recognized that some process outcomes are related primarily to certain aspects of content. For instance, on a social studies examination, an objective related to map reading might be testable primarily in a content unit on natural resources rather than in one on human resources. Cell entries need to be modified to make the content and process congruent. Furthermore, it is probably desirable to indicate a range of items for each cell, as our example does, to provide flexibility if difficulty is encountered in writing acceptable items for certain cells. The number of items planned for each cell should be viewed as a guide rather than as a straitjacket.

Appropriate Level of Difficulty of the Items.   *Difficulty* implies something different for an essay than it does for a short-answer or objective test. An item that is of appropriate difficulty for an essay test is one for which each member of the class can produce a credible answer and which elicits responses varying in completeness, thoughtfulness, and quality of organization of ideas.

Difficulty can be thought of in terms of individual items or the whole test. The difficulty of an item is determined by dividing the number of students getting an item correct by the total number of students attempting the item. The difficulty of the entire test is determined by dividing the mean of the test by the total number of items on the test, and it can be thought of as the average difficulty for all of the items on the test. For example, if a particular item on a test is answered correctly by 40% of all the students who take the test, we say the item has a 40% or 0.40 difficulty. An item that 75% of the students get correct would have a difficulty of 0.75. (This system can be confusing because the larger the difficulty index the easier the test. The value used could more logically be called the "easiness" of a test.) The difficulty of the whole test is the average of the individual item difficulties.

The appropriate average difficulty and spread of difficulty differs for norm- and criterion-referenced tests. In general, criterion-referenced tests are easier than norm-referenced tests. On a diagnostic test intended to locate isolated individuals who are having special difficulty, it is reasonable to expect a large number of perfect scores or near-perfect scores and very few relatively low scores. On the other hand, if we administer a test before beginning instruction on a new topic to find out how much students already know, we should not be surprised to get a large number of near-zero scores because the material has not yet been taught.

On criterion-referenced tests, diagnostic tests, or pretests administered prior to instruction, we are not concerned about maximizing variability. Even if everyone gets a perfect score or if everyone gets a zero score, we are obtaining the information that we were seeking. On the other hand, when the purpose of the test is to discriminate levels of achievement among different members of the class and for the results to serve as a basis for ranking or grading, then we want the test to yield a spread of scores. We want to be able to separate the really high achiever from the next highest achiever and the really low achiever from the next lowest achiever. Ideally, we would like to have every student get a different score on the test because that would increase variability and facilitate ranking. It is undesirable for anyone (or more than one person) to get a perfect score on such a test because that would decrease variability and make ranking more difficult. It would also mean that the test lacked sufficient ceiling to allow the really able students to demonstrate their knowledge. On the other hand, we would not want to get a zero or chance-level score, indicating that the student could not successfully answer any items, because then we would not have gotten down to his or her level. On such a test, we would not want an item that everyone got correct or an item that everyone got incorrect simply because neither of these items contributes to making discriminations among students according to their levels of achievement.

In general, the difficulty of a test should be halfway between the number of items a student could get correct by guessing and 100%. Because the effect of guessing adds chance variability to test scores, it is generally better to have the test be slightly easier than this guideline would suggest rather than more difficult. For a multiple-choice test with four options, the preferred level of difficulty would be 0.62; for a true-false test, the optimum difficulty level would be 0.75. Because the probability of getting an item right by chance is 1 divided by the number of answer choices, this rule leads to the conclusion that the average difficulty for items with five alternatives should be about 0.60. (Chance variability is 20%, and halfway between chance variability and a perfect score is 0.60.)

Continuing with our example (Table 7.3), suppose the 60 items on the health test were all completion items. We would want the average score for the class to be 30 items correct (0.50×60) because the probability of guessing the correct answer to a supply response item is assumed to be zero. If the 60 items had been five-choice multiple-choice items, we would have wanted the average score to be about 36 items correct (0.60×60).

Difficulties as low as this sometimes bother teachers who are accustomed to thinking of "passing" scores or "failing" scores in terms of the percentage of the items that a student gets correct on a test. The above suggestions have nothing to do with passing or failing; assigning marks or grades to students is an entirely different problem that should be kept separate from the proportion of items correctly answered. The percentages that are suggested here will tend to yield a set of scores that will be maximally useful to a teacher who wants to discriminate levels of achievement among students.

In the process of achieving the desired average level of difficulty, the teacher is likely to produce some difficult items that are passed by as few as 30% or 40% of the students (assuming a four-choice multiple-choice item) and some easy ones that are passed by 80% to 90% of the students. We would hope that many of the items would approach the desired average level of about 62% to 65%, and they should be written with that goal in mind. However, achieving optimum difficulty levels is less important than ensuring that the items provide a good coverage of content and that each one is answered correctly more often by able than by less able students (a matter that will be considered later). Ensuring proper content coverage require a process similar to that used in establishing content validity, which was discussed in Chapter 5.

Suggestions for Writing Objective Items

In this section we will discuss suggestions and recommendations for writing objective test items.

1. Keep the reading difficulty and vocabulary level of the test item as simple as possible. It is best to avoid complex sentence structure or unnecessarily difficult words that can prevent a student from showing what he or she knows. When technical vocabulary has been emphasized in a course and knowledge of that vocabulary is one of the objectives of instruction, it may appropriately be used, but obscure general vocabulary should be avoided. In the example here, which was written for eighth graders, the sentence posing the item is unnecessarily wordy and complex, and the words "promiscuous," "pernicious," and "deleterious" are unnecessarily difficult for this grade level. (For each example, the correct answer is underlined. Also, for true-false items, T indicates true and F indicates false.)

EXAMPLE

Poor: The promiscuous use of sprays, oils, and antiseptics in the nose during acute colds is a pernicious practice because it may have a deleterious effect on:
A. the sinuses.
B. red blood cells.
C. white blood cells.
D. the olfactory nerve.

Better: Frequent use of sprays, oils, and antiseptics in the nose during acute colds may result in:
A. the spreading of the infection to the sinuses.
B. damage to the olfactory nerve.

C.   destruction of white blood cells.
D.   congestion of the mucous membranes in the nose.

2. Be sure each item has a correct or best answer on which experts would agree. Ordinarily, statements of a controversial nature do not make good objective items, although there are instances when knowledge of different viewpoints on controversial issues may be important. When this is the case, the item should clearly state whose opinion or what authority is to be used as the basis for the answer. The student should not be placed in the position of having to endorse a particular opinion or viewpoint as an indisputable fact.

Poor:	T	F	Alcoholism is a disease.	EXAMPLE
Better:	T	F	According to your textbook, alcoholism is a disease.	

3. Be sure each item deals with an important aspect of the content area, and not with trivia. Sometimes teachers try to increase the difficulty of a test by basing items on obscure or trivial details such as the content of a footnote or an obscure fact from a table. The example that follows, written for the eighth-grade health test, asks for a trivial detail, the knowledge of which could not possibly make any difference in an eighth grader's level of competence in health. Example 2 consists of a statement lifted from the textbook that is of little importance. Any student would know that it was true whether they were familiar with the course content or not. The only way that someone would get this item incorrect would be if they thought it was so obvious that it must be a trick question.

Poor: In 1987, the death rate from accidents of all types per 100,000 population in the age group 15–24 was: EXAMPLE 1

    A.   59.0.
    B.   59.1
    C.   59.2.
    D.   59.3.

Better: In 1987, the leading cause of death in the age group 15–24 was:

    A.   respiratory diseases.
    B.   cancer.
    C.   accidents.
    D.   rheumatic heart disease.

Poor: T   F   The manufacture of prescription drugs is a highly scientific industry.   EXAMPLE 2

4. Be sure each item is independent. The answer to one item should not be required as a condition for solving the next item. Every student should have a fair chance at each item on its own. In the example shown next, the person who does not know the answer to the first item is unlikely to get the second one correct.

EXAMPLE

Poor: 1. Scurvy is caused by the lack of:
     A. vitamin A.
     B. vitamin B−1.
     C. vitamin B−12.
     <u>D.</u> vitamin C.
    2. A good source of this vitamin is:
     <u>A.</u> orange juice.
     B. cod-liver oil.
     C. liver.
     D. whole rice.

It is also important to make sure that the statement of one question does not provide the answer to some other question.

5. Avoid the use of trick items. Objective items tend to be trick items when the student has to pick one word or number out of a sentence that appears to be focusing on an entirely different point. In the poor example that follows, the item is keyed "false" because the immunizing agent for diphtheria is either a toxoid or an antitoxin, not a vaccine. However, the statement conveys the idea that the student is to react to the effectiveness of immunization procedures against diphtheria. If the purpose of the item is to test whether a student knows the correct use of the word "vaccine," the item should be rephrased as indicated. Trick questions are likely to mislead the better student who attempts to focus on the meaning of the statement rather than to check each word.

EXAMPLE

Poor: T <u>F</u> The use of diphtheria vaccine has contributed to the decline in death rate from this disease between 1900 and 1988.

Better: T <u>F</u> The immunizing material used to prevent diphtheria is called a vaccine.

---

6. Be sure the problem posed is clear and unambiguous. This is a general admonition and somewhat like "Sin no more!" It may be just as ineffective. However, it is certainly true that ambiguity of statement and meaning is the most pervasive fault in objective test items. Let us look at two examples of this problem.

EXAMPLE 1

Poor: <u>T</u> F Diabetes develops after 40.

The statement is keyed "true." But what does it mean? Does it mean "only after 40 years of age" or does it mean "more frequently after 40"? What does "develop" mean in this context? You can obtain data on the relative frequency of diagnosis of diabetes in people of different ages, but the time of diagnosis and the time of development are not the same. To which type of diabetes is the item writer referring, diabetes mellitus, diabetes insipidous, or some other form? Items such as this one are likely to trouble the student who knows the most and not the less informed student. The item cannot be revised to make it an adequate item and should be dropped from the test.

EXAMPLE 2

Poor: Which of the following substances is most essential to human life?
   A. protein
   B. water
   C. vitamins
   D. minerals

The keyed answer to the question is B, but all of the substances are essential to human life. To answer the question, the examinee has to guess what the item writer meant by "most essential." In this question, the item writer was trying to determine whether the students knew that healthy people could survive for a fairly long period of time without food but could survive for only a few days without replenishing water lost from the body. The revised question tests for this knowledge with greater clarity.

EXAMPLE 2–
REVISED

Better: A healthy person is marooned on a deserted island. To survive, the person needs almost immediately to find a source of:
   A. protein to maintain body cells.
   B. water to drink.
   C. vitamins to maintain body metabolism.
   D. carbohydrates or fats to supply energy.

Writing True-False Items

True-false tests owe much of their popularity to objectivity in scoring and ease of construction. Their use also permits the inclusion of a larger number of items on a test than do other item formats. Despite these advantages, the true-false test is not considered to be a sound method of assessing student performance because it is hard to write items that are neither too difficult nor too easy or items that are not so ambiguous or tricky that they provide a poor assessment of knowledge. This approach is appropriate for only a limited amount of course material, and in many fields there are no statements, except for the trivial, that can be said to be unambiguously true or false.

The true-false item is best suited to knowledge that is categorical—for example, bacteria are either pathogenic or nonpathogenic and diseases are either communicable or noncommunicable. Around this type of knowledge it is possible to write reasonable true-false items. But only a small fraction of the knowledge in any field is of this type, and much that fits the pattern is relatively unimportant. Because the statement that constitutes an item typically appears in isolation, with no frame of reference, judgments about truth or falsity are difficult.

Because a student has a 50% chance of getting a true-false item correct by guessing, this format yields less accurate information per item about a student's performance than do other forms of items. As a result, a large number of items are needed to provide a precise appraisal of each student's competence.

Suggestions for Writing Better True-False Items.   The true-false item format has serious limitations, and its use is not recommended. However, there are rules that, when applied, can result in better true-false items for teachers who insist on using them.

1. Ensure that the item is unequivocally true or false. Each statement should be true enough or false enough that experts would unanimously agree on the answer. Many statements cause problems because the well-informed student can build a case for why any statement is true or why it is false. Consider the following:

EXAMPLE   Poor: T̲ F   Penicillin is an effective drug for the treatment of pneumonia.

Although the item is keyed "true," the student with the most knowledge about penicillin will know that this antibiotic is more effective against certain types of pneumonia than others. Such a student might mark the statement false. The revised statement removes the amibugity.

EXAMPLE   Better: T̲ F   Penicillin is an effective drug for the treatment of streptococcal
                                         pneumonia.

---

2. Avoid the use of specific determiners or qualified statements. Statements that include such words as "all," "never," "no," "always," and other all-inclusive terms represent such broad generalizations that they are likely to be false. Qualified statements involving such terms as "usually," "sometimes," "under certain conditions," and "may be" are likely to be true. The testwise student knows this and will use such cues to get credit for knowledge he does not possess.

EXAMPLE   Poor: T F̲   All bacteria cause disease.
                       Better: T̲ F   Pathogenic bacteria are parasites.

---

3. Avoid ambiguous and indefinite terms of degree or amount. Expressions such as "frequently," "greatly," "to a considerable degree," and "in most cases" are not interpreted in the same way by everyone who reads them. When the student is left to guess what the item writer had in mind, the result is likely to be frustration and poor measurement. In the poor example that follows, the students may be troubled by the word "frequently" because this method of preserving food is used extensively today only for fruits.

Poor:	T F	Drying is frequently used to preserve foods.	EXAMPLE
Better:	T F	Fruits can be preserved by drying.	

4. Avoid the use of negative statements and particularly double negatives. Wason (1961), working with adults, and Zern (1967), working with elementary school children, have each shown that the time needed to answer a negatively stated item is greater than that needed for an equivalent positively stated item. Furthermore, more errors are made in response to negatively phrased items. Both investigators used pairs of statements such as "36 is not an even number" and "36 is an odd number." The negative statement requires an involved, reverse process of reasoning to untangle its meaning and is semantically more difficult. In addition, students under the time pressure of the examination can easily overlook the negative. Double negatives present even greater problems of interpretation.

Poor:	T F	Resistance to smallpox obtained through the use of smallpox vaccine is not called active immunity.	EXAMPLE 1
Better:	T F	Resistance to smallpox obtained through the use of smallpox vaccine is called passive immunity.	

Poor:	T F	Tuberculosis is not a noncommunicable disease.	EXAMPLE 2
Better:	T F	Tuberculosis is a communicable disease.	

5. Limit true-false statements to a single idea. Complex statements that include more than one idea are difficult to read and understand. A statement that contains one true idea and one false idea is usually inappropriate because it is likely to be more a measure of test-taking skills than of true knowledge of the target subject matter. Complex statements may be used if the student's attention is directed toward the one part of the statement that he or she is to judge to be true or false.

Poor:	T F	Bleeding of the gums is associated with gingivitis, which can be cured by the sufferer himself by brushing his teeth daily.	EXAMPLE
Better:	T F	Daily brushing of the teeth will cure gingivitis.	

6. Make true and false statements approximately equal in length. There is a tendency for true statements to be longer than false ones. Generally, the greater length of true statements results from the need to include qualifications and limitations to make the statement unequivocally true. An occasional long true statement will not cause a problem if it is matched by an occasional long false one and if there is no consistent difference in length between the two categories of statements.

7. Include the same number of true statements as false ones. Teachers are sometimes tempted to include more true statements than false ones because of their concern that students will remember false statements and therefore be learning course content that is wrong. A problem arises when students discover this tendency and learn to answer "true" to statements when they are in doubt.

8. Write statements in your own words. The use of verbatim quotes from the textbook encourages rote memory. In most cases, this is not a legitimate instructional goal.

9. Include the source for statements based on opinion. It is not really fair to force a student to make a decision about whether a statement is true or false if experts in the field are undecided. Listing the source will make the item a more reasonable measure of student understanding and knowledge.

Variations in the Format of True-False items. Several variations in the format of true-false items have been suggested as ways of improving them. Most of these variations endeavor to accomplish one or more of the following: (1) reduce the ambiguity of the items, (2) reduce the effects of guessing on the scores, and/or (3) provide more specific information about how much a student knows. The three most frequently used variations are described below.

1. Underlining a word or clause in the statement. This variation is the simplest one, and it is used to reduce ambiguity by focusing the attention of the examinee on the most important part of the statement.

EXAMPLES

1. <u>T</u> F   Malaria is transmitted by the <u>Anopheles</u> mosquito.
2. T <u>F</u>   If foods are frozen, harmful bacteria in them will be <u>killed</u>.

The instructions for such items should clearly indicate that the student is to judge the truth of falsity of the underlined portion in relation to the rest of the statement. Underlining also permits the use of more complex statements.

2. Requiring students to correct false statements. A student who correctly marks a statement "false" may have made a lucky guess or he or she may have chosen the answer on the basis of misinformation. For example, for the item "Insulin is secreted by the pituitary gland," a student could indicate that it is false because he or she thinks insulin is secreted by the adrenal glands. In this case, incorrect information leads to a correct answer. To make sure that the student knows the facts underlying a false statement and to reduce guessing, the student can be instructed to provide the correct answer to all statements that are marked false. The above example can be corrected by changing "insulin" to one of the pituitary hormones, by changing "is secreted" to "is not secreted," or by changing "the pituitary gland" to "an endocrine gland" or "the pancreas." For this reason, it is advisable when this variation is used, to underline the key word or words in all statements both true and false. The part of the statement that is underlined should be the specific content that the teacher is trying to appraise. Thus, in the example, if the teacher were trying to determine whether students knew the name of a hormone secreted by the pituitary gland, they should be instructed to underline the word "insulin." If the teacher were interested in determining whether students knew the name of the gland that secretes insulin, they should be instructed to underline "the pituitary gland."

3. *Basing true-false items on specific stimulus material provided for the student.* True-false items tend to be most effective and most useful when they are based on specific stimulus material such as a chart, map, graph, table, or reading passage. In this situation, the student is instructed to respond to the item only in terms of the given material. Under these circumstances, the student will have a frame of reference that is better defined. This type of true-false item can be effectively used to appraise comprehension, interpretation, extrapolation, and logical reasoning. An example of this item type is given here.

Directions: The pie graph below shows how each dollar for medical care is spent. Look at the graph carefully. Statements are given following the graph.   EXAMPLE

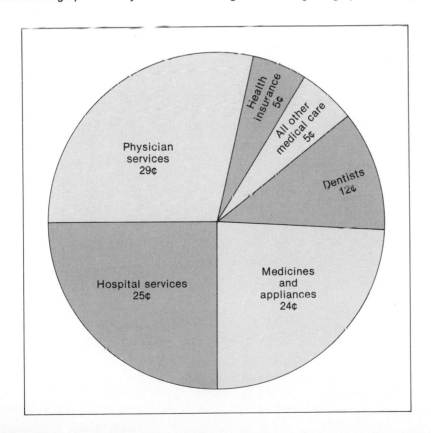

Read each statement carefully.

Mark T, if the data in the graph support the statement.

Mark F, if the data in the graph contradict the statement or no data are provided in the graph to either support or contradict the statement.

(T)   1. More of the medical care dollar is spent for physicians' services than for any other single category of the expense.

(F)   2. Few Americans have health insurance.

(F)   3. Americans spend 24 cents out of every dollar they make on medicines and appliances.

(T)   4. Hospital and physicians' services together account for slightly more than half of the money spent for medical care.

(T)   5. Less money is spent on dental care than on physicians' services.

(T)   6. About 25 percent of the medical care dollar is spent on nursing service in hospitals.

This form of item is sometimes made more complex by requiring the student to answer in four or five categories such as "definitely true," "probably true," "insufficient data to determine whether it is true or false," "probably false," and "definitely false." In this format, the item becomes a multiple-choice item rather than a true-false item.

4. Grouping short true-false items under a common question or statement heading. Two examples of this variation are given here.

EXAMPLES

Directions: Place a T in front of each choice that is a correct answer to the question. Put an F in front of each choice that is NOT a correct answer to the question.

A. Which of the following diseases are caused by viruses?

(T) 1. chicken pox	(T) 5. measles
(F) 2. diphtheria	(T) 6. mumps
(T) 3. influenza	(F) 7. tuberculosis
(F) 4. malaria	(F) 8. typhoid fever

B. A girl, 14 years old, ate the following food during a 24–hour period.

Breakfast	**Lunch**	**Dinner**
Cup of black coffee	1 glass Coca-Cola (8 oz)	Roast rib of beef (9 oz)
	1 hamburger (4 oz) with bun	Mashed potatoes (½ cup)
	French fried potatoes (20 pieces)	1 glass milk (8 oz)
		Apple pie (1 piece)

In which of the following was her diet deficient?

(T)   1. calcium   (F)   5. niacin

(F)   2. calories   (F)   6. protein
(F)   3. carbohydrates   (T)   7. vitamin A
(T)   4. iron   (T)   8. vitamin C

The format of this variation makes it look like a multiple-choice item, but the task for the student is to judge whether each choice is true or false in relation to the original question; therefore, it is basically a series of true-false items. The variation can be an efficient way to test for knowledge of categories, classifications, or characteristics and for simple applications. It is particularly effective for testing a specific part of a topic in depth. The format reduces the reading load for the student, and the question serves as a frame of reference for judging truth or falsity that removes some of the ambiguity in true-false statements. An alternative to this approach is to have the students place a check mark next to the statements that are true and to leave the others unmarked.

Writing Multiple-Choice Items

The multiple-choice item is the most flexible of the objective item types. It can be used to appraise the achievement of any of the educational objectives that can be measured by a paper-and-pencil test except those relating to skill in written expression and originality. An ingenious and talented item writer can construct multiple-choice items that require not only the recall of knowledge but also the use of skills of comprehension, interpretation, applications, analysis, or synthesis to arrive at the keyed answer.

It should be noted that not all multiple-choice items are of high quality and that it takes a great deal of time and skill to write good items. Perhaps the most important characteristic of the multiple-choice test is the way that the options can be altered or replaced. Because he or she can change distractors, the test author has flexibility in adjusting the difficulty of the test item. In this way, tests can be constructed that are at the optimum difficulty level, which maximizes their capacity to differentiate among those taking the test.

The multiple-choice item consists of two parts: the stem, which presents the problem, and the list of possible answers or distractors. In the standard form of the item, one of the options is the correct or best answer and the others are foils or distractors. The stem of the item may be presented either as a question or as an incomplete statement. The form of the stem seems to make no difference in the overall effectiveness of the item as long as the stem presents a clear and specific problem to the examinee.

The number of options used in the multiple-choice item differs from test to test, and there is no real reason why it cannot vary for items in the same test. An item must have at least three answer choices, or options, to be classified as a multiple-choice item, and the typical pattern is to have four or five answer choices to reduce the probability of guessing the answer. A distinction should be made between the number of options presented for a multiple-choice item and the number of effective or functioning options that the item has. In the poor example that follows, written for that eighth-grade test on health, the item will really function as a two choice item because no one is likely to choose Option A or D. The revised item still presents four answer choices but is now more likely to function as a four-option item because Options A and D have been made more reasonable.

EXAMPLE

Poor: About how many calories are recommended daily for a girl, age 14, height 62 in., weight 103 lb, moderately active?
    A. 0
    B. 2,000
    C. 2,500
    D. 30,000

Better: About how many calories are recommended daily for a 14-year-old girl who is 62 in. tall, weighs 103 lb, and is moderately active?
    A. 1,500
    B. 2,000
    C. 2,500
    D. 3,000

The revised item will probably be more difficult than the original one because the options are closer in value. The difficulty of a multiple-choice item depends on the cognitive processes required by the item as well as the closeness of the options. Consider the set of three items shown in the next example, all relating to the meaning of the term "fortified food." We can predict that Version 1 will be relatively easy, Version 2 somewhat more difficult, and Version 3 still more difficult. In Version 1, the stem is a direct copy of the definition of "fortified food" in the textbook and the distractors are not terms used to indicate the addition of nutrients to foods. The difference between Versions 1 and 2 is that the stem of Version 2 recasts the text book definition into a novel form and calls for a different mental process than Version 1 does. The difference between Versions 2 and 3 is in the closeness of the options.

EXAMPLES

1. When a nutrient has been added that is not present in natural food, the food is said to be:
    A. fortified.
    B. processed.
    C. pasteurized.
    D. refined.

2. In the processing of milk for sale, Vitamin D concentrate has been added to provide at least 400 U.S.P. units per quart. The carton can then legally state that the milk is:
    A. fortified.
    B. processed.
    C. pasteurized.
    D. refined.

3. In the processing of milk for sale, Vitamin D concentrate has been added to provide at least 400 U.S.P. units per quart. The carton can then legally state that the milk is:

A. fortified.

B. enriched.

C. irradiated.

D. restored.

Suggestions for Writing Better Multiple-Choice Items. The construction of good tests requires the allocation of an adequate amount of time, proper planning, and adherence to a set of well-recognized rules for item construction. The rules for writing better multiple choice items are included in this section.

1. Be sure the stem of the item clearly formulates a problem. The stem should be worded so that the students clearly understand what problem or question is being asked before they read the answer choices. Look at the poor example that follows. When you finish reading the stem, you know only that the item is related to a part of the pancreas. You have no idea what the problem is until you read each of the options. The answer choices that are provided are heterogeneous in content; that is, one relates to structure, one to function, one to permanence, and one to location. The poor item is really nothing more than four true-false items with the words "The cell islets of the pancreas" in common. The revised item provides both a clearly formulated problem in the stem and a more homogeneous set of answer choices.

EXAMPLES

Poor: The cell islets of the pancreas:

A. contain ducts.

B. produce insulin.

C. disappear as one grows older.

D. are located around the edge of the pancreas.

Better: The cell islets of the pancreas secrete the substance called:

A. trypsin.

B. insulin.

C. tryptophan.

D. adrenalin.

---

2. Include as much of the item as possible in the stem and keep options as short as possible. In the interests of economizing space, minimizing reading time, and providing a clear statement of the problem, try to word and arrange the item so that the answer choices can be kept relatively short. If the same words and phrases are repeated in all or most of the options, as in the poor example given next, rewrite the stem to include the repetitious material. Answer choices that are long in relation to the stem frequently occur because of failure to formulate a problem clearly in the stem.

EXAMPLE   Poor: The term "empty-calorie" food designates:
                                     A.   a food that has few essential nutrients but high caloric value.
                                     B.   a food that has neither essential nutrients nor caloric value.
                                     C.   a food that has both high nutritive value and high caloric value.
                                     D.   a food that has high nutritive value but low caloric value.
                    Better: The term "empty-calorie" applies to foods that are:
                                     A.   low in nutrients and high in calories.
                                     B.   low in both nutrients and calories.
                                     C.   high in both nutrients and calories.
                                     D.   high in nutrients and low in calories.

3. Include in the stem only the material needed to make the problem clear and specific. Items with long, wordy stems that contain material that is irrelevant to the problem are likely to reduce the efficiency of the test. This loss of efficiency occurs because the added material increases the amount of reading needed for an item, which makes it more difficult to separate generalized skill in reading from knowledge of the subject matter. It also causes a student to spend more time on each item, which means fewer items can be included on a test. Sometimes, material unrelated to the item is included in the stem in the mistaken belief that tests should be made to teach as well as assess. Tests appropriately teach as well as test when they (1) reflect accurately the objectives of instruction, (2) pose clear and meaningful questions or problems, and (3) are returned promptly to the students with appropriate comments, not when new material is introduced in the test item.

EXAMPLE   Poor: Cells of one kind belong to a particular group performing a specialized duty.
                                   We call this group of cells a tissue. All of us have different kinds of tissues
                                   in our bodies. Which of the following would be classified as epithelial tissue?
                                   A.   tendons
                                   B.   adenoids and tonsils
                                   C.   mucous membranes
                                   D.   cartilage
                    Better: Which of the following would be classified as epithelial tissue?
                                   A.   tendons
                                   B.   adenoids and tonsils
                                   C.   mucous membranes
                                 D.   cartilage

4. Use the negative only sparingly in an item. Just as was true for true-false items, negatively stated multiple-choice items increase the reading difficulty of an item and require the student to perform difficult reasoning tasks. Negative items also provide little information about exactly what a student knows.

There are times when it is important for the student to know the exception to a general rule or to be able to detect errors. For these purposes, a few items with the words "not" or "except" in the stem may be justified, particularly when overinclusion is a common error for students. When a negative word is included in a stem, it should be underlined and/or capitalized to call the student's attention to it.

The poor example that follows was written to measure whether students knew the function of the semicircular canals, but the item as written does not measure this aspect of the students' knowledge. The revised examples measure more directly what the teacher wanted to assess. There are two reasons why the second "better" example shows a more appropriate use of the negative stem: (1) The most common error made by students about the duties of the Food and Drug Administration is the inclusion of meat inspection, a duty of the Department of Agriculture, and (2) it would be difficult to get three plausible misleads if the item were stated in a positive form.

EXAMPLES

Poor: Which of the following structures of the ear is NOT concerned with hearing?
    A. eardrum
    B. oval window
    C. semicircular canals
    D. cochlea

Better: 1. Which one of the following structures of the ear helps to maintain balance?
        A. eardrum
        B. oval window
        C. semicircular canals
        D. cochlea

      2. Which of the following activities is NOT the responsibility of the U.S. Food and Drug Administration?
        A. inspection of warehouse storing food for interstate shipment
        B. inspection of slaughter houses that ship meat across state lines
        C. initiation of court action to remove spoiled food from the market
        D. testing samples of foods for interstate sale

---

5. *Use novel material in formulating problems to measure understanding or ability to apply principles.* Most teacher-made tests place too much emphasis on rote memory and neglect the measurement of application skills. The multiple-choice item is well adapted to measuring simple recall, but a novel situation must be presented to the student if more than rote memory is to be required to answer the question. Two examples are given here to illustrate how an item can be structured to appraise the ability to use information.

EXAMPLES

Rote memory: Which of the following foods will yield the largest number of calories when metabolized in the body?

A.   1 gram of fat
B.   1 gram of sugar
C.   1 gram of starch
D.   1 gram of protein

Application: Which of the following would result in the greatest reduction of calories if it were eliminated from the daily diet?

A.   1 tablespoon of butter
B.   1 tablespoon of granulated sugar
C.   1 slice of white, enriched bread
D.   1 boiled egg

Rote memory: Death from pneumonia and influenza is most frequent among:

A.   infants and aged people.
B.   infants and elementary school children.
C.   teenagers and aged people.
D.   teenagers and young adults.

Interpretation: Look at the graph below, which shows the death rate from Disease A by age group.

Which of the following diseases could be Disease A?

A.   pneumonia

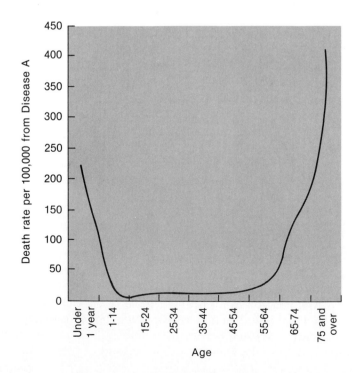

        B.   cancer
        C.   tuberculosis
        D.   heart disease

    6. *Be sure that there is one and only one correct or clearly best answer.* In the typical multiple-choice item, the examinee is instructed to choose one and only one answer. Having instructed the examinee to choose the answer that is best, the test maker is obligated to provide one and only one correct answer for each item. Although this may seem obvious, many items on classroom tests either have two or more equally good answers or no good answer. In the following example, Option B is keyed as the correct answer but there is also a large element of correctness for Options C and E. The revised version eliminates this fault but it may be too easy.

Poor: A color-blind boy inherits the trait from a: **EXAMPLE**
        A.   male parent.
        B.   female parent.
        C.   maternal grandparent.
        D.   paternal grandparent.
        E.   remote ancestor.

Better: A color-blind boy most probably inherited the trait from his:
        A.   father.
        B.   mother.
        C.   paternal grandfather.
        D.   paternal grandmother.

    In addition to making sure that there is only one correct answer, the item writer should make sure that the one answer is unequivocally best. It is the teacher's responsibility to use the very best scholarship, as well as his or her skill in phrasing stem and answer choices, to produce a problem and answer with which experts in the field will agree.

    7. *Be sure distractors are plausible.* One of the major advantages of the multiple-choice item is its capacity to require choices, which permits control of item difficulty. However, the distractor must be attractive to examinees who are lacking in knowledge about the material the item is intended to assess. To make distractors attractive, the incorrect answer choices should be logically consistent with the stem and should represent common errors made by students in a particular grade or at a particular ability level.

    In the first poor example that follows, Options A and C are compounds, not elements, and thus inconsistent with the stem. In the second poor example, Options C and D are implausible.

EXAMPLES

Poor: Which of the following elements is found in proteins but not in carbohydrates or fats?
   A. carbon dioxide
   B. oxygen
   C. water
   D. nitrogen

Poor: The gas that is formed in the cells after the oxidation of food and is taken to the lungs and expelled is:
   A. oxygen.
   B. carbon dioxide.
   C. helium.
   D. chlorine.

One good way to develop plausible distractors, particularly with items that measure quantitative concepts and skills, is to determine what answer a student would get if he or she made a particular error at some point in analyzing or solving the problem. It is sometimes possible to identify specific informational or procedural deficiencies in this way.

8. Be sure no unintentional clues to the correct answer are given. Inexperienced test constructors frequently give away the correct answer to an item or give clues that permit the examinee to eliminate one or more of the incorrect answer choices from consideration.

Examples of items containing some types of unintentional clues are given here in Item 1, which is an example of a clang association, that is, a repetition of a word, phrase, or sound in the keyed answer and in the stem. Item 2 contains specific determiners that have the same effect in multiple-choice options as in true-false statements. In Item 3, the keyed answer is much longer than the other options. Item 4 is an example of a grammatical inconsistency; the word "a" in the stem implies a singular word, but Options A and C are both plural.

The revised items show how each of these faults can be corrected to make the items more effective in measuring knowledge rather than testwiseness.

EXAMPLES

Poor: Clang association
   1. The function of the platelets in the blood is to help in:
      A. carrying oxygen to the cells.
      B. carrying food to the cells.
      C. clotting of the blood.
      D. fighting disease.

Poor: Specific determiners
   2. Which of the following is characteristic of anaerobic bacteria?
      A. They never live in soil.
      B. They can live without molecular oxygen.

       C. They always cause disease.

       D. They can carry on photosynthesis.

Poor: Length clues

    3. The term "side-effect" of a drug refers to:

       A. additional benefits from the drug.

       B. the chain effect of drug action.

       C. the influence of drugs on crime.

       D. any action of the drug in the body other than the one the doctor wanted the drug to have.

Poor: Grammatical inconsistency

    4. Penicillin is obtained from a:

       A. bacteria.

       B. mold.

       C. coal tars.

       D. tropical tree.

Better:

    1. Which of the following structures in the blood helps in forming blood clots?

       A. red blood cells

       B. lymphocytes

       C. platelets

       D. monocytes

    2. The one characteristic that distinguishes all anaerobic bacteria is their ability to:

       A. withstand extreme variation in air temperature.

       B. live without molecular oxygen.

       C. live as either saprophytes or parasites.

       D. reproduce either in living cells or nonliving culture media.

    3. Which of the following, if it occurred, would be a side-effect of aspirin for a man who had been taking two aspirin tablets every 3 hours for a heavy cold and slight fever?

       A. normal body temperature

       B. reduction in frequency of coughing

       C. easier breathing

       D. ringing in the ears

    4. Penicillin is obtained from:

       A. bacteria.

       B. molds.

       C. coal tars.

       D. tropical trees.

---

9. Use the option "none of these" or "none of the above" only when the keyed answer can be classified unequivocally as correct or incorrect. This option can be appropriately used by experienced test writers on tests of spelling, mathematics, and study skills. In these types of tests an absolutely correct answer can be given. On other types of tests, where the student is to choose the best answer and where the keyed answer is the best answer, but not necessarily absolutely correct, the use of "none of these" or "none of the above" is inappropriate.

The option "none of the above," if used, works better when the stem is stated as a question rather than a sentence to be completed. An incomplete sentence seldom works because the "none of the above" statement seldom makes any sense because it does not complete the stem grammatically. An example of this is illustrated in the following item, which appeared on a tenth-grade biology test.

EXAMPLE

Poor: Of the following, the one that is never a function of the stem of plants is:
    A.   conduction.
    B.   photosynthesis.
    C.   support.
    <u>D.</u>   none of the above.

Not only is the option "none of the above" grammatically inconsistent with the stem, but it is also logically inconsistent with the stem. Option D does not name a function of the plant, and the double negative effect of the option and the "never" in the stem makes comprehension of the meaning of the item difficult. There is no way of revising the item to make it better because any function of a plant is performed by the stem in some plant.

Some studies of the use of "none of these" as an option have indicated that the use of the option makes items more difficult and more discriminating, but other studies have failed to confirm this finding (Rimland, 1960; Wesman & Bennett, 1946).

If "none of these" or its equivalent is used as an option in items requiring quantitative solutions or in spelling tests, it should be used as frequently for the correct option as any other answer choice and the stem of the item should be phrased as a question. On such tests, the option functions best if it is used as the correct answer on some of the easier items at the beginning of the test to reinforce the instructions that "none of the above" is sometimes the correct answer.

The example given next represents a poor use of the "none of the above" option in an item calling for a numerical answer because only approximations are given rather than exact quantities. Option B is keyed as the correct answer, but Option E is better because the estimates of the blood volume for an average adult range from a low of 10 pints to a high of 16 pints. One could also question the importance of a junior high school student knowing this particular fact.

EXAMPLE

Poor: How many pints of blood does a normal human adult of average weight have?
    A.   3 pints
    <u>B.</u>   13 pints

C. 30 pints
D. 50 pints
E. None of the above

Better: Approximately what percentage of the body weight of a healthy human adult is blood?

A. 3% to 5%.
B. 8% to 9%.
C. 12% to 15%.
D. 20% to 25%.

10. Avoid the use of "all of the above" in the multiple-choice item. This type of item is used either when only three options can easily be generated and a fourth option is needed or when there is an easily obtained list of characteristics or traits of something and it is difficult to come up with three incorrect distractors. In this latter case, it is easy to list three of the characteristics along with an "all of the above" statement. Usually, when the option "all of the above" is used on teacher-made tests, it is the correct answer. Items using this option tend to be easy because the examinee will be led to the correct answer even though he or she has only partial information. Look at the poor example that follows. Assume that the student has been instructed to mark only one answer and that he or she knows that both age and weight are used to compute basal energy requirements. He must then mark D for his answer; thus, he gets credit for having complete information even though he does not. In the revised version, the student must have full information to arrive at the keyed answer.

The option "all of the above" is much more effective if it is used in the variation of the complex multiple-choice item described in the next section.

Poor: Which of the following factors must be considered in computing basal energy requirements?

A. age
B. height
C. weight
D. all of the above

Better: Which of the following factors must be considered in computing basal energy requirements?

A. weight only
B. age only
C. height and weight only
D. age and weight only
E. age, height, and weight

Variations in the Format of Multiple-Choice Items. A number of variations of the standard multiple-choice items have been suggested. Gerberich (1956) gives illustrations of most of these variations. One commonly used variation is the matching item that will be discussed in a separate section. In this section, we discuss two other variations that are sometimes used.

Complex Multiple-Choice Items. This variation gets its name from the format and the combinations of options that are used as answer choices. It is most effective when it is used to appraise knowledge of or ability to apply or interpret multiple causes, effects, functions, or uses. The following example illustrates a poor use of the complex multiple-choice item and several faults of item construction. Although there are multiple signs of impaired circulation, the options are short; therefore, the knowledge could be tested more efficiently in the usual format. The technical problems with the item are as follows: (1) No specific problem is presented to the examinee, (2) Signs 1, 2, and 3 are used in all the answer choices so that the student is required only to determine whether signs 4 and 5 are correct, and (3) the method of presenting choices (contrast between Option C and Options B and D) is varied, which creates unnecessary difficulty for the student.

The following example then illustrates an effective use of the item type because it requires the student to discriminate between both the kind of food and the kind of commerce that come under the jurisdiction of the Food and Drug Administration. Hughes and Trimble (1965) have shown that this type of item is both more difficult and more discriminating than the typical form of multiple-choice item that tests for the same knowledge.

EXAMPLE

Poor: If a bandage or cast on the arm is too tight, it might interfere with the circulation in the arm. Signs of interference with circulation include:

1. cold.   3. numbness.   5. loss of motion.
2. blanching.   4. swelling.

    A. all of these
    B. 1, 2, 3 and 4
    C. all except 5
    D. 1, 2, 3 and 5

Better: Look at each of the food processing or producing activities below.

1. A housewife makes jellies and sells them in her home town.
2. A butcher makes scrapple and pork sausage and sells them only in the state of Maryland.
3. A food processor makes jellies in California and sells them in New York.
4. A slaughterhouse in Chicago ships meats to all states.
5. A citrus grower produces oranges in Florida and ships them to all Eastern States.

Which of the above would be subject to the regulations and supervision of the U.S. Food and Drug Administration?

    A. 2 and 4 only
    B. 3 and 5 only
    C. 3, 4, and 5 only

D. 1, 3, and 5 only
E. all of them

The complex multiple-choice item should be used very sparingly on teacher-made tests.

Paired Item Format.   This format is an efficient and effective way of measuring judgment of relative amounts or quantities, relative effects of changing conditions, or relative chronology. This format preferably should be used for content having established quantitative values. For example, the use of the pair of statements, (I) "The number of hours of sleep needed by a 14-year-old boy" and (II) "The number of hours of sleep needed by a 30-year-old man" would be undesirable because there is no empirically determined value for the number of hours of sleep required for any age group.

Directions: Items 1 through 3 are based on pairs of statements. Reach each state-
              ment carefully. On your answer sheet, mark:

A   if the amount in Statement I is greater than that in Statement II.
B   if the amount in Statement II is greater than that in Statement I.
C   if the amount in Statement I is equal to that in Statement II.

(B) 1. I Caloric value of 1 tablespoon of cane sugar.
         II Caloric value of 1 tablespoon of butter.
(A) 2. I The daily requirement of calories for a 25-year-old male
            lumberjack who is 73 in. tall and weighs 190 lb.
         II The daily requirement of calories for a 25 year-old male
            office clerk who is 73 in. tall and weighs 190 lb.
(A) 3. I The daily requirement of iron for a 16-year-old girl.
         II The daily requirement of iron for a 16-year-old boy.

EXAMPLE

Writing Matching Items

The matching item can best be thought of as a series of multiple-choice items presented in a more efficient manner. For example, a series of items is listed down the left-hand column of the test paper and a series of options are listed down the right-hand column. The student picks the option that goes with each item. The matching item has most frequently been used to measure factual information such as meanings of terms, dates of events, achievements of people, symbols for chemical elements, and authors of books. Effective matching items can be constructed by basing the set of items on a chart, map, diagram, or drawing. Features of the figure can be numbered and the examinee can be asked to match names, functions, and so on with the numbers on the figure. This type of item is useful in tests dealing with study skills, science, or technology; for example, such items might require biology students to identify and match cell structures.

When there is a need to assess a student's ability to make associations, matching items are more efficient than a series of multiple-choice items. The major disadvantage of this approach is that it is suitable only for measuring associations and not for assessing higher levels of understanding. Another disadvantage of this method is that such a test cannot easily be machine scored because the number of options often exceeds the five spaces allocated to each item on standard machine-scorable answer sheets. Of course, answer sheets can be customized for this type of item.

Matching items, like other types of test items, must be carefully constructed to be useful. Teacher-made tests often have technical faults and poorly constructed matching items can be superficial measurement devices. Look at the following matching exercise, which appeared on a test in health and hygiene for an eighth-grade class.

The example illustrates some of the most common mistakes made in preparing matching items. First, the directions are vague and fail to specify the basis for matching. Second, the set of stimuli is too heterogeneous for a good matching exercise. How many answer choices in Column II are logically possible answers for the first statement in Column I? For the second? The statements in Column I have very little in common except that they relate to teeth and dental health in general. Third, the set is too long, and the answer choices in Column II are not arranged in any systematic order. Even examinees who know the answer to a statement, have to search through the entire list in Column II to find it, which is time consuming. Fourth, some of the entries are vague, for example, Entries 9, 11, and 12 in Column I and Entries i, l, and m in Column II. The vagueness makes it difficult to justify the answer keyed as correct by the teacher; furthermore, the accuracy of number 12 can be questioned. Fifth, there are 16 statements in Column I and 16 answer choices in Column II. If the student knows 15, he or she automatically gets the 16th correct.

EXAMPLE

Poor:

Directions: Place the correct letter to the left of each number. Use each letter only once.

	Column I		Column II
(p)	1. Number of permanent teeth	a.	Malocclusion
(i)	2. Vitamin D	b.	Tear and rip food
(n)	3. Vitamin C	c.	Trench mouth
(k)	4. Enamel	d.	Straightening teeth
(o)	5. Bleeding gums	e.	Jawbone socket
(c)	6. Vincent's Angina	f.	Contains nerves and
(d)	7. Orthodontia		blood vessel
(e)	8. Alveolus	g.	Grind food
(a)	9. Lower jaw protruding	h.	Crown
(f)	10. Pulp	i.	Sunshine
(m)	11. Acid	j.	Cleaning device

(l)	12. Low percentage of decay	k.	Hardest substance
(b)	13. Cuspids	l.	Primitives
(g)	14. Molars	m.	Decay
(h)	15. Visible part of tooth	n.	Citrus fruits
(i)	16. Dental floss	o.	Gingivitis
		p.	32

Note: The "correct" answers are those designated by the teacher who constructed the exercise.

Suggestions for Writing Better Matching Items. Matching items can be thought of as a condensed series of multiple-choice items. Many of the same rules for writing better items apply to both. In this section, we discuss the specific rules for writing matching items.

1. Keep the set of statements in an single matching exercise homogeneous. The last example would have been better if all of the choices were parts of a tooth, diseases of the teeth and gums, or methods of promoting oral hygiene. Homogeneous choices force the student to make genuine discriminations to arrive at correct answers.

2. Limit the number of entries in any matching exercise. Limiting the number of entries makes it easier to keep the content homogeneous. Short-answer lists also put less of a clerical burden on the examinee.

3. Have the students choose answers from the column with the shortest statements. The reason for this suggestion is that the answer column will be read several times by the student and it takes less time to read short statements than long ones. Having the student select from the shortest column helps to minimize the already important influence of reading ability on test performance.

4. Use a heading for each column that accurately describes its content. A descriptive heading helps to define the task for the examinee. If the test maker is unable to identify a heading that specifically defines the content, the entries are probably too heterogeneous.

5. Have more answer choices than the number of entries to be matched unless answer choices can be used more than once. The larger number of answer choices reduces the influence of guessing on test scores. It also prevents students from arriving at correct answers through a process of elimination that does not require the student always to know the associations.

6. Arrange the answer choices in a logical order if one exists. If a student knows the answer, he or she should be able to find it easily. Arranging names in alphabetical order or dates in chronological order reduces the time required to find the answer.

7. Specify in the directions the basis for matching and whether answer choices can be used more than once. This practice will tend to reduce ambiguity and make the task more uniform for all examinees.

Variation in the Format of Matching Items.   A variation in the matching item format is the classification or master list. This variation can be used quite effectively to appraise application, comprehension, or interpretation. It is an efficient way of exploring the range of mastery of a concept or related set of concepts. An illustration of this type of item is given here.

EXAMPLE,
MASTER
MATCHING

Instructions: Below are given four kinds of appeals that advertisers of health and beauty products make.

A.   Appeal to fear or a sense of insecurity
B.   Appeal to snobbery or identification with a particular small group or individual
C.   Appeal to desire to be like others, that is, to join the "bandwagon"
D.   Appeal to authority

Statements 1 to 6 are advertisements of imaginary products. Read each statement carefully. For each statement, mark the letter of the appeal that is being used. Answer choices may be used more than once.

(A)   1. Don't let iron-tired blood get you down. Keep your verve and vivacity. Take Infantol.
(D)   2. Research shows Lucy's Little Lethal Pills are 10 times more effective than ordinary pain killers.
(B)   3. Duchess Poorhouse, the international beauty, bathes her face twice a day with Myrtle's Turtle Oil.
(B)   4. Men, are you tired of a woman's deodorant? Be a man. Use No-Sweat. Leave the weaker stuff to the weaker sex.
(B)   5. At $1,629.21, the Inside Jogger is not for everyone. Only a select few can be proud owners of one! Are you one of these?
(C)   6. Be one of the crowd. Drink and serve Popsie's Cola.

Preparing the Objective Test for Use

Each examinee should have his or her own copy of the test. This practice is particularly important for multiple-choice tests. Oral administration of objective tests does not work well. The teacher should always try to obtain the best quality copies possible. More important than the process of duplication is the quality of work, both the organization of the layout of the test and the typing. The most important points to consider in arranging the items of the test will be discussed in the paragraphs that follow.

1. Arrange items on the test so that they are easy to read. In the interest of those taking the test, items should not be crowded together on the test paper because spreading out the items makes them more easily read and understood. Items also are easier to read if each response is on a separate line. Furthermore, items should not be split between pages because such an arrangement may confuse the examinees. If several items all refer to a single diagram or chart, try to arrange the test so that the diagram or chart and all of the items are on the same page. An alternative when it is impossible to fit the stimulus material (chart, diagram, etc.) and the questions on a single page is to put the stimulus material on a separate sheet that is not stapled with the rest of the test. On the downside, optimum arrangement of items to facilitate a student's ability to read and understand the items can add to the cost of reproducing copies of the test because more pages will be needed for each test.

2. *Plan the layout of the test so that a separate answer sheet can be used to record answers.* The use of a separate answer sheet may make the test-taking process a bit more difficult but there is a considerable gain in ease of test scoring. Most standardized tests require separate answer sheets, but many students in the first two grades may find the use of a separate answer sheet too difficult. By the third grade, students can easily learn to use a separate answer sheet. The ability to use a separate answer sheet is a test-taking skill that should be taught to students, and practice in the skill should be provided to students early. Although the appropriate equipment can be expensive and not simple to operate, the use of a machine scorer is highly recommended. The simplest machines will score the answer sheets and print the scores on them, but there are more sophisticated scanners available that will capture the data and store it on a disk. This type of equipment can greatly facilitate item analysis procedures.

3. *Group items of the same format (true-false, multiple choice, or matching) together.* Each different kind of objective item requires a different set of directions. Grouping items of the same format together makes it possible to write a concise and clear set of directions that will apply throughout that part of the test. Each item type requires a different response set or approach on the part of the examinee. The examinee will be better able to maintain an appropriate response set if the items of the same type are grouped together.

4. *Within item type, group items dealing with the same content together.* This practice makes the test more coherent and provides a reasonable context for the student. It can also help both the student and the teacher to see the student's strong and weak points.

5. *Arrange items so that difficulty progresses from easy to hard.* This practice is of particular importance on a test for which testing time is limited and some items on the test will not be attempted by all students. Those unattempted items should be the more difficult ones that the examinee would have been less likely to answer correctly even if he or she had reached them. On a power test on which most students answer all of the items, this arrangement can encourage students, particularly young children and less able students by ensuring some early success. This practice may motivate them to attempt all of the items on the test rather than to give up. The practice is supported more by professional judgment than by empirical evidence.

6. *Write a set of specific directions for each item type.* A good set of directions will provide information about how the examinees are to record their answers, the basis on which they are to select their answers, and the scoring procedures

that will be used. For a test made up of multiple-choice items that will not be corrected for guessing and for which separate answer sheets are used, the teacher might use the following set of directions.

EXAMPLE

Directions: Read each item and decide which choice best completes the statement or answers the question.

Mark your answers on the separate answer sheet. Do not mark them on the test itself. Indicate your answer by darkening in the letter on the answer sheet the letter corresponding to your choice. That is, if you think that Choice B is the best answer to Item 1, darken in the B in the row after No. 1 on your answer sheet.

Your score will be the number of correct items, so it will be to your advantage to respond to every item, even if you are not sure of the correct response.
Be sure your name is on your answer sheet.

For a test made up of true-false items in which answers are to be recorded on the test paper and the total score will be corrected for guessing, the following set of directions could be used.

EXAMPLE

Directions: Read each of the following statements carefully.

If all or any part of the statement is false, circle the F in front of the statement.

If the statement is completely true, circle the T in front of the statement.

Your score will be the number of correct answers minus the number of incorrect answers, so do not guess blindly. If you are not reasonably sure of an answer, omit the item.

Be sure your name is on your test.

---

7. *Be sure that one item does not provide clues to the answer of another item or items.* Unless one is very careful in assembling items for a test, the answer to an item may be given away by a previous item. All of the items that are finally selected should be carefully checked because it is possible for a true-false or completion item to give clues to the answer of a multiple-choice item or vice versa. For example, in the example that follows, the true-false item provides a clue to the answer to the objective item.

EXAMPLES

1. <u>T</u> F   The spores of the bacteria causing botulism are present in soil and air.

2.   Which of the following bacteria form spores?
    A. Staphylococus causing "food poisoning"
    <u>B.</u> Bacillus causing botulism
    C. Bacillus causing typhoid fever
    D. Pneumococcus causing pneumonia

8. Be sure that the correct responses do not form a pattern. Some classroom teachers attempt to make their job of scoring easier by establishing a regular pattern of correct answers. For example, on a true-false test, they use a repetitive pattern such as T, T, F, F, F, or on a multiple-choice test, they use a pattern such as A, C, B, D. When a pattern is used, some testwise students may discover the pattern and use it as a means of answering items that they really do not know. On four-option multiple-choice tests, there is a tendency for the correct answers to appear more frequently in the second and third positions than in the first and last positions. On a multiple-choice test the correct answer should appear in each of the possible response positions about the same percentage of the time. For example, on a four-option multiple-choice test of 50 items, the teacher might check to see that each response position contains the keyed answer in not less than 10 and not more than 15 items.

Scoring the Objective Test

Once the test has been constructed, typed, reproduced, administered, and scored, the assessment procedure is still not complete. The scores must be interpreted. The transformation of raw scores into standard scores was discussed in Chapter 3 and the interpretation of test scores for the purpose of assigning grades was presented in Chapter 6. The interpretation of scores can also be influenced by the interpretation of error caused by guessing, which is discussed in the following section. Another important set of activities that takes place after a test has been scored are item analysis procedures. It is important that this step not be omitted because only through this process can subsequent tests be improved. This topic will be covered later in this chapter.

Correction for Guessing

It is well known that there are differences among students in their tendency to guess on an objective test when they are not sure of the answer. The more they guess, the less reliable the test will be because some students will be luckier than others. Willingness to guess is particularly important when tests are speeded because not every student has enough time to finish. Under these conditions, students who guess on items when there is not enough time to answer carefully will obtain higher scores than those students who leave the items blank. These differences in willingness to guess introduce variations in scores that are not related to real differences in achievement among students.

One reason for instructing examinees not to guess and for imposing a penalty for incorrect answers is to try to make the guessing behavior more alike for all examinees.

Controlling Guessing.   One approach to dealing with the problem of guessing is to adjust scores with the correction for guessing equation. This equation is based on the assumption that all incorrect responses result from guessing. Students are expected either to get an item correct or to omit it. The correction for guessing equation works by subtracting points from the score of the student who guesses, equivalent to the gain that can be expected from guessing. On a multiple-choice test with four alternatives, a student can be expected, by chance alone, to get one out of four answers correct by guessing. Therefore, for every three questions a students gets incorrect, he or she can be expected to get one correct by guessing. To put this logic into mathematical terms, the following equation is used:

$$\text{Corrected score} = R - \frac{W}{(n-1)}$$

where

R is the number of items answered correctly,
W is the number of items answered incorrectly, and
n is the number of answer choices for an item.

Items for which examinees do not give an answer, that is, items they omit, do not count in this formula for guessing. On a true-false test (where there are only two possible answers), $n - 1$ in the formula becomes $2 - 1$, or 1, and the correction for guessing is the number of correct answers minus the number of incorrect answers.

The two examples that follow, the first based on a true-false test and the second on a multiple-choice test, illustrate how the equation works.

EXAMPLE 1

STUDENT PERFORMANCE

Type of Test	n	R	W	Skips
True-false	2	48	20	7

Corrected score = 48 − 20/(2 −1) = 48 − 20/1 = 28

EXAMPLE 2

STUDENT PERFORMANCE

Type of Test	n	R	W	Skips
Multiple-choice	5	48	20	7

Corrected score = 48 − 20/5 − 1 = 48 − 20/4 = 43

Criticism of the Correction for Guessing Equation.   The correction for guessing formula has been criticized both because its assumptions are difficult to meet and because it generally fails to do what it purports to do, which is to correct for guessing. The formula is based on the following two assumptions: (1)

that all guesses are blind, with each response having an equal probability of occurring, and (2) that every incorrect answer results from guessing. The first assumption rejects the possibility that a student might make an educated guess based on partial information or eliminate some options. If this happens, the probabilities in the formula would change. On a four-option multiple choice test, the probability that a student will obtain a correct answer becomes greater than 1 in 4. Only when you have a highly speeded test, where it is not possible to give a reasoned response to all questions, will you have students engaged in truly blind guessing. The second assumption precludes the possibility that a student might make an incorrect response based on faulty or misunderstood knowledge.

Undercorrection.   On a four option multiple-choice test, the formula will un dercorrect to the extent that a student chooses answers based on partial information or can eliminate responses and guess which of the remaining responses is correct. Under these circumstances, the student is well advised to guess because the penalty for guessing is less than the expected increase in score that would accrue to the student if he or she guessed. If even one alternative can be eliminated, guessing will help the student's score. On the other hand, students who are not testwise are likely to be intimidated by the knowledge that the correction for guessing formula is being employed, and for this reason they may refrain from guessing.

Overcorrection.   The correction for guessing formula is most likely to overcorrect on tests that emphasize higher level thought processes. On such a test, there will be a larger proportion of students who get items incorrect because they were unable to employ correctly the cognitive processes required. For instance, in solving a problem requiring mathematical computations, a student may make arithmetic errors. Although such errors really should not be classified as guesses, they are with this formula, which causes overcorrection.

When the Assumptions Are Met.   Even under ideal circumstances where the test is highly speeded and guessing is blind and random, the correction for guessing formula does not punish the student for guessing. The formula only penalizes the student the number of items that they would be expected to get correct by chance, which brings them to the point where they would have been had they not guessed. Under these circumstances some students will be lucky and get more than their fair share of items correct by guessing, while others will be unlucky and get fewer items correct. The formula can do nothing to correct for this occurrence. This formula corrects for guessing but not for the luck of the guesser.

Technical Limitations.   Another drawback to the use of this formula is that it does not change the rank order of students if no questions are omitted. Under these circumstances, there is a perfect correlation between raw scores and corrected scores. Only when there are omitted responses does the correlation become less than 1.0, and even then it remains in the 0.90s (Ebel, 1979) unless there is a great deal of variability in the number of items omitted.

Reliability and validity are increased by correcting for guessing only if there is a positive correlation between omitted responses and the raw score (Ebel,

1979). Of course, this circumstance would not normally be expected to occur because the student who works most quickly and answers the most questions is usually the better student. Additionally, the more testwise students are likely both to answer more questions and also do better on the test overall.

It would be possible to employ a correction for guessing formula that would be even stricter. For instance, on a four-option multiple-choice test, one point could be deducted for every incorrect answer, rather than one-third of a point, as is done with the original formula.

Students who were made aware of this procedure would be more likely to leave a question blank unless they were sure of their answer than to risk the large penalty for guessing. Such an approach would certainly diminish guessing, but it is not clear that it would yield a more reliable test because the ability to make educated guesses is an important skill closely related to a student's overall grasp of the subject matter. Thus, an increased number of omitted questions would have the effect of shortening the test and lowering reliability. There is little to be gained from discouraging guessing this way.

Why the Correction for Guessing Equation Is Used.   You might, at this point, ask why, given the previous discussion, the correction for guessing equation is ever employed. The motivations of those using this formula may be more related to discouraging guessing than to correcting for guessing. Because guessing contributes directly to error variance, it is believed that the use of this equation might increase reliability. Reliability coefficients are the most easily obtainable and objective evidence of the quality of a test, so a great deal of emphasis is placed on these indices, and even a slight increase in reliability will be hailed as improvement in a test.

With this increased reliability, the importance of testwiseness increases. The testwise student guesses to his or her advantage, whereas the student who is not testwise is afraid to guess and ends up with a lower score. Because it is anticipated that testwiseness correlates with the total score on the test, the introduction of this factor may enhance rather than detract from reliability.

Guessing on a test presents the most serious problem for tests that are highly speeded or that have items with only two answer choices. The scores obtained from such tests will probably be more dependable if they are corrected for guessing. In multiple-choice tests that have four or five answer choices (or options) and liberal enough time limits to permit all or most examinees to attempt every item, a score that is simply the number of correct answers is quite satisfactory, and there is little or no gain from correcting for guessing.

Using Item Analysis to Improve Objective Tests

Good classroom testing practice generally requires the reuse of test items because of the enormous amount of work involved in generating items. If the same tests are used over and over with no change, there will not only be no improvement in the test, there will also be an increased liklihood of a breach in test security. Once the teacher has constructed, administered, and scored a test, he or she needs to know which items to include on the next test, which to modify, and which to eliminate. These decisions cannot be made by determining the proportion of students getting a particular item correct. Although as a general rule it is better to avoid items that nearly everyone gets correct or incorrect, it is possible to have an item that many students answer incorrectly that assesses something useful and should be retained. At the same time, if an easy item covers a particularly important point, you may be pleased that everyone correctly answered it and want to know this fact.

Categorizing items as good and poor by inspection is also of limited value. Except to identify clearly flawed items, this practice seldom provides much insight into item usefulness. On the other hand, students can sometimes offer useful feedback about items that are flawed in some way, and their comments and suggestions should not be ignored.

The most sophisticated item analysis procedures are generally associated with large-scale standardized tests, where the test publishers have sizable resources that can be devoted to elaborate item analysis. In that setting, these techniques are indispensable. The use of item analysis procedures by classroom teachers is less common. The procedures are seldom employed because they require technical support, specialized skills, and the investment of a great deal of time. If optical scanning is available at a particular school, the item analysis procedures described later in this chapter can be used to evaluate, improve, and correct test items. However, even when this service is not available, the classroom teacher can implement some of the procedures described below without an unreasonable amount of effort. As personal computers and optical scanners have become more available, it has become easier for teachers to conduct more elaborate item analyses.

Item Analysis Assumptions

Item analysis procedures are intended to maximize test reliability. Because maximization of test reliability is accomplished by determining the relationship between individual items and the test as a whole, it is important to ensure that the overall test is measuring what it is supposed to measure. If this is not the case, the total score will be a poor criterion for evaluating each item.

Need for Item Analyses

The analysis of the responses that students make to the items on a test can serve several important purposes, such as the following:

1. The most important function of item analysis procedures is the provision of information about how the quality of test items compare. This comparison is necessary if subsequent tests of the same material are going to be better.

2. Item analysis can provide diagnostic information about the types of items that students most often get incorrect, and this information can be used as a basis for making instructional decisions.

3. Item analysis procedures can provide the teacher with a rational basis for discussing test results with students. There is tendency for such discussions to degenerate into special pleadings by students who believe that any item they answered incorrectly must be flawed.

4. In addition to communicating to the test developer which items need to be improved or eliminated, item analysis provides feedback that can enhance a teacher's item-writing skills. This process is much more effective for enhancing skills than merely reading about how to write better items.

Methods of Conducting Item Analyses

There are several different methods of conducting an item analysis. In terms of sophistication, the methods range from those based on complex item response theory to fairly simple ones that can easily be employed by a teacher with minimal training and without access to a computer. With the appropriate equipment and software, it is possible to set up procedures that can easily provide a wealth of item analysis information to the teacher with minimal effort on his or her part. Unfortunately, the equipment and technical expertise are not generally available to the classroom teacher.

Simplified Procedures for Conducting Item Analyses

The first step in performing an item analysis is the tabulation of the responses that have been made to each item of the test. You will need to know how many students got each item correct, how many chose each of the possible incorrect answers, and how many skipped the item. You must have this information for the upper and lower sections of a class based on the total test score. From this type of tabulation, you will be able to answer the following questions about each item:

1. How difficult is the item?

2. Does the item distinguish between the better and the poorer students?

3. Do some students respond to all the options? Or are there some options that no students choose?

To illustrate the type of information that is provided by an item analysis, in Examples 1–4 of this section, four items from a social studies test are presented along with the analysis of responses for each item. This test was given to 100 high school seniors who enrolled in a course called Current American Problems. There were 95 multiple-choice items on the test, each with four options. The highest score on the test was 85, and the lowest score was 14. The test papers were arranged in order, by the total score, starting with the score of 85 and ending with the score of 14. The top 25 papers were selected to represent the upper group (scores ranged from 59 to 85) and the last 25 papers were selected to represent the lower group (scores ranged from 14 to 34). The item analysis is based only on those in the upper and lower group. The responses made to each item by each student in the upper and lower groups were tallied to give the frequency of choosing each option. These frequencies are shown on the right. The correct option is underlined. Each item is followed by a brief discussion of the item data.

The first thing we can learn about the test comes from the total score distribution. The test was quite difficult. The 3rd quartile is located at the point where the median should be, 62% correct $[(59/95) = 0.62]$. A second indication that the test is too hard is that at least one student scored 10 points below the chance level of 24. When this happens, it is necessary to inspect the score distribution to determine whether this was an isolated case or if several other students scored well below chance. Such poor scores could result from misinformation or a motivation to do poorly. Under such circumstances, the teacher should talk to the students and try to determine the cause. The test also shows a wide range of scores. The range is 72 points out of a possible 95, and the interquartile range is 25; therefore, the test has been successful in spreading out the students.

The following example is an easy item because everyone in the upper groups and 20 students in the lower group got it correct. However, it does differentiate in the desired direction because the incorrect answers that occurred fall in the lower group. The item is also good in that all of the incorrect options are functioning; that is, each incorrect answer was chosen by at least one student in the lower group. Two or three easy items like this one would be good icebreakers with which to start a test.

	EXAMPLE 1

"Everyone's switching to Breath of Spring Cigarettes!" is an example of the propaganda technique called:

	Upper	Lower
A. glittering generality.	0	2
B. bandwagon.	25	20
C. testimonial.	0	2
D. plain folk.	0	1
Item omitted.	0	0

The next example is a difficult but effective item because only 13 out of 50 students got it correct. It is also effective because all 13 students getting the item correct were in the upper group. All of the incorrect options attracted some students in the lower group, and all of the incorrect options attracted more of the lower group than of the higher group. Incidentally, an item such as this one diminishes the effect of guessing on test scores. When an item is provided that is attractive and plausible enough for members of the lower group to choose it, there is that much less guessing occurring. In fact, on a properly constructed test, the average score of a theoretical group of students who do not know the answers to any questions should be less than the chance level. For example, on a 40-item, four-option multiple-choice test, the average score of this theoretical group of students should be less than 10 items correct.

EXAMPLE 2	There were no federal income taxes before 1913 because prior to 1913:		
		Upper	Lower
	A. the federal budget was balanced.	3	5
	B. regular property taxes provided enough revenue to run the government.	9	15
	C. a tax on income was unconstitutional.	13	0
	D. the income of the average worker in the U.S. was too low to be taxed.	0	5
	Item omitted	0	0

The next example turned out to be a poor item. First, the item is very difficult; only 8 out of the 50, or 16% of the students got it correct. Second, the item is negatively discriminating; that is, correct answers were more frequent in the lower group than in the upper group. There are two possible explanations for these results: (1) The item was ambiguous, especially for students who knew the most, or (2) the students have not learned the provisions of the "correct practices act." The second explanation is the more probable. The concentration of responses of the upper group at Option A and the apparently random responses of the lower group that indicate random guessing suggest that the class, as a whole, did not understand the meaning of the "corrupt practices act." To arrive at the correct answer to the item, the student would have to know (1) the limit placed on contributions to the national committee of a political party, (2) who is forbidden to make contributions, and (3) what kind of organization the National Association of Manufacturers is. The teacher would have to discuss the item with the class to determine where the difficulty lies, but you might guess that it is Points 1 and 3 that are causing difficulty in the upper group.

EXAMPLE 3	Under the "corrupt practices act" the national committee of a political party would be permitted to accept a contribution of:		
		Upper	Lower
	A. $10,000 from Mr. Jones.	15	6
	B. $1,000 from the ABC Hat Corporation.	4	6
	C. $5,000 from the National Association of Manufacturers.	2	6
	D. $500 from union funds of a local labor union.	4	7
	Item omitted	0	0

This next item shows some discrimination in the desired direction (21 v. 17), but the differentiation is not very sharp. The response pattern is one that is quite common. Only two of the four choices are functioning at all. Nobody selects either Option B or Option C. If we wished to use this item again, we might try substituting "wages paid for easy work" for Option B and "money paid to people on welfare" for Option C. The use of the adjective "easy" in Option B (it is also in the stem) and the idea of getting money for not working in Option C might make the item more difficult and therefore more discriminating.

The term "easy money" as used in economics means:		
	Upper	Lower
A. the ability to borrow money at low interest rates.	21	17
B. dividends that are paid on common stocks.	0	0
C. money that is won in contests.	0	0
D. money paid for unemployment.	4	8
Item omitted	0	0

EXAMPLE 4

Formal Item Analysis Procedures

The previous section included a discussion of an informal, straightforward approach to conducting an item analysis that had the virtue of conceptual simplicity. The lack of a concrete discrimination index is its most important limitation. Two methods of indicating the discriminating power of an item are discussed next.

Item Discrimination.   As in the previous section, which discussed simplified procedures for conducting an item analysis, the item discrimination method requires that each student's test be scored and that a total score for each student be computed and used to put the test scores in rank order. Next, 27% of the students at the top and a like number at the bottom are then separated for the analysis. The middle group is set aside and is not used in the subsequent analysis. Twenty-seven percent is used because it is desirable to maximize two characteristics of the two groups of test papers. You want as many students as possible in each group to promote stability; at the same time it is desirable to have the two groups be as different as possible to make the discriminations clearer. It has been determined that the use of 27% maximizes these two characteristics. In actual practice, if you have less than 40 students in your class, it is probably better to place 10 student test papers each in the top and in the bottom group because this simplifies the mathematical computations without degrading the stability of the discrimination index.

The discrimination index *(D)* is computed by subtracting the number of students who got the item correct in the lower group *(CL)* from the number who got it correct in the upper group *(CU)* and dividing the difference by the number in one group. The equation is as follows:

$$\text{Discrimination index } (D) = \frac{CU - CL}{N}$$

For example, suppose that 74 students took a test. Twenty-seven percent of that number is 20 *(N)*, so you would select the 20 students who did best on the test and the 20 who did poorest. The responses by the two groups of students to one item are shown in Table 7.4. (Option C is the correct answer.) Fifteen students got the item correct in the upper group, and only three got it correct in the lower group. The difference between the two is 12; when that is divided by 20, you obtain a discrimination index of 0.60. This procedure is used to compute discrimination indexes for each item.

The higher the discrimination index, the better the item because such a value indicates that the item discriminates in favor of the upper group, which should get more items correct. An item that everyone gets correct or that everyone gets incorrect will have a discrimination index equal to zero. If more students get an item correct in the lower group than in the upper group, the item will have a negative value and is probably flawed. A negative discrimination index is most likely to occur with an item covering complex material written in such a way that it is possible to select the correct response without any real understanding of what is being assessed. A poor student may make a guess, select that response, and come up with the correct answer. Good students may be suspicious of a question that looked too easy and will take the harder path to solving the problem and may end up being less successful than those who guess.

The item discrimination method of conducting an item analysis is straightforward and not too computationally complex for any classroom teacher. But, even with 30 students and a 50-item test, it is necessary for the person conducting the item analysis to examine 1,000 items (20 students [10 in the top and 10 in the bottom group] × 50 items = 1,000). This is more effort than most teachers are likely to be willing to put forth.

TABLE 7.4
Item Discrimination Analysis for a Sample Item

	OPTION			
	A	**B**	**C**	**D**
20 best students	3	2	15	0
20 poorest students	12	3	3	2
Difference			12	
Computation of discrimination index	$D = \dfrac{CU - CL}{N} = \dfrac{15 - 3}{20} = 0.60$			

Note. The difference is given for the correct answer, Option C, only.

Item-Total Score Correlations.   To conduct an item analysis using the item-total score correlation method, you need a computer and the software to permit the computation of correlations. It is also necessary to enter each student's response to every item. This analysis can be an arduous task, and for this reason the item-total score correlation method is usually employed only when machine scoring is available. Once the data are entered into the memory, they can be analyzed using available item analysis packages, a special program written specifically for the analysis, or an existing statistical analysis program. The outcome that is of most interest is the correlation between the item and the total score, but it is also possible to have the computer generate item difficulties, item means, standard deviations, and the frequencies of responses to distractors. The correlations are interpreted in the same way the discrimination index is.

Interpreting Discrimination Indexes

Despite differences in their computation, both methods of determining the discrimination of an item can be interpreted in the same way. The larger the index, the better the item. Guidelines specifying (1) how high the discrimination index or the item-total score correlation should be to justify the retention of an item or (2) how low it could be before the item is rejected are difficult to specify because the sample size in a classroom will generally be small, which causes these indexes not to be stable. An item might be effective in one class and not work in another. Subtle differences in the presentation of material or the responses made by different teachers to a specific question can alter the difficulty and effectiveness of an item. Another important consideration is the variability of the class in the construct being measured by the test. If most students are about the same, it will be difficult to obtain items that have high discrimination indexes. In a class with a wide disparity in performance, the indexes will tend to be higher.

The simplest way to interpret the size of the index is to retain the items with the highest discrimination index (over 0.50), to eliminate the ones with the lowest index (below 0.20), and to consider modifying those in between. Items between these two points should be examined for possible modifications. In trying to determine why an item has a low index, look first at item difficulty. Items that are too easy or too hard are almost always poor discriminators. Sometimes an item is a poor discriminator because it is too hard even though the computed difficulty might be in an acceptable range. This discrepancy can occur when two of four distractors are completely implausible, leaving the correct answer and a plausible distractor. Even if the item is so difficult that only a few students know the correct answer, many more students will get the correct answer by guessing because they need only to guess between the two plausible responses. Of course, the test maker also needs to determine whether the item is flawed in some other way and if its construction violates the rules of good item writing set forth in this chapter. It is also important to see that all of the distractors are functioning effectively. Distractors that are not plausible make items too easy, and those that are too close to the correct answer make an item too difficult. This possibility of manipulating item difficulty is an advantage to and sometimes a frustration of multiple-choice tests.

Test Construction in the Age of Computers

The availability of computers has had an enormous impact on test construction, item bank construction, and item analysis procedures. Anyone involved in the construction of objective tests that require the reuse of items should be working with a set of items stored in computer memory. This computer storage can be accomplished in several ways. Perhaps the most efficient approach is to use item bank software that enables the test maker to specify the items he or she wishes to include; then a test will be printed in the desired format. Most programs permit the addition of new items and the modification of existing items in the pool.

Tests can also be constructed using word processing programs. The teacher has more direct control using these techniques, but the test construction process can be more time consuming. Old tests can be modified by adding, deleting, or changing items. One annoyance encountered when tests are modified in this manner concerns item numbering. Every time changes are made that affect the number of items, all subsequent items must be renumbered. One way to get around this problem is to use outlining programs; these programs can be used to construct tests, and they have the additional capacity to renumber items while maintaining the outline format of the objective test.

The computer technology necessary to conduct a complete item analysis may require more sophistication on the computer than the average teacher possesses. The ideal arrangement is to make one person who possesses the necessary expertise responsible for conducting the analyses for one or several schools. With such a system, teachers need only to submit the answer sheets from their students and to pick up the completed item analyses after the more expert person has computed them.

Supply Response Tests

Our attention so far has been directed toward tests made up of selection type items. There may also be occasions when it is appropriate to include supply type items on teacher-made tests. The distinguishing feature of supply type items is that the answer is produced by the examinee in response to the question or problem that is presented. The response may be very brief—a single word or a number—in which case the item approaches the objectivity of a selection type item. Or, at the other extreme, the response may be an extended essay.

There are certain educational objectives that can be more successfully appraised by extended essay responses. These objectives focus on selecting, arranging, organizing, and expressing ideas, or they focus on producing original or ingenious solutions to problems. In practice, the evaluation of essays does not

TABLE 7.5
Summary of Evaluation of Test Types

Factor	Essay	Short Answer and Completion	Objective
Can measure ability to solve novel problems	+ +	+	+ +
Can measure ability to organize, integrate, or synthesize	+ +	+	− −
Can measure originality or innovative approaches to problems	+ +	+	− −
Can isolate specific abilities in subject area through general skills of writing, spelling, and language usage	− −	−	+ +
Has potential value for diagnosis	− −	+	+ +
Can sample adequately the objectives of instruction	− −	−	+ +
Is free from opportunities for guessing answer	+ +	+ +	− −
Gives consistent scores from scorer to scorer	− −	−	+ +
Is accurate in differentiating levels of competencey among examinees	− −	−	+ +
Can be scored by unskilled clerk or machine	− −	−	+ +
Takes little time to write items	+	+	−

Note. The pluses and minuses indicate the degree to which each type of test can measure a quality: + + = measures well; + = measures somewhat; − = measures slightly; − − = does not measure.

always focus on the mastery of these types of objectives. The evaluation is also influenced by knowledge of facts, correctness and effectiveness of English usage, and legibility of handwriting. Furthermore, reading a pile of essay examinations is a laborious and a subjective undertaking.

The biggest disadvantage of essay tests is their low reliability, partially resulting from variations within and among readers and partially from the small number of questions that can be included on such a test. A table listing the advantages and disadvantages of essay, short-answer, and objective test items is presented in Table 7.5.

Restricted Response Items

The restricted response item can be in the form of a question (short-answer type) or of a statement with blanks that must be filled in. The blanks can either be at the end of the item, which makes it a completion item, or be embedded in the statement. Generally, these forms are interchangeable; that is, the same problem could be presented either as a short-answer, fill-in-the blank, or completion type of item. To be classified as a restricted response item, the question or statement must be answerable with a word or phrase, a date, a number, a list of several words, or a maximum of two or three sentences. The restricted response item is not very flexible and should be used sparingly on locally made tests. Items of this type are best suited for testing knowledge of vocabulary, names or dates, simple comprehension of concepts, and ability to solve quantifiable problems. Quantitative problems that yield a specific numerical solution are "short answer" by their very nature.

Although short-answer items have a simple, straightforward structure, it is common to encounter poorly written items of this type. The most common faults found in teacher-made items are ambiguity, lack of precision, and triviality.

Completion items are too often constructed from sentences lifted directly from a textbook with one or two words removed. This practice is undesirable for two reasons: (1) A sentence out of context loses much of its meaning, and (2) such an approach places too great a premium on the rote memorization of textbook material.

Suggestions for Writing Better Restricted Response Items.   Although the use of restricted response items is recommended for assessing a limited range of objectives, when such items are used they should be constructed according to the following rules.

1. Be sure that each item deals with important content and does not measure trivia. The information that a student is required to recall on a test should be important. Avoid the type of item that could quite justifiably be answered, "Who cares?" Ask yourself in each case whether knowing or not knowing the answer is an indication of a student's competence in the area being appraised. Both of the examples of poor items given next measure trivial information, but both appeared in a teacher-made eighth-grade health test. No revision is suggested for the items because the information called for is of no relevance to an eighth graders' understanding of health or health practices.

EXAMPLES	Poor:	
	Short answer	How many cases of smallpox occurred in the United States in 1950? (<u>39</u>)
	Poor:	
	Completion	In 1985, only 1 out of (<u>10</u>) Americans were provided adequate dental care.

2. Be sure the question or statement poses a specific problem to the examinee. A short-answer or completion item should be written so that a student who knows the material will be likely to provide the correct answer. Look at the following examples of short-answer and completion items. For the first two items, the correct answer is nicotine. However, the way that the items are written, many words or phrases other than nicotine would be factually correct and reasonably sensible: Chlorophyll, pigments, veins, moisture, starch, cells, leaf tissue, and poison are all possibilities. The problem needs to be more specifically defined as is done in the revised examples.

Poor:

Short answer   What does the tobacco leaf contain? (Nicotine)

Completion   The tobacco leaf contains (nicotine).

Better:

Short answer   What is the name of the poisonous substance found in tobacco leaves? (Nicotine)

Completion: The poisonous substance found in tobacco leaves is named (nicotine).

---

3. *Be sure the answer that the student is required to produce is factually correct.* Examine the poor examples given next. The answer the test maker wanted was cirrhosis of the liver, but alcohol per se does not cause cirrhosis of the liver; it is the nutritional deficiency that is frequently associated with excessive drinking of alcohol that leads to cirrhosis of the liver.

Poor:

Short answer   What organic disease of the liver is caused by alcohol? (Cirrhosis of the liver)

Completion   Alcohol causes an organic disease called (cirrhosis) of the liver.

Better:

Short answer   What organic disease of the liver is common among people who drink large amounts of alcohol and have inadequate diets? (Cirrhosis of the liver)

Completion   People who drink large amounts of alcohol and have inadequate diets frequently suffer from an organic disease called (cirrhosis) of the liver.

---

4. *Be sure the language used in the question is precise and accurate in relation to the subject being tested.* The following completion item appeared on an eighth-grade health test. The use of the term "particles" is imprecise, and the teacher should have used the term "genes." In addition, the adjectives "stronger" and "weaker" are less appropriate than "dominant" and "recessive." The revision of the question shows how it could have been stated in a more precise way without giving the answer away.

Poor: Some of the small particles inside chromosomes are stronger than others. These stronger ones are said to be (dominant) while the weaker ones are said to be (recessive).

Better: A mother has Type A blood and a father has Type O blood. Four children are born in the family, all of whom have Type A blood. From this one would conclude that the genes for Type A blood are (dominant) in comparison to those for Type O.

5. *If the problem requires a numerical answer, indicate the units in which it is to be expressed.* This practice will simplify the problem of scoring and will remove one source of ambiguity in the examinee's answer. In the poor example that follows, 4 cups, 2 pints, or 1 quart can be the answer, and if the student does not designate the units in which he or she is expressing the answer, the teacher may find it difficulty to determine whether the student really knows the answer.

EXAMPLE

Poor: What is the recommended daily minimum requirement of milk for a 14-year-old boy?

Better: The recommended daily requirement of milk for a 14-year-old boy is (4) cups.

6. *In a completion item, omit only key words.* The blank in a completion item should require the student to supply a fact or term that is relevant to what is being assessed. Do not leave the verb out of a completion statement unless the purpose of the item is to measure knowledge of verb forms. In the example that follows, the teacher should decide whether he or she wants to test for knowledge of the word "glycogen," of the place where excess glucose is stored in the body, or of a function of the liver and write the item accordingly.

EXAMPLE

Poor: The liver (stores) excess glucose as glycogen.

Better: In normal body metabolism, excess glucose in the blood is stored in the liver in the form of (glycogen).

7. *In an achievement test, do not leave too many blanks in a completion statement.* Overmutilation of a statement reduces the task of the examinee to a guessing game. Overly mutilated statements may be appropriate when you are trying to appraise creativity or originality with words but not when you are trying to appraise factual knowledge.

EXAMPLE

Poor: The ___(1)___ whose primary ___(2)___ is ___(3)___ are the ___(4)___. (Answer: 1, teeth; 2, function; 3, cutting; 4, incisors).

Better: The teeth whose primary function is cutting are called the (incisors).

8. In a completion item, put blanks near the end of the statement rather than at the beginning. The student should know what question is being asked before encountering the blank.

Poor: The _____ gland is an example of an endocrine gland.
Better: An example of an endocrine gland is the _____ gland.

Preparing the Test for Use

In preparing a restricted response test for use, it is important to select a test format that is easy for examinees to understand and convenient for the test maker to score. Some suggestions that will help to achieve these goals are provided here.

1. If both completion and short-answer items are used on the same test, put items of the same type together. Each type of question requires a different set of directions and a somewhat different frame of mind on the part of the students.

2. Have students write their answers on a separate answer sheet. Students should have ample space for recording their answers. The size of handwriting varies from student to student, so it is very difficult to judge how much space each student will need. The teacher will also find it easier to score papers if the answers are recorded in a uniform manner. For short-answer questions, blue books or blank sheets of paper can be used, and the students can be instructed to number their answers to correspond to the questions. The teacher should state whether answers have to be in the same order as the questions are in. For completion items, an answer sheet can be a copied sheet containing the number of each question, with a line on which the student can record his or her answer extending from the number.

3. Write a set of directions for each item type that is used on the test. The directions should be simple but complete. They should include such things as how and where the students are to record their answers, the score value of each item, and whether spelling will be considered in judging the adequacy of the answer. For quantitative problems, students should be told whether they are to show all of their work or whether they can merely record the answer. For short-answer items, students should be told whether their answers must be written in complete sentences.

4. Try to group items dealing with the same content or skill together. Following this practice may help to reduce the feeling by students that the test is made up of unrelated bits and pieces. The examinees will also be able to concentrate on a single area of content at a time rather than shift back and forth among areas of content. Furthermore, the teacher will have an easier job of analyzing the test results for the group or for the individual student because the teacher will be able to see at a glance whether the errors are more frequent in one content area than in another.

Scoring the Test

Once the test has been completed, the teacher will need to score it. Suggestions for the best ways of scoring a test are included in this section.

1. Check the answer key against a sample of papers before scoring any paper. Checking the prepared key against a few papers, preferably of those who are known to be good students, may disclose one or more items to which students have consistently given a response different from that in the key. This occurrence may arise either from a clerical error in preparing the key or from students interpreting the question differently than the instructor intended. When this problem occurs, and if the alternative interpretation is defensible, the key should be corrected or extended to include the alternate response. In an item such as "give an example of a communicable disease," a number of answers could be correct. Sometimes in making the original key, the teacher does not think of some possible answers, and the key may need to be extended as scoring proceeds.

2. If spelling, grammar, and sentence structure, as well as accuracy of content, are to be scored, provide a separate score for each. Although it may be difficult for graders, spelling, grammar, and sentence structure should not be factors in a student's score. They may be scored separately, but this is seldom done.

3. Correct errors and make comments on each item as it is scored or provide a complete set of answers for each student when the papers are returned. This practice helps students learn the correct answer, and it has also been shown to increase motivation for student learning.

4. Score each item either correct or incorrect and assign an equal weight. A well-written restricted response item will pose a very specific problem to the student and should be scored either 0 for incorrect or 1 for correct. Awarding partial credit can make scoring unnecessarily complex. The issue of partial credit generally arises with those items presenting a quantitative problem or in completion items that include more than one blank. Although awarding partial credit for the using the correct methodology in a quantitative problem or for correctly filling in some of the blanks in a multiple-blank completion item may seem more fair to students, it contributes little or nothing to the psychometric qualities of a test. If a teacher believes that some content or skills are more important than others, more questions based on that content or requiring that skill should be included.

Essay Questions

Although students at all levels of education need practice to develop writing skills, it is doubtful that an examination is the appropriate place to provide this practice. Instead, the major advantage of the essay type of question is its potential for measuring a student's abilities to organize, integrate, and synthesize knowledge; to use information to solve novel problems; and to be original or innovative in approaches to problem situations. To realize this potential, each question must be carefully phrased to require the student to reveal these kinds of abilities. Merely casting a question in essay form does not automatically ensure that these abilities will be assessed. Consider the following two essay questions.

EXAMPLES

1. What methods have been used in the United States to prevent and control communicable diseases?

TABLE A
Causes of Death and Rate for Each in 1900 and 1987

	DEATH RATE PER 100,000 PEOPLE	
Cause of Death	1900	1987
1. Pneumonia	175.4	21.8
2. Diarrhea and enteritis	139.9	2.0
3. Diseases of the heart	137.4	399.9
4. Cancer	64.0	160.9
5. Diphtheria	40.3	0.02

2. Examine the data provided in the table shown here. Explain how changes in knowledge, in medical practice, and in the conditions of life in the United States between 1900 and 1987 account for the changes in death rate shown in the table.

To answer the question in Example 1, the student need only recall the information and write it down in much the same form in which it was presented in the textbook or in class. On the other hand, the task in Example 2 requires that the student recall facts about the characteristics of each of the diseases and disease conditions and facts about methods of transmission or conditions that affect the incidence of disease. The student must then relate these to such things as immunization, chemotherapy, improvements in sanitation, and the increasing proportion of older people in the population. Example 2 seems more clearly appropriate for an essay question.

To realize the potential of the essay question to appraise a student's ability to use information, to organize materials, or to use language effectively requires not only appropriately written questions but also a situation structured such that other factors do not obscure the desired appraisal. In the typical essay examination, differences in knowledge of basic factual material may obscure differences in the ability to use and organize those facts. Time pressures also may prevent students from producing their best writing.

The "open-book" examination has been suggested as one means of partially evening out differences in factual knowledge. In this form of examination, the students have access to any data in their texts or their notes. Realistically, we cannot expect to eliminate all of the effects of differences in knowledge with an open-book examination. The able student knows what to look for in the book and where to find it; the poor one can spend a whole period aimlessly leafing through the pages. However, there seem to be other advantages to the open-book examination. Feldhusen (1961) reported that college students who were given open-book examinations felt that this type of examination was more effective in promoting learning, reducing worry and tenseness about the examination, and reducing cheating. He also reported that although students spent less time memorizing factual material in preparing for an open-book examination than for a closed-book one, they spent as much or more time on general review of the material.

The time pressures of the typical essay testing situation can be eased by assigning essay questions as an out-of-class examination or by having very liberal time limits. If the former suggestions is taken, the teacher not only minimizes time pressures but also gains the advantages of the open-book examination. Under these conditions, students have time not only to write carefully but also to edit their writing, and the teacher can get samples of their best writing under optimal conditions. An out-of-class examination does introduce certain problems, such as the possibility of help from parents or others. We can never be sure how much the final product is a result of the student's own efforts and how much should be attributed to others. For this reason, some essay testing must continue to be administered under supervised conditions, but the out-of-class essay examination can be a valuable teaching device. It is in effect, a highly structured paper written out of class.

Suggestions for Writing Better Essay Questions

The following suggestions are presented as suggestions for writing more effective essay questions.

1. Have clearly in mind what mental processes you want the student to use in responding to the question before starting to write it. The teacher or test author must understand as fully as possible the kinds of ability or abilities that are to be measured by an essay question and the type of responses that would indicate their existence. Once these characteristics have been identified, the stimuli needed to elicit these responses can be selected. For example, a teacher who wants to use the essay question to evaluate eighth-graders' ability to think critically about health information may identify the following abilities as evidence of critical thinking: to evaluate the adequacy of an authority, to recognize bias or emotional factors in the presentation, to distinguish between verifiable and unverifiable data, to recognize the adequacy of data, to check statements against other known data, and to determine whether data support the conclusion. Once it has been decided that these competencies should be appraised, the stimulus materials required to elicit these abilities can be selected.

2. Use novel material or organization of material in phrasing essay questions. The purpose of most essay items is to appraise students' ability to use information. To assess this ability, we put students in a situation where they must do more than merely reproduce the material from their text or from the classroom lecture or discussion.

3. Start essay questions with such words or phrases as "compare," "contrast," "give the reasons for," "give original examples of," "explain how," "predict what would happen if," "criticize," "differentiate," and "illustrate." The use of words or phrases such as these, combined with novel material, will help to present tasks requiring students to select, organize, and use their knowledge. Avoid beginning essay questions with such words as "what," "who," "when," and "list" because these words direct students merely to reproduce information.

4. Write the essay question in such a way that the task is clearly and unambiguously defined for each examinee. We want the score that a student gets to be a reflection of how well a specified task can be performed, not a measure of his or her skill in interpreting what the task is. Furthermore, in large-scale testing programs, we want the task to be perceived in the same way by all graders, so that a student's score will be affected as little as possible by who scores the paper. Luck in guessing what is wanted for an answer and disagreements in the quality of answers produced can be reduced by writing essay questions that set a clearly defined task for the examinee.

An item such as "Discuss the organizations that contribute to the health of the community" is global, vague, and ambiguous. First, what is meant by the word "discuss"? Does it imply listing organizations and their activities? Criticism and evaluation of what they do? Identification of gaps in the organizational structure? Second, does the teacher expect students to consider only government organizations? Or does the teacher expect students to consider the whole gamut of public and private organizations that contribute to the health of a community? Third, what does the teacher mean by "contribute to the health of the community"? Does the teacher intend for students to confine the answer to the kinds of contributions that involve enforcement of health regulations, direct treatment of illness, and preventive medicine? Or should students include contributions through education and research? The item could also be interpreted to refer to factors of economics, political stability, social justice, and a variety of other dimensions. The item as written requires students to guess what the teacher wanted for an answer, and the scores are likely to depend on how lucky each student is in guessing.

A better way to phrase the question so that each student will interpret it the same way follows:

Using tuberculosis as an example, indicate how each of the following organizations could be expected to contribute to the prevention of the disease or to the cure or care of people with the disease.

A. Local and state health departments
B. U.S. Public Health Service

EXAMPLE

C. Department of Agriculture
D. The National Lung Association
E. The American Public Health Association

The item as it has been rephrased provides a more common basis for response without sacrificing the freedom of each student in answering it. (The revised question also would be difficult for the typical eighth-grade student.)

5. A question dealing with a controversial issue should ask for and be evaluated in terms of the presentation of evidence for a position, rather than the position taken. On many issues that individuals and society face, there are no generally agreed-upon answers. At the same time, these controversial issues constitute much of what is genuinely vital in education. In these areas, it is indefensible to demand that students accept a specific conclusion or solution. However, it is reasonable to appraise students in terms of what they know and how well they can marshal and use the evidence on which a specific conclusion is based. Thus, the question, "What laws should Congress pass to improve the medical care of all citizens in the United States?" has no generally accepted answer. But, we could reasonably ask a student to respond to a question such as the following: "It has been suggested that the cost of all medical care provided by physicians and the cost of all medications be borne by funds provided by the federal government. Do you agree or disagree? Support your position with logical arguments." In this type of question, the teacher should grade the student on the basis of how well the position is defended.

6. Be sure the essay question asks for the behavior that you really want the student to display. Teacher-made essay tests quite frequently have questions such as "Give your best definition of good health"; "What do you think is the difference between active and passive immunity?"; and "In your opinion, what factors have contributed to the decreasing number of cases of diphtheria between 1900 and 1987 in the United States?" Usually, for such questions, the teacher is not interested in what the student's opinion is but in whether the student knows the factual material. Rewritten, the questions would read, "Define good health"; "Explain the differences between active and passive immunity"; "What factors have contributed to the decreasing number of cases of diphtheria in the United States between 1900 and 1987?" (The revisions make it clear that the questions are too factual in nature to be good for essay testing.)

7. Adapt the length and complexity of the answer to the maturity level of the students. At all levels, the distinctive value of the essay question is the way it requires respondents to select and organize their own ideas in their own ways. The organization and expression that we can reasonably expect an elementary or junior high school student to produce is quite restricted in amount and conceptual level. The teacher learns from experience what to expect from typical students in his or her classes.

In addition, the teacher should make sure that students do not have too many questions or questions that are too long to respond to in the time available.

8. Require all students to answer the same questions. Giving students a choice of items makes grading more difficult because student responses are not directly comparable. If students answer different combinations of questions, the scorer will be forced to make difficult judgments. He or she will have to decide how to compare the student who writes a good answer to an easy question with the student who writes a less adequate response to a harder question.

9. Provide an indication of how questions are weighted by indicating the number of points or the amount of time to be spent on each question. If all questions are to be weighted the same, students should be told this. If a different amount of credit is to be given to different questions, the weighting should be indicated next to each question. Such procedures prevent students from either spending too much time on an unimportant question or too little time on a more important one.

Evaluating Essay Tests

Adequate appraisal of student achievement with an essay test requires not only well-formulated essay questions but also sound and consistent procedures for assessing the quality of the answers.

Formal research provides little systematic guidance for improving the scoring of essay tests, but the following suggestions, derived from accumulated professional experience, are offered. These suggestions should help the teacher maintain a consistent standard for judging the answers across all students. It will also result in the teacher being more aware of the basis for his or her ratings, making it possible to provide specific comments to the students on their performance and to reduce the likelihood of irrelevant factors influencing the judgment of the quality of answers.

1. Decide in advance what qualities are to be considered in judging the adequacy of the answer. If more than one distinct quality is to be appraised, make separate evaluations of each. If a student is to be evaluated on the basis on the structural aspects of an essay test, each aspect should be given a separate score.

2. Determine what you will consider a correct answer for each question before grading the test. In many cases, students provide answers that are not anticipated by the teacher. Finding that the first papers graded have quite different answers can be disconcerting. It is helpful for the teacher to have already determined what he or she considers correct or acceptable.

3. Cover students' names before scoring the responses. This procedure prevents personalities from interfering with objectivity. It may also stop the teacher from thinking, despite how poorly the response is written, "Mary Jane must really know the answer" or "Johnny Jones just thinks he is smart, but I don't think his answers are so great."

4. Score each question for all students before going to the next question. This procedure allows the scorer to concentrate on each question separately and provides a clearer idea of how students' responses compare. There is also less chance for the scorer's evaluation of one answer to generalize to other answers.

5. *Decide on your scoring method before you start to score.* There are two primary approaches to scoring essay tests. The *analytic approach* requires the grader to outline what will be considered a correct answer prior to seeing how the students have responded. The scorer then determines the number of points that each type of response will receive. Tests also can be scored using a *global approach*. With this approach, the scorer reads all of the papers quickly, to get some general impressions, and then divides them into categories according to the overall impression of how good they are. Second, and even third, readings are used to verify and adjust the ratings obtained (Hopkins, Stanley, and Hopkins, 1990).

The analytical approach is systematic and conveys to the students the idea that their grades are not determined capriciously. This approach has the disadvantage of being time consuming both to set up and to implement, and it may also result in an overemphasis on the trivial. The reliability of the global approach has been shown to be satisfactory, but it is a difficult approach to defend to students who usually like their teachers to be specific about why their examinations were graded the way they were.

6. *Either reread the test papers a second time—before returning them—or have someone else read them.* One limitation of essay tests is the difficulty in maintaining consistency across a large number of papers. Responses that get low marks when they are the first graded may become quite acceptable after the scorer has waded through a great many papers. The scorer might be outraged at the inadequacy of one of the first papers read and score it accordingly, only to find that the rest of the class did little better, and end up giving higher marks to the later papers. Also, the teacher might start out with great energy and resolve to read carefully, but when it is late at night and the papers must be returned the next day, it is easy to succumb to the temptation to read less carefully. The less attention the teacher is able to give to a test, the more willing he or she may be to give the student the benefit of the doubt, causing scoring to be less consistent. A final rereading of all of the papers can help increase fairness in scoring.

7. *Put comments on the examinations.* This practice forces the scorer to read students' responses and provides proof to students that he or she has actually done so. There is something very disconcerting to the student about having a paper returned with a grade but without any indication of how or why that particular grade was assigned.

Summary

When cognitive instructional objectives are assessed, the conventional teacher-made or locally constructed paper-and-pencil test is appropriate. The more important the decisions, the more likely a conventional teacher-made test will be used. Teacher-made tests can be divided into two types, selection and recall. True-false, multiple-choice, and matching are examples of selection items. Their unifying characteristic is that they require the student to choose between or among alternatives. It is important with all three of these item types that the items be written in a straightforward manner. The test maker should avoid trick questions, items that depend too much on reading ability, and items that depend too much on "testwiseness" skills. Recall items include short-answer and essay type formats. Although it is relatively easy to assemble a set of items for recall tests, it takes time and planning to construct good essay and short-answer tests. The advantage of selection type items comes from the ease and objectivity of their scoring, while their disadvantages include the time and effort required for their construction. Recall tests are easier to construct but time consuming to grade and difficult to evaluate objectively. After a test has been constructed, administered, and scored, the work of the teacher is not complete. At a minimum, he or she should compute descriptive statistics on the results, including the mean and standard deviations. Teachers are also strongly urged to perform item analysis procedures on their tests to differentiate between good and poor items and to increase the likelihood that future tests will be better.

Questions and Exercises

1. Why do teachers so often use poor test development procedures when they construct tests for their own classes?
2. What are the requirements for good test construction?
3. Under what circumstance would a criterion-referenced test be more appropriate than a norm-referenced test?
4. A teacher writes 10 objectives for a biology class. For each objective, five items are written. An objective is considered mastered if a student correctly answers four out of five items. What is the most appropriate label for this approach to testing?
5. Present an argument for using criterion-referenced tests and then an argument for not using them.
6. Prepare a set of objectives for a course or a unit of a course that you are teaching or hope to teach.
7. Construct a domain specification for one of the objectives from Problem 6.
8. Which of the objectives in Problem 6 could be measured effectively by a written test? Which objectives can be measured either partially or not at all? Why is a written test inadequate for appraising the objectives given for the last question? How might these objectives best be appraised?
9. Based on the objectives identified in the first question in Problem 8 and a course outline, prepare a blueprint for a test to evaluate the unit of course.
10. In a junior high school, one teacher takes complete responsibility for preparing the common final examination for all the classes in general science. This teacher develops the examination without consulting the other teachers. What advantages and disadvantages do you see in this procedure? How could it be improved?
11. One objective that is often proposed for the social studies program in secondary schools is to increase the students' "critical reaction to the news in different news media." How could the formulation of this objective be improved so that progress toward it could be measured?
12. The following objectives were included in a school system's formulation of the

objectives of a unit on health. Critique each, revising it if there are ways to improve it.

(a) Makes posters illustrating good health habits.

(b) Demonstrates health consciousness.

(c) Points out relationships between improvements in sanitation and the drop in occurrence of disease.

(d) Appreciates the critical role of bacteria in sickness and in health.

(e) Shows knowledge of and a lasting improvement in health habits.

13. Look at the blueprint for the examination on a unit on health that appears under Preparing the Test Blueprint. For which of the cells in this blueprint would it be appropriate to use (a) recall or (b) selection exercises? What factors influenced your decisions?

14. Construct four multiple-choice items designed to measure understanding or application in some subject area with which you are familiar.

15. Write a series of true-false items to assess the same outcomes assessed in Problem 14. Which approach seemed to assess student knowledge most effectively?

16. Prepare a short objective test for a small unit that you are teaching or plan to teach. Indicate the objectives that you are trying to evaluate with each item.

17. For which of the following tests would correcting scores for guessing be justified? Give the reason or reasons for your decision.

(a) A 100-item true-false test. All students answered all questions.

(b) A 70-item multiple-choice test of spatial relations. Each item has five answer choices. For each item, one or more answer choices may be correct. All students answered all questions.

(c) A 50-item multiple-choice test with four answer choices for each item, one of which is the keyed answer. Only 40% of the examinees completed all items.

(d) A 60-item multiple-choice test with four answer choices for each item, one of which is the keyed answer. Ninety percent of the students answered all items.

18. A college professor has given an objective test to a large class, scored the papers, and entered the scores in the class record book. What additional steps might the teacher take before returning the papers to the students? Why?

19. Collect five examples of poor items you have seen on tests. Indicate what is wrong with each item.

20. Critique the following features of an essay test planned for a ninth-grade social studies class:

(a) The test will consist of 10 items.

(b) Each student will answer any five items.

(c) Each item will have a value of 20 points.

(d) One point will be subtracted for each misspelled word and each grammatical error.

(e) A five-point bonus will be added for neatness.

(f) Forty minutes will be allowed for the test.

21. Critique each of the following essay questions:

(a) Instead of talking just about France's industry and agriculture, we talked about both as part of the Common Market. What are the advantages to France as a member of the Common Market? What products, raw materials, and agricultural products does France contribute to the Common Market? (9th-grade social studies)

(b) What should scientists do to make sure that scientific discoveries are used for the benefit of mankind rather than for its destruction? (8th-grade science)

(c) Select a character from a novel or short story that you have read this year. Give the character's name and the title and author of the work. In a well-written paragraph, explain how this character has influenced your life. (12th-grade English literature)

(d) Discuss essay-type tests. (College undergraduate class in tests and measurements)

Suggested Readings

Albanese, M. A. (1988). The projected impact of the correction for guessing on individual scores. *Journal of Educational Measurement, 25*(2), 149–157.

Albanese, M. A., & Sabers, D. L. (1988). Multiple true-false items: A study of interitem correlations, scoring alternatives, and reliability estimation. *Journal of Educational Measurement, 25*(2), 111–123.

Berk, R. A. (Ed.). (1984). *A guide to criterion-referenced test construction.* Baltimore: Johns Hopkins University Press.

Cunningham, G. K. (1986). *Educational and psychological measurement.* New York: Macmillan.

Gronlund, N. E. (1982). *Constructing achievement tests.* Englewood Cliffs, NJ: Prentice-Hall.

Gronlund, N. E., & Linn, R. L. (1990). *Measurement and evaluation in teaching* (6th ed.). New York: Macmillan.

Gullickson, A. R., & Ellwein, M. C. (1985). Post hoc analysis of teacher-made tests: The goodness of fit between prescription and practice. *Educational Measurement: Issues and Practices, 4*(1), 15–18.

Kubiszyn, T., & Borich, G. (1987). *Educational testing and measurement.* Glenview, IL: Scott, Foresman and Company.

Mager, R. F. (1975). *Preparing instructional objectives.* (2nd ed.). Belmont, CA: Fearon.

Nitko, A. J. (1983). *Educational tests and measurement.* New York: Harcourt, Brace, Jovanovich.

Sax, G. (1989). *Principles of educational and psychological measurement and evaluation.* Belmont, CA: Wadsworth.

Thissen, D., Steinberg, L., & Fitzpatrick, A. R. (1989). Multiple-choice models: The distractors are also part of the item. *Journal of Educational Measurement, 26*(2), 161–176.

Wainer, H. (1989). The future of item analysis. *Journal of Educational Measurement, 26*(2) 191–208.

CHAPTER 8
Performance and Product Evaluation

Introduction

To most people, in and out of education, the word "testing" means the sort of paper-and-pencil assessment methods that are customarily used to assess cognitive objectives. Such tests usually employ the type of item formats discussed in Chapter 7. Experience has shown that clever teachers and test writers can construct cognitive tests for assessing almost any learning outcome, and for most instructional objectives, this is appropriate. However, there are many types of objectives for which a paper-and-pencil assessment is too abstract from the instructional objective that it is intended to measure to be useful.

Artificiality of Conventional Cognitive Tests

All testing is to some degree artificial because we seldom directly measure instructional goals. Test standardization exacerbates this problem by increasing the need to use selection type items to facilitate machine scoring and computer analysis. Even with cognitive material, such as reading comprehension, that we think of as most appropriate to be assessed with an objective test format, there can be a problem with matching the assessment task to the instructional goal. Reading comprehension is usually measured by assessing a student's ability to answer multiple-choice items about the meaning of short paragraphs. This method of assessing reading comprehension contrasts with the conventional definition for comprehension, which is based on the capacity of students to understand, to relate to previously learned material, and to critically evaluate long passages of reading. Artificiality also occurs with objective spelling tests that require a student to select the correctly spelled word from among three or four misspelled words or English usage tests that require the student to distinguish between grammatically correct and grammatically incorrect sentences. Instruction in English composition classes is generally intended to bring students to the point where they can write grammatically correct paragraphs with a minimum of misspelled words. This task is most directly accomplished by evaluating paragraphs that students have written. The mere identification of grammatical errors or misspelled words is not an equivalent form of cognitive functioning. Despite the indirectness of paper-and-pencil tests, educators are usually willing to accept the artificiality of them in exchange for their objectivity and ease of administration.

Inappropriate Use of Conventional Cognitive Tests

There are, however, important instructional objectives that cannot be appropriately assessed by paper-and-pencil tests. Included among these are objectives associated with subject matter that calls for a product or a process—for example, the performances required in a music, physical education, speech, or drama class or the projects required in art, industrial arts, and home economics classes.

Evaluating student performance in such classes can be quite difficult; as a result, teachers may avoid this activity. This tendency to deemphasize grades is exacerbated by the perception that processes and products are not academic and are therefore less important. This is sometimes used as a justification for a lack of emphases on assigning grades in these settings.

The reluctance of teachers to evaluate educational products in the same critical manner as they evaluate more academic activities may partially stem from the belief that performances in areas such as music, art, and physical education are strongly influenced by prior ability. It is widely believed that the quality of the products and the performance of students is to a great degree a function of skills and abilities that the student possessed prior to entering a class and not necessarily the result of instruction. There are art students, for instance, who can produce the best painting in their class on the first day and others who can never paint anything acceptable no matter how much instruction they receive. Of course, this phenomenon might also apply to English composition or the solving of calculus problems, but there is a reluctance to believe that success in these areas is also the result of ability and not just effort. A poor singing voice, therefore, is more likely to be attributed to factors outside of the control of the student than is an inability to solve arithmetic problems.

Assessing Products

In the past, it was useful to distinguish between a concrete product such as a sculpture made in art class and performances such as a speech or an interpretive dance; however, with video cameras now available in most schools, performances can be transformed into concrete products.

In most cases, it is the product rather than the process by which it was produced that is the focus of assessment. For example, a teacher is usually more interested in the poem a student has written than the process of its composition. In addition, it is usually easier to evaluate a product than a process. With a product, there is a single object (or performance) that can be compared to others. A process is made up of many parts, each of which must be weighted to obtain a summary evaluation. Standards also must be established for each step in the process. However, sometimes the process and the product are not easily distinguishable, such as for a speech or a dance. There are also three situations for which the process itself is as important if not more important than the product: (1) when safety is a primary concern; (2) when the student's product can be considered transitory; (3) when it is particularly difficult to evaluate a product.

Safety.   When the process can be dangerous, there is a necessary emphasis on ensuring that it is carried out correctly. Examples of such a process would be the procedures used in a chemical experiment, a gymnastic performance, or the use of power tools in a woodworking shop. The evaluation of a student in these situations would be influenced to a considerable degree by the student's adherence to specified safety procedures.

Transitory Performance.   There are circumstances in which the particular product or performance of a student is secondary to the process because the product is just a step in the direction of better products and performances. An example of this would be a tennis serve. A good athlete might be able to serve more effectively than any one else in his or her class despite a lack of correct form. Even if such a serve wins points, a tennis instructor would not give it high marks. A good serve cannot be evaluated in terms of its success alone because improvement in a serve cannot occur without learning to use the correct form. Most tennis instructors would be happier with a serve based on correct form that was going into the net than with a serve that, while winning points, was the product of incorrect form. Computer programming is another area where there may be a need to emphasize proper procedures. Just because a computer program is capable of performing a designated task, does not necessarily mean that the program is acceptable. Appropriate procedures and efficiency of programming might also be considered important.

Difficult-to-Evaluate Product.   When the evaluation of a product is subjective, it may be more practical to evaluate the components of the process rather than the product. For example, it is easier to evaluate the process of teaching than to evaluate its products because no satisfactory system of evaluating the effectiveness of teaching has yet been devised. However, there are systems for evaluating the process of teaching—for example, systems based on the results of process-product research. Counseling is another activity for which the process is more easily evaluated than the product.

Applying Performance and Product Evaluation to Cognitive Tasks

Although in the past, cognitive skills typically were not evaluated using performance and product evaluation techniques, there is increased interest in using these techniques in this context. Some of the recent calls for educational reform are based on new developments in the role of cognitive psychology in education. These new developments have led to an increased interest in assessing the products of cognitive functioning. The interest in cognitive psychology also stems from criticisms of current educational practice, which relies heavily on objective paper-and-pencil tests as the sole criterion for measuring educational effectiveness (Nickerson, 1989). The increasing interest in implementing principles of cognitive psychology in the classroom has resulted in the need to encourage the development of higher order thought processing and critical thinking skills. There is a general belief that these should be assessed with performance and product evaluation techniques.

In addition, Fredericksen and Collins (1989) point out the increasing use of statewide writing assessment. With trained scorers and carefully delineated standards, these techniques can produce accurate and dependable results.

Assessing Processes

A process is always made up of a number of parts or steps, and therefore, unlike a product, it cannot be evaluated globally. The emphasis is instead on evaluating the steps in the process. Checklists are the primary instruments used to assess the steps.

Using Checklists

The preferred method of evaluating whether a student has used the appropriate process is to use a checklist or rating scale. In general, the checklist is preferred to the rating scale. With a checklist, the observer is required only to observe the behavior and to mark on the observation form whether the behavior was present or absent. In contrast to a checklist, when using a rating scale, the observer must make decisions about how often the behavior occurs or the quality of the behavior. Also with a rating scale, judging is time consuming, which can severely limit the number of response categories.

When constructing a checklist, the developer should do the following:

1. Designate the appropriate performance or product
2. List the important behaviors and characteristics
3. Include common errors that the individual being evaluated might make
4. Put the list into an appropriate format

Designate an Appropriate Performance or Product.   The construction of a checklist should always begin with the designation of what the end-product will be. In most cases when the focus is on a checklist to evaluate a process, it was not possible to define the product itself precisely, but it is necessary to specify it. The purpose of this step is to provide a focus for delineating the important behaviors and characteristics.

List the Important Behaviors and Characteristics.   Developing a list of behaviors and characteristics is the critical part of constructing a checklist. It is important to include all of the important and relevant behaviors and characteristics necessary to achieve the final product or performance. Behaviors and characteristics that are exhibited by all students and those that cannot be assessed for any student should be excluded because they contribute no additional useful information and they can clutter the checklist. The statements designating the behaviors should be worded in such a way that the need for interpretations by the observers is minimized. The list should be as inclusive as possible without being so lengthy and detailed that the process of judging becomes unwieldy. An example of a partial list of behaviors that an individual who is able to play tennis effectively should exhibit follows. An effective tennis player should be able to

1. Use the correct grip
2. Have his or her feet in the correct position when hitting the ball
3. Keep the elbow straight

4. Hit a forehand to the opposite court

5. Hit a backhand to the opposite court

6. Serve the ball to the correct part of the opponent's court

7. Volley effectively

8. Hit overheads

Of course, each of these behaviors could be broken down even further. There are numerous steps associated with, for example, serving correctly or hitting an overhead.

Associated with any such list of behaviors and characteristics, either implicitly or explicitly, are standards. These standards can be as formal as the distance in fractions of an inch that a student's hand can deviate from the ideal in his or her grip on a tennis racket or as informal as a consensus among judges about what would be considered a correct grip. The intent of standards is to increase the probability that all judgments have the same basis and meaning.

Include Common Errors that the Individual Being Evaluated Might Make. It is not sufficient to determine that a student is performing all of the requisite steps in a procedure; it is important to identify specific behaviors that are considered inappropriate as well. For instance, in observing a teacher, it might be found that he or she exhibits most of the behaviors associated with good teaching but, in addition, responds to student misbehavior with sarcasm. It is important to have such negative behavior noted along with all of the positive ones.

Put the List into an Appropriate Format. Once the list of desired and undesired behaviors and characteristics has been formulated, it should be organized into the sequence that is most likely to be encountered by the observers. The list should be placed on the observation forms in such a way that it is easily readable. Also, space should be provided for the observer to mark a check if the behavior is present. The observer can merely place a checkmark if the behavior occurred over a designated period of time, indicate the number of times the behavior occurred, or record the amount of time that a given activity took. Appropriate space for the specific type of response should be provided.

Once the checklist has been completed, the results must be interpreted. As long as the results are to be used to provide feedback to students about their performance or to help teachers improve their teaching, the components (behaviors and characteristics) can be interpreted separately. If the results of the checklist are to be used to make summative evaluations, the components must be summarized into a total score. This summarizing can be accomplished by summing the items, taking into account, of course, those that refer to behaviors to be avoided. It might also be desirable to weight the items according to their importance.

Constructing Rating Scales

Rating scales can be used to evaluate a set of behaviors and characteristics in much the same way that checklists are used. Rating scales differ by having the observer provide a number, or rating, for each behavior to indicate either how often the behavior occurs or to indicate its quality. For purposes of evaluating processes that are ongoing, checklists are usually preferred because of the additional time required to respond to a rating scale. Additional information about the construction of rating scales is included in Chapter 9.

The simplest rating scale would consist of a set of behaviors and characteristics and instructions to the observers to respond to each with a number within a designated range to indicate some quality of the behavior. But, more often the scale is presented in a graphic form, with anchors at either end and numbers designating the points on the scale. Scales can take many forms, including approaches as simple as the following ones:

Uses proper safety procedures in the chemistry laboratory.

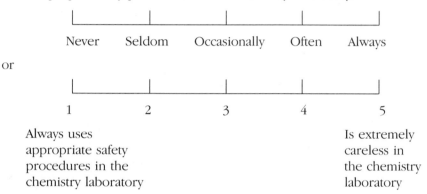

or

Always uses
appropriate safety
procedures in the
chemistry laboratory

Is extremely
careless in
the chemistry
laboratory

Another option is to have the observers imagine an individual who was the best possible exemplar of a particular behavior or characteristic and put him or her on one end of the scale and then to imagine the worst possible examplar and put that individual on the other end. The observer has the task of indicating where along the continuum the individual observed should be placed. An example of this approach follows:

Rate the quality of the student's introduction to his or her speech.

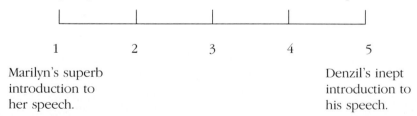

Marilyn's superb
introduction to
her speech.

Denzil's inept
introduction to
his speech.

Evaluating Products and Processes

Fitzpatrick and Morrison (1971) list nine areas in which performance testing is likely to be used because the structure of the content of what is being assessed. Included are tests of secretarial skills, language, and vehicle operation, as well as tests used in art, music, industrial arts, agriculture, sports, and physical education.

As was true for essays, products and processes can be evaluated either globally or in terms of their parts. The advantage of a global approach is that it facilitates making normative comparisons. When we try to evaluate the separate parts of, or steps in, a product or performance, we need to make subjective decisions about the quality of these parts, and making these discrete decisions is difficult. It is better to be able to judge the product or performance in comparison with other products and performances.

A critical aspect of products and performances are the instructions that accompany them. In many cases, projects place a premium on originality and creativity, which makes their evaluation more difficult. When the products of students are different in many dimensions, it is difficult to make legitimate comparisons among the products. Any two products can be different in many different ways, and each may be superior in some aspects and inferior in others. For instance, in a science project, the teacher or judges must consider originality, scientific contribution, neatness, sturdiness, creativity, extensiveness and quality of narrative explanations, the use of references, and so forth. How do you weight these qualities? How do you compare a bold and unusual, yet somewhat awkwardly presented project with a more conventional, less creative one that is neat, carefully constructed, and meticulously documented? Under these circumstances, it is obviously difficult to compare two such different products. In this situation, a set of rules that can standardize the project as much as possible and specify the qualities to be considered most important can help. This set of rules given to the students makes it possible to limit the number of dimensions along which comparisons must be made.

Using Observers

When a teacher creates a checklist, he or she will usually be the only person to administer it. However, there are distinct advantages to using multiple observers. First, comparisons can be made among them to obtain information about their reliability. If the responses are the same, the indication is that the judgments are reliable. Naturally, when two observers are in disagreement, the suggestion is that there is something wrong with their observations. The particular items for which there is disagreement can be examined to decide whether the items need to be defined more clearly. Using more than one observer has other advantages. For example, by pooling the responses of several observers, it is possible to obtain a more accurate score than could be obtained from a single observer because the errors of each observer tend to compensate for the errors of others.

Systematic Observation

Some instructional objectives require neither cognitive behaviors nor a product but instead focus on changes in personality traits and attitudes. Information about personality traits and attitudes can be obtained using systematic observations.

There are important advantages to observing behavior in the naturally occurring settings of daily life, although these situations are often not uniform from person to person. Avoiding the need to stage special events just for testing purposes makes observation of real life situations appealing and more accurate reflections of behavior.

Of course, we observe the people with whom we associate every day, noticing what they do and reacting to their behavior. Our impressions of people are continuously formed and modified by our observations. But these observations are casual, unsystematic, and undirected. If asked to document with specific instances our judgments that Helen is a leader in the group or that Henry is undependable, most of us would find it difficult to provide more than one or two concrete observations of actual behavior to back up our general impressions. Observations must be organized, directed, and systematic if they are to yield dependable information about an individual.

It is appropriate at this point to note a distinction between the observational procedures that we are currently discussing and the rating procedures described in Chapter 9. In collecting observations, we want the observer to function as an objective and mechanical recording instrument, whereas in using ratings, we want the rater to synthesize and integrate the evidence that he or she has. With systematic observations, the function of the observer is strictly that of providing an accurate record of the number of social contracts, suggestions, aggressive acts, or whatever is the behavioral category of interest. The observer serves as a camera or recording device with enhanced flexibility and versatility. In ratings, however, the human instrument must judge, weigh, and interpret the information.

Systematic observational procedures have been most fully developed in connection with studies of young children. They seem particularly appropriate in this setting. Young children have not learned to camouflage or conceal their feelings as completely as older individuals, so there is more to be learned from observing them. They also may be less able to tell us about themselves in words. For these reasons, observational procedures have had their fullest development in the study of infants and young children.

Conducting the Systematic Observation

Extracting a meaningful, dependable, and relatively objective appraisal of some aspect of an individual's personality from observing a sample of behavior is far from easy. First, behavior flows continuously without any clear breaks. A preschooler is at the sand table making a "cake" at one moment, moves on to listen to the teacher talking to a group, and again moves on to build a house with the giant blocks. On the way, he or she sits down for a short rest, takes a playful poke at some other child, and shouts to the teacher (or the world in general), "See me! See what I've made." But, this report is only partial. No verbal description can capture the full details of even 5 minutes of the life of an active child. What should be observed? What behaviors represent a personality attribute? When and for how long should observations be made? How should observers be trained? How should the observations be organized?

What Should be Observed?   If anything meaningful is to emerge from observing the complex flow of behavior, the observations must have some focus. We must be looking at something or for something—for indications of leadership, insecurity, sociability, emotional strain, energy level, aggressiveness, dependency, or indicators of several such personal attributes at the same time. The research or practical problem with which we start specifies what aspect or aspects of behavior should be observed, and our plan for observing follows from a definition of the aspects of behavior that will be relevant to the problem.

What Behaviors Represent a Personality Attribute?   Even after we have selected an attribute to study, we still have to decide what behaviors will be acceptable indicators of that attribute. Consider the following behaviors:

o Sitting alone
o Kicking another child
o Holding onto a teacher's hand or apparel
o Calling attention to a mess on the floor
o Tattling on another child
o Volunteering information in a discussion

Which of these behaviors should be tallied as indicators of "dependency" in a kindergartner? What behaviors should be added? This type of decision must be made with knowledge of typical childhood behavior and the dynamics underlying it, if the observational data are to have real meaning.

When and for How Long Should Observations Be Made?   When we begin a program of systematic observations, we must decide where, when, and for how long each person is to be observed. These decisions will reflect a compromise between the cost of extended observations and the need for a representative and reliable picture of the person. Because people and situations vary from day to day, it is generally preferable to have a number of relatively brief periods of observation on different days than to have only one or two long periods of observation. Under these conditions, the sample of the person's behavior will be more representative and the score we obtain will be more reliable. We must be careful not to make the observation too brief a sample of behavior, or it may be difficult to judge what a particular action signifies. Practical considerations such as travel time and the administrative tasks associated with it also may limit the number of observations that we can make on a particular child or group.

It might even be useful to break daily 5-minute observation sessions into still shorter segments of, say, no more than 1 minute or even 30 seconds. The observation made can then consist of an indication of whether the behavior occurred. For instance, we might observe each child for ten 5-minute periods, each on a different day. Each 5-minute period might be subdivided into ten 30-second periods. For each of the 30-second periods, we would observe whether the particular child did or did not exhibit any of a set of defined aggressive behaviors. Assuming that we decide to count only the number of observation periods in which children engaged in the target behavior, each child would receive a score, with a possible range from 0 to 100, indicating the number of periods in which he or she engaged in aggressive acts. We would obtain a somewhat different result if we recorded the number of aggressive acts in each period. In either case, such scores, based on an adequate number of short samples of observed behavior, have been found to show satisfactory reliability.

The interpretation of the reliability of behavioral observations can be somewhat misleading. Under these circumstances, reliability is often defined in terms of the agreement between two observers, and the size of the coefficient depends on the method used to determine the degree of agreement. The percentage of agreement, which reflects the percentage of times that two observers agree, tends to be inflated when the rate of the behavior is either very high or very low. When a behavior occurs often, it is likely that two observers will both record it and therefore will agree. Therefore, with a very high or low behavior rate, the reliability will always be high. Statistical techniques can be used to correct for this tendency, but they also have limitations (Foster, Bell-Dolan, & Burge, 1988).

Naturally, it is desirable to plan to make observations in settings where the target behavior is likely to occur. Observations of aggressive acts, for example, can best be made during a period devoted to free-play than during one devoted to listening to stories or watching television.

How Should Observers Be Trained? Disagreements among observers can occur even when the behaviors have been carefully defined. In one extreme case, a researcher reported the rate of interobserver agreement on the gender of the teacher in a classroom where the observations were taking place to be 95%. To some extent, discrepancies are unavoidable because of fluctuations in attention and/or legitimate differences of opinion about whether a behavior occurred. Reliability can be increased, however, by training. Training sessions in which two or more observers record the same sample of behavior, compare notes, discuss discrepancies, and reconcile differences are a good means of increasing uniformity of observations. It can also be useful to have previously trained observers sit in on these sessions to offer suggestions. Such procedures can enhance the (1) uniformity of interpretation and observation and (2) placement of subjects into correct observation categories.

How Should the Behavior Be Organized? It is of primary importance that the observation be recorded immediately after it occurs. Recent research on the observations of witnesses regarding events that they have observed has shown that the errors and selectivity of memory can bias the reporting of even outstanding and unusual events. In terms of the rather ordinary and highly repetitive events that are observed in watching a child in preschool, for example, an adequate account of what occurred is possible only if the behaviors are recorded immediately. There is so much to see and one event is so much like others that relying on memory to provide an accurate after-the-fact account of a child's behavior is likely to lead to serious omissions and distortions of what really happened.

Any program of systematic observation must, therefore, provide a method for immediate and efficient recording of observed events. Many possibilities exist for facilitating recording of behavioral observations. One that has been widely used is a systematic code for the behavioral categories of interest. For example, in recording aggressive behavior, preliminary observations will have defined the range of aggressive acts that can be expected from 3-and 4-year-old children. Part of the code might be set up as follows: h = "hits," p = "pushes," g = "grabs materials from others," c = "calls a nasty name," and so forth. A blank observation form can be prepared and divided to represent the time segments of the observations, and code entries can be made quickly while the child is observed almost without interruption.

If the observer is skilled in standard shorthand, of course, fuller notes of the observation can be taken. (Space would have to be provided on the form for such notes.) These notes can be transcribed and coded or scored later. Another effective approach is videotape or audiotape recordings of the observations. This procedure provides a permanent record of the behaviors in a relatively complete form. The tapes can be analyzed at a later date, and ambiguous behavior can be examined repeatedly to obtain accurate observations.

Laptop computers also have promise for easier, more accurate recording of behavior. They can be programmed to accept a set of codes, or information can be entered on templates. Such a procedure not only can ease the burden on the observer and increase accuracy but also can make data analysis by computer much easier. The most important consideration at this point is to minimize the dependence on memory, to get a record that will preserve as much as possible of the significant detail in the original behavior, and to develop a recording procedure that will interfere as little as possible with the process of observing.

Study Using Systematic Observation

The study (Birns, 1965) described here deals with a rather straightforward question (but not necessarily one that is easy to answer): are there consistent differences in children at or near the time of birth? We are limited in what we can observe in neonates, but responsiveness to stimulation seemed to be one observable trait. The babies observed were stimulated with a soft tone, a loud tone, a cold disk, and a pacifier several times during the first 4 or 5 days of life. Each stimulus was presented three times during each of four different sessions, and three trained observers recorded the babies' responses as (1) inhibition or diminution of activity then underway, (2) no response, or (3) a response rated on a five-point scale from one, indicating small eye, toe, or finger flicker or movement of only one body part, to five, indicating hard crying or major intense overall activation.

Two types of evidence were offered to support the proposition that there are consistent individual differences in responsiveness. First, responsiveness to the four stimuli was examined. The finding was that the typical correlation among intensities was about 0.50. Second, responsiveness was compared across the four separate test sessions, and the finding was that the typical correlation between separate sessions was about 0.40. These two findings were interpreted as supporting the position that consistent individual differences in an aspect of personality already exist within the first few days of life.

Advantages and Disadvantages of Systematic Observation

Systematic observations of behavior have a number of features that make them attractive as a method of assessing personality characteristics as well as some significant limitations. Some of the advantages and disadvantages of direct observations are summarized here.

Advantages of Systematic Observation.   The advantages to systematic observation are as follows: (1) It provides a record of actual behavior, (2) it can be used in real-life situations, and (3) it can be used with young children.

1. A Record of Actual Behavior. When we observe an individual, we obtain a record of what he or she does rather than rationalizations and protestations. If our observational procedures have been well planned and our observers carefully trained, the scores obtained will be to a large degree free from the biases and idiosyncrasies of the observers. Our record of the behavior of individuals is not a reflection of what they think they are, or of what others think they are; their actions speak to us directly. If, as is so often the case, we are primarily concerned with changes in behavior, observations are the most direct and, in most cases, the most useful way of obtaining information.

2. Use in Real-Life Situations. Observational techniques can be applied in the naturally occurring situations of life and are not restricted to laboratory settings. Observations can be carried out in the nursery school, in the classroom, in the cafeteria, on the playground, at camp, in the squadron day room, on the assembly line, or any place individuals work or play. There are practical difficulties and limitations associated with observations, which we will discuss in a later section, but in spite of some disadvantages, direct observation is a widely applicable approach to studying individual personalities in a natural environment.

3. Use with Young Children. Observation is possible with small children, no matter how young, the youngest being the easiest to observe. Infants are not self-conscious, which makes it easy for the observer to sit and watch what he or she does without special procedures or precautions. With older children, it is sometimes necessary to screen the observer from the child being observed, perhaps by using a one-way vision screen that permits the child or children to be seen while the observer is hidden from view. Of course, using this type of physical arrangement seriously restricts the type of setting in which observation may take place. It may be simpler and more effective to have the observer function unobtrusively and be present long enough for those being observed to ignore him or her, accepting the observer as a natural part of the surroundings.

The value of direct observation is greatest where its application is most feasible—with young children. Young children are limited in their ability to communicate through language, they have little experience or facility in analyzing or reporting their feelings or the reasons for their actions, and they are often shy with strangers. For this group, systematic observation provides an important method of learning about personality.

Disadvantages of Systematic Observation.   In contrast to the positive aspects of observations as an information gathering technique, there are a number of factors that seriously limit the usefulness of observational techniques. These limitations, or disadvantages, range from practical considerations, which we will consider first, to issues of theory.

1. Cost of Making the Observations.   Observations are costly primarily because of the demands they make on the time of trained observers. In most applications, each individual must be observed for a number of observation periods extending in some instances to several hours. When observations are made of a substantial number of individuals or a particular group, the hours rapidly add up. Therefore, systematic observation as well as recording of behavior is usually limited to research projects in which the necessary time commitments can be made. In routine school operations, it is seldom possible to find the resources needed to make direct observations of each student.

The cost of direct observation goes beyond the expenditure of time needed to record information. The need for special settings or mechanical recording requires additional funds. Furthermore, when the original record is a running diary account or a videotape of an individual's or a group's actions, analysis of the record is likely to be time consuming, and thus costly.

2. Problems in Fitting the Observer into the Setting.   There is always a concern about whether having an observer present, watching and taking notes of what happens, will actually change what happens. In many of the situations we wish to observe, it is not practical to have the observer hidden from view. We hope with justification, that after an initial period in which the presence of the observer is noticeably intrusive, the individual being observed will gradually begin to ignore the presence of the observer. Getting subjects to ignore the observer may be easier in some situations than in others. When the group is small, when it is necessary for the observer to see the activities closely, or when the group meets for too short a time to get used to being observed, the members may not come to think of the observer as part of the normal environment.

3. Difficulties in Eliminating Subjectivity and Bias.   When observational procedures are used, it is necessary to use precautions to keep the observer's interpretations and biases out of the observation. The observer should not know much about the study being conducted, or know about the experimental treatment the individual being observed is receiving, or know test scores or other facts about that individual. It is best for the observer to function as a recording instrument that is sensitive to and makes a record of certain categories of behaviors. However, the observer is human. We may minimize subjectivity in the observations, but we cannot eliminate it. We must be aware of the role of the observer in the final result, especially when the phenomena being studied are complex or involve an element of interpretation.

4. Difficulties in Determining a Meaningful and Productive Set of Behavior Categories.   Observations are always selective. Only certain limited aspects of an individual's behavior can be observed and recorded. Furthermore, if observations are to be treated quantitatively, they must be classified, grouped, and counted. Any system of classification is a somewhat arbitrary framework that we impose on the infinitely varied events of life. It is not always easy to set up a framework that serves our purposes well. There will never be complete agreement about the categories of behavior used in a particular observation scheme or the types of activities included under a given heading. For one purpose, we might decide to classify aggressive acts in terms of overt behaviors like hitting, pushing, or grabbing. For other purposes, it might be better to note the precipitating event (if we can observe it): aggression in response to conflict over property, as a reaction to verbal disparagement, or after the thwarting of some activity in progress. In any event, scores based on observations of behavior can be no more significant and meaningful than the categories devised for recording and analyzing the behavior.

5. Difficulties in Determining the Significance of Isolated Behavior.   To make the assessment reliable and objective, systematic observations usually focus on rather small and discrete acts or break the observations and analyses into small parts. There is a real danger here for the meaning of the behavior, the true significance of the action, to be lost. We observe a 3-year-old hugging another 3-year-old. Is this an act of aggression or affection? In isolation, we have no way of telling. Or, suppose that one child hits another. This behavior is obviously an aggressive act, but what does it signify in a child's life? Is it a healthy reaction to earlier domination by another child? Or is it a displaced aggression resulting from events occurring at home? Or does it signify something else? Or nothing?

6. The External Character of Observation.   Observations are external; that is, they focus only on what can be seen. Observations are not intended to inform us about internal states. The "outsideness" is exaggerated when little bits of behavior are analyzed out of context. But the outsideness is a fundamental feature of any observational approach to studying behavior. We always face the problem of determining the meaning of the behavior and must recognize that what we have before us is only what the individual does, not what it signifies.

Summary

Although most instructional objectives can be evaluated using conventional cognitive tests, there are circumstances in which other techniques should be used. Alternative methods are particularly important when performances, products, attitudes, or personality traits are assessed. When there is a choice, it is generally easier to assess products than to assess processes, but there are circumstances when the focus of assessment efforts must be on processes. Processes are usually evaluated either with checklists or with rating scales.

Checklists should include the following elements: (1) designation of the appropriate performance or product, (2) listing of the important behaviors and characteristics,

(3) inclusion of common errors, and (4) placement of the list into an appropriate format. Rating scales are more effectively used with products than with processes because their use requires more time. With processes, there is usually much to evaluate and little time to do it.

Behavior in naturally occurring situations can best be assessed by systematic observations. To make systematic observation more effective, the following questions must be answered: What should be observed? What behaviors represent a personality attribute? When and for how long should observations be made? How should observers be trained? How should the observations be organized?

Systematic observation has the advantages of (1) representing actual behavior, (2) being applicable to real-life situations, and (3) being usable with young children and others with whom verbal communication is difficult. However, observational procedures present a number of problems and thus have the following disadvantages: (1) cost of making the observations, (2) problems in fitting the observer into the setting, (3) difficulties in eliminating subjectivity and bias, (4) difficulties in determining a meaningful and productive set of behavior categories, (5) difficulties in determining the significance of isolated behavior, and (6) the external character of observation.

Questions and Exercises

1. Consider the following objectives from a general science class at a junior high school. Specify the most appropriate type of assessment: paper-and-pencil test, process evaluation, or product evaluation. Provide a justification for your selection. Each student will:
   (a) prepare a project for the science fair.
   (b) demonstrate a knowledge of the taxonomic classification of vertebrates.
   (c) conduct a successful titration experiment.
   (d) make a presentation on one local threat to the ecology.
2. Construct a checklist that would be appropriate for judging a science fair project.
3. Construct a rating scale that could be used to evaluate performance in a unit on softball in a physical education class.
4. Design a behavior test to measure a personality trait desired of students in music appreciation class.
5. How could a classroom discussion serve as the basis for systematic observation? Make a plan for recording these observations.
6. In a research study, you propose to use systematic observations of school children as a method of studying their social adjustment. What problems would you encounter? What precautions would you need to take in interpreting the results?
7. What advantages do systematic observations have over the observations of everyday life?

Suggested Readings

Barrios, B. A. (1988). On the changing nature of behavioral assessment. In A. S. Bellack & M. Hershon (Eds.), *Behavioral assessment: A practical handbook* (pp. 3–41). New York: Pergamon.

Berk, R. A. (Ed.). (1986). *Performance assessment: Methods and applications.* Baltimore: Johns Hopkins University Press.

Evertson, C. M. (1986). Observation as inquiry and method. In M. C. Witrock (Ed.), *Handbook of research on teaching* (pp. 162–213). New York: Macmillan.

Fitzpatrick, R., & Morrison E. J. (1971). Performance and product evaluation. In R. L. Thorndike (Ed.), *Educational measurement* (pp. 237–270). Washington DC: American Council on Education.

Foster, S. L., Bell-Dolan, D. J., & Burge, D. A. (1988). Behavioral observation. In A. S. Bellack & M. Hershon (Eds.), *Behavioral assessment: A practical handbook* (pp. 119–160). New York: Pergamon.

Kubiszyn, T., & Borich, G. (1987). *Educational testing and measurement.* Glenview, IL: Scott, Foresman and Company.

Sax, G. (1989). *Principles of educational and psychological measurement and evaluation.* Belmont, CA: Wadsworth.

CHAPTER 9
Attitudes and Rating Scales

Introduction

As was emphasized in Chapter 8, there are important instructional objectives that cannot be assessed with conventional cognitive tests. Some of these instructional objectives refer to processes and products and others to changes in personality traits and attitudes. This chapter will emphasize the assessment of these latter characteristics.

A music appreciation class may be concerned with the attitudes and feelings students have toward music as well as their cognitive knowledge about the subject. Instructional objectives for social studies classes may emphasize the development of good citizenship as well as knowledge of how government works. It is always more difficult to gain knowledge about personality traits and attitudes than about cognitive characteristics, because with cognitive tests we are measuring maximum performance. When assessing personality, we are measuring typical performance. It is much easier to structure a test to elicit maximum performance than to elicit typical performance.

We can learn about personality traits in three main ways: (1) by observing the behavior of the individual, as discussed in Chapter 8, (2) by obtaining information indirectly through another person, or (3) by gaining information directly from the individual—that is, by measuring attitudes. The last two approaches, are covered in this chapter.

Learning About Personality from Others

One important way in which an individual's personality is manifested is through the impression that it makes on others. The second person serves as a source of information about the personality of the first. We can have a teacher rate students on the degree to which they have learned to appreciate music or the degree of their opposition to drug use. Alternatively, other students can be asked to make this evaluation.

These techniques for learning about the personality of others have proved useful in other situations as well. We might want answers to any of the following questions: How well does Person A like Person B? Does Person A consider Person B to be a pleasing individual to have around? An effective worker? A good job risk? Does Person A consider Person B to be conscientious? Trustworthy? Emotionally stable? Questions of this sort are continuously asked of teachers, supervisors, former employers, ministers, and even friends of individuals being rated.

Rating scales can be used to learn about an individual's cognitive characteristics, that is, abilities and achievement. Usually such abilities are measured with paper-and-pencil tests, but rating scales can also provide useful information about cognitive functioning. Under some circumstances, they may even replace paper-and-pencil tests. Of course, we need to be sure that these ratings provide accurate estimates if they are to be used to make important decisions.

Letters of Recommendation

Information from letters of recommendation can be used for different purposes, but it is most commonly used to evaluate a candidate for something: admission to a school, a scholarship or fellowship, a job, membership in a club, or a security clearance. How useful and how informative is the material that is included in free, unstructured communications describing a person? Actually, there is very little that is known about the adequacy of letters of recommendation or their effectiveness. Opinions about their value vary widely.

One analysis (Siskind, 1966) of 67 letters written for 33 psychology internship applicants found 958 statements distributed as follows:

Type of Statement	Number	Percentage
Positive statements	838	87
"Don't know" statements about a characteristic	17	2
Statements referring to natural shortcomings, the result of inexperience or youth	44	5
Other statements indicative of shortcomings	59	6

Reviewers do use such letters, and there is a moderate degree of consistency (reliability = 0.40) among letters written about a given person. One clue as to why this relationship occurs comes from a study of adjectives used in a series of letters written in support of applicants for engineering jobs (Peres & Garcia, 1962). Of 170 different adjectives extracted from the letters, almost all were positive in tone, but when the "best" employees were compared with the "worst" employees, the adjectives differed enormously in the degree to which they differentiated these groups. An applicant might be called "congenial," "helpful," and "open" or he or she might be called "ingenious," "informed," and "productive." The first three adjectives were applied about equally as often to the best and to the poorest workers, while the last three adjectives were used only to describe the best workers. Apparently, the validity of the inferences drawn from a letter of recommendation depends to a considerable extent on the degree to which the reviewer has learned to "read between the lines," weighting the nice things that are said by an appropriate *discrimination factor* that identifies whether it is the job-relevant or the tangential virtues that are mentioned. Similar findings were obtained by Baxter, Brock, Hill, and Rozelle (1981) in a study of letters of recommendation for graduate school applicants.

In addition, writers of letters of recommendation are free to write whatever they choose, so there is no core of content common to letters about a single person or to the letters dealing with different people. One letter may deal with a person's social charm, a second with his or her integrity; and a third with his or her originality.

An additional consideration is the part that the applicant usually is free to select the people who will write the letters and certainly can be expected to select people who will support him or her. Furthermore, writers of recommendations differ profoundly in their propensity for using superlatives.

The extent to which a letter of recommendation provides a valid appraisal of an individual and the extent to which it is accurately diagnostic of outstanding points, strengths, or weaknesses are almost completely unknown. However, there is little reason for optimism in terms of their validity.

Rating Scales

The extreme subjectivity of the unstructured statement, the lack of a common core of content or standard of reference from person to person, and the extraordinary difficulty in attempting to quantify unstructured materials gave impetus to the development of rating scales. Rating scales were developed to obtain appraisals on a common set of attributes for all raters and all individuals being rated and to have the attributes expressed on a common quantitative scale.

We have all had experience with ratings, both in the capacity of rating others or being rated ourselves. Rating scales appear on many report cards, particularly in sections reporting nonacademic performance. An example of the use of this type of rating follows:

Student Characteristic	First Period	Second Period	Third Period	Fourth Period
Effort	_____	_____	_____	_____
Conduct	_____	_____	_____	_____
Citizenship	_____	_____	_____	_____
Adjustment	_____	_____	_____	_____

H = superior   S = satisfactory   U = unsatisfactory

Many civil service agencies and industrial firms send rating forms out to people listed as references by job applicants, asking for evaluations of the individual's "initiative," "originality," "enthusiasm," and "ability to get along with others." These same companies or agencies often require supervisors to give merit ratings of their employees, rating them as "superior," "excellent," "very good," "good," "satisfactory," or "unsatisfactory" on a variety of traits or on overall performance. Colleges, medical schools, fellowship programs, and various agencies require ratings as a part of their selection procedure. Beyond these practical uses, ratings are used in many research projects; vast numbers of ratings are completed, often reluctantly, every day.

Often ratings are retrospective, summarizing the impressions developed by the rater over an extended period of contact with the person being rated. Sometimes ratings are concurrent, arising out of an interview or a period of observation. Almost universally, a rating involves an evaluative summary of past or present experiences in which the "internal computer" of the rater processes the data in complex and unspecified ways to arrive at the final assessment.

The most common rating procedure involves presenting the rater with a set of traits and a range of numbers, adjectives, or descriptions that represent levels

FIGURE 9.1
Rating scale for rating leadership.

Leadership
Consider the individual's ability to inspire confidence. How much respect does he or she command as an individual, not merely because of the individual's position? Do people look to this person for decisions? Is this person a team-worker?

Completely lacking. Definitely a follower with equals. Does not try to convince others that his or her way is best.	Tries to lead with some success, but has never achieved a strong position. Is passive in directing his or her subordinates.	Good leader, people wait to hear what he or she has to say. Respected by colleagues. People call for his or her opinion.	Exceptional leader, able to take over and pull things into shape. People seem to enjoy going along on his or her side. Is respected by subordinates and colleagues.

or degrees of the traits. The rater is asked to evaluate one or more people on the trait or traits by assigning a number, letter, adjective, or description to the trait. Figure 9.1 contains a two rating scale that assesses the trait of leadership; qualities of the trait are provided along with definitions of various levels of leadership.

Problems in Obtaining Sound Ratings

For two primary reasons—willingness and ability—it is difficult to obtain accurate and valid appraisals of an individual through ratings.

Factors Affecting the Rater's Willingness to Rate Conscientiously. Two circumstances affect a rater's willingness to do a good job: (1) the rater's unwillingness to put forth the effort that is called for by the appraisal procedure and (2) the rater's identification with the person being rated to such an extent that the rater is unwilling to render a rating that may be harmful to that person.

1. Unwillingness to put forth sufficient effort. The careful and thoughtful rating of an individual requires considerable effort. If the rating form is long and the number of individuals to be rated is large, the task may be so overwhelming that it seems not to be worth the effort. When ratings are carried out in a perfunctory manner, the rating process is less effective. Unless raters are really "sold" on the importance of the ratings, the judgments are likely to be hurried and superficial, with more emphasis on finishing the task than on making accurate analytical judgments.

2. Identification with the person being rated. Ratings are often requested by distant administrators and impersonal agencies. The Civil Service Commission, the Military Personnel Division of a commanding general's headquarters, the personnel director of a large company, or the central administrative staff of a school system are all far removed from the first-line supervisor, the squadron commander, or the classroom teacher—the ultimate raters. The rater usually feels greater connection to the people being rated—the workers in the office, the junior officers in the outfit, or the pupils in the class—than to the agency requesting the ratings. One of the first principles of supervision or leadership is that "the good officer looks out for his men." Morale in an organization depends on the conviction that the leader of the organization takes care of its members. When ratings come along, "taking care of" becomes a matter of seeing to it that one's own people fare as well as—or a little better than—those in competing groups.

As a result, in too many situations, the rater is more interested in ensuring that those with whom he or she works closely get high ratings than in providing accurate information. This situation is made even worse by the policy of allowing the rated person access to the ratings and mandating explanations of any unfavorable results. Administrative rulings that specify the minimum rating necessary for promotion or a pay increase pose another threat to rating accuracy. It should come as no surprise that ratings tend to climb or to pile up at a single scale point. A tendency exists for the typical rating, accounting for a very large proportion of all ratings given, to be "excellent." "Very good" almost becomes an expression of dissatisfaction, while a rating of "satisfactory" is reserved for a person who the rater would like to get rid of at the earliest opportunity.

It is important to understand that a rater cannot always be depended on to work wholeheartedly at giving valid ratings for the benefit of the requesting agency, that making ratings is usually a nuisance to the rater, and that there is likely to be more of a commitment to the rater's own subordinates than to an outside agency. A rating program must be continuously "sold" and policed if it is to remain effective. However, there are limits to the extent to which even an active campaign can overcome a rater's natural inertia and interest in the group with which he or she identifies.

Factors Affecting the Rater's Ability to Rate Accurately. Even when raters are well motivated and try to do their best to provide valid judgments, a number of factors still operate to limit the validity of their judgments. These factors center on the lack of opportunity to observe the person to be rated, the covertness of the trait to be rated, ambiguity in the meaning of the dimension to be rated, lack of a uniform standard of reference, and specific rater biases and idiosyncrasies.

Lack of Opportunity to Observe. Raters often have limited opportunities to observe the person being rated. For example, a high school teacher with five classes of 30 students each may be required to judge the "initiative" or "flexibility" of all his or her students. A college professor who has taught a particular class of 100 students may receive rating forms from an employment agency or from the college administration asking for similar judgments on some of the students. Under such circumstances, there has usually been insufficient contact with individual students to provide adequate bases for the judgments being requested. The person being rated may physically have been in the presence of the rater for many hours, possibly several hundred, but these were very busy hours in which the rater, as well as the person being rated, was concerned with more pressing matters than observing and forming judgments.

In a civil service or industrial setting, the same problems arise. The primary concern is getting the job done. Even though, in theory, a supervisor may have a good deal of time to observe each worker, in practice, he or she has been busy with other things. We may be able to "sell" supervisors on the idea of devoting more of their energy to observing and evaluating the people working for them, but there are very real limits on the amount of effort—thus time—that most supervisors can withdraw from their other functions and apply to this one.

The problem is not only a lack of opportunity to observe but also a lack of opportunity to observe a particular aspect of a person's personality. Each person sees others in limited contexts, and these contexts reveal only some aspects of behavior. The teacher sees a child primarily in the classroom, the foreman sees a worker primarily on the production line, and so forth. In a *conventional* classroom it is doubtful whether the teacher has seen a child under circumstances that might be expected to elicit "initiative" or "originality." The college professor who teaches mainly through lectures is not well situated to rate a student's "presence" or "ability to work with individuals." The supervisor of a clerk doing routine work is not in a position to appraise "judgment." Whenever ratings are proposed, either for research purposes or as a basis for administrative actions, we should ask whether the rater has had an adequate opportunity to observe the people to be rated in enough situations for the ratings to be meaningful. If the answer is "no," we should not rate this trait.

Each rater sees a person in different roles and is therefore likely to focus on quite different aspects of the person. Students see a teacher from a different vantage point than does the principal. Classmates in Officer Candidate School have a different view of other potential officers than does their tactical officer. In deciding who should be the rater, it is appropriate to ask who has had the best opportunity to see the relevant behavior displayed. Normally, that person should be the rater.

Covertness of the Trait. A trait can be appraised only if it shows on the outside. Such characteristics as appearing at ease at social gatherings, having a pleasant speaking voice, and participating actively in group projects are characteristics that are essentially social. They appear in interactions with other people and are directly observable. By contrast, attributes such as "feelings of insecurity," "self-sufficiency," "tension," or "loneliness" are inner personal qualities. They are private aspects of personality and can be inferred only crudely from what the person does. We refer to these as covert characteristics.

An attribute that is largely covert can be judged by an outsider only with great difficulty. Inner conflict, or tension, may not show on the surface, and when it does, it may reveal itself indirectly. Furthermore, it is unlikely to manifest itself in the same way for each person. For example, deep insecurity may express itself as aggression against other students in one child or as withdrawal into an inner world in another. Insecurity may not be revealed in overt behavior. It is instead an underlying trait that may be manifested in different ways by different people or in different ways by the same person at different times. Only with a thorough knowledge of the person, combined with psychological insight, is it possible to infer from overt behavior the nature of underlying trait.

For these reasons, rating procedures for covert aspects of personality are generally unsatisfactory. Qualities that depend both on a thorough understanding of a person and on the generation of inferences from behavior are measured with low reliability and poor validity. Ratings are more accurate for those qualities that show outwardly as a person interacts with other people than for covert ones.

Ambiguity in the Meaning of the Dimension. Many rating forms require ratings of broad and abstract traits. For example, see the rating scale presented earlier that includes "citizenship" and "adjustment," as well as other attributes. Agreement among raters regarding the meanings of these terms is unlikely. What do we mean by "citizenship" in an elementary school student? How is "good citizenship" shown? Does "good citizenship" mean not marking on the walls? Or not spitting on the floor? Or not pulling little girls' hair? Or does it mean bringing newspaper clippings to class? Or joining the Junior Red Cross? Or staying after school to help the teacher clean up the room? No two raters are likely to have exactly the same things in mind when they rate a group of students on "citizenship."

Consider "initiative," "personality," "supervisory aptitude," "mental flexibility," "executive influence," or "adaptability." Although there is certainly some core of uniformity in the meaning that each of these terms will have for different raters, there is a great deal of variability in meaning from one rater to another. The more abstract a term, the more variable its meaning from person to person, and such qualities as those just listed are conspicuously abstract. The rating that a given child receives for citizenship will depend on what citizenship means to the rater. If to one teacher citizenship is indicated by a child conforming to school regulations, he or she will certainly rate children who comform high. If to a different teacher citizenship is indicated by a child taking a active role in school projects, high ratings may go to quite different children. The first step in getting consistent ratings is to establish a minimal level of agreement among raters about the meanings of the qualities being rated. One way to accomplish this task is to provide the desired definition on the rating form. If a good citizen is defined as "child who follows the school rules," then a common understanding of the term will be fostered if the definition is made explicit in the directions for the rating scale.

Lack of Uniform Standard of Reference. Many rating scales call for judgments of the people being rated in sets of categories such as the following:

○ Outstanding, above average, average, below average, unsatisfactory
○ Superior, good, fair, poor
○ Best, good, average, fair, poor
○ Outstanding, superior, better than satisfactory, satisfactory, unsatisfactory
○ Superior, excellent, very good, good, satisfactory, unsatisfactory

How good is "good"? Is a person who is "good" in "judgment" in the top 10% in judgment for the group with whom he or she is being compared? The top 25%? The top 50%? Or is this person just not one of the bottom 10%? And, what is the composition of the group with which this comparison is made? Are all members the same age? Are all employees of the same company? Are all members in a particular job? Are all employees in the same job with the same length of service? If the latter, how is the rater supposed to know the level of judgment that is typical for people in a particular job with a given amount of experience?

The problem that all these questions bring up is the need for a standard against which to appraise a person being rated. Variations in interpretation of terms and labels, variations in definition of the reference population, and variations in experience with the members of that background population all contribute to variability from rater to rater in their standards of rating. The phenomenon is familiar to those involved in academic grading. There are enormous variations among faculty members in the percentages of As, Bs, and Cs awarded in comparable courses. The same situation holds for any set of categories, numbers, letters, or adjectives that may be used. Standards are highly subjective interpretations, and they can therefore be expected to vary widely from one rater to another.

Raters differ not only in the level of ratings that they assign but also in how much they spread out their ratings. Some raters are conservative and rarely rate anyone very high or very low; others tend to go to both extremes. Differences in variability in ratings reduce their comparability from one rater to another. These differences among raters appear not to be a chance matter but to be a reflection of the personal characteristics and value structure of individual raters. Thus, one study (Klores, 1966), found that supervisors who placed importance on a supervisor's personal relationships with subordinates gave higher and less variable ratings than supervisors who placed importance on providing structure in the work situation.

Specific Rater Biases and Idiosyncrasies. Raters not only differ in general toughness or softness but also may be characterized by other idiosyncrasies as well. Life experiences have provided each of us with likes and dislikes and an assortment of individualized interpretations of the characteristics of other people. You may distrust people who do not look at you when they are talking to you. Your teenage son may consider anyone who listens to folk music to be "not with it." Your boss may consider a firm handshake to be a guarantee of strong character. Your tennis partner may be convinced that people with shifty eyes are not trustworthy. The behaviors that are believed to indicate the presence of these traits are concrete, and the descriptions of these behaviors can be clearly verbalized by the person making judgments.

There are myriad other biases that we each have and that influence our ratings. These biases help to form our impression of a person and influence all aspects of our reaction to that person. In some cases, our rating of one or two traits may be affected. But often the bias is one of general liking for or an aversion to the person, and this generalized reaction influences all of our ratings. Ratings, therefore, reflect not only the general subjective rating standard of the rater but also any biases about the characteristics of the person being rated.

A different type of idiosyncrasy that is likely to influence overall judgments of effectiveness on a job (or in an educational program) is individual differences in the types of behavior considered desirable. Barrett (1966) found wide differences among supervisors of employees in closely similar jobs in the attributes that were considered important. Some raters considered "solving problems on one's own initiative" among the most important traits a subordinate could have, and others considered it among the least important. To the extent that such differences in values prevail, it is inevitable that supervisors will fail to agree on who are their more effective subordinates.

The Outcome of Factors Limiting Rating Effectiveness

The effects of factors limiting rating effectiveness are manifested in systematic distortions of the ratings, in relatively low reliabilities, and in questionable validity of rating procedures. We summarize these problems under four headings:

1. the generosity error
2. the halo effect
3. low reliability
4. questionable validity

The Generosity Error.   The rater usually identifies more with the people being rated than with the agency for which ratings are being prepared. There also seems to be a widespread unwillingness to give others low ratings. The net result is that ratings tend generally to pile up at the high end of any scale. The unspoken philosophy of the rater seems to be "everyone is at least equal if not better," so that the term "average" in practice is not the midpoint of a set of ratings but instead a point at the lower end of the group. It is a little like the commercial classification of olives, where the tiniest ones are called "medium," and the classification continues from there through "large" and "extra large" to "jumbo" and "colossal."

If the generosity error operated uniformly for all raters, it would not be particularly disturbing; we would merely have to remember that ratings cannot be interpreted in terms of their verbal labels and that "average" means "low" and "very good" means "average." Makers of rating scales have even countered this humane tendency with some success by having several extra steps on their scale on the plus side of average, so that there is room for differentiation without the rater having to be negative by labeling a person or trait "average." The differences between raters in their degrees of "generosity error" are more troublesome than the fact that there is "generosity error." Corrections for such differences are difficult to implement.

The Halo Effect.   Limitations in experience with the person being rated, lack of opportunity to observe the specific qualities that are called for in the rating instrument, and the influence of personal biases that affect general liking for the person all conspire to produce another type of error in ratings. This factor is the tendency of raters (1) to evaluate in terms of an overall impression without differentiating among specific aspects of personality and (2) to allow the total reaction to the person to color judgment of each specific trait. This factor is called the *halo effect*.

This propensity is illustrated in Table 9.1, which contains ratings of World War II student pilots by their instructors (Army-Air Force Aviation Psychology Program, 1947). The table provides two kinds of information: (1) the intercorrelations among four distinct characteristics when ratings are given by the same instructor, and (2) reliabilities as determined by the correlations obtained when the same trait is rated by two different instructors.

While the average between-rater reliability of the judgments was 0.47, the average correlation among different traits (intercorrelations) by the same rater was 0.71. What this tells us is that the same instructor tended to see the same level of performance for each pilot across all traits. On the other hand, different instructors did not agree about ratings of pilots on these traits. This tendency indicates that an individual instructor was more likely to see disparate traits as similar for the same pilot than several instructors were to rate the same trait similarly for the same pilot.

Of course, a relationship among desirable traits is to be expected. We find correlation among different abilities when these abilities are assessed by objective tests and do not speak of the halo effect that produces a correlation between verbal and mechanical ability. Just how much of the relationship between the different qualities on which we get ratings is genuine and how much is spurious is hard to determine, but when correlations among traits exceed the reliability of a trait, there is need for concern.

Low Reliability. The between-raters reliability of conventional rating procedures has generally been found to be low. When two ratings are uncontaminated, which means the raters have not discussed the people being rated, and when the usual type of numerical or graphic rating is used, the resulting appraisals can be expected to have a low correlation. However, evidence exists that

TABLE 9.1
Ratings of World War II Student Pilots

Trait	INTERCORRELATION[a]			Between-Rater Reliability[b]
	2	3	4	
1. Eagerness	.77	.77	.59	.39
2. Foresight		.66	.62	.61
3. Leadership			.66	.56
4. Instrument flying				.32

[a]Intercorrelation are from ratings by same instructor.
[b]Between-rater reliability is based on the ratings of two different instructors.

when great care is taken in structuring rating scales through a careful delineation of the end-points, or anchors, on the scale, and when the raters are well trained and have had ample opportunity to observe those being rated, the reliability of ratings can be improved (Landy & Farr, 1980).

If it is possible to pool the ratings of a number of independent raters who know the people being rated about equally well, the reliability of the appraisal can be substantially increased. Pooling ratings has the same effect as lengthening a test, and the Spearman-Brown Prophecy Formula (discussed in Chapter 4) can legitimately be applied in estimating the reliability of pooled independent ratings. Thus, if the reliability of a single rater is represented by a correlation of 0.55, we have the following estimates for the reliability of pooled ratings:

- 0.71 for 2 raters
- 0.79 for 3 raters
- 0.86 for 5 raters
- 0.92 for 10 raters

Unfortunately, in many situations, obtaining additional equally qualified raters is impractical if not impossible. An elementary school student has only one regular classroom teacher; a worker has only one immediate supervisor. Adding other raters who have more limited acquaintance with the person being rated may weaken rather than strengthen the ratings.

Reliability data on some of the newer types of rating instruments (to be discussed later in this section) appear more promising. The reliability data for these instruments will be presented as the methods are discussed. We hope that one of the gains from basing ratings on specific tangible behaviors will be increased objectivity, and hence increased reliability, of ratings.

Questionable Validity.   All the limiting and distorting factors that we have considered—in particular, rater biases and low reliability—tend to suppress the validity of rating instruments. However, it is seldom possible to determine the validity of ratings empirically. The fact that we are using ratings suggests that no better measure of the quality in question is available, and usually there is no data with which we can verify the accuracy of ratings.

In one context, the validity of ratings is axiomatic. If we are interested in appraising how a person is perceived by other people, that is, whether a child is well liked by his classmates or a foreman by his work crew, ratings are the reactions of the other people and are directly relevant to the trait or behavior in question.

When ratings are used as predictors, it is sometimes possible to obtain statistical data that can be used to quantify the accuracy of the prediction. In some cases, ratings may be the most valid available predictors. One example of this validity comes from studies of the ratings from aptitude tests that have been given at the U.S. Military Academy at West Point (Adjutant General's Office, Personal Research Section, 1953). These ratings by tactical officers and fellow cadets were shown to correlate better with later ratings of performance as officers than with any other aspect of the candidates' records at the U.S. Military

Academy at West Point. The problem with this study and similar ones is that the variables being compared in both cases are ratings, and the reliability and the validity of each or both has a sizable effect on the outcome.

Ratings usually are used as a criterion measure. When this is the case, everything possible should be done to ensure the accuracy and reliability of the ratings because they represent the standard against which other procedures will be judged.

Improving the Effectiveness of Ratings

Thus far we have painted a rather gloomy picture of rating techniques as measurement devices. It is certainly true that there are many hazards and pitfalls in rating procedures. But, for all their limitations, there are and will continue to be a host of situations in which we will have to rely on the judgments of other people as a means of appraisal. The sincerity and integrity of a potential medical student, the social skills of a would-be salesperson, or the conscientiousness of a private secretary can probably be evaluated only through the judgment that someone makes of these qualities in the people in question. What can be done, then, to mitigate the defects of rating procedures? First, we will consider the design of the rating instrument and then the planning and conduct of the ratings.

Refinements in the Rating Instrument. The usual rating instrument has two main components: (1) a set of stimulus variables (the qualities to be rated) and (2) a pattern of response options (the ratings that can be given). In the simplest and most conventional forms, the stimulus variables consist of trait names and the response options consist of numerical or adjectival categories. Such a form was provided earlier. This type of format appears to encourage most of the shortcomings discussed in the preceding section; consequently, many variations and refinements of format have been tried in an attempt to overcome or at least to minimize these shortcomings. The variations have manipulated the stimulus variables, the response options, or both. Some of the main variations are described next.

Refinements in Presenting the Stimulus Variables. Simple trait names themselves represent unsatisfactory stimuli for two reasons. First, the words mean different things to different people. The child who shows "initiative" to Teacher A may show "insubordination" to Teacher B, whereas Teacher B's "good citizen" may seem to Teacher A to be a "docile conformist." Second, trait names are abstract and far removed from the realm of observable behavior. Consider "adjustment," for example. We obviously cannot directly observe a child's adjustment. Instead, we can observe only the reactions of the child to situations and people. Some of these reactions may be indicative of poor adjustment. But the judgment about the child's adjustment is an inference based on what we have a chance to observe.

Users of ratings have tried to maintain greater uniformity in the meaning of traits to be rated by basing the ratings more closely on observable behavior.

These attempts have modified the stimulus aspect of rating instruments in three ways.

1. Traits have been defined. "Social adjustment" is a rather nebulous label. It can be given somewhat more substance by elaborating on what the label is intended to mean, as in the following example.

> *Social adjustment.* Interest in and skills of interacting with both children and adults in work and play situations. Willingness both to give and to take in interpersonal situations. Conformity to basic social norms of behavior.

The elaboration attaches more substance to an intangible concept and should provide greater uniformity of meaning among different raters and between the raters and the rating form designer.

There is no question that an expanded definition of each attribute to be appraised is a desirable first step in improving rating procedures. However, it is doubtful that a brief verbal definition will do very much to overcome the raters' individual differences in the meanings that they attach to terms.

2. Traits have been replaced by several more limited and concrete descriptive phrases. For example, the abstract and inclusive term "social adjustment" might be broken down into several components, each relating to a more limited aspect of behavior. Thus, for that one term, we might have the following components:

○ Works in groups with other children
○ Plays with other children
○ Interacts with teacher and other adults
○ Obeys school rules

Of course, judgment would now be called for with respect to each of these more restricted and more tangible aspects of student behavior.

3. Each trait has been replaced with a substantial number of descriptions of specific behaviors. This practice carries the move toward concreteness and specificity one step farther. Thus, the descriptor "works in groups with other children" might be enhanced with something like the following list of descriptions of the behavior:

○ Takes an active part in group enterprises
○ Makes and defends suggestions
○ Accepts majority decisions
○ Does his or her share of the work
○ Helps others with their work

A similar subdivision would be carried out for each of the three other components listed in the previous step. The descriptions used to define "works in groups with other children" make the behavior more concrete. But there is still an element of interpretation in deciding, for example, what level of involvement constitutes "takes an active part."

Replacing one general term with many specific behaviors allows more uniformity in meaning from one rater to another. It may also bring the ratings closer to the observations that the rater has had an opportunity to make. The process of identifying specific observable behaviors will often elucidate problems with indicators of traits that raters have not had an opportunity to observe.

The gains that a list of specific behaviors achieves in uniformity of meaning and concreteness of behavior judged are not without cost. The cost lies in the greatly increased length and complexity of the rating instrument. There are limits to the number of different judgments that a rater can be asked to make. Furthermore, the lengthy, analytical report of behavior may be confusing to the person who tries to use and interpret it. The lengthy list of specific behaviors will probably prove most effective when (1) judgments are in very simple terms, such as "present" or "absent" and (2) there are provisions for organizing and summarizing the specific judgments into one or more scores for broad areas.

Refinements in Response Categories. Expressing judgments about a person being rated by selecting one of a set of numbers, letters, or adjectives is still common on school report cards or in civil service and industrial merit rating systems; however, these procedures have little except simplicity to commend them. The categories are arbitrary and undefined. No two raters interpret them in exactly the same way. A rating of "superior" may be given to 5% of employees by one supervisor and to 25% by another. One teacher's A is another teacher's B. Subjective standards reign supreme.

Attempts to achieve a more meaningful scale or greater uniformity from rater to rater have included use of the following:

1. percentages
2. graphic scales
3. behavioral statements
4. person-to-person scales
5. present or absent scales
6. frequency of occurrence or degree of resemblence

1. Percentages. In an attempt to produce greater uniformity from rater to rater and better discrimination among the ratings given by a particular rater, judgments are sometimes called for in terms of percentages of a particular defined group. Thus, a professor rating an applicant for a fellowship is instructed to rate each candidate according to the following scale:

- In the top 2% of students at his or her level of training
- In top 10%, but not in top 2%
- In top 25%, but not in top 10%
- In top 50%, but not in top 25%
- In lower 50% of students at his or her level of training

Presumably, the specified percentages of a defined group provide a uniform standard of quality for different raters; however, the strategy is usually only partially successful. Individual differences in generosity are not that easily suppressed, and we may still find 25% of the people being rated placed in the top 10% category.

2. Graphic scales. Rating scales are often prepared so that judgments can be recorded by the rater making a checkmark at some appropriate point on a line instead of choosing a number, letter, or adjective that approximates the level of the trait. These instruments are called "graphic scales," and an example is given here.

Responsibility for completing work

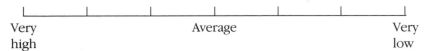

Very   Average   Very
high   low

The use of graphic scales results in an attractive page layout and seems somewhat less forbidding than a form that is all print. However, this variation on rating scales uses more space than a series of statements would, which results in rating scales that require more pages. For sophisticated users, the simplicity of a graphic presentation makes little difference, but it may help newer users to visualize the construct as being on a continuum.

3. Behavioral statements. We have seen that the stimuli may be in the form of relatively specific behavioral statements. Statement of this sort may also be used to present the rating alternatives. Thus, we might have an item of the following type:

Participation in school projects

| Volunteers to bring in materials. Suggests ideas. Often works overtime. | Works or brings materials as requested. Participates but takes no initiative. | Does as little as possible. Resists attempts to get him or her to help. |

Here, three sets of statements describing behavior are listed on a graphic scale; they are used to define three points on the scale. The descriptions can be expected to make the task more concrete and the scale steps more uniform. However, the use of behavioral statements does not ensure that all raters will see things the same way because raters must still make subjective decisions on how to interpret these behavioral statements.

A whimsical development of a rating form that provides a fairly clear illustration of behavioral statements is shown in Table 9.2.

4. Person-to-person scales. An early attempt to add uniformity of meaning to the response scale, developed as far back as World War I, used a scale person instead of numbers, adjectives, or descriptions to represent the scale points. The rater is asked to think of someone he or she has known well who is very high on the quality being rated. That person's name is entered on the rating form to

TABLE 9.2
Employee Performance Appraisal

Level of Performance	Degree of Performance				
	Far exceeds job requirements	Exceeds job requirements	Meets job requirements	Needs Improvement	Does not meet minimum requirements
Quality of work	Leaps tall buildings in a single bound	Leaps tall buildings with a running start	Can leap short buildings with prodding	Bumps into buildings	Fails to recognize buildings
Promptness	Is faster than a speeding bullet	Is as fast as a speeding bullet	Would you believe a slow bullet?	Misfires frequently	Wounds self when handling guns
Adaptability	Walks on water	Readily keeps head above water	Washes with water	Drinks water	Chronically waterlogged
Communication	Talks with God	Talks with the angels	Talks to himself or herself	Argues with himself or herself	Loses arguments with himself or herself

define the "very high" point on the scale. In the same way, the names of other people known well by the rater are entered in spaces to define "high," "average," "low," and "very low." The five names then define levels for the trait. When a person is to be rated, the rater is instructed to compare him or her with the five people defining the levels of the trait. The rater then judges which person the person being rated most closely resembles on the trait in question. The value assigned to the person being rated on that trait corresponds to the position on the scale that the scale person occupies.

The developers thought that the person-to-person scale would lend concreteness to the comparisons and overcome the tendency of some raters to be consistently generous. When all raters have a wide range of acquaintances, so that their scale people may be expected to be fairly comparable, the procedure may add more uniformity from rater to rater. Unfortunately, raters seldom have both a broad and similar range of acquaintances. Ratings almost always involve implicit comparisons with other people, but explicit use of particular people to define the steps on a rating scale has never been widely adopted.

5. Present or absent scales. When a large number of specific behavioral statements are used as the stimuli, the responses could just be checks to indicate which statements apply to the individual being rated. The rating scale then takes the form of a behavior checklist.

If this type of appraisal procedure is to yield a score, the statements must be scaled or assigned score values in some way. The simplest way is to score each statement is +1, −1, or 0, depending on whether it is favorable, unfavorable, or neutral, respectively, in terms of a particular attribute (e.g., perseverance, integrity, or reliability) or a particular criterion (e.g., success in academic work, success on a job, or responsiveness to therapy). A person's score can then be the sum of the scores for the items checked.

6. *Frequency of occurrence or degree of resemblance.* Instead of reacting in an all-or-none fashion to an item, as with checklists, the rater can be given choices such as "always," "usually," "sometimes," "seldom," or "never." In formulating items to be responded to with these categories, you must take care that no term expressing frequency is included in the statement of the item. Otherwise, you might be faced with the syntactic atrocity of judging that Johnny "always" "usually accepts majority decisions." Another approach is to have the person being rated characterized as "very much like," "a good deal like," "somewhat like," "slightly like," or "not at all like" the behavior described in the statement.

Indefinite designations of frequency or degree of the sort suggested here will not be interpreted the same way by different raters, so the old problem of differences in rater biases and idosyncrasies reappears. When asked to indicate what percentage of the time each was implied by several terms, a class of introductory psychology students gave a wide range of answers. For some students "always" meant "more than 80% of the time," while for others it meant *every* time. Words like "usually" and "frequently" were taken to mean somewhere between 50% and 95% of the time. Similar variation has been found for other frequency terms. Moreover, when the number of specific behaviors being checked is substantial, a simple checking of presence or absence correlates quite highly with the more elaborate form.

Improving the Accuracy of Ratings

The best designed instrument cannot give good results if it is used under unsatisfactory rating conditions. Raters cannot give information they do not have, and they cannot be made to give information they are unwilling to give. We must, therefore, try to select raters who have had close contacts with the people being rated and ask them for judgments on attributes they have had an opportunity to observe. We also must give raters guidance and training in the type of judgment we expect them to make and ensure that they have an ample opportunity to observe the people being rated. When there are several people who know the people being rated equally well, ratings should be gathered from each person and then pooled.

Selecting Raters.   For most purposes, the ideal rater is the person who has had the most extensive opportunity to observe the person being rated in those situations in which he or she would be likely to show the qualities being rated. (Occasionally, it may be desirable to get a rating of the impression that a person makes on brief contact or in a limited experimental situation.) It is also desirable that the rater maintains an impartial attitude toward the person being rated. The desirability of these two qualities, thorough acquaintance and impartiality, is generally recognized in the abstract. However, the goals may be only partially realized in practice because knowing someone well and being impartial may be mutually exclusive.

Administrative considerations usually dictate that the rating and evaluation function be assigned to the teacher in a school setting and to the supervisor in a work setting. The relationship in each case is one of teaching or direct supervision. There is generally a continuing and fairly close personal relationship. But the relationship is one-directional and partial. The teacher or supervisor sees only one aspect of the student or worker.

Deciding Who Should Choose the Raters.   The applicant may be asked to supply a specific number of references or to submit evaluation forms filled out by a predetermined number of others. The choice of the raters is usually left up to the applicant, and we may anticipate that he or she will select people who will furnish favorable ratings. It might be more satisfactory if the applicant were asked to supply the names and addresses of people with whom there is a particular relationship and who can therefore be requested to supply relevant information. A job applicant might be asked to give the names of immediate supervisors in his or her most recent jobs; a fellowship applicant might be asked to list the names of his or her major advisors and of any instructors from whom two or more courses have been taken. Thus, we would shift the responsibility of determining who will provide the ratings from the applicant to the agency using them. Such a shift should reduce the amount of positive bias for the applicant.

Educational Program for Raters.   Good ratings do not just happen, even with motivated raters and good instruments for recording the ratings. Raters must be "sold" on the importance of making good ratings and taught how to use the rating instrument. As was indicated earlier, unwillingness to put forth the necessary effort on the one hand and identification with the person being rated on the other are powerful motives for providing inadequate ratings. These problems can only be overcome by education and indoctrination to convince the raters that their tasks are important.

Raters should have practice with the specific rating instrument that they will use. A training session, in which the instrument is used under supervision, is desirable. The meanings of the attributes can be discussed, sample rating sheets can be prepared, and the resulting ratings can be reviewed. The prevailing generosity error can be noted, and raters can be cautioned to avoid it. Additional practice can be given, in an attempt to generate a more symmetrical distribution of ratings. Training sessions will not eliminate all the shortcomings of ratings, but they should reduce the more common distortions.

Selecting Qualities to be Rated.   Two principles appear to apply in determining the types of information to be sought through rating procedures.

First, it is undesirable to use rating procedures to get information that can be provided by a more objective and reliable indicator. A score on a well-constructed aptitude test is a better indicator of cognitive ability than is a supervisor's rating of intellect. When accurate production records exist, they should be preferred over a supervisor's rating for productivity. We resort to ratings when we do not have better indicators available.

Second, we should limit ratings to relatively overt qualities—ones that can be expressed in terms of actual observable behavior. Furthermore, we must bear in mind the extent and nature of the contact between the rater and the person being rated. For example, a set of ratings to be used after a single interview should be limited to the qualities that can be observed in an interview. The interviewee's neatness, composure, manner of speech, and fluency in answering questions are qualities that should be observable in a single interview. Industry, integrity, initiative, and ingenuity are not directly observable in such a limited encounter, although these qualities might be appraised with some accuracy by a person who has worked with the interviewee for a time. Ratings should be of behavior observable in the setting in which the rater has known the person being rated.

Focusing Raters on Behaviors Prior to Ratings.   One objection to ratings is that they are usually made after the fact and are based on general, unanalyzed impressions about the person being rated. Dependence on memory to complete a rating scale is sometimes supplemented by specifying the focus of observations prior to the actual ratings. A record form can be developed in which critical areas of performance are identified in space provided for recording instances of desirable as well as undesirable actions of the person being rated. A section from such a form, designed to be used for evaluating student nurses (Fivars & Gosnell, 1966), is shown in Figure 9.2. A final rating for each section would be based on a review of the incidents, both positive and negative, that were observed and recorded by the rater. Recordings of this type require a high level of commitment to, and cooperation with, the rating program. When such a level of involvement is achieved, advance notice and systematic recording can improve the rating process. However, situations of this sort are probably rare.

Pooling Independent Ratings from Several Raters.   One of the limitations of ratings is low reliability. If several people have had a reasonably good chance to observe the person being rated, reliability can be improved by pooling their independent ratings. Unfortunately, the number of persons well placed to observe a person in a particular setting—school, job, camp, and so forth—is usually limited. Often, only one person has been in close contact with the person being rated in a particular relationship. A student has had only one homeroom teacher, a worker only one foreman, and a camper only one tent counselor. Others have had some contact with the person, but the contact may have been so much more limited that pooling their judgments add little to the information of the rater most intimately involved.

Note that we specified the pooling of *independent* ratings. If the ratings are independently made, the "error" components will be independent and will tend to cancel out. If, however, the judgments are combined through some sort of conference procedure, we do not know what will happen. Errors may cancel out, wisdom may win, or the prejudices of the most dogmatic may prevail. Pooling independent ratings is the only sure way to cancel out individual errors.

One study (Adjutant General's Office, Personnel Research Section, 1952) has found this procedure to be more satisfactory than conference type procedures.

Improving Rating Procedures

There have been a number of refinements on the student rating approaches, including the following: (1) adaptive behavior scales, (2) ranking procedures, (3) rating scales based on input from raters, and (4) the forced-choice format.

Adaptive Behavior Scales.   Checklists using information gathered from an informant can also be used to combine some of the characteristics of the rating procedures with the characteristics of ability tests. Examples of such instruments are the Adaptive Behavior Scale (ABS) of the American Association of Mental Deficiency (Nihira, Foster, Shellhaas, & Leland, 1974), the Adaptive Behavior Scale-School Edition (Lambert, Windmiller, Tharinger, & Cole, 1981), the Adaptive Behavior Inventory for Children (ABIC) (Mercer & Lewis, 1978), and the Vineland Adaptive Behavior Scale (Sparrow, Balla, & Cicchetti, 1984).

The four instruments have similar formats—a set of items that are based on developmental tasks typical of children at different ages. An informant (usually a parent or teacher) is then asked to indicate whether the child has accomplished the task. The items can be scored either "yes" or "no" along a range indicating how typical the behavior is. The responses are summed, and the total scores are compared to normative standards to indicate the child's developmental age. The following items might be found on such a scale:

○ Uses toilet
○ Uses knife and fork
○ Throws ball
○ Stacks three blocks
○ Uses irregular verbs
○ Makes friends

Clearly, the number of potential items is enormous. The items can also be subdivided into categories such as motor, self-grooming, social, language, and school-related skills.

Adaptive behavior scales are most appropriately used when there is a need to obtain information about a child's level of functioning either to supplement what can be learned from mental ability tests or to substitute for them. These instruments are most frequently used to assess children with learning problems, and they are particularly appropriate for trainable and young educable mentally retarded children.

Concern about the disproportionate numbers of minority children enrolled in special education classes has increased interest in using such instruments. There is concern that standardized intelligence tests may be unfairly labeling some minority children as mentally retarded. The precept of unfairness stems from the ability of many of these student to function normally in nonschool settings. Adaptive behavior scales can be used to understand better the func-

FIGURE 9.2

Observational record form to serve as a basis for rating. (Adapted from Fivars and Gosnell, 1966.)

Student's Name

_____

Behaviors Needed Improvement

1. *Planning, organizing, and adapting nursing care*
   a. Failed to organize nursing care for maximum patient benefit.
   b. Failed to collect all equipment necessary for patient care.
   c. Took unwise shortcuts in giving nursing care.
   d. Failed to adapt procedure to situation.
   e. Used inadequate or improper substitute equipment.

Date	Item	What happened

2. *Checking*
   a. Failed to check Kardex in administering medication, treatment.
   b. Did not check cards, labels, or names in medication procedure.
   c. Failed to see that laboratory orders were carried out.
   d. Did not question inconsistent medication, treatment, diet order.
   e. Failed to check requisition, equipment, or supplies.
   f. Neglected to check patient's condition.

Date	Item	What happened

3. *Meeting the patient's adjustment and emotional needs*
   a. Refused request, was unkind, tactless, or indifferent.
   b. Did not provide recreational or diversional activity.
   c. Failed to recognize social service, spiritual, other needs.
   d. Did not explain or reassure patient about test, treatment, or policy; or misinformed patient.

Date	Item	What happened

FIGURE 9.2
(Continued)

Behaviors to Be Encouraged
1. *Planning, organizing, and adapting nursing care*
    a. Organized nursing care plan or equipment efficiently.
    b. Anticipated needs of others.
    c. Adapted nursing care plan to overcome difficulties.
    d. Adapted nursing care procedures to patient's needs.
    e. Used adequate substitute equipment when necessary.
    f. Devised or suggested new technique for welfare of patient or for ward efficiency.

Date	Item	What happened

2. *Checking*
    a. Checked Kardex frequently for new orders.
    b. Made special checks in medication procedure.
    c. Checked to see that laboratory orders were carried out.
    d. Noted inconsistency in medication, treatment, diet order.
    e. Checked equipment and supplies for shortage or defects.
    f. Made special checks on signs and condition of patient.

Date	Item	What happened

3. *Meeting the patient's adjustment and emotional needs*
    a. Was reassuring, kind, and considerate to patient.
    b. Made arrangements for recreational or diversional therapy.
    c. Noted social service, home nursing, spiritual, other needs.
    d. Adapted explanation of teaching to patient's understanding.
    e. Effectively taught patient health principles or home care.

Date	Item	What happened

tioning of students in a wide range of settings and to help diagnostic teams make better decisions about placement.

Although the administration of one of these instruments can be a useful part of the overall diagnosis of a child with learning or developmental problems, the four share important limitations. The norming is not considered entirely adequate for any of these instruments. For the ABIC, the inadequacy of norms is a particularly serious problem because the norm sample was selected exclusively from California children, and there are indications that the norms may be inappropriate for other parts of the country (Buckley & Oakland, 1977). A major deficiency of these instruments is their dependence on the ability of the informants to provide accurate information. A related problem concerns the intrusive nature of the items and the appropriateness of asking the questions as well as the willingness of informants to give the information to individuals who are, in many cases, strangers. The use of these tests as substitutes for standardized measures of intelligence has not proved successful because the scores from these tests tend not to be strongly related to performance in school.

Ranking Procedures.   When each rater knows a substantial number of people being rated, raters may be asked to place them in rank order with respect to each attribute being rated. Thus, a teacher might be asked to indicate the child who is most outstanding for contributing to class projects and activities "over and beyond the call of duty," the one who is second, and so on. Usually, the rater is instructed to start at the extremes and work toward the middle because the extreme cases are usually easier to discriminate than the large group of average ones in the middle. This procedure is sometimes formalized as *alternation ranking,* that is, picking the highest and then the lowest, the next highest and then the next lowest, and so on. To ease the task of the rater, tie ranks (where people being rated seem equal) may be permitted. If tie ranks are not permitted, the rater may feel that the task is an unreasonable one, especially for a large group.

Ranking is an arduous task, but it achieves two important objectives. First, it forces the rater to discriminate among those being evaluated. The rater is not permitted to place all or most of the people being rated in a single category, as may happen with other reporting systems. Second, ranking washes out individual differences among raters in generosity or leniency. No matter how generous the rater is, someone must be last, and no matter how ungenerous he or she is, someone must come first. Individual differences in biases and idiosyncrasies are minimized in the final score.

If scores based on rankings by different judges are to be combined, one assumption is introduced in ranking that may be as troublesome as the individual differences in judging biases and idiosyncrasies that have been minimized. If we are to treat rankings by different judges as comparable scores, we must assume that the quality of the group ranked by each rater is the same. That is, we must assume that being second in a group of 20 represents the same level on the trait being appraised, in all the groups of 20. Usually, there is no direct way to compare the subgroups, so we have to assume that they are comparable. If the subgroups are fairly large (e.g., 30 or more people) and chosen more or less at random from the same sort of population, this assumption may be reasonable. But, with groups of less than 30 people or groups selected from different sorts of populations, the failure to meet the assumption of comparability may introduce substantial errors into scores based on ranking. Of course, when two raters rank the same people, this issue should not arise.

Ranks in their raw form do not provide a useful type of score because their meaning depends on the size of the groups, that is, being third in a group of 3 is quite different from being third in a group of 30. Furthermore, steps of rank do not represent equal units of a trait. As we saw in our discussion of percentile norms (Chapter 3), with a normal distribution, one or two places in the rank order at the extremes of a group represent much more of a difference than the same number of places in rank order near the middle of the group. Therefore, a common practice is to convert ranks into normalized standard scores to obtain a type of score that has uniform ranks and meaning regardless of the size of the group, throughout the score range.

Rating Scales Based on Input from Raters.   A method that has become popular for developing instruments to evaluate performance is based on involving raters in developing the rating scales that they will eventually use. Development on such instruments proceeds in three stages.

1. A group of future raters agrees on the dimensions that can be distinguished as aspects of performance on a given job. In an early application of the method (Smith and Kendall, 1963), head nurses agreed on the following dimensions as applicable to medical-surgical nurses:

- Knowledge and judgment
- Conscientiousness
- Skill in human relations
- Organizational ability
- Objectivity
- Observational ability

2. The potential users generate a pool of *critical incidents,* or examples of actually observed behavior, to illustrate superior, average, and inferior performance in each of the selected dimensions. Raters in a second group are then called on to assign each incident to the appropriate dimension. For further analysis, only when the second group of raters agrees on the assignment of critical incidents to a dimension are these incidents retained in the final instrument.

3. Each person in the second group of raters indicates where on a scale of excellence each statement falls. The average level and the consistency of these judgments are scrutinized, and a subset of items is retained that shows good agreement among raters and for which the complete set shows a wide range of average scale values. The following items are taken from a scale titled Interpersonal Relations with Students that is used to evaluate college faculty (Harari & Zedeck, 1973). The scores on the scale range from 1 (low) to 7 (high).

Scale Value	Statement
6.8	When a class doesn't understand a certain concept or feels "lost," this professor could be expected to sense it and act to correct the situation.
3.9	During lectures, this professor could often be expected to tell students with questions to see him during his office hours.
1.3	This professor could be expected to embarrass or humiliate students who disagree with him.

To apply this methodology, the set of statements for each dimension is provided, and the rater indicates which statement comes closest to describing the person being rated. Users have reported (Campbell, Dunnette, Arvey, & Hellervik, 1973) that this procedure yielded less method variance, less halo error, and less leniency error than more conventional rating procedures.

The procedures for scale development are quite time consuming, and the resulting instrument tends to be a little cumbersome. More experience with rating scales based on input from raters is needed before we can judge whether gains from using the scales are maintained in further use and whether the gains are sufficient to justify the additional effort required in developing the scales.

The Forced-Choice Format.   All the variations considered so far operate on the same basic pattern, the rater considers one attribute at a time and assigns the person being rated to one of a set of categories or places him or her in a position relative to others on the particular attribute. Now, we will consider a major departure from that pattern. The essence of this procedure is that the rater must choose from a *set* of attributes and decide which one (or ones) most accurately represents the person being rated. For example, an instrument developed for evaluating technical school instructors for the air force (Highland & Berkshire, 1951) included sets of items such as the following:

1. Is patient with slow learners

2. Lectures with confidence

3. Keeps interest and attention of class

4. Acquaints classes with objective for each lesson

The rater's assignment is to select the two items from the set that are *most descriptive* of the person being rated.

All of the statements in this set are positive because they were carefully matched, on the basis of information from a preliminary investigation, to be about equally positive in their description of an instructor. They do differ, however, in the extent to which they distinguish between people who have been identified on other evidence as good or poor instructors. The most discriminating statement is Statement 1 and the least discriminating one is Statement 2. That is, good instructors were identified as being patient with slow learners and poor instructors were not. Both good and poor instructors were equally likely to be identified as lecturing with confidence. Thus, we could assign a score value of two to Statement 1, one to Statements 3 and 4, and zero to Statement 2. An instructor's score for the set would be the sum of the scores for the two items marked as most descriptive of him or her. The score for the whole instrument would be the sum of the scores for 25 or 30 such blocks of four statements. Such a score was found to have good split-half reliability (0.85 to 0.90), so this type of instrument can provide a reliable score on the individual's desirability as an instructor, at least in the eyes of one rater. Of course, this score does not tell us anything about the agreement or lack of agreement that might be found between different raters.

By casting the evaluation instrument into a forced-choice format, the test maker hopes to accomplish three things.

1. To eliminate variation in rater standards of generosity or kindness. Because the items in a set include equally favorable statements about a person, those who prefer to be positive in their evaluations of others will not be inclined to choose any particular statement. Thus, a more accurate picture of the person being rated should emerge.

2. To minimize the possibility of a rater intentionally biasing the score. With most rating scales, the raters control the process. They can rate a person high or low as they please. In a forced-choice instrument, the rater should be unable easily to identify positive and negative statements and should therefore be unable to raise or lower a score at will. The success of this approach will depend on the skill of the scale constructor to equate the attractiveness of the grouped items. Although there are some indications that a forced-choice format is less susceptible to intentional biasing than other rating scales are, it is still far from tamper proof in the hands of a determined rater.

3. To produce a better spread of scores and a more nearly normal distribution of ratings. Making all options equally attractive minimizes the effect of the generosity error, which results in a better spread of scores.

Disadvantages of the Forced-Choice Format.   The most important disadvantage of this format is that raters dislike using this approach, largely because it takes control away form them. They cannot easily rate an individual high or low depending on their overall feelings, which leads to frustration often manifested in an unwillingness to work diligently at the task of rating.

Forced-choice formats generated a good deal of interest, some research, and a certain amount of practical use during the period from 1945 to 1965, but the burden of preparing them and negative reactions to them by raters have resulted in a gradual decline in interest in recent years.

Measuring Attitudes

In the previous sections, we discussed methods of learning about people, their abilities, as well as their personality traits and attitudes, by obtaining information from others who know them well, in terms of the type of information sought. It is also possible to obtain this kind of information directly from the individuals being rated.

In attitude measurement, we are interested in obtaining a reliable score that can represent the intensity of an individual's sentiments toward or against something. Like other self-report measures, attitude assessments are limited by what the individuals know and are willing to communicate about themselves. Most people have similar perceptions about the social desirability of the items measuring personality traits, so there is a tendency for everyone to respond to items on such instruments in a similar fashion—generally, in a way that makes them look good; this tendency is a limitation inherent in such instruments. Because the social desirability of attitude measures differ, they are affected less by this tendency.

When we seek the overall attitude level of a group and do not need to know about the attitudes of individuals, it is possible to keep responses anonymous. This practice increases the probability that responses will represent a more genuine reflection of attitudes.

The biggest problem with attitude assessment instruments is the apparent ease with which they can be constructed. Just because items can be collected quickly and an instrument put together easily does not mean that the instrument will measure the constructs it is intended to measure in a reliable fashion. Unless attitude scales are created in a systematic fashion, using what is known about good scale construction, the results probably will be meaningless.

The construction of an attitude rating scale usually begins with a catalog of statements covering possible views on the target concept drawn from readings, associates, and the recesses of the author's consciousness. The goal of this process is to select a broad range of statements that is representative of all of the possible items that could be used to measure an attitude. These items should range from the most positive and favorable to the most negative and unfavorable and should cover all aspects of the attitude. Each statement should be clear and brief, present a single idea, and focused on a feeling rather than on a fact, that is, an attitude rather than information. Edwards (1957) provides a useful list of suggestions for selecting statements to include in an attitude rating scale:

1. Avoid statements that refer to the past rather than to the present.
2. Avoid statements that are factual or capable of being interpreted as factual.
3. Avoid statements that may be interpreted in more than one way.
4. Avoid statements that are irrelevant to the psychological object under consultation.
5. Avoid statements that are likely to be endorsed by almost everyone or by almost no one.
6. Select statements that are believed to cover the entire range of the affective scale of interest.
7. Keep the language of the statements simple, clear, and direct.
8. Statements should be short, rarely exceeding twenty words.
9. Each statement should contain only one complete thought.

10. Statement-containing universals such as *all, always, none* and *never* often introduce ambiguity and should be avoided.

11. Words such as *only, just, merely* and others of a similar nature, should be used with care and moderation in writing statements.

12. Whenever possible, statements should be written in simple sentences rather than compound or complex sentences.

13. Avoid the use of words that may not be understood by those who are to be given the completed scale.

14. Avoid the use of double negatives. (p. 14)

Summative Ratings

Attitude scales usually require the subject to respond to the statements with a numerical indication of the strength of his or her feeling toward the statement. The responses are summed to estimate the strength of the attitude. The most often used technique for obtaining a numerical indication of the strength of an attitude is to have respondents indicate their level of feeling toward statements, often in terms of the degree to which they agree or disagree with them. This technique is called a "summative rating," or "Likert scale," after Reneis Likert, who first introduced the use of the technique. The following key is an example of the options that might be provided to an individual responding to the scale.

- 5 — Strongly agree
- 4 — Mildly agree
- 3 — Somewhat agree
- 2 — Mildly disagree
- 1 — Strongly disagree

If you wanted to measure attitudes toward grouping students, you might include statements such as the following:

1. I favor grouping students.

2. Students achieve more when they attend class with other students of similar ability.

3. Gifted students should be taught in classes made up of other gifted students.

4. Special education students should be assigned to regular classes.

The respondents place a number adjacent to each statement, indicating their degree of agreement with the statement. Items may be stated both positively and negatively to correct for the tendency of respondents to agree with most statements presented to them, a tendency called "acquiescence." For example, on a scale intended to measure attitudes toward grouping students in classes according to their ability, the following item might be included: "Grouping students by ability results in higher achievement." Reversed it would read, "Grouping students by ability results in lower achievement." (Please note that it is extremely difficult to reverse statements without substantially changing the meaning.) During the process of summing across items to attain the assessment of the attitude, the scoring of negatively stated items is reversed by subtracting the value that a subject assigned to an item from one point more than the highest value that can be assigned. For example, on a six-point scale, a score of five would be subtracted from seven, making it a two.

Number of Steps

The number of steps in the scale is important. The more steps, the greater the reliability of the scale. This increase is noticeable up to 7 steps, but the increase in reliability declines as 20 steps are reached. Items with more than 7 steps are seldom used because the increase in reliability resulting from the additional steps is slight. It is easier to increase reliability by adding more items.

Types of Anchors

Even though the agree-disagree anchors are particularly flexible, other anchors could be used when they fit the meaning of the statements. For instance, anchors such as "effective–ineffective," "important–unimportant," or "like me–not like me" have been used successfully.

An Odd or an Even Number of Steps

The scale constructor must also decide whether to use an odd or an even number of steps. Most people seem to prefer an odd number, so that they have an appropriate response when they feel neutral toward a statement. With an even number of steps, they might feel as if they are being forced to make a distinction where none exists. On the other hand, repeated selection of the neutral position can be an easy way out for the person unwilling to devote an appropriate amount of time to the task of responding to all items. In support of an even number of steps, there is some evidence that, when forced to make a commitment other than the neutral one, most people can make reliable decisions (Nunnally, 1967).

One drawback to using an even number of steps and denying the individual responding the opportunity to make a neutral response is a possible increase in the number of statements not responded to because some respondents may refuse to give any response if they cannot pick the midpoint.

Single-Item Scales

Although single-item scales are common, they provide a poor measure of attitudes. They prevent the assessment of internal consistency, and if the one item is misunderstood, the results of the assessment become invalid. There is also the danger that the single item may be written in a way that biases the results. Consider the following two statements:

1. Parents should be forced to bus their children long distances for the purpose of achieving school desegregation.

2. The courts should use any reasonable means for achieving school desegregation.

Even though in the mind of the author, both statements are related to the use of busing as a means of achieving school desegregation, used as single items, each could be expected to yield quite different results. This instability is often a problem in opinion polls used by candidates for public office and the reason that two candidates can both claim the support of most of the public. This type of bias could occur to some degree with any attitude scale, but with a large number of items, the likelihood exists that the positive and negative items will cancel each other out.

Another problem with single-item attitude rating scales is that they can be constructed in such a way that there is no variability among the respondents. For instance, if you ask respondents to agree or disagree with the statement "The subject of abortion is controversial," there will be little variability.

Example of an Attitude Rating Scale

The attitude rating scale shown in Figure 9.3 is intended to assess attitudes toward the equality and liberation of women. The first task in developing the scale was to gather a large number of items representing a range of topics and views on the subject. For women's liberation, the topics cover equal employment opportunities, child care, sexual freedom, personal independence, degree of role differentiation, and so forth. Each statement should be clear and brief, present a single idea, and focused on a feeling rather than on a fact, that is, an attitude rather than information.

The total pool of items is usually much too large to use as a measuring instrument, so it is necessary to select a subset of items. This subset is selected by having the items reviewed and rated by judges. The judges' function is not to indicate agreement or disagreement with the item but rather to assess where the statement falls on a "for and against" scale in relation to the target concept. The scale points might range from 9, indicating very strongly favorable toward women's liberation and status, to 1, indicating very strongly hostile toward women's liberation and status. The purpose of the rating is to find (1) where on the "for and against" scale a given statement falls and (2) how well a group of judges agree on the statement's meaning. We wish eventually to select a set of statements that represent all degrees of favorableness and unfavorableness and statements that convey nearly the same meaning to everyone. The position of any item on the scale of "favorableness-unfavorableness" is indicated by the median rating that it receives from the the judges and its ambiguity by the spread of ratings as indicated by the standard deviation. Consider the following two statements:

	Median	Standard Deviation
A wife's job and career are just as important as her husband's.	8.1	1.0
Feminine fashions are a device to hold women in an inferior role.	7.0	3.1

FIGURE 9.3

Sample of an attitude scale.

ATTITUDE TOWARD WOMEN'S LIBERATION

Read each statement. Then circle the symbol that best represents your reaction to the statement, according to the following scale:

> AA — strongly agree with the statement.
> a — tend to agree with the statement.
> ? — undecided. Neither agree nor disagree.
> d — tend to disagree with the statement.
> DD — strongly disagree with the statement.

AA a ? d DD   1. Men and women should receive the same pay for the same work.

AA a ? d DD   2. No woman should have to bear a child unless she chooses to.

AA a ? d DD   3. Most women are unsuited by temperament for supervisory or administrative jobs.

AA a ? d DD   4. There should be no clubs or public places that are restricted to a single sex.

AA a ? d DD   5. A woman's place is in the home.

AA a ? d DD   6. Standards for promotion should be the same for men and women.

AA a ? d DD   7. A woman's job and career are just as important as her husband's.

AA a ? d DD   8. Men and women are basically different in their makeup and are suited to fill different roles.

AA a ? d DD   9. A woman who follows a career can seldom expect to have a satisfactory home life.

AA a ? d DD   10. There are no inborn psychological differences between men and women.

AA a ? d DD   11. Men should share equally in housework—getting meals, cleaning, etc.

AA a ? d DD   12. Every woman should have an independent career if she wants one.

AA a ? d DD   13. In matters of sex, there should be a single standard for men and for women.

AA a ? d DD   14. The workers for women's liberation are frustrated female failures.

AA a ? d DD   15. Except for physical strength, anything a man can do, women can do equally well.

AA a ? d DD   16. Women's liberation is of interest only to a few women on the lunatic fringe.

AA a ? d DD   17. It doesn't make sense to make a large investment in a woman's education, because she is likely to marry and not use her advanced training.

AA a ? d DD   18. By nature, women are submissive and men are dominant.

AA a ? d DD   19. The natural role for a woman is a secondary, supporting one.

AA a ? d DD   20. In all respects, men and women should receive the same treatment.

The first statement seems to be promising for inclusion in the final attitude scale. It is a strongly "pro" statement, and judges agree about where it falls on the attitude dimension. The second statement is a poor choice for the scale. Although on the average it is rated as implying a moderately favorable position toward women's liberation, there is disagreement among raters on what the statement signifies.

Given the judges' ratings, we can select a reasonably brief set of statements that have clear meanings, that represent all degrees of intensity of views "for and against," and that cover the main facets of the domain being studied. The statements can usually best be presented to subjects in the format shown in Figure 9.3, on which the respondent indicates the degree of acceptance of each statement. Responses can be scored 4, 3, 2, 1, 0, with AA getting a score of 4 and DD, a 0. The scores could all be entered into the computer in this way, and the negative items could be reversed by computer. The total score could range from 0 to 80, with a neutral score near 40, depending on the sample to which it was administered.

A sample of the results obtained from administering the scale to 133 students in a measurement classes is shown in Table 9.3. The scale shows quite satisfactory reliability. In general, these students tended to endorse statements favorable to womens's rights, and the more strongly favorable positions (above the median) appeared most often among women, students under 30, unmarried respondents, and non-Catholics.

Item Analysis

Once a set of statements is collected and assembled into an instrument, using the preceding suggestions, they should be administered to a pilot group. Ideally, responses should be made on a machine-scorable answer sheet, which facilitates

TABLE 9.3
Selected Results for an Attitude Scale on Women's Liberation

SCORES FOR SELECTED PERCENTILES		PERCENTAGES BY DEMOGRAPHIC VARIABLES	
Score	**Percentile**	**Group**	**Percentage Above the Median**
75	90th	Women	61
		Men	29
68	75th	30 and over	41
		Under 30	57
61	50th	Single	55
		Other	46
51	25th	Catholic	39
		Other	57
40	10th		

entering the responses into computer memory where it is accessible to the statistical analysis program being used. The responses should be summed making sure that any negative items are reversed. This reversal of items is done by subtracting the numerical response from a value equal to the number of steps on the scale plus one. If you have a six-point scale, subtract each reversed score from 7. In this way, a one becomes a six ($7 - 1 = 6$) and a six becomes a one ($7 - 6 = 1$). The value of each item is then correlated with the total score, and the coefficient obtained indicates how much each item contributes to the overall reliability of the test. The higher the correlation, the better the item. The size of of the correlation necessary for a good item depends on the subject matter and test length. A negative correlation may indicate that the item needs to be reversed. By deleting, replacing, or revising bad items, the reliability of the test can be greatly improved. The item analysis of an attitude rating scale is all but impossible without the aid of a computer.

Reliability

It is important to determine the internal consistency reliability of the attitude rating scales. This determination should be made using coefficient alpha, a computation which requires the use of a computer. As is true with other measures of reliability, the size of coefficient alpha is a function of variability in the dimension being measured within the sample. Therefore, it is important for the scale to be administered to a sample that differs along the dimension being measured. For instance, if you are measuring attitude toward the value of higher education among a group of highly educated people, you will find little variability and consequently low internal consistency reliability. Internal consistency is an indication that we can make discriminations in the sample as well as evidence that we are measuring a one-dimensional trait. If several traits are measured on a single scale and only one score is reported, the traits will cancel each other out and the scale will have low variability and low reliability.

Summary

To gain insight into the personality and attitudes of others, you can obtain information directly from individuals, observe their behavior, or obtain information from someone who is in a position to provide it. Personality and attitude assessments are usually accomplished either informally through letters of recommendation or formally in a structured manner using rating scales. Both methods have similar limitations centered on the raters' willingness and/or inability to provide accurate assessments. In spite of the limitations of ratings, evaluations of an individual through ratings will undoubtedly continue to be widely used for administrative evaluations in schools, civil service, and industry, as well as in educational and psychological research. Every attempt should be made to minimize the limitations.

The limitations of rating procedures result from the following characteristics of the assessment technique:

1. Raters' unwillingness to make unfavorable judgments about others (generosity error), is particularly pronounced when the raters identify with the person being rated.

2. Wide individual differences among raters in "humaneness" (differences in rater standards) or in leniency or severity of rating.

3. Rater's tendency to respond to other persons as a whole in terms of general liking or aversion and difficulty in differentiating among specific aspects of the individual personality (halo error).

4. Limited contact between the rater and person being rated—limited both in amount and in type of situation in which the person being rated is seen.

5. Ambiguity in meaning of the attributes to be appraised.

6. The covert and unobservable nature of many of the inner aspects of personality dynamics.

7. Instability and unreliability of human judgment.

In view of these limitations, the ratings will provide a more accurate picture of the person being rated when the following criteria are met:

1. Appraisal is limited to those qualities that appear overtly in interpersonal relations.

2. The qualities to be appraised are analyzed into concrete and relatively specific aspects of behavior, and judgments are made of these aspects of behavior.

3. The rating form forces the rater to discriminate and/or has controls for rating differences in judging standards.

4. Raters are selected who have had the greatest opportunity to observe the person being rated in situations in which the qualities to be rated are displayed.

5. Raters are "sold" on the value of the ratings and trained in using the rating instrument.

6. Independent ratings of several raters are pooled when there are several people qualified to conduct ratings.

Evaluation procedures in which the significance of the ratings is concealed to some extent from the rater present an interesting possibility for civil service and industrial use, particularly when controls on rater bias are introduced through forced-choice techniques.

Attitude scales have been developed to score the intensity of favorable or unfavorable reactions to a group, institution, or issue. Although these reactions represent only verbal expressions of attitude and may be inconsistent with actual behavior, such expressions may presage behavioral changes.

Questions and Exercises

1. If you were writing to someone who had been given as a reference by an applicant for a job in your company or for admission to your school, what should you include in your letter to obtain the most useful evaluation of the applicant?

2. Make a complete list of the different ratings used in the school that you are attending or the school in which you teach. What type of a rating scale or form is used in each case?

3. How effective are the ratings that you identified in the previous question? How adequate is the spread of ratings obtained? How consistently is the scale used by different users? What is your impression of the reliability of the ratings? What is your impression of their freedom from the halo effect and other errors?

4. What factors influence a rater's willingness to rate conscientiously? How serious is this issue? What can be done about it?

5. Why would three independent ratings from separate raters ordinarily be preferable to a rating prepared by the three raters working together as a committee.

6. In the personnel office of a large company, employment interviewers are required to rate job applicants at the end of the interview. Which of the following characteristics would you expect to be rated most reliably? Why?
   (a) Initiative
   (b) Appearance
   (c) Work background
   (d) Dependability
   (e) Emotional balance

7. In a small survey of the report cards used in a number of communities, the following four traits were most frequently mentioned on the cards: (a) courteous, (b) cooperative, (c) good health habits, (d) works with others. How might these traits be broken down or revised so that the classroom teacher could evaluate them better?

8. What advantages do ratings by peers have over ratings by superiors? What disadvantages?

9. What are the advantages of ranking in comparison with rating scales? What are the disadvantages?

10. Suppose a forced-choice rating scale is developed to use in evaluating teacher effectiveness in a city school system. What advantages will this rating procedure have over other types of ratings? What problems will be likely to arise in using it?

11. Suppose you are placed in charge of a merit rating plan being introduced in your company. What steps will you take to try to get the best possible ratings?

12. What factors limit the usefulness of paper-and-pencil attitude scales? What other methods might a teacher use to evaluate attitudes?

13. Prepare a rough draft for a brief attitude scale to measure teacher's attitudes toward objective tests.

Suggested Readings

Egan, O., & Archer, P. (1985). The accuracy of teachers' ratings of ability: A regression model. *American Educational Research Journal, 22*(1), 25–34.

Kubiszyn, T., & Borich, G. (1987). *Educational testing and measurement.* Glenview, IL: Scott, Foresman and Company.

Morrison, R. L. (1988). Structured interviews and rating scales. In A. S. Bellack & M. Hershon (Eds.), *Behavioral assessment: A practical handbook* (pp. 252–278). New York: Pergamon.

Saal, F. E., Downey, R. G., & Lahey, M. A. (1980). Rating the ratings: Assessing the psychometric quality of rating data. *Psychological Bulletin, 88*(2), 413–428.

Sax, G. (1989). *Principles of educational and psychological measurement and evaluation.* Belmont, CA: Wadsworth.

CHAPTER 10

Sources of Information About Tests

Introduction

There were 2,672 published tests in print in 1983. In addition, there are many more than this number that are out of print, were produced locally, or were developed for one or another specific research project. Many of these are available from one source or another. A single text cannot even begin to list, much less describe, the instruments that have been developed that might interest you. A few of the best known and most widely used tests will be reviewed in later chapters as illustrations of different types of tests. For the rest, we try in this chapter to provide you with some tools to find the tests you need and information about them. We have organized the sections of this chapter around the questions that you are likely to ask, in the order that you will ordinarily ask them, and we try to give useful answers to these questions.

What Tests Exist?

What tests of reading comprehension are suitable for fourth graders? What tests of vocational interests exist for high school seniors? What measures of attitude toward nuclear power are available? First, we need to know what already exists. When we have a catalog of possibilities, we can begin to pick and choose. Or, if nothing satisfactory is available, we can undertake to construct something from scratch. Where should we go to assemble a catalog of possibilities?

The first source to turn to is *Tests in Print III* (Mitchell, 1983). This book, which is due to be revised shortly, provides an alphabetical listing of 2,672 instruments that were available from publishers at that time and information on when each was published and by whom. A subject matter index is provided to help the reader locate the tests in a given category. *Tests in Print* is a companion volume to the *Mental Measurements Yearbook* series (hereafter referred to as *MMY*), which is described in a later section. *Tests in Print* includes references to entries in the *MMY*s dealing with the test in question. It also brings up to date the bibliography of references relating to that test.

A companion source to *Tests in Print* is *Tests: A Comprehensive Reference for Assessments in Psychology, Education and Business* (hereafter referred to as *Tests*) (Sweetland & Keyser, 1986). The entries in *Tests* are alphabetically arranged within topic areas, and the volume has the advantage over *Tests in Print* that it provides a brief description of each entry as well as information about the publisher and price. The descriptions are not evaluative; they closely follow the author's or publisher's statement of what the test measures. The information is somewhat sketchy, in that it does not identify the author, give the date of publication of an instrument, or give any statistical information about it. There are about 2,500 entries for current tests and an index of out-of-print tests and their publishers.

Tests in Print and *Tests* are useful for finding tests, but they fall short in two respects. They do not give information on *the most recent tests,* and they do not give information about *unpublished* instruments. (By unpublished instruments, we mean tests that are not offered for sale. An attitude scale that is given in full in a book or article is, for our purposes, unpublished unless its author offers it for sale.)

To find the most recent published tests, you need to obtain a copy of test publishers' current catalogs. They describe the tests that the publisher is currently promoting, and even some expected to be published in the near future. A large number of publishers produce an occasional test, but relatively few are regular and substantial producers of testing instruments. A complete listing of test publishers can be found in *Tests in Print,* and we provide the names and addresses of a number of the major publishers in Appendix 3. (Also, in Appendix 4, we provide an annotated list of tests.) A file of current test catalogs may sometimes be available through the measurement facility of your university or through the testing center in your local school system.

In addition to test catalogs, there is a newsletter *News on Tests,* which is published quarterly by the Educational Testing Service (ETS). In this newsletter, you may find announcements by test publishers of forthcoming tests and revisions, citations of test reviews, and other up-to-date information about tests and testing practices.

Locating unpublished instruments that have been locally developed or that have been used only in research studies can be a bit tricky. However, several source books and directories have been prepared since 1975 that provide useful assistance in such an undertaking. Probably, the most useful of these sources is the test collection, *Tests in Microfiche,* developed by ETS. Beginning with 1975, ETS started distributing not only an index of unpublished tests but also copies of the tests on microfiche. ETS also accumulates references to publications using these tests. At this time, the Test Collection Bibliographies service at ETS can provide a bibliographic search for 203 topics on a test collection comprising over 16,000 titles.

Several summaries of the ETS test collection have been published. One of these is the *ETS Test Collection Cumulative Index to Tests in Microfiche, 1975–1987* (hereafter referred to as *Cumulative Index*) (Hepner, 1988), which lists the tests in the collection by title, author's name, and Educational Research Information Center (ERIC) identification number as well as provides a brief abstract of the test. There is also an annual *Tests in Microfiche Annotated Index* (hereafter referred to as *Annotated Index*) (Educational Testing Service, Test Collection, 1975–1989) which updates the information in the *Cumulative Index* each December.

The ETS collection *Tests in Microfiche* is a service to which many university libraries subscribe. However, the subscription contains the following restriction (printed in the *Annotated Index,* p. iii):

> The materials included in the microfiche may be reproduced by the purchaser for his or her own use. Permission to use these materials in any other manner must be obtained directly from the author. This includes modifying or adapting the materials or selling or distributing them to others.

A number of other sources also provide references to unpublished tests. The *Directory of Unpublished Experimental Mental Measures* (Goldman & Busch,

1978, 1982, Goldman & Mitchell, 1985; Goldman & Osborne, 1990; Goldman & Sanders, 1974) includes over a thousand entries describing such instruments, while *Tests and Measurements in Child Development: Handbook II* (Johnson, 1976) and *Tests and Measurements in Child Development: A Handbook* (Johnson & Bommarito, 1971) are other sources for unpublished instruments for use with young children. Several volumes cover the field of attitude measurement and reproduce the actual scales used (Robinson, Athanasion, & Head, 1969; Robinson, Rusk, & Head, 1968; Robinson & Shaver, 1973; Shaw & Wright, 1967). More recently, O'Brien (1988) has published a bibliography of selected references on testing that includes 2,759 sources, categorized by the topic or subject covered in the article. In addition to the sources already mentioned, the Sources of Test Information list at the end of this chapter presents several references that cover more limited areas.

An additional resource that may be useful in certain circumstances is the *Directory of Selected National Testing Programs* (Educational Testing Service Test Collection, 1987). This three-volume series gives the names, publishers or producers, addresses, and general descriptions of a wide range of national testing programs. Volume 1 covers selection and admission programs for secondary and postsecondary institutions, government service, graduate and professional schools, and health-related programs. Volume 2 lists academic credit and advanced placement testing programs, and Volume 3 gives the testing programs for certification and licensing. The tests covered in this series generally are not available for public review, but one of them might serve your purpose.

Finally, there are computerized data bases that will be described more fully later in the chapter. They represent extended data files that can be searched to locate additional tests as well as to locate research using a known test or research on a problem of interest.

Exactly What Is Test X Like?

Once you have identified a promising reading test, interest inventory, or attitude measure (called, say, Test X), you will want to find out more about it. Where should you turn?

A certain amount of descriptive information about the test will appear in some of the sources listing tests and in evaluations that appear in the *MMY*s. However, there is really no substitute for examining the test firsthand. So, the first thing to do is to obtain a copy of the test and look at it. A specimen set may be available through your university—in the library, in the counseling center, or in the measurement area files for published tests. Or, the testing office of your school system may be able to provide one. If not, you may have to order a specimen set from the publisher—the catalog will indicate the price.

A publisher is likely to require some credentials to show that you are an appropriate person to have access to the testing materials. A letter from your instructor or from a supervisor in the school system where you work may suffice. However, some types of instruments that call for special training or skills will have further restrictions on their distribution, and you may have to complete a form to verify that you have the required qualifications. In a few cases, it may be necessary to have a person with the required professional credentials order the test for you and supervise your examination of it.

Many of the unpublished instruments are reproduced in full in the compendia listed in Sources of Test Information at the end of this chapter, particularly in the *Tests in Microfiche* collection of ETS. Others are produced in full in articles reporting their development and use. If an unpublished test you wish to examine is not available from one of these sources, you may have to try to get a copy from its author.

Now you have a copy of the test or inventory. What information should you try to get from it? The answer depends on the type of test. If it is a test of school achievement, you should examine the items and ask yourself if the content covered and the processes called for match the objectives you have set for your teaching. For all kinds of tests, you should ask whether the items are clearly stated and the answer choices plausible. For all types of tests, you should ask whether the directions are clear and the page layouts attractive and legible. Of course, for unpublished tests, the quality of the test materials may ultimately be up to you because you are likely to have to produce your own copies of the test.

Of equal importance to the test itself are the supporting materials that describe the test's statistical properties, the form in which test results will be reported, and the aids that will be provided for test use and interpretation. For tests available from commercial publishers, this information should appear in one or more test manuals—possibly a manual for test administrators, a manual for counselors or supervisors, and a technical manual that gives, in considerable detail, the statistical properties of the test. These manuals should be examined thoroughly.

For unpublished tests, the primary sources of technical material about the tests will be in articles or books reporting studies in which the tests were used. The quality of this information is likely to be much lower than that which you will find in a good test manual. For relatively new tests or tests that have not been widely used, it is often necessary to contact the author. It is not uncommon to encounter a measuring instrument, developed to be used in a research study, for which there is no information about reliability or validity except the findings from that one study.

Most commercially published tests provide accompanying scoring and reporting services. The services range from simply scoring the test answer sheets and reporting raw scores and percentiles or standard scores to providing extended narrative interpretations of each individual's test results. Examples of some of these reports were given in Chapter 3. The specimen set should describe, and perhaps illustrate, the types of reports that are available, and you should determine how adequately these will serve your needs.

The evidence on reliability and validity should be scrutinized with a particularly critical eye. Remember that the specimen set is primarily a promotional piece. You can expect the publisher to accentuate the positive, so try to cut through the puffery and get down to the basic evidence; be suspicious if evidence is incompletely or vaguely reported. Chapters 4 and 5 indicate what evidence you can reasonably expect to find.

What Do Critics Think of Test X?

Because materials from the test publisher focus on selling the test—some blatantly, some subtly—it is highly desirable to get an evaluation by a competent and unbiased reviewer. The one source to which one automatically turns for such critical reviews is the series of *Mental Measurements Yearbooks.* This series was initiated by the late Oscar Buros in 1936 and published by him until 1978. Preparation of *The Ninth Mental Measurements Yearbook* (Mitchell, 1985), *The Tenth Mental Measurements Yearbook* (Conoley & Kramer, 1989), and future *MMYs* is in the hands of the Buros Institute of Mental Measurements of the University of Nebraska. The *MMYs* provide reviews, by presumably competent and disinterested people, of each published test of any significance. In recent *Yearbooks,* the publishers have obtained at least two independent reviews of each new test.

The volumes of this series are cumulative. That is, a test is reviewed when it first comes out; it is generally not reviewed again unless there has been a significant change in the test or the material supporting it or unless it is a test of unusually widespread and continuing use. An index giving the volume and page numbers for reviews in the first eight volumes for tests still in print is provided in *Tests in Print III.*

In 1988, the Buros Institute of Mental Measurements began a new schedule for producing the *MMYs*. That year saw the publication of a *Supplement to The Ninth Mental Measurements Yearbook* (Conoley, Kramer, & Mitchell, 1988), which gave full *MMY* treatment to 89 new tests that had been published since 1985. *The Tenth Mental Measurements Yearbook* was published in 1989, and the staff of the Buros Institute has announced plans to publish a complete volume in alternate years thereafter, with supplements in the intervening years.

Each of the 10 *MMYs* includes tests of all types, but in the mid-1970s, a number of volumes were produced, each bringing together all the reviews of tests in a specific area, such as reading tests or personality inventories. One of these volumes may be an efficient source for the evaluations in which you are interested. The *MMYs* and *Tests in Print* should be available at the reference desk of any good university library, at many larger public libraries, and at the testing bureau in many school systems. The *MMYs* provide the most important source for evaluative reviews of tests. They also include reviews of books and monographs on testing, a listing of test publishers, and nearly complete bibliographies of published material on each of the tests. Reviews that have been received for upcoming editions of the *MMY* are available in a computer data base described in a later section.

Another source of critical reviews of tests is the seven-volume series *Test Critiques* (Keyser & Sweetland, 1984). Each volume in the series contains a single review of each of several hundred tests. The reviews are often somewhat longer and more detailed than those in the *MMYs*, but lack the contrasting opinions that multiple reviews provide. Unfortunately, the organization of the volumes is less than obvious. Each of the last five volumes contains a subject index to all preceding ones, but within a single volume, the tests are arranged alphabetically by title without regard to topic. This system may make it more difficult to find a specific test.

Reviews of some American tests and a large number of tests published in Great Britain may be found in *Tests in Education: A Book of Critical Reviews* (Levy & Goldstein, 1984). The tests are organized into six general categories: early development, language, mathematics, achievement batteries, general abilities, and personality and counseling. The reviews are brief.

Reviews of new and important tests will occasionally be found, along with book reviews, in some psychological and educational journals. However, they appear sporadically, and there does not seem to be any journal that has a policy of systematically and regularly reviewing new published tests. At this time, the best source of evaluative information seems to be the *MMYs* and their supplements, particularly now that they are updated in print annually and on the computer data base monthly.

What Research Has Been Conducted on Test X?

What studies have been made of the test's reliability? Its validity as a predictor of Z? The influence of coaching on its score? Its relation to measures of Y?

Of course, some material will appear in the technical manual for the test. Manuals vary widely in the amount of statistical information that they report. Some of the better ones become almost a full-length book and report a wide range of analyses of the test's reliability, correlations with other instruments, and predictive validity for academic or job criteria. The manual will also often include a bibliography, providing references to specific research studies. But, for widely used tests, the manual can hardly provide complete information; for example, in the course of its 75-year career, over 6,000 studies have been carried out with the Stanford-Binet Intelligence Scale, and in only 50 years, almost as many have been carried out with the Minnesota Multiphasic Personality Inventory. It is also difficult for a manual to be up-to date with recent studies. In fact, it is rare for a test publisher to bring out a revision of a test manual that does not correspond to a revision of the test itself, so even the manuals for the best commercially produced tests may be 5–8 years old.

As already noted, for published tests, very comprehensive bibliographies appear in the *MMYs* and *Tests in Print*. As is the case with the reviews of the tests themselves, these reference sources include only references to articles and books published since their last editions. Even so, for a number of the popular and widely used tests, the bibliography is *so* extensive, running to thousands of entries, that it becomes almost unusable. However, these bibliographies permit you to scan through titles with the hope of identifying ones that deal with the specific problem of interest.

The bibliographic service associated with the Test Collection of ETS is another potential source of research about tests. The bibliographic search is by topic rather than by a specific test name, so it may produce unusable entries as well as ones that pertain to your test. ETS welcomes inquiries concerning their collection and bibliographic services at the address given in Sources of Test Information.

The other main avenue for locating research on tests and testing is through the index and abstract services that appear as monthly journals and are then combined into annual volumes. The ones most likely to be useful for a person interested in testing are *Dissertation Abstracts International,* the *Education Index,* and the *Psychological Abstracts*. A useful recent resource is the *Index to Tests Used in Educational Dissertations* (Fabiano, 1989). Although *Dissertation Abstracts International* has had an online computer search service since 1980, finding earlier references to tests has been difficult. This reference categorizes over 50,000 tests alphabetically by title. The entries for each test include the type of examinees, the volume and page number of the abstract, and the author's name. Dissertations in psychology are not covered.

A relatively new development in sources of information about testing is the appearance of computerized data bases. There are several data bases that can help you find information about a type of test or a testing problem. One is the computerized update of the *MMY*. Now, it is possible to obtain from the computerized data base of the *MMY*s any reviews or other information that have been assembled in preparing the next edition or supplement.

Finally, there is the computerized access to the *Psychological Abstracts*. Each year this series includes, usually with an abstract, a fairly complete listing of publications in the field of psychology. The entries for the last several years are stored in the computer's memory and may be accessed through appropriate key words.

In using any data base, the secret of a successful search is a shrewd selection of key words that serve to guide the computer in identifying relevant entries. In most instances, preparers of a data base provide a glossary of terms that the computer will recognize. It is the responsibility of the user to generate or to select from the glossary the entries that are most likely to elicit the relevant items from the data base. Although test titles are unlikely to appear as key words, the general traits measured by the instrument may well give access to publications in which the test is referenced.

Generally, a person who wishes to search one of the data bases will find it desirable, and perhaps necessary, to work through the reference division of a university or public library. The library is likely to have a computer terminal with direct access to the data files in question. If not, the reference librarian should be able to help arrange such access. There will be a charge for the search, and the user will want to get an estimate of cost before starting this undertaking.

Questions and Exercises

1. Using the resources listed in the text, prepare as complete a list as you can of currently available standardized tests for a specific purpose (i.e., tests in first-year French, tests of reading achievement, inventories to measure adjustment to college life, etc.).
2. For some characteristic that interests you (e.g., self-concept, attitude toward pollution, creativity, etc.), determine what *research* tests are available in the literature, using the compilations and bibliographic sources referred to in this chapter.
3. Using the volumes of *Mental Measurements Yearbooks,* find out what reviewers think of a particular test that interests you. Do the reviewers agree?
4. To what sources would you go to try to answer each of the following questions? To which would you go first? What would you expect to get from each?
   (a) What test should you use to study the progress of two classes in beginning Spanish?
   (b) What kinds of norms are available for the Metropolitan Achievement Tests?
   (c) Is the Rorschach Test of any value as a predictor of academic success in college?
   (d) Has a new revision of the Wechsler Intelligence Scale for Children been published yet?
   (e) What measures of verbal ability have been published for use with the blind?
   (f) What are the significant differences between the Iowa Tests of Basic Skills and the Metropolitan Achievement Tests?
   (g) How much does the Cognitive Abilities Test cost?
   (h) What do testing people think of the Career Occupational Preference System?
5. Look at two or three publishers' catalogs. Compare the announcements of tests of the same type. How adequate is the information provided? How objective is the presentation of the tests' values and limitations?

Sources of Test Information

Of General Interest

Buros, O. K. (Ed.). (1978). *The eighth mental measurements yearbook.* Highland Park, NJ: The Gryphon Press. (This and previous *Mental Measurement Yearbook* volumes are now handled by the Buros Institute of Mental Measurements at the University of Nebraska, Lincoln, NB.)

Conoley, J. C., & Kramer, J. J. (Eds.). (1989). *The tenth mental measurements yearbook.* Lincoln, NB: Buros Institute of Mental Measurements.

Conoley, J. C., Kramer, J. J., & Mitchell, J. V., Jr. (Eds.). (1988). *Supplement to the ninth mental measurements yearbook.* Lincoln, NB: Buros Institute of Mental Measurements.

Fabiano, E. (1989). *Index to tests used in educational dissertations.* Phoenix, AZ: Oryx Press.

Goldman, B. A., & Busch, J. C. (1978). *Directory of unpublished experimental mental measures.* Volume 2. New York: Human Sciences.

Goldman, B. A., & Sanders, J. L. (1974). *Directory of unpublished experimental mental measures.* Volume 1. New York: Behavioral Publications.

Hepner, J. C. (1988). *ETS test collection cumulative index to tests in microfiche, 1975–1987*. Princeton, NJ: Educational Testing Service.

Johnson, O. G. (1976). *Tests and measurements in child development: Handbook II*. San Francisco: Jossey-Bass.

Johnson, O. G., & Bommarito, J. W. (1971). *Tests and measurements in child development: A handbook*. San Francisco: Jossey-Bass.

Keyser, D. J., & Sweetland, R. C. (1984). *Test critiques*. Kansas City, MO: Test Corporation of America.

Lake, D. G., Miles, M. B., & Earle, R. B. (1973). *Measuring human behavior: Tools for the assessment of social functioning*. New York: Teachers College Press.

Levy, P., & Goldstein, H. (1984). *Tests in education: A book of critical reviews*. London: Academic Press.

Mauser, A. J. (1977). *Assessing the learning disabled: Selected instruments* (2nd ed.). Novato, CA: Academic Therapy Publications.

Miller, D. C. (1983). *Handbook of research design and social measurements* (4th ed.). New York: Longman.

Mitchell, J. V. Jr. (Ed.). (1983). *Tests in print III*. Lincoln, NB: Buros Institute of Mental Measurements.

Mitchell, J. V., Jr. (Ed.). (1985). *The ninth mental measurements yearbook*. Lincoln, NB: Buros Institute of Mental Measurements.

O'Brien, N. P. (1988). *Test construction: A bibliography of selected resources*. New York: Greenwood.

Robinson, J. P., Athanasion, R., & Head, K. B. (1969). *Measures of occupational attitudes and occupational characteristics*. Ann Arbor, MI: University of Michigan.

Robinson, J. P., Rusk, J. G., & Head, K. B. (1968). *Measures of political attitudes*. Ann Arbor, MI: University of Michigan.

Robinson, J. P., & Shaver, P. R. (1973). *Measures of social psychological attitudes* (rev. ed.). Ann Arbor, MI: University of Michigan.

Shaw, M. E., & Wright, J. W. (1967). *Scales for the measurement of attitudes*. New York: McGraw-Hill.

Sweetland, R. C., & Keyser, D. J. (Eds.). (1986). *Tests: A comprehensive reference for assessments in psychology, education and business* (2nd ed.). Kansas City, MO: Test Corporation of America.

Publications and Collections Available from the Educational Testing Service

For information regarding the Test Collection Data Base, *Tests in Microfiche,* the *Tests in Microfiche Annotated Index,* and the Test Collection Bibliographies, write:

> Test Collection
> Educational Testing Service
> Princeton, NJ 08541

Other publications related to the test collection include:

Educational Testing Service Test Collection. (1986). *The ETS test collection catalog* (3 vols.). Phoenix, AZ: Oryx Press.

Educational Testing Service Test Collection. (1987). *Directory of selected national testing programs*. Phoenix, AZ: Oryx Press.

In Specific Subject Areas

Braswell, J. S. (compiler). (1981). *Mathematics tests available in the United States and Canada.* Reston, VA: National Council of Teachers of Mathematics.

Grommon, A. H. (Ed.). (1976). *Reviews of selected published tests in English.* Urbana, IL: National Council of Teachers of English.

Johnson, T. F., & Hess, R. J. (1970). *Tests in the arts.* St. Ann, MO: Central Midwestern Regional Education Laboratory.

Mangen, D. J., & Peterson, W. A. (Eds.). (1982). *Research instruments in social gerontology.* Minneapolis, MN: University of Minnesota Press.

Northwest Regional Educational Laboratory, Center for Bilingual Education. (1978). *Assessment instruments in bilingual education: A descriptive catalog of 342 oral and written tests.* Los Angeles: National Dissemination and Assessment Center.

Savard, J-G. (1969). *Analytical bibliography of language tests.* Quebec: International Center for Research on Bilingualism.

Scholl, G., & Schnur, R. (1976). *Measures of psychological, vocational and educational functioning in the blind and visually handicapped.* New York: American Foundation for the Blind.

Valette, R. M. (1977). *Modern language testing* (2nd ed.). New York: Harcourt Brace Jovanovich.

Wall, J. (1981). *Compendium of standardized science tests.* Washington, DC: National Science Teachers Association.

CHAPTER 11
Standardized Achievement Tests

Introduction

In Chapter 7, tests prepared by a teacher or group of teachers for their own use in their own classes were discussed. This chapter focuses on centrally produced tests, published commercially or by a state or national testing agency for use in a large number of schools and across school districts. Although the items used in both categories of tests may be similar, the overall design and function of these two types of tests may be quite different.

Distinctive Features of Centrally Produced Tests

Centrally produced tests differ from those constructed locally by a teacher or groups of teachers in three ways: (1) the amount of time and professional skill available for their development, (2) breadth of objectives, and (3) the inclusion of norms.

Time and Professional Skill Required

In anticipation that the product will achieve widespread acceptance and use over a period of several years, there is a willingness on the part of test publishers to invest substantial amounts of time and money in developing centrally produced tests and test batteries. The development of such tests requires such processes as reviewing current curricula, preparing blueprints of content and skill, writing test exercises, reviewing items to eliminate ambiguities, eliminating biased items, completing item analyses to provide objective verification of item quality, and assembling the items that survive review into the resulting test.

Breadth of Objectives

Because centrally produced tests are designed to be marketable as widely as possible—across districts, states, and the nation as a whole, standardized achievement tests can include only material that every student at the level assessed has had the opportunity to learn. Test authors must examine the objectives for all potential school districts and select only those objectives common to all. As a result, standardized achievement tests do not emphasize the recall of facts, as is commonly believed, because this sort of content is not likely to be similar across curricula.

Inclusion of Norms

The most distinctive feature of centrally produced tests is the availability of norms. The term "standardized test" implies the availability of normative data, and publishers of these tests provide a range of normative information to help give meaning to test scores.

Normative data provide meaning through comparisons with other students at the same grade level. They permit statements about how a student is doing in relation to others of the same age or grade or from the same type of school system. They also permit statements about how students do in mathematics in comparison with their performance in reading or on tests of scholastic aptitude. They tell how a particular school compares with schools all over the country, with schools of a particular type, or with schools in a particular type of community.

The quality of the norm sample is largely a function of how much the publisher is willing to spend. Because norm samples may include hundreds of thousands of subjects, they can be expensive. When reading the manual to a standardized achievement test, it is easy to be impressed by the effort and expense that goes into ensuring a large representative sample. It is, of course, impossible to obtain a truly random sample because test publishers must conduct pilot testing in those school districts where they can obtain permission to do so. These pilot school districts usually turn out to be the districts that already use a particular publisher's tests (Baglin, 1981).

Use of Standardized Achievement Tests

In considering the characteristics of standardized achievement tests just discussed and the information from Chapter 7 on locally constructed tests, we come to the following conclusions about the types of decisions for which standardized achievement tests are likely to be helpful:

1. Day-to-day instructional decisions should depend primarily on locally constructed rather than standardized tests.

2. Grading decisions should be based primarily on locally constructed tests covering what has been taught in a given unit or course.

3. Diagnostic and remedial decisions can be based on information from locally constructed as well as from centrally produced diagnostic tests.

4. Placement decisions require a broad appraisal of achievement, and standardized tests can be useful in identifying entry-level performance.

5. Guidance decisions are usually based on the type of normative comparisons that standardized tests make possible.

6. Selection decisions imply comparison with others, and for these decisions, norms are often important.

7. Curricular decisions between alternative programs imply a broadly based comparison in which standardized measures can play a role, often supplemented by measures developed locally for distinctive special objectives.

8. Public policy decisions require, as do curricular decisions, a comprehensive view of how well a school is doing. The sort of broad survey that standardized tests provide is useful for this purpose.

Types of Standardized Tests

The early objective achievement tests generally measured performance in individual subjects. A school district that wanted to measure the achievement of students in several subjects such as reading, mathematics, and social studies had to administer a different test for each use. The use of so many different tests was expensive and time consuming, and it required that teachers be familiar with the norming and administrative procedures for a number of different tests. Later, these separate, uncoordinated tests were replaced by test batteries, which could be administered together using a single test booklet.

These coordinated batteries have several important advantages. Planning is comprehensive, and the components are designed to provide an integrated coverage of the major academic skills and curricular areas. Each part is planned with an awareness of the other parts, so that duplication can be minimized and joint coverage of important material guaranteed.

More important than these advantages is the fact that all of the subtests of such batteries have been standardized on the same sample of students. Comparisons within and between individuals and comparisons within and between groups are more direct and straightforward when norms for all parts of a battery are based on the same group of students; the batteries become much more "iffy" when the reference group changes from test to test. Of course, there are possible drawbacks to using achievement test batteries. Comparing different batteries, we may prefer a mathematics test from one, a language test from another, and a reading test from still another on the basis of correspondence of each to our local curriculum and objectives. But, for the types of comparisons for which standardized tests are appropriately used, the gains from unified norms (and test design) seem to outweigh any losses from having to accept a package in which one or two elements are judged to be less than ideal.

Available Standardized Achievement Tests

There are six *major* large-scale achievement test batteries: the California Achievement Test (CAT), published by McGraw-Hill; the Comprehensive Test of Basic Skills (CTBS), also published by McGraw-Hill; the Iowa Tests of Basic Skills (ITBS), published by the Riverside Publishing Company; the Metropolitan Achievement Tests (MAT), published by the Psychological Corporation; the Science Research Associates (SRA) Achievement series published by Science Research Associates, Inc.; and the Stanford Achievement Test (SAT), published by the Psychological Corporation. These tests are appropriate for use from kindergarten to 12th grade, except for the ITBS, which is appropriate for use through the 9th grade. However, the Riverside Publishing Company also publishes the Iowa Tests of Educational Development, for students in Grades 9–12. All of these tests include reading, language, and mathematics subtests; the CTBS, MAT, and SAT also have science and social studies subtests.

These tests are similar in terms of the time and effort that has gone into their development, and their overall quality is high. They cover the same range of students and have similar content areas. The test development and norming procedures are generally exemplary. The tests differ in terms of specific items, subscales, and techniques of test development. Of greatest importance are the specific objectives assessed by each. Anyone involved in making decisions concerning which test to use needs to compare tests carefully to determine which objectives are most appropriate.

To illustrate how the form and content of a test changes from the elementary to advanced levels, Figure 11.1 (pp. 338–339) contains sample items similar to those used in the reading subtest of the MAT.

An examination of the different levels illustrates how the presentation shifts from a teacher-paced, oral format to a student-paced, entirely written format. Pictures are used frequently at the lower levels, at the point where basic decoding skills are still being established. Emphasis is placed on word analysis and decoding skills at the lower levels, while at the higher levels, more emphasis is on knowledge of word meanings and the reading of continuous text followed by questions that assess reading comprehension.

Two aspects of these changes in the test over time are particularly notable. First, there is a progressive shift in the nature of what is tested to match the capabilities of the maturing students. Second, at the higher levels, the test provides a broad survey of complex skills rather than a specific analysis of sharply defined competencies.

The Comprehensive Test of Basic Skills, Fourth Edition

In this section, a more detailed discussion of a specific test, the fourth edition of the CTBS (CTBS/4) is provided. This particular test is of interest because it uses some of the most sophisticated test development and norming techniques.

The purpose of the CTBS/4 is to measure basic skills that are developed from exposure to varied curricula. It is intended to be independent of the particular course content taught in any one school district. However, the test cannot be made entirely independent of the effect of the year that specific subjects are introduced into the local curriculum.

The CTBS/4 does not endeavor to measure specific knowledge or content directly. The emphasis is instead on more general skills. Although modern curricular methods are considered, items were rejected if students enrolled in traditional programs could not answer them correctly.

The current version of the CTBS, CTBS/4, was first administered in the spring of 1989 in Kentucky and New Mexico and in 1990 in Tennessee. The previous edition was in Forms U and V, originally published in 1981. Three versions of the CTBS/4 are offered: the complete battery, the benchmark, and the survey test. The complete battery is intended to provide both norm-referenced and curriculum-referenced scores. The benchmark test is intended to provide information about only norm-referenced scores. The two survey tests, which make up the halves of the benchmark test, provide shorter and somewhat less precise estimates of the scores obtained by the benchmark test. The norm-referenced version of the complete battery consists of one of the survey tests. A version of the CTBS/4 is planned that will be curriculum-referenced only. Table 11.1 (p. 340) lists the grade levels and corresponding CTBS levels. Note that there is more than one grade associated with a given level.

Determining the Appropriate Level.   An examination of Table 11.1 indicates that there is always more than one level that can be administered to each grade. For ease of administration and prevention of confusion in scoring, all students in one class or all classes of the same grade are often given the same level of the test. This practice tends to make the test less reliable for individual students because their ability is not matched with the difficulty of the test. A better procedure would be to make decisions concerning which level to administer according to the following rules. For average students, the lower of the two levels should be given during the first half of the year and the higher level during the second half. Bright students should be given higher levels and below-average students lower levels.

This procedure also reduces the frustration students experience when given a test that is too far above or below their level of achievement. Locator tests consisting of twenty vocabulary and twenty mathematics items are available to assist in the selection of the most appropriate test level. A discussion of locator or screening tests is provided in the discussion of the fourth edition of the Stanford-Binet in Chapter 12.

Content Covered.   The test is divided into seven content areas: reading, spelling, language, mathematics, study skills, social studies, and science. These content areas in turn are further subdivided. Each content area is not administered on every level of the test. The technical manual for the CTBS/4 provides the objectives associated with each test.

Norming.   The CTBS/4 was developed to provide fall and spring norms and was based on the school population of the entire United States. The total sample included approximately 222,000 students selected from public, parochial, and private schools. A stratified random sampling procedure was employed that took into account geographic region, size, and socioeconomic level.

Reporting Results.   The item analysis and scaling of the CTBS/4 is based on a highly sophisticated application of item response theory (IRT). The methods used represent the state of the art of standardized test development, and this technique for interpreting results makes computer analyses essential. This interpretation must be done either by the test publisher, McGraw-Hill, or by programs leased from that company. The use of a computer for test scoring makes available a wide array of derived scores, such as normal curve equivalents, scaled scores, grade equivalents, and percentiles based on local, state, and national norms.

Reliability.   The preliminary technical manual (Comprehensive Test of Basic Skills, 1988) includes both reliability coefficients and standard errors of mea-

FIGURE 11.1
Sample items similar to those on the Metropolitan Achievement Test.

Primer Level (Grade K to 1.4)

Listening for sounds

Picture sounds (22 items): Look at the pictures of the ball, the kite, and the tree. Which one starts with a sound like *cat?* Put a mark under it.

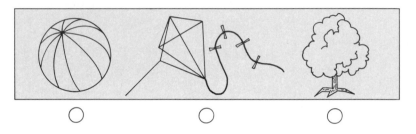

    ○   ○   ○

Letter sounds (8 items):   Mark under the letter that stands for the beginning sound in *top*.

g	n	t	s
○	○	○	○

Word sounds (9 items):   Mark under the word *tall*. He is a *tall* boy.

fall	**tell**	**tall**	**talk**
○	○	○	○

Reading

Letter recognition (11 items):   Mark under the letter R.

R	**P**	**B**	**W**
○	○	○	○

Word-picture matching (17 items):   Which word tells what the picture is about?

○ **mouse**
○ **house**
○ **hat**
○ **howl**

FIGURE 11.1 continued

Sentence-picture matching (5 items): Mark in the space beside the sentence that tells about the picture.

○ The birds are flying.

○ The bird is sitting.

○ The boys are jumping.

Primary I (Grade 1.5—2.4)
Word Knowledge
  Word-picture matching (see Primer) (35 items)
Word Discrimination
  Word sounds (see Primer) (35 items)
Reading
  Sentence-picture matching (see Primer) (13 items)
  Stories (33 items):
  John and Mary like to play ball.
  John throws the ball.
  Mary catches the ball.

What does Mary like to play?

○ ball

○ dolls

○ jacks

Primary II (Grade 2.5—3.4)
Word Knowledge
  Word-picture matching (see Primer) (17 items)
  Synonyms (23 items):
    To *strike* is to ○ hit ○ cry ○ fall ○ jump
Word Analysis
  Word sounds (see Primer) (35 items)
Reading
  Sentence-picture matching (see Primer) (13 items)
  Stories (see Primary I) (31 items)

Elementary (Grade 3.5—4.9)
Synonyms (see Primary II) (50 items)
Word Discrimination-Sentence Completion (36 items):
  Please_____and lock the door.
            clothes   close   cause   class

Reading
  Stories (see Primary I) (44 items)

Intermediate (Grade 5.0—6.9)

Advanced (Grade 7.0—9.5)
Synonyms (50 items)
Stories (45 items)

TABLE 11.1
Grade Levels and Corresponding Levels of the Comprehensive Test of Basic Skills (CTBS)

Grade Level	CTBS Level
K.0–K.9	K
K.6–1.6	10
1.0–2.2	11
1.6–3.2	12
2.6–4.2	13
3.6–5.2	14
4.6–7.2	15
5.6–8.2	16
6.6–9.2	17 and 18
8.6–11.2	19 and 20
10.6–12.9	21 and 22

Note. K=kindergarten. Grade-level notations are interpreted as follows: K.0=beginning of kindergarten; K.9=ninth month of kindergarten; 1.6=sixth month of first grade, and so forth.

surement. These are all respectably high although they are based on administrations of the benchmark test, which can be expected to have higher reliabilities than the other forms of the test because it has more items. The technical manual provides information that emphasizes the degree to which the standard error of measurement is smallest at the midranges of performance and largest at the floor and ceiling of each level of the test. They also illustrate the advantage of IRT techniques over the "number correct" approach to computing scaled scores. (For a description of IRT techniques, see Chapter 16.) The reporting of complete data on standard errors of measurement is useful because it permits estimations of the amount of error associated with scores across the range of student ability. This information demonstrates why we can place more confidence in the scores of students in the midrange of performance than in those at upper or lower levels.

Validity.   The section on validity in the Comprehensive Test of Basic Skills Pre-publication Technical Bulletin (1988) is introduced with the following definition: "Validity of an achievement test has to do with the degree to which it measures well what it purports to measure." It further states, "Care was taken during the development of CTBS/4 to provide a valid measurement of basic academic skills in the areas of reading, spelling, language, mathematics, and study skills." Nothing more is said about validity except in references to the chapters that deal with test development and item analysis. Such a limited discussion of validity is typical of most technical manuals for standardized achievement tests, which tend to include numerous tables of reliability data but barely mention validity.

Additionally, the definition of validity given in the CTBS/4 manuals is quite different from the one found in Chapter 5. Furthermore, it is not consistent with the definition found in the *Standards for Educational and Psychological Testing* (American Psychological Association, American Educational Research Association, & National Council on Measurement in Education, 1985). The simplistic definition found in the CTBS/4 technical manual contrasts sharply with the otherwise highly sophisticated treatment of the technical aspects of achievement testing found in the rest of the manual.

In the past, this practice might have been defended by arguing that tests of this kind are judged primarily on the basis of their content validity. The use of content validity in this context would mean that the case for validity could be contained in sections describing the development of the test and the match between the objectives of the agency adopting the test and those built into the test. However, the publication of the *Standards* renders this treatment of validity inadequate. The standards included in this publication require that tests be evaluated not only in terms of one type of validity (in this case content validity) but also in terms of the other types. This requirement means it is not enough to establish that the science subtest of the CTBS/4 covers the appropriate content; it is necessary to establish that this subtest measures the construct underlying the objectives in this subtest.

Secondary School and College-Level Achievement Tests

At the elementary school level, standardized tests tend to focus on the basic skills of operating with words and numbers. At the secondary school and college levels, the emphasis shifts to the substance of particular curricular areas and even to particular courses. Because the curriculum becomes more differentiated, with the core that is common to all students representing a smaller fraction of the total, there is less need for a uniform comprehensive assessment. However, there are situations where a standardized achievement test battery can appropriately be used.

At the end of World War II, there was a need to evaluate and give credit for educational experiences obtained in the armed forces, so the Iowa Tests of Educational Development were developed. Like all general ability tests, this battery was designed to be appropriate for individuals who come from varied backgrounds. The test, therefore, tends to emphasize general knowledge and ability to read material from different fields of knowledge with understanding. The present version, the eighth edition of the Iowa Tests of Educational Development (1988), has two forms (Forms X-8 and Y-8) and two levels (Level I for Grades 9 and 10 and Level II for Grades 11 and 12) and contains the following subtests:

1. Correctness and appropriateness of expression
2. Ability to do quantitative thinking
3. Analysis of social studies materials

4. Analysis of natural sciences materials

5. Ability to interpret literary materials

6. Ability to use sources of information

In addition, it provides a composite reading test score. The emphasis on getting, using, and interpreting material of various types and from various sources is apparent in the test titles. Almost all of the subtests make a substantial demand on reading skills, and most of the subtests are highly correlated with each other. As a result, although the test provides a good prediction of later academic performance, the subtests are not effective diagnostic tools. They also do not correspond closely enough to what is taught in any specific course to have value in indicating how effective a total school program has been.

More conventional and more representative of other high school batteries is the Tests of Achievement and Proficiency—Forms G and H (Scannell, 1986). In the basic battery, there are eight subtests:

1. Reading comprehension

2. Mathematics

3. Written expression

4. Using sources of information

5. Total

6. Applied proficiency skills

7. Minimum competency in reading

8. Minimum competency in mathematics

In addition to these scores, the complete battery has a social studies and science score. As can be seen from the titles, the battery is a mixture of basic skills (reading, writing, and mathematics) and of content (social studies, science, and literature). However, even in the content areas, there is a fair amount of emphasis on functional knowledge, for example, interpretation of data and of experimental designs in science. Such adaptations bring the tests closer to the common core of secondary education and make them more useful for comparing different schools and curricula and for making guidance decisions relating to a particular student. However, the emphasis on functional knowledge renders the tests less useful as measures of what has been taught in any specific course.

In addition to batteries such as those just described, there are series of tests whose titles correspond rather closely to those of specific courses. One extensive series was developed by the Cooperative Test Division of the Educational Testing Service. The nature of the tests is suggested by the types of tests in mathematics: structure of the number system; arithmetic; algebra I, II, and III; geometry; trigonometry; analytic geometry; and calculus. Another series is the Evaluation and Adjustment Series published by Harcourt, Brace, Jovanovich. This series includes tests in chemistry, physics, biology, American history, algebra, geometry, listening comprehension, and other areas. Typically, the tests in these series are designed for students who have completed some specific course—beginning algebra, biology, world history, or the like. Norms are usually based on samples of students who have completed such a course. Individual factors that may affect the integrity of the norming procedures influence a student's decision to enroll in a course. Little attempt has been made to maintain comparability of the score scale from one field to another, so comparisons across fields are rather questionable. Test content may in some cases match course content well enough that the test can play a role in the end-of-year evaluation of each student, but such a step should be taken with care to ensure that the course objectives are covered by the test.

One role suggested for tests designed to match specific courses is that of exempting particular students from specific course requirements. In part because many young people have received various kinds of training in the armed forces and in part in recognition of the fact that some individuals may have been educated through media other than formal schooling—for example, through reading, radio and television, and/or work experience—it seems desirable to some educators to provide through examinations a channel for accreditation of such experience. The College Level Examination Program of the Educational Testing Service is such a channel.

The College Level Examination Program was established to provide a uniform nationwide procedure for evaluating experience claimed as the equivalent of specific college courses. Examinations have been prepared for 35 areas ranging from accounting and African American history to tests and measurements, trigonometry, and western civilization. Normative data have been obtained from college students who have completed the designed course, as well as from the population samples who have taken the equivalency test. Scores are presented as standard scores that range from 200 to 800, with 500 representing the average score for the basic reference population. The way that the results from such a test will be used is determined by the college to which the student is applying and from which he wishes equivalency credit. As with any accrediting or licensing examination, the decision on what constitutes a minimum acceptable level is quite arbitrary. Although general normative data may be available for those who have taken the course for which the examination is a substitute, it is likely that no data will be available specifically for the college to which an individual is applying. The score at which the balance shifts in favor of the gain in time saved and away from the risk of misclassifying a student as having mastered a course must be determined intuitively. The use of examinations for licensure and certification is widespread in our society, but the system for setting cutoff scores generally falls far short of being rational.

Statewide Administration of Achievement Test Batteries

An increasing number of states are mandating statewide testing programs. Typically, in these programs, all public schools in a state are required to administer the same test or battery of tests for all or a selected number of grade levels.

Currently, 26 states administer statewide a commercially available standardized achievement test, 6 use locally developed tests, and 18 allow school districts to test independently (Cannell, 1988). John Jacob Cannell reports the following breakdown of test use by state:

Iowa Tests of Basic Skills
    Arizona
    Colorado
    Georgia
    Idaho
    Iowa
    North Dakota

Stanford Achievement Test
    Alabama
    Hawaii
    Mississippi
    Nevada
    South Dakota
    Tennessee

Comprehensive Test of Basic Skills
    Delaware
    Kentucky
    New Mexico
    South Carolina
    Utah
    West Virginia
    Wisconsin

California Achievement Test
    Maryland
    New Hampshire
    North Carolina

Metropolitan Achievement Tests
    Arkansas
    Oklahoma
    Washington

Science Research Associates
    North Dakota
    Virginia

Locally Developed Tests
    California
    Maine
    Oregon
    Pennsylvania
    Rhode Island
    Texas

Test Chosen by School Districts
>Alaska
>Connecticut
>Florida
>Illinois
>Indiana
>Kansas
>Louisiana
>Massachusetts
>Michigan
>Minnesota
>Missouri
>Montana
>Nebraska
>New Jersey
>New York
>Ohio
>Vermont
>Wyoming
>(North Dakota used both the ITBS and SRA series in 1988, but has now adopted CTBS)

Where the tests have been developed by state departments of education, they are usually based on a systematic formulation of relatively specific objectives. These objectives are selected by committees of educators within that state to fit the testing more closely to the objectives and sequence of instruction within the state. Teachers are involved in the design of the test blueprint to overcome the objection that the test exercises do not match what the schools are teaching.

The "Lake Wobegon Effect"

Several years ago, Cannell, a physician in West Virginia, became concerned when the results of the administration of the CTBS in his state were announced (Cannell, 1988). It seemed that his state was above the national average in all grade levels tested. These results were reported in the face of convincing evidence that West Virginia had serious educational problems. The state has the highest percentage of adults without college degrees, the second lowest per capita income, and the third lowest scores on the tests of the American College Testing (ACT) Program. When Cannell began to check the results of standardized achievement test administrations around the country, what he found was even more disconcerting. He discovered that none of the 50 states were below average at the elementary level. This phenomenon was quickly labeled the "Lake Wobegon Effect" after Garrison Keillor's description of his hometown on the American Public Radio program, A Prairie Home Companion, as a place "where all the women are strong, all the men are good-looking, and all the children are above average."

The discovery that all states are above average should cause the same alarm as the sound of a clock striking 13. There is certainly something wrong; basic rules of statistics dictate that it is impossible for every child or every state to be above average. Test publishers and the school districts that use these tests are quick to defend themselves against charges that they are guilty of any wrong-doing.

The most often heard explanation for these high scores is that the achievement of students has increased since the tests were standardized. With a 7- to 8-year turnaround between revisions, there is a sizable gap between standardization and use. The available evidence, however, fails to support this explanation. ACT and Scholastic Aptitude Test scores have declined, National Assessment of Educational Progress scores show no increase nor do Armed Services Vocational Aptitude Battery scores. The hypothesis that overall achievement has increased since the tests were most recently normed would be supported if test results were much lower the first year the test was introduced. The MAT—Form 6, the CAT—Form E, and the ITBS—Form G and H were all introduced during the 1985–1986 school year, and for each, states that immediately administered the test reported scores that were quite high. The high scores were not the result of teacher's teaching to the test because the teacher's had not seen the test before the test date. The high scores also could not have resulted from improvement since the last norming because not enough time had passed since that norming.

A second explanation for the high proportion of students who score above average on standardized achievement tests is that the students taking these tests differ from the norm sample. Although the test publishers spend enormous sums norming their tests, including samples that typically exceed 100,000, there is no way to ensure that the sample is truly representative because the administration of the test, for norming purposes, can take place only where permission can be obtained. For this reason, these samples may be different in important ways from the students that are assessed when the tests are administered. This problem is exacerbated by the tendency of many school districts to exclude students from testing who might be expected to obtain low scores, such as special education and other special program students. Some school districts or specific teachers within a district might exclude or at least not encourage the participation of students who are not expected to do well. When low performing students are excluded, classroom teachers or districts that engage in such practices can expect to improve their performance relative to the norming population.

A third explanation for the high proportion of students who score above average relates to changes in the curriculum that are the direct result of the testing process. As more importance is placed on test results, the likelihood that the curriculum will be altered to fit what is being tested will increase. Some such alterations may be considered legitimate—to the extent that they do not involve teaching the test. But, even in its most legitimate forms, altering curriculum to increase the match with test objectives will violate the sampling assumptions of the test, and the resulting standard scores will lose their meaning.

If a teacher realizes that a class is consistently failing to answer correctly an item that requires the capitalization of the name of the state of "Arizona," it would obviously be inappropriate for the teacher to tell his or her students to always capitalize the word "Arizona." On the other hand, it seems acceptable for a teacher to alter the lesson plan to emphasize the need to capitalize the names of *all* states. But such a practice can change the meaning of scores derived from norms because standardized achievement tests are intended to sample student behavior, which permits generalizations about a wide range of behaviors. If the teachers do not know what is included on a test, they have to make sure that they cover everything that could be included. On the other hand, if a teacher knows the general categories included on the test and teaches only these categories, the content sampling of the test will be compromised. Students taking the test under these circumstances will be taught and assessed only over a narrow range of content, that covered on the test. This narrowing of the curriculum focus occurs, for example, when a teacher focuses on the capitalization of states because items assessing this knowledge are known to be on the test. A major deficit in learning occurs when the teacher fails to teach the students to capitalize the names of countries because this type of item is not assessed by the test.

Another possible explanation for the high proportion of above average students is that teachers could actually be teaching the items from the test or administering the test in a nonstandard way that causes scores to be inflated. For instance, a teacher could provide inappropriate assistance when the test is administered or give students too much time to complete sections of the test that they have trouble completing in the allotted time. At the elementary level, the teachers administer the tests. When undue importance is placed on student performance and there is an absence of supervision of the test administration, the likelihood that cheating will take place increases. Two factors contribute to this problem. First, there are pressures on teachers to have their students do well on tests because the teachers may be evaluated on the basis of the test results. Second, all the way up the chain of command, those who are responsible for seeing that proper test administration procedures are maintained have a second and perhaps more important interest in seeing the scores rise because they are often evaluated on this basis of the scores. As a result, the individuals face a serious conflict of interest and may be tempted to overlook inappropriate practices that may lead to inflated scores.

Obviously, a teacher who is giving students too much time to complete a section of a test or actually helping students answer questions is guilty of cheating. Likewise, a teacher who drills students on actual items from a test is involved in a practice that is generally perceived to be inappropriate. On the other hand, a teacher concerned about her students' performance on an achievement test who worked extremely hard to get her students to learn more or who encouraged students to work hard on the test is not engaged in cheating. In fact, such behaviors would probably be viewed as exemplary. Gray areas, such as the following, cause problems: Teachers using similar items to those that appear on a test to be administered, or focusing instruction on those topics that are known to appear on the test, are engaged in practices that are generally considered unethical, but unfortunately are common.

Some school districts have even implemented systemwide programs that involve a curricular emphasis on the specific content of the achievement tests that they use. Test publishers also make available instructional materials that can have a similar impact on student performance.

Interpreting Standardized Achievement Test Batteries

The survey achievement test is designed to yield a reliable score for each of the skill areas. (Reliability coefficients in the high 80s or low 90s would be fairly typical.) Interest tends to focus on these subtest scores and their profile of strengths and weaknesses. We not only want to know how Peter's achievement in mathematics compares with national norms, but also how it compares with other areas of achievement as well. We may also want to know how Ms. Albertson's class is progressing in mastery of mathematics concepts in comparison with computational skills. There also may be a need to know in what respects schools of the Peterboro district appear better than average and in what respects they show deficiencies. There may be a further interest in knowing whether these differences reflect the desired curricular emphasis; if school administrators, teachers, parents, and the public should be concerned; and if remediation efforts should be initiated.

When it comes to classroom instructional decisions, the subtest scores on a survey achievement battery are of limited value. If Peter's achievement is a full grade below his current grade placement in capitalization skills, what is to be done about it? If Ms. Albertson's class shows an average grade equivalent a half grade lower in mathematics concepts than in mathematics computation, what steps should Ms. Albertson take? What should she teach or reteach? One way to answer these questions is to look at the individual questions on the capitalization test that Peter answered incorrectly or the specific mathematics concepts that many of the children in Ms. Albertson's class did not know. This information about student performance can be provided by the scoring services made available by test publishers.

Because large-scale testing programs are scored and interpreted by computer, only fairly simple modifications in the scoring program are required to permit more detailed information about the responses of individual children and classes. Report forms are available that will indicate which items Peter answered incorrectly on the capitalization subtest. The items can even be grouped by the capitalization rule that they exemplify. Information about the types of mathematics skills which the class as a whole is experiencing difficulty also can be identified. From this information, Ms. Albertson can determine whether Peter made errors in capitalizing at the beginning of a sentence, at the beginning of a quotation, for names of persons, for names of places, or so forth. She can also see the frequency of errors in various concept and computational mathematical skill areas for the entire class. This analysis of the test results has the potential for identifying specific difficulties and giving clues for instruction. Through these reports, the test author can assist teachers in what they have always been urged to do, that is, dig beneath the normative test score to identify the specific test exercises with which individuals and the class as a whole are encountering difficulty.

This type of detailed analysis of successes and failures on specific items can be quite useful for the teacher. However, there are some important cautions about such an approach. First, these tests do not contain enough items to assess each specific skill adequately. Usually there are only one or two items per skill, making it possible for a child to answer items correct and thereby "pass an objective" by making a lucky guess or to answer items incorrectly because of some distraction or reason that is not relevant to the basic skill the item is designed to test. One or two items are insufficient to permit a reliable mastery/nonmastery decision about a child. Failure to answer an item correctly can alert the teacher to the need to test the skill being measured more fully, perhaps with a short teacher-made test that focuses specifically on the skill covered by the item answered incorrectly. Similarly, failure on an item by a substantial percentage of students in a class suggests the need to test that skill more thoroughly to determine whether some part of the class lacks mastery of the skill involved in that item.

The previous section highlights a still more serious problem with the practice of assessing objectives with one or two items. If teachers are familiar with the specific items students are missing and are under pressure to have their students improve their scores, they may be tempted to teach the specific items or at least the specific type of items, a practice that leads to inflated test scores.

If the analysis of test results is to be helpful to a teacher, it should be in the teacher's hands as soon after testing as possible. Because modern computer-based test scoring usually must be done centrally, there inevitably will be a lag of several weeks between testing and receipt by the teacher of the report of the test results. Each added week of delay makes the results less timely for instructional decisions concerning specific children or the whole class. New learning has taken place, previously learned material may have been forgotten, and the details of the descriptive picture have become less accurate. For these reasons, it is important to expedite completion of a testing program, assembly of answer sheets from the participating schools, and shipment of the materials to the processing agency. From that point on, teachers are at the mercy of the U.S. Postal Service and the agency conducting the scoring and report preparation. The problem of turnaround time is likely to be particularly serious in statewide testing programs if there is a requirement that returns from all school systems be received before test analysis can be conducted. In some cases, processing problems resulting from technical and/or political issues have delayed reporting beyond the year in which the test results were obtained. By the time these results are in the hands of the teachers, it is too late for any use to be made of them for instructional planning for specific students.

Diagnostic Achievement Tests

Diagnosis relates primarily to the single individual. Why does Sarah get a low score on a survey test of reading comprehension? Why does Peter get a low score on the mathematics subtest of the achievement battery? What are the sources of difficulty? Much, probably most, diagnostic testing is conducted with single students after it has been determined from a survey test or from the observations of the teacher that a student is not making satisfactory progress in reading, mathematics, or some other segment of the school program. Some tests are available that are intended to serve a diagnostic function and to be administered to a group. We will describe one of these, indicating what it undertakes to do and the problems that arise in its use and interpretation.

An example of a diagnostic test is the third edition of the Stanford Diagnostic Mathematics Test (1984), Forms G and H, which is designed for use in Grades 1–12. Levels are designated by colors. The red level is for use with students at the end of first grade and in the second and third grades as well as with low performing students in fourth grade. The green level is for fourth-, fifth-, and low performing sixth-grade students. The brown level is for sixth-, seventh-, and low performing eighth-grade students. The blue level is for 8th–12th graders. All four levels assess three areas of mathematical competence. Test 1 measures the concepts of the number system and numeration, Test 2 measures computation, and Test 3 measures the application of these concepts and skills. For each test, a series of skills is measured. For example, at the green level of Test 2, computation, the following skills are measured: addition with whole numbers (9 items), subtraction with whole numbers (12 items), multiplication with whole numbers (15 items), and division with whole numbers (9 items).

Raw scores, scaled scores, grade equivalents, percentiles, and a total score are reported for each of the three subtests. Information on the performance of students on each separate skill measured within each of the three subtests is also provided in the form of raw scores and an indication of whether the child was above or below a cutoff score.

The test has been normed for both fall and spring administration, but for maximum value it is recommended that the test be administered in the fall. In selecting which level to administer, both the grade and the level of functioning of the student should be considered. Little diagnostic information can be derived from a test that is either too easy or too difficult. The test is structured so that one test can be administered each day or so that two can be administered on the same day. If two tests are administered on the same day, a 10-minute rest period between tests is recommended.

The subtest scores provide only an initial step in diagnosis. Performance on the specific skills that are subsumed by the subtests must also be examined. But even analysis at this level may not be sufficient. If Peter's scores are compared with the norms for his grade group and it is found that his lowest score is in multiplication of whole numbers, we still do not know what aspect of multiplication is giving him trouble. We have some guidance on where we should focus further scrutiny, but we still need to analyze Peter's errors in multiplication problems to see if we can determine whether his problem is errors in conception or procedure or a deficit in the mastery of number facts. Having tentatively identified an area of weakness, we need to observe the process of Peter's functioning in that area to determine exactly what he does incorrectly and to generate hypotheses on why he does it. A thorough diagnostic study typically requires observation of the process as well as the product of student performance.

If a weakness on a particular subtest characterizes an individual student in a class, we first look for deficits in his or her acquisition of knowledge. If the class as a whole performs poorly on some subtest, we should ask whether the quality of instruction was as it should have been or whether the introduction of certain topics has been delayed in the local curriculum. A discrepancy between local performance and national norms signifies a problem only to the degree that the local curriculum agrees with the assumptions made by the publisher regarding when topics are introduced. If a topic (such as fractions) has not been taught to a particular class at the time of testing, obviously there is no reason to be concerned if the topic has not been mastered. Interpretation of class-average profiles on such a diagnostic battery must be made in light of the group's past instructional history and instructional emphasis.

Because the subtests in a battery provide meaningful diagnostic clues only when the material covered by a subtest has been taught to the students, we may question whether the material on fractions and decimals provides useful diagnostic information for fourth- and fifth-grade groups. We cannot identify deficient performance on a subtest if the average performance is very close to a zero score. In general, the better adapted a test is for displaying a serious deficiency, the poorer it will be for identifying levels of excellence. There is an essential incompatibility between the functions of diagnosing deficiency and assessing all degrees of excellence. The test that is good for one of the purposes is unlikely to be good for the other. Usually, a diagnostic test should be designed more like a criterion-referenced or mastery test, so that the expected score is close to a perfect score and so that there is a wide range of below-par scores to express degrees of deficiency.

Criterion-Referenced Standardized Achievement Tests

The enthusiasm that surrounded the introduction of criterion-referenced approaches to classroom tests generated a parallel interest in the application of the approaches to standardized achievement tests. There are two ways to construct a criterion-referenced standardized achievement test: (1) objectives can be associated with items from existing norm-referenced achievement tests to give them the appearance of a norm-referenced test, or (2) achievement tests can be constructed from the ground up as criterion-referenced tests. The first approach is employed on a widespread basis; however, the availability of criterion-referenced tests of the second type is more limited.

Examples of Criterion-Referenced Achievement Tests

The Psychological Corporation has two reading achievement subtests that are part of the MAT series: (1) the reading survey tests and (2) the reading diagnostic tests. The first subtest is a survey battery similar to other norm-referenced survey achievement batteries, and the second is a criterion-referenced test covering basic reading skills. The SRA Achievement Series has 34 criterion-referenced diagnostic tests available covering instructional objectives included in the curriculum for children in Grades 1–4. Houghton Mifflin, in its School Curriculum Objective-Referenced Evaluation, provides 5,000 items that can be put together in various combinations for criterion-referenced tests to meet the specific needs of teacher and classroom settings.

A criterion-referenced standardized achievement test that has received a considerable amount of attention is the IOX Basic Skills Test (1978). What makes this test unique is the use of the domain-referenced methodology developed by James Popham. There are elementary (5th- and 6th-grade) and secondary (9th- through 12th-grade) versions of the test. At the elementary level, seven skills are assessed in reading, eight in writing, and six in mathematics. At the secondary level, five skills are assessed in reading, four in writing, and four in mathematics. Each skill is assessed by about 10 items. The internal consistency of the 10 items measuring each skill is not very high. A form of content-related validity is reported, and the authors assert that the test has such validity.

Problems with Criterion-Referenced Standardized Achievement Tests

In general, it is not possible for a single test to serve the purposes of both a norm-referenced and a criterion-referenced test because criterion-referenced tests need to be tied closely to the specific instructional objective of the classroom or school district. The publishers of nationally distributed achievement tests must avoid any objectives that are not found in the curricula of most school districts. This need to focus on common objectives works better in the early grades in reading and mathematics, where the greatest consensus exists among school districts concerning which objectives should be emphasized. The demand for criterion-referenced achievement tests has led some test publishers to associate instructional objectives with existing items and to claim that these new tests have the properties of, or can be used as, criterion-referenced tests. As was pointed out in Chapter 7, such tests are better described as objective-referenced tests and are considered to be poor forms of assessment. The criterion-referenced approach to assessment is attractive because it seems to avoid some of the negative associations that surround testing, by avoiding the labeling of students as failures, and it is more constructive because it provides more specific information about student performance.

Although there are important advantages to using criterion-referenced tests, such as those just cited, the use of criterion-referenced techniques with standardized achievement tests is fraught with logistic problems. To assess reliably a large number of objectives, it is necessary to administer many items. For instance, the Metropolitan Reading Diagnostic Test includes over 200 items at most grade levels but assesses some objectives with only 3 items. The MAT, on the other hand, uses only 60 items to obtain an overall reading score. To measure something, whether it is a skill such as reading comprehension or an objective such as "can add two-digit numbers," an adequate number of items is required. That is, a test reporting performance on a large number of objectives must be much longer than one reporting seven subtest scores.

Summary

Most standardized testing involves the use of survey test batteries selected from a small number of similar tests. Testing is also conducted using diagnostic and criterion-referenced tests. Survey tests are useful primarily in connection with selection, placement, guidance, curricular, and public policy decisions. Diagnostic tests are used to determine a student's strengths and weaknesses. Diagnostic testing is difficult and time consuming to implement.

At the secondary and college levels, centrally produced achievement tests are called on to provide evidence both of outstanding competence— to serve as a basis for advanced placement—and of minimal competence. An important controversy in statewide achievement testing is the existence of the "Lake Wobegone Effect," which, because it inflates scores, makes the interpretation of the results of such tests difficult. Another problem is the tendency by educators to vacillate between attempts to make objective-referenced interpretations of achievement in local schools and attempts to make global appraisals of the effectiveness of different schools and school systems at the state level.

Questions and Exercises

1. For which of the following purposes would a standardized test be useful? For which purposes should a teacher expect to make his or her own test? Why?
   (a) To determine which students have mastered the addition and subtraction of fractions.
   (b) To determine which students are below the expected skill level in mathematics computation.
   (c) To determine the subjects in which each student is strongest and weakest.

      (d) To determine for a class which punctuation and capitalization skills need to be taught further.

      (e) To form subgroups in a class for the teaching of reading.

2. Obtain a curriculum guide covering the content and objectives of a subject that you are teaching, plan to teach, or someday might want to teach. Examine a standardized achievement test for that subject. Which of the objectives in the curriculum guide are adequately measured by the test? Which ones are not? How adequately is the content covered by the test?

3. Make a critical comparison of two achievement test batteries for the same grade. How do they differ? What are the advantages of each from your point of view?

4. The manual for a test states that it can be used for diagnostic purposes. What criteria could you use to determine whether it has any real value as a diagnostic tool?

5. Why should we be concerned about the reliability of the scores resulting from a set of diagnostic tests? What implications does the reliability have for using and interpreting such tests?

6. A senior high school that draws from three feeder junior highs has a special accelerated program in mathematics. What are the advantages and disadvantages of selecting students for this program on the basis of a standardized achievement test in mathematics given at the end of the ninth grade (the last year in junior high)?

7. You have given a standardized achievement battery in October to your fourth-grade class. How might you, as a teacher, use the results?

8. Using a centralized scoring service, a school buys item analysis data that show the percentage of students answering each item correctly for each grade and each classroom in the school. How could the school as a whole use these results? How could individual teachers use them?

9. Miss Carson, a sixth-grade teacher, says, "I am not as much interested in a student's level of performance as I am in the growth that he or she shows while in my class." In terms of measurement, what problems does this point of view raise?

10. The school system of Centerville is proposing to introduce a revised mathematics curriculum on an experimental basis in selected elementary schools. It wishes to evaluate the effectiveness of the program before introducing it throughout the system. How adequate would a standardized achievement test in elementary school mathematics be for this type of evaluation? What problems are likely to arise? How might these problems be dealt with?

11. A state legislature has passed a law requiring all students to show adequate competency in skills needed for everyday living before they are awarded a high school diploma. To implement the legislation, what is the first problem that needs to be solved? To determine adequate competency, what would be the advantages and disadvantages of using the following types of tests?

      (a) Centrally produced tests by the state education department

      (b) Locally constructed tests by each school

      (c) A nationally published achievement test

Suggested Readings

Cannell, J. J. (1988). Nationally normed elementary achievement testing in America's public schools: How all 50 states are above the national average. *Educational Measurement: Issues and Practice, 7*(2), 5–9.

Cunningham, G. K. (1986). *Educational and psychological measurement*. New York: Macmillan.

Gronlund, N. E. & Linn, R. L. (1990). *Measurement and evaluation in teaching*. New York: Macmillan.

Hall, B. W. (1985). Survey of the technical characteristics of published educational achievement tests. *Educational Measurement: Issues and Practice, 4*(1), 6–14.

Kubiszyn, T., & Borich, G. (1987). *Educational testing and measurement*. Glenview, IL: Scott, Foresman and Company.

Mehrens, W. A. (1987). *Using standardized tests in education*. New York: Longman.

Nitko, A. J. (1983). *Educational tests and measurement*. New York: Harcourt Brace Jovanovich.

Sax, G. (1989). *Principles of educational and psychological measurement and evaluation*. Belmont, CA: Wadsworth.

CHAPTER 12
Aptitude Tests

Introduction

An aptitude test measures a person's present performance on selected tasks to provide information that can be used to estimate how the person will perform at some time in the future or in a somewhat different situation. The situation about which you wish to predict may be school performance, job performance, or some more general adaptation to life's demands. An aptitude test differs somewhat from an achievement test in the tasks that it presents, but the differences are often small and technical. For example, measures of reading comprehension or of arithmetic problem solving may be found both in aptitude and in achievement measures. Generally, aptitude measures depend *more* on general life experiences and *less* on specific instruction, but the difference is frequently one of degree and not one of kind. The one respect in which the two classes of tests *do* clearly differ is the function that they are designed to serve. An achievement test is typically given to find out how much a student has profited from past instruction; an aptitude test is given to estimate how the examinee is likely to perform in the future. The key difference is one of purpose and function.

The first aptitude tests were designed to assess broad, general cognitive ability, and much of aptitude testing still is and probably always will be conducted with the purpose of appraising general ability to carry out cognitive tasks. Subsequently, emphasis shifted somewhat, and a number of tests of more specialized abilities were developed, intended to identify more specific strengths (and weaknesses) in the examinee. First, we will devote our attention to tests that focus on general cognitive ability, often familiarly labeled "IQ tests." Then, we will turn our attention to tests of more specialized abilities. Within the field of general ability tests, we will look first at those that are designed to be given on a one-on-one basis by a trained examiner. After that, we will look at tests designed for group administration.

Individual General Ability Tests

The latter part of the 19th century saw widespread interest in testing human abilities. The recent international movement toward universal compulsory education had created, in the minds of many educators, a need to be able to identify two groups of children—those who *could* not learn because of low ability and those who *would* not learn because of poor motivation or other causes. The first widely acknowledged instrument to accomplish this separation was produced in France in 1905 by Alfred Binet and Theodore Simon.

Stanford-Binet Intelligence Scale: Fourth Edition

Early Binet-Type Scales. At the time of Binet and Simon's work, Charles Spearman proposed a theory of intelligence that has had a directing influence on the development of all tests of ability. Spearman suggested that there is a single global intellectual function, which he called general intelligence, or *g*, and which underlies each individual's performance on all tests of ability. Many of the early tests were constructed either with this idea as their theoretical base or in an attempt to refute the theory of general intelligence. The scales that Binet created, and those developed in his intellectual tradition, were generally consistent with the theory of general intelligence.

Several adaptations of the Binet-Simon scales were shortly brought out in the United States, but the version that has survived is the one published by Lewis Terman in 1916 and known as the Stanford Revision of the Binet-Simon Scales. It has since come to be called the Stanford-Binet Intelligence Scale, or simply the Binet. The Stanford-Binet was extensively revised in the 1930s. In 1960, a third edition was released that included the best items from the 1938 version. New norms were prepared in 1972, but the test itself was not changed. In 1986, the first real revision of the test in almost 50 years was published, the Stanford-Binet Intelligence Scale: Fourth Edition.

As originally developed by Terman, and revised by Terman and Maud Merrill, the Stanford-Binet was organized by age levels and consisted of six quite different tests at each age level. The tests also varied from level to level, but collectively the levels included, among other tasks, ones involving picture and oral vocabulary; memory for objects, for sentences, and for digits; comprehension of what to do in practical situations; analogies; picture and verbal absurdities; similarities and differences; bead chain copying; arithmetical problem solving; and sentence completion. In the fourth edition of the Stanford-Binet, the items are grouped by type so that the examinee attempts vocabulary items as one set of tasks, comprehension items as a second, separate set of tasks, and so forth.

With the first three versions of the Stanford-Binet, the examiner usually started testing with tests a year or so below the examinee's current age. If all tests at this level were passed, the examiner continued up to the next age level and so on until a "ceiling" was reached—an age level at which all the tasks were failed. If one or more tests were failed at the initial entry level, the examiner dropped back until a "basal" age, the highest age at which all the tasks were passed, was found. The examiner then proceeded with testing to determine the child's ceiling. The result was a single score expressing the general ability of the examinee.

A mental age (MA) was determined by taking the basal age and adding to it months of mental age credit for each test passed beyond the basal level. For tests at the 5-year level and below, each test was worth 1 month because the tests were arranged in half-year increments. From Levels 6 through 14, 2 months were awarded for each success. Above that level, the tests received greater weight "in order to make IQs for the upper levels comparable to IQs for the lower age levels" (Terman & Merrill, 1960, p. 62). By way of illustration, suppose a child passed all tests at the 6-year level, three at 7 years, one at 8 years, and none beyond that point. Then the mental age would have been determined as follows:

Test Performance	Mental Age Credit
Basal age	6 years, 0 months
Passed three out of six 7-year tests	6 months
Passed one out of six 8-year tests	2 months
Passed zero out of six 9-year tests	0 months
MA =	6 years 8 months

An index of brightness was obtained by relating mental age to chronological age (CA) to yield an IQ. Originally, the procedure was one of division, in which mental age was divided by chronological age. An IQ was obtained using the formula

$$IQ = (MA/CA)\ 100$$

This ratio yielded values with a mean of 100 (hence the origin of the idea that an IQ of 100 is average) and a standard deviation of about 16 (actual values ranged from about 12 to 20 points). The ratio IQ was used with the first two editions of the instrument. However, since the 1960 revision, the Stanford-Binet has reported results as standard scores, adjusted to yield the same population mean (100) and standard deviation (16) for IQs at all ages. (The values of 100 and 16 were chosen for continuity with earlier practice.) These standard scores produce nearly the same numerical scale as the original ratio IQs and have the advantage of uniformity for all ages. They also avoid the problem that we pointed out in Chapter 3, namely, that age equivalents become meaningless when the rate of development changes significantly.

The 1986 Stanford-Binet has largely avoided the term IQ, substituting the phrase "standard age score" (SAS) instead. This term is more descriptive of what the index really is, and it is possible that the change in terminology will eventually eliminate some of the connotations that have grown over the years around the term *IQ*. However, the numerical scale is essentially identical (mean of 100 and standard deviation of 16). The relationship between SAS of the Stanford-Binet and percentile rank within the individual's age group is approximately as follows:

Stanford-Binet SAS	Percentile Rank
130	97
120	89
110	73
100	50
90	27
80	11
70	3

Subtests of the Stanford-Binet.   The 1986 revision of the Stanford-Binet is composed of many of the same item types as the earlier editions, but as already noted, the items are grouped by type into 15 subtests. The items are graded in difficulty from the simplest item that it was possible to construct up to items of a high level of difficulty. There are two items at each level of difficulty. The 15 types of items included in the current form of the Stanford-Binet are listed and briefly described here. They may be combined to yield four ability scales or an overall measure of ability.

Verbal Reasoning Tests

1. Vocabulary (23 levels—test given at all ages). At the 7 lowest levels, items are pictures that the examinee is required to name. In the 16 higher levels, words are presented, and the examinee must tell what the word means.

2. Comprehension (21 levels—test given at all ages). The three lowest levels require the examinee to point to named parts of a picture of a unisex, ethnically ambiguous child. The higher levels ask the examinee the "why" of things, starting with why people use umbrellas and going up to why it is advantageous to be able to amend a constitution.

3. Absurdities (16 levels—test given from age 2 years to about age 14 years). Each item consists of a picture that has something definitely wrong with it (e.g., a bicycle with square wheels or a person with two right hands). The examinee must tell what is wrong—what is silly in the picture.

4. Verbal Relations (9 levels—test begun at about age 11 years). This test calls for identification of the basis on which three terms are alike but different from a fourth term. An easy item might read

cat   fox   horse   but not pigeon

Abstract/Visual Reasoning Tests

5. Pattern Analysis (21 levels—test given at all ages). The lowest levels of this test use a three-hole form board that looks like this one.

The subject must replace the pieces in the holes. Difficulty is increased by rotating the board and by dividing the three pieces into halves.

Higher levels are based on adaptation of the classic Kohs Blocks. Each block is a black and white cube with a different design on each face. These six faces are displayed here.

Starting with the task of the examinee matching the face shown by the examiner, the test progresses to assembling from two to nine blocks to produce a design, such as that shown here.

6. *Copying* (14 levels—test given from age 2 years to about age 8 years). The lowest levels require matching arrangements of two or three blocks presented by the examiner. The higher levels call on the child to copy a simple figure, such as the one displayed here.

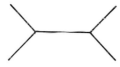

7. *Matrices* (13 levels—test begun at about age 6 years). The task presents the examinee with an incomplete matrix, and requires that the correct entry be selected to complete it. A relatively simple item is illustrated here.

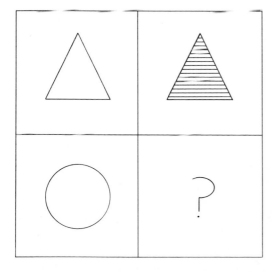

8. *Paper Folding and Cutting* (9 levels—test begun at about age 11 years). The task presents the examinee with a demonstration of how a rectangle of paper has been folded and one or more pieces cut out of it. The examinee must

indicate how the paper will look when unfolded. A relatively simple item is illustrated here.

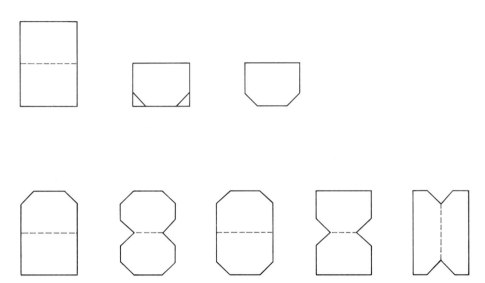

Quantitative Reasoning

9. Quantitative (20 levels—test given at all ages). The easiest items involve counting and adding or subtracting the spots on what are essentially dice. From this task, the test goes to a series of pictures, each involving a quantitative question, graded in difficulty. An early item might read, "These are Mary's six marbles. If she gave three to Jane, how many would be left?"

10. Number Series (13 levels—test begun at about age 6 years). Starting at about age 6, sequences of numbers are presented, and the examinee is required to state the two numbers that should come next. A very easy and a more difficult item are shown here.

$$3 \quad 4 \quad 5 \quad 6 \quad 7 \quad \underline{\quad} \quad \underline{\quad}$$
$$4 \quad 6 \quad 5 \quad 8 \quad 6 \quad 10 \quad \underline{\quad} \quad \underline{\quad}$$

11. Equation Building (9 levels—test begun at about age 11 years). This test presents the examinee with a set of numerals and operational signs. The examinee is required to rearrange them to produce a true number sentence or equation. Again, a very easy item and a more difficult one are illustrated here.

$$2 \quad 2 \quad 4 \quad - \quad = \quad \underline{\quad}$$
$$1/2 \quad 1 \quad 5 \quad 7 \quad - \quad \times \quad (\quad) \quad = \quad \underline{\quad}$$

Short-Term Memory Tests.

12. Memory for Sentences (21 levels—test given at all ages). The examiner reads a sentence to the examinee, who is instructed to repeat it exactly as it was read. The test starts with two-word sentences at the lowest level, and progresses to sentences of more than 20 words at the top level.

13. Bead Memory. (21 levels—test given at all ages). The test involves a stack of beads of four shapes and three colors. At the lowest levels, the examinee is shown a bead for 2 seconds and then must find it on a card showing beads with all the shapes and colors. For most of the test, the examinee is shown for 5 seconds the picture of a stalk with a sequence of beads on it and then must correctly reproduce from memory the sequence on his or her own stalk.

14. Memory for Digits (7 levels forward, 6 levels reversed—test begins at about age 6 years). The examiner reads a sequence of digits at a rate of approximately one per second. In the first section of the test, the examinee must repeat the digits in the order that they are read. In the second section, the examinee must recite them in reverse order.

15. Memory for Objects (7 levels—test begins at about age 6 years). A sequence of pictures of objects is shown to the examinee, one at a time. Then a picture is shown that includes all the objects that were shown in the series plus several others. The examinee must point to all objects that had been shown to him or her in the order that they had previously been shown.

Organization of the Stanford-Binet. The current version of the Stanford-Binet represents a marked shift from the theoretical position held by Binet and Terman. Until 1986, the Stanford-Binet yielded only a single global score for general intelligence. The fourth edition is grounded in a much more recent theory developed by Raymond B. Cattell and John Horn. This theory postulates two basic types of abilities—*fluid abilities,* which are free of reliance on specific learning, and *crystallized abilities,* which depend on specific experiences. The tests of the new Stanford-Binet are organized to yield scores in four areas, or dimensions, of ability. The vocabulary, comprehension, absurdities, and verbal relations tests are combined to yield a score for *verbal reasoning.* Pattern analysis, copying, matrices, and paper folding and cutting are summed to give an *abstract/visual reasoning* score. A *quantitative reasoning* scale is derived from the combination of the quantitative, number series, and equation building tests. Finally, the four memory tests yield a score for *short-term memory.* The verbal reasoning and quantitative reasoning scales are intended to represent the crystallized abilities of the Cattell-Horn theory and may be combined to give a score for such abilities, while abstract/visual reasoning is seen as a fluid ability. Short-term memory, although included in the test, was not derived from the Cattell-Horn theory. When all four area scores are combined, the resulting composite score is essentially equivalent to the general intellective dimension proposed by Spearman and measured by earlier forms of the Stanford-Binet.

Administration of the new Stanford-Binet is somewhat more complex than its predecessors. Testing starts with the vocabulary test, and the examiner begins with the items at or just below the examinee's chronological age. (A basal level is defined as the point where the child passes both items at two successive ages.) Then, more difficult items are given until the point is reached where three out of four or all four items at two successive ages are failed, which yields a ceiling.

The raw score is determined by giving credit for all items below the basal level and one additional point for each item attempted and passed. The vocabulary score and the child's age are then used to determine a starting point for each of the remaining tests. A basal level and a ceiling are found for each test in the same manner as that used for vocabulary.

A raw score is assigned in each subtest, giving the examinee credit for having passed all the easier items below the basal level. Raw scores on each of the subtests are then converted to standard scores for that age level, with a mean of 50 and a standard deviation of 8. These can be combined to yield the four area scores or a composite of all of the subtests. The scores for areas and for the total are expressed as SASs—normalized standard scores for that age level—with a mean of 100 and a standard deviation of 16.

It is possible to combine results from all of the subtests into a single score that resembles and has many of the same properties as the mental age and IQ of the earlier versions of the Stanford-Binet. However, it is also possible to work with the four area scores: verbal reasoning, abstract/visual reasoning, quantitative reasoning, and short-term memory. These area scores are all related to one another and contribute to an overall measure. But, they are sufficiently distinct so that each describes a somewhat different aspect of a person's cognitive functioning.

In the current version of the Stanford-Binet, a major effort has been made to adapt the testing to the ability level of the person being tested, so that the tasks presented are closely matched to his or her ability level. This adaptation is accomplished by using the vocabulary "routing test" to determine, in combination with chronological age, the level at which the examinee is likely to succeed. Thus, the design is to bracket the examinee's ability level as efficiently as possible to minimize time wastage on items that are too easy and frustration on items that are too hard for the examinee.

Even though the individual tests of the Stanford-Binet are quite short, they are reasonably reliable. Median Kuder-Richardson Formula 20 (KR-20) reliabilities computed within age groups for the individual tests run from 0.73 to 0.94, with all but memory for objects exceeding 0.83. Within-age-group reliabilities for the area scores are higher, and the composite score based on four area scores generally yields a KR-20 reliability in excess of 0.95.

The individual tests show moderate to high correlations with each other. Median within-age-group correlations range from 0.29 between paper folding and cutting and memory for objects to 0.73 between vocabulary and comprehension, with most in the 30s, 40s, and 50s. In general, the tests within an area correlate more highly with other tests in the same area than they do with tests in other areas. The area scores all correlate in the 60s and 70s with each other, indicating that they measure somewhat discrete concepts that share a common core. These correlations are consistent with the theory that guided the development of the instrument. Recent studies of the structure of the Stanford-Binet (Boyle, 1989; R. M. Thorndike, 1990b) have confirmed that the individual tests generally relate to each other in the manner predicted by the theory used in test development.

Wechsler Scales

The other major series of individually administered tests of general ability is the Wechsler series, the first of which, the Wechsler-Bellevue, was published in 1939. Periodically, the tests have been extended and revised. The series currently is composed of three test levels: the newly released Wechsler Preschool and Primary Scale of Intelligence Revised (WPPSI-R), the Wechsler Intelligence Scale for Children Revised (WISC-R), and the Wechsler Adult Intelligence Scale Revised (WAIS-R). These are intended, for ages 4 to 6-1/2, 6 to 16, and 16 and above, respectively. The scales were developed from the start as a set of subtests, each containing items graded in difficulty. They were also designed from the beginning to produce two subscores (verbal ability and performance ability) as well as an overall ability score. The titles of the subtests from the WISC-R, together with their arrangement into subscales and an illustrative item (similar to those included in the actual test) are shown here.

Verbal Scale

1. *General Information.* What day of the year is Independence Day?

2. *Similarities.* In what way are wool and cotton alike?

3. *Arithmetic Reasoning.* If eggs cost 60 cents a dozen, what does 1 egg cost?

4. *Vocabulary.* Tell me the meaning of corrupt.

5. *Comprehension.* Why do people buy fire insurance?

6. *Digit Span.* Listen carefully, and when I am through, say the numbers right after me.

7   3   4   1   8   6

Now, I am going to say some more numbers, but I want you to say them backward.

3   8   4   1   6

Performance Scale

7. *Picture Completion.* I am going to show you a picture with an important part missing. Tell me what is missing.

				1990		
S	M	T	W	T	F	S
		1	2	3	4	5
6	7	8	9	10	11	12
13	14	15	16	17	18	19
20	21	22	23	24	25	26
27	28	29	30	31		

8. Picture Arrangement. The pictures below tell a story. Put them in the right order to tell the story.

9. Block Design. Using the four blocks that I have given you make a design just like this one.

10. Object Assembly. If these pieces are put together correctly, they will make something. Go ahead and put them together as quickly as you can.

11. Coding. In the top row, each figure is shown with a number. Write the number that goes with each figure in the second row.

Code

Test

etc.

12. Mazes. This is a supplementary test for the performance scale. It includes pencil mazes like those found in newspapers.

Each subtest yields a separate score, which is then converted into a standard score with a mean of 10 and a standard deviation of 3 for that subtest, based on a sample of individuals of the same age as the examinee. The subtest standard scores are combined in three different groupings to yield total scores for verbal, performance, and overall abilities, and from these total scores, three different types of IQ may be read from norm tables. The three IQs are (1) a verbal IQ from subtests 1 through 6, (2) a performance IQ from subtests 7 through 11, and (3) a total IQ from the combined subtests. The separate verbal and performance IQs may have diagnostic significance in the case of certain individuals with verbal, academic, or cultural handicaps; however, such interpretations should be made only by individuals with extensive clinical training. Studies of the value of such diagnoses have yielded conflicting results. The verbal, performance, and overall IQ scores on the WPPSI-R and WAIS-R are also standard scores. The scale on all the Wechsler instruments is set to make the mean of the normative sample 100 and the standard deviation 15.

The Wechsler scales report internal consistency reliabilities generally in the 90s for the individual subtests. Test-retest reliabilities are somewhat lower, but generally in the 80s. Correlations of the verbal and performance Wechsler IQs with the area standard age scores of the Stanford-Binet are all above 0.60 except for correlations of the WPPSI scales with abstract/visual reasoning. Wechsler full-scale IQs correlate from 0.80 to 0.91 with the Stanford-Binet composite (R. L. Thorndike, Hagen, & Sattler, 1986a). Thus, although the two instruments were independently developed, they yield a consistent assessment of general intellectual ability.

Kaufman Assessment Battery for Children

A recent addition to the field of individual ability testing, introduced with considerable fanfare in 1982, is the Kaufman Assessment Battery for Children (K-ABC). The battery is composed of three sections, one stated to measure "sequential processing," one to measure "simultaneous processing," and one to measure "achievement." The sequential processing tests are three tests of short-term memory for a sequence of unrelated items—hand movements, digits, and unrelated words, respectively. The examinee must simply reproduce these items in the order that they were presented. The simultaneous processing tests are substantially all nonverbal. Of the seven tests, two involve encoding and memory of a visual pattern—faces in one case and spatial arrangement in the other. Two involve perceptual synthesis of incomplete visual material, with the task being to name the object partially displayed. Three require analyzing a pattern or sequence of visual material—a design, a matrix, or a picture sequence. The achievement scale includes six tests, two that test basic reading skills, a general information test requiring the naming of pictures, an "expressive vocabulary" test, a riddles test, and a test of arithmetical skills. For those tests calling for a verbal response, a key is provided for scoring responses given in Spanish.

The 16 tests in the battery yield five scores, sequential and simultaneous processing scores, an achievement score, a mental processing composite score that is a combination of sequential and simultaneous processing, and a nonverbal score that combines 6 of the 10 processing scales. Each score is scaled to have a mean of 100 and a standard deviation of 15.

The battery is designed to cover the age range from 2−6 (2 years-6 months) to 12−6. However, average performance for age 2−6 is only 3 items passed out of the 40 items on the sequential processing scale and 6 out of 55 on simultaneous processing, so the test seems better suited to children 3−6 and over. Test-retest reliabilities, over an average interval of 18 days were as follows:

	Ages 2−6 to 4−11	Ages 5−0 to 8−11	Ages 9−0 to 12−5
Sequential processing	.77	.82	.88
Simultaneous processing	.77	.88	.91
Processing composite	.83	.88	.93
Achievement	.95	.95	.97

Correlations among the above scales for the three age groups were

	Ages 2−6 to 4−11	Ages 5−0 to 8−11	Ages 9−0 to 12−5
Sequential/ Simultaneous	.41	.49	.52
Sequential/ Achievement	.46	.63	.62
Simultaneous/ Achievement	.64	.63	.69

The authors (Kaufman & Kaufman, 1983) provide a commendable amount of data on the correlations of the Kaufman scales with other established ability and achievement tests.

Taking account of its correlations with other tests, as well as the correlations among the three sections and 16 subtests, we judge that the simultaneous processing scale of the K-ABC is primarily a measure of fluid and nonverbal intelligence. The sequential processing scale also to some degree measures this ability, but in addition it provides a measure of short-term memory of a series of disconnected stimuli. The achievement scale seems to measure developed or crystallized intellectual abilities, because its highest correlations are with verbal scales on the WISC-R and the Cognitive Abilities Test (CogAT) (a group test of intellectual ability discussed in the next section) rather than with scores on school achievement batteries. The authors imply that the distinctions between the three scales, and to some extent the distinctive features each of the 16 subtests, will be useful for educational diagnosis and remediation, but in large part, these values remain to be demonstrated.

Abbreviated Individual Tests

A major problem in using individually administered tests of aptitude is that they are very costly. A trained examiner must spend at least 1 hour with each examinee. This costliness has led to three responses, the development of group-administered tests such as those described in the next section, the use of short forms of the Stanford-Binet and Wechsler scales in which only some of the tests are given, and the preparation of some short individual tests.

Various short forms of the Wechsler scales have been proposed. Sattler (1982) provides a table containing estimates of the correlations between various combinations of two to five subtests with the composite IQ on the WPPSI and WISC-R. The two-test combinations generally yield correlations in the 0.80s, and using more subtests produces higher correlations.

Several authors provided suggested selections of tests to use as a short form in earlier versions of the Stanford-Binet. With the publication of the new edition, it has become possible to use individual subtests as well. Based on the median correlations reported in the technical manual (R. L. Thorndike, Hagen, & Sattler, 1986a) of the individual subtests with the full composite score, the best two tests to use to represent the full test are vocabulary (correlation coefficient $[r] = 0.81$) and quantitative ($r = 0.82$). An optimum four-test composite that samples all four areas would be vocabulary, quantitative, pattern analysis ($r = 0.74$), and bead memory ($r = 0.72$) (R. L. Thorndike, Hagen, & Sattler, 1986b). Each of these tests is used at all age levels. The authors suggest adding memory for sentences and comprehension to these four to give "a reasonably accurate estimate of overall cognitive level and pattern of cognitive abilities" (p. 35).

The consistent finding that verbal tests show high correlations with broader measures of intellectual ability has led to the development of various short tests based entirely on verbal material. A particularly popular type, because of its inherent interest to children, is the picture vocabulary test, of which the Peabody Picture Vocabulary Test (Dunn & Dunn, 1981) is probably the best known. Each of the two forms of the test has 175 plates, each containing four pictures. The examiner gives a word, and the examinee indicates the picture that relates to the word. The test takes about 15 minutes and provides an indication of general verbal ability.

Group General Ability Tests

There are certain advantages to having a test administered to a person in a one-on-one relationship by a trained examiner. No reading need be required on the part of the examinee, so it is possible to test young children and people of limited literacy. An empathic and perceptive examiner can maintain a continuing high level of motivation on the part of the examinee.

Furthermore, the examiner can observe aspects of the examinee's behavior in the testing session that are not reflected in the numerical score. However, there are also disadvantages. Examiners may vary in their presentation of tasks and their evaluation of responses. Some examinees may be self-conscious in a face-to-face situation and block on responses that they really know. But the most critical point is that individual testing is expensive—prohibitively so if information is desired on each child in a school or on each applicant for admission to an educational institution or a training program. Primarily because of cost considerations, most ability testing has become group testing, using paper-and-pencil testing instruments that can be scored objectively.

There are a number of series of group tests on the market. Three relatively widely used series are the Test of Cognitive Skills produced by the California Test Bureau (CTB) and McGraw-Hill, the Otis-Lennon School Ability Test published by the Psychological Corporation, and the School and College Ability Tests prepared by the Educational Testing Service and CTB/McGraw-Hill. However, we will illustrate this category of test with the series with which we are intimately acquainted—the CogAT, with which two of the authors of this book (RLT and EPH) have been associated for the past 30 years. Like many other group-administered tests of general ability, these are multiscore tests providing one score for verbal ability, one for quantitative ability, and one for nonverbal ability. The most recent edition (R. L. Thorndike & Hagen, 1987) of these tests is composed of nine subtests; see sample test items in Figures 12.1, 12.2, and 12.3.

The tests are organized in a multilevel format and printed in a single booklet that covers the range from Grade 3 to Grade 12. (There are also primary level tests for kindergarten through Grade 3, and the publisher will provide booklets containing only a single level of the tests at a user's request.) The multilevel booklet is arranged so that testing can be carried out at any one of eight levels of difficulty, depending on where an examinee is started and stopped. The pattern is illustrated here for the sentence completion subtest and a similar pattern is used for each of the other subtests.

Pattern of item ranges for the sentence completion subtest of the CogAT

Level	Start at Item	End at Item	Usual Grade Level
A	1	25	3
B	6	30	4
C	11	35	5
D	16	40	6
E	21	45	7
F	26	50	8–9
G	31	55	10–11
H	36	60	12+

FIGURE 12.1

Sample verbal test items like those used in the Cognitive Abilities Test.

Vocabulary
Impolite:
    A. unhappy   B. angry   C. faithless
        D. <u>rude</u>   E. talkative

Sentence Completion
Mark was very fond of his science teacher, but he did not
__ _____his mathematics teacher.
A. obey   B. discuss   C. regard   D. desire   E. <u>like</u>

Verbal Classification
Dove   Hawk   Wren   Sparrow
A. moth   B. bat   C. <u>gull</u>   D. bee   E. squirrel

Verbal Analogy
Pea is to **bean** as **peach** is to
A. pit   B. tree   C. eat   D. skin   E. <u>apple</u>

FIGURE 12.2

Sample quantitative test items like those in the Cognitive Abilities Test.

Quantitative Comparison
I. 4 dimes   Mark **A** if I is more money than II.
II. 5 nickels   Mark **B** if I is less money than II.
                    Mark **C** if I is the same amount of money as II.

Number Series
18   16   14   12   10
          A. 7   <u>B. 8</u>   C. 9   D. 10   E. 12

Equation Building
1   8   9   +   –
        <u>A. 0</u>   B. 3   C.8   D. 9   E. 18

FIGURE 12.3
Sample nonverbal items like those in the Cognitive Abilities Test.

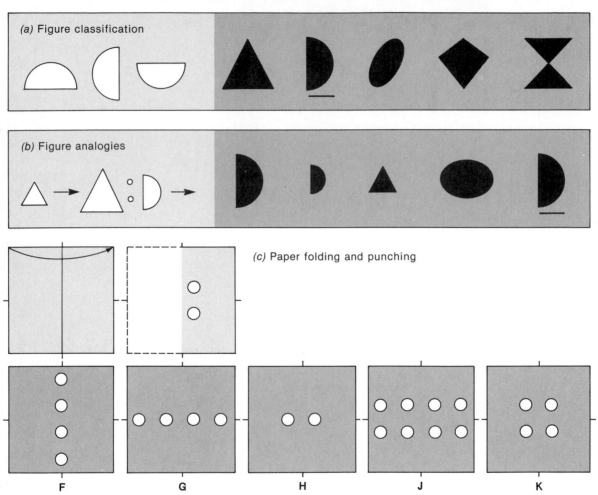

(a) Figure classification

(b) Figure analogies

(c) Paper folding and punching

F   G   H   J   K

Responses are marked on a separate answer sheet, and a different answer sheet is provided for each level, with spaces for only the items that are to be answered at that level. The test exercises get progressively more difficult, so the format permits a good deal of flexibility in selecting a test level that is appropriate in difficulty for a given class or even a particular individual. Thus, for a school located in a disadvantaged community, more accurate information about pupils would be likely to result if an easier level of the test were used, so that sixth graders, for example, might be tested with Level C rather than with Level D. More accurate information is obtained from testing when the difficulty of the test tasks closely matches the ability level of the people being tested.

Non-reading group tests can be prepared, as evidenced by the types of tasks represented in Figure 12.3. For very young children, it is, of course, necessary to avoid requiring them to read. It is also desirable to monitor rather closely the progress of children to be sure that they continue to work on the tasks—and to work on the proper tasks. The use of group testing is more questionable with young children, but it is possible after they have been in school for a while and have gotten used to following directions.

Two levels of a primary test have been prepared for the CogAT to extend downward the range of the multilevel version. These levels are intended for use from late kindergarten to Grade 3. In most instances, directions for each item are read aloud by the examiner, who proceeds at a pace that permits each child to respond by marking the test booklet. (A separate answer sheet is not used at these levels.) At these levels, the tests are composed of only two verbal, two quantitative, and two nonverbal subtests. Illustrations of some of the types of items are provided in Figure 12.4.

The CogAT provides three separate scores—verbal, quantitative, and non verbal. As was the case with the fourth edition of the Stanford-Binet, while these scores represent distinguishable dimensions of individual differences, they are not unrelated. In fact, the correlations among the three scores are quite high, averaging about 0.70. Thus, although what each measures is somewhat different from what the others measure, all three scores have a good deal in common; this commonality can be thought of as a general intellectual factor.

This point can be brought out more clearly by looking at the results from a factor analysis of the 9 subtests that compose the CogAT. Factor analysis is a procedure that undertakes to analyze the relationships among a number of different tests (or other types of measures) to identify a smaller number of more basic, underlying variables that can account for the observed pattern of relationships. The results are shown in Table 12.1.

A factor loading can be interpreted as the correlation of a test with an underlying dimension. In Table 12.1 to simplify the picture, values less than 0.10 have been omitted because such values can be considered negligible.

The pattern that emerges in this factor analysis is quite clear. For *each one* of the subtests, the predominant loading is on the general factor shared by all of them. In addition, a verbal factor of moderate size appears in all the subtests of the verbal scale and a somewhat smaller figural visualization factor in the subtests of the nonverbal scale. The quantitative subtests are not very successful in defining a quantitative factor; they tend to load almost solely on the general ability factor. In addition, each of the nine subtests involves some elements of ability that are unique to that subtest (specific factors), the nature of which is not made clear by a factor analysis.

The question that you might raise next is, how much of whatever validity is found for the CogAT is to be attributed to the common general ability factor and how much to the less extensive factors, that is, verbal and spatial. A partial answer to this question can be obtained by looking at a set of data available from one large suburban school district. The CogAT had been given in Grades 5, 7, and 9 of this school system, and it was possible to compare the results with teachers' grades in specific courses and with grade point averages in Grade 9. Selected results based on about 4,300 cases are shown in Table 12.2.

In this table, the higher correlations are generally those for the verbal and quantitative scores, with nonverbal scores tending to be a rather poor third.

FIGURE 12.4
Items like those in the Cognitive Abilities Test—Primary Levels.

Verbal

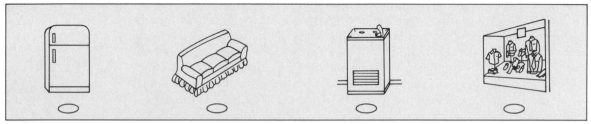

Fill the oval under the <u>refrigerator</u>.

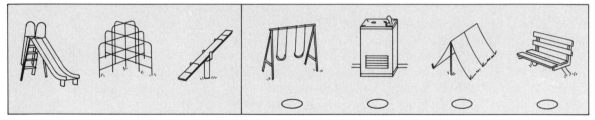

See the slide, the jungle gym and the teeter-totter. Which one belongs with them?

Quantitative

Mark the oval under the <u>biggest</u> piece of pie.

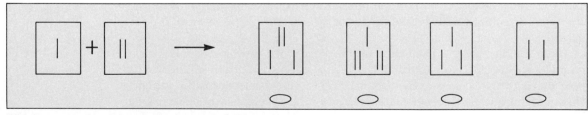

Which one on the right equals the <u>sum</u> of the two boxes on the left?

FIGURE 12.4
continued

Nonverbal

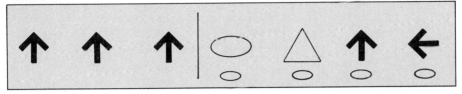

Which one on the right belongs with the three on the left?

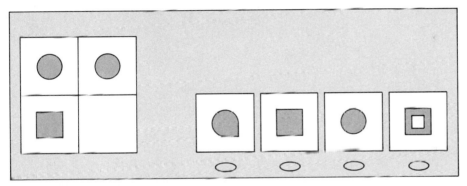

Which one on the right belongs in the empty box on the left?

Such a result might be expected because education relies heavily on the symbol systems of words and numbers. But you should note that the highest correlation is almost universally that for the simple sum of the three scores. Such a simple sum accentuates and is a reliable measure of the general factor that is shared by all three tests.

TABLE 12.1
Median Factor Loadings of the Multilevel Battery of the Cognitive Abilities Test

Subtest	General	Verbal	Quantitative	Nonverbal
Verbal classification	.71	.48		
Sentence completion	.72	.48		
Verbal analogies	.76	.42		
Quantitative relations	.82		.14	
Number series	.81		.16	
Equation building	.71		.18	
Figure classification	.72			.30
Figure analogies	.77			.34
Figure analysis	.62			.36

Note. Values less than 0.10 deleted.

TABLE 12.2

Correlations of the Cognitive Abilities Test (CogAT) Scores in Grades 5, 7, and 9 with Class Marks in Grade 9

CogAT Score	English	Social Studies	Mathematics	Science	Overall
		COURSE GRADES			
Grade 5—V	.46	.49	.34	.46	.51
Q	.45	.49	.39	.50	.54
NV	.38	.39	.34	.42	.45
Total	.48	.52	.40	.52	.56
Grade 7—V	.49	.53	.36	.49	.55
Q	.51	.54	.45	.56	.61
NV	.41	.43	.38	.46	.49
Total	.53	.56	.45	.57	.62
Grade 9—V	.52	.56	.39	.52	.58
Q	.52	.57	.48	.59	.63
NV	.42	.45	.41	.48	.52
Total	.55	.59	.48	.60	.65

Note. V = verbal; Q= quantitative; NV = nonverbal.

You can also ask what validity there would be for a *difference* score that brings out what is distinctive to one or another of the three scores. The answer for these data is the following: Across the group as a whole, almost none; the validity of a difference score for predicting relative academic performance in particular subjects is never as much as 0.05. So, in the pure prediction of academic performance, it is almost exclusively the common general ability factor that forecasts performance.

The value of the three separate scores will be found primarily when they call attention to a certain (usually small) number of children who display an uneven pattern of scores on the three tests. For *most* children, SASs, on the three tests will be similar, differing by not more than 10 points, as is indicated by the relatively high correlations among the scores. Differences of this magnitude generally have little predictive or descriptive value. However, a few individuals will be found who show differences of 20 or even 30 points. Thus, a child may be encountered who has a verbal SAS of 80 but a nonverbal score of 105. You might then be moved to ask what produced this dramatic difference. Was English not the language of the home? Some groups of Hispanic students have been found to exhibit this pattern. By contrast, some groups of Asian children have shown much higher performance on the quantitative scale than on the verbal or nonverbal scales. Was the child dyslexic? Or had there been some failure in early teaching of reading skills? And what can be done to help the child's school progress? Would remediating the verbal deficit or exploiting the nonverbal capabilities accomplish the desired goal? One can raise similar questions about other patterns of high and low scores. The key is to use marked discrepancies in scores as a warning light that there may be a nonstandard situation and that developing the best educational program for the child may require further exploration.

One way to judge whether the difference between two scores is large enough to attract attention is to consider the standard errors of measurement of the two scales. The standard error of measurement, you will remember, is an index of the random variation that we would expect in a person's score if we retested them with equivalent tests several times. Unless the difference between two scores is substantially larger than the standard error of measurement, it should probably be ignored as resulting from random fluctuations in test performance. A reasonable standard to apply is that the difference should be at least three times as large as the larger of the two standard errors. Thus, if the standard errors of measurement for verbal and nonverbal scores are 4.3 and 5.7, respectively, we should probably not interpret a score difference of less than about 18 points as important. The score difference of 25 points mentioned earlier exceeds this criterion and may therefore indicate an important inconsistency.

Tests of Multiple Abilities

Over the past 40 years, a number of test batteries have been developed that are designed to provide differential predictions of success in specific jobs or training programs. These grew out of job analyses suggesting that different jobs called for quite different abilities. Thus, each of the armed forces developed a classification battery to be used in helping to assign each recruit to a military occupational speciality in which he or she could perform effectively. Because of the large samples that accumulate in military training programs, studies based on these batteries provide some of the most substantial bodies of data that have ever been available on tests as predictors of training success and, to a lesser extent, of job success. We will refer to some of these data in the sections that follow. However, of more practical interest to people in civilian settings are batteries that have been developed for civilian use. We will describe and illustrate two of these: the Differential Aptitude Tests (DAT), designed primarily for use in high school guidance programs and the U.S. Employment Service General Aptitude Test Battery (GATB), designed for vocational counseling services and job placement.

The Differential Aptitude Test Battery

This battery was originally published by the Psychological Corporation in 1947 as a guidance battery for use at the secondary school level, and revised and streamlined forms were produced in 1963, 1972, and 1982. In the design of the battery, some attention was paid to having separate tests with low intercorrelations, but the main focus was on getting measures that would be meaningful to high school counselors. As a result, with the exception of the test of clerical speed and accuracy, intercorrelations are about 0.50. However, because the reliabilities of the parts are about 0.90, it is clear that more than one ability is being measured. The eight subtests are briefly described and illustrated here.[1]

1. Verbal Reasoning. Items are of the double-analogy type, that is,

_____ is to A as B is to _____.

Five pairs of words are provided to complete the analogy.

_____ is to night as breakfast is to _____.
- A.   supper—corner
- B.   gentle—morning
- C.   door—corner
- D.   flow—enjoy
- E.   supper—morning

2. Numerical Ability. This subtest consists of numerical problems emphasizing comprehension rather than simple computational facility.

$3 = $ _____% of 15
- A.   5
- B.   10
- C.   20
- D.   30
- E.   none of these

3. Abstract Reasoning. A series of problem figures establishes a relationship or sequence, and the examinee must pick the choice that continues the series.

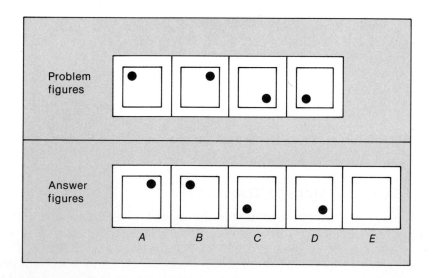

4. Spatial Relations. A diagram of a flat figure is shown. The examinee must visualize and indicate which solid figure could be produced by folding the flat figure, as shown in the example here.

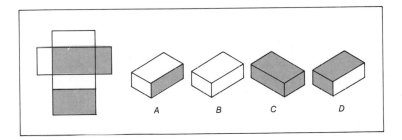

5. Mechanical Reasoning. A diagram of a mechanical device or situation is shown, and the examinee must indicate which choice is correct for the situation.

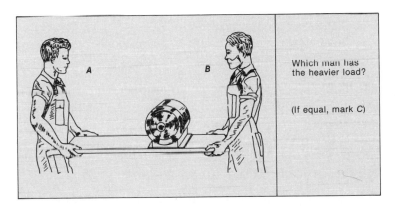

6. Clerical Speed and Accuracy. Each item is made up of a number of combinations of symbols, one of which is underlined. The examinee must mark the same combination on his or her answer sheet.

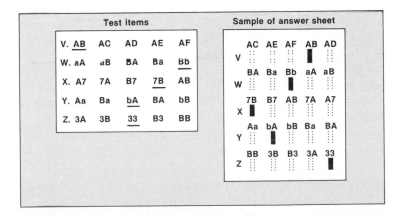

7. *Language Usage: Spelling.* A list of words is given, some of which are misspelled. The examinee must indicate for each word whether it is correctly or incorrectly spelled.

8. *Language Usage: Sentences.* A sentence is given, divided by marks into four subsections. The examinee must indicate which section—A, B, C, or D—contains an error; if there is no error, he or she marks E.

<table>
<tr><td></td><td>A</td><td>B</td><td>C</td><td>D</td><td>E</td></tr>
<tr><td>1. Ain't we / going to / the office / next week?</td><td>||</td><td>||</td><td>||</td><td>||</td><td>||</td></tr>
<tr><td>   A   B   C   D</td><td></td><td></td><td></td><td></td><td></td></tr>
</table>

The tests of the DAT are essentially power tests, with the exception of the clerical speed and accuracy test, and time limits in most cases are 30 minutes. Total testing time for the battery is about 5 to 5.5 hours, and the test requires at least two separate testing sessions. Percentile norms are available for each grade from Grade 8 through Grade 12. Norms are provided for each of the subtests and also for the sum of verbal reasoning and numerical ability, which may be used as a general appraisal of scholastic aptitude.

The General Aptitude Test Battery

The GATB was produced by the Bureau of Employment Security of the U.S. Department of Labor in the early 1940s. It was based on previous work in which experimental test batteries had been prepared for each of a number of different jobs. Analysis of more than 50 different tests that had been prepared for specific jobs indicated that there was a great deal of overlap among some of them and that only about 10 different ability factors were measured by the complete set of tests. The GATB was developed to provide measures of these different factors. In its most recent form, the GATB includes 12 tests and gives scores for nine different factors. One is a factor of general mental ability, resulting from scores on three tests (vocabulary, arithmetic reasoning, and three-dimensional space) that are also scored for more specialized factors. The other factors and the tests that contribute to each are described here. Each factor is scaled to yield scores with a mean of 100 and a standard deviation of 20.

1. *Verbal Aptitude.* The score is based on one test, Number 4—Vocabulary. This test requires the examinee to identify the pair of words in a set of four that are either synonyms or antonyms. For example,

a. cautious   b. friendly   c. hostile   d. remote
a. hasten   b. deprive   c. expedite   d. disprove

2. Numerical Ability. The appraisal of this aptitude is based on two tests. The first of these, Number 2—Computation, involves speed and accuracy in simple computation with whole numbers. For example,

Subtract (−)   256   Multiply (X)   37
                    83   8

The second test entering into the numerical ability score, Number 6—Arithmetic Reasoning, involves verbally stated quantitative problems, such as

John works for $1.20 an hour. How much is his pay for a 35-hour week.

3. Spatial Aptitude. One test, Number 3—Three-Dimensional Space, enters into appraisal of this aptitude. The examinee must indicate which of 4 three-dimensional figures can be produced by folding a flat sheet of a specified shape, with creases at indicated points.

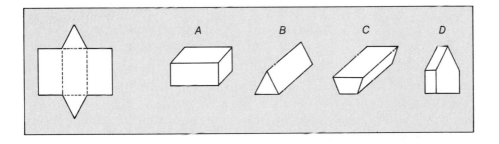

4. Form Perception. This aptitude involves rapid and accurate perception of visual forms and patterns. It is appraised in the GATB by two tests, (1) Number 5—Tool Matching and (2) Number 7—Form Matching, which differ in the type of visual stimulus provided. Each requires the examinee to find from among a set of answer choices the one that is identical with the stimulus form.

Tool Matching

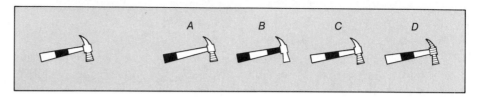

Form Matching

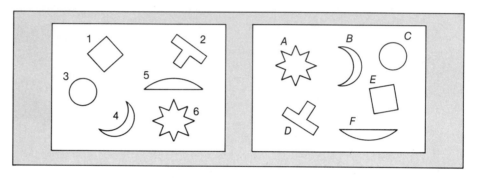

5. Clerical Perception. This aptitude also involves rapid and accurate perception, but in this case, the stimulus material is linguistic instead of purely spatial. The test, Number 1—Name Comparison, presents pairs of names and requires the examinee to indicate whether the two members of the pair are identical or whether they differ in some detail.

John Goldstein & Co.—John Goldston & Co.
Pewee Mfg. Co.—Pewee Mfg. Co.

6. Motor Coordination. This factor has to do with speed of simple but fairly precise motor response. It is evaluated by one test, Number 8—Mark Making. The task of the examinee is to make three pencil marks within each of a series of boxes on the answer sheet to yield a simple design. The results appear approximately as follows:

etc.

The score is the number of boxes correctly filled in a 60-second test period.

7. *Manual Dexterity*. This factor involves speed and accuracy of fairly gross hand movements. It is evaluated by two pegboard tests, (1) Number 9—Place and (2) Number 10—Turn. In the first of these tests, examinees use both hands to move a series of pegs from one set of holes in a pegboard to another. In the second test, examinees use their preferred hand to pick a peg up from the board, rotate it through 180°, and reinsert the other end of the peg in the hole. Three trials are given for each of these tests, and score is the total number of pegs moved or turned.

8. *Finger Dexterity*. This factor represents a finer type of dexterity than that covered by the previous factor, calling for more precise finger manipulation. Two tests, Number 11—Assemble and Number 12—Disassemble, use the same pieces of equipment, a board with 50 holes in each of two sections. Each hole in one section is occupied by a small rivet. A stack of washers is piled on a spindle. During "assemble," the examinee picks up a rivet with one hand and a washer with the other, puts the washer on the rivet, and places the assembly in the corresponding hole in the unoccupied part of the board. The task is to assemble as many rivets and washers as possible in 90 seconds. During "disassemble," the examinee removes the assembly and returns the washer to its stack and the rivet to its original place. The score is the number of items assembled or disassembled as the case may be.

The apparatus tests (non–paper-and-pencil tests)—motor coordination, manual dexterity, and finger dexterity—are all arranged so that at the completion of testing the equipment has been returned to its original condition and is ready for the testing of another person.

A comparison of the GATB and the DAT reveals that the DAT has tests of mechanical comprehension and language that the GATB lacks, while the GATB includes form perception and several types of motor tests that are missing in the DAT. Thus, the GATB is more work oriented and less school oriented in its total coverage. Inclusion of the motor tests results in somewhat lower correlations, on the average, among the GATB scales, although the "intellectual" tests correlate about as highly as those of the DAT. The correlations among the different aptitude scores of the GATB are shown in Table 12.3 for a group of 100 high school seniors. Excluding the correlations of the verbal, numerical, and spatial scores with the score for general intelligence (G) (which is composed of verbal, numerical, and spatial scores), the correlations range from -0.06 to 0.66. The three motor tests show fairly marked correlations, but they are only moderately related to the perception tests and are practically unrelated to the tests that make up the general intelligence scale. The perceptual and intellectual scores also relate closely to one another, and there is a strong relationship between the two types of perceptual ability.

There are quite substantial correlations between the corresponding factors of the DAT and the GATB. Representative values from one study (U.S. Employment Service, 1967) are as follows:

Scale	Correlation
Verbal	.74
Numerical	.61
Spatial	.65
Clerical	.57

However, the correlations are low enough so that it is clear that the tests cannot be considered identical. One important difference in the two tests is the fact that the DAT tests are in most cases purely power tests, while the GATB tests are quite highly speeded.

We must now ask how useful batteries such as these are and how much they enable us to improve the prediction of educational and occupational success over what is possible from a general measure of cognitive ability. These questions are easily raised but are very difficult to answer satisfactorily.

There have been hundreds, probably thousands, of studies in which test scores have been related to some criterion measure of success on a job. Results were found to vary from study to study and from job to job. As a consequence, personnel psychologists tended to emphasize the specificity of jobs in the abilities that they required and the need to carry out local job analyses and specific validation studies not only for each category of job but even for each local setting in which the job appeared. This demand, given the force of law in the guidelines of the federal Equal Employment Opportunity Commission, becomes a counsel of despair for using tests in vocational selection, placement, and counseling decisions because relatively few employment situations provide a flow of new employees sufficient in number to generate stable validity data. But more recently, this doctrine of specificity has been seriously questioned. It has been pointed out by Schmidt and Hunter (1981) that much of the variation in results from one study to another can be attributed to a combination of (1) small sample size, (2) differences in degree of curtailment or preselection in the group studied, and (3) differences in the nature and reliability of the criterion measure.

TABLE 12.3
Intercorrelations of Aptitude Scores (from the General Aptitude Test Battery) for 100 High School Seniors

	G	V	N	S	P	Q	K	F	M
G—Intelligence	—	.73	.74	.70	.43	.35	−.04	−.05	−.06
V—Verbal		—	.42	.40	.34	.29	.13	−.03	.06
N—Numerical			—	.34	.42	.42	.06	−.03	.01
S—Spatial				—	.48	.26	−.03	.01	−.03
P—Form perception					—	.66	.29	.27	.23
Q—Clerical perception						—	.29	.20	.16
K—Motor coordination							—	.37	.49
F—Finger dexterity								—	.46
M—Manual dexterity									—

Schmidt, Hunter, and their associates (e.g., Schmidt, Hunter, Pearlman, & Hirsh, 1985) have carried out a number of "meta-analyses" of existing data. Meta-analyses are reanalyses that pool data from the large number of existing studies, trying to correct for the deficiencies just mentioned, and to extract the findings that transcend the individual studies. The following general conclusions appear to emerge from their work.

1. General cognitive ability has significant validity for practically all jobs. The level of validity is related to the complexity of the job, being higher for more complex jobs and lower for simpler jobs.

2. The true validity is quite high, after making allowance for the depressing effects of preselection in those studies and for the unreliability of criterion measures.

3. General psychomotor ability also has some validity, its validity tending to be greater for the simpler jobs (such as machine tending or packing and wrapping) for which the validity of cognitive ability is lowest.

4. Measurement of mechanical or technical understanding adds to validity for a range of occupations in which one works with machines or repairs mechanical, electrical, or electronic devices.

5. Beyond the conclusions just listed, there is little evidence for the validity of other and more specific abilities.

The term that Schmidt and Hunter (1981) apply to their approach is *validity generalization.* Although they may have tended to overstate the uniformity of validity patterns across a range of jobs and the size of "true" test validity, their work provides a healthy corrective influence to the job specificity doctrine that was prevalent in the period from 1950 to 1980. And one thing that becomes abundantly clear from their work and some of our own (R. L. Thorndike, 1985) is that groups used in validation studies must be *much* larger than those that have appeared in validation studies in the past if data on the distinctive validity patterns for specific educational programs or specific jobs are to be demonstrated at an acceptable level of confidence.

One earlier attempt was made by Ghiselli (1973) to pool validity data for general categories of tests and fairly broad groupings of jobs. A summary of his results is presented in Table 12.4.

Ghiselli (1973) made no attempt to correct for the attenuating effects of curtailment and of criterion unreliability that tend to make reported correlations less than the true validity of predictor measures. Thus, the values shown in Table 12.4 are underestimates of the true validity by an uncertain amount. However, the values do provide some picture of the relative validity of different categories of tests in different categories of jobs.

We have looked at ability tests as predictors of educational and vocational success. We can look at the relationship between test scores and occupations in another way. We can ask how and to what extent people in different occupations differ in their test scores. We can designate this a *taxonomic,* as contrasted with

TABLE 12.4
Average Validity of Different Types of Tests for Job Performance in Broad Categories of Jobs

Jobs	Intellectual Abilities	Spatial and Mechanical Abilities	Perceptual Accuracy	Motor Abilities
Executives and administrators	.30	.23	.24	.13
Foremen	.26	.22	.27	.15
Clerical	.28	.17	.29	.16
Sales clerks	−.03	.14	−.02	.09
Salesperson	.19	.18	.04	.12
Protective service	.22	.18	.21	.14
Personal service	.27	.13	.10	.15
Vehicle operators	.16	.20	.17	.25
Trades and crafts	.25	.23	.14	.19
Industrial occupations	.20	.20	.20	.22

Note: Adapted from Ghiselli, 1973.

a *predictive,* view of test validity. That is, if we give a test to individuals employed in different occupations, will we find that their patterns of abilities differ?

Let us look first at the level of general cognitive ability. A number of data sets provide information here, but U.S. Employment Services data on the GATB have certain advantages in terms of the number and variety of occupations covered, so we will focus on those data. Among the over 400 different occupations that have been studied with the GATB, there were clearly substantial differences in average score on the *G* scale. These ranged from a high of 143 for mathematicians to a low of 55 for tomato peelers. But, before we look at the differences, let us ask how consistent they were from one sample to another in the same job. Among the jobs studied by the U.S. Employment Service, for 48 jobs there were two or more independent samples of 50 or more cases. And across these jobs, the correlation between Sample A and Sample B was 0.93. Clearly, average *G* score was a very reliable, very stable characteristic of people in a given occupation.

At the same time that we find these quite stable differences *between* occupations, we also find quite a wide range of scores *within* a given occupation. In Figure 12.5, we have shown the average *G* score for a selection of occupations and have also shown the ±1 standard deviation range, the range that includes about two-thirds of all the persons in that occupation. You can see that although the differences in average score are quite dependable, the overlapping is considerable for all but the extreme groups. It is also true that among the occupations studied by the U.S. Employment Service, most fall within a fairly narrow range in average *G* scores. This fact is shown in Table 12.5,

FIGURE 12.5
Mean general intelligence score (*G* scores) on the General Aptitude Test Battery for selected occupations. Bar around mean shows ±1 standard deviation range.

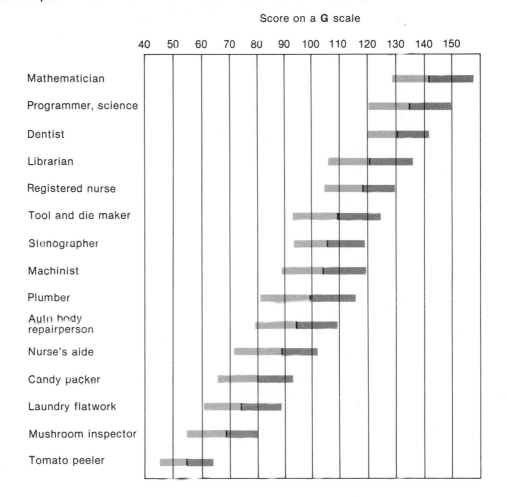

where one sees that 246 out of the 442 jobs have average *G* scores falling between 90 and 109 or within half a standard deviation of the overall population mean of 100. A minority of occupations are highly restrictive in the level of *G* score required to enter a particular occupation and then to survive in it. Thus, only 30 of the occupations were characterized by average *G* scores of 120 or over. A person of near average ability can fit into a wide range of occupational niches.

We may ask to what extent occupations display distinct and stable *patterns* of abilities. To what extent do we find occupations in which the members are especially high (or low) in verbal ability? In quantitative ability? In motor coordination or finger dexterity? The GATB data also help to answer these questions.

TABLE 12.5
Frequency Distribution of Average General Intelligence (G) Scores in Different Occupations

Score Level	Frequency
140 +	1
130–139	6
120–129	23
110–119	57
100–109	107
90–99	139
80–89	89
70–79	18
60–69	1
Below 60	1

We have taken the 48 jobs with at least duplicate samples and for each job computed the correlation between the paired samples across the eight primary scores of the GATB (excluding G). The 48 correlations ranged from very slightly negative (-0.02) to $+0.97$. The distribution of correlations is shown in Table 12.6, where the median value is 0.72. Figure 12.6 shows the pattern of scorers for duplicate samples for three jobs, one highly consistent, one of average consistency, and one completely lacking in consistency. The conclusion that may be drawn is that questions about consistency of patterning can only be answered on a job-by-job basis. Some jobs do show consistency, but others can only be characterized by general level.

TABLE 12.6
Profile Correlations for Pairs of Job Samples

Correlation	Frequency
.90–.99	11
.80–.89	9
.70–.79	7
.60–.69	6
.50–.59	6
.40–.49	1
.30–.39	3
.20–.29	1
.10–.19	1
.00–.09	2
Negative	1

FIGURE 12.6
Profiles of mean scores for pairs of job samples from the General Aptitude Test Battery (GATB). Dashed lines are for Sample 1; solid lines are for Sample 2.

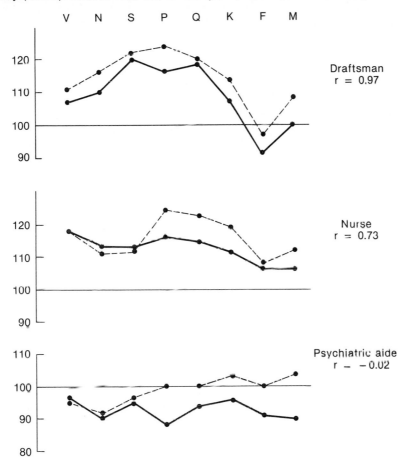

Summary

Individual tests of aptitude were first developed near the turn of the century in response to educational problems. The Stanford-Binet soon became the leading test in the United States. The demands of World War I led to the development of group aptitude tests. The Wechsler series of tests was produced first to measure adults and, later, people of all ages. Currently, the fourth edition of the Stanford-Binet, the WPPSI, the WISC-R, and the WAIS-R are the most widely used individually administered aptitude tests. Many group tests have descended in one way or another from those of World War I, of which the CogAT is a good example.

Test batteries were introduced in the early 1940s to give better differential prediction of occupational and training potential. Two of the major current batteries are the

DAT, which is designed for school counseling, and the GATB, which is used primarily in employment situations. The two batteries are similar, but the GATB places more emphasis on speed and on perceptual and clerical abilities. Recent evidence suggests that it is primarily the general ability measured by each of these batteries that is responsible for their ability to predict scholastic and occupational success.

Questions and Exercises

1. It has been proposed that all intelligence tests be called scholastic aptitude tests. What are the merits and limitations of this proposal?
2. In what respects is it preferable to rely on a good aptitude test for an estimate of a student's intelligence rather than on ratings by teachers? Are there situations where teacher ratings would be preferable?
3. In each of the following situations, would you elect to use a group intelligence test or an individual intelligence test? Why?
    (a) You are studying a boy with a serious speech impediment.
    (b) You are selecting students for admission to a nursing program.
    (c) You are preparing to counsel a high school senior on educational and vocational plans.
    (d) You are studying the academic progress of Hispanic children in a school system in Texas.
    (e) You are working with a group of boys, in a state institution, who have been convicted of criminal offenses.
    (f) You are trying to identify the sources of difficulty for a child who is a nonreader.
4. Are the usual group intelligence tests more useful for those students who are considering professional occupations or for those considering occupations in the skilled trades? Why?
5. A newspaper article reported that a young woman who had been placed in a mental hospital with an IQ score of 62 had raised her IQ score to 118 during the 3 years she spent there. What is misleading about this statement? What factors could account for the difference between the two IQ scores?
6. In what respects are intelligence tests better than high school grades as predictors of college success? In what respects are they less good?
7. Why do intelligence tests show higher correlations with standardized achievement tests than they do with school grades?
8. You are a fourth-grade teacher, and you have just received the results for your class from a citywide administration of the Cognitive Abilities Test in all fourth-grade classes. What use might you make of the results? What additional information would you need?
9. An eighth-grade student received the following standard age scores on the Cognitive Abilities Test—Verbal: Grade 4—98, Grade 6—116, Grade 8—104. What would be the best figure to represent the child's "true" scholastic ability level?
10. During the first 2 weeks of school, a school in a well-to-do community gave the Kaufman Assessment Battery for Children to all entering kindergarteners and all first graders who had not been tested in kindergarten. How desirable and useful is this procedure? Why?
11. A school system wanted to set up procedures for identifying students to receive remedial instruction in reading. Students whose reading achievement was seriously

behind their potential for learning to read were the target group. What would be a sound procedure for accomplishing this goal?

12. There have been a number of aptitude test batteries developed for use at the secondary school level and with adults but few for use at the elementary school level. Why? Is this a reasonable state of affairs?

13. What are the advantages of using a battery such as the Differential Aptitude Tests instead of tests selected from a number of different sources? What are the limitations?

14. A vocational high school offers programs to train bookkeepers, cosmetologists, dental assistants, and stenographers. Studies with the General Aptitude Test Battery have yielded data on the means (*M*s), standard deviations (*SD*s) and correlations (*r*s) with supervisory ratings shown here for these four occupations. As a counselor in the school, how would you use this information in helping students to choose among the four programs?

	Verbal			Numerical			Spatial			Manual Dexterity		
Occupation	*M*	*SD*	*r*	*M*	*SD*	*r*	*M*	*SD*	*r*	*M*	*SD*	*r*
Bookkeeper	106	16	.51	112	15	37	103	20	.38	105	21	.36
Cosmetologist	96	15	.24	92	13	.31	100	16	.25	98	17	.07
Dental assistant	106	13	.26	102	14	.34	107	16	.30	115	19	.36
Stenographer	105	12	.21	105	14	.24	106	16	.06	103	21	.09

15. How sound is the statement, "The best measure of aptitude in any field is a measure of achievement in that field to date"? What are its limitations?

16. What are the differences between a reading readiness test and an intelligence test? What are the advantages of using the readiness test rather than the intelligence test for first-grade students?

17. In what ways could a follow-up study of graduates of a high school help in improving the school guidance program?

Suggested Readings

Anastasi, A. (1988). *Psychological testing* (6th ed.). New York: Macmillan.

Bolton, B. (Ed.). (1987). *Handbook of measurement and evaluation in rehabilitation.* Baltimore: Paul Brookes.

Bond, L. (1989). The effects of special preparation on measures of scholastic ability. In R. L. Linn (Ed.), *Educational measurement* (3rd ed., pp. 429–444). New York: Macmillan.

Eysenck, H. J. (1986). Inspection time and intelligence: A historical perspective. *Personality and Individual Differences, 7,* 603–607.

Eysenck, H. J. (1988). The concept of "intelligence": Useful or useless? *Intelligence, 12,* 1–16.

Garber, H. L. (1988). *The Milwaukee Project: Preventing mental retardation in children at risk.* Washington, DC: American Association on Mental Retardation.

Gregory, R. J. (1987). *Adult intellectual assessment.* Boston: Allyn and Bacon.

Guilford, J. P. (1985). The structure-of-intellect model. In B. B. Wolman (Ed.), *Handbook of intelligence* (pp. 225–266). New York: Wiley.

Horn, J. L. (1985). Remodeling old models of intelligence. In B. B. Wolman (Ed.), *Handbook of intelligence* (pp. 267–300). New York: Wiley.

Kaufman, A. S., & Kaufman, N. L. (1983). *Kaufman Assessment Battery for Children. Interpretive Manual.* Circle Pines, MN: American Guidance Service.

Newmark, C. S. (Ed.). (1985). *Major psychological assessment instruments.* Boston: Allyn and Bacon.

Sattler, J. M. (1988). *Assessment of children's intelligence and special abilities* (3rd ed.). San Diego: Author.

Snow, R. E., & Lohman, D. F. (1989). Implications of cognitive psychology for educational measurement. In R. L. Linn (Ed.), *Educational measurement* (3rd ed., pp. 263–331). New York: Macmillan.

Sternberg, R. J. (1985). *Beyond IQ: A triarchic theory of intelligence.* Cambridge: Cambridge University Press.

Thorndike, R. L., Hagen, E. P., & Sattler, J. M. (1986). *The Stanford-Binet Intelligence Scale: Fourth edition. Technical manual.* Chicago: Riverside Publishing Company.

Woodcock, R. W. (1978). *Development and standardization of the Woodcock-Johnson Psycho-Educational Battery.* Hingham, MA: Teaching Resources Corporation.

CHAPTER 13
Interests, Personality, and Adjustment

Introduction

We turn now to published instruments and procedures that assess interests, personality traits, and personal adjustment. Our focus shifts from what a person is capable of doing with best effort to what that person is likely to do under the day-to-day circumstances of living. For example, will Mary be more content working as a lawyer or working as a laboratory technician? Does Walter have the sociability, aggressiveness, and persistence that will make him a successful salesman? Will Ellen tend to be depressed and withdraw from social contacts? Such questions as these refer to a person's typical patterns of responding to the circumstances that arise and the choices that must be made daily.

We have already seen (in Chapter 9) that one approach to appraising personality characteristics is through observation and rating by those who come into contact with the person being appraised. This approach provides a view from the outside—the impression that the person's actions make on others. A contrasting approach is to seek the person's own view of his or her feelings, likes and dislikes, and typical modes of reacting. This approach is carried out most frequently through self-report inventories that present to the examinee a standard and usually fairly extensive set of statements or questions to which he or she responds. We will describe in detail two widely used interest inventories and two of the best-known inventories that assess personality and personal adjustment. These inventories illustrate the different item formats and rationales for test development that have been used in this field, and they will introduce you to the problems and issues that arise in this area of measurement.

Interest Measurement

Strong-Campbell Interest Inventory

The Strong-Campbell Interest Inventory (SCII) is the current version of an instrument originally developed by E. K. Strong and first published in 1927 as the Strong Vocational Interest Blank (SVIB). (The original instrument was called the SVIB. A major revision of the SVIB was published in 1974 under the title, Strong-Campbell Interest Inventory. With the most recent revision of the test in 1985, the name was changed again, this time to the Strong Interest Inventory. Some of the materials related to the instrument also bear the name Strong Interest Inventory of the Strong Vocational Interest Blanks. The various names refer to relatively minor variations on the same theme. We have chosen to use the label SCII, because much of the literature of the past 15 years, including the manual for the test, has SCII in the title.) The rationale for the original development was that people who are in different occupations and who say they are satisfied in their occupations have distinctive patterns of interests. If you can determine how closely an examinee's interests match the distinctive pattern of those persons in a specific occupation, you should be able to predict how content the examinee will be in that occupation and to some extent whether he or she will actually enter and stay in the occupation. The Strong-Campbell, which follows quite closely the design of the original SVIB, is made up primarily of items in the following format (sometimes called the LID format, for Like [L] Indifferent [I], or Dislike [D]):

L	I	D	Lawyer
L	I	D	Automobile mechanic
L	I	D	Go camping
L	I	D	Chair a meeting

The examinee responds to 325 items, distributed among the following categories:

Category	Number of Items
Liking for occupations	131
Liking for activities	51
Liking for amusements	39
Liking for school subjects	36
Preference between activities	30
Liking for types of people	24
Personal characteristics	14

Items that have survived to appear in the present form are ones that show a wide range among occupational groups in terms of percentage of people choosing a given response.

Occupational Scales. The original type of score scale, which continues to be used in the present version, indicates how closely the examinee's pattern of responses matches that of people in a specific occupation. The scoring key for an occupation such as, for example, chemist, was developed by administering the inventory to several hundred employed chemists who met certain standards of length of employment and stated satisfaction with and success in the occupation. For each item, the percentage of chemists who indicated liking (or disliking) for the topic or activity was compared with the percentage making that choice in a large group of people in general assembled from many different occupations. If the two percentages differed substantially, the item was scored in the key for chemist. A person's raw score on the chemist scale would be the number of items on which he or she responded the way typical chemists did. The raw score would then be converted to a standard score in which the mean of the occupational group (chemist in this example) was set at 50 and the standard deviation at 10. For purposes of interpretation, the standard scores are characterized on the report form as follows:

55 or over	Very similar
46–54	Similar
40–45	Moderately similar
28–39	Midrange (neither similar nor dissimilar)
22–27	Moderately dissimilar
13–21	Dissimilar
12 or below	Very dissimilar

In the Strong-Campbell, scores are provided for 81 occupational groups of men and 81 occupational groups of women. Seventy-seven of the occupations are common to the two sexes, but each scale is based on a group within one sex because the pattern of interests characteristic of men in a certain occupation, for example, physical education teachers, may be different from the pattern characteristic of women in that same occupation. For eight occupations, it did not prove feasible to obtain samples of sufficient size from each sex to establish a scoring key; therefore, in those occupations, a key is provided for only one sex.

The occupational scoring keys of the Strong-Campbell are examples of a strictly empirical, atheoretical approach to interest assessment. The original pool of items was assembled with no clear rationale other than to include a wide range of stimuli that would be likely to elicit "liking" in some people and "disliking" in others. The scoring keys were developed solely on the basis of group differences, with no psychological constructs in mind on what the specific occupations represented. This method of key development is often referred to as *empirical scale construction.*

The sample from each occupation was quite large, typically over 200, so that the scoring keys are unlikely to include many items that just happened to differentiate in that particular sample of cases. Each score tells how similar an individual's interest pattern is to that typical of individuals in a specific occupation. But, it is not easy to tell what an individual is like from the fact that he received a 45 on the scale for chemist (male). What sort of individuals' interests are similar to those of male chemists? What are male chemists like anyhow?

Of course, the SCII provides a score not just for chemist but also for numerous other occupations. Quite early in the history of the SVIB, the author provided data on the correlations among the scales, finding that some of these correlations were decidedly high. Correlations for one group of science-related scales are shown here.

Job Title	1	2	3	4	5	6
1—Psychologist		.77	.72	.40	.71	.74
2—Mathematician	.77		.91	.66	.80	.72
3—Physicist	.72	.91		.85	.93	.78
4—Engineer	.40	.66	.85		.88	.52
5—Chemist	.71	.80	.93	.88		.73
6—Physician	.74	.72	.78	.52	.73	

The finding of correlations such as these encouraged grouping the scales into clusters and paying attention to the scores of an individual for all the scales in a cluster rather than to those for single occupations considered in isolation. The cluster "physical scientist" may carry somewhat more breadth of meaning than "chemist" considered by itself, especially because the scales in the "physical scientist" cluster all tend to show negative correlations with scales in the "sales" cluster. The pattern of an individual's high and low values on a scale in relation to the occupational clusters begins to generate a psychological as well as a vocational picture of that individual. However, the correlations among the scales of the SCII are difficult to interpret for two reasons.

First, scales in an occupational cluster are likely to include the same items, scored in the same direction. Likewise, scales in different clusters may well include some of the same items, but scored in opposite directions. This situation is quite a different matter from what we had in the case of a high correlation between two ability tests that included different items. The chemist and physicist scales are alike because, for some reason, the chemist and physicist reference groups responded in a similar way to the rather small set of statements that compose the SCII. The scales for other occupational groups show negative correlations because they include some of the same items, but the items are keyed in opposite directions because the members of one reference group marked "like" and the other marked "dislike."

A second confounding feature of correlations among scales on the SCII is that many people tend to mark "like" to roughly the same number of items. There is no profound meaning to be drawn from this, but it has the consequence, for purely statistical reasons, of making many of the correlations between scales negative. Thus, it would be unwise to attempt to draw substantive conclusions about the nature of interests as constructs from the fact that many of the scales for dissimilar occupations are negatively correlated.

Holland Occupational Themes.   A more focused attempt to give psychological meaning to expressions of like and dislike for occupations is found in Holland's (1985) conception of "general occupational themes." Growing out of his experience with the SVIB and reviews of previous factor analytic studies of interests, Holland concluded that there are six foci, or themes, of vocational interest that represent six sorts of individuals, which he designated realistic, investigative, artistic, social, enterprising, and conventional. Holland felt that the salience of one or more of these themes in an individual could be identified through the individual's expressed likes and dislikes for occupations. Starting with his a priori rational analysis, he assembled clusters of occupations to represent each focus. He refined the clusters through analysis of the correlations of single occupations with cluster scores in their own and the other clusters until cluster scores were developed that showed reasonably high reliability, both internal consistency and stability over time, and that were largely unrelated to one another. The foci were visualized as the apexes of a hexagon, as shown here.

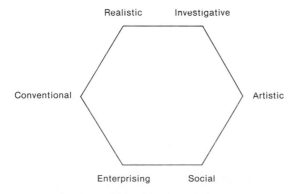

Holland viewed his six foci as a way of representing not merely groups of occupations but also patterns of personality. Support for this view was gathered from an analysis of terms used to describe individuals high on each of the six foci. Some of the frequently mentioned terms are listed here.

Realistic	Investigative	Artistic
robust	task oriented	expressive
rugged	introspective	original
practical	analytical	intuitive
strong	curious	creative
athletic	independent	nonconforming
mechanical	reserved	introspective
direct	unconventional	independent
persistent	intellectual	
aggressive		

Social	Enterprising	Conventional
sociable	aggressive	conscientious
responsible	popular	efficient
humanistic	self-confident	obedient
group oriented	cheerful	calm
understanding	sociable	orderly
idealistic	energetic	practical
helpful	verbal	possession and
	power and status	status oriented
	oriented	

In an ambitious tour de force, Gottfredson and Holland (1989) have classified all 12,860 occupations from the *Dictionary of Occupational Titles* (*DOT*) (U.S. Department of Labor, 1977, 1986) according to where each belongs in the above system. The classification was developed on the basis of the job analyses that had been carried out by the U.S. Employment Service on the full range of *DOT* occupations. This represents an impressive attempt to provide an extended catalog of occupations appropriate for individuals who display a certain profile on Holland's general occupational themes.

Because of the great overlap in item content between the older SVIB and the SCII, it was quite easy for Campbell and Hansen (1981) to incorporate the Holland structure in the scoring and interpretation of the SCII. Scores for the six general occupational themes were added to the report, supplementing the scores for the specific occupations. The correlations among the six general occupational themes of the SCII are shown in Table 13.1.

The correlations in this table tend to confirm the hexagonal structure in that the larger correlations tend to be between adjacent foci. Most of the correlations in the table are quite low, indicating that each of the six scores provides new information about an examinee.

TABLE 13.1
Intercorrelations of General Occupational Themes (Based on 300 Males and 300 Females)

Occupational Theme	Realistic	Investigative	Artistic	Social	Enterprising	Conventional
Realistic		.43	−.11	.10	.31	.29
Investigative	.43		.33	.16	−.02	.11
Artistic	−.11	.33		.21	−.09	−.18
Social	.10	.16	.21		.40	.30
Enterprising	.31	−.02	−.09	.40		.52
Conventional	.29	.11	−.18	.30	.52	

A sense of the relationships of specific occupations to the general themes can be obtained from Table 13.2, in which correlations are shown for selected occupations. For each theme, the three or four occupational scales have been included that showed the highest correlations with the theme scores. Only correlations of 0.30 or greater are reported in the table.

If you examine the two types of scales in relation to each other, you can get a better feel for each. Thus, the navy officer scale exemplifies the "realistic" theme, the mathematics and science teacher scale exemplifies the "investigative" theme, the art teacher scale exemplifies the "artistic" theme, and so forth. The manual for the SCII gives the complete table of correlations of the six themes with all the occupational scales, separately for males and females, from which Table 13.2 was extracted. Moreover, in the report form provided to counselors and clients, separate occupations are grouped according to the theme or themes considered to be salient for the occupation. Thus, the user is provided with the empirically based occupation scores, arranged according to the general themes, as well as the theme scores themselves.

Basic Interest Scales.   Scores of still a third type are also provided. These are 23 "basic interest scales," each composed of a set of homogeneous items. (Each scale is composed of 24 items). The items are homogeneous both in manifest content and in the statistical sense that the items entering into a given scale all have substantial correlations with each of the other items in that scale. The basic interest scales were derived directly from the items of the SVIB without reference to any theory. They address more specifically vocational themes than do the themes of Holland's model, but they are broader in content than the occupational scales and reflect some of the high correlations among those scales.

Table 13.3 lists all the basic interest scales and shows all correlations of 0.30 or greater between these and the scales for Holland's general occupational themes. The basic interest scales are also shown on the SCII report form. Thus, the counselor and the counselee are encouraged to proceed from the quite broad and theory-based occupational themes through the content-based homogeneous area scores to the empirically determined scales for specific occupations. The instrument is now eclectic in the foundations on which its scor-

TABLE 13.2

Correlations of Selected Occupational Scales with General Occupational Themes (Average of Male (m) and Female (f) Groups)

Occupational Scale[a]	GENERAL OCCUPATIONAL THEME					
	Realistic	Investigative	Artistic	Social	Enterprising	Conventional
Navy officer (m)	.74	.36				.48
Vocational agriculture teacher (m)	.62	.54		.42	.42	.54
Engineer (m)	.60	.54				
Mathematics and Science teacher (m)	.54	.82				
Chemist (m)	.73				−.47	
Medical technician (m)	.48	.76				.32
Physician (m)	.35	.80	.30			
Art teacher (f)		.32	.78			
Musician (f)			.66	−.36	−.40	−.58
Sociologist (m)		.57	.66		−.38	−.30
Guidance counselor (m)				.81	.59	.42
YMCA director (m)				.80	.57	
Special education teacher (m)			.30	.77	.30	
Buyer (m)		−.31		.37	.86	.46
Life insurance agent (m)				.52	.80	.38
Purchasing agent (f)		.32			.87	.54
Realtor (f)					.81	.34
Restaurant manager (f)				.30	.84	.54
Banker			−.50		.50	.78
Credit manager (m)			−.46		.70	.72
Internal Revenue Service agent (m)				.47	.71	.72

Note. Only correlations of 0.30 or greater are reported here.

[a]m = male; f = female.

TABLE 13.3

Correlations of Basic Occupational Scales with General Occupational Themes (Average of Male and Female Groups)

Basic Occupational Scale	GENERAL OCCUPATIONAL THEME					
	Realistic	Investigative	Artistic	Social	Enterprising	Conventional
Agriculture	.58					
Nature	.45	.38				
Adventure	.40					
Military	.39					.31
Mechanical	.89	.50				.31
Science	.42	.91				
Mathematics	.38	.60				.48
Medical science	.32	.66	.30	.34		
Medical service	.30	.34		.44		
Music and drama		.32	.86			
Art			.88			
Writing		.34	.78			
Teaching		.32	.32	.64		
Social service				.84	.32	
Athletics				.44	.30	
Domestic arts				.43		
Religious				.58		.31
Public speaking			.34	.52	.50	
Law and Politics				.40	.40	
Merchandising				.41	.88	
Sales					.89	.44
Business management					.82	.60
Office practice				.50	.46	.81

Note. Only correlations of .30 or greater are reported here.

ing systems have been based and comprehensive in the information that it provides.

A replica of the SCII profile form is shown in Figure 13.1. The authors suggest that the interpretation of the profile of a counselee start with consideration of the general occupational themes. These themes are reported as standard scores (mean is 50 and standard deviation is 10) based on a people-in-general group composed of equal numbers of males and females. Verbal characterizations ranging from "very high" through "high" and "moderately high" to "very low" are also presented. The comments are based on the percentile rank of the score within the individual's own sex group. A letter code is assigned to the counselee that reflects his or her highest themes. For example, a counselee who was described as "high" on enterprising (designated E) and "high" on realistic (designated R) would be coded ER.

The basic interest scales and the occupational scales are grouped according to the general occupational theme with which they have shown the highest correlations. Inspection of high scores on these two types of scales can confirm or modify the coding for an individual and provide a more specific picture of content areas and single occupations that stand out within the broader theme categories. Thus, high scores on the scales for interest in sales and business management activities would add detail to a high score on the enterprising theme. Likewise, high scores for scales in the areas of adventure, military activities, and mechanical activities would add substance to the realistic theme. Further exploration with the individual would be needed to determine whether the military and protective service activities had any realism in light of the young person's circumstances and family tradition. Each area in which high scores occur provides occupational possibilities to be investigated.

On the profile, each occupation has been assigned a theme code consisting of one to three letters, based on the high point or points of the group average on the general occupational themes for the sample of individuals on which the scale was based. An expanded list of 285 occupations, grouped by their code designation, is shown in an appendix of the SCII manual (Hansen & Campbell, 1985), and, of course, 12,860 occupations are coded in Gottfredson and Holland's book (1989), to which reference was made earlier. These sources make it easy to display to a counselee an extended list of occupations that have been attractive to people with interests similar to those that he or she has expressed. Thus, in the list of 285 occupations, there are 42 that are coded either E, R, ER, or RE (as well as many others coded E or R followed by some other secondary theme). The 42 occupations include the following:

○ Agribusiness manager	○ Rancher
○ Auctioneer	○ Retailer
○ Building contractor	○ Secret service agent
○ Corrections officer	○ Sports reporter
○ Electrician	○ Stockbroker
○ Funeral director	○ Traveling salesman.

So a long list is provided of possibilities that appear to be congruent with the client's interests. These possibilities may be considered in light of the coun-selee's individual abilities, training, and cultural background.

We turn now to the reliability and validity of SCII scores. The evidence reported on reliability consists primarily of test-retest correlations over various time intervals. The manual for the SCII reports average values as shown here for the three types of scores:

	Test-Retest Interval		
Scale	2 Weeks	30 Days	3 Years
General occupational themes	.91	.86	.81
Basic interest scales	.91	.88	.82
Occupational scales	.91	.89	.87

All three types of scales show reasonable stability, although over the longer time period, the scales for specific occupations held up somewhat better than the others. Studies of the original SVIB provide information on stability of the occupational scales over extended periods of time as well as some indication of the relationship of stability to age at the time of original testing. The data have been summarized in the manual (Hansen & Campbell, 1985) as follows:

	Test-Retest Interval					
Age at First Testing	2 Weeks	1 Year	2–5 Years	6–10 Years	11–20 Years	20+ Years
17–18		.80	.70	.65	.64	
19–21	.91	.80	.73	.67	.67	.64
22–25			.78	.69	.75	.72
25+			.77	.81	.80	

Note. No data exist for time spaces where cells are blank.

The data indicate that interests become increasingly stable during adolescence and early adulthood and that, as one might expect, shifts are more common over longer intervals but that there is still a substantial core of consistency over even the longest intervals.

It is not entirely clear what a prospective user should offer as evidence of the validity of an interest inventory. First, he or she can inquire into the meaning-fulness of the constructs on which the inventory is based. For the occupational scales, the case has rested in large part on the effectiveness of the scales in differentiating members of a specific occupation from the broad reference group of people in general. Although the situation varies somewhat from one occupation to another because some occupational groups are more distinctive than others, a rough but reasonably accurate overall summary would be that approximately 10% of people in general would be rated "high" or "very high" on an occupational scale, in comparison with 65%–70% of those people actually in the occupation.

The meaningfulness of the constructs implied by Holland's six general occu-pational themes lies in the manner in which each relates to a number of occu-

FIGURE 13.1
Strong Interest Inventory

Source: Reproduced by special permission of the distributor, Consulting Psychologists Press, Inc., Palo Alto, CA, for the publisher, Stanford University Press, from the Strong Interest Inventory, Form T325 of the Strong Vocational Interest Blank by David Campbell, E. K.

pational scales, to item content areas expressed in the basic interest scales, and to characterization of people high on each of the six themes.

Of special interest in the appraisal of the validity of interest measures is the effectiveness of such measures as predictors of subsequent occupational histories. What percentage of individuals end up in occupations for which their inventory scores indicated high or very high interest? In view of the thousands

FIGURE 13.1
continued

STRONG INTEREST INVENTORY OF THE
STRONG VOCATIONAL INTEREST BLANKS   PAGE 2

PROFILE REPORT FOR: DATE TESTED:

ID: DATE SCORED:
AGE: SEX:

OCCUPATIONAL SCALES	STANDARD SCORES F M	VERYDISSIMILAR	DISSIMILAR	MODERATELYDISSIMILAR	MID-RANGE	MODERATELYSIMILAR	SIMILAR	VERYSIMILAR

SOCIAL

GENERAL OCCUPATIONAL THEME - S 30 40 50 60 70

	F M	Occupation	Std
	SA (AS)	Foreign language teacher	(AS)
	SA SA	Minister	
	SA SA	Social worker	
	S S	Guidance counselor	
	S S	Social science teacher	
	S S	Elementary teacher	
	S S	Special education teacher	
	SRI SAR	Occupational therapist	
	SIA SAI	Speech pathologist	
	SI (ISR)	Nurse, RN	(ISR)
	SCI N/A	Dental hygienist	N/A
	SC SC	Nurse, LPN	
	(RIS) SR	Athletic trainer	(RIS)
	SR SR	Physical education teacher	
	SRE SE	Recreation leader	
	SE SE	YWCA/YMCA director	
	SEC SCE	School administrator	
	SCE N/A	Home economics teacher	N/A

BASIC INTEREST SCALES (STANDARD SCORE)
- TEACHING F M
- SOCIAL SERVICE F M
- ATHLETICS F M
- DOMESTIC ARTS F M
- RELIGIOUS ACTIVITIES F M

ENTERPRISING

GENERAL OCCUPATIONAL THEME - E 30 40 50 60 70

	F M	Occupation	Std
	E ES	Personnel director	
	EE E	Elected public official	
	ES ES	Life insurance agent	
	EC E	Chamber of Commerce executive	
	EC EC	Store manager	
	N/A ECR	Agribusiness manager	N/A
	EC EC	Purchasing agent	
	EU E	Restaurant manager	
	(AR) EA	Chef	(AR)
	EC E	Travel agent	
	ECS E	Funeral director	
	(CSE) ESC	Nursing home administrator	(CSE)
	EC ER	Optician	
	E E	Realtor	
	E (AR)	Beautician	(AE)
	E E	Florist	
	EC E	Buyer	
	EI EI	Marketing executive	
	EIC ECI	Investments manager	

BASIC INTEREST SCALES (STANDARD SCORE)
- PUBLIC SPEAKING F M
- LAW/POLITICS F M
- MERCHANDISING F M
- SALES F M
- BUSINESS MANAGEMENT F M

CONVENTIONAL

GENERAL OCCUPATIONAL THEME - C 30 40 50 60 70

	F M	Occupation	Std
	C C	Accountant	
	C C	Banker	
	CR IS	IRS agent	
	CES CES	Credit manager	
	CES CES	Business education teacher	
	(CS) CES	Food service manager	(CS)
	(ISR) CSE	Dietitian	(ISR)
	CSE (ESC)	Nursing home administrator	(ESC)
	CSE CSE	Executive housekeeper	
	CS (CES)	Food service manager	(CES)
	CS N/A	Dental assistant	N/A
	C N/A	Secretary	N/A
	C (R)	Air Force enlisted personnel	(R)
	CRS (RC)	Marine Corps enlisted personnel	(RC)
	CRS CR	Army enlisted personnel	
	CIR CIR	Mathematics teacher	

BASIC INTEREST SCALES (STANDARD SCORE)
- OFFICE PRACTICES F M

ADMINISTRATIVE INDEXES (RESPONSE %)

OCCUPATIONS	%	%	%
SCHOOL SUBJECTS	%	%	%
ACTIVITIES	%	%	%
LEISURE ACTIVITIES	%	%	%
TYPES OF PEOPLE	%	%	%
PREFERENCES	%	%	%
CHARACTERISTICS	%	%	%
ALL PARTS	%	%	%

Strong Jr. & Jo-Ida Hansen. Copyright 1974, 1981, and 1985, by the Board of Trustees of Leland Stanford Junior University.

of specific occupations and the limited number of scales of the SVIB and the SCII, serious problems arise in trying to estimate congruence between actual occupation entered and interest scale scores. In spite of these problems, however, studies by different investigators are in reasonably good agreement in indicating that about 50% of individuals end up in occupations consistent with their interests expressed at about 20 years of age. This agreement certainly represents a substantial relationship and, in view of the many life factors in addition to interest that can influence an individual's choice of occupation, can be considered evidence of rather good predictive validity for the instrument.

Career Assessment Inventory

A recent inventory, frankly modeled on the Strong-Campbell, is Johansson's Career Assessment Inventory (CAI). The CAI, like the SCII, provides general theme scales, basic interest scales, and occupational scales, but the primary focus is on nonprofessional occupations. A total of 91 occupational scales are provided covering occupations varying widely in type and level; for example, the CAI has scales for accountant as well as for waiter/waitress. Many of the occupational samples on which the keys are based were relatively small (under 100) and included both males and females, the proportions varying from job to job, so that you feel that the scales are generally not as firmly established as those for the SCII. However, the CAI offers advantages in the occupations covered if you are working with high school students who do not plan to go to college or train for a professional or executive career.

Self-Directed Search

An instrument that was derived directly from Holland's model of occupational themes is the Self-Directed Search (SDS) (Holland, 1973, 1985). In this inventory, 228 items are used to provide scores on the six themes, realistic, investigative, artistic, social, enterprising, and conventional. Three-letter codes are based on the pattern of these scores and then used to enter an "occupation finder" containing over 1,100 occupations. Those occupations that correspond to the code are suggested for further consideration.

As its name implies, one feature of the SDS is that it is designed to be used by an individual without the aid of a counselor. The directions for filling out, scoring, and interpreting the inventory are intended to be sufficiently complete that individuals can use the results directly. For example, it could be administered by a classroom teacher to help students explore possible career options. The purpose of the SDS is to simulate a career counseling interview. However, it is doubtful whether completely naive students can reach useful interpretations without assistance.

Kuder Preference Record and Kuder Occupational Interest Survey

Another early entrant into the field of interest measurement was the Kuder Preference Record (KPR). This inventory contained major differences from the original SVIB both in its item format and in its underlying rationale. The items were organized in sets of three that appeared somewhat like this:

Like most	Like least	Go for a hike in the woods
Like most	Like least	Play a musical instrument
Like most	Like least	Analyze data on a computer

The examinee was required to choose from each triad which of the three activities he or she would enjoy most and which least. Thus, the choices were *forced* and each examinee had to express the same total number of likes and dislikes. Whenever one activity was chosen, the competing activities in the set had to be rejected. This process produces what are called *ipsative* scores—scores that express relative preference *within* that person. In fact, the sum of the scale scores for a person who responds to every item will be the same, regardless of the pattern of likes and dislikes chosen. As a consequence, every person's interest profile must have both peaks and valleys, and every person must show the same average level of interest as every other person. This fact accentuates the tendency that we mentioned earlier for the scales to be artificially negatively correlated. With fully ipsative scales, roughly two-thirds of the scale intercorrelations will be negative.

Interest Measurement and Response Sets.   In a test format such as that of the Strong-Campbell, there is no *necessary* limit to the number of likes (or dislikes) that a person can express. (Although, as we noted earlier, there seem to be rough interpersonal consistencies.) This free-choice format raises problems with what have been called *response sets*. We will mention two. One is called *acquiescence,* or "yea-saying." This response set is simply a propensity for accepting statements. In the context of the Strong-Campbell, it would show up as a record in which a great many of the items were marked "like." In an attitude questionnaire, it would appear as a tendency to agree with statements, regardless of their content. A second response set is called *social desirability.* Here, the tendency is to choose responses that would be approved (or acceptable) in the wider society, that is, to say the "right" thing. Interest statements are relatively neutral in value, so a social desirability set is not likely to become a serious problem with them. However, we will see that this type of response set can become a problem in inventories dealing with measures of personal adjustment.

Response sets are undesirable because they cause scores to be influenced by factors other than those that we are trying to assess. The forced-choice format, such as that in the Kuder Preference Record, immediately rules out individual differences in acquiescence, and if the choices in a set are carefully matched, it can minimize any effects of social desirability response set as well.

The rationale on which the KPR was developed is similar in many respects to that used by Holland—an a priori identification of a number of categories of interest and the selection, partly on rational and partly on statistical grounds, of a set of items to represent each. The 10 categories included in the KPR were outdoor, mechanical, computational, scientific, persuasive, artistic, literary, musical, social service, and clerical. While copies of the KPR can still be found, it is no longer offered for sale. It has been replaced by the Kuder Occupational Interest Survey (KOIS).

The Kuder Occupational Interest Survey.   The KOIS, in contrast to the KPR, applies the Kuder forced-choice triads directly to occupational interpretations. The KOIS is composed of 100 triads. It was administered to samples from various occupations, and for each occupational group, the percentage selecting a given member of the triad as most, intermediate (neither most nor least), or least preferred was determined. These percentages can be stored in the memory of a computer so that the choices made by an examinee can be compared with them. In effect, the examinee's responses are correlated with those of each occupational group, and the correlations are reported as scores. Thus, scores can theoretically range from -1.00, indicating perfect disagreement between the client and an occupational group, to $+1.00$, indicating perfect agreement. The highest correlations identify the occupations to which the examinee's pattern of responses is most similar.

On the KOIS record form, correlations of the individual's responses with those of a reference group are reported for 126 occupations and 48 college majors. Some of the scales have been developed for males, some for females, and some for both groups. In addition, a verification score and eight scores for research purposes are reported. These scores are printed out on the record form in order from high to low. A typical range of values for an examinee might be 0.25–0.55. The publisher recommends that special attention be paid to all scales within a range of 0.06 from the highest scale, and these are starred on the report form. The most recent form of the KOIS has added 10 broad homogeneous scores labeled vocation interest estimates. These are similar to the interest area scores from the original KPR and can also be converted into Holland's themes.

A further type of analysis, focusing on specific pairs of occupations, would be possible if there were certain pairs about which the examinee particularly wanted feedback. For each response made by Examinee X, you would look at the difference between Job A and Job B in percentage of examinees selecting that response (i.e., percentage of Job A − percentage of Job B). These differences could be summed over the whole set of Examinee X's responses. If the sum was positive, Examinee X would have responded in a pattern more like that of people in Job A, while if it were negative, Examinee X would have responded more like those in Job B. The size of the sum would reflect the decisiveness of the difference or similarity. With modern computers, such comparisons can readily be made, and they will give a focused answer (i.e., one that is precise and relates directly to the question asked) to such counselee concerns as, do my interests match more closely those of a lawyer or those of an accountant? However, the publishers do not currently provide such an analysis.

Personality Assessment

We shift now from measures of interest to measures of temperament and personal adjustment. Instead of asking how well the person's tendencies and preferences match those of particular groups of people, we wish to ask how well the person is likely to be able to cope with the stresses of everyday life or with exceptional life events. Does this person tend to be anxious or calm, outgoing or reserved, trusting or suspicious?

Measures of personality have been developed for two somewhat different purposes. Some inventories, such as the Sixteen Personality Factor (16PF) Questionnaire, seek to describe the normally functioning person and to give guidance in dealing with minor problems of adjustment. Others, such as the Minnesota Multiphasic Personality Inventory (MMPI), focus on persons with more severe problems and attempt to diagnose serious mental disorders.

Sixteen Personality Factor Questionnaire

In our first personality measure, the 16PF, we see yet another approach to inventory development—that of *factor analysis*. Factor analysis provides a way of analyzing the pattern of correlations among the scores on a number of different measures to identify a limited number of more fundamental variables that can account for the complete pattern of observed relationships. In the 1940s, R. B. Cattell carried out a series of studies of personality ratings, self-report inventories, and behavioral personality measures and arrived at a set of 16 dimensions that he felt were needed to describe a person's personality fully. To be useful, each such personality dimension must show a fair degree of homogeneity within its own domain and be clearly distinct from the other dimensions in the personality description. Soon, we will look at some data that indicate how well the 16PF meets that standard.

Scales of the Sixteen Personality Factor Questionnaire.   Items on the 16PF are in a three-choice format such as that illustrated in the following four examples:

I can find enough energy to face my difficulties
(a) always
(b) generally
(c) seldom

I hold back from criticizing people and their ideas
(a) yes
(b) sometimes
(c) no

I prefer semiclassical music to popular tunes.
(a) True
(b) Uncertain
(c) False

On social occasions, I
(a) readily come forward
(b) respond in between
(c) prefer to stay quietly in the background

Each of the 16 scales is composed of either 10 or 13 items formated like these examples. The item is scored either 0, 1, or 2, depending on the alternative chosen, so raw scores can extend from 0 to 20 or 26. Raw scores are converted to standard scores on a 1–10 scale. With single scales as short as these, it is not surprising that the reliability of the scores is rather low. However, alternate forms are available and can be added if time permits and it is important to get more reliable measures.

The scales of the 16PF provide an example of *bipolar scales;* that is, each scale is characterized by the two extremes of a trait dimension. Each scale is also given a one- or two-character designation. Thus, one of the scales measures the bipolar dimension of tense-relaxed, and it has the label Q_4. The names used for these traits in the 16PF are often special terms coined by Cattell for use in his personality theory. In Table 13.4, and the discussion that follows, we have substituted commonly understood terms for the actual scale titles. Also, we have adopted the convention of referring to each scale by the label of its positive or socially desirable pole. "Tense" people would earn high scores on scale Q_4, so the label Q_4- indicates that the scale has been reversed to give high scores to relaxed people. Scales O (self-assured), Q_4 (relaxed), L (trusting), Q_2 (group

TABLE 13.4
Scales for Sixteen Personality Factor Questionnaire, with Reliabilities and Significant Intercorrelations

Trait[a]	Reliability (Form A with B)	Significant Correlations[b]
C, Emotionally stable	.54	$(O-)$ .97, (Q_4-) .95, $(L-)$ .78, (Q_3) .77
O−, Self-assured	.59	(C) .97, (Q_4-) .94, $(L-)$ .81, (Q_3) .69, (H) .55
Q_4-, Relaxed	.62	(C) .95, $(O-)$ .94, $(L-)$ .81 (Q_3) .79
L−, Trusting	.37	(C) .78, $(O-)$ .57, (Q_4-) .81 (Q_3) .56, (E) −.69
Q_3, Controlled	.43	(C) .77, $(O-)$ .69, (Q_4-) .79 $(L-)$ .56, (G) .90
G, Conscientious	.47	(Q_3) .90
A−, Outgoing	.57	(Q_2-) .69, (F) .51
Q_2-, Group dependent	.39	(A) .69, (F) .51, (H) .62
F, Happy-go-lucky	.61	(A) .51, (Q_2-) .69, (H) .78 $(N-)$ .70, (E) .69
H, Venturesome	.71	(Q_2-) .62, (F) .78, (E) .65, $(O-)$ .55
E, Assertive	.52	(F) .69, (H) .65, $(N-)$ .94, (Q_1) .79, (M) .57, $(L-)$ −.69
N−, Artless	.21	(E) .94, (F) .70
Q_1, Radical	.34	(E) .79, (M) .82
M, Imaginative	.40	(E) .57, (Q_1) .82
I, Tender minded		
B, Intelligent		

[a]Trait names are given in common terminology rather than by the scale names used in the instrument. Traits have been rearranged to show groupings. Trait names with a minus sign have been reversed to make the "favorable" end the positive end of all traits.
[b]Correlations have been corrected for unreliability (see Chapter 4).

dependent), and N (artless) have been reversed. Table 13.4 also shows the reported reliabilities of the scales and identifies other scales on the instrument with which the given scales have significant overlap, that is, a correlation corrected for unreliability of 0.50 or higher.

It is clear that there are several clusters of related scores. The five traits labeled, emotionally stable, self-assured, relaxed, trusting, and controlled (with their opposite extremes designated easily upset, apprehensive, tense, suspicious, and undisciplined, respectively) are so highly correlated that you may question whether they should be thought of as separate scores. Collectively, they seem to define a broad factor of level of emotional adjustment. Cattell identifies such a factor in further analyses of his instrument. Certainly, the five scores should be looked at together in any interpretation of an individual's record.

A second cluster of scales, but with somewhat less complete overlapping, is composed of the scales designated outgoing, group dependent, happy-go-lucky, and venturesome (as opposed to reserved, self-sufficient, serious, and shy, respectively). Collectively, these seem to represent the polarity of extroversion versus introversion, referring to related but still distinguishable aspects of this familiar personality dimension.

A third possible grouping is composed of assertive, artless, radical, and imaginative (as opposed to submissive, shrewd, conservative, and conventional, respectively.) This cluster suggests an assertiveness, in relation to both people and ideas However, there remains a reasonable amount of uniqueness in each of the component scales, so that this grouping is less well defined and each component scale makes some distinctive contribution to the personality description.

The other three scales (conscientious unconscientious, tender minded-tough minded, and intelligent-unintelligent) do not have patterns of significant correlations with other scales that would indicate their inclusion in one of the clusters.

All in all, we may question how useful the full set of 16 personality dimensions is, because of the noted overlapping. Just as we found overlapping in ability dimensions, a degree of overlapping appears in certain of these personality dimensions. Three or four broad aspects of personality stand out clearly, but further detail needs to be interpreted with a good deal of caution. Other analyses have suggested as many as five broad personality dimensions: extroversion, agreeableness, conscientiousness, emotional stability, and intelligence or openness.

Personality Description.   The orientation of the 16PF is primarily toward describing patterns of normal personality. As in all self-descriptive inventories, the validity of the scores as a *description* of a person depends on the willingness of the examinee to respond with what he or she believes to be the truth and to some extent on the examinee's self-insight. The precision of the description is limited by the low reliability of some of the scores, but reliability can be increased if time permits by also giving an alternate form of the inventory and pooling the results from the two forms.

Even if one accepts the descriptive validity of the obtained personality profile, the question of *external* validity remains. For what sort of real-life decisions is a personality profile useful? The manual for the 16PF provides a substantial number of profiles showing the average scores, relative to a general norm group, of people who were in different occupations. The occupational groups highest and lowest on certain of the scales are shown here.

Trait Label	High	Low
(C) Emotionally stable	Airline pilot	Farmer
	Olympic athlete	Artist
	Airline hostess	Supermarket manager
	Air cadet	Employment counselor
(O−) Self-assured	University administrator	Farmer
	Garage mechanic	Priest, Roman Catholic
	Olympic athlete	Supermarket manager
	Psychologist	Employment counselor
(A) Outgoing	Social worker	Physicist
	Business executive	Artist
	Traveling salesperson	Research scientist
	Sales manager	Junior high school teacher
(H) Venturesome	Air cadet	Nursing student
	Airline hostess	Artist
	Garage mechanic	Farmer
	Olympic athlete	Priest, Roman Catholic
(E) Assertive	Air cadet	University professor
	Writer	Farmer
	Psychologist	Priest, Roman Catholic
	Olympic athlete	Supermarket manager
(M) Imaginative	Artist	Electrician
	Employment counselor	Cook
	Writer	Miner
	Editorial worker	Police Officer

Evidence about the personality characteristics of people in particular occupational settings might be used in much the same way that interest profiles have been used, to suggest possible occupations that an individual might find congenial or ones that would be clearly inappropriate. For example, a score at the "reserved" end of the outgoing-reserved scale might suggest that a person should not plan a career as a traveling salesperson because people in this occupation tend to be outgoing. However, there has been no systematic attempt to develop occupational personality scores for the 16PF or to validate the use of the instrument for this purpose.

Results are also presented for various groups identified as having some type of psychopathology, and certain of these groups tend to display rather extreme and deviant personality profiles. The most extreme scores (on average) appeared for a group of individuals classified as neurotic. They gave scores that would characterize them, in order of extremeness, as apprehensive, tense, easily upset, sober, submissive, and sensitive. A group of criminals showed less extreme patterns but tended to represent themselves as easily upset, apprehensive, imaginative, tense, seeking expedient solutions, and less intelligent. Psychotic groups seemed, in general, to show less distinct personality patterns. Although only certain groups show profiles that have these distinct features, perhaps for individuals the personality profile will be useful to clinicians in providing quick impressions of the type of individuals with whom the clinicians will be dealing. We will return soon to systematic computer-based procedures that have been developed for communicating such a picture.

Minnesota Multiphasic Personality Inventory

A concern for different forms and degrees of psychopathology leads naturally to the Minnesota Multiphasic Personality Inventory or MMPI. This instrument originated and was developed with the purpose of providing objective scales to yield insight into aspects of psychological disorders. The authors of the MMPI approached assessment of pathology from a completely empirical perspective. From texts describing symptoms of pathology and similar sources, a large pool of items (555) was assembled and organized for presentation to examinees in a "yes-no" format. A reference group was obtained of 724 presumably "normal" individuals (similar to Strong's people in general). Then, smaller groups of individuals, chosen to be, as far as possible, clear exemplars of particular types of disturbances, were tested. Scoring keys were developed by identifying those items that differentiated the pathological groups from the "normal" reference group.

Scales of the Minnesota Multiphasic Personality Inventory. The 10 basic scores established on this empirical basis carry the labels shown next. The labels are followed by a characterization of the group on which the scale was based. Although each scale has a label that associates it with the type of disorder that characterized the group for which its items were selected, current clinical practice does not identify any clinical syndrome with any single scale. Instead, interpretation of an MMPI profile is based on the pattern formed by the scores on several scales. The scales are numbered from 1 to 0 as shown here, and most interpretations are based on the pattern of elevated scores an individual shows:

1. *Hypochondriasis (Hs).* Individuals showing excessive worry about health, often accompanied by reports of obscure pains and disorders, but with no organic basis for the symptoms. (32 items)

2. *Depression (D).* Individuals suffering from chronic depression, feelings of uselessness, and inability to face the future. The items on this scale also reflect high personal standards and intrapunitiveness. (57 items)

3. *Conversion Hysteria (Hy).* Individuals who have reacted to personal problems by developing physical symptoms such as paralysis, cramps, gastric complaints, or cardiac symptoms or who show denial of problems. (60 items)

4. *Psychopathic Deviate (Pd).* Individuals showing lack of deep emotional response, irresponsibility, and disregard of social pressures and the regard of others. (50 items)

5. *Masculinity-Feminity (Mf).* Individuals, particularly males, tending to identify with the opposite sex rather than their own. The items also differentiate stereotypic sex role perceptions. (56 items)

6. *Paranoia (Pa).* Individuals tending to be excessively suspicious of others' motives and to be interpersonally sensitive, with feelings of being picked on or persecuted. (40 items)

7. *Psychasthenia (Pt).* Individuals troubled with excessive fears (phobias) and compulsive tendencies to perform certain acts. Item content reflects high moral standards, self-blame, and rigid impulse control. (48 items)

8. *Schizophrenia (Sc).* Individuals characterized by bizarre and unusual thoughts or behavior and a subjective life tending to be divorced from the world of reality. (78 items)

9. *Hypomania (Ma).* Individuals tending to be physically and mentally overactive, with rapid shifts in ideas or actions. (46 items)

0. *Social Introversion (SI).* High scores characterize individuals who tend to keep to themselves and not to seek the company of large numbers of other people. Low scores indicate extroversion and ascendance. (69 items)

The item pool and the empirical technique of the MMPI have appealed to psychologists interested in a wide variety of specialized problems, and over 200 different scoring keys have been developed for all kinds of special groups ranging from alcoholics to underachievers. The MMPI is alleged to be the most extensively used self-descriptive instrument in clinical practice and has been applied in a wide range of other settings. For example, Butcher (1981) has described its application in personnel selection for jobs involving a high degree of responsibility or stress.

The MMPI item pool is a somewhat unusual mixture of statements, some that have a clearly pathological import and some that are neutral and innocent sounding. These statements are spoken of, respectively, as "obvious" and "subtle" items. The mixture of the two leads to certain problems. Where a scale has a mixture of both, the two types tend to be almost completely uncorrelated, so that you have, in effect, two unrelated scores combined into one. Furthermore, many of the subtle items have been found to fail to discriminate the appropriate pathological group in new cross-validation samples (see Duff, 1965). It appears that the bulk of the continuing validity of the original scales lies in the obvious items and in the profiles.

The clearly pathological implication of many of the obvious items makes them subject to avoidance by any examinee who wants to give an impression of good personal adjustment. Recognizing this possibility, the authors were moved very early to develop a number of *validity* scales designed to identify and, in part, to correct for various types of invalidity in an examinee's response record. Four scales of this type are regularly used:

1. *?*   The number of items on which an individual refuses to mark either "yes" or "no," seen as an indication of defensiveness and withdrawal from the task.

2. *L*   The number of obviously "good" but extremely improbable behaviors that the examinee claims, seen as an indication of rather naive defensiveness and overclaiming. (15 items)

3. *F*   The number of very rare and unusual responses that the individual makes, seen as a sign that the respondent may have failed to understand or to follow the directions. (60 items)

4. *K*   The tendency to choose responses given by individuals clinically identified as exhibiting psychopathology who have shown normal profiles on the test, seen as a sign of subtle defensiveness and the tendency to describe oneself in a "socially desirable" light. (30 items)

Of these validity scales, the most interesting and controversial is the *K* scale. It is not entirely clear to what extent this scale does indeed represent defensiveness and to what extent it is an expression of a genuine, and often legitimate, positive self-image. Elevated scores on the *K* scale are characteristic of various groups of successful individuals who appear to be getting on well in life, as well as certain clinical populations. To "correct" for this defensiveness, the authors of the MMPI suggest adding a portion of the *K*-scale score to the raw scores of five of the clinical scales.

Experience has accumulated with the MMPI for almost 50 years. In the 1980s, the body of research served as a basis for a revision of the instrument (Hathaway & McKinley, 1989). The revision was intended to correct a number of deficiencies that had been noted in the original instrument. For example, new norms based on a national sample of 1,138 males and 1,462 females and with minority group representation have been developed. The original items were culled and edited to correct items with outdated or offensive content, and 154 new items were tried out. The final form of the MMPI, the MMPI-2, contains 567 items, although the "basic scales are scored from the first 370 items" (Hathaway & McKinley, 1989, p. 15).

Both test-retest and internal consistency reliability information is given for clinical scales of the new MMPI. Retest reliabilities over an average interval of 1 week ranged from 0.67 to 0.92 for a sample of 82 males and from 0.58 to 0.91 for 111 females. Coefficient alpha reliabilities from 0.33 to 0.85 are reported for males, while the female sample yielded values from 0.36 to 0.87. Because most of the item content of the revised MMPI is essentially unchanged from its predecessor, many of the same reservations about its quality as a psychometric instrument still apply.

As we already noted, interpretation of the MMPI is usually based on patterns of elevated scale scores rather than on the values of individual scales. The MMPI manual (Hathaway & McKinley, 1989) contains extensive directions on how to use eight special symbols to code the scores by their elevation to yield a profile. Generally, the pattern of the highest two or three scales, known as two-point and three-point codes, are used in interpretation to find one of 426 recognized clinical profiles.

In spite of its psychometric limitations, the MMPI has had wide acceptance and use, especially by clinical psychologists. In a sense, it can be thought of as a standardized and comprehensive, although impersonal, psychiatric interview. Thus, in addition to the scores and overall profile, the clinician may look at the responses to specific questions or groups of questions as part of the search for insights about and understanding of a client. However, such use should be limited to individuals with extensive clinical training and should serve only as the starting point for diagnosis. The test authors set completion of graduate courses in testing and in psychopathology as minimum educational standards for using the MMPI, but we would suggest higher standards unless you are working under the direct supervision of a trained clinician.

Problems with Personality and Interest Measures

We have commented on several problems in using self-descriptive inventories for insight into personality and adjustment. These problems include limitations of (1) ability and willingness to read through and to understand the extensive list of items, (2) ability to stand back and view one's own behavior and decide whether a particular statement applies, and (3) willingness to give frank and forthright answers. Validity indicators such as those on the MMPI help in identifying and, to some extent, in controlling the operation of these factors, but these limitations still present problems. In addition, especially in employment situations, ethical issues arise relating to invasion of privacy and the requirement that the individual give testimony that may be against his or her own interest. Consequently, these instruments have a limited role in education and should be used in educational settings only when the results are to benefit the examinee and will be interpreted by a person with adequate clinical training and experience.

Interest and personality measures are notably different from cognitive ability measures in that the former are often composed of a number of dimensions that are largely independent. As was pointed out in Chapter 12, cognitive ability tests tend generally to show positive correlations, often fairly substantial ones. The result of this tendency is that most of the validity of ability measures for academic, and even for job, success is carried by the common general ability factor, and additional valid and useful information is obtained only with difficulty and in limited amounts. With interest and personality measures, the situation is rather different. As was shown in Table 13.1, most of the correlations among Holland's general interest areas are quite small. Thus, each score provides largely new and distinct information about an individuals interests. All six scores are then useful in describing an individual, in describing an occupation, and in describing the match between them.

Somewhat the same situation holds for the 16PF, although the number of useful dimensions appears to be less than 16 because of the clustering of certain scales. By contrast, many of the MMPI scales are highly correlated, and interpretation of an individual's scores is complicated by this fact. Some analyses of the instrument suggest that it has really only two main dimensions, anxiety level and repression. (The scores for these dimensions are typically reported by scoring services, along with the original 10 scales.) And, it might be suggested that interpretation should be limited to these two dimensions if you are not inclined to interpret the profile of extremely high and low scores.

Computerized Scoring and Interpretation

Because of the number of different scales for which they can be scored and because the scoring often includes differential weighting of the items (either some positive and some negative or some weighted more heavily than others), hand-scoring of interest and personality inventories is particularly laborious, so their scoring has largely been taken over by organizations that provide optical scanning of the answer sheets and computerized scoring and in some cases computerized interpretation of the results. A directory of such services, with descriptions and illustrations of the report forms, can be found in a volume entitled *Psychware Sourcebook* (Krug, 1988). (It is likely that this publication from the Test Corporation of America will be updated frequently, in light of the rapid changes occurring in computer applications to test interpretation.) Examples of many types of computerized interpretive reports are provided by Herman and Samuels (1985).

The report outputs from computerized scoring services can be divided into four rather distinct types, although more than one type of material may appear in a given report:

1. Generation of a set of scores for specific scales, such as the occupational scales of the Strong-Campbell Interest Inventory

2. Generation of narrative reports that closely follow the quantitative results, giving, in effect, a verbal paraphrase of the score profile

3. Generation of synthetic and interpretive narrative reports that go considerably beyond and are not readily identifiable with particular scales of the original instrument

4. Generation of predictive statements about probable satisfaction or success in specific vocations, likelihood of specific adjustment problems, or probable response to specific educational or therapeutic interventions

The first type of report has been illustrated by the record form for the Strong-Campbell displayed earlier in this chapter and the individual and class reports shown in Chapter 3. With respect to this type of reporting, the only questions that arise are the universal questions of reliability and validity that we need to address for any type of test score. The computer program introduces no new problems or issues.

The second type of reporting begins to bring into focus the major advantage, and a possible significant limitation, of computerized reporting. On the one hand, the procedure is standardized and the reporting avoids variations and limitations in the experience and language of different interpreters. The same set of scores or of item responses will in every case generate the same set of narrative responses. (Some of the more sophisticated systems select a statement at random from a pool of equivalent statements.) To the extent that the terminology has been carefully chosen and reviewed, this type of reporting should be a good representation of the constructs included in the scales of the instrument. But, the standardization tends to isolate the report from any other facts known about the examinee and to make it more mechanical and more removed from the functioning individuals than a report by a clinician who has other contacts with the examinee. However, to the extent that the narrative report provides a close semantic parallel to the scale scores, no substantial new issues of validity arise.

Material of the third type becomes more interpretive and less a simple summary of the test scores. Here, the potential advantages of standardization become more salient because with a standard output you are protected from the limited experience and expertise and the biases of any one test interpreter. But, the further the interpretations go beyond the separate scores, and whatever validity had been shown for those scores, the more crucial it becomes to obtain (and to make publicly available) evidence of the validity of each interpretive statement. Interpretations are based in part on the accumulation of data showing the relationship between the level of scores on certain scales, taken singly or in combination, and descriptive statements that have actually been made about individuals obtaining those scores. In some cases, the statements have been made by close associates and in others by counselors who have worked with the individuals. These empirical data may in some cases be supplemented by the interpreter's particular theoretical model of human personality or pathology. Based on this background, a complex set of rules is generated and stored in the computer. These rules govern the statements that are printed out in the report on the examinee. In some applications, the same score always generates the same text. In other, more complicated systems, a particular score or pattern of scores causes one passage to be selected at random from a group of passages that have been written to represent equivalent interpretations for that score or profile. The advantage of the latter method is that it reduces the appearance of mechanical interpretation and the risk of boredom if you must read a large number of reports, as would be the case for a teacher.

To illustrate the kind of interpretive material that these programs produce, we provide paragraphs printed out for the scores on the Millon Adolescent Personality Inventory (Millon, Green, & Meagher, 1982) taken by a 14-year-old girl who showed high scores on the scales designated forceful (assertive, dominating, and tough minded), sensitive (dissatisfied with self, moody, and unpredictable), and inhibited (socially uncomfortable and withdrawing):

> The behavior of this young adolescent is typified by her highly variable and unpredictable moods, a resentful irritability, an untrusting and pessimistic outlook, and the feeling of having been cheated, misunderstood, and unappreciated. An intense conflict between dependency and self-assertion contributes to her impulsive and quixotic emotionality. She expresses momentary thoughts and feelings impulsively and can be provoked by outside stimuli into sudden and unpredictable reactions. The pattern of negativism, sullen pouting, fault-finding and stubbornness is punctuated periodically by belligerent and querulous outbursts. Notable here is that ex-

pressions of guilt and contrition often follow these negative and impulsive behaviors.

This youngster anticipates being disillusioned in relationships with others and for this reason often behaves obstructively and, thereby, creates the expected disappointment. Though desperately seeking closeness and intimacy with both peers and family members, she is deeply untrusting, fearful of domination, and suspiciously alert to efforts which might undermine her desires. Family and social relationships are fraught with wrangles and antagonism, often provoked by her touchiness, and her complaining and passive-aggressive behaviors. The struggle between feelings of resentment and guilt and the conflict between dependency and autonomy permeate most of her relationships. She displays an unpredictable and rapid succession of moods, and is offended quickly by mere trifles. Her low tolerance for frustration is notable, as is her vacillation between being distraught, at one time, and contentious another. As a result, she may already have been stereotyped as a person who dampens the spirits of everyone, a teenage malcontent who obstructs the pleasure of others.

Central to her difficulties and behavior is the struggle between acting out and curtailing resentments. Her sulking, unpredictable, blowing hot and cold behavior induces others to act in a similar inconsistent manner. As a consequence, she feels misunderstood or unappreciated, and tends to be overly sensitive, defensive, and suspicious. Unfortunately, her behaviors set in motion a self-fulfilling prophecy, driving away potential well-wishers and thereby confirming and justifying her disappointment and hostility.

Clearly, there is considerable elaboration in the report, and the relationship of some of the statements to the scale designations is not immediately apparent. Individuals with a conservative psychometric bent may be concerned about the empirical basis for such an elaborate interpretation. However, the extended reports appear to be congenial to the clinically oriented. Millon (1983) reports that clinicians found that reports interpreting configural patterns of scores, as is done for Millon's inventories and for certain systems of MMPI interpretation, more adequately confirmed their own knowledge, added relevant information, and clarified the case than did reporting procedures that only dealt with scales one at a time. This type of "testimonial" validation is somewhat unsatisfying, but it may do as much as is possible to establish the validity of such an elaborated report.

As you move into the fourth type of reporting—reports that project into the future and predict specific behaviors or success or failure in particular occupations or endeavors—the need for validation of each type of prediction becomes even more imperative. We have a right to expect that the author or publisher will obtain evidence to support each type of forecast that is made and will make that evidence available to us. We should have access to evidence on which we can legitimately judge not only how much confidence to place in the *existence* of an asserted relationship, but also how strong and general the relationship is. What proportion of children who show Configuration X become truants from school? How does the incidence of reading disability among children with Configuration Y compare with the incidence for those who fail to show this configuration?

Computerized reporting, especially configural reporting, such as is used with the MMPI, is relatively new. We hardly know how to proceed in determining the validity of the multiple descriptions and predictions that it provides. We certainly do not have substantial organized body of validity information on which to judge it. At a minimum, the *Standards for Educational and Psychological Testing* (American Psychological Association [APA], American Educational Research Association [AERA], & National Council on Measurement in Education [NCME], 1985) state that "organizations offering automated test interpretation should make available information on the rationale of the test and a summary of the evidence supporting the interpretation given. This information should include the validity of the cut scores or configural rules used and a description of the samples from which they were derived" (APA, AERA, & NCME, 1985, Standard 5.11, p. 37).

Summary

Inventories to assess personality traits and personal adjustment are of interest primarily to the clinician rather than to the educator. In the clinical context, they provide a jumping-off point and a set of initial hypotheses to serve in further indepth study of an individual. Their other use is likely to be primarily in research.

Interest inventories are important tools for a school or college guidance program or for the vocational counselor in individual practice. They can help explicitly to make an individual aware of the likes and dislikes that he or she had sensed previously in a somewhat diffuse way (i.e., through unfocused feelings). And, they can relate those likes and dislikes concretely to the world of work.

Questions and Exercises

1. Consider the following interest inventories: (1) the Strong-Campbell Interest Inventory; (2) the Kuder Occupational Interest Survey; (3) the Career Assessment Inventory; and (4) the Self-Directed Search. Which one (or ones) would you recommend in each of the following situations? Give reasons for your choices.
   (a) A college sophomore wants counseling on his or her choice of major and on vocational plans.
   (b) A counseling program is being set up for students entering a vocational high school that has several different trade programs.
   (c) An inventory is needed for a course for 10th graders exploring careers and the process of occupational choice.
   (d) A counseling service for adults wants an inventory to use with college graduates.
2. The scales for the same or very similar occupations on the Strong-Campbell Interest Inventory and the Kuder Occupational Interest Survey often show low correlations with one another. Why might this happen? What is its theoretical significance? What is its practical significance?
3. Most studies outside the military have failed to find interest or adjustment inventories very useful in personnel selection. What might be reasons for this occurrence?
4. What is meant by the term "response set"? What are some potentially important

response sets? How might they affect the results on an interest inventory? On a personality inventory?

5. What conditions must be met if a self-report inventory is to be filled out accurately and give meaningful results?

6. How much trust can we place in adjustment inventories given to elementary school children? What factors limit their value?

7. What important differences did you notice between the Minnesota Multiphasic Personality Inventory and the Sixteen Personality Factor Questionnaire? For what purposes would each be more suitable?

8. What types of distortion of the image of a person are the validity scales (*L, K, F,* and *?*) of the Minnesota Multiphasic Personality Inventory intended to identify and correct for? What would be the analogous problems in the ratings of one person by another? How might you adapt the ideas of the control scales to ratings by other people?

9. What benefits are to be derived from computerized interpretations of personality inventories? What are the hazards or disadvantages?

Suggested Readings

Anastasi, A. (1988). *Psychological testing* (6th ed.). New York: Macmillan.

The ASVAB workbook. (1986). Washington, DC: U.S. Government Printing Office. (No. 642–413).

Butcher, J. N., Keller, L. S., & Bacon, S. F. (1985). Current developments and future directions in computerized personality assessment. *Journal of Consulting and Clinical Psychology, 53,* 803–815.

Gottfredson, G. D., & Holland, J. L. (1989). *Dictionary of Holland occupational codes* (2nd ed.). Odessa, FL: Psychological Assessment Resources.

Hansen, J. C., & Campbell, D. P. (1985). *The Strong manual* (4th ed.). Palo Alto, CA: Consulting Psychologists Press.

Holland, J. L. (1985). *Making vocational choices: A theory of vocational personalities and work environments* (2nd ed.). Englewood Cliffs, NJ: Prentice-Hall.

Jackson, D. N. (1985). Computer-based personality testing. *Computers in Human Behavior, 1,* 225–264.

Jackson, D. N., Holden, R. R., Locklin, R. H., & Marks, E. (1984). Taxonomy of vocational interests of academic major areas. *Journal of Educational Measurement, 21,* 261–275.

Kaplan, R. M., & Saccuzzo, D. P. (1989). *Psychological testing: Principles, applications, and issues* (2nd ed.). Pacific Grove, CA: Brooks/Cole.

McAllister, L. W. (1986). *A practical guide to CPI interpretation.* Palo Alto, CA: Consulting Psychologists Press.

Moreland, K. L. (1985). Validation of computer-based test interpretations: Problems and prospects. *Journal of Consulting and Clinical Psychology, 53,* 816–825.

Newmark, C. S. (Ed.). (1985). *Major psychological assessment instruments.* Boston: Allyn and Bacon.

Walsh, W. B., & Osipow, S. H. (Eds.) (1986). *Advances in vocational psychology: Vol. 1. The assessment of interests.* Hillsdale, NJ: Erlbaum.

CHAPTER 14
Testing in Special Situations

The Assessment of Exceptional Children

The latter half of the 1960s was a time when attitudes about dropping out of school began to change and students were urged to stay in school. During this time, the belief that the inequities that exist in our society could best be addressed through education became increasingly clear, and again, students were urged to stay in school.

Keeping more students in school has led to greater diversity in the school population and increased enrollment in special education classes because students who must be enticed to stay in school are generally from the low end of the ability distribution. The policy of encouraging students to stay in school has also had the indirect effect of increasing the reliance on grouping and tracking.

A major impetus for legislation that increased funding for exceptional children came from the parents of handicapped children. They were successful in mobilizing their supporters and in lobbying for legislation that increased funding for special education programs.

In 1975, the Education for All Handicapped Children Act (Public Law 94-142) was passed. Although there are many facets to this law, the overriding theme is entitlement. It specifies that every child who qualifies as handicapped has a right to special education services. The services, however, can come at a high cost for the identified child because according to PL 94-142, students are not eligible for special education services unless they have been certified as handicapped. This label can be a heavy burden for a child or an adult to carry. Shepard (1989) points out that the connotations of permanence the term carries seem more appropriate for the sensory impaired or trainable mentally handicapped child.

Measurement issues arise mainly in the context of decisions about whether a child is mentally handicapped, learning disabled, or emotionally disturbed. In general, parents want to avoid having their children classified as mentally handicapped, so the assessment procedures are structured to prevent a child from being erroneously placed in this category. The same approach is used with emotionally and behaviorally handicapped children. Parents are less likely to object to having their children labeled learning disabled than mentally handicapped or emotionally disturbed, and they sometimes try to pressure their school system into admitting their child into programs for the learning disabled. It may be to the advantage of local school districts to increase the number of special classes for the learning disabled. The funding support received from the state and federal governments may further encourage the local school systems not to restrict the number of students in such classes.

Trainable Mentally Handicapped Students

Trainable mentally handicapped children are defined by their inability to perform more than the most rudimentary academic tasks. As adults, they can be employed only in a sheltered environment and are generally incapable of living independently. For the most part, these individuals' subnormal mental functioning is caused by some known factor such as a chromosomal anomaly (e.g., Down syndrome), an illness of the mother during pregnancy (e.g., rubella), a lack of sufficient oxygen during the birth process (anoxia), an early childhood disease with an accompanying temperature high enough to permanently impede neurological development, or another of a number of misfortunes that can cause diminished brain functioning. The most important characteristic of this category is that the reason for the diminished intellectual capacity is known. This mental handicapping classification is also referred to as organic, or exogenous, mental retardation.

There tends to be little controversy about whether these individuals should be classified as mentally handicapped, and the cultural fairness of using individual intelligence tests to diagnose this mental handicapping classification is seldom questioned. It is evident that this group is mentally handicapped not only from performance on mental ability tests and in the classroom but also from interpersonal, social, and motor skills as well.

The parents of these children come from the full range of socioeconomic, income, educational, and ethnic backgrounds. However, the incidence of the syndrome among children from lower socioeconomic backgrounds might be expected to be higher than it is as a result of the mother's poor nutrition and inadequate medical and prenatal care. At the same time many such children can survive only through the intervention of heroic and expensive medical treatments that are available only to financially secure parents. At any rate, parents of trainable children have been aggressive in asserting their children's rights and have made themselves more visible than the parents of other mentally handicapped children. This visibility has tended to reinforce the view that the trainable child is typical of all children labeled mentally handicapped. Despite this, such children represent only a small proportion of all children who are labeled mentally handicapped.

Educable Handicapped Students

At one time, this category was by far the most populous special education category, but its numbers declined as more lower functioning children were identified as having learning disabilities. Educable handicapped children have the capacity to do some academic work, albeit at a low level. They can learn to read and compute but seldom can progress beyond elementary school level. They are able to master certain educational skills only with a great deal of help and over a long period of time. They are capable of being good employees and functioning independently as adults if given the opportunity. In many cases, they are able to "disappear" (i.e., blend into the mainstream) and shed the label of "mental retardation," becoming "normal" when not in a school setting. On the down side, these individuals are over-represented in prison populations and among the homeless.

The cause of this mental handicap is seldom obvious, and there usually is no illness or physical concomitant that can be identified. The most notable characteristic that these children share is that they typically have brothers, sisters, and other near relatives with the same problem, and their parents do not generally function at a much higher intellectual level. Individuals in this category tend to come from lower socioeconomic backgrounds, have parents who have had little educational success, and are likely to be members of a minority group. There is also the likelihood of the individual having had poor prenatal and postnatal nutrition and medical care. It must be emphasized that not all minority children or ones from lower socioeconomic backgrounds are educable mentally handicapped. Most such children are successful in school.

Considerable controversy has surrounded the assessment procedures used to identify children as educable handicapped. There are large numbers of children who might be considered candidates for inclusion in this group. There is no clear demarcation between the child who is doing poorly in school but is otherwise considered normal and the child who is operating at the upper reaches of being educable handicapped. Included in this group is a disproportionately high number of minority children, particularly black children. Because they can function normally outside of the classroom, it seems wrong to label them "mentally handicapped." With some prodding from litigation, the initial response was to move the minority children in this group from self-contained classrooms to resource rooms, regular classes with resource teachers, and other forms of mainstreaming. Another solution to this problem was to certify such children as learning disabled rather than mentally handicapped.

Providing special education services is expensive, and if left to local funding, few school districts can afford it. The funds to support such programs come from the federal government and are administered through the states, which have a responsibility to see that the funds are spent correctly. The states must remain vigilant to prevent any local school district from obtaining more funds than it is entitled to. One way for states to exert control is for them to see that no funds go to any children who have not been certified and thus labeled as deserving special education. The onus of the label mentally handicapped cannot be removed without the risk of losing services. School officials are therefore caught in a quandary; they must continuously ask themselves whether the quality of special education services justifies the risk of erroneously labeling a child as mentally handicapped.

Learning Disabled Students

The term "learning disability" was defined as a separate learning problem in the early 1960s. However, even before the term was introduced, there were children identified as suffering from mild forms of brain damage. They had been in accidents, contracted illnesses, or had some other misfortune that led to an unambiguous diagnosis of brain damage or neurological atypicality. There can be many manifestations of this syndrome, but learning disabled individuals typically are distractible and hyperactive, tend to repeat words and behaviors (perseverate), and experience difficulty in separating a figure from its background. Although this minimal brain damage is a low incidence syndrome, some school districts set up classes for these children, which emphasized individual attention and the use of study areas that minimized distractions.

As the number of school dropouts declined, the existence of students unable to succeed academically became more apparent. In particular, there was a group of students, predominantly male, who were failing to acquire basic reading skills in the early grades despite average or even above average tested intelligence. It was not unusual to find among this group, individuals who manifested the same behavioral characteristics that were typically observed among children with mild forms of brain damage. These poor readers displayed these characteristics in the absence of any medical history documenting actual brain damage. So, a new special education category was initiated that included children who had normal or above average intelligence but were unable to learn in the usual way. It was assumed that there were underlying neurological impairments causing the problems. A number of different names were used to describe this syndrome, most of which referred to neurological impairment. Among these were "minimal brain damage," "minimal cerebral dysfunction," "minimal brain dysfunction," "perceptually impaired," "psychoneurological learning disorder," and "neuropsychological disorder." Currently, the accepted term among educators is "learning disabled," with the term "dyslexia" referring specifically to the inability to read or, as in the popular press, as a synonym for learning disabilities.

Initially, treatment focused on the neurological impairment, and it was believed that the neurological problems should be addressed before any attempt was made to correct the educational deficits. The treatment involved activities intended to improve neurological function such as balance beam walking, cross-lateral crawling, and visual motor skill training.

During the early 1970s, there was a change in the way that this syndrome was defined and treated. A much larger number of children than originally anticipated were being identified as unable to succeed in school. At the same time, there was increased concern about the disproportionate number of minority children being placed in classes for the mentally handicapped. This concern led to a series of court cases and policy shifts leading to a tightening of the requirements for eligibility for placement in classes for the mildly handicapped and a concomitant loosening of the definition of learning disabilities. The requirement that the learning disabled child have normal or above normal intelligence was deemphasized. This move was justified by the assertion that the disability itself tended to suppress test performance. Any academically unsuccessful child who was not obviously mentally handicapped became a candidate for classification as learning disabled.

At the same time that the criterion was being changed, the learning disability field began to shift from viewing learning disabilities as a neurological impairment to an emphasis on deficits in academic performance. This shift occurred because the treatments that focused on neurological impairment tended to be unsuccessful and because the number of students given this label was so broad that the emphasis on underlying brain damage was no longer justified.

Parents of children who were unable to succeed in school began to demand the inclusion of their children under this heading because it made their children eligible for otherwise unavailable services. Most states have experienced a proliferation of such classes and the loss of any clearly identifiable syndrome. This tendency persists because there is often no place else to put these students, and the learning disability label does not carry as many negative associations as other special education categories. It is estimated that at least 40% of all students in learning disabilities classes are misdiagnosed (Shepard, 1983) and that 80% of all students could be classified as learning disabled by some diagnostic procedure now in use (Ysseldyke, Algozzine, & Epps, 1983)

What harm is there in "overidentification"? The students enrolled in classes for the learning disabled undoubtedly have academic problems, and through these classes, they receive more individual attention than would otherwise be available. So, it could be argued that such classes cause no harm. There are, however, a number of problems associated with mislabeling children as learning disabled:

1. Even though the connotations associated with this label are less pejorative than those associated with mental retardation, the label can have negative consequences for treatment. The use of this label implies that the problem stems from a central nervous system disorder. If this is not the problem, the treatment may be inappropriate. Furthermore, there may be a tendency for a student to stop trying once he or she has the excuse of having a learning disability.

2. Programs for the learning disabled are expensive, and the learning disability model of delivering instruction may not be the one that is most efficient. Given a finite and relatively fixed pool of money for education, spending more on some individuals or groups implies spending less on others.

3. Because learning disabilities is a special education category that falls under the control of PL 94–142, the diagnostic and assessment procedures required before a child can be placed in a special class are expensive. Currently, nearly half of the money available for educating learning disabled children is spent on testing and other bureaucratic requirements for placement.

Federal funding for special education is dispersed through state-level education departments. Each state must submit proposals to the U.S. Department of Education in which they request funding. Because of the trend over the past 10 years for increased enrollments in classes for the learning disabled, state offices are under pressure to limit inclusion in these classes. The problem has generally been approached by tightening eligibility requirements through the use of more restrictive definitions based on objective scores. Only students who meet the strict criteria are supposed to be certified as having a learning disability.

It is relatively easy, using test scores, to identify children who are doing poorly in school and in particular that group that is so far below its peers that its members cannot succeed in a regular class. The difficult task is to separate the learning disabled child from the child who is mildly handicapped. The two criteria most often used to make this decision are (1) the relationship between how much a student achieves and his or her score on a mental aptitude test and (2) test score scatter. The latter criterion refers to the difference between a student's strong and weak areas. Shepard (1983) describes a number of technical problems that are encountered when these approaches are used. First, most of the tests used to make such decisions are technically deficient, and those charged with making the differentiation often cannot adequately separate good tests from bad ones. Second, the field of measurement is replete with failed attempts to distinguish achievement from aptitude. The problem is that achievement and aptitude tests measure essentially the same things, and the two are highly correlated. Attempts to interpret discrepancies meaningfully between aptitude and achievement are doomed by the low reliability of the differences. Similar problems plague attempts to define learning disabilities in terms of test score scatter (marked differences among subscale scores). There is a great deal of scatter among the scores of most children, and before it can be considered unusual, the scatter has to be quite extreme. In addition, no evidence systematically links scatter with neurological damage.

An even more fundamental problem stems from the main assumption underlying this syndrome, the existence of an underlying neurological deficit. Every child who is mentally handicapped, by definition, has a neurological deficit, or he or she would not be mentally handicapped. The difference between the mentally handicapped and the learning disabled child can be defined as follows: the learning disabled child has specific damage, while the neurological damage suffered by the mildly handicapped child is more general. This assertion is not easily supported by evidence, and there is no existing testing procedure that can reliably make the distinction just noted. Learning disabilities and a mild mental handicap might very well differ in terms of the types of neurological dysfunction that cause them, but there is currently no way to demonstrate this difference.

The diagnostic team charged with the task of placing a child into a diagnostic category often must face a dilemma. The team must often choose between a diagnosis that is correct in terms of the syndrome and the more immediate need to find an appropriate educational setting. If a child is failing in a regular class and it is believed that the child's chances of avoiding failure rest in special education assistance, it is likely that the child will be placed into a category that will make the provision of such services possible. This placement will occur even if the identification is inconsistent with accepted definitions of the syndrome. Such classification practices are most often found with learning disabled children. This tendency to place students in classes for the learning disabled despite the students' characteristics is the major reason for the divergence between practice and theory in identifying learning disabled children.

These considerations illustrate how difficult it is to solve the problem of overidentifying learning disabled children through the use of tighter, more technologically correct definitions of the syndrome. Shepard (1983) noted the futility of these solutions and proposed that states designate a permissible percentage of learning disabled students. She believes that this would force school districts to tighten their selection processes. She asserts that where this approach has been tried, the tendency has been to place students with characteristics that agree most with accepted definitions in the special classes.

Emotionally Disturbed Students

The problems associated with identifying emotionally disturbed children are even more daunting than those encountered in the previously discussed categories. For both mildly handicapped and learning disabled children, it is possible to formulate some rules, however imperfect, for determining eligibility using standardized tests. Decisions on designating children as emotionally disturbed are, for the most part, based on clinical judgments.

According to PL 94–142 (Federal Register, 1977), a child is considered to be emotionally disturbed if one or more of the following characteristics are exhibited over a long period or to a marked degree: (1) an inability to learn that cannot be explained by intellectual, sensory, or health reasons, (2) an inability to build or maintain satisfactory interpersonal relations, (3) inappropriate behaviors, (4) a pervasive mood of depression or unhappiness, and/or (5) physical symptoms or fears. Included in this group are children who are schizophrenic or autistic but not those who are merely maladjusted. Definitions and procedures that lead to implementing these guidelines are left to state governments.

This description of the syndrome introduces a problem in terminology. The usual term is "emotionally disturbed," but behaviorists often prefer "behaviorally disturbed." As such, the terms mean essentially the same thing and can be used interchangeably or in tandem. Others in the field use the term "behaviorally disturbed" to refer to the children who are socially maladjusted and who get into trouble—in short, children who misbehave. Unless the behavior is a symptom of a deeper emotional problem, such children would not be eligible for special education placement. In this chapter, we will use the term "emotionally disturbed."

A perusal of the characteristics just discussed should make it clear that diagnosing emotional disturbance is subjective. Parents are not anxious to have their children labeled emotionally disturbed, and school systems do not want large numbers of students to be placed in this category. For this reason, the diagnostic procedures tend to err on the side of not making a child eligible unless the diagnosis is quite certain. This tendency is in contrast with the tendency to overdiagnose children as learning disabled. Assessment is typically based on four types of data: (1) informal observations, (2) systematic behavioral observations, (3) interpretation of standardized test scores, and (4) responses on projective tests.

Typical evaluation procedures for determining whether a child is emotionally disturbed consist of the following steps, from the "State and Federal Requirements for Programs for Exceptional Children and Youth" for Kentucky (Kentucky Department of Education, Office of Education for Exceptional Children, 1990):

a. A health screening which would indicate there are no primary visual, auditory or physical handicapping conditions;

b. A written account of specific behavioral data collected over a period of time by the referral source describing the behavior(s) of concern;

c. A written compilation of data from direct observations of the referred child in familiar surroundings by a person other than the referred source;

d. An individual educational assessment of the referred child's specific strengths and weaknesses in basic skill areas;

e. An individual psychological or psychiatric evaluation;

f. A developmental and social history; and

g. A written record or evidence of previous educational and behavioral intervention strategies that have been utilized. (pp. 4–5, 4–6)

The determination of the relative weight that should be placed on behavioral observations and on psychological test performance is the most controversial aspect of the diagnostic procedures used for determining whether a child is emotionally disturbed. All school psychologists have been trained to use individual intelligence tests to make inferences about the cognitive functioning of children, and some are trained to make more in-depth personality assessments. Other instruments such as the Bender Visual-Motor Gestalt Test (otherwise used as a means of assessing levels of visual-motor functioning) and sentence completion and drawing tasks can also be used to generate hypotheses about the existence of emotional problems. In addition, projective techniques such as the Rorschach Test and the Thematic Apperception Test are used to diagnose emotional disturbances.

Inferences about school-related ability based on scores from the established ability tests such as the Wechsler scales and the Stanford-Binet Intelligence Scale are considered to be valid. No strong claims for the validity of inferences about psychodynamic functioning can be supported.

Shepard (1989) asserts that when the responses on these instruments are so bizarre that they can be viewed as certain indicators of emotional disturbance, the individual's behaviors are likely to be such that observations alone would be sufficient for identification. She advocates diagnosing this syndrome on the basis of behavioral observations. This view, which has become increasingly accepted in the special education field, is based on a rejection of the medical model. That model defines the syndrome in terms of the existence of an underlying psychological disturbance that may or may not be easily discernible through observations but that may be detected with the aid of psychological tests. In contrast, the emphasis in Shepard's approach is on outward symptoms and behaviors.

Emotional disturbance is difficult to diagnose because an understanding of psychodynamic functioning falls outside of the usual expertise of educators. Physical handicaps present few measurement problems, and instruments exist that can diagnose visual and auditory impairments with a high degree of accuracy. The diagnosis of mental retardation and learning disabilities is based primarily on educational evaluations, behavioral observations, and objective test scores. Emotional disturbance is not only an elusive and inherently difficult phenomenon to measure but also a phenomenon whose identification depends on recognizing a set of behaviors with which educators are neither familiar nor comfortable.

The most important attribute that diagnosticians involved in identifying emotional disturbance can have is a thorough knowledge of the range of normal behavior. Behaviors such as crying or tantrums that might not be considered unusual for a child in the first grade might be a much greater cause for concern when exhibited by a child in the ninth grade.

The Future of Special Education Assessment

Some drastic solutions to the problems encountered in placing children in special education classes and in the structure of this field in general have been proposed (Wang, Reynolds, & Walberg, 1988). The abolition of special education, or what is referred to as the "second system," has even been advocated. It is asserted that the classification systems now in use are flawed, the bureaucracy is wasteful, the use of labels hurts children, and funds used for special education could better be spent modifying the regular instruction system to benefit all children.

The problems of special education cannot be solved by dismantling the "second system" and reallocating the vast sums of money that the system now receives because it is the system that attracts the money. Once the institution of special education is gone, the money that once supported it will also go. When parents and lobbyists address congressional committees to request special education funds, they must base their arguments on the severity, high incidence rate, and permanence of the handicaps. It is unlikely that Congress will be willing to allocate funds for a less clearly defined group of children.

Demographic analysis of the types of students that can be expected to attend school in the future suggests that the number of those unable to succeed in school will increase. To date, our schools have not had much success in dealing with this problem. The dissolution of the "second system" would not be likely to usher in a renaissance in the way low-performing and at-risk students are helped to succeed in school. Criticisms of the existing special education structure do appear to have merit. However, despite the problems of labeling, inaccurate classification, and wastefulness, this structure has brought resources to the students with the greatest need in our school systems. For this reason, the movement to dismantle the special education system is premature. As laudatory as such a goal might be, its implementation will have to await the development of programs to take its place.

Identifying the Academically Gifted

Although most proposals for educational reform have focused on the academically deficient and the goal of keeping all students in school, there has been continued interest in identifying and providing special programs for the gifted, or academically talented, student. A school system wishing to accommodate the gifted child has four choices: (1) enrichment, (2) promotion to higher grades, (3) separate classes, or (4) some combination of the first three. Decisions about whether a child is eligible for placement in a class for the academically gifted involve the most measurement issues.

As school districts strive to keep more students in school, schools and school districts are more likely to deal with increased diversity in their student populations by relying on grouping and/or tracking students. Special education placement and separate classes for the gifted child illustrate grouping on opposite ends of the continuum. The increased use of all forms of grouping has been accompanied by controversies regarding the effect that this practice has on achievement and the negative impact that it can have on the self-esteem of students. Despite the controversies that surround it, grouping seems to be an educational practice that will remain a part of the classroom structure in most school systems for a long time.

There are three main criteria used to identify the gifted child: (1) achievement, (2) creativity, and (3) level of intelligence. Achievement is relatively easy to assess either by means of achievement tests, grades, or teacher ratings. It is not often used as the sole criterion for determining eligibility for gifted classes, possibly because educators sense that "giftedness" means something more than high academic achievement.

The importance of creativity as a criterion for eligibility to participate in gifted classes is often promoted, but it has proved to be an elusive concept to measure. Creativity cannot be easily assessed with standardized tests because of their emphasis on convergent thinking, which is by definition not a creative act. The goal of convergent thinking is the identification of an established correct answer. Creativity, on the other hand, is related to divergent thinking, the goal of which is the generation of answers that differ from the expected. Consider a simple test of creativity such as asking a child to name all of the possible uses for a brick. The task is divergent in that all reasonable uses would be acceptable, but it is convergent in that the goal is the listing of many uses; the child who lists the most uses is considered the most creative. Creativity tests tend not to be reliable or valid; therefore, heavy reliance on them will result in the misidentification of students for gifted programs. Thus, some students are placed in such programs, despite not being gifted, while other students who could benefit from such programs may be ruled ineligible.

The method most often used to identify the gifted student is an assessment of general intelligence, usually by means of a group intelligence test. Individual intelligence tests are not usually used because they are impractical, requiring excessive amounts of time and a high level of expertise on the part of the examiner. Anyway, we do not need a test that minimizes the need for reading when trying to identify gifted children.

If intelligence is to be either the sole criterion or a major one, several problems emerge. Cutoff scores must be set that bring into play all of the complexities of setting standards. (We will discuss setting standards later in this chapter.) Black and other minority students tend not to perform as well as white students on intelligence tests and thus are underrepresented in classes for the gifted just as they are overrepresented in special education classes. Furthermore, a high intelligence quotient score does not ensure superior performance in all areas. Teachers can become impatient with a child placed in a class for the gifted on the basis of a high level of tested general intelligence who lacks an aptitude for mathematics even though this sort of variance in abilities should be expected

Minimum Competency Testing

Assessing Student Competency

A series of events—from Sputnik in 1957 to failures in compensatory education programs to declining scores on the Scholastic Aptitude Test and the ascendancy of Japanese technology—has eroded public faith in the nation's educational system. This erosion was translated into political action when the decline in the quality of our educational institutions was recognized by the public. Politicians realized that educational reform was an issue on which a career could be built. The result has been a series of calls for reform at the local, state, and national levels.

One important aspect of educational reform proposed in the 1970s was minimum competency testing. Performance at an unacceptable level mandated remediation or retention and, ultimately, denial of a diploma. These competency testing programs have three main purposes: (1) to identify students in need of remediation, (2) to ensure that graduates and/or those who are promoted to the next grade have all reached some minimum level of competency, and (3) to provide additional motivation to students to increase their achievement. This approach has great appeal to politicians and the public in general because it appears to be an effective way to improve public schools, which is less expensive than other proposed reforms.

The impetus for developing minimum competency testing did not come from educators. It was a political movement supported, for example, by editorial writers, state legislatures, candidates for all sorts of public office, recommendations of blue-ribbon committees studying education, and public opinion polls. The attitude of educators tends to range from open hostility to a willingness to accede to public and political pressure. Occasionally, educators have even expressed strong support.

The Proliferation of Minimum Competency Testing.   Interest in minimum competency testing seems to have touched nearly every state. The particular manifestation in each has differed because of uncertainty about the best approaches to implementation. Additionally, such programs are the result of complex political processes. There are many forces within a state pulling a program in different directions: local school boards may want to maintain control, the legislature may want to assess functional literacy, and the governor may want to focus on academic skills.

Minimum competency testing programs range from centralized programs, where instructional objectives and tests are developed at the state level, to those where the local school districts are either permitted to test or are mandated to do so. Remedial programs are sometimes funded at the state level or made the sole responsibility of the local school district. Some states have created their own tests, while others have contracted with outside agencies. Most states use what they describe as criterion-referenced tests, but in most cases, the tests used do not satisfy the definition of criterion-referenced testing given in Chapters 3 and 7.

Legal Issues Surrounding Minimum Competency Testing.   Since the 1970s, when the minimum competency testing movement began, there have been many questions raised about the legality of minimum competency tests. The problem is not with implementing the tests to determine which students need remediation. When test results are used for making what are called "high stakes" decisions, such as determining which children will be given diplomas, the legality of minimum competency testing is most likely to be challenged. Currently, most of the legal issues have been resolved, generally in favor of minimum competency testing. Much of this legal clarification took place in Florida because of its statewide program for determining who could graduate; Florida was one of the first states to implement such a program.

Florida's Functional Literacy Test (which is what the test was originally called) was announced in 1977 and was slated to go into effect in 1979. Students were required to pass the test to receive a high school diploma. The requirement was challenged in a class action suit brought by a group of parents whose children had failed the test. In *Debra P. v. Turlington* (1979), Judge George Carr of the Federal District Court ruled that there must be a sufficient amount of time between the announcement of such programs and the date when diplomas are actually denied to allow students enough time to remedy deficiencies.

There was also concern about what is called "disparate racial impact," the higher failure rate by minority students than by white students. The court ruled that it was not necessary to prove discriminatory intent because the differential test scores were the result of past discriminatory policies of school segregation that had been corrected only a few years earlier. The students and the school system had not been given enough time to correct the results of past discrimination. For this reason and to give students time to remedy deficiencies, the test was not made mandatory until the 1982–1983 school year.

In 1981, *Debra P. v. Turlington* was appealed to the Court of Appeals for the Fifth Circuit. The Court of Appeals upheld Judge Carr on the issue of fair warning and the requirement that minimum competency testing not carry forward the effects of racial segregation. The Court of Appeals added one further condition: The test had to have content validity. For minimum competency testing, content validity is usually of two types (McClung, 1979). There is *curricular validity,* which refers to the match between the competency test and the curriculum. To establish curricular validity, it is necessary to demonstrate agreement between the curricula of the various school districts and the state curriculum and to compare both with the test content. Because competency tests are generally built from sets of instructional objectives that are developed to provide guidance concerning curriculum, it is not difficult to establish this sort of validity. The biggest problem is that teachers may not teach exactly what is listed in the curriculum, which leads to a concern about a more stringent type of validity—*instructional validity.*

Instructional validity requires the establishment of a match between what is assessed on the minimum competency test and what happens in the classroom. "Opportunity to learn," which involves the match between what is taught and what is measured on these tests, is a major a concern of the critics of minimum competency testing. This type of validity is what the Court of Appeals for the Fifth Circuit required, although it did not use this terminology. At the time, this was a controversial decision among the members of the court because it had impli cations for all testing conducted by a school system; the courts have traditionally left such judgments in the hands of educators.

Florida was required to go to great lengths and expense to satisfy the courts that the students had in fact been taught what was included on the test. When the court first ordered the state to establish instruction validity, it seemed like an impossible task. In a state the size of Florida, how do you determine the extent to which something has been taught? The state took a lot of time, spent a great deal of money, and was able to survey administrators, teachers, students, and curricular guides to provide sufficient documentation. In 1983, Judge Carr found that Florida had met all required conditions, including content validity, and the injunction was lifted, allowing the state to deny diplomas to students who did not pass the test.

When minimum competency testing was first introduced, there was a widely held view that a likely successful legal challenge to this form of testing would come from critics who believed that such programs were unfair to special education students. The courts, however, have consistently ruled that school systems could require special education students to take such a test and deny them a diploma if they did not pass. They have also ruled that it is not necessary for those requiring such a test for students in special education programs to establish curricular and instructional validity (Jaeger, 1989). They also have not been required to defend the existence of disparate impact on special education students, which stands in interesting contrast to the judicial response to testing students from minority backgrounds.

Problems Associated with Minimum Competency Testing.   The first problem concerns content, or what to include on a competency test. Without a statewide curriculum, these tests cannot be specific without being unfair to some students who will have not been exposed to the subject matter of the test. As a result, we see the same tendencies in these instruments that we see in standardized achievement tests, an emphasis on basic skills such as reading and mathematics. This emphasis is appropriate for the lower grades, where a great deal of in-structional time is devoted to teaching this subject matter, but in high school, this content would usually be taught in remedial classes only. Too often, the public, school administrators, the media, and politicians place so much importance on performance on these tests that high school teachers alter their curricula to emphasize basic skills to the point that other important knowledge and skills expected of students at this level are ignored.

The emphasis on basic skills also raises the concern that everyone is being brought down to the same level. The "minimum" in minimum competency testing is criticized because students should be encouraged to function at higher levels than the minimum. This emphasis on minimum performance exists at the same time that the tests are being criticized by those who believe the tests unfairly deny important credentials in the form of diplomas to some students.

Perhaps the biggest problem associated with minimum competency testing is agreeing on what constitutes a minimum level of competence. Consider a topic such as mathematics, for which it should be easy to set minimum standards, because at the secondary level it is concrete and straightforward. However, it is not as easy to set minimum standards as it appears. Someone must decide whether competency should be represented by mastery (at some specified level) of a catalog of specific skills such as "addition of three two-digit whole numbers" or "conversion of such fractions as halves, thirds, quarters, and fifths to decimals," or whether it should be defined normatively as performance on a representative arithmetic test at a level equal to that of the average sixth-grade student. Or, should competency be defined in still some other way?

Designing the Test.   Designing minimal competency tests presents no special problems once a definition of the domain and level has been determined. However, such tests need to be different from the usual ability tests. Because we are interested only in a decision at one specific ability level, the level chosen to represent minimum competence, the test should be designed to be maximally sensitive at that level. There is no need to include those difficult items that differentiate between average and superior competence nor to include very easy items that can be correctly answered even by those of low competence in the skill in question. The items should be targeted at a narrow band of difficulty and be able to differentiate between those falling just below and those just above the minimum passing score. It is impossible to determine this point with complete precision, and inevitably the test will differentiate over a fairly wide range of competence. It is difficult to construct a test in such a way that it can effectively serve two functions. The better job a minimum competency test does in differentiating the minimally competent from those who fall just below this point, the less effective it will be in differentiating among students across the full range of abilities.

The Future of Minimum Competency Testing for Students.   A major problem with minimum competency testing programs is that they do not seem to focus as much on educating students—although this outcome is hoped for—as they do on ensuring that students below a certain level do not obtain degrees. Thus, the tests and the programs are punitive.

Interest in minimum competency testing has begun to fade as it has become apparent that the tests have failed to do what they were intended to do. They were announced with great fanfare—glowing promises to improve greatly the level of student performance by their advocates and predictions of the direst consequences by their critics.

When minimum competency tests are implemented, a similar process seems to occur. During the first year of implementation, as expected, there will be a large number of failures and an accompanying outpouring of concern about how the high failure rate reflects negatively on the school system. As a result, remediation programs are initiated; teachers become familiar with the content of the test and adjust their teaching accordingly. Modifications are made to the content of the test to bring it more in line with curriculum content that seems more appropriate or easier, and the standards may even be adjusted downward. As a result, within a year or so, the passing rates increase and eventually very few students fail.

Under these circumstances, an interplay might be expected between those who want to have higher standards, and therefore a higher cutoff score, and those who want fewer students to fail, and therefore argue for a lower cutoff score. The resulting criteria should fall between the goals of the two groups. Instead of the process just discussed occurring, nearly all the interest groups favor a very low failure rate, and thus no interplay occurs. Ultimately, the most salient criticism of minimum competency testing is its irrelevance to the educational process and student competency.

Assessing Teacher Competency

Growing out of the need for educational reform and following the increase in interest in minimum competency testing of students came an interest in assessing the competency of teachers. Rudner (1988) observed that every state except Alaska has either implemented or plans to implement some sort of competency testing for teachers. Twenty-seven states have tests for admission to teacher education, and 44 require tests for initial certification. But, only three have testing programs for practicing teachers as a condition for renewal of teaching certificates.

When legislators, blue-ribbon committees, and governor-appointed task forces meet to generate ideas about how best to improve the educational system, their attention naturally turns to teachers. After all, they have the greatest control over how much students learn. Teachers have the most contact with students, and any successful educational reform must be implemented through them. In addition, the public's most important contact with schools is through teachers. Everyone has had extensive experiences with teachers, at least as students. These experiences are likely to include a broad range of recollections, from fond memories of teachers who were wonderful to not so fond memories of teachers who were pretty awful. There is the belief that some of our schools' failures are caused by unqualified teachers. Evidence exists that students admitted to teacher education programs are likely to be among the least qualified of all students enrolled in a college, based on scores on the Scholastic Aptitude Test. All things considered, it seems appropriate that proposals to improve education would focus on strategies to maximize the skills and qualifications of teachers.

Competency Testing for Practicing Teachers.   Currently only Georgia, Arkansas, and Texas have instituted competency testing programs for practicing teachers. In addition to questions about appropriateness and effectiveness, the reasons for the lack of implementation are political. Teachers are strongly opposed to being tested for competency. They consider themselves to be professionals and are insulted by competency tests, which currently assess only literacy. In most states, teacher organizations constitute powerful political action groups. Not only can they vote for and funnel large amounts of money to those politicians who oppose this sort of testing, but they can also influence other voters because of their influence in the community. Few politicians are willing to challenge this sort of power. In two of the states in which these programs were implemented, the decision to adopt competency testing for teachers occurred as part of a compromise over state funding of education. The state legislatures were willing to approve increases in the state education budgets only if practicing teachers were tested. This strategy tends to fragment the opposition to assessing practicing teachers. Some opponents have been willing to accept such testing to gain the needed additional funding.

The intention of competency testing programs is to change the public's negative image of teachers by eliminating incompetent teachers. Shepard and Kreitzer (1987), in their study of the Texas Examination of Current Administrators and Teachers (TECAT), provide some excellent reasons for this sort of competency testing not being adopted by more states.

The test was supposed to cost about $3 million, a modest expenditure given the number of the teachers and the magnitude of improvement in teaching that was expected to result from the elimination of poor teachers. Although the exact cost is difficult to determine because of the many expenses associated with this program, such as the cost of workshops and training materials used to help prepare the teachers to take the test and the cost of the in-service day when teachers actually took the test, Shepard and Kreitzer (1987) estimate that the TECAT cost at least $35 million. The test was first envisioned as a competency test to determine which teachers had the skills to succeed as teachers or administrators. As so often happens, it did not take long for those responsible for developing the test to realize that a focus on teaching skills was not feasible. If these competencies can be identified (experience suggests that they cannot), a separate test would be needed for each grade and each subject-matter area. There would have to be different tests for administrators and teachers because it would not be fair or legal, because of Constitutional guarantees of due process, to test different specialties with the same test. Hundreds of tests would have to be developed, which was not possible. As a compromise, a literacy test was chosen. It seems reasonable to assume that all teachers need some minimal level of basic literacy and numeracy. It is difficult to defend the renewal of a teacher's certificate if he or she is a poor reader who cannot complete simple computations. It is, however, difficult to determine how high that minimum level should be. It is also fairly obvious that it does not need to be the same for all teachers. Certainly, the reading level required of a high school English teacher should be higher than that required of a kindergarten or vocational teacher. Because the same standard had to be used for all teachers on the TECAT, the cutoff score was set very low.

From the results of the field trials, state department officials charged with monitoring the program anticipated a 12% failure rate on the TECAT. But, this estimate was made without considering the preparation programs and the massive array of training materials made available to teachers. After the first administration, the passing rate was 96.7%. Those who failed the test the first time were given the opportunity to retake the test, which increased the passing rate to 99%. Out of 202,000 teachers and administrators who originally took the test, only 1,950 lost their certificates. Of these, 887 had what could be considered academic teaching jobs, and 1,063 were in nonacademic teaching roles in such areas as vocational and physical education (Shepard & Kreitzer, 1987).

The higher than expected passing rate was attributable to the extensive inservice instruction, tutoring, and preparation on the part of the teachers. Shepard and Kreitzer (1987) concluded that the purpose of most of this instruction was to help the teachers to obtain a passing score by teaching to the tests because information about the test specifications was available and by providing information on test taking tricks. These activities did not seem likely to increase the teachers' mastery of the underlying constructs the test was intended to assess.

In conclusion, the implementation of the TECAT was not successful. It cost a great deal of money, far more than was originally anticipated, and it eliminated relatively few teachers. Of those that it did eliminate, most were in nonacademic teaching positions. Disproportionately large numbers of special education, vocational education, and minority teachers were removed. In terms of the major purpose of the test, increasing the esteem in which teachers were held by the public, the test seems to have had the opposite effect. Texas teachers and their professional organizations fought a bitter fight in opposition to the test, which created the unfortunate impression that they were afraid to be tested. When examples of test content were published, it was obvious that the test was embarrassingly easy, which made the teachers look foolish for being afraid to take it. Unfortunately, the implementation of the test probably resulted in the public's having a less positive attitude toward teachers in that state.

Preservice Tests. As was noted earlier, most states have adopted programs for screening prospective teachers. This screening can take place either prior to admission to teacher education programs or as a condition of being awarded a teaching certificate or both. These programs face the same limitations that apply to tests administered to practicing teachers; it is almost impossible to construct a test that measures skills that are actually prerequisites for being an effective teacher. No list of such skills exists, and even if such a list did exist, it would be impossible to get consensus among experts that the list was accurate. Additionally, there is no agreed-upon set of objectives, materials, or methods to which all teacher candidates are exposed in their training. As a result, both the tests that are administered prior to admission and those required as a condition for the awarding of a teaching certificate tend to be measures of basic literacy skills. These tests also have the same problems with standard setting that are associated with all types of competency tests. (We will discuss this topic later in this chapter.)

The Effect of Competency Tests on Minorities.   Perhaps the most troubling outcome of the implementation of teacher competency tests is their disastrous effect on the certification of minority teachers, both in terms of high failure rates and the tendency for prospective minority teachers not to enroll in teacher education programs. Projections of enrollment patterns suggest that over half of the students enrolled in public school will be minorities by the year 2000 (which may cause some concern about the semantic meaning of the term "minorities"). At the same time, the percentage of minority teachers is expected to drop to 5% (Smith, 1987). Rudner (1988) reports that only 23% of blacks and 34% of Hispanics passed the teacher education admissions test in Texas between March 1984 and March 1985. According to Smith (1987), the rate of certification for blacks in that state was expected to drop to 1% of all teachers being certified. Only 10% of students graduating from black colleges in Louisiana between 1978 and 1984 were able to pass that state's teacher certification test. Smith (1987) concludes that cutoff scores in all states are set at a level such that most minority students are denied entry to teacher education programs or denied teaching certificates. He reviewed 19 states and found that the typical first time passing rates for white students ranged from 71% to 96%, while the first time passing rate for blacks ranged from 15% to 50%.

Setting Standards

The biggest problem associated with minimum competency testing is the setting of a standard in the form of a cutoff score because the skills being measured do not occur in discrete states. A child does not either know or not know how to read at an appropriate level for his or her grade. We cannot walk into a classroom and easily divide the students into those who can read third-grade vocabulary and those who cannot. There is always a range: some can read well, some cannot read at all, and the rest fall somewhere between the two extremes. To draw an arbitrary line and say that those above a certain point have reached mastery while those below have not is quite difficult. The problem is made worse by the fact that the performance of students in a class or teachers in a state can be expected to approximate a normal distribution, at least to the extent that most are in the middle and few are at the extremes. This tendency makes decisions about competency difficult.

If a distinction is to be made between those who are competent and those who are not, a standard must be set. There are a number of computational approaches to setting standards. Hambleton and Eignor (1980) list 18 approaches. They all depend on the use of judges, and even though they appear to be objective psychometric procedures, they depend on judgments. With the Nedelsky method (1954), for each item, judges decide how many distractors the lowest passing student should be able to eliminate. The minimum passing level is the reciprocal of the remaining choices. On a four-option multiple-choice test, for an item on which the minimum-level student could be expected to eliminate two incorrect options, the minimum passing level would be one-half, or 0.5 (the reciprocal of $4 \div 2$ is $\frac{1}{2}$, or 0.5). The minimum passing levels are averaged across judges and items to obtain a cutoff score for the entire test. Ebel's method (1972) involves setting up a 3×4 matrix based on three levels of difficulty (easy, medium, and hard) and four levels of relevance (essential, important, acceptable, and questionable). Judges place each item in the appropriate cell and also determine the minimum percentages of questions in each cell that a student should get correct. The number of questions is multiplied by the percentages in each cell. This value is summed and then divided by the total number of items to yield the minimum passing score.

Angoff (1971) proposed a simpler approach. He suggested that judges estimate the probability that a minimally competent person would correctly answer each item or the proportion of a group of minimally competent people who would correctly answer it. These percentages are summed to determine the standard. It is, of course, necessary to ensure, in some way, that all judges have the same idea about the level of functioning required of a minimally competent person.

Jaeger (1989) examined 32 studies that compared different methods of standard setting. He concluded that different approaches to the problem produced quite different results when applied to the same test. He computed the ratio between the most stringent and least stringent standards. In one case, the ratio was 1.0, which means that the standards were the same regardless of the method. The largest ratio was 52.0. The median was 1.5 and the mean was 5.0. The mean was much larger because there were three studies with very high ratios (34.0, 42.0, and 52.0), which caused the distribution to be positively skewed. Glass (1977), after conducting comparisons with similar results, concluded that you can obtain widely divergent results depending on the method selected and that in the absence of a strong rationale for deciding which to use, none should be used. The real problem is that when such different standards result from different methods, there is the temptation to make the decision about which method to use on the basis of what cutoff score is perceived to be most desirable. It is not difficult to find examples of the manipulation of cutoff scores through the creative selection of methods of setting standards.

An example of the way standard-setting procedures can be manipulated comes from the description of the procedures used to set the standard for the National Council Licensure Examination for Nurses (NCLEX) (*Issues,* 1988). In

1988, the test was substantially changed, and there was a need to establish a new minimum passing score for it. A modification of the Angoff procedure was used. In this application, judges are given normative information about the performance of a pilot group prior to evaluating any items. When the standard for the NCLEX was set, it was projected that there would be an unacceptably high failure rate. Another panel, presumably identical to the first, was appointed and given the same instructions and information as the first panel. They set the standard too low. The cutoff scores from the two panels were then combined so that the second panel was weighted more heavily than the first. This procedure resulted in a final cutoff score at a point where the passing rate was 84%, which was similar to the passing rate on the previous version of the test. This final cutoff score was the score that was wanted in the first place.

Ethics in Testing

Ethics are discussed throughout this book in the context of the topics covered in different chapters. This section summarizes the ideas already presented and places special emphasis on those aspects of the ethics of measurement that are of greatest importance.

Ethics can be viewed as a set of rules for conduct that fall between morals and values, which are personal, and laws, which are the result of a legislative process and are enforced by the state. Ethics are rules of conduct supported and enforced by a group or its organization for its own members. Punishment for violating a law is generally spelled out in the law itself. The violation of an ethical precept does not imply a violation of the law although the difference between the two can become blurred. We may obey laws because we think that is the right thing to do or because we support the system that promulgates them, but ultimately, we obey them because the society provides punishments for those who do not. Ethics are also enforced, but much more loosely. The most important mode of enforcement is the group pressure that can be applied by the organization that promulgates the ethical code. Organizations such as the American Psychological Association (APA) and the American Association for Counseling and Development (AACD) have ethical guidelines that all members are required to follow, on pain of sanctions or even expulsion from the organizations.

Unfortunately, the ethics of testing tend to be rather loosely defined, and there is a lack of concrete sanctions for those who violate them. The single most important source of information about the ethics of testing can be found in the *Standards for Educational and Psychological Testing* (American Psychological Association, American Educational Research Association, & National Council on Measurement in Education, 1985). Additional information on this subject can be found in textbooks devoted to testing and in articles published by the professional organizations most involved with testing.

Misunderstandings about fundamental issues in testing contribute most to disagreements about what is ethical in testing. Any attempt to increase adher-

ence to ethical precepts must begin with a better understanding of the funda-
mentals of testing.

The Importance of Testing

Any discussion of the ethics of testing needs to begin with an emphasis on the
importance of testing in our society and the magnitude of the role it plays in
people's lives. If it were not such an important endeavor, the ethics of its use
would be of less concern. Tests can have powerful influences on the lives of
both individuals and subgroups within the population. They have the capacity to
do great good or cause harm. Which of the outcomes occurs often depends on
the ethics of those involved. There are relatively few legal limits on testing and
the amount of governmental oversight is minimal. This makes ethics all the
more important.

Basic Issues in the Ethics of Testing

In this section we will discuss the following six basic issues related to the ethics
of testing:

1. Tests must be valid for their intended purpose.
2. Tests should not be biased.
3. Only people competent to administer and interpret tests should be permitted
   to do so.
4. Access to test materials should be restricted to those who are competent to
   use them and have a legitimate need to possess them.
5. Standardized achievement tests should be constructed and administered so
   that the scores accurately reflect the achievement of the students taking them.
6. Test results and interpretations belong to the person tested.

Tests Must Be Valid.   Tests must be valid for their intended purpose. The most
basic rule in the ethics of testing is the requirement that the interpretation of
tests be valid. The 1985 edition of *Standards for Educational and Psychological
Testing* defines validity in terms of the inferences made from test scores. At one
time, it was considered correct to discuss validity in terms of "test validity."
However, now the validity of the interpretation of tests is deemed most important. According to Tittle (1989), the ethical use of tests requires another step. It
is necessary to evaluate the validity of inferences made about test scores in terms
of the context of the use of the test.

The test publisher and author(s) must take responsibility for ensuring that the
manuals and promotional materials that accompany tests claim or imply validity
only where such inferences can legitimately be made. The user must ensure that
inferences about test scores are valid.

Tests Should Not Be Biased.   One particularly important issue related to validity is the assessment of minorities. It is important to determine not only if the

inferences made from test scores are valid, but also whether the inferences are valid for the particular cultural or ethnic groups with which they are being used. Tests are samples of behavior, and behavior is affected by culture; therefore, membership in a particular cultural or ethnic group can be expected to have some effect on test scores. The critical issue is the degree to which this status affects the criterion behavior. If cultural background affects test scores but not criterion behavior, then the test is unfair. For example, mechanical aptitude on the Armed Services Vocational Aptitude Battery is assessed by requiring the test taker to match tools with their names. Males outperform females on this test, but there is no evidence that they surpass females in job performance. If females are denied access to certain occupations as a result of low scores on this test of mechanical aptitude, then the test is unfair to females. A test is considered more fair if cultural background affects both the test score and the criterion. Even if both the test score and the criterion are affected, the following ethical question remains: Should we use the particular test? Answers to this question would depend on the purposes of the test. Ethical problems concerning the assessment of minorities do not stem so much from the tests themselves as from the ways the tests are used and in particular the inferences that are drawn from the test scores.

There are certain legal restrictions on the use of tests on minorities. For instance, the Uniform Guidelines on Employee Selection Procedures developed jointly by the Equal Employment Opportunity Commission, the U.S. Civil Service Commission, the U.S. Department of Labor, and the U.S. Department of Justice (1978) and the Equal Employment Act (Title VII of the Civil Rights Act of 1964 and its subsequent amendments) place some restrictions on test use in relation to their impact on minorities. Any time the use of tests has an adverse racial impact, the users are required to defend the validity of the inferences made about the test.

Test publishers do not want their tests to be biased. Not only does such a practice raise questions of ethics but it also is bad for business. These publishers spend enormous amounts of money and put forth extraordinary efforts to prevent biases in their tests, but there are few issues in measurement that are more technically complex than those determining whether items are biased. There is no easy way to make these determinations. They cannot be done by inspection. Experience shows that just because an item appears biased does not mean that it actually is. Empirical studies of test items often identify biased items that on the surface appear to be completely fair. The test user is often placed in a dilemma in making decisions about whether a test is biased because determining bias or the lack of it is exceptionally difficult.

Competent People Should Administer and Interpret Tests.   Not everyone is equally qualified to administer and interpret tests, and just because a person is qualified to administer one test does not mean that he or she is qualified to administer other tests. For example, most states place restrictions on who can use psychological tests. In general, only licensed psychologists or psychiatrists can administer these instruments for a fee, although state laws differ and there are many exceptions to the guidelines. Included under the rubric of psychological tests are individual intelligence tests, the major projective tests, and the Minnesota Multiphasic Personality Inventory from among the group-administered personality tests. Although there is general agreement that the use of other tests should be restricted to those who are competent, decisions about competency are left in the hands of the publisher or user. Diagnostic decisions made by people who are not qualified or by those who are operating outside of their areas of expertise are clearly unethical, but determining who is qualified is not easy. Each individual must decide whether the use of a particular test is within his or her range of expertise and understand that not everyone who is legally qualified to use a test is competent to do so. At the same time, there may be individuals who are quite competent to administer a particular test (perhaps because of training or supervised experience) but are not otherwise qualified; these individuals might be legally restricted from administering the particular test.

Access to Test Materials Should Be Restricted.   Access to psychological test materials is straightforward. Access should be restricted to those who are qualified by law and by training to use them. For other tests, access raises sometimes difficult ethical questions. Extensive training is not required for the administration of standardized ability and achievement tests but their dissemination could have a marked impact on their validity. In the hands of the parents of children who are candidates for admission to advanced and gifted classed, copies of group ability tests used to determine admission compromise the validity of the tests. If teachers have access to the achievement tests their students are required to take, the possibility exists that cheating will occur. As a rule, it is not difficult for the public to get access to standardized tests, and some publishers suggest that teachers take the tests themselves. Most schools now have copying machines, which increases access and opportunities for the inappropriate use of tests.

Test publishers generally have policies to control who is to have access to tests, but they sometimes are faced with conflicts of interest. They have a need to be successful as businesses, and their business is to sell tests. The more they restrict who can buy tests, the fewer sales they are likely to make. To control access to tests, test publishers generally provide some or all of the following in their catalogs: a purchaser qualification form, information about who is and who is not qualified to order the different types of tests included in the catalog; and information from the 1985 edition of *Standards for Educational and Psychological Testing* specifying the requirements for ethical testing. It is still necessary for a worker at the publishing house to make a decision about whether to ship a particular test to an individual.

Scores Should Accurately Reflect Achievement.   Recently, concern has been expressed about the high scores being reported on standardized achievement tests. As was described in Chapter 11, in virtually every state and school district that reports scores, mean student performance has been above average; this phenomenon has been called the "Lake Woebegon Effect."

Everyone associated with this phenomenon, from test publishers to public school officials, has proffered explanations. One alleged cause for the high scores is the propensity for teachers to teach the test (Mehrens & Kaminski, 1989). To the extent that this activity leads to higher performance on intended instructional objectives, the instructional time is well spent. If the instruction has no other purpose than to raise test scores, with no effect on the learning objectives, such instruction is inappropriate, unethical, and a waste of instructional time.

The honest and accurate assessment of students using standardized achievement tests depends on the ethics of the test developers, users, and administrators. Unfortunately, there is a lack of agreement regarding just what these ethics are, or should be, which leaves open a great many inappropriate practices. Mehrens and Kaminski (1989) provide points on a continuum ranging from practices that are generally considered to be acceptable to practices that are generally viewed as unacceptable. The most difficult ethical decisions concern the points in between. Mehrens and Kaminski suggest the following descriptive headings for the continuum:

1. general instruction on objectives not determined by looking at the objectives measured on standardized tests;

2. teaching test-taking skills;

3. instruction on objectives generated by a commercial organization where the objectives may have been determined by looking at objectives measured by a variety of standardized tests. (The objectives taught may, or may not, contain objectives on teaching test taking skills.);

4. instruction based on objectives (skills, subskills) that specifically match those on the standardized test to be administered;

5. instruction on specifically matched objectives (skills, subskills) where the practice (instruction) follows the same format as the test questions:

6. practice (instruction) on a published parallel form of the same test; and

7. practice (instruction) on the same test. (p. 16)

According to Mehrens and Kaminski (1989), Activity 1 is always ethical, Activities 6 and 7 are never ethical, and the other activities are open to debate and discussion. In many instances, test preparation activities go beyond what is considered ethical. Providing inappropriate assistance to students is partially the result of the tremendous pressure felt to obtain higher scores at any cost and partially a function of a lack of understanding of the basic measurement principles involved.

Another big problem in making a clear delineation between what is ethical and what is unethical in helping students improve their performance on achievement tests is the difference in orientation between norm-referenced and criterion-referenced tests. With criterion-referenced tests, it is considered desirable to focus instruction on the specific objectives of a test. This focused instruction would not be appropriate for norm-referenced tests. Often tests that are not really criterion referenced (according to accepted definitions), because they do not permit reference to a well-defined domain, are made to look like criterion-referenced tests for marketing purposes. As a result, some users may feel that it is legitimate to focus instruction on the specific objectives of the tests.

Test Results and Interpretations Belong to the Person Tested. Confidentiality of test results constitutes a fundamental and important aspect of test ethics. With some notable exceptions, tests should be administered for the benefit of the person being tested, and the responses and interpretations belong to that person.

Tests should not be administered to anyone unless he or she (or his or her parent or guardian) agrees to the testing. This permission should come in the form of informed consent from the person being tested (or the person's parent or guardian if he or she is a minor).

Informed consent refers to explanations, in comprehensible language of (1) the reasons for testing, (2) the content of the test, (3) who will have access to results, and (4) how the results will be used. The explanation also must make it clear that the person to be tested has the option to deny consent. Permission to release the test results at some time in the future, if not included in the original consent form, must be obtained before the results are released to another agency.

Informed consent is not required for school-related tests or employment-related testing, where permission is implicit in the employment application. But, even if it is not required, the examiner should inform the test taker of the purpose of the test and how it is to be used.

Test takers or their legal representatives should be given explanations of test results in terms that they can understand. It is generally possible to frame even complex test results so that they can be understood at some level by any person being tested.

The test user has a responsibility to maintain the security of files that contain test results. Only individuals with a legitimate need to see these files and with permission through informed consent should have access to files that contain test results. Special care must be taken with computer networks, data bases, and electronic mail to ensure that test security is maintained.

Summary

During the last 30 years, there has been an increase in the interest in as well as ser-vices for exceptional children. With the increase in services came the need for better and more highly refined assessment techniques for making decisions about the eligi-bility of students for special programs. Although the procedures for identifying stu-dents with sensory deficits (hearing and visual impairments) is relatively straightfor-ward as is the identification of trainable mentally handicapped children, the identification of educable handicapped, learning disabled, and emotionally handi-capped children is fraught with difficulties. There is a lack of agreement regarding the definition of who belongs in each of these categories and the criteria that should be applied for eligibility. These problems are exacerbated by the need to control eligibility for placement in these classes both to conserve limited special education resources and to prevent the tragedy that misidentification can cause. The identification of the academically gifted poses a different set of problems, but these problems do relate to those of special education placement. Difficulties exist in obtaining consensus regarding who should be identified as belonging in this category. As with special education programs, concern exists about limited resources.

Minimum competency testing is used to determine whether a student should be awarded a high school diploma, whether a prospective teacher should receive a teaching certificate, or whether a practicing teacher should keep his or her certification and to make competency decisions about licensing and certification in other occupations. Although there is considerable agreement that the tests serve valid purposes, the technical problems in implementing the tests are overwhelming. There is also a tendency for passing rates on such tests to escalate gradually to the point that virtually nobody fails, and the administration of the test becomes essentially meaningless.

Ethics in testing represents an important but sometimes neglected aspect of measurement. Because tests in many cases are used to make critically important decisions about people and because there is often sizable financial involvement by those publishing tests, selling tests, using tests, administering tests, and taking tests, it is important that care and thought go into their appropriate use. The need for care in the use of tests is made even more crucial because there are few legal restrictions on the sale, claims of the sellers, and uses of such tests.

Some of the basic issues in the ethics of testing follow:

1. Tests must be valid for their intended purpose.

2. Tests should not be biased.

3. Only people competent to administer and interpret tests should be permitted to do so.

4. Access to test materials should be restricted to those who are competent to use them and have a legitimate need to possess them.

5. Standardized achievement tests should be constructed and administered so that the scores accurately reflect the achievement of the students taking them.

6. Test results and interpretations belong to the person tested.

Questions and Exercises

1. Describe the impact of the Education for all Handicapped Children Act (Public Law 94–142) on the testing of children for placement in special education programs.
2. What are the major problems of assessment associated with each of the following special education populations?
   (a) Trainable mentally handicapped
   (b) Educable mentally handicapped
   (c) Learning disabled
   (d) Emotionally disturbed
3. Describe how you would set up a procedure for selecting students for a class for academically gifted students.

4. Present the case for maintaining separate programs for exceptional children. Present the case for the integration of such students into the regular program.
5. What are the benefits of requiring students to pass a minimum competency test as a prerequisite for graduation?
6. Why did minimum competency programs become so popular? Why did their popularity decline following implementation?
7. Currently, only three states have implemented statewide testing programs that result in the canceling of teaching certificates for teachers who do not pass a competency test. Why haven't other states adopted such programs?
8. What have been the results of legal challenges requiring students to pass minimum competency tests to receive high school diplomas?
9. What ethical responsibilities does the director of testing of a school district have in the administration of a systemwide achievement test?
10. What are the ethical limitations placed on a teacher in preparing students to take a standardized achievement test?
11. What restrictions are placed on who has access to standardized test materials that are centrally produced?

Suggested Readings

Cunningham, G. K. (1986). *Education and psychological measurement*. New York: Macmillan.

Diamond, E. E., & Fremer, J. (1989). The Joint Committee on Testing Practices and the Code of Fair Testing Practices in Education. *Education Measurement: Issues and Practice 8*(1), 23–24.

Eyde, L. D., Moreland, K. L., Robertson, G. J., Primoff, E. S., & Most, R. B. (1988). *Test user qualifications: A data-based approach to promoting good test use*. Washington DC: American Psychological Association.

McGuinness, D. (1986). Facing the "learning disability" crisis. *Education Week, 5*(21), 22, 28.

Mehrens, W. A., & Kaminski, J. (1989). Methods for improving standardized test scores: Fruitful, fruitless, or fraudulent. *Educational Measurement: Issues and Practice, 8*(1), 14–22.

Reis, S. M. (1989). Reflection on policy affecting the education of gifted and talented students: Past and future perspectives. *American Psychologist, 44*(2), 399–408.

Roth, R. (Ed.). (1985). Special issue on teacher testing [Special issue]. *Educational Measurement: Issues and Practice 4*(3).

Rudner, L. M. (1988). Teacher testing—An update. *Education Measurement: Issues and Practice, 7*(1), 16–19.

Shepard, L. A. (1989). Identification of mild handicaps. In R. L. Linn (Ed.), *Education measurement* (3rd ed., pp. 545–572). New York: Macmillan.

Shepard, L. A., & Kreitzer, A. E. (1987). The Texas teacher test. *Educational Measurement: Issues and Practice 16*(6), 22–31.

Shepard, L. A., Smith, M. L., & Vojir, C. P. (1983). Characteristics of pupils identified as learning disabled. *American Educational Research Journal, 20*(3), 309–331.

CHAPTER 15
Social and Political Issues in Testing

Introduction

In the brief history of testing provided in Chapter 1, we offered the opinion that testing is in a renewed period of criticism that began in the 1960s with rising concerns over tests as instruments of the invasion of privacy and discrimination. The recent history of psychological and educational measurement has been quite turbulent, with these two major public policy issues making the waves. As a result of the perceived threat of tests as invasions of privacy and their impact— either intended or not—on social equity, government agencies and the courts have come to play a major role in regulating tests and testing practices. The issue of discrimination based on race, ethnic background, or gender has led to a widespread concern with bias in test content and use. In this chapter we explore both issues briefly and provide guidelines for responsible testing practices.

Invasion of Privacy

Legal and political concern about all types of inroads into individual privacy has been increasing for over two decades. The widespread and sometimes irresponsible use of credit bureaus, the advent of data bases in which information about individuals can be mechanically and impersonally stored (and sometimes retrieved by unauthorized people for illegal or inappropriate purposes), and a growing belief that people's lives are their own business have all sensitized society to using any procedure that might probe into a person's private life and reveal it to others. Personality inventories have been the most frequent targets of this concern because the questions that they ask are often highly personal and revealing. Consider the following questions:

○ Do you have trouble making new friends?

○ Did you ever want to run away from home?

○ Do you sometimes have thoughts that are too bad to talk about?

These questions certainly ask the individual to make public—to whomever may have access to the responses—some quite personal aspects of his or her inner life. We may well ask under what circumstances and to whom such revelations appropriately may be called for.

Although the personal exposure may be less obvious, a mathematics test that causes a person, in effect, to say "I don't do mathematics very well" can also be seen as calling for a personal revelation that the individual might prefer not to make. When is it reasonable to demand such information? Under what circumstances may a societal need to know override individuals' rights to keep their own secrets—that is, their rights to privacy? Here, we offer a number of considerations that can be used to judge when it is reasonable to require people to demonstrate what they can do or what they believe or feel.

1. For whose benefit will the information be used? When information is assembled to provide specific help to the individual to whom it relates, objection

tion to collecting it will be minimal. Such a situation arises when classroom tests are given and used to identify specific skills on which individual students need further practice or when diagnostic tests are given as guides to planning remedial work. Such a situation also arises when a student goes to a counselor to seek help in career planning or with a personal problem and questionnaires or inventories are used to provide the counselor *and* the student with information to help in the counseling process. When some general social good is anticipated from the information, such as using achievement test data to guide a state or school district in the allocation of resources for education, we are not generally inclined to be too critical as long as the demands on the time and effort of the examinees are reasonable. Another type of social good is found in licensing examinations that protect the public from incompetent practitioners of important functions—from driving a truck or selling real estate to practicing law or performing brain surgery.

A less obvious case of who may benefit from information arises when tests are used for placement. Suppose, for example, an aptitude test is used to assign students to sections of a course. The objective of the testing may be to provide instruction focused on the level at which these children function; in this case, the children should benefit from a program that proceeds at their pace. But, children may also be identified as "second class" in some way if they do not make it into the "top" group. In such cases, the educational benefits for the children should be made clear to them and their parents before the testing is undertaken.

The most severe restriction to placement testing would seem to be indicated when the information sought will be used solely for the benefit of some individual or group other than the one supplying the information (and perhaps to the detriment of the latter). The most obvious illustration is the use of tests and self-report inventories by employers. However, even here, it can be argued that society benefits if the individuals in each job are those who are likely to be most effective and most satisfied in the position.

2. How relevant is the information for the decisions to be made?   What evidence is there that test scores will lead to correct decisions? Even when the goal is worthwhile, there is no point in gathering evidence whose relevance is so limited that it provides almost no improvement in the decisions to be made. Conversely, the more clearly relevant the information is, the more one is justified in calling on the individual to provide it—always assuming the uses to be made of the information are themselves defensible.

3. If the information is being gathered for the social good rather than for the good of the individual, how crucial is that social good?   A group of students was asked whether it would be acceptable to gather information on the emotional stability of candidates for each of several jobs. The percentages of students saying "yes" were as follows:

Clerical employee	34
Airline pilot	75
Astronaut	83

These differences may reflect in part a judgment of the relevance of emotional stability to functioning in the three jobs. But they also probably reflect a perception of the amount of social damage or loss that might result from having a person "come unglued"—become unable to function—in each of the three settings. Society is well advised to be more demanding in the standards it sets for surgeons than in those it sets for sausage sellers. The rights of one individual may have to yield more when the rights of others are crucially involved.

4. How "personal" is the information being sought? Some questions are perceived as much more "nosy,"or invasive, than others. In a questionnaire study used in the context of personnel selection, Rosenbaum (1971) asked which items people felt were an invasion of privacy. Five broad factors were identified in the set of 66 items, and most of the items could be placed in one of these five clusters. The designation of the clusters, the number of items pertaining to each cluster, and the average percentages of participants considering items of the kind in each cluster an invasion of privacy were as follows:

Cluster	No. of Items	Percentage
Family background and influences	17	49
Personal history data	19	3
Interests and values	11	12
Financial management data	7	52
Social adjustment	7	16

It appears from these results that tests of ability, which might fall in the same category as interests or personal history, and assessments of interests are seen by these participants as acceptable in an employment context, although probing personality inventories dealing with matters of politics, religion, finances, and other personal matters are inappropriate. Of course, when the interest is in group rather than individual results and provisions are made to ensure the anonymity of examinees, issues of invasion of privacy are likely to be defused. However, most situations not relating to research *do* require the examinees to be identified. Under these circumstances, adequate provision for the security of the information is essential. The data should be available only to those who need it for legitimate decision-making purposes.

5. Has provision been made for informed consent? One way to minimize the offensiveness of any invasion of privacy is to give the test, questionnaire, or other procedure only after obtaining the *informed consent* of the person or of a parent or guardian of a minor child. Informed consent implies that the person to be tested has been told what information will be collected, why it is being collected, and how it will be used. It also implies that the consenter is competent to understand what information is being provided and has the right to decide whether to participate or not without prejudice. Meeting these conditions may be difficult when the consenter is of limited ability or is from a limited or different background from that of the investigator. Increasingly, informed consent is required in federally funded psychological and/or medical research and service programs. The American Psychological Association has also adopted guidelines to protect the rights of people participating in such studies.

Informed consent raises problems both for the person seeking the information and for the person providing the information. For the person being tested, there must exist a genuine freedom to refuse to participate if the act of consent is to mean very much. Applicants who desperately want particular jobs or prisoners who feel their privileges will depend on whether they cooperate are under considerable pressure to consent to whatever procedures are requested. Under such circumstances, it is especially important that the demands be justifiable without the need to resort to informed consent—that is, the good to be achieved is clear to all.

From the point of view of the investigator, two problems arise: one from the word "informed" and one from the fact that you invite refusal to participate by making consent an explicit positive act.

The first problem is encountered when it is essential that participants remain somewhat naive about the nature and purpose of the procedure. Sometimes, the process of fully informing them can make their scores meaningless because their behavior on the tests may be radically altered. This problem arises whenever the purpose of the test—or of a psychological experiment—is to some degree covert or devious. In some situations, informing the participants may destroy that person's usefulness for the investigation. In such cases, it is essential for the purpose of the study to be fully justified, that all possible precautions be taken to ensure the safety and well-being of the participants, and that participants be informed of the true nature of the study as soon after participation as possible.

The other problem in requiring explicit consent is that it invites refusal, a refusal that might never have been contemplated if acquiescence had been taken for granted. Particularly in such projects as norming tests or the conduct of surveys of abilities or attitudes, in which the representativeness of the sample is critically important, refusals and dropouts are a serious problem. If, as we suspect is often the case, those who refuse differ in important ways from those who consent, the resulting sample is biased, and the nature and amount of that bias is usually unknown. The consequent distortion of results may seriously reduce or even destroy their meaning and usefulness.

Self-Incrimination and Right to Rebuttal

A concern related to invasion of privacy, but still distinguishable from it, is that of self-incrimination. In words from the Fifth Amendment to the Constitution of the United States, no person shall "be compelled in any criminal case to be a witness against himself," and modern American culture has tended to extend this notion to many noncriminal contexts. We view with concern procedures that *force* people, either through pressures brought to bear on them or through concealed and indirect inferences that are made from their responses, to give information that will be used to their own disadvantage. Yet we recognize that the individual who seeks some special personal gain—for example, entry into an education program, a job, or even a bank credit agreement—has some responsibility to justify receipt of that special consideration and that the attempt to justify might involve some risk. Perhaps a reasonable view would be that the potential gains for the person should at least balance the possible harm from information that may prove derogatory. Unfortunately, assigning value to the gains and risks is a subjective process fraught with the possibility for error and misunderstanding. But it is probably better to try to consider such factors than to leave the issues unaddressed.

People who stand accused in a court of law have the right to face their accusers, hear the evidence against them, and offer evidence to refute the accusations. One concern with some uses of test data is that this situation does not prevail. The examinees do not see their test results, do not know how they are being interpreted, and are not aware of what decisions are being based on them. (Of course, this concern is not specific to test results. It applies in equal measure to any dossier that is maintained on a person.)

In view of the less than perfect reliability of test scores, the occasional day when an individual performs poorly for irrelevant reasons, and the occurrence, albeit rare, of errors in scoring, score conversion, or score handling, the possibility that a person may be condemned by an erroneous, or flawed, score is sufficiently real for the investigator to wish to give the examinee (or a parent or guardian) an opportunity to see the score and to react to it. The reaction might take the form of a description of mitigating circumstances, a request for a retest, or presentation of other compensating information. In any event, if the results are made available to and perhaps discussed with the concerned person (or his or her representative), you avoid the impression of star chamber proceedings in which a person is forced to provide information that is then kept secret and used in secret ways. This concern about the secrecy of academic records, including test results, has been crystallized in the Buckley-Pell Amendment, which specifies that school records must be made available to parents or students. Implementing this requirement has generated some practical problems for schools— and may perhaps encourage them to do less testing and to keep less complete records—but the requirement does provide a safeguard against the types of faulty test results mentioned above. And, computerized recordkeeping may make it easier for school personnel to access records when they are requested by parents or students.

Another reaction to the secrecy that has surrounded testing in education is the New York state law regarding "truth in testing." This law, which was enacted in 1979, largely in response to the aptitude testing programs of the Educational Testing Service, requires companies that produce tests administered in the state of New York to do three things.

First they must disclose the results of all studies of each test's validity. This provision is not particularly controversial except that testing companies might wish to suppress studies that question the validity of their products.

Second, the law requires that students be informed of how their scores were calculated (any item weights used and the types of transformations applied) and what the scores mean (what norm groups were used). Although this second provision may require participants to learn more about testing than they really wanted to know, it has not presented any real problems for the testing companies.

The third provision of the law requires that a copy of the test questions, the answer key, and the participant's answers be provided to any examinee who requests them. Because part of the meaning of test scores of this nature depends on all examinees having equal pretest access to the test questions (up to now, none), this provision carries the implication that if even one student obtains a copy of the test, all of the items must be replaced for future testings. Otherwise, different examinees may have had differential access to the items, making their scores noncomparable.

One objective of this law was to enable people who felt that their test scores might be inaccurate to check one potential source of error and to rebut the test score if errors were found. This is a laudable purpose. Unfortunately, from the point of view of quality and economy of measurement, the law has several adverse consequences. There has been an increase in the cost of testing because of the need to write new items for each test. Because new items must be written for each test, the validity of a particular set of items is less well established than was the case prior to enactment of the law. In addition, because the items change each year, it is much more difficult to equate the meaning of scores over a period of years. It remains to be seen whether the potential benefits of the law to individuals will offset the losses to the educational system. Preliminary reports indicate that there have been very few requests for copies of the tests.

Physical or Psychological Risk

In addition to concerns about testing as an invasion of privacy and as potentially self-incriminating, a third concern that has been expressed is that testing may invade the rights of the individual by subjecting the person tested to "physical or psychological risk." It is hard to see how any of the standard educational or psychological tests of the type we have considered in this book could subject the examinee to *physical* risks beyond the normal hazards of living. However, there may be some possibility of increased psychological risk. Tests can be somewhat anxiety provoking. Personality inventories may raise issues and set the person to thinking about aspects of his or her feelings that lead the person to worry. Poor performance on an ability test may be damaging to a person's self-esteem. If some extra anxiety, worry, or self-derogation are considered to represent psychological hazards, it must be acknowledged that test taking and test results may at times contribute to these hazards. The problem is to judge the severity of the hazard and to balance it against the countervailing benefits either to the person tested or to the larger society.

A somewhat different type of risk is that which may result from classifying or categorizing individuals. All of us have a natural, but sometimes regrettable, tendency to try to simplify the infinite complexity of the world by placing people and events in categories to which we attach labels. We then deal with the person or event as a representative of a class rather than as a unique individual. This labeling carries with it a cluster of implications as to what people in this category are like, can do, and can be expected to become. A host of such implications attaches to the labels "mentally retarded," "emotionally disturbed," or "delinquent," and the labels carry with them prospects for the way that person may be treated in the educational and social system.

Labeling is at best an oversimplified description, even when the label is appropriately applied. Furthermore, many labels are likely to be thought of as explanations rather than simply as descriptive classifications. Instances of mislabeling are a particular matter of concern, and the prospect that test results may frequently play a role in mislabeling people from economically disadvantaged or culturally different backgrounds is one basis for concern about the hazards to the individual as a result of testing.

Those of us who make tests and those of us who use them must be continuously on guard against the tendency to label and to categorize glibly. We must continuously insist and remind others that a test score is simply *one descriptive* fact about a person and that this fact can be fully understood only in terms of the total past and present context of the person. It is an exacting challenge for all who work in education and the helping professions— for example, teachers, counselors, social workers, and psychologists—to know each student or client thoroughly enough and to put all of the information together wisely enough that the person is understood and helped, not merely labeled.

Possible Hazards to the Rights of Groups

One of the most prevalent themes in popular discussions of testing is that tests are unfair to certain groups. The term that is used is *bias*. It is often asserted that standardized tests are used to deprive certain groups of access to educational opportunities and jobs. To the extent that tests are used mechanically as selection and placement devices and to the extent that some groups in our society — most commonly ethnic and racial minorities or poor people more generally— do less well on tests, tests *do* become instruments through which access to education and jobs is disproportionately barred to members of these groups. The question that must be addressed is whether they are unjustly barred and, more generally, what constitutes fair and equitable use of tests for the selection, placement, and classification of individuals for educational or occupational purposes.

Test Bias and Equal Opportunity

The issue of bias in testing has probably been the most hotly debated topic relating to psychological and educational measurement over the last 25 years. When Congress passed the Civil Rights Act of 1964, Title VII of the Act expressly prohibited the use of tests for the purpose of discriminating against individuals for employment on the basis of race, creed, color, sex, or national origin. However, the framers of the Act expressly permitted the use of tests to make job-related decisions when test scores could be shown to be related to an individual's level of job performance. Thus, the Act required that the test be a valid predictor of job performance for all individuals with whom it was to be used, and a test would be considered unbiased if it gave equally accurate predictions for members from any racial, ethnic, or gender group.

The situation changed dramatically for the use of tests in employment in 1971 when the U.S. Supreme Court, in the case of *Griggs v. Duke Power Co.,* held that a test could be *presumed to be* biased if it gave differential predictions *for groups.* This decision, subsequent amendments to the Civil Rights Act of 1964, and various federal administrative directives led to the development of the 1978 Equal Employment Opportunity Commission Uniform Guidelines for Employee Selection Procedures. Thus, if the members of one group, almost always minority group members or women, tended to score lower on a particular measurement, it became the responsibility of the employer to demonstrate that the test was a valid predictor of job performance. The principle developed by the Supreme Court in *Griggs* is called *adverse impact;* a demonstration of adverse impact by the plaintiff shifts the burden of proof to the employer to show that discrimination did not occur.

A 1976 suit in Illinois by the Golden Rule Insurance Company against the Educational Testing Service led to one solution to the bias issue. Golden Rule alleged that differential passing rates for blacks (52%) and whites (77%) on the Illinois Insurance Licensing Examination was proof that the test was racially biased. In an out-of-court agreement in 1984, in which the Educational Testing Service did not admit guilt, the parties agreed to a revised criterion for selecting items for the examination. The Educational Testing Service agreed to use items for which the success rate for blacks and whites differed by no more than 15%. The principle adopted in the Golden Rule case has been used in several other situations in an effort to equate passing rates on selection tests. (See Gottfredson and Sharf (1988) for a series of papers that comment on bias and the use of tests for employment decisions.)

A number of court actions have addressed the use of tests in educational settings as well as in employment. Perhaps the most well known is *Larry P. v. Nelson Riles,* in which a group of black children who had been placed in a class for the educable mentally retarded sued the school district and the State of California, claiming that the tests used to make the placement decisions were racially biased. After heated debate in which both sides called on expert witnesses in psychology and education, the judge ruled that the tests, the Wechsler Intelligence Scale for Children and the Stanford-Binet Intelligence Scale, were racially biased. As a result of the suit, the use of standardized tests for educational placement of minorities was banned in California. (It is interesting to observe that at almost the same time that this final judgment was being rendered in California, a judge in Illinois was hearing a case with very similar conditions and arguments. In *Parents in Action on Special Education v. Hannon,* the judge, after hearing the arguments and reviewing the test items personally, concluded that the same tests that had been found to be biased against blacks in California were not biased against blacks in Illinois!)

Barring the use of tests of aptitude or ability may have unintended consequences. W. B. Allen (1988), a member of the U.S. Commission on Civil Rights in California, has described such a situation.

> In the case of Mary Amaya, a California mother, the state refuses to her son [sic] an IQ test on the grounds that it is "protecting" him from bias inherent in the test. . . .
>
> Consider the irony: Mrs. Amaya's son has been recommended for assignment to remedial courses. She believes that he may not require them. In an earlier, less enlightened era, an older son of hers had a similar experience. In that case the IQ test refuted the psychologist's subjective evaluation and the lad was spared a potentially damaging assignment. Mrs. Amaya would like to have such an opportunity for her youngest son as well. It has been denied. . . . Thus, a family of at best modest means is placed in a position of having to fight off the entire legal edifice of its state and federal courts in order to guarantee an opportunity for its son. (pp. 368–369)

Allen (1988) notes further that in California " 'there is no fundamental civil right to be able to take an IQ test.' Where such a test may be a means to establish one's eligibility for an opportunity, therefore, it may nevertheless be denied to a black child by the state" (p. 368). Thus, protection can be a mixed blessing.

There have been a number of other court challenges to the use of tests and other objective measures to aid in decision making in education and employment. The challenged procedures have included everything from aptitude and achievement tests to height and strength requirements. In general, until recently, the courts have tended to find in favor of the plaintiffs and against the tests and objective decision rules. However, following is a summary of a 1988 U.S. Supreme Court decision (*Watson v. Fort Worth Bank and Trust*):

> Seven justices agreed that a statistical disparity is not always sufficient to make out a prima facie case [of discrimination]. . . . In addition, a majority of the justices would require a plaintiff to identify the *specific* decision-making practice being challenged and then to prove that this practice *caused* the exclusion of applicants for jobs or promotions because of their membership in a protected group [minority or female]. (Sharf, 1988, p. 242)

Attempts to Reduce Bias

Challenges to the use of tests have had the beneficial effect of causing test developers to be much more careful in the selection of test items and the composition of norm groups. For example, in the preparation of the fourth edition of the Stanford-Binet, the authors used a panel of judges that included members of the larger minority groups to screen items for content that might be gender or race biased before the items were ever tried out. A second panel reviewed the items and item statistics from the initial tryouts to eliminate any items that were clearly biased. Similar procedures have been taken for recent editions of the Cognitive Abilities Test, the Iowa Tests of Basic Skills, and the Tests of Achievement and Proficiency. In addition, the publishers of all of these tests carried out careful statistical analyses of the performance of each item further to ensure that bias in test content had been minimized. Other test developers use similar procedures, with the result that the tests often show smaller group differences without the loss of predictive validity. However, even with elaborate precautions to eliminate bias, some differences remain between the average test performance of members of different ethnic groups unless an extreme application of the "Golden Rule" principle (coined from the agreement reached in the Golden Rule Insurance Company case), that only items with zero difference in passing rates are used, forces the mean scores to be equal.

The question of test bias is inextricably bound to test validity. Remember that validity relates to the use that will be made of a test score. A test may be valid for one use and not for another. A claim of test bias is really a claim that the use of the test for a particular decision or type of decision is not appropriate for a given group of individuals. But accurate prediction or description is only part of the story. Test use takes place in a social context and has particular social consequences. As Cole and Moss (1989) and Messick (1989) point out, it is also a matter of social policy whether a given test should be used for a given purpose in light of the likely results of that use. There is relatively little question that tests can improve efficiency and productivity in educational and occupational contexts, but we must also ask how much weight should be given to maximizing the productivity of educational and occupational establishments (in whatever terms that "productivity" is defined). On the other hand, how much weight should be given to balancing opportunity between different segments of the society or to eliminating any existing educational or occupational differences? Psychometric research may be able to provide some crude estimates of the cost in productivity of forcing numerical equality among groups in selection and placement decisions (see Schmidt, 1988b), but psychometric research alone cannot determine whether the cost in relation to one type of value is justified by the gain in quite a different value. That judgment must be made by the larger society, with some understanding of the costs and benefits involved. To state an extreme case, measures of Characteristic X might yield perfect predictions of performance in Job Y but might reveal large mean differences between left-handed and right-handed people. The test is not biased from a statistical point of view, but the society might choose not to use it because of the real or imagined negative social consequences of having all jobs of Type Y performed by left-handed employees. It is important to differentiate between matters of validity in test use (in the sense of the accuracy of the predictions that are made) and the social desirability of using the information thus exposed.

Benefits that Testing Is Designed to Achieve

To this point, we have considered primarily the hazards and problems for individuals and groups that may arise from the use of tests. However, there is another side of the coin. Testing is carried out to a considerable extent to achieve positive outcomes (benefits) both for the individual and for the larger society. In this section, we will consider those positive outcomes. In a later section we will compare the hazards and the benefits and see what kind of approach to the use of tests is likely to yield the most in terms of positive values at the least cost in terms of hazards.

Individual Benefits that Testing May Achieve

At various points in this book, we have spoken of testing in relation to decisions—the decisions that are inevitably going to be made by a person, for a person, or about a person in the course of education and life. Those of us who construct tests or teach about tests generally believe that the use of tests will permit (but certainly not guarantee) better, wiser decisions.

Decisions About Educating Individuals. For over 100 years, educators and psychologists have recognized that individuals show substantial differences in learning styles and learning capabilities. Educators have tried various ways to adapt to these differences and to individualize instruction. Any attempt to adapt instruction to the characteristics of a specific individual requires a series of decisions on what pattern of instruction is best suited to that person at that moment. How rapidly and in what way should a particular child be introduced to reading? Should that child be taught mathematics primarily by a "discovery" approach or by practice and drill? Should an eighth grader be taught algebra? And if so, when and at what rate? These are decisions that have to be made if instruction is to be anything but a lock-step process carrying everyone through the same sequence at the same pace with the same instructional materials.

Of course, these decisions can be based wholly on the subjective judgments of teachers, aided by such tests as they may choose to construct and employ in their individual classrooms. But there seem to be advantages to supplementing those judgments with objective appraisals based on a uniform set of exercises that are systematically related to critical skills or aptitudes and that permit comparison with the performance of groups of learners with defined characteristics (e. g., of age, grade, or sex). It has become increasingly clear that the relationships between human characteristics on the one hand and optimal patterns of instruction on the other are more complex than our theories had indicated previously and that we still have much to learn about how and how much to modify instructional materials, methods, or goals to optimize the learning experiences of a particular individual or group. But the problems exist, and the decisions must be made. Tests comprise one source of information that a wise and thoughtful person can use to make better decisions, and these better decisions constitute one of the important values that we try to achieve through the use of tests.

One consequence that tests can have is that by setting objective standards for performance, the academic achievement of minority individuals can be raised. That is, people generally rise to meet the standards that are set for them. When standards such as minimum proficiency criteria on standardized tests are maintained for all students, those who initially are unable to reach the required level soon raise their achievement enough to realize success, particularly if their efforts are supported by the larger society. An example of such an outcome from implementing a minimum competency testing program at the college level may be found in the experience of the State of Florida. When passing an objective test of academic skills such as reading, mathematical computation, and writing was imposed as a requirement for students to get a degree from a community college or to begin upper division work at an undergraduate institution, the failure rate was initially much higher among minority students than among white students. However, with instruction focused on the skills measured by the tests, the minority students soon raised their achievement levels to those required by the tests, and their success rate improved dramatically (see Gottfredson & Sharf, 1988).

We have much to learn about the ways in which human characteristics interact with instructional modes for individuals to learn most effectively. We also have a good deal to learn about techniques of instructional management that will permit different instructional modes to flourish side by side in the same classroom. There is room for improvement of our techniques of diagnosis and prescription for children who have shown specific learning difficulties. But progress is being made, and in this progress, testing has played a key role.

Other Treatment Decisions.   Decisions about the treatment that a person is to receive are, of course, not limited to educational contexts. To the extent that the staffs of mental hospitals, prisons, and other custodial institutions accomplish more than a purely custodial function, they must determine what each person in their care is like and the focus of each person's problems to plan a treatment program that is best for that person. Testing is one tool to help complete the picture.

In addition to treatment decisions, there are also selection, classification, and placement decisions that are made by business and government agencies, including the military. Objective measures of developed abilities can help to eliminate past preferential practices that have supported discrimination against minority individuals. These measures can also help to maximize the effectiveness of training programs by placing individuals in positions where they have a high probability of success.

Personal Decisions Concerning Choices and Future Plans.   It is obvious that every person has many choices to make that depend on the individual knowing what sort of person he or she is. And, without question, many people feel that they need help in making those choices. Help may take the form of information on what the world is like—what careers there are and what each implies in terms of abilities, preparation, and interest; what types of educational programs exist; and what demands each program will make. Help may also take the form of information provided to people about themselves—how their interests, abilities, or temperaments match the demands of different training or career options. This help to the individual in achieving better self-knowledge represents one of the important benefits that test makers hope to achieve.

Social Benefits that May Come from Testing

Psychological and educational tests function not only in the interests of specific individuals for whom the test results may provide useful information and guidance in their educational and vocational careers, but also in the interests of the larger social groups to which those individuals belong. There are a number of social problems in which testing can play a constructive role.

Protection from Incompetence and Ineptitude. There is a wide range of occupations and services in which it is important that all of us be protected from those who cannot perform the occupation or service competently. The need is perhaps most obvious in the field of medicine. We would all agree that it is socially desirable that medical practitioners, physicians, nurses, and therapists of all sorts, be competent and that some guarantees be set up to protect the public from practitioners who lack the requisite knowledge and skills. Of the various bases for ensuring the competence of practitioners in some field, tests to assess knowledge and application of that knowledge represent one important component. The field of medicine has seen some very interesting developments in examinations; these examinations involve assessing not only the individual's mastery of the content of the field but also his or her ability to demonstrate that mastery in diagnosing individual cases and in prescribing proper treatment. In one such examination, a computer is used to simulate a patient. The medical student taking the examination can ask initial questions, call for various tests, and ask more questions based on the results of answers to previous questions before diagnosing the case (Fredericksen, 1986). Obviously, no test can provide a perfect assessment of performance in a professional or occupational speciality, but a test can provide one important safeguard against the individual who is uniformed, incompetent, or inept.

Efficient Use of Social Resources. Related to the protection of people from incompetent practitioners is the protection of society from the waste of its resources in training individuals who are unlikely to master the specialized skill that is required in certain fields. Again, we can take medicine as an example. Medical training is a scarce and heavily subsidized resource, and providing the necessary faculty and laboratories for training medical students is a costly demand on society. With places for training practitioners at a premium, it becomes important to society that those who are given the opportunity to receive this training be people who are likely to learn the skills involved and to succeed in the speciality for which they are being trained. The problem is less acute in areas in which the training is less costly and in which shortages are less severe. However, efficient use of social resources is an important good that we hope to achieve by applying valid selection and placement procedures.

Efficient use of social resources can be thought to apply not only to training programs but also to efficient use of the means of production. If a worker is ineffective in using expensive equipment for industrial production, this inefficiency represents a social cost, one that is perhaps less recognized as a general concern to society than is the allocation of positions in medical schools. However, over the years, improved efficiency in operating our whole production establishment has been one of the goals of personnel testing. The economic gains from applying selection procedures, even ones with modest validity, can be substantial; Schmidt (1988b) cites estimates that run into the tens of billions of dollars annually. Production losses of such a magnitude would seriously affect the price and competitiveness of U.S. products in world markets.

Efficient Educational Procedures.   Education is an expensive enterprise, and its costs have been mounting faster than those of most other segments in society. "Productivity" is not easy to assess in education. Performance on well-designed achievement measures provides one indication of the "yield" from our educational investment, but this performance is a partial indication at best. Attention has been centered on educational standards and accountability in recent years, but good assessments of the more general "output" (such as socialization and critical thinking) of the educational system are lacking. However, we have an uncomfortable feeling that there is nothing in education to match the gains in industrial productivity that have been realized in the last 75 years. Thus, it becomes increasingly important to monitor and guide the educational enterprise so that it can be as effective as possible.

Testing has a role in appraising the outcomes of education, particularly in evaluating curricular innovations and instructional changes. It has a role in routinely monitoring a school's or a school system's overall effectiveness. Additionally, it has a role in adjusting the program of instruction to the individual learner. For example, during the last 25 years, there has been a good deal of research directed toward the idea of "learning style" and particular patterns of learning, implying that information about a specific individual can help to provide an educational treatment that is more appropriate for that individual, one that will foster greater learning gains. We must admit that, to date, the amount of clear, verifiable information on the relationship between learning style and educational treatment is disappointingly slim and limited, but the basic notion is attractive. With the increasing availability of microcomputers in classrooms, truly individualized learning programs become more possible, and we can expect research in this area to lead to significant improvements in instructional efficiency.

Discovering Talent in All Segments of the Population.   One beneficial characteristic of tests is that they are "colorblind"; they characterize each person as an *individual*, not as a member of any group. The test does not know whether the person taking it is black or white; rich or poor; or male or female. It has no preconceptions about who should do well or poorly, and it will recognize the abilities it measures by anyone who displays them. This colorblindness is more than generally can be claimed for teachers and other human evaluators, who may entertain strong convictions that the poor generally or minority individuals specifically should not aspire or be encouraged to pursue higher levels of education or certain types of careers. Although total reliance on objective measures in selection and placement is neither possible nor desirable, objective evidence can temper the natural human tendency to prefer members of one's own social or ethnic group, resulting in fairer treatment for all (see Ryanen, 1988).

As we indicated in an earlier section, there are legitimate concerns that the different backgrounds of some groups in our society may tend to limit the general level of performance of those groups. But *individual* differences still remain. In every group, there are individuals whose test scores are near the top of the total distribution of talent, and in every group, there are individuals who test near the bottom. Tests are designed to recognize individual talent wherever it occurs, without regard to other factors. Thus, test results may be a liberating force to open up opportunities to talented individuals who, because of their group membership, might otherwise have been denied them.

Additions to Knowledge. A fifth benefit to which testing can contribute is the store of potentially useful knowledge about individuals. The science of psychology and the science of education, so far as education can be considered a science, depend on knowing how human beings develop, how they learn, how they react to stress and crisis, and what factors influence the processes of growth, learning, and response. Through science, we observe relationships, manipulate conditions, and measure outcomes. Measurement is central to all scientific enterprise. Advances in science often depend on advances in measurement techniques. Psychology and education are no exceptions. If we wish to study the conditions that favor mental development, we must be able to measure the product of that development—probably by some type of test. If we wish to map the factors that foster hostility toward certain groups in our society, we must be able to measure that hostility—probably with some type of attitude scale; that is, with a test. With all their shortcomings, tests of one sort or another continue to play a central role in research on human growth and learning.

Maximizing the Positive

We have tried to make it clear in the previous sections that although there are certain legitimate concerns about the uses of test results, there are significant advantages to be gained from testing. Under what circumstances will we most likely realize the gains while minimizing the risks of negative effects? The prescription we offer sets a high standard for test use, at best only approximated by fallible human beings, but it seems to us to define a goal for which we should strive. We will use test results constructively in decision making to the extent that we do the following things.

1. Examine and be clear about all values involved. Most decisions, whether they relate to one individual or to a whole class or category of individuals, involve a complex of interacting and competing values. The decision to place a student in a special class might mean more efficient learning for that child and a higher ultimate level of achievement, but the decision might also result in a degree of social isolation from the mainstream of the school. The decision of a student to apply for admission to a particular law school might involve such satisfying consequences as personal prestige and future economic benefits if admitted but might result in such costs as the loss of self-esteem or missed opportunities at other institutions if the candidate is rejected or fails to meet the demands of the program. A personnel selection system may achieve benefits for the employer of money saved through shorter training programs, reduced personnel turnover, and higher worker productivity at a cost to the larger society of reduced employment opportunities for young persons from the inner city.

Choices would exist for individuals and society whether tests had been invented or not, and the decision to ignore the possibility of alternatives is itself a decision. Only as the competing values are recognized and weighed can you decide whether or how tests can contribute to better decisions.

2. Recognize that test scores are only indicators or signs. Score on a mathematics test is an *indicator* of mathematics ability, not the mathematics ability itself. A score on a scholastic aptitude test is one partial indicator of readiness to undertake school learning. The sign is at best an imperfect representation of reality, but the underlying reality is only accessible through the signs that it gives. We become aware that a person has a fever through a clinical thermometer or more crudely through a hot and flushed face, but neither the thermometer nor the person's physical appearance is itself the fever. All measurement is more or less indirect, but when distorting physical, cultural, or social factors intervene, the significance of the indicator may become modified or blurred. Proper interpretation of the measurement requires a sensitivity to possible distortions.

3. Recognize test results as only one type of descriptive information. The key words in this statement are *one* and *descriptive*. In any type of decision, many other types of information are relevant in addition to test scores. A score for the Stanford-Binet or the Wechsler Intelligence Scale for Children-Revised may provide one item of information useful for prescribing a learning program for a poor reader, but an assessment of visual abilities, information about home circumstances, or knowledge about interests and hobbies may provide other equally relevant data. And, the ability test score can do no more than *describe* one aspect of the person's current functioning. Alone, it does not tell *why* the person performs in a particular way, nor does it reveal what causal relationships that performance has, for example, to the difficulties the person is having with reading. Test users must always guard against inferring more than is warranted from a test score.

4. Relate test results to whatever else is known about the person or group. Test scores do not exist in a vacuum. A score only gains maximum meaning when it is fitted into a complete and comprehensive constellation of information about the person. This constellation includes information about the cultural context of the individual, family background, personal history, physical and health status, and much, much more. Computers are being programmed to handle and summarize some portions of this information, but even so, there is a very real question of how fully and soundly the human mind can synthesize such a complex of information about an individual case. The problem becomes more complex when you have to deal with substantial numbers of individuals, for example, school and employment personnel. However, decisions must be made, and wise decisions will result when *all* the available evidence can be weighed, digested, and applied to the problem at hand.

5. Recognize the possibilities of error in all types of descriptive information. We have discussed the measurement error in test scores. We have even pointed out the possibility of gross errors in test administration, scoring, or reporting. The users of test results need continuously to be aware of the approximate nature of any score and to bracket the score, at least mentally, with a band of uncertainty. But it is at least as true, although perhaps less explicitly recognized, that all the other kinds of information that we have about a person are also subject to error. The teacher's impression of how well Joyce reads, how popular Joyce is with her classmates, or how interested her parents are in her school success are all rough and fallible judgments. The physician's appraisal of her health or the social worker's characterization of her home environment are both subjective, approximate, and fallible. We always arrive at decisions on the basis of partial and imperfect information, test scores being imperfect along with everything else. They have the advantage that they are usually more objective than other information and their fallibility has often been carefully studied and quantified.

6. Acknowledge the limits of human wisdom, and maintain tentativeness about the basis for decisions. Decisions *have* to be made, even though we have to make them on the basis of partial and fallible data. We make them as best we can with what wisdom is given to us. Some decisions are tactical day-to-day decisions, such as those made while instructing or guiding a specific child, and the possibility exists of promptly changing direction on the basis of new information from a continuous monitoring of progress. Other decisions are instrumental decisions that only partially commit one to the future, such as the decision to take mathematics courses because of a tentative commitment to enter an engineering program in college. The tentative nature of such decisions should be recognized; redirection can readily be undertaken in light of future evidence. With some decisions, redirection is more difficult than it is for this student taking mathematics courses, and the decision may have permanent consequences. But for all decisions, no matter what role test results had in guiding them, we should always remember that a given decision might be wrong. The conscientious test user will always strive to minimize this possibility.

Summary

The use of tests in psychology and education has faced a number of challenges in recent years. Tests have been viewed as invading the privacy of the people who take them, as forcing people to reveal aspects of themselves that may work to their own detriment, and as exposing people to unnecessary psychological risks. The most strident criticism of tests has been that they are biased against minority groups and women. Both the courts and government agencies have taken an active role in controlling the use and abuse of tests.

The psychological profession and testing companies have attempted to reduce possible harmful side effects of testing programs, both by setting standards for appropriate test use and by reducing bias in the scores. Because tests can help to achieve many societal and individual benefits in the form of helping individuals and groups to make better decisions, it is important that tests be used wisely and carefully. When tests are used properly for their intended purposes, they can help to improve individual well-being and social equity.

Questions and Exercises

1. How serious is the problem of invasion of privacy with ability measures? With personality measures? What uses of measures of each type are acceptable? What controls on their use should be introduced? How and by whom?
2. Does an employer have the right to require all prospective employees to provide certain basic information as part of the process of applying for a job? Under what circumstances? What kinds of information are appropriate? What safeguards should be required?
3. Comment on the statement: College admissions officers should discount scholastic aptitude test scores of applicants who come from low socioeconomic groups.
4. There are many potential situations involving the use of tests where the rights of one individual or group come into conflict with the rights of another individual or group. Identify two such situations, and list the factors that support the claims of each side in the argument.

Suggested Readings

American Psychological Association. (1981). *Ethical principles of psychologists.* Washington DC: Author.

American Psychological Association, American Educational Research Association, & National Council on Measurement in Education. (1985). *Standards for educational and psychological testing.* Washington, DC: American Psychological Association.

Berk, R. A. (Ed.). (1982). *Handbook of methods for detecting test bias.* Baltimore: Johns Hopkins University Press.

Cole, N. S., & Moss, P. A. (1989). Bias in test use. In R. L. Linn (Ed.), *Educational measurement* (3rd ed., pp. 201–220). New York: Macmillan.

Frederickscn, N. (1984). The real test bias: Influences of testing on teaching and learning. *American Psychologist, 39,* 193–202.

Gottfredson, L. S., & Sharf, J. C. (1988). Fairness in employment testing [Special issue]. *Journal of Vocational Behavior, 33*(3), 225–477.

Howard, G. S. (1985). The role of values in the science of psychology. *American Psychologist, 40,* 255–265.

Osterlind, S. J. (1983). Test item bias. Sage University Paper Series on Quantitative Applications in the Social Sciences, 007–030. Beverly Hills, CA: Sage Publications.

Scheuneman, J. D. (1984). A theoretical framework for the exploration of causes and effects of bias in testing. *Educational Psychologist, 19,* 219–225.

Thorndike, R. L. (1982). *Applied psychometrics.* Boston: Houghton Mifflin.

CHAPTER 16
Emerging Trends in Measurement

Introduction

From 1900 to about 1950, the rate of development and the rate of increase in use of tests and testing procedures were dramatic. Starting from practically nothing, standardized tests were developed to appraise all aspects of educational skills, to assess generalized intellectual ability and specialized aptitudes, and to evaluate many aspects of interest and temperament. By midcentury, almost all of the patterns for objective test items had been developed and were being widely used. The basic statistical procedures for analyzing test reliability and validity and for developing test norms were generally available. With a few exceptions, a general reader would find it difficult to distinguish between a test (or test manual) published in 1950 and one published in 1990. As Linn (1989) observes,

> . . . on inspection of three versions of a well-established, standardized achievement test battery, one published around the time of each of the three editions of this book [*Educational Measurement*, 1951, 1971, 1989] one might easily wonder if there had been any progress in the field of educational measurement since the early 1950s. The multiple-choice items, grade-equivalent scores, and percentile ranks would give quite a sense of constancy. (p. 1)

Developments during the past 40 years have primarily involved (1) an increased interaction between testing and the general field of cognitive psychology, (2) new models of test performance based on item response theory, (3) the pervasive impact of computers on all aspects of test preparation and use, (4) the application of Bayesian statistics to the analysis and interpretation of test results, and (5) the application of concepts of meta-analysis to the accumulated body of test validation research. Some of these developments are likely to continue to influence testing procedures over the next 10 or 20 years, so we will discuss them in this concluding chapter. In addition, as we saw in Chapter 15, the concern of the society with bias in educational and employment contexts has had a major impact on both the content of test items and the way that they are evaluated prior to general use.

Testing and Cognitive Psychology: A Computer Analogy

Historically, educational and psychological measurement developed rather separately from the general course of psychological research. Testing was concerned primarily with the *products* that people produced rather than the mental *processes* by which these products were achieved. Furthermore, emphasis was on *differences* between people in their ability to produce these products rather than on the common principles of human learning and behavior that concerned researchers in the psychology of learning and problem solving. More recently, at least at the frontiers of research, this separation has started to break down. Cognitive psychologists have started to investigate individual differences in cognitive processes, and psychometricians have begun to analyze the processes underlying the solutions to the problems that appear on their tests (see R. L. Thorndike, 1984).

Underlying this trend is, at least in part, a common focus on *information processing* that has been fostered by the spread of computers and by research with computers in simulating human problem solving. A whole branch of computer science has grown up, to which the label *artificial intelligence* has been attached, in which the possibility of modeling human problem solving with a computer has been investigated. Following the steps in processing information through a computer has suggested analogous stages in human problem solving, and this line of research has suggested processes that might be studied by the test maker to provide a better understanding of individual differences in ability and achievement. We will consider a few of these steps here.

Encoding Information

Just as the computer receives inputs of data through its keyboard or from magnetic tape or disk, humans receive and encode sensory inputs. When we attempt to measure the effectiveness of an individual's encoding processes, we can do so only by recording that individual's *responses*. This restriction introduces one of the dilemmas of measures that try to isolate one element of the information processing sequence for study. You can only observe the outcomes in behavior, making it difficult to determine where in the sequence failures were generated. Thus, given the task, "Find one that is just like this one" (pointing),

does the child fail because of (1) the inability to understand the directions, (2) imperfect encoding of

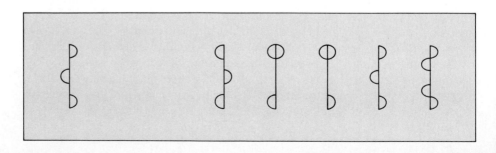

(3) the inability to remember the sample while looking for its match, (4) noncooperation in the task, or some other reason. To test for one process component, the difficulties of the other components must be held to the lowest possible level. Then, if the encoding part of the task is made progressively more difficult by using the same task with more abstract figures such as

the investigator may hope that failures on such items represent encoding deficiencies. Encoding tasks involving matching single letters, combinations, and short words appear in reading tests at the preprimer level, such as the Metropolitan Achievement Tests.

Encoding capabilities develop rapidly during the preschool and initial school years and have been assessed as an aspect of readiness for schooling. One recent line of research (Hunt, 1987; Jensen, 1982) suggests that speed of encoding (and responding to) quite simple stimuli may be an indicator of the effectiveness of the information processing sequence for even quite difficult tasks and may be predictive of the individual's level of performance in the higher level cognitive tasks that appear in general ability tests. This line of investigation, which tries to relate speed of simple information processing to the limit of ability in complex tasks, is one that is likely to be pursued actively in the years ahead. Snow and Lohman (1989) provide a review of developments in this area.

Processing in Short-Term Memory

A limited amount of the material that has been entered into a computer may be held in what is called a "memory buffer," ready for immediate use in whatever processing the computer has been programmed to carry out. Similarly, a small amount of encoded material may be stored in human short-term memory for immediate use in a task, such as calling a repairman on the telephone, that the individual has undertaken. Unfortunately, in comparison with the memory buffer of a computer, the capacity of human short-term memory is sharply restricted. Research suggests that about six to eight discrete units of information is as much as can be held in human short-term memory at any one time. If more is loaded in, much of the input may be lost. So one practical limit on human information processing is the meager storage capacity of short-term memory.

Test tasks, such as digit span or verbatim memory of a series of disconnected words or of a sentence, have been designed to reflect primarily the capacity of short-term memory. On such tests, we find both individual differences and an increase in average score with age during childhood. Furthermore, these tests show moderate correlations with other measures of cognitive functioning, leading researchers to suspect that failures and errors in solving complex problems arise in some cases from failure to keep alive in working memory one or more components of the problem. This cause of failure is not readily isolated in problem solutions but might be identified if the efforts to solve the problem were verbalized in detail.

Long-Term Memory Storage and Retrieval

Computers are built with outstanding resources for storing information in auxiliary memory devices, tapes, and especially disks, from which the information can be recalled on demand. Similarly, long-term memory storage is a prominent feature of human memory, although the details of human memory appear to differ in significant ways from computer memory. On the one hand, human memory is not 100% dependable; we all have had the experience of being unable to retrieve an elusive item at one moment that pops up spontaneously a little later. Furthermore, human memories are linked in a complex network, so that the memory of a given fact or event may be elicited by any one of a variety of other mental events, in contrast to the specificity of the memory organization of a computer. But, whether by computer or human processes, retrieval of material from long-term memory and processing it together with current inputs in working memory is central to information processing and to problem solving.

Past and present ability tests have given undue emphasis to assessing what material can be retrieved from long-term memory. At test of factual knowledge is, after all, one of the easiest tests to prepare. Such a test does not, of course, determine what is *in* the memory storage bank, but only what can be retrieved on demand. Although sheer information can easily be overemphasized in a test, factual knowledge should not be derogated. To think, you must have something to think about, so factual knowledge in any subject is a basic requirement. But it is retrievable knowledge that is valuable, so perhaps future testing should probe the linkages within the memory store—what is related to what—rather than just the elements of knowledge per se. One attribute of an expert in any field appears to be not just that he or she has more knowledge about the field than others do but also that the knowledge is more complexly and logically organized. An instructive exercise to explore, at a relatively simple level, the nature of long-term memory structures and the process of retrieval might be to ask someone to "Tell me everything you can about the number *nine.*" Try this exercise—on yourself, a friend, or a student. The diversity of responses should give you some sense of the complexity of long-term memory structures.

Various types of free- and controlled-association tests have been used in the past as research tools to study the structure of human memories and human knowledge. Somewhat related are the fluency and flexibility tests that have been designed to assess "creativity" or "divergent thinking." These tests can be thought of as attempts to tease out some of the complex linkages in long-term memory.

Executive Programs.   At the heart of the information processing capabilities of a computer are the executive programs that tell it what to do with its information inputs, what information to retrieve from its memory storage, and how to combine the old and the new information to arrive at the required answer. In the same way, executive programs represent the heart of human information processing and problem solving activities. (Sternberg, 1985, has called these programs "meta-components" in his theory of intelligence.) These programs can be thought of as strategies that guide the attack on the problem and the search for a solution. At a simple level, in arithmetic problem solving an explicit or implicit strategy might start with the following questions: What is given? What do I know? What is required to be found out? What model does the required answer fit into? What relationships do I know of between the "givens" and the "required?"

Effective problem solving, as well as effective learning, depends on using good strategies (1) for organizing what is known, (2) for seeking information, either in your own memory store or in external sources, and (3) for applying information in new contexts. Gross deficiency in executive programs, or strategies, is one of the most apparent limitations of the mentally retarded. To the degree that test tasks present novel and problematic situations, the answers require strategies of search and synthesis rather than of simple recall. But, the strategies are usually implicit in the solution rather than clearly displayed.

Sometimes, defective strategies can be identified by analyzing errors that an examinee makes. Thus, a pupil who adds the following numbers,

$$
\begin{array}{r}
17 \\
25 \\
+19 \\
\hline
\end{array}
$$

and arrives at the answer 421 is presumably using a strategy of adding the right-hand column and writing down the sum on the right and then adding the left-hand column and writing down that sum on the left. Or, a pupil who gives 4 as an answer to $8/\frac{1}{2}$ appears to be using the strategy that "divide means make smaller." When individuals are tested individually, the examinee can be asked to "think out loud"; that activity can provide further evidence of ineffective strategies. We hope that additional testing procedures can be developed that will enable us to focus more directly on the nature and effectiveness of the strategies that an examinee employs in attacking a variety of problems (see Snow & Lohman, 1989, for a review of recent studies of problem solving strategies).

Output.   The end-product of computer information processing is some sort of output. Likewise, the end-product of human information processing is output in the form of behavior. Sometimes the motor aspects of the output are of interest in their own right. Thus, the performance on a copying test may depend in part on the accuracy of encoding the form to be copied, and in part, as well, on the motor coordination that permits accurate copying. Or, in evaluating handwriting, the motor skill is the skill primarily being assessed.

More often, the cognitive structure of the output is of primary interest. Thus, you may be concerned with the completeness and precision of a definition, the accuracy and idiomatic appropriateness of a translation, or the coherence and clarity of an exposition. Multiple-choice questions are poorly suited to appraising the output side of an individual's information processing. The behavior involved almost never permits an assessment of the process of interest. Here, open ended tasks requiring a constructed response come most clearly into their own. Some of the steps taken to improve reliability and to eliminate biases from the appraisal of performances and products are described in Chapter 8.

Of course, the adequacy of the output as a solution to a substantive problem depends on the effective execution of all the prior stages of information processing. It is far from easy to judge to what extent a deficient end-product reflects inadequate encoding of the task, a meager working memory span that is inadequate to keep all aspects of the task in mind, a meager and poorly organized stock of information in long-term memory, a lack of effective strategies for seeking and organizing the relevant material, or poor skills for producing the appropriate response. The advantage of the computer as an analogy for human information processing is that it draws our attention to the stages that are integral parts of solving any problem. A challenging task for the designers of tests is to develop effective and efficient measures that permit the localization of the reasons for poor performance so remedial measures can be undertaken.

Impact of Computers on Testing

One of the most significant influences on testing over the past 20 years has been the rapid spread of computers, as well as the increase in their information processing capabilities and the decrease in their cost. Computerization has had an impact on test construction, on test scoring and reporting, on procedures for test administration, and on the presentation and interpretation of test results.

There is little doubt that computers will occupy an even more prominent place in educational and psychological measurement in the years to come. Computing power is becoming so inexpensive and so readily available that it is easy to imagine a time when every classroom will have a computer to assist the teacher in all sorts of recordkeeping and administrative tasks. Some of these uses will relate to testing and evaluation.

Computers and Test Development

In the course of producing a well-designed standardized test, the test maker generates masses of data. After items have been written, they must be tried out on adequate samples, and the results must be analyzed to verify that the items are of appropriate difficulty and that they do differentiate between more and less capable individuals with respect to the domain that the items represent.

After items have been assembled into a test and scored, the scores must be converted into a continuous scale, often extending over several levels of a test, that is expressed in equal units of the ability in question. Norms must be developed that are applicable to the groups with which the test is to be used. Reliability estimates must be calculated, and correlations of the test with other measures or with background variables must be determined. All of these analyses are facilitated by computers, and some, such as the more elegant procedures for item analysis and test scaling, become feasible only when adequate computers are available. The computer has both expedited and changed the nature of testing and item analysis.

Commercial programs are now available that allow the teacher to employ similar analyses on locally developed tests. Although it is unrealistic to expect local tests to undergo the rigorous development and analysis to which commercially produced tests are subjected (or should be subjected), computers and optical scanning equipment are likely to become sufficiently widely available that classroom teachers will be able to get item analyses on their tests at little cost in time or effort. These analyses will allow teachers to improve the tests and their test-writing skills as a result of feedback received from the analyses.

Computers and Test Scoring and Reporting

Test scoring services have been operating for so many years that few people even remember when all test processing was done by hand. Even the IBM test-scoring machines of the 1940s are only a dim memory. Optical scanners that read the marks on an answer sheet are taken for granted, together with the computers that receive the electrical inputs from the scanners and analyze them. The variety of these analyses continuously increases, so that the computer is programmed to generate not only raw and converted scores for individuals but also, as indicated in Chapter 3, summary statistics for class groups, for schools, and for school systems. Results are provided not only for tests and subtests but also for individual items.

Computerized test processing was originally limited to large centralized computer installations. In recent years, with the proliferation of microcomputers, systems have been developed that combine optical scanning and a microcomputer and bring the capability of preparing computerized scoring reports within the reach of local school systems. Many large schools and school districts also process their enrollment and attendance information with scanner and computer hardware. There is every reason to believe that test and information processing equipment will become more compact, more affordable, and more powerful in the years to come.

Computers and Test Administration

Computers are also used for the actual administration of tests. Computerized testing was a natural adjunct to computer assisted instruction, in which formative testing occurred as an integral part of the instructional program. But use of a computer terminal as the medium for test administration has other advantages as well. Whenever pupils are working on a subject individually at different rates and at different levels, it is advantageous to be able to have a specific pupil take a specific test at just the time when she or he is ready for it. If the library of tests is stored on disks in the memory file of the computer, ready to be called up when needed, the pupil can be seated at the terminal, call up the specified test, be tested, and receive immediate feedback of the test results. The pupil and the teacher can use this feedback to guide the next phase of instruction.

The type of testing for which the computer is uniquely well suited is computer-adaptive testing (CAT). In this assessment technique, the test is specially tailored to the individual examinee on the basis of his or her prior responses to provide the maximum amount of information about that examinee. The basis for designing CAT is considered in more detail later in this chapter.

Computers and Test Interpretation

Increasingly, test authors and publishers have relied on computers to prepare narrative reports of test results that interpret the numerical scores for the user. A catalog of statements is stored in computer memory, and the computer is programmed so that a score falling in a given range, a particular combination of two or more scores, or even a combination of responses to specific questions triggers the production of one or more of these statements. The elements in the narrative may be as simple and as directly related to a particular score as "Henry is somewhat below the average in arithmetic problem solving" or as extended as the interpretive personality picture provided in Chapter 13. The report may focus solely and very specifically on one examinee's scores, or it may include an extended general discussion of the conceptual basis for the instrument. For example, National Computer Systems produces a report for the Strong-Campbell Interest Inventory that is 20 pages long and provides, as a basis for interpreting the examinee's scores, a full exposition of the general nature of the instrument and of the rationale for the different types of scores that it produces, together with suggested sources for further information about occupations that appear congruent with the examinee's pattern of interests.

Narrative computer printouts can be no better than the wisdom and clinical experience on which they are based. However, they do permit the distillation of that experience, as it has accumulated in the professional literature and in the pooled background of a number of experts. They protect the examinee from possible bias or inexperience in a local practitioner, while expediting what can be a time-consuming and tedious chore of report writing. They guarantee that aspects of the record dealt with by the narrative will not be inadvertently over-looked by a current interpreter and ensure uniformity and consistency in inter-pretation. The narrative *does* need to be evaluated by a counselor or clinician who knows other facts about the client, but it can serve as a useful foundation for such an evaluation.

Bayesian Thinking in Test Interpretation and Use

Intuitively, most people would agree that how we interpret a person's perfor-mance on some present test task or testing instrument that we have adminis-tered should be influenced by other things that we already know about that person. Thus, if a child has been doing acceptable work in the fifth grade and then receives a deviation intelligence quotient (IQ) of 80 on a verbal ability test, the teacher should suspect that some extraneous influence has lowered the child's score on the test. The teacher has a *prior estimate* that the child is of at least average ability, and when the test results fail to confirm this prior estimate, the result should become suspect.

During the past 20 years, considerable attention has been directed toward systematizing the use of prior and collateral information in arriving at the most reasonable belief about a person's true status on some trait. Bayes' theorem (a theorem about probability developed by the British theologian Thomas Bayes in the 18th century) provides a basis for arriving at a final estimate of a person's status *(posterior estimate)* based on an initial estimate *(prior estimate)* and ad-ditional information. For example, suppose an ability test given 2 years ago in the third grade yielded an IQ equivalent for Joe of 100, while one just given in the fifth grade shows an IQ of 80. What is our best estimate of Joe's true current IQ? It seems reasonable that we should not *completely* ignore the result from the earlier test, but how much weight should we give it? The answer depends on two variances—(1) the variance error of *estimate* of the fifth-grade test from that of the third-grade test, which is the square of the standard error of estimate for predicting fifth-grade scores from third-grade scores (see Chapter 5), and (2) the variance error of *measurement* of the fifth-grade test, which is the square of the standard error of measurement of the fifth-grade test (see Chapter 4). Suppose the correlation of the third-grade test with the fifth-grade test is 0.80, the reliability of the fifth-grade test is 0.09, and the standard deviation of the fifth grade test is 16 points. The variance error of estimate then is $(16^2)(1 - 0.80^2) = 92.16$, and the variance error of measurement is $(16^2)(1 - 0.90) = 25.60$. The two items of information should be weighted in proportion to the reciprocals of these error variances, thus giving not quite four times as much weight to the current as to the earlier test. The weighted average gives 84.35 as our best estimate of Joe's true current IQ. This value has a variance error of 20.04 in comparison with 25.60 for the current test taken alone. So we gain some precision by also considering the earlier test. (For an introduction to Bayes' theorem and Bayesian thinking, see R. L. Thorndike, 1982, pp. 288–299.)

One important application of Bayesian thinking is to *adaptive testing,* which is described in a later section. Here, we start with a prior estimate of the individual's ability level and present a test task selected to match that prior estimate. If the examinee passes the item, our posterior estimate is raised somewhat to reflect this success. This posterior estimate after Item A becomes the prior estimate for Item B, and so on through the test, adjusting the estimate of ability level to take account at each point of the information obtained from the earlier test items. As more information accumulates, the posterior estimate stabilizes, and the examinee's ability level is determined within narrow limits.

Bayesian procedures can become somewhat involved, but Bayesian thinking is basically simple. What it says is that we should frequently—possibly always—take account of what we already know in interpreting new information about an individual or about a group. What we already know may be the results of an earlier test; it may be information stemming from other sources, such as a teacher's day-to-day contacts; or it may at times be information about the performance of *other* individuals in the same group or receiving the same treatment. This inclusion of prior data, of course, is what counselors, clinicians, and sometimes teachers have done for years when using test information. The difference here is that Bayesian procedures make the process of assigning importance to the prior information objective. The question is *how much* weight to give to this prior or collateral evidence; developments from Bayes' theorem help to answer that question. The need to use this other information and procedures for doing so are likely to become more widely known and accepted in the years ahead.

Testing and Item Response Theory

Many of the recent developments in testing stem from what has come to be called *item response theory,* or *latent trait theory.* The practical application of this theory has depended on the availability of computers and has in turn shaped the ways in which computers are used in testing. Let us look at a set of interlocking developments that stem from the interaction of these theoretical models and the availability of computers to implement them.

Latent trait theory assumes the existence of a relatively unified underlying trait or characteristic that determines an individual's ability to succeed with some particular type of cognitive task. Possible attributes might be "knowledge of word meanings," "arithmetical reasoning," or "spatial visualizing." We can represent a trait as a linear scale (as shown in Figure 16.1) on which both tasks and people can be placed.

For the *tasks,* the scale can be thought of as a scale of difficulty, so the words in the illustration go from very easy on the left to quite difficult on the right. The difficulty of an item is defined as the ability level at which half of the examinees will get the item correct. For *people,* the scale can be thought of as a scale of ability. A person's ability level is defined by the tasks that she or he can just about do—that is, the difficulty level at which the examinee would get half of the items correct. Thus, Joe can most likely define "borrow" because his ability exceeds the difficulty of the item, but he is unlikely to be able to define "incision" because its difficulty exceeds his ability. The likelihood that Billy can correctly define "borrow" is relatively low.

It is important to note that in this model, a person's ability level is subject to change over time. That is, if Billy is 6 years old, we can expect that his position on the scale of ability will change as he matures. Conversely, we would expect the relative difficulty of the words to remain nearly constant for long periods of time. The stability of the difficulty scale is what gives meaning to the ability scale.

The ability/difficulty scale is an arbitrary one, just as the Fahrenheit scale of temperature is. You could use a scale with different sized units (for example, Centigrade) or a different zero point (for example, Centigrade or Kelvin). But, for a given scale, the units are presumably equal and the *relative* position of a person or task does not depend either on the size of the units or on the placement of the zero point.

The relationship between ability level and passing an item of a given difficulty is not an all-or-none matter but instead is a question of probability. The form of the relationship between ability and probability of passing an item is shown in Figure 16.2. The graph in this figure is called the item characteristic curve, or

FIGURE 16.1
Scale of world knowledge.

FIGURE 16.2

Item characteristic curve for the meaning of the word "incision."

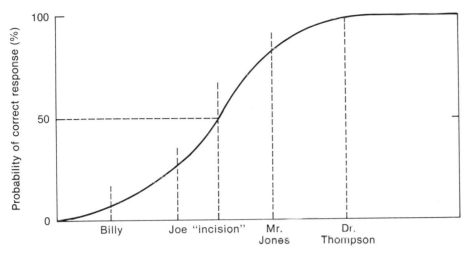

item trace line, and there is one such curve for every item. Thus, if we include the word "incision" on a test given to a group of people at Joe's level of ability, about 25% would know the meaning, while among those at Mr. Jones' level, about 85% would be able to provide a definition. Turning things around, Joe could define 25% of the words whose difficulty was the same as "incision," while Mr. Jones could provide definitions for about 85% of them.

As we see from Figure 16.2, the probability of passing an item as a function of ability level is expressed by a curve that is quite flat at the two extremes, but rises steeply around the level that matches the difficulty of the item. The test item differentiates effectively between those whose abilities are somewhat above and those whose abilities are somewhat below the difficulty level of the task but provides very little differentiation among those whose abilities are very high or among those whose abilities are very low. Dr. Thompson would pass almost all the items at the difficulty level represented by "incision," and we would know that she had very high verbal ability, but we would not know *how* high. We would need words in the difficulty range from "prologue" to "tenet" to locate Dr. Thompson's ability with any precision.

The trace line of an item is a characteristic of the item that does not depend on the people taking the test, but our ability to reveal the entire curve depends on applying the item to a sufficiently heterogeneous group that people over the full range of ability are represented. If we gave items like "incision" only to people like Joe and Mr. Jones, we could only see that part of the curve that falls between them. Because this range covers the difficulty level of the item, the result would not be too serious, but if only people like Billy or like Dr. Thompson were included, we would be able to tell very little about the item.

Each item has its own characteristic curve that is defined by its difficulty level (the 50% point) and its discrimination. Discrimination was discussed in Chapter

7, but here it takes on a slightly different meaning. The ability of an item to discriminate those at different levels of ability is a function of the rate at which the probability of getting the item correct changes with ability. Graphically, this rate of change can be seen as the slope of the item characteristic curve. Figure 16.3 shows curves representing items that differ in difficulty but are equal in discrimination and also items that are of equal difficulty but differ in discrimination. For items of the multiple-choice or selected response variety, the curve has a third feature, the probability of getting the item correct by chance, or guessing. This effect is seen when the curve flattens out at some probability greater than zero. Figure 16.4 provides an example of such a curve.

FIGURE 16.3
Item characteristic curves for items that differ in difficulty (top) or discrimination (bottom).

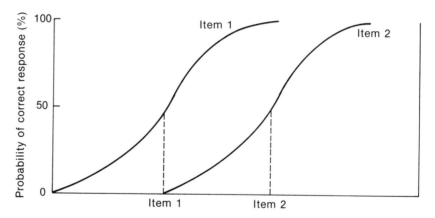

Two items of equal discrimination that differ in difficulty

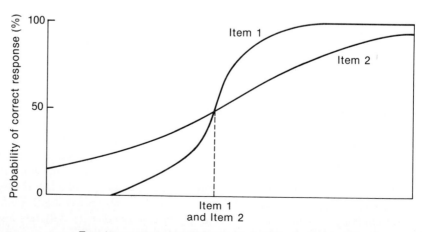

Two items of equal difficulty that differ in discrimination

FIGURE 16.4

Effect of guessing on the item characteristic curve.

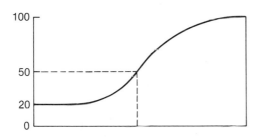

If we have determined the difficulty values on a common scale for a sufficient pool of items, we can use items from that pool to do a number of useful and interesting things. We outline some of them here.

1. Estimating ability level from any set of items. If the difficulty scale values are available for a large pool of items measuring a common trait, an unbiased estimate (unbiased in a statistical sense, not in the social policy sense discussed in Chapter 15) of a person's ability level on that trait can be obtained from *any* set of items drawn from that pool. The precision of the estimate will depend on the number of items, increasing as the number increases. It will also depend on how closely the difficulty of the items matches the ability level of the person, with accuracy increasing with the closeness of the match. But there will be no systematic error in the estimate in any case, assuming the probability of a correct response is not zero (chance level for selected response items) or 1.0 In these two cases, the item gives no information about the person's ability.

2. Preparing equivalent test forms. By drawing from the pool sets of items having the same average difficulty value, the same spread of difficulty values, and the same average discrimination, we can prepare test forms that are equivalent in the sense that any given raw score signifies the same level of examinee ability, irrespective of the test form on which it is based. We could use the test forms to measure gains from instruction, giving one form before and another after some instructional period. Or, in situations in which test security or pupil copying is likely to be a problem, different forms could be given to pupils in alternating seats. If, for some reason, one test were invalidated for a person, an alternate, equivalent form could be administered.

3. Matrix sampling in testing. At times, a researcher may wish to cover some domain of content very completely. If he or she is not interested in making decisions about specific pupils but instead in assessing the performance level of a class, a school, or a school system, it is then not necessary that every test item be administered to every person. Each person can be given a fraction of the items as long as each item has been given to some of the people. The investigator can then think of the class, or school, or school system as a composite "person." Determining the proportion of items passed at known difficulty scale values, he or she can estimate an ability level for the group, either with respect to the complete domain or with respect to specific limited segments of that domain. This approach makes it possible to hold testing time within reasonable limits and yet to cover completely the domain of content which the investigator is interested.

Computer-Adaptive Testing

The rapid development and widespread availability of computers has combined with item response theory to lead to the development of computer adaptive testing. By adaptive testing, we mean the rapid adjustment of the difficulty level of the test tasks to the ability level of the person being tested. As we indicated earlier, tasks that are much too difficult or much too easy give little new information about the ability level of an examinee. For example, if the examinee is an applicant for college admission, that he or she knew the meaning of the word "dig" would tell us essentially nothing about whether the applicant was a promising candidate. "Dig" is a word that *any* high school senior could be expected to know. We would also learn relatively little if he or she failed on "fracedinous." Probably not 1 high school senior in 100,000 would know the meaning of the word. (*Webster's Unabridged Dictionary* defines it as "producing heat by putrefaction [obsolete]".) We gain useful information by testing with tasks on which we *do not* know in advance whether the examinee will succeed.

Ideally, in adaptive testing, we start at a difficulty level at which we are *most uncertain* whether the examinee can pass the item. This point would usually be an item of about 50% difficulty for that age or grade group. If he or she *does* get the item correct, this fact causes us to raise our posterior estimate of the person's ability level somewhat and makes it appropriate to present next a somewhat more difficult item. As long as the examinee continues to get items correct, we continue to raise our estimate of the ability level and to raise the difficulty level of the next item presented. If our prior information was accurate, and thus our starting level was close to the examinee's ability level, the examinee should quickly get an item incorrect, and we would lower our posterior estimate slightly and drop back to a slightly easier item. With a sequence of passes and failures, we will soon zero in with items near the examinee's ability level, and the record of passes and failures will give a good final estimate of the examinee's ability level. Any given level of precision in the estimate can be achieved by well-designed adaptive testing using perhaps half as many test items as would be required in a conventional test designed for use with a complete age or grade group.

To be really effective, a procedure for adaptive testing must be able to search the pool of items and find one that is of appropriate difficulty, given the current estimate of the examinee's ability level. This searching is something that only a computer can do efficiently. The complete pool of items can be stored on a disk in the computer memory, coded by difficulty level and, if need be, by discrimination level and content category. The computer can be programmed to adjust its estimate of the examinee's ability level by an appropriate amount after each pass or failure and to seek out the yet unused item that best matches that new estimate. An ongoing record is maintained of the examinee's estimated ability level and of the precision of that estimate. The computer can be programmed to terminate testing either after a specified number of items has been administered or when a specified precision of estimate has been reached.

Early developmental work on adaptive testing was conducted for organizations such as U.S. Navy and the U.S. Civil Service Commission with the expectation that testing would be carried out at local terminals connected to a massive mainframe computer. However, this type of adaptive testing, or a close approximation to it, is now well within the capability of the better microcomputers that are becoming widely available in local school systems. Where testing time is at a premium, as when it is important to assess several different aspects of a person's ability, the possibility of using a shorter test without losing precision can be very attractive. Organizations such as the College Board are now making computer adaptive tests in various subjects available for college placement, and it seems highly likely that publishers of curricular materials for use in the public schools will soon follow suit.

Two-Stage Testing.   A rougher approximation to fully adaptive testing can be achieved by what may be called two-stage testing. In this procedure, a short test is given, probably one that takes no more than 10 minutes. This test is scored, and on the basis of the score, the examinee is routed to one of two, three, or possibly more levels for the main testing. Those examinees with the highest scores on the short test are routed to the most difficult form of the main test; those in the middle range, to the test of average difficulty; and those with lowest scores, to the easiest form. Such a procedure would be useful if you were working with a heterogeneous group about whom you knew very little in advance, such as, for example, a group of refugees from East Asia or a miscellaneous group of job applicants.

One of the interesting potential applications of item response theory and adaptive testing is the linking of grading procedures between classes or sections of a course. One of the motivating forces that has led to the creation of standardized tests such as the Scholastic Aptitude Test is the desire for comparable information for students from different schools. If some items that had been calibrated by item response methods were included in locally developed tests in different schools or in different sections of a course where, for example, ability grouping had been used, the tests could be equated and the relative performance of pupils in different classes assessed on a common scale. The different levels of the Cognitive Abilities Test use item response theory to achieve a common scale, called a universal scale score, for the different levels of the test. The American College Testing Program also uses the theory to create a common scale for several different tests that have no items in common.

As computers become more generally available, we can anticipate development of a wide range of tests in one or another of the adaptive formats. The development is likely to proceed slowly at first because both users and regulating bodies (courts, legislatures, and the like) must be persuaded of the essential soundness of the procedures, but we anticipate that these developments will be one of the major changes in testing during the coming years.

Meta-Analysis and Validity Generalization

In psychology and education, studies are often carried out with rather small samples of cases, and, partly as a consequence of this fact, different studies have often given quite inconsistent results. In the past decade, researchers have sought better ways of distilling an essence of truth from a mass of seemingly contradictory results. The term "meta-analysis" was coined (Glass, 1977) to apply to the systematic pooling and integration of results from many different studies of the same phenomenon.

A specific example of meta-analysis is the integration of test validity data for different groups and from different sources. As soon as ability tests became available, researchers started to collect data on the validity of those tests for both educational and vocational criteria. Validity coefficients were found, for any given test or type of test, to vary rather substantially for the same school subject or for what appeared to be the same job. For example, the validity coefficient for English grades on the verbal reasoning test of the Differential Aptitude Tests (DAT) ranged, in different groups, from 0.07 to 0.76.

People came to accept the doctrine, especially in relation to vocational prediction, that validity must be established in each specific location. However, more recently, Schmidt and associates (Schmidt, 1988a, 1988b; Schmidt & Hunter, 1981; Schmidt, Hunter, Pearlman, & Hirsh, 1985) have demonstrated that much of the variation in results from one study to another can be attributed to a variety of statistical artifacts—sampling error in small samples, criterion unreliability, or differing degrees of restriction in the range of ability in the sample studied. They propose that meta-analysis be applied to the accumulated data, thus pooling results from separate studies and arriving at an average value that may be taken as a generally applicable estimate of test validity, one that is closer to the "true" value than the value obtained from a local sample, usually of quite modest size. Thus, unless the English program in School System X is *radically* different from the program in most schools, the median validity coefficient of 0.49, based on pooling the results from many schools, will probably be a more appropriate value for School System X to use in thinking about the validity of the verbal reasoning test of DAT for predicting English grades than will be whatever value might be obtained from a limited local study. To this application of meta-analysis, Schmidt and Hunter have attached the name *validity generalization*.

The procedures for meta-analysis and validity generalization are still controversial, but the methods are being applied to an increasingly wide variety of topics in education and occupational psychology. We may anticipate that the next 10 or 20 years will see a more systematic synthesis of the validation research that has accumulated over the past 50 years, leading to stable generalized estimates of test-criterion relationships. We may hope that these relationships will be accepted by the Equal Employment Opportunity Commission, other government agencies, and the courts as superior replacements for local studies on necessarily small samples and that objective testing procedures will again become a practical procedure for appraising job applicants.

Summary

In Chapter 1, we suggested that the pace of development in psychological and educational measurement has been uneven. In the first third of the 20th century, there was rapid progress in the development of new measurement instruments and techniques. Most features of human behavior were exposed to tests, and there was great enthusiasm for testing as a key to the social millenium.

By contrast, the middle third of this century was a period of relative stagnation. Few real advances were made in either techniques or instruments, and some of the innovations of the period, such as ability batteries, have generally failed to live up to their original promise.

As this chapter suggests, the last third of this century seems to be a period of renewed activity and achievement in testing, coupled with greater sensitivity by test developers and users to the impact that tests can have. Although it is probably impossible to eliminate all bias in all test items, both concern about the problem of bias in tests and the development of techniques of item response theory should help to minimize its impact. There is a much more sophisticated view of tests and of the cognitive processes that underlie test behavior. Computers are making possible new kinds of testing and the rapid interpretation and reporting of test results. The trends seem decidedly positive, and we may look forward to more progress in the coming decades.

Suggested Readings

Baker, F. B. (1985). *The basics of item response theory*. Portsmouth, NH: Heinemann.

Baker, F. B. (1989). Computer technology in test construction and processing. In R. L. Linn (Ed.), *Educational measurement* (3rd ed., pp. 409–428). New York: Macmillan.

Bunderson, C. V., Inouye, D. K., & Olsen, J. B. (1989). Four generations of computerized educational measurement. In R. L. Linn (Ed.), *Educational measurement* (3rd ed., pp. 367–408). New York: Macmillan.

Cook, L. L., & Eignor, D. R. (1983). Practical considerations regarding the use of item response theory to equate tests. In R. K. Hambleton (Ed.), *Applications of item response theory* (pp. 175–195). Vancouver: Educational Research Institute of British Columbia.

Green, B. F. (1988). Critical problems in computer-based psychological measurement. *Measurement in Education, 1,* 223–231.

Green, B. F., Bock, R. D., Humphreys, L. G., Linn, R. L., & Reckase, M. D. (1984). Technical guidelines for assessing computerized adaptive tests. *Journal of Educational Measurement, 21,* 347–360.

Hambleton, R. K. (1989). Principles and selected applications of item response theory. In R. L. Linn (Ed.), *Educational Measurement* (3rd ed., pp. 147–200). New York: Macmillan.

Hedges, L. V., & Olkin, I. (1985). *Statistical methods for meta-analysis.* New York: Academic Press.

Ronning, R. R., Glover, J. A., & Conoley, J. C. (1987). *The Influence of cognitive psychology on psychological testing.* Hillsdale, NJ: Erlbaum.

Skaggs, G., & Lissitz, R. W. (1986). IRT test equating: Relevant issues and a review of recent research. *Review of Educational Research, 56,* 495–529.

Wright, B. D., & Bell, S. R. (1984). Item banks: What, why, how. *Journal of Educational Measurement, 21,* 331–345.

REFERENCES

Adjutant General's Office, Personnel Research Section. (1952). *A study of officer rating methodology, validity and reliability of ratings by single raters and multiple raters* (PRS Report No. 904). Washington, DC: Author.

Adjutant General's Office, Personnel Research Section. (1953). *Survey of the aptitude for service rating system at the U.S. Military Academy, West Point, New York.* Washington, DC: Author.

Aiken, L. R. (1985). *Psychological testing and assessment* (5th ed.). Boston: Allyn and Bacon.

Albanese, M. A. (1988). The projected impact of the correction for guessing on individual scores. *Journal of Educational Measurement, 25,* 149–157.

Albanese, M. A., & Sabers, D. L. (1988). Multiple true-false items: A study of interitem correlations, scoring alternatives, and reliability estimation. *Journal of Educational Measurement, 25,* 111–123.

Alexander, L., & James, H. T. (1987). *The nation's report card: Improving the assessment of student achievement.* Washington, DC: National Academy of Education.

Allen, W. B. (1988). Rhodes handicapping, or slowing the pace of integration. *Journal of Vocational Behavior, 33,* 365–378.

American Psychological Association. (1981). *Ethical principles of psychologists.* Washington, DC: Author.

American Psychological Association, American Educational Research Association, & National Council on Measurement in Education. (1985). *Standards for educational and psychological testing.* Washington, DC: American Psychological Association.

Anastasi, A. (1986). Evolving concepts of test validation. *Annual Review of Psychology, 37,* 1–15.

Anastasi, A. (1988). *Psychological testing* (6th ed.). New York: Macmillan.

Angoff, W. H. (1971). Scales, norms, and equivalent scores. In R. L. Thorndike (Ed.), *Educational measurement* (2nd ed., pp. 508–600). Washington, DC: American Council on Education.

Angoff, W. H. (1988). Validity: An evolving concept. In H. Wainer & H. Braun (Eds.), *Test validity* (pp. 19–32). Hillsdale, NJ: Erlbaum.

Army-Air Force Aviation Psychology Program. (1947). *Psychological research on operational training in the continental air forces* (Research Report No. 16, pp. 101–105). Washington, DC: U.S. Government Printing Office.

THE ASVAB workbook (No. 642–413). (1986). Washington, DC: U.S. Government Printing Office.

Baglin, R. F. (1981). Does "nationally" normed really mean nationally? *Journal of Educational Measurement, 18,* 97–107.

Baird, L., & Feister, W. J. (1972). Grading standards: The relation of changes in average student ability to the average grades awarded. *American Educational Research Journal, 9,* 431–442.

Baker, F. B. (1985). *The basics of item response theory.* Portsmouth, NH: Heinemann.

Baker, F. B. (1989). Computer technology in test construction and processing. In R. L. Linn (Ed.), *Educational measurement* (3rd ed., pp. 409–428). New York: Macmillan.

Barrett, R. S. (1966). The influence of supervisor's requirements on ratings. *Personnel Psychology, 19,* 375–388.

Barrios, B. A. (1988). On the changing nature of behavioral assessment. In A. S. Bellack & M. Hershon (Eds.), *Behavioral assessment: A practical handbook* (pp. 3–41). New York: Pergamon.

Baxter, J. C., Brock, B., Hill, P. C., & Rozelle, R. M. (1981). Letters of recommendation: A question of value. *Journal of Applied Psychology, 66,* 296–301.

Berk, R. A. (1980). A consumer's guide to criterion-referenced test reliability. *Journal of Educational Measurement, 17,* 323–349.

Berk, R. A. (Ed.). (1982). *Handbook of methods for detecting test bias.* Baltimore: Johns Hopkins University Press.

Berk, R. A. (1984). Selecting the index of reliability. In R. A. Berk (Ed.), *A guide to criterion-referenced test construction* (pp. 231–266). Baltimore: Johns Hopkins University Press.

Berk, R. A. (Ed.). (1986). *Performance assessment: Methods and applications.* Baltimore: Johns Hopkins University Press.

Birns, B. (1965). Individual differences in human neonates' responses to stimulation. *Child Development, 36,* 249–256.

Blatchford, C. H. (1970). *Experimental steps to ascertain reliability of diagnostic tests in English as a second language.* Unpublished doctoral dissertation, Columbia University, Teachers College, New York.

Blixt, S. L., & Shama, D. B. (1986). An empirical investigation of the standard error of measurement at different ability levels. *Educational and Psychological Measurement, 45,* 545–550.

Bloom, B. S. (Ed.) (1956). *Taxonomy of educational objectives, Handbook I: Cognitive domain.* New York: Longman, Green and Company.

Bloom, B. S., Hastings, J. T., & Madaus, C. F. (1971). *Handbook on formative and summative evaluation of student learning.* New York: McGraw-Hill.

Blumberg, H. H., De Soto, C. B., & Kuethe, J. L. (1966). Evaluation of rating scale formats. *Personal Psychology, 19,* 243–260.

Bolton, B. (Ed.). (1987). *Handbook of measurement and evaluation in rehabilitation.* Baltimore: Paul Brookes.

Bond, L. (1989). The effects of special preparation on measures of scholastic ability. In R. L. Linn (Ed.), *Educational measurement* (3rd ed., pp. 429–444). New York: Macmillan.

Boyle, G. J. (1989). Confirmation of the structural dimensionality of the Stanford-Binet Intelligence Scale (Fourth Edition). *Personality and Individual Differences, 10,* 709–715.

Boynton, B. (1936). The physical growth of girls. *University of Iowa Studies in Child Welfare, 12* (4).

Braswell, J. S. (Compiler). (1981). *Mathematics tests available in the United States and Canada.* Reston, VA: National Council of Teachers of Mathematics.

Brennan, R. L. (1984). Estimating the dependability of the scores. In R. A. Berk (Ed.), *A guide to criterion-referenced test construction* (pp. 292–334). Baltimore: Johns Hopkins University Press.

Buhler, R. A. (1953). *Flicker fusion threshold and anxiety level.* Unpublished doctoral dissertation, Columbia University, New York.

Bunderson, C. V., Inouye, D. K., & Olsen, J. B. (1989). Four generations of computerized educational measurement. In R. L. Linn (Ed.), *Educational measurement* (3rd ed., pp. 367–408). New York: Macmillan.

Buros, O. K. (Ed.). (1978). *The eighth mental measurements yearbook.* Highland Park, NJ: The Gryphon Press. (This volume and previous *Mental Measurement Yearbook* volumes are now handled by the Buros Institute of Mental Measurements at the University of Nebraska, Lincoln, NB.)

Butcher, J. N., Keller, L. S., & Bacon, S. F. (1985). Current developments and future directions in computerized personality assessment. *Journal of Consulting and Clinical Psychology, 53,* 803–815.

California Achievement Tests (CAT). (1985). New York: McGraw-Hill.

Campbell, J. P., Dunnette, M. D., Arvey, R. D., & Hellervik, L. V. (1973). The development and evaluation of behaviorally based rating scales. *Journal of Applied Psychology, 57,* 15–22.

Campbell, D. P., & Hansen, J. C. (1981). *Manual for the SVIB-SCII* (3rd ed.). Stanford, CA: Stanford University Press.

Cannell, J. J. (1988). Nationally normed elementary achievement testing in America's public schools: How all 50 states are above the national average. *Educational Measurement: Issues and Practice, 7*(2), 5–9.

Cohen, J., & Cohen, P. (1983). *Applied multiple regression for the behavioral sciences* (2nd ed.). Hillsdale, NJ: Erlbaum.

Cole, N. S., & Moss, P. A. (1989). Bias in test use. In R. L. Linn (Ed.), *Educational measurement* (3rd ed., pp. 201–220). New York: Macmillan.

Comprehensive Tests of Basic Skills (4th ed.). (1988). New York: McGraw-Hill.

Comprehensive Test of Basic Skills pre-publication technical bulletin. (1988). Monterey, CA: McGraw-Hill.

Comrey, A. L., Bott, P. A., & Lee, H. B. (1989). *Elementary statistics: A problem-solving approach* (2nd ed.). Dubuque, IA: Wm. C. Brown.

Conoley, J. C., & Kramer, J. J. (1989). *The tenth mental measurements yearbook.* Lincoln, NB: Buros Institute of Mental Measurements.

Conoley, J. C., Kramer, J. J., & Mitchell, J. V., Jr. (Eds.). (1988). *Supplement to the ninth mental measurements yearbook.* Lincoln, NB: Buros Institute of Mental Measurements.

Cook, L. L., & Eignor, D. R. (1983). Practical considerations regarding the use of item response theory to equate tests. In R. K. Hambleton (Ed.), *Applications of item response theory* (pp. 175–195). Vancouver: Educational Research Institute of British Columbia.

Cook, T. D., & Campbell, D. T. (1979). *Quasi-experimentation: Design and analysis issues for field settings.* Chicago: Rand McNally.

Cronbach, L. J. (1975). Five decades of public controversy over mental testing. *American Psychologist, 30,* 1–14.

Cronbach, L. J. (1988). Five perspectives on validation argument. In H. Wainer & H. Braun (Eds.), *Test validity* (pp. 3–17). Hillsdale, NJ: Erlbaum.

Cunningham, G. K. (1986). *Educational and psychological measurement.* New York: Macmillan.

Debra P. v. Turlington, 78–892 Civ. T–C (M. D. Fla. July 12, 1979) at 2380.

Diamond, E. E., & Fremer, J. (1989). The Joint Committee on Testing Practices and the Code of Fair Testing Practices in Education. *Educational Measurement: Issues and Practice, 8*(1), 23–24.

DuBois, P. H. (1970). *A history of psychological testing.* Boston: Allyn and Bacon.

Duff, F. L. (1965). Item subtlety in personality inventory scales. *Journal of Consulting Psychology, 29,* 565–570.

Dunn, L. M. & Dunn, L. M. (1981). *Peabody Picture Vocabulary Test—Revised: Manual for Forms L and M.* Circle Pines, MN: American Guidance Services.

Ebel, R. L. (1972). *Essentials of Educational Measurement* (2nd ed.). Englewood Cliffs, NJ: Prentice-Hall.

Ebel, R. L. (1979). *Essentials of educational measurement* (3rd ed.). Englewood Cliffs, NJ: Prentice-Hall.

Ebel, R. L. (1983). The practical validation of tests of ability. *Educational Measurement: Issues and Practices, 2*(2), 7–10.

Educational Testing Service, Test Collection. (1975–1989). *Tests in Microfiche Annotated Bibliography* (Set A–Set O). Princeton, NJ: Author.

Educational Testing Service, Test Collection. (1986). *The ETS test collection catalog* (3 vols.). Phoenix, AZ: Oryx Press.

Educational Testing Service, Test Collection. (1987). *Directory of selected national testing programs.* Phoenix, AZ: Oryx Press.

Edwards, A. L. (1957). *Techniques of attitude scale construction.* New York: Appleton.

Egan, O., & Archer, P. (1985). The accuracy of teachers' ratings of ability: A regression model. *American Educational Research Journal, 22*(1), 25–34.

Embretson (Whitely), S. (1983). Construct validity: Construct representation versus nomothetic span. *Psychological Bulletin, 93,* 179–197.

Equal Employment Opportunity Commission, U.S. Civil Service Commission, U.S. Department of Labor, & U.S. Department of Justice. (August 1978). Uniform Guidelines on Employee Selection Procedures. 43 Fed. Reg. 166, 38290–38309. Washington, DC: U.S. Government Printing Office.

Evertson, C. M. (1986). Observation as inquiry and method. In M. C. Witrock (Ed.), *Handbook of research on teaching* (pp. 162–213). New York: Macmillan.

Eyde, L. D., Moreland, K. L., Robertson, G. J., Primoff, E. S., & Most, R. B. (1988). *Test user qualifications: A data-based approach to promoting good test use.* Washington DC: American Psychological Association.

Eysenck, H. J. (1986). Inspection time and intelligence: A historical perspective. *Personality and Individual Differences, 7,* 603–607.

Eysenck, H. J. (1988). The concept of "intelligence": Useful or useless? *Intelligence, 12,* 1–16.

Fabiano, E. (1989). *Index to tests used in educational dissertations.* Phoenix, AZ: Oryx Press.

Federal Register, 42(163), 42474–42518. (1977). Regulation implementing Education for All Handicapped Children Act of 1975 (PL 94–142).

Feldhusen, J. F. (1961). An evaluation of college students' reactions to open-book examinations. *Educational and Psychological Measurement, 21,* 637–646.

Feldt, L. S., & Brennan, R. L. (1989). Reliability. In R. L. Linn (Ed.), *Educational measurement* (3rd ed., pp. 105–146). New York: Macmillan.

Ferguson, G. A., & Takane, Y. (1989). *Statistical analysis in psychology and education* (6th ed.). New York: McGraw-Hill.

Fitzpatrick, R., & Morrison E. J. (1971). Performance and product evaluation. In R. L.

Thorndike (Ed.), *Educational measurement* (2nd ed., pp. 237–270). Washington DC: American Council on Education.

Fivars, G., & Gosnell, D. (1966). *Nursing evaluation: The problem and the process.* New York: Macmillan.

Flynn, J. R. (1984). The mean IQ of Americans: Massive gains 1932 to 1978. *Psychological Bulletin, 95,* 29–51.

Foster, S. L., Bell-Dolan, D. J., & Burge, D. A. (1988). Behavioral observation. In A. S. Bellack & M. Hershon (Eds.), *Behavioral assessment: A practical handbook* (pp. 119–160). New York: Pergamon.

Fredericksen, N. (1984). The real test bias: Influences of testing on teaching and learning. *American Psychologist, 39,* 193–202.

Fredericksen, N. (1986). Construct validity and construct similarity: Methods for use in test development and test validation. *Multivariate Behavioral Research, 21,* 3–28.

Fredericksen, J. R., & Collins, A. (1989). A systems approach to educational testing. *Educational Researcher, 18*(9), 27–32.

Garber, H. L. (1988). *The Milwaukee Project: Preventing mental retardation in children at risk.* Washington, DC: American Association on Mental Retardation.

Gardner, E. F. (1983). Intrinsic rational validity: Necessary but not sufficient. *Educational Measurement: Issues and Practice, 2*(2), 13.

Gerberich, J. R. (1956). *Specimen objective test items: A guide to achievement test construction.* New York: Longman, Green and Company.

Ghiselli, E. E. (1973). The validity of aptitude tests in personnel selection. *Personnel Psychology, 26,* 461–477.

Glass, G. V. (1977). Integrating findings: The meta-analysis of research. *Review of Research in Education, 5,* 351–379.

Glass, G. V. (1980). Minimum competence and incompetence in Florida. *Phi Delta Kappan, 59,* 602–605.

Goldman, B. A., & Busch, J. C. (1978). *Directory of unpublished experimental mental measures: Vol. 2.* New York: Human Sciences.

Goldman, B. A., & Busch, J. C. (1982). *Directory of unpublished experimental mental measures: Vol. 3.* New York: Human Sciences Press.

Goldman, B. A., & Osborne, W. L. (1985). *Directory of unpublished experimental mental measures: Vol. 4.* New York: Human Sciences Press.

Goldman, B. A., & Mitchell, D. F. (1990). *Directory of unpublished experimental mental measures: Vol. 5.* Dubuque, IA: Wm. C. Brown.

Goldman, B. A., & Sanders, J. L. (1974). *Directory of unpublished experimental mental measures: Vol. 1.* New York: Behavioral Publications.

Gottfredson, G. D., & Holland, J. L. (1989). *Dictionary of Holland occupational codes* (2nd ed.). Odessa, FL: Psychological Assessment Resources.

Gottfredson, L. S., & Sharf, J. C. (1988). Fairness in employment testing [Special issue] *Journal of Vocational Behavior, 33*(3), 225–477.

Green, B. F. (1988). Critical problems in computer-based psychological measurement. *Measurement in Education, 1,* 223–231.

Green, B. F., Bock, R. D., Humphreys, L. G., Linn, R. L., & Reckase, M. D. (1984). Technical guidelines for assessing computerized adaptive tests. *Journal of Educational Measurement, 21,* 347–360.

Gregory, R. J. (1987). *Adult intellectual assessment.* Boston: Allyn and Bacon.

Griggs v. Duke Power Co., 401 U.S. 424 (1971).

Grommon, A. H. (Ed.). (1976). *Review of selected published tests in English.* Urbana, IL: National Council of Teachers of English.

Gronlund, N. E. (1982). *Constructing achievement tests.* Englewood Cliffs, NJ: Prentice-Hall.

Gronlund, N. E. (1985). *Measurement and evaluation in teaching* (5th ed.). New York: Macmillan.

Gronlund, N. E., & Linn, R. L. (1990). *Measurement and evaluation in teaching* (6th ed.). New York: Macmillan.

Guilford, J. P. (1959). Three faces of intellect. *American Psychologist, 14,* 459–479.

Guilford, J. P. (1985). The structure-of-intellect model. In B. B. Wolman (Ed.), *Handbook of intelligence* (pp. 225–266). New York: Wiley.

Gullickson, A. R., & Ellwein, M. C. (1985). Post hoc analysis of teacher-made tests: The goodness of fit between prescription and practice. *Educational Measurement: Issues and Practice, 4*(1), 15–18.

Gullickson, A. R., & Hopkins, K. D. (1987). The context of educational measurement instruction for preservice teachers: Professor perspectives. *Educational Measurement: Issues and Practice, 6*(3), 12–16.

Haertel, E. (1985). Construct validity and criterion-referenced testing. *Review of Educational Research, 55,* 23–46.

Hall, B. W. (1985). Survey of the technical characteristics of published educational achievement tests. *Educational Measurement: Issues and Practice, 4*(1), 6–14.

Hambleton, R. K. (1984). Validating the test scores. In R. A. Berk (Ed.), *A guide to criterion-referenced test construction* (pp. 199–230). Baltimore: Johns Hopkins University Press.

Hambleton, R. K. (1989). Principles and selected applications of item response theory. In R. L. Linn (Ed.), *Educational measurement* (3rd ed., pp. 147–200). New York: Macmillan.

Hambleton, R. K., & Eignor, D. R. (1980). Test score validity and standard-setting methods. In R. A. Berk (Ed.), *Criterion-Referenced Measurement: The State of the Art.* Baltimore: Johns Hopkins University Press.

Haney, W. (1981). Validity, vaudeville, and values: A short history of social concerns over standardized testing. *American Psychologist, 36,* 1021–1034.

Hansen, J. C., & Campbell, D. P. (1985). *The Strong manual* (4th ed.). Palo Alto, CA: Consulting Psychologists Press.

Harari, O., & Zedeck, S. (1973). Development of behaviorally anchored scales for the evaluation of faculty teaching. *Journal of Applied psychology, 58,* 261–265.

Hathaway, S. R., & McKinley, J. C. (1989). *The Minnesota Multiphasic Personality Inventory II.* Minneapolis, MN: University of Minnesota Press.

Hedges, L. V., & Olkin, I. (1985). *Statistical methods for meta-analysis.* New York: Academic Press.

Hepner, J. C. (1988). *ETS test collection cumulative index to tests in microfiche, 1975–1987.* Princeton, NJ: Educational Testing Service.

Herman, K., & Samuels, R. (1985). *Computers: An extension of the clinician's mind—A sourcebook.* Norwood, NJ: ABLEX.

Hieronymus, A. N., Hoover, H. D., Oberly, K. R., Cantor, N. K., Frisbie, D. A., Dunbar, S. B., & Lewis, J. C. (1990). *Iowa Tests of Basic Skills teacher's guide: Form J.* Chicago: Riverside Publishing Company.

Highland, R. W., & Berkshire, J. R. (May 1951). *A methodological study of forced choice performance rating* (Research Bull. 51–9). San Antonio, TX: Human Resources Research Center, Lackland Air Force Base.

Holland, J. L. (1973). *Making vocational choices: A theory of vocational personalities and work environments* (1st ed.). Englewood Cliffs, NJ: Prentice-Hall.

Holland, J. L. (1985). *Making vocational choices: A theory of vocational personalities and work environments* (2nd ed.). Englewood Cliffs, NJ: Prentice-Hall.

Holland, P. W., & Rubin, D. B. (Eds.). (1982). *Test equating.* New York: Academic Press.

Hoover, H. D. (1984). The most appropriate scores for measuring educational development in the elementary schools: GE's. *Educational Measurement: Issues and Practice, 3,* 8–14.

Hopkins, K. D., & Stanley, J. C. (1981). *Educational and psychological measurement and evaluation* (6th ed.). Englewood Cliffs, NJ: Prentice-Hall.

Hopkins, K. D., Stanley, J. C., & Hopkins, B. R. (1990). *Educational and psychological measurement and evaluation* (7th ed.). Englewood Cliffs, NJ: Prentice-Hall.

Horn, J. L. (1985). Remodeling old models of intelligence. In B. B. Wolman (Ed.), *Handbook of intelligence* (pp. 267–300). New York: Wiley.

Howard, G. S. (1985). The role of values in the science of psychology. *American Psychologist, 40,* 255–265.

Hughes, H. H., & Trimble, W. E. (1965). The use of complex alternatives in multiple-choice items. *Educational and Psychological Measurement, 25,* 117–126.

Hunt, E. (1987). Science, technology, and intelligence. In R. R. Ronning, J. A. Glover, J. C. Conoley, & J. C. Witt (Eds.), *The influence of cognitive psychology on testing and measurement: The Buros-Nebraska Symposium on Measurement and Testing* (Vol. 3, pp. 11–40). Hillsdale, NJ: Erlbaum.

Iowa Tests of Basic Skills. (1986). Chicago: Riverside Publishing Company.

Iowa Tests of Educational Development (8th ed.). (1988). Chicago: Riverside Publishing Company.

IOX Basic Skills Test (1978). Los Angeles: IOX Assessment Associates.

Issues. (1988). NCLEX: Keeping pace with practice. *Issues, 9*(3), 3–6.

Jackson, D. N. (1955). Computer-based personality testing. *Computers in Human Behavior, 1,* 225–264.

Jackson, D. N., Holden, R. R., Locklin, R. H., & Marks, E. (1984). Taxonomy of vocational interests of academic major areas. *Journal of Educational Measurement, 21,* 261–275.

Jaeger, R. M. (1989). Certification of student competence. In R. L. Linn (Ed.), *Educational measurement* (3rd ed., pp. 545–572). New York: Macmillan.

Jarjoura, D. (1985). Tolerance intervals for true scores. *Journal of Educational Measurement, 10,* 1–17.

Jensen, A. R. (1982). The chronometry of intelligence. In H. J. Eysenck (Ed.), *A model for intelligence.* New York: Springer.

Johnson, O. G. (1976). *Tests and measurements in child development: Handbook II.* San Francisco: Jossey-Bass.

Johnson, O. G., & Bommarito, J. W. (1971). *Tests and measurements in child development: A handbook.* San Francisco: Jossey-Bass.

Johnson, T. F., & Hess, R. J. (1970). *Tests in the arts.* St. Ann, MO: Central Midwestern Regional Educational Laboratory.

Jones, L. V. (1971). The nature of measurement. In R. L. Thorndike (Ed.), *Educational measurement* (2nd ed., pp. 335–355). Washington, DC: American Council on Education.

Kane, M. T., & Wilson, J. (1984). Errors of measurement and standard setting in mastery testing. *Applied Psychological Measurement, 4,* 107–115.

Kaplan, R. M., & Saccuzzo, D. P. (1989). *Psychological testing: Principles, applications, and issues* (2nd ed.). Pacific Grove, CA: Brooks/Cole.

Kaufman, A. S., & Kaufman, N. L. (1983). *Kaufman Assessment Battery for Children. Interpretive Manual.* Circle Pines, MN: American Guidance Services.

Kentucky Department of Education, Office of Education for Exceptional Children. (1990). *The Manual of Local Education Requirements Related to Exceptional Children.* Frankfort, KY: Author.

Keyser, D. J., & Sweetland, R. C. (1984). *Test critiques.* Kansas City, MO: Test corporation of America.

Kirk, R. E. (1990). *Statistics: An introduction* (3rd ed.). Fort Worth, TX: Holt, Rinehart, and Winston.

Klores, M. S. (1966). Rater bias in forced-distribution performance ratings. *Personnel Psychology, 19,* 411–421.

Kolen, M. J. (1988). Defining score scales in relation to measurement error. *Journal of Educational Measurement, 25,* 97–110.

Krathwohl, D. R., Bloom, B. S., & Masia, B. B. (1964). *Taxonomy of educational objectives, The classification of educational goals, Handbook II: Affective domain.* New York: David McKay.

Krug, S. E. (Ed.). (1988). *Psychware sourcebook* (3rd ed.). Kansas City, MO: Test corporation of America.

Kubiszyn, T., & Borich, G. (1987). *Educational testing and measurement.* Glenview, IL: Scott, Foresman and Company.

Lake, D. G., Miles, M. B., & Earle, R. B. (1973). *Measuring human behavior: Tools for the assessment of social functioning.* New York: Teachers College Press.

Lambert, N. M., Windmiller, M., Tharinger, D., & Cole, L. J. (1981). *AAMD adaptive behavior scale—school edition.* Monterey, CA: CTB/McGraw-Hill.

Landy, F. J., & Farr, J. L. (1980). Performance rating. *Psychological Bulletin, 87,* 72–107.

Larry P. v. Nelson Riles. 343 F. Supp. 1306 (N.D. Cal. 1972), affirmed 502 F2d 963 (9th Cir. 1979).

Levy, P., & Goldstein, H. (1984). *Tests in education: A book of critical reviews.* London: Academic Press.

Linn, R. L. (1989). Current perspectives and future directions. In R. L. Linn (Ed.), *Educational measurement* (3rd ed., pp. 1–10). New York: Macmillan.

Livingston, S. A., & Zieky, M. J. (1982). *Passing scores: A manual for setting standards of performance on educational and occupational tests.* Princeton, NJ: Educational Testing Service.

Lord, F. M. (1984). Standard errors of measurement at different score levels. *Journal of Educational Measurement, 21,* 239–243.

Lord, F. M., & Novick, M. R. (1968). *Statistical theories of mental test scores.* Reading, MA: Addison-Wesley.

Mager, R. F. (1975). *Preparing instructional objectives.* (2nd ed.). Belmont, CA: Fearon.

Mangen, D. J., & Peterson, W. A. (Eds.). (1982). *Research instruments in social gerontology.* Minneapolis, MN: University of Minnesota Press.

Mauser, A. J. (1977). *Assessing the learning disabled: Selected instruments* (2nd ed.). Novato, CA: Academic Therapy Publications.

McAllister, L. W. (1986). *A practical guide to CPI interpretation.* Palo Alto, CA: Consulting Psychologists Press.

McClelland, D. C., Atkinson, J. W., Clark, R. A., & Lowell, E. L. (1953). *The achievement motive.* New York: Appleton-Century-Crofts.

McClung, M. S. (1979). Competency testing programs: Legal and educational issues. *Fordham Law Review, 47,* 652.

McGuinness, D. (1986). Facing the "learning disability" crisis. *Education Week, 5*(21), 22–28.

Mehrens, W. A. (1987). *Using standardized tests in education.* New York: Longman.

Mehrens, W. A., & Kaminski, J. (1989). Methods for improving standardized test scores:

Fruitful, fruitless, or fraudulent. *Educational Measurement: Issues and Practice, 8*(1), 14–22.

Mercer, J. R., & Lewis, J. F. (1978). *System of multicultural pluralistic assessment.* San Antonio, TX: Psychological Corporation.

Merian, E. M., Stefan, D., Schoenfeld, L. S., & Kobos, J. C. (1980). Screening of police applicants: A five-item MMPI research index. *Psychological Reports, 47,* 155–158.

Messick, S. (1989). Validity. In R. L. Linn (Ed.), *Educational measurement* (3rd ed., pp. 13–103). New York: Macmillan.

Metropolitan Achievement Tests. (1985–1988). San Antonio, TX: Psychological Corporation.

Michell, J. (1986). Measurement scales and statistics: A clash of paradigms. *Psychological Bulletin, 3,* 398–407.

Miller, D. C. (1983). *Handbook of research design and social measurements* (4th ed.). New York: Longman.

Millon, T. (1983). The DSM-III: An insider's perspective. *American Psychologist, 38,* 804–814.

Millon, T., Green, C. J., & Meagher, R. B. (1982). A new psychodiagnostic tool for clients in rehabilitation settings: The MBHI. *Rehabilitation Psychology, 27,* 23–35.

Mitchell, J. V., Jr. (Ed.). (1983). *Tests in print III.* Lincoln, NB: Buros Institute of Mental Measurements.

Mitchell, J. V., Jr. (Ed.). (1985). *The ninth mental measurements yearbook.* Lincoln, NB: Buros Institute of Mental Measurements.

Moreland, K. L. (1985). Validation of computer-based test interpretations: Problems and prospects. *Journal of Consulting and Clinical Psychology, 53,* 816–825.

Morrison, R. L. (1988). Structured interviews and rating scales. In A. S. Bellack & M. Hershon (Eds.), *Behavioral assessment: A practical handbook* (pp. 252–278). New York: Pergamon.

National Education Association. (1967). Report to parents. *NEA Research Bulletin, 45,* 51–53.

Nedelsky, L. (1954). Absolute grading standards for objective tests. *Educational and Psychological Measurement, 14,* 3–19.

Newmark, C. S. (Ed.). (1985). *Major psychological assessment instruments.* Boston: Allyn and Bacon.

Nickerson, R. S. (1989). New directions in educational assessment. *Educational Researcher, 18*(9), 3–7.

Nihira, K., Foster, R., Shellhaas, M., & Leland, H. (1974). *AAMD adaptive behavior scale* (rev. ed.). Washington, D.C.: American Association of Mental Deficiency.

Nitko, A. J. (1983). *Educational tests and measurement.* New York: Harcourt Brace Jovanovich.

Nitko, A. J. (1984). Defining "criterion-referenced test." In R. A. Berk (Ed.), *A guide to criterion-referenced test construction* (pp. 8–28). Baltimore: Johns Hopkins University Press.

Northwest Regional Educational Laboratory, Center for Bilingual Education. (1978). *Assessment instruments in bilingual education: A descriptive catalog of 342 oral and written tests.* Los Angeles: National Dissemination and Assessment Center.

Nunnally, J. C. (1967). *Psychometric theory.* New York: McGraw-Hill.

Oakland, T. (1983). Joint use of adaptive behavior and IQ to predict achievement. *Journal of Consulting and Clinical Psychology, 51*(2), 298–301.

O'Brien, N. P. (1988). *Test construction: A bibliography of selected resources.* New York: Greenwood.

Osterlind, S. J. (1983). Test item bias. *Sage University Paper Series on Quantitative Applications in the Social Sciences, 007–030*. Beverly Hills, CA: Sage Publications.

Osterlind, S. J. (1989). *Constructing test items*. Boston: Kluwer.

Page, E. B. (1984). Struggles and possibilities: The use of tests in decision making. In B. S. Plake (Ed.), *Social and technical issues in testing* (pp. 11–38). Hillsdale, NJ: Erlbaum.

Parents in Action on Special Education v. Hannon. U.S.D.C. NI11; J. Grady Pub. (July 7, 1980).

Pedhazur, E. J. (1982). *Multiple regression in behavioral research* (2nd ed.). New York: Holt, Rinehart, and Winston.

Peres, S. H., & Garcia, J. R. (1962). Validity and dimensions of descriptive adjectives used in reference letters for engineering applicants. *Personnel Psychology, 15,* 279–286.

Petersen, N. S., Kolen, M. J., & Hoover, H. D. (1989). Scaling, norming, and equating. In R. L. Linn (Ed.), *Educational measurement* (3rd ed., pp. 221–262). New York: Macmillan.

Pinchak, B. M., & Breland, H. M. (1974). Grading practices in American high schools: National longitudinal study of the high school class of 1972. *Education Digest, 39,* 21–23.

Popham, W. J. (1980). Domain specification strategies. In R. J. Berk (Ed.), *Criterion-referenced measurement*. Baltimore: Johns Hopkins University Press.

Popham, W. J. (1981). *Modern educational measurement: A practitioner's perspective* (1st ed.). Englewood Cliffs, NJ: Prentice-Hall.

Popham, W. J. (1990). *Modern educational measurement: A practitioner's perspective* (2nd ed.). Englewood Cliffs, NJ: Prentice-Hall.

Reis, S. M. (1989). Reflection on policy affecting the education of gifted and talented students: Past and future perspectives. *American Psychologist, 44,* 399–408.

Rimland, B. (1960). The effects of varying time limits and of using right answer not given in experimental forms of the U.S. Navy arithmetic test. *Educational and Psychological Measurement, 20,* 533–539.

Robinson, J. P., Athanasiou, R., & Head, K. B. (1969). *Measures of occupational attitudes and occupational characteristics*. Ann Arbor, MI: University of Michigan.

Robinson, J. P., Rusk, J. G., & Head, K. B. (1968). *Measures of political attitudes*. Ann Arbor, MI: University of Michigan.

Robinson, J. P., & Shaver, P. R. (1973). *Measures of social psychological attitudes* (rev. ed.). Ann Arbor, MI: University of Michigan.

Rogosa, D. R., & Willett, J. B. (1983). Demonstrating the reliability of the difference score in the measurement of change. *Journal of Educational Measurement, 20,* 335–343.

Ronning, R. R., Glover, J. A., & Conoley, J. C. (1987). *The influence of cognitive psychology on psychological testing*. Hillsdale, NJ: Erlbaum.

Rosenbaum, B. L. (1971). *An empirical study of attitude toward invasion of privacy as it relates to personnel selection*. Unpublished doctoral dissertation, Columbia University, Teachers College, New York.

Roth, R. (Ed.). (1985). Special issue on teacher testing [Special issue]. *Educational Measurement: Issues and Practice, 4*(3).

Rudner, L. M. (1988). Teacher testing—An update. *Educational Measurement: Issues and Practice, 7*(1), 16–19.

Ryanen, I. A. (1988). Commentary of a minor bureaucrat. *Journal of Vocational Behavior, 33,* 379–387.

Saal, F. E., Downey, R. G., & Lahey, M. A. (1980). Rating the ratings: Assessing the psychometric quality of rating data. *Psychological Bulletin, 88*(2), 413–428.

Sattler, J. M. (1982). *Assessment of children's intelligence and special abilities* (2nd ed.). Boston: Allyn and Bacon.

Sattler, J. M. (1988). *Assessment of children's intelligence and special abilities* (3rd ed.). San Diego: Author.

Savard, J. G. (1969). *Analytical bibliography of language tests.* Quebec: International Center for Research on Bilingualism.

Sax, G. (1989). *Principles of educational and psychological measurement and evaluation* (3rd ed.). Belmont, CA: Wadsworth.

Scannell, D. P. (1986). *Tests of Achievement and Proficiency, Forms G/H: Manual for school administrators.* Chicago: Riverside Publishing Company.

Scheuneman, J. D. (1984). A theoretical framework for the exploration of causes and effects of bias in testing. *Educational Psychologist, 19,* 219–225.

Schmidt, F. L. (1988a). The problem of group differences in ability test scores in employment selection. *Journal of Vocational Behavior, 33,* 272–292.

Schmidt, F. L. (1988b). Validity generalization and the future of criterion-related validity. In H. Wainer & H. Braun (Eds.), *Test validity* (pp. 173–189). Hillsdale, NJ: Erlbaum.

Schmidt, F. L., & Hunter, J. E. (1981). Employment testing: Old theories and new research findings. *American Psychologist, 36,* 1128–1137.

Schmidt, F. L., Hunter, J. E., Pearlman, K., & Hirsh, H. R. (1985). Forty questions about validity generalization and meta-analysis. *Personnel Psychology, 32,* 697–798.

Scholl, G., & Schnur, R. (1976). *Measures of psychological, vocational and educational functioning in the blind and visually handicapped.* New York: American Foundation for the Blind.

Sharp, J. C. (1988). Litigating personnel measurement policy. *Journal of Vocational Behavior, 33,* 235–271.

Shaw, M. E., & Wright, J. W. (1967). *Scales for the measurement of attitudes.* New York: McGraw-Hill.

Shepard, L. A. (1984). Setting performance standards. In R. A. Berk (Ed.), *A guide to criterion-referenced test construction* (pp. 169–198). Baltimore: Johns Hopkins University Press.

Shepard, L. A., Smith, M. L. & Vojir, C. P. (1983). Characteristics of pupils identified as learning disabled. *American Educational Research Journal, 20*(3), 309–332.

Shepard, L. A. (1989). Identification of mild handicaps. In R. L. Linn (Ed.), *Educational measurement* (3rd ed., pp. 545–572). New York: Macmillan.

Shepard, L. A., & Kreitzer, A. E. (1987). The Texas teacher test. *Educational Measurement: Issues and Practice, 16*(6), 22–31.

Shepard, L. A., Smith, M. L., & Vojir, C. P. (1983). Characteristics of pupils identified as learning disabled. *American Educational Research Journal, 20,* 309–331.

Siskind, G. (1966). "Mine eyes have seen a host of angels." *American Psychologist, 21,* 804–806.

Skaggs, G., & Lissitz, R. W. (1986). IRT test equating: Relevant issues and a review of recent research. *Review of Educational Research, 56,* 495–529.

Slavin, R. E. (1987). Mastery learning reconsidered. *Review of Educational Research, 57*(2), 175–213.

Slavin, R. E. (1988). *Educational psychology: Theory into practice.* Englewood Cliffs, NJ: Prentice-Hall.

Smith, G. P. (1987). The effects of competency testing on the supply of minority teachers. A report prepared for the National Education Association and the Council of Chief State School Officers. Jacksonville, FL: University of North Florida.

Smith, M. L., & Glass, G. V. (1977). Meta-analysis of psychotherapy outcome studies. *American Psychologist, 32,* 752–760.

Smith, P. C., & Kendall, L. M. (1963). Retranslation of expectations: An approach to the construction of unambiguous anchors for rating scales. *Journal of Applied Psychology, 47,* 149–155.

Snow, R. E., & Lohman, D. F. (1989). Implications of cognitive psychology for educational measurement. In R. L. Linn (Ed.), *Educational measurement* (3rd ed., pp. 263–331). New York: Macmillan.

Sparrow, S. S. Balla, D. A., & Cicchetti, D. V. (1984). *Vineland Adaptive Behavior Scales.* Circle Pines, MN: American Guidance Services.

Spence, J. T., Cotton, J. W., Underwood, B. J., & Duncan, C. P. (1990). *Elementary statistics* (5th ed.). Englewood Cliffs, NJ: Prentice-Hall.

SRA Achievement Series. (1978). Chicago: Science Research Associates.

Stanford Diagnostic Mathematics Test (3rd ed.). (1984). San Antonio, TX: Psychological Corporation.

Sternbeg, R. J. (1985). *Beyond IQ: A triarchic theory of intelligence.* Cambridge: Cambridge University Press.

Stiggins, R. J., & Bridgeford, N. J. (1985). The ecology of classroom assessment. *Journal of Educational Measurement, 22,* 271–286.

Stiggins, R., Conklin, N. F., & Bridgeford, N. J. (1986). Classroom assessment: A key to effective education. *Educational Measurement: Issues and Practice, 5*(2), 5–17.

Stiggins, R. J., Frisbie, D. A., & Griswold, P. A. (1989). Inside high school grading practices: Building a research agenda. *Educational Measurement: Issues and Practice, 8*(2), 5–14.

Subkoviak, M. J. (1984). Estimating the reliability of mastery—Non-mastery classifications. In R. A. Berk (Ed.), *A guide to criterion-referenced test construction* (pp. 267–291). Baltimore: Johns Hopkins University Press.

Sweetland, R. C., & Keyser, D. J. (Eds.). (1986). *Tests: A comprehensive reference for assessments in psychology, education and business* (2nd ed.). Kansas City, MO: Test Corporaton of America.

Terman, L. M., & Merrill, M. A. (1960). *Stanford-Binet Intelligence Scale: Manual for third edition.* Boston: Houghton Mifflin.

Terwilliger, J. S. (1989). Classroom standard setting and grading practices. *Educational Measurement: Issues and Practice, 8*(2), 15–19.

Thissen, D., Steinberg, L., & Fitzpatrick, A. R. (1989). Multiple-choice models: The distractors are also part of the item. *Journal of Educational Measurement, 26,* 161–176.

Thorndike, R. L. (1982). *Applied psychometrics.* Boston: Houghton Mifflin.

Thorndike, R. L. (1984). *Intelligence as information processing: The mind and the computer.* Bloomington, IA: Center on Evaluation, Development and Research.

Thorndike, R. L. (1985). The central role of general ability in prediction. *Multivariate Behavioral Research, 20,* 241–254.

Thorndike, R. L., & Hagen, E. P. (1986). *Cognitive Abilities Test* (Form 4). Chicago: Riverside Publishing Company.

Thorndike, R. L., & Hagen, E. P. (1987). *Cognitive Abilities Test: Technical manual.* Chicago: Riverside Publishing Company.

Thorndike, R. L., Hagen, E. P., & Sattler, J. M. (1986a). *Guide for administering and scoring the Stanford-Binet Intelligence Scale: Fourth edition.* Chicago: Riverside Publishing Company.

Thorndike, R. L., Hagen, E. P., & Sattler, J. M. (1986b). *The Stanford-Binet Intelligence Scale: Fourth edition. Technical manual.* Chicago: Riverside Publishing Company.

Thorndike, R. M. (1987). Reliability. In B. Bolton (Ed.), *Handbook of measurement and evaluation in rehabilitation* (2nd ed., pp. 21–36). Baltimore: Paul Brookes.

Thorndike, R. M. (1990a). *A century of ability testing.* Chicago: Riverside Publishing Company.

Thorndike, R. M. (1990b). Would the real factors of the Stanford-Binet (fourth edition) please come forward. *Journal of Psychoeducational Assessment.*

Tittle, K. T. (1989). Validity: Whose construction is it in the teaching and learning context? *Educational Measurement: Issues and Practice, 8*(1), 5–13).

U.S. Department of Labor. (1977). *Dictionary of occupational titles* (4th ed.). Washington, DC: U.S. Government Printing Office.

U.S. Department of Labor. (1986). *Dictionary of occupational titles: Fourth edition supplement.* Washington, DC: U.S. Government Printing Office.

U.S. Employment Service. (1967). *Manual for the General Aptitude Test Battery, Section III: Development.* Washington, DC: U.S. Department of Labor.

Valette, R. M. (1977). *Modern language testing* (2nd ed.). New York: Harcourt Brace Jovanovich.

Vold, D. J. (1985). The roots of teacher testing in America. *Educational Measurement: Issues and Practice, 4*(3), 5–8.

Wainer, H. (1989). The future of item analysis. *Journal of Educational Measurement, 26,* 191–208.

Wall, J. (1981). *Compendium of standardized science tests.* Washington, DC: National Science Teachers Association.

Walsh, W. B., & Osipow, S. H. (Eds.). (1986). *Advances in vocational psychology: Vol. 1. The assessment of interests.* Hillsdale, NJ: Erlbaum.

Wang, M. C., Reynolds, M. C., & Walberg, H. J. (1988). Integrating the children of the second system. *Phi Delta Kappan, 70*(3), 248–251.

Wason, P. (1961). Response to affirmative and negative binary statements. *British Journal of Psychology, 52,* 133–142.

Watson v. Fort Worth Bank and Trust, U.S. Sup. Ct., No. 86–6139 (June 29, 1988).

Wesman, A. G., & Bennett, G. K. (1946). The use of "none of these" as an option in test construction. *Journal of Educational Psychology, 37,* 533–539.

Wigdor, A. K., & Garner, W. R. (Eds.). (1982). *Ability testing: Uses, consequences, and controversies: Part I. Report of the committee.* Washington, DC: National Academy Press.

Wike, E. L. (1985). *Numbers: A primer of data analysis.* Columbus, OH: Merrill.

Willett, J. B. (1988). Questions and answers in the measurement of change. In E. Z. Rothkopf (Ed.), *Review of research in education* (Vol. 15, pp. 345–422). Washington, DC: American Educational Research Association.

Woodcock, R. W. (1978). *Development and standardization of the Woodcock-Johnson Psycho-Educational Battery.* Hingham, MA: Teaching Resources Corporation.

Wright, B. D., & Bell, S. R. (1984). Item banks: What, why, how. *Journal of Educational Measurement, 21,* 331–345.

Yalow, E. S., & Popham, J. H. (1983). Content validity at the crossroads. *Educational Researcher, 12*(8), 10–14, 21.

Yen, W. M. (1986). The choice of scale for educational measurement: An IRT perspective. *Journal of Educational Measurement, 23,* 299–325.

Ysseldyke, J. E., Algozzine, B., & Epps, S. (October, 1983). A logical and empirical analysis of current practice in classifying students as handicapped. *Exceptional Children,* 160-166.

Zern, D. (1967). Effects of variations in question phrasing on true-false answers by grade-school children. *Psychological Reports, 20,* 527–533.

APPENDIX 1

Calculating the Mean, Standard Deviation, and Correlation Coefficient

The Mean for Grouped Data

In Chapter 2, we described the procedures for calculating the mean—from the original set of scores, the raw data. When the scores have been placed in a frequency distribution, we can use a shortcut to calculate the mean. If the data have not been assembled into groups, the following procedure will yield exactly the same answer that would be obtained from the original scores; however, if the scores have been summarized in a grouped frequency distribution, the results may be slightly different because of the inaccuracies introduced by grouping.

Suppose we have the following small frequency distribution of scores on a five-item test. The values in the X column are the possible scores, and the values in the f column are the frequencies.

X	f
5	6
4	12
3	30
2	8
1	3
0	1

The values in the f column, of course, represent the number of people who got each score. Six people answered all items correctly, 12 people missed only one item, and so on. If we added the scores of the people who scored 5, we would have $5 + 5 + 5 + 5 + 5 + 5 = 30$. If we multiplied the score 5 by the number of people who earned that score (5×6), we would get the same answer. The same is true for every score value. Adding twelve 4s is the same as multiplying 4 by 12, and so forth. We can therefore get the sum of all 60 scores by multiplying each score by the number of people who earned it and adding these products. In symbols, for individual score totals, that is

$$\Sigma X = \Sigma f X$$

For our problem, we add $(6 \times 5) + (12 \times 4) + (30 \times 3) + (8 \times 2) + (3 \times 1) + (1 \times 0) = 187$. We would have gotten the same answer if we had been working with the original 60 scores, but then we would have had to add a column of 60 numbers. We get the mean by dividing ΣX by the number of individuals, represented by Σf or N. The mean is

$$M = \frac{\Sigma X}{N} = \frac{187}{60} = 3.12$$

Now suppose the same 60 people had taken a 50-item test and that the results had been entered into a grouped frequency distribution with an interval of three. In working with a grouped frequency distribution, we use the midpoint (X in the tabulation that follows) of each interval to stand for all scores in the interval (see Chapter 2). The results might look like this:

Interval	Midpoint (X)	f	fX
48–50	49	3	147
45–47	46	7	322
42–44	43	13	559
39–41	40	20	800
36–38	37	11	407
33–35	34	6	204
			$\Sigma fX = 2{,}439$

Because the midpoint of each interval stands for all scores in the interval, regardless of what those scores actually are, we use the midpoint just like we used the score values above. That is, instead of adding $49 + 49 + 49$ to get the sum of scores for the three people in the top interval, we use $3 \times 49 = 147$. The sum for the seven people in the next interval is found to be $7 \times 46 = 322$. Each of the other products of f and X is found in the same way. These values have been placed in the last column. The sum of these entries gives a value of 2,439 for ΣfX that, when divided by the number of individuals (60), yields a mean of 40.65. Note that the equation used here is identical to the one used earlier except that X stands for the midpoint of an interval rather than for a single score value.

The Standard Deviation for Grouped Data

We can approach the computation of the standard deviation *(SD)* for grouped data in the same way that we approached the computation of the mean. Recall from Chapter 2 that we needed the sum of squared scores to find the standard deviation. We can square each score individually and add them, or we can place them in a frequency distribution as we did in the previous section. Here, we have the same distribution just used for our five-item test, but the third column contains the square of each score value, and the last column contains X^2 multiplied by its frequency.

X	f	X^2	fX^2
5	6	25	150
4	12	16	192
3	30	9	270
2	8	4	32
1	3	1	3
0	1	0	0

$$\Sigma fX^2 = 647$$

The sum of the values in the last column, 647, is the same value we would obtain if we squared each of the 60 scores individually. Putting this value into the equation for the standard deviation, we get

$$SD = \sqrt{\frac{\Sigma fX^2}{N} - M^2}$$

$$= \sqrt{\frac{647}{60} - 3.12^2}$$

$$= \sqrt{1.05} = 1.02$$

We can carry out the same procedure for computing the SD on the second set of data used as an example for computing the mean if we substitute the interval midpoints for the scores, as shown here.

Interval	Midpoint (X)	f	X^2	fX^2
48–50	49	3	2,401	7,203
45–47	46	7	2,116	14,812
42–44	43	13	1,849	24,037
39–41	40	20	1,600	32,000
36–38	37	11	1,369	15,059
33–35	34	6	1,156	6,936

$$\Sigma fX^2 = 100,047$$

The value of ΣfX^2 is 100,047. Using this value in the equation for standard deviation gives the following:

$$SD = \sqrt{\frac{100,047}{60} - 40.65^2} = \sqrt{15.03} = 3.88$$

Many calculators allow for grouped-data entry. The procedure usually works in the following way. You enter a score value on the keyboard and then push a special key, often having a capital sigma on it, to enter the value. Next, you enter the frequency for that score and push a second key, often the "equal" key. The calculator computes and stores fX and fX^2. This sequence is repeated for each score value and its frequency, and at each step, the calculator adds the new values to those already in memory. When all the data have been entered, you can either recall the sums or, on most calculators, simply press a key for the mean and a second one for the standard deviation.

Computing the Correlation Coefficient

The correlation coefficient (r) was introduced in Chapter 2 as an index that expresses the extent to which two variables (say, X and Y) go together, or correlate. It indicates the extent to which high X scores go with high Y scores and vice versa. But "high" and "low" must be expressed in some uniform terms from one set of data to another if the index is to have the same meaning for different sets of data. Standard scores (z scores) provide just such a framework because they express position as so many standard deviations above or below the mean of the distribution of scores.

The correlation coefficient between X and Y (or, more precisely, the *Pearson product-moment* correlation coefficient—there are other kinds of correlations) is defined as the mean product of standard scores. If each X and Y is expressed as so many standard deviations above or below its mean, the product of the standard scores for each individual is found, and the mean of these products is found, the result is the correlation between X and Y. Expressed as an equation,

$$r = \frac{\Sigma z_X z_Y}{N}$$

where r is the correlation coefficient, x_x and z_y are standard scores on X and Y, and N is the number of individuals.

This is the *definition* of the correlation coefficient. However, it does not provide an efficient or convenient routine for calculation. If we substitute the raw score definitions of the z scores in the equation just given, we get something that looks harder but is really much easier to work with.

In most cases, we would already have computed the mean and standard deviation of both X and Y. The only additional step then is to find the sum of the products of X and Y across all individuals. Once, we find this quantity, ΣXY, we can use the following equation for r.

$$r = \frac{\dfrac{\Sigma XY}{N} - M_X M_Y}{SD_X SD_Y}$$

That is, to find the correlation coefficient, follow these steps:

1. Find the product X times Y for each individual.
2. Find the sum of these products.
3. Divide this sum by the number of individuals.

4. Find the product of the means of the two variables.

5. Subtract the quantity in Step 4 from the quantity in Step 3.

6. Find the product of the standard deviations of the two variables.

7. Divide the quantity in Step 5 by the quantity in Step 6.

The result is the correlation between X and Y.

The procedures for computing the correlation coefficient can be illustrated with the following small set of data. Each row gives X, Y, X^2, Y^2, and XY for a different individual. The values in the last row are the sums.

X	Y	X^2	Y^2	XY
10	12	100	144	120
8	6	64	36	48
13	10	169	100	130
11	11	121	121	121
14	11	196	121	154
12	14	144	196	168
68	64	794	718	741

The column sums are used to compute the various quantities required to calculate the correlation coefficient as follows:

$$M_x = 68/6 = 11.33$$
$$M_y = 64/6 = 10.67$$
$$SD_x = \sqrt{(794/6) - 11.33^2} = 1.99$$
$$SD_y = \sqrt{(718/6) = 10.67^2} = 2.41$$

$$r = \frac{(741/6) - (11.33)(10.67)}{(1.99)(2.41)} = \frac{123.5 - 120.89}{4.80}$$
$$= 0.54$$

Again, many calculators have a program that will compute the correlation with the press of a single key, once you have entered the data. Ordinarily, they will accumulate the five required quantities—XY, X, Y, X^2, and Y^2—in particular memory locations (which are listed in the user's manual). These quantities can be recalled, one at a time, to compute the means and standard deviations of the two variables and the correlation between them while entering the data into the calculator only once. It is also likely that the calculators will have keys that can be used to compute each of these statistics automatically.

APPENDIX 2
Percent of Cases Falling Below Selected Values on the Normal Curve

Deviation in Standard Deviation Units	Cases Falling Below (%)	Deviation in Standard Deviation Units	Cases Falling Below (%)
+3.0	99.9	−.1	46.0
2.9	99.8	−.2	42.1
2.8	99.7	−.3	38.2
2.7	99.6	−.4	34.4
2.6	99.5	−.5	30.9
2.5	99.4	−.6	27.4
2.4	99.2	−.7	24.2
2.3	98.9	−.8	21.2
2.2	98.6	−.9	18.4
2.1	98.2	−1.0	15.9
2.0	97.7	−1.1	13.6
1.9	97.1	−1.2	11.5
1.8	96.4	−1.3	9.7
1.7	95.5	−1.4	8.1
1.6	94.5	−1.5	6.7
1.5	93.3	−1.6	5.5
1.4	91.9	−1.7	4.5
1.3	90.3	−1.8	3.6
1.2	88.5	−1.9	2.9
1.1	86.4	−2.0	2.3
1.0	84.1	−2.1	1.8
.9	81.6	−2.2	1.4
.8	78.8	−2.3	1.1
.7	75.8	−2.4	.8
.6	72.6	−2.5	.6
.5	69.1	−2.6	.5
.4	65.6	−2.7	.4
.3	61.8	−2.8	.3
.2	57.9	−2.9	.2
.1	54.0	−3.0	.1
.0	50.0		

APPENDIX 3

Sources for Educational and Psychological Tests

Many agencies publish one or two tests, questionnaires, or other measurement instruments; however, most of the widely used tests are handled by a relatively small group of publishers. The list that follows includes publishers of the tests described in Appendix 4 and a few other publishers that have a substantial list of titles.

Addison Wesley Publishing Company
2725 Sand Hill Road
Menlo Park, CA 94025

American College Testing Program
P.O. Box 168
Iowa City, IA 52243

American Guidance Services, Inc.
Publishers Buildings
Circle Pines, MN 55014

Bobbs-Merrill Company, Inc.
4300 East 62nd Street
Indianapolis, IN 46268

College Entrance Examination Board
P.O. Box 592
Princeton, NJ 08540

Consulting Psychologists Press
577 College Avenue
Palo Alto, CA 94306

CTB/McGraw-Hill
Del Monte Research Park
Monterey, CA 93940

Educational Testing Service
Rosedale Road
Princeton, NJ 08540

Houghton Mifflin Company
1 Beacon Street
Boston, MA 02107

Institute for Personality and Ability Testing
1602 Coronada Drive
Champaign, IL 61820

Jastak Associates, Inc.
P.O. Box 4460
Wilmington, DE 19807

Psychological Assessment Resources
P.O. Box 998
Odessa, FL 33556

Psychological Corporation
555 Academic Court
San Antonio, TX 78204

Psychometric Affiliates
P.O. Box 3167
Munster, IN 46321

Riverside Publishing Company
8420 Bryn Mawr Drive
Chicago, IL 60631

Scholastic Testing Service
480 Meyer Road
Bensenville, IL 60106

Science Research Associates, Inc.
155 North Wacker Drive
Chicago, IL 60606

Sheridan Psychological Services
P.O. Box 6101
Orange, CA 92667

Stoelting Company
1350 South Kostner Avenue
Chicago, IL 60623

Teachers College Press
Teachers College, Columbia University
525 West 120th Street
New York, NY 10027

Western Psychological Services
12031 Wilshire Boulevard
Los Angeles, CA 90025

APPENDIX 4

Commercially Available Psychological and Educational Tests and Inventories

Introduction

In this appendix, we present lists and brief descriptions of some of the commercially available psychological and educational tests and inventories. The appendix is organized by topic, and the tests within a topic are arranged alphabetically. Each entry contains the test title, publisher, intended age range or grade of test takers, testing time, a notation of the most recent review of the test in the *Mental Measurements Yearbook (MMY),* and a brief review of the test. Of course, there are thousands of tests that we have not included here.

Section A—Tests of General Ability

Several measures of general cognitive ability are distributed only under programs controlled by their publishers, including the Scholastic Aptitide Test of the College Board and the American College Testing (ACT) Program's ACT Assessment. The latter is described as an achievement test, but it is used for making college admissions decisions. These instruments are revised for every administration and are of uniformly high quality. However, their restricted distribution makes them of limited value for use with any but their narrow target group. We note the existence of these instruments, but do not include them for review.

Cognitive Abilities Test (CogAT)—Form 4
Riverside Publishing Company
Grades: Primary battery, Kindergarten–Grade 3
       Multilevel, Grades 3–13
Testing time: Primary, 2 sessions of about 30 minutes each
       Multilevel, 30 minutes for each of 3 sections
Last *MMY* review: 10th

The Nonreading primary battery has two levels; the multilevel battery is composed of eight overlapping levels of difficulty. The multilevel battery provides separate scores for verbal, quantitative, and nonverbal sections. These batteries are jointly normed with the Iowa Tests of Basic Skills and the Tests of Achievement and Proficiency. Results are reported as standard age scores (mean = 100 and standard deviation (SD) = 16), percentile rank by age and grade, and stanine by age and grade. (See Chapter 12.)

Culture Fair Intelligence Tests
Institute for Personality and Ability Testing
Ages: Scale 1, 4–8 and older learning disabled
        Scale 2, 8–14 and average adults
        Scale 3, Grades 9–16 and superior adults
Testing time: Scale 1, 22 minutes
                Scales 2 and 3, 15 minutes
Last *MMY* review: 6th
    Scale 1 consists of eight subtests, four of which must be administered individually. Scales 2 and 3 contain four subtests involving different perceptual tasks: completing progressive series, classifying, solving incomplete designs, and evaluating conditions. Raw scores on Scale 1 are converted into mental ages and IQ scores; on Scales 2 and 3, they are converted into percentile ranks by ages and IQ scores. The stimulus materials were revised in 1977, but the test manuals were last revised in 1973. A Spanish language version of Scales 2 and 3 is available.

Goodenough-Harris Drawing Test
Psychological Corporation
Ages: 3–15
Testing time: Untimed (usually 10–15 minutes)
Last *MMY* review: 7th
    This is a nonverbal test of mental ability, suitable as either a group or an individual test. The current version of the test is the 1963 revision of the original Draw-a-Man test. The examinee is required to draw a picture of a man, a woman, and himself or herself. Prospective users of the test should have a copy of Dale B. Harris's *Children's Drawings as Measures of Intellectual Maturity* in addition to the examiner's kit. The test was standardized on 2,975 children from families representative of the occupational distribution of the United States in 1950. Raw scores are converted to standard scores (mean = 100 and *SD* − 15), and these scores may be converted into percentile ranks. Reliability and validity information is extremely dated.

Henmon-Nelson Tests of Mental Ability
Riverside Publishing Company
Grades: Kindergarten–Grade 2, and Grades 3–6, 6–9, 9–12
Testing time: Kindergarten–Grade 2 untimed (approximately 25–30 minutes)
                Grades 3–12, 30 minutes
Last *MMY* review: 8th

This test provides a quick measure of general intellectual ability at a modest cost. Scores are reported as age and grade percentiles and stanines as well as deviation IQ Scores. The last standardization was 1973. Scores correlate well with other group tests of intelligence, with teachers' grades, and with achievement test results. Reliabilities are in the range of 0.85–0.95.

Kaufman Assessment Battery for Children (K-ABC)
American Guidance Service
Ages: 2½–12½
Testing time: 35–85 minutes (longer for older examinees)
Last *MMY* review: 9th

This test was first published in 1983 to answer some of the deficiencies ascribed at that time to older instruments such as the Stanford-Binet Intelligence Scale and the Wechsler scales. There are 10 "mental processing" subtests and 6 "achievement" subtests, with different combinations given at different ages. A particular child may take as many as 13 of the tests. Special scales are included to enable the assessment of children with hearing impairment or speech or language disorders or non-English speaking children. (See Chapter 12.)

Kuhlmann-Anderson Intelligence Tests, (KA) Eighth Edition
Scholastic Testing Service, Inc.
Grades: Kindergarten and Grades 1, 2–3, 3–4, 5–6, 7–9, 9–12
Testing time: 25–60 minutes
Last *MMY* review: 9th

The KA consists of eight subtests at all levels. The lower levels yield a single overall score; the higher levels produce three scores, verbal, quantitative, and total. Percentile ranks and deviation IQ scores within age are reported. Reliability coefficients are generally satisfactory. The difference score between verbal and quantitative subtests does not appear to have high enough reliability to be useful. Data on concurrent validity are satisfactory, but few predictive validity coefficients are reported in the technical manual. The subtests have very short time limits, making this a highly speeded test and placing heavy demands on examinees for fast work and on examiners for accurate timing.

McCarthy Scales of Children's Abilities
Psychological Corporation
Ages: 2½–8½
Testing time: Varies with age
Last *MMY* review: 9th

The instrument consists of 18 tests grouped into six overlapping scales: general cognitive, verbal, perceptual performance, quantitative, memory, and motor. The scores for the latter five scales are reported as normalized standard scores with a mean of 50 and an *SD* of 10. The general cognitive scale, based on 15 of the 18 tests, is reported as a general cognitive index (GCI), a normalized standard score with a mean of 100 and an *SD* of 16. The standardization sample was carefully designed to include equal numbers of males and females and proportional representation by race, geographical region, father's occupational level, and urban or rural residence. The median split-half reliability for the GCI is about 0.93 within age levels. Split-half reliabilities for the other five scales range from 0.79 to 0.88. Retest reliabilities over a 1-month interval for 125 children in three age groups were about 0.90 for the GCI and ranged from 0.69 to 0.89 for the other scales. Factor analyses support the usefulness of reporting six separate scores, and GCIs show reasonable agreement with scores from other instruments.

Otis-Lennon School Ability Test (OLSAT)
Psychological Corporation
Grades: 1, 2–3, 4–5, 6–8, 9–12
Testing time: 60–85 minutes depending on level
Last *MMY* review: 9th

This test is a revision of the Otis-Lennon Mental Ability Tests. There are two forms at each of five levels. Form R (1979) was standardized concurrently with the Metropolitan Achievement Tests and Form S (1982) with the Stanford Achievement Test. The instrument yields a single score, called a school ability index, which is a normalized standard score with a mean of 100 and *SD* of 16. Internal consistency reliabilities range from 0.88 to 0.96. Six-month test-retest reliabilities were 0.84–0.92. A 3- to 4-year retest interval yielded values of 0.75–0.78. Equivalent form correlations were in the 0.82–0.92 range, depending on test level. Standard errors of measurement are reported to be about four points. (Scores are also reported in stanines and percentiles.) Correlations with other measures of scholastic aptitude are in the 0.50s and 0.60s.

Peabody Picture Vocabulary Test Revised (PPVT-R)
American Guidance Service, Inc.
Ages: 2½ to adults
Testing time: 15–20 minutes
Last *MMY* review: 9th

The PPVT-R is an individually administered test of vocabulary consisting of a graduated series of 175 plates, each containing four pictures. The examiner gives an oral stimulus word and the examinee points to, or otherwise indicates, the picture on the plate that best illustrates the meaning of the stimulus word. The PPVT-R is frequently used as an abbreviated test of general ability. Norms are based on 4,200 children, ages 2–18 years, and 828 adults. Raw scores can be converted to age equivalents, standard scores with a mean of 100 and an *SD* of 15, and percentile ranks. Alternate form reliabilities range from 0.71 to 0.91, with a median of 0.82, while internal consistency coefficients run from 0.61 to 0.88. Correlations of the PPVT-R with various measures of intellectual ability range from about 0.40 to 0.60.

Progressive Matrices (Raven's Matrices)
Psychological Corporation

Ages: 5 and over
Testing time: Untimed (approximately 15–45 minutes, depending on form)
Last *MMY* review: 6th

This test has three forms: Standard (in black and white for 6 year olds to adult), Advanced (in black and white for ages 11 and over of superior ability), and Coloured (in color for ages 5–11, mental patients, and the elderly). It represents an attempt to appraise the general ability factor, Spearman's *g*. The tasks consist of abstract designs with missing parts. The examinee chooses from the given options the design that best fits. Although the test is claimed by some to be "culture fair," there is little evidence to support this claim. The test is untimed. Evidence on reliability and validity is limited and inconsistent. The manual for the test is inadequate, and normative data are sketchy at best. Most of the norms are based on British samples.

Schaie-Thurstone Adult Mental Abilities Test
Consulting Psychologists Press
Ages: 22–84
Testing time: 50–60 minutes
Last *MMY* review: 10th

This instrument was published in 1985 as a revision and updating of the Primary Mental Abilities Test (PMA). There are two forms, one essentially equivalent to the PMA and one for older adults. There are seven scales. Long-term stability data are impressive, with 7-year retest coefficients of about 0.80 for all scales. Validity is assessed in terms of conformity of the scales to Thurstone's theory of mental abilities. Scale scores are reported as *T* scores (normalized standard scores with a mean of 50 and an *SD* of 10), and there is a composite IQ with a mean of 100 and an *SD* of 15.

Short Form Test of Academic Aptitude (SFTAA)
CTB/McGraw-Hill
Grades: 1.5–12
Testing time: 31–38 minutes
Last *MMY* review: 8th

The SFTAA was designed so that it could be administered in one class period. It is a 1974 revision of the California Tests of Mental Maturity and yields three scores: language, nonlanguage, and total. It consists of four subtests: vocabulary, analogies, sequences, and memory. There are five levels of the test spanning Grades 1.5–12. Scores are presented in the form of a standard score called the reference scale score with a mean of 100 and an *SD* of 16.

Slosson Intelligence Test
Slosson Educational Publications
Ages: 2 weeks–27 years
Testing time: Untimed (approximately 10–30 minutes)
Last *MMY* review: 9th

This is a quick screening test of general mental ability for use primarily with younger children. Reliability and validity information is sketchy and inconsistent. The test was designed as a short form of the 1960 Stanford-Binet.

Stanford-Binet Intelligence Scale, Fourth Edition
Riverside Publishing Company
Ages: 2 to adults
Testing time: Varies with level
Last *MMY* review: 10th
    See the discussion of this instrument in Chapter 12.

Wechsler Adult Intelligence Scale Revised (WAIS-R)
Psychological Corporation
Ages: 16 and over
Testing time: 50–75 minutes
Last *MMY* review: 9th
    See the discussion of the instrument in Chapter 12.

Wechsler Intelligence Scale for Children Revised (WISC-R)
Psychological Corporation
Ages: 6–16
Testing time: 50–75 minutes
Last *MMY* review: 9th
    See the discussion of this instrument in Chapter 12. A new revision of this instrument is in preparation.

Wechsler Preschool and Primary Scale of Intelligence Revised (WPPSI-R)
Psychological Corporation
Ages: 4–6½
Testing time: 50–75 minutes
Last *MMY* review: *MMY* reviews can be expected in the supplement to the 10th
                edition. (This is a new edition released in 1989.)
    See the discussion of this instrument in Chapter 12.

Woodcock-Johnson Psycho-Educational Battery
DLM Teaching Resources
Ages: 3–80
Testing time: Part 1, 60–90 minutes
                Part 2, 30–45 minutes
                Part 3, 15–30 minutes
Last *MMY* review: 9th
    Published in 1978, the Woodcock-Johnson battery is composed of three parts:
Part 1—cognitive ability, 12 scores; Part 2—achievement, 10 scores; Part 3—

scholastic interest, 5 scores. There are 13 derived scores: 4 scholastic aptitude clusters, 4 cognitive factor clusters, 4 achievement clusters, and a broad cognitive ability score. It is administered individually and is the only instrument to assess ability, achievement, and interests. Reliabilities are generally in the high 0.80s and 0.90s for the cluster scores, and a median reliability of 0.97 was found for broad cognitive ability. Correlations with other measures of general ability are in the 0.70s and 0.80s.

Section B—Aptitude Test Batteries

Armed Services Vocational Aptitude Battery (ASVAB)
U.S. Military Enlistment Processing Command
Grade level: High school
Testing time: 135 minutes
Last *MMY* review: 9th
This aptitude battery is designed for use in high school vocational guidance programs and in armed services recruitment centers. The battery has 12 subtests and provides 6 composite scores: verbal, mathematics, perceptual speed, mechanical, trade technical, and academic ability. Median Kuder-Richardson Formula 20 reliabilities are 0.82 for the subtests and 0.92 for the composites. Validity correlations are reported for various military training programs and for high school grades. The test is given and scored without charge by personnel from the U.S. Department of Defense.

Structure of Intellect Learning Abilities Test (SOI)
Western Psychological Services
Level: Preschool to adult, 7 forms
Testing time: Forms A and B, 150–180 minutes
                    Forms G, M, P, R, and RR, 60–90 minutes
Last *MMY* review: 10th
Forms A and B are alternate forms, each with 26 tests that assess the five cognitive operations of Guilford's Structure of Intellect model: cognition, memory, evaluation, convergent production, and divergent production. Scores include the five cognitive dimensions; the figural, symbolic, and semantic contents, and the units, classes, relations, systems, transformations; and implication products from the SOI model. The other five forms (G, M, P, R, and RR) contain selected tests from Form A or similar tests intended for lower levels. Median reliability for the individual subtests is 0.57 (the range is 0.35–0.88). Reliabilities for general ability scores range from 0.65 to 0.90, with most in the 70s. Validity of the battery depends on the validity of the SOI model, which has been questioned. Norms are not as complete as for most batteries, but the tests cover a wider age range.

U.S. Employment Service General Aptitude Test Battery (GATB), 1983 Edition
U.S. Employment Service

Grades: 12 and above and adults
Testing time: 120–150 minutes for group tests
Last *MMY* review: 9th
    See Chapter 12 for a discussion of this battery. It is only available for use by state employment offices.

U.S. Employment Service Nonreading Aptitude Test Battery (NATB), 1982 Edition
U.S. Employment Service
Level: Educationally limited students in Grades 9–12 and adults
Testing time: 107 minutes
Last *MMY* review: 9th
    This battery is an adaptation of the GATB designed for use with high school students and adults with limited reading ability.

Section C—Interest Inventories

Kuder Occupational Interest Survey (KOIS) Revised—Form DD
Science Research Associates, Inc.
Grades: 10–12 and adults
Testing time: Untimed (approximately 30–40 minutes)
Last *MMY* review: 10th
    The instrument consists of 100 triads. In each triad, the examinee selects one activity that is most liked and one that is least liked. The instrument yields 119 occupational scores (79 with male norms and 40 with female norms), 48 college major scores (29 with male norms and 19 with female norms), 10 vocational interest estimates (preferences for different kinds of activities), and a dependability (verification) score. Twenty occupations and 12 majors have norms for both males and females. Scores are reported in terms of the relationship between the examinee's responses and those of successful and satisfied groups in the occupations and college majors. A new supplement allows conversion of interest scores to Holland codes. Answer sheets must be machine scored, but scoring services are quick and efficient. Evidence of reliability and validity is accumulating. See Chapter 13 for further discussion.

Kuder Preference Record—Vocational (KPR-V)
Science Research Associates, Inc.
Grades: 9–12 and adults
Testing time: Untimed (approximately 40–50 minutes)
Last *MMY* review: 8th
    The KPR-V yields 10 interest area scores: outdoor, mechanical, computational, scientific, persuasive, artistic, literary, musical, social service, and clerical. In addition, there is a verification score. See Chapter 13 for further discussion.

Kuder General Interest Survey—Form E
Science Research Associates, Inc.

Grades: 6–12
Testing time: Untimed (approximately 30–40 minutes)
Last *MMY* review: 7th

A revision and downward extension of the Kuder Preference Record—Vocational), this instrument measures the individual's relative preference for activities in 10 job categories: outdoor, mechanical, scientific, computational, persuasive, artistic, literary, musical, social service, and clerical. Percentile scores are available for four norm groups: (1) males and (2) females in Grades 6–8 and (3) males and (4) females in Grades 9–12.

Ohio Vocational Interest Survey, Second Edition (OVIS-II)
Psychological Corporation
Grades: 7 to college and adults
Testing time: Untimed (approximately 60 minutes)
Last *MMY* review: 9th

The instrument is divided into two sections, a student information questionnaire and an interest inventory. The student information questionnaire gathers information about the examinee's occupational plans, school subject preferences, curricular plans, post-high school plans, and vocational course interests. The interest inventory consists of 253 work activity items. Scores are given for 23 occupational area scales that are linked to the *Dictionary of Occupational Titles*. There is also a score called a scale clarity index, which is supposed to reflect the carefulness and consistency of the examinee's answer choices. Raw scores are converted to percentile ranks and stanines by grade and gender.

Self-Directed Search (SDS), 1985 Revision
Psychological Assessment Resources
Level: High school, college, and adults
Testing time: Untimed (approximately 40–60 minutes)
Last *MMY* review: 10th

The SDS was developed to simulate a vocational counseling experience. It is designed to be self-administered, self-scored, and self-interpreted. Scores are provided for the six personality/interest types of Holland's model (realistic, investigative, artistic, social, enterprising, and conventional) on each of three scales (activities, competencies, and occupations). The SDS can be administered and scored by microcomputer. Scores are linked to the *Dictionary of Occupational Titles* codes through the Holland codes. Internal consistency reliabilities for the scales are in the 80s and 90s. Validity evidence is derived primarily from association with Holland's model. See Chapter 13 for further discussion.

Strong Interest Inventory of the Strong Vocational Interest Blank (SII-SVIB)
Consulting Psychologists Press
Grades: 11–12, college, and adults
Testing time: Untimed (approximately 40–60 minutes)
Last *MMY* review: 9th

See the discussion of this instrument in Chapter 13.

Vocational Preference Inventory (VPI), 1985 Revision
Consulting Psychologists Press
Grades: 12–16 and adults
Testing time: Untimed (approximately 30 minutes)
Last *MMY* review: 10th

The VPI consists of 160 occupational titles to which the examinee indicates "like" or "dislike." The inventory yields 11 scores, 6 of which are the Holland types and can be used as vocational interest scales: realistic, investigative, artistic, social, enterprising, and conventional. The remaining 5 scales are personality scales for self-control, masculinity, status, infrequency, and acquiescence. The inventory is probably most useful as a vocational interest inventory. Many reviewers consider the VPI to be a good instrument for vocational counseling or research. It can be administered and scored by Apple or IBM computers. Vocational scales can be linked to Holland's *Occupations Finder* and the *Dictionary of Holland Occupational Codes.*

Section D—Reading Tests

Gates-MacGintie Reading Test
Riverside Publishing Company
Grades: 1–12
Testing time: Varies by level
Last *MMY* review: 9th

This tests has seven levels: Basic R for Grades 1.0–1.9, Level A for Grades 1.5–1.9, Level B for Grade 2, Level C for Grade 3, Level D for Grades 4–6, Level E for Grades 7–9, and Level F for Grades 10–12.

For many years, this instrument has been the most often administered reading test. It was first published in 1926. It provides only three scores: vocabulary, comprehension, and total. Unlike rival reading tests, it does not provide information about separate skills. It is intended to provide an overall estimate of reading level and does not aspire to be diagnostic. Reliability is quite satisfactory ranging from the high 0.80s to the mid 0.90s.

Iowa Silent Reading Test
Harcourt Brace Jovanovich Inc.
Grades: 6–12 and college
Testing time: Varies with level
Last *MMY* review: 8th

This test has three levels: Level 1 for Grades 6–9, Level 2 for Grades 9–14, and advanced for accelerated high school and college students. All levels of the test appraise vocabulary, reading comprehension, and speed of reading with comprehension. Levels 1 and 2 also appraise the use of reference materials and skimming and scanning for specific information. Two forms of the tests are available at each level. Raw scores can be converted to standard scores, percentile ranks, and stanines. A reading efficiency index and an index of reading speed and accuracy are also provided.

Metropolitan Readiness Test (MRT), Fifth Edition
Harcourt Brace Jovanovich
Grades: Prekindergarten–Grade 1
Testing time: 80–100 minutes
Last *MMY* review: The most recent edition has not been reviewed yet in the *MMY*.

This test is intended to asses the underlying or enabling skills that are necessary for early school learning, in particular reading; to determine readiness for instruction; and to identify instructional needs. The test has two levels. Level 1 is intended for use with 4-year-olds prior to their entry into kindergarten and with students already in kindergarten. Level 1 includes auditory memory, beginning consonants, letter recognition, visual matching, school language, and listening, and quantitative language. Level 2 is intended for use with students in the second half of kindergarten and the beginning of first grade. Assessed in this level are beginning consonants, sound-letter correspondence, visual matching, finding patterns, school language, listening, quantitative concepts, and quantitative operations. A full range of standard scores and norms are provided.

Nelson-Denny Reading Test—Forms E and F
Riverside Publishing Company
Grades: 9 to adults
Testing time: 35–50 minutes
Last *MMY* review: 9th

This test provides four scores: vocabulary, comprehension, total, and rate. It is intended for use with high school, college, and adult students as a means of obtaining summary norm-referenced survey scores. There are two subtests: vocabulary with 100 items and comprehension with 36 items. The test is intended to be used to screen students, to predict college success, and to diagnose reading difficulties. There is little evidence provided in the manual to support the validity of the test for these purposes, however. The test has the high reliability one expects of tests of this type. This instrument is a valuable and useful test because it is one of the few reading tests appropriate for use with older students.

Nelson Reading Test
Riverside Publishing Company
Grades: 3.0–9.9
Testing time: Varies with level
Last *MMY* review: 9th

This test has three levels. Level A, for Grades 3.0–4.5, includes five scores, word meaning, reading comprehension, sound-symbol correspondence (optional), root words (optional), and syllabication (optional). Level B, for Grades 4.6–6.9, includes three scores, word meaning, reading comprehension, and reading rate (optional). Level C, for Grades 7.0–9.9, includes three scores, word meaning, reading comprehension, and reading rate (optional). Reliabilities are mostly in the high 0.80s and the low 0.90s. Some attention is given to establishing validity in the manual but a lack of validity evidence must be considered a weakness.

Stanford Diagnostic Reading Test (SDRT), Third Edition
Harcourt Brace Jovanovich
Grades: 1.5–12
Testing time: Varies with level
Last *MMY* review: 9th

This test is intended to provide diagnostic-prescriptive information to teachers both to help individual students and to assist in decision making about grouping students who have the same instructional needs. There are four levels. Red level (Forms A and B), for Grades 1.6–3.5, has six scores: auditory vocabulary, auditory discrimination, phonetic analysis, and three comprehension scores (word reading, reading comprehension, and total). Green level (Forms A and B), for Grades 2.6–5.5, has seven scores: auditory vocabulary, auditory discrimination, phonetic analysis, structural analysis, and three comprehension scores (literal, inferential, and total). Brown level (Forms A and B), for Grades 4.6–9.5, has seven scores, which are the same as those of the green level except that reading rate replaces auditory discrimination. Blue level (Forms A and B), for Grades 9.0–13.0, has 12 scores: three for comprehension (literal, inferential, and total), three for vocabulary (word meaning, word parts, and total), three for decoding (phonetic analysis, structural analysis, and total), and three for rate (fast reading, scanning and skimming, and total). A wide range of normative scores are available along with an impressive array of computer scoring and interpretation services. Extensive use of intraindividual differences are emphasized, but these should be interpreted with caution because of the unreliability inherent in such comparisons.

Section E—Achievement Test Batteries

California Achievement Tests (CAT)
CTB/McGraw-Hill
Grades: Kindergarten–Grade 12
Testing time: Varies with level
Last *MMY* review: 10th

This achievement test battery has been available and used extensively for over 50 years. Forms E and F of the 1985 version are intended to replace forms C and D. Form E consists of 11 levels (Levels 10–20) covering kindergarten through Grade 12, while Form F contains 8 levels (Levels 13–20) and ranges from the second half of Grade 2 to Grade 12. The two forms can be used together for fall and spring testing. The test covers the usual topics for an achievement test battery: word analysis, vocabulary, comprehension, language expression, mathematics computation, concepts, and applications. Test development including item selection, norming, and scaling represents the state of the art in test development. Extensive use is made of item response theory. Particularly useful are standard error of measurement curves, which make it possible to evaluate the capacity of a test to make discriminations anywhere along the ability scale.

Comprehensive Tests of Basic Skills, Fourth Edition (CTBS/4)
McGraw-Hill
Grades: Kindergarten–Grade 12
Testing time: Varies with age
Last *MMY* review: The most recent edition has not been reviewed yet in the *MMY.*

There are currently three options available to the schools choosing to adopt the CTBS/4. (1) Complete battery tests are similar to the previous editions, Forms U and V. The complete battery provides norm-referenced and curriculum-referenced information. (2) Benchmark tests are intended to provide the most reliable and valid norm-referenced scores. This option is most suitable for schools that do not need curriculum-referenced information. (3) There are two survey tests, each half as long as the benchmark tests; they are intended to provide a quicker measure of the achievement level of students than the benchmark tests do. Of course, because the survey tests are shorter, their item coverage and statistical characteristics are inferior to those obtained from the benchmark tests. A curriculum-referenced version of the CTBS/4 has also been planned.

Scales included in CTBS/4 are visual recognition (kindergarten), word analysis (Grades 1–3), vocabulary (kindergarten through Grade 12), comprehension (kindergarten through Grade 12), language mechanics and language expression (Grades 1–12), spelling (Grades 2–12), study skills (Grades 4–12), mathematics computation and mathematics concepts and applications (kindergarten through Grade 12), science (Grades 1–12), and social studies (Grades 1–12). The CTBS/4 differs from earlier editions by placing greater emphasis on the assessment of higher order thinking skills. Item selection, norming, and scaling represent the state of the art in test development, effectively employing item response theory techniques. The CTBS/4 is similar in its psychometric properties to the California Achievement Tests, which is not surprising because they share the same publisher and the same test development staff.

Iowa Tests of Basic Skills (ITBS)
Riverside Publishing Company
Grades: Kindergarten–Grade 9
Testing time: Varies with level
Last *MMY* review: 10th

This test is a highly regarded achievement test battery that uses all of the most accepted techniques of test development that might be expected of such a venerable test. It differs from the other two most often used achievement test batteries, the Comprehensive Tests of Basic Skills and the California Achievement Tests, in eschewing the use of item response theory. The early primary battery is available for Form G only and has two levels: Level 5 for Grades

K.1–1.5 and Level 6 for Grades K.8–1.9. The primary battery has two levels: Level 7 for Grades 1.7–2.6 and Level 8 for Grades 2.5–3.5. For Grades 3–9, there are multilevel and separate level editions. The basic battery has 6 tests, and the complete battery has 11 tests. In addition, there are supplemental science and social studies tests that use an essay format.

Iowa Tests of Educational Development (ITED)
Riverside Publishing Company
Grades: 10–12
Testing time: Level I, 250 minutes
                    Level II, 280 minutes
Last *MMY* review: 10th
    This test has two forms, Forms X8 and Y8, and two levels, Level I for Grades 9 and 10 and Level II for Grades 11 and 12. There are nine tests and therefore nine scores provided:

> Test E—Correctness and appropriateness of expression
> Test Q—Ability to do quantitative thinking
> Test SS—Analysis of social studies materials
> Test NS—Analysis of natural sciences materials
> Test L—Ability to interpret literary materials
> Test V—Vocabulary
> Test SI—Uses of sources of information
> Composite
> Reading total

    Unlike other achievement batteries, the ITED assesses secondary school students differently than elementary school students. The ITED focus is on neither basic skills nor the specific course content found in high school curricula. The focus is instead on long-term educational goals and higher order thinking skills. The reliability of the separate tests ranges from the mid-0.80s to the high 0.90s. Strong evidence that the test is unspeeded is provided. Completion rates are in the .90s and all items are answered by 95% of the students who take the test.

Metropolitan Achievement Tests (MAT), Sixth Edition
Psychological Corporation
Grades: Kindergarten–Grade 12
Testing time: Varies with level
Last *MMY* review: 10th
    This test focuses on eight basic skills: vocabulary, reading, mathematics, spelling, language, science, social studies, and writing. It has eight levels:

> Preprimer, K.0–K.9
> Primer—K.5–K.9
> Primary 1, 1.5–2.9
> Primary 2, 2.5–3.9
> Elementary, 3.5–4.9

Intermediary, 5.0–6.9
Advanced 1, 7.0–9.9
Advanced 2, 10.0–12.9

Also included are three diagnostic batteries: reading, language, and mathematics.

The sixth edition of the MAT is intended to serve as both a norm-referenced survey and a diagnostic test. It endeavors to accomplish this formidable task by relating survey tests to diagnostic tests. The test emphasizes basic skills, with less emphasis placed on higher level skills. Reliabilities are in the high 0.80s.

Sequential Tests of Educational Progress (STEP)—Series III
Educational Testing Service
Grades: 3.5–12.9
Testing time: Varies with level
Last *MMY* review: 9th

This test has six levels: Level E for Grades 3.5–4.5, Level F for Grades 4.5–5.5, Level G for Grades 5.5–6.5, Level H for Grades 6.5–7.5, Level I for Grades 7.5–10.5, and Level J for Grades 10.5–12.5. These tests include measures of reading vocabulary, mathematics computation, mathematics basic skills, writing skills, study skills/listening, science, and social studies. A great deal of effort has been expended to ensure that representative curricula and state lists of objectives are assessed. It is, however, not always easy to distinguish the mastery of this specific subject matter from general ability. Of course, this problem exists with all standardized achievement tests.

SRA Achievement Series
Science Research Associates, Inc.
Grade: Kindergarten–Grade 12
Testing time: Varies with level
Last *MMY* review: 9th

This test has eight levels. Level A (for kindergarten and Grade 1) has 11 scores: 8 achievement test scores and 3 educational abilities series (EAS) scores (verbal, nonverbal, and total). Level B (for Grades 1 and 2) has 13 scores: 10 achievement scores and 3 EAS scores. Level C (for Grades 2 and 3) has 16 scores: 13 achievement test scores and 3 EAS scores. Level D (for Grades 3 and 4) has 14 scores: 11 achievement scores and 3 EAS scores. Levels E (for Grades 4–6), F (for Grades 6–8), G (for Grades 8 and 9), and H (for Grades 9–12) each provide 18 scores: 15 achievement scores and 3 EAS scores. Both norm-referenced and criterion-referenced scores are reported, but what are called criterion-referenced scores are in reality norm-referenced scores for subsections of the test. The technical information provided for the SRA is excellent, and the reliabilities of the test are at an expected and acceptably high level. As is the case for all achievement tests, the establishment of validity is difficult, and the technical manual for the SRA does not succeed in establishing the validity of the battery any better than the manuals for other tests do.

Stanford Achievement Tests
Psychological Corporation
Grades: 1.5–9.9
Testing time: Varies with level
Last *MMY* review: 9th

This test has six levels. Primary Level 1, for Grades 1.5–2.9, yields 13 scores: five reading scores (word reading, reading comprehension, word plus comprehension, word study skills, and total reading), three mathematics scores (concepts of number, computation and applications, and total mathematics), three listening scores (vocabulary, comprehension, and total listening), a spelling score, and an environment score. Primary Level 2, for Grades 2.5–3.9, yields 14 scores: the same scores provided by Level 1 except that separate scores are reported for mathematics computation and applications. Primary Level 3 and Intermediate Levels 1 and 2 yield 16 scores: three reading scores (comprehension, word study skills, and total reading), four mathematics scores (concepts of number, computation, applications, and total mathematics), three language scores (spelling, language, and total language), three listening scores (vocabulary, comprehension, and total listening), a science score, a social science score, and a using information score. The Advanced Level, for Grades 7.0–9.9, yields a reading score for reading comprehension and the 13 nonreading scores provided by the intermediate levels. Like the other major achievement test batteries, the Stanford Achievement Test Series employes sophisticated test development procedures, and like several other tests, it has succumbed to the entreaties of the market and provided criterion-referenced type scores despite the fact that there is general agreement among testing specialists that this practice is inappropriate.

Test of Academic Progress
Riverside Publishing Company
Grades: 9–12
Testing time: 160–280 minutes
Last *MMY* review: 10th

This test has two forms and two overlapping levels. The basic battery has eight scores: reading comprehension, mathematics, written expression, using sources of information, total, applied proficiency skills, minimum competency—reading, and minimum competency—mathematics. The test includes a writing test, a listening test, and a 15-item questionnaire. The lowest reliability coefficient is 0.82, with most reliabilities over 0.90. No validity data are provided to establish the legitimacy of the applied proficiency skills tests or the two minimum competency tests.

Section F—Individually Administered Tests of Achievement

Gates-McKillup-Horowitz Reading Diagnostic Test, Second Edition
Teachers College Press
Grades: 1–6

Testing time: Untimed (highly variable depending on tests used)
Last *MMY* review: 9th

The purpose of this test is to identify strengths and weaknesses within the individual student and not to provide normative comparisons. Twenty-three scores are provided: omissions, additions, repetitions, mispronunciations (directional errors, wrong beginning, wrong middle, wrong ending, wrong in several parts, accent errors, and total), reading sentences, words flash, words untimed, word attack (syllabication, recognizing and blending common word parts, reading words, giving letter sounds, naming capital letters, and naming lowercase letters), vowels, auditory blending, auditory discrimination, and spelling. The use of the test is predicated on the assumption that reading can be analyzed from a reductionistic framework and that oral phonic skills are of primary importance: both assertions are dubious.

KeyMath Revised
American Guidance Service
Grades: Kindergarten–Grade 9
Testing time: 35–50 minutes
Last *MMY* review: Not yet reviewed

This test is an individually administered diagnostic mathematics test that can be administered quickly and easily and that is used quite often in conjunction with special education assessment. This test includes three domains with different subtests subsumed under each: basic concept (numeration, rational numbers, and geometry), operations (addition, subtraction, multiplication, division, and mental computation), and applications (measurement, time and money, estimation, interpreting data, and problem solving). Four types of scores are available: (1) total test, the student's performance on all subtests combined; (2) area, the student's performance in each area; (3) subtest, performance on each subtest; and (4) domain, performance in each domain. A variety of scores are provided, including standard scores, percentiles, normal curve equivalents, age and grade equivalents, and stanines. Confidence intervals are also provided. This revision is a major improvement over the previous version, which provided only grade equivalents and an insufficient amount of additional information to compute any other type of score. With the exception of the kindergarten level, where some of the reliabilities are very low, the reliabilities are within an acceptable range, 0.80s and 0.90s for the upper grades.

Peabody Individual Achievement Test Revised (PIAT-R)
American Guidance Service, Inc.
Grades: Kindergarten–Grade 12
Testing time: Untimed, power test (The only timed test is the written expression subtest, which takes 20 minutes.)
Last *MMY* review: Not yet reviewed

The PIAT-R includes the following subscales: general information, reading recognition, reading comprehension, mathematics, spelling, total reading, total test, and written expression. It is individually administered with user friendly materials such as easels, making this test an easy one to administer. Scores that reflect overall student performance on subscales are provided, but this test is not intended to be diagnostic or used as the sole criterion for high stakes decisions about students. The PIAT-R, like the Wide Range Achievement Test (WRAT), is a good screening test for use in circumstances where a quick estimate of academic functioning is needed.

Wide Range Achievement Test Revised (WRAT-R)
Jastak Associates, Inc.
Grades: Kindergarten to adults
Testing time: 15–30 minutes
Last *MMY* review: 10th

   This test, which covers reading, spelling, and arithmetic, is frequently used because it can be easily and quickly administered. Its psychometric characteristics have often been criticized. The weakest of the three scales is reading, which is assessed by having the student read a list of words orally that have been placed in ascending order of difficulty. The revised version of this test does little to allay these concerns because, except for changes in format and the manner of presentation, there is little difference between this test and the previous edition.

Woodcock Reading Mastery Test
American Guidance Service, Inc.
Grades: Kindergarten to adults
Testing time: 40–45 minutes for the entire battery
Last *MMY* review: 10th

   This test consists of six individually administered reading tests all contained in an easel kit. Six test scores are provided, four of which are reading achievement scores (word identification, word attack, word comprehension, and passage comprehension) and two of which are readiness scores (letter identification and visual auditory learning). There is also a supplementary letter checklist. Five derived scores are provided from clusters: readiness, basic skills, reading comprehension, total reading (full scale), and total reading (short scale). Two forms, G and H, are available. A software package called ASSIST is available to aid in the complex process of converting raw scores to standard scores. Split-half reliabilities are provided, and they range from 0.34 to 0.98.

Section G—Personality Inventories

Adjective Checklist (ACL)
Consulting Psychologists Press
Grades: 9–16 and adults
Testing time: Untimed (approximately 15–20 minutes)
Last *MMY* review: 9th

   The ACL is an alphabetic list of 300 adjectives from "absent-mined" to "zany." The examinee responds by marking the adjectives that are self-descriptive. The instrument can be scored for 3 control scales and 34 variables that include 15 needs (from Murray's system), measures of personal adjustment, counseling readiness, self-confidence, self-control, lability, and the types associated with transactional analysis. Scoring is complicated because different norm tables are required depending on the number of adjectives checked. Median scale alpha coefficients were 0.76 for males and 0.75 for females. Retest correlations were lower. Validity data are rather meager; therefore, the instrument is most appropriate for research.

California Psychological Inventory (CPI)
Consulting Psychologists Press
Ages: 13 and over
Testing time: Untimed (approximately 45–60 minutes)
Last *MMY* review: 9th

The CPI was developed as a personality assessment instrument for use with normal populations. It consists of 480 items to be answered "true" or "false." About half of the items on the CPI were taken from the Minnesota Multiphasic Personality Inventory. The CPI yields 18 scores, three of which are check scales to determine test-taking attitudes. Items on 11 of the 15 scales were selected for their ability to discriminate among contrasting groups. Retest reliabilities for high school groups over a 1-year interval averaged 0.65 for males and 0.68 for females. Retest reliabilities for an adult group over a 1- to 3-week interval averaged about 0.80. Correlations among the scales tend to be moderate to high. Current development efforts are focusing on the interpretation of patterns of scale scores. Separate norms are provided by gender for high school and college samples. Some of the validity data based on differences between extreme groups are questionable.

Comrey Personality Scales (CPS)
Educational and Industrial Testing Service
Ages: 16 and over
Testing time: Untimed (approximately 30–50 minutes)
Last *MMY* review: 8th

Eight personality scales are reported for this inventory (trust, orderliness, social conformity, activity, emotional stability, extroversion, masculinity, and empathy) as well as scales for validity of responding and response bias. The scales were developed to be homogeneous using factor analysis. Median scale internal consistency was 0.93. Correlations among the scales are generally modest. Evidence for the validity of the scales as measures of personality dimensions for normal individuals is increasing.

Eysenck Personality Inventory (EPI)
Educational and Industrial Testing Service
Grades: 9–16 and adults
Testing time: Untimed (approximately 10–15 minutes)
Last *MMY* review: 8th

The EPI yields three scores: extroversion, neuroticism, and lie. Two forms are available, and the author recommends administration of both forms to obtain adequate reliability for individual measurement. The items require a "yes" or "no" response. Each form consists of a 24-item extroversion (e) scale, a 24-item neuroticism (n) scale, and 9-item lie scale. Normative information is weak.

Fundamental Interpersonal Relations Orientation (FIRO) Scales
Consulting Psychologists Press
Grades: 9–16 and adults
Testing time: Untimed (approximately 120 minutes for combined scales)
Last *MMY* review: 9th

The FIRO Scales are self-report questionnaires designed to assess a person's need for inclusion, control, and affection in various aspects of interpersonal situations. There are six subscales, each of which focuses on a different inter-personal situation: behavior toward others (FIRO-B), feelings toward others, retrospective childhood relationships with parents, coping operations prefer-ence enquiry (COPE), marital attitudes evaluation, and educational values. A downward extension of the behavior scale for Grades 4–8 is available. In all subscales except the COPE, the subscales contain nine single-statement items, each of which is answered on a six-point scale. In the COPE subscale, the examinee rank orders the defense mechanisms that he or she uses for each interpersonal situation. Only the FIRO-B subscale is well enough developed to be used for other than exploratory studies.

Gordon Personal Profile (GPP)
Psychological Corporation
Grades: 9–16 and adults
Testing time: Untimed (approximately 15–20 minutes)
Last *MMY* review: 10th

The items in this instrument are arranged in sets of four statements, two favorable and two unfavorable, from which the examinee is to select the state-ment that is "most" like him or her and the one that is "least" like him or her. The GPP yields five scores: ascendancy (A), responsibility (R), emotional stability (E), sociability (S), and self-esteem (SE). Although the five traits were selected as being independent, the correlations between the A and S scales and between the R and E scales are 0.60 or higher. Reliability is adequate. Validity data reported in the manual include correlations between scores and peer ratings and coun-selor's ratings for college groups. Additional validity data are presented for groups in industrial and training situations. Percentile norms are provided for high school and college students, low- and middle-level employees, managers, salespeople, and supervisors.

Gordon Personal Profile Inventory (GPP-I)
Psychological Corporation
Grades: 9–16 and adults
Testing time: Untimed (approximately 20–25 minutes)
Last *MMY* review: 10th

This inventory uses the same format as the GPP. It produces four scores: cautiousness, original thinking, personal relations, and vigor. Internal consistency reliability coefficients (split-half) of the four scales range from 0.77 to 0.84. Validity data consist primarily of correlations between scores on the subtests and performance criteria. However, because there is no theoretical basis for predicting either the magnitude or direction of the correlations, these data must be viewed somewhat skeptically unless they appear for several groups. Most of the validity information comes from studies conducted in the 1960s and is therefore quite dated. Percentile norms are provided by gender for high school and college groups.

Guilford-Zimmerman Temperament Survey (GZTS)
Sheridan Psychological Services
Grades: 9–16 and adults
Testing time: Untimed (approximately 45 minutes)
Last *MMY* review: 9th

This inventory provides 10 scores: general activity, restraint, ascendance, sociability, emotional stability, objectivity, friendliness, thoughtfulness, personal relations, and masculinity. There are 300 items, with 30 items per scale. All items are affirmative statements to which the respondent answers "yes," "no," or "?." Scales have reasonable internal consistency (80s) and temporal stabilities. There are over 500 studies contributing to the interpretation of GZTS scores. It is one of the better inventories for describing aspects of the normal personality. Experience is needed to determine whether the dimensions are of practical importance for personal or vocational counseling.

IPAT Anxiety Scale Questionnaire (ASQ)
Institute for Personality and Ability Testing
Ages: 14 and over
Testing time: Untimed (approximately 5–10 minutes)
Last *MMY* review: 8th

The ASQ consists of 40 items that yield five part scores and a total score. In addition, the 40 items yield separate "covert" and "overt" anxiety scores. Construction of the scale was based on extensive factor analytic studies. Empirical validity of the scale is based on (1) correlations of total scores with psychiatric ratings (range of 0.30–0.40 uncorrected for attenuation), (2) differences in mean scores between anxiety neurotics and the standardization population, and (3) differences in mean scores among other clinically diagnosed groups. Reliability coefficients for the part scores, based on subtests with as few as 4 and as many as 12 items, are too low to justify the use of the part scores with individuals. The ASQ is probably most useful as a quick screening device for literate adults and as a research instrument.

Minnesota Multiphasic Personality Inventory Revised (MMPI-II)
University of Minnesota Press

Ages: 16 and over
Testing time: Untimed (approximately 30–90 minutes)
Last *MMY* review: 9th

This instrument is oriented toward abnormal rather than normal groups. It was designed to differentiate between clinical groups, but there is some question on how well it does this. It is too long to be used as a screening test, but the profile based on the separate scale scores provides a good deal of material for interpretation by the sophisticated clinical psychologist. It is the most widely used and cited objective personality measure. A Spanish translation is available. See Chapter 13 for further discussion.

Myers-Briggs Type Indicator (MBTI), 1985 Revision
Consulting Psychologists Press
Grades: 9–16 and adults
Testing time: Untimed (approximately 50–60 minutes)
Last *MMY* review: 10th

The MBTI is a forced choice self-report inventory that is based on a modification of the Jungian theory of types. It yields four bipolar scores: extraversion versus introversion; sensation versus intuition; thinking versus feeling; judgment versus perception. The universe of all combinations of types yields 16 possibilities. The instrument was originally published in 1943 and has undergone a number of revisions. There are currently three forms available, all of which can be administered by computer. The MBTI has been extensively used in counseling and research.

Omnibus Personality Inventory (OPI)
Psychological Corporation
Level: College students
Testing time: 45–60 minutes
Last *MMY* review: 8th

Most items on the OPI have been drawn from other personality inventories. The OPI was developed to assess the personality characteristics of college students, especially those who are intellectually superior. The inventory yields 15 scores. Internal consistency (Kuder-Richardson Formula 21) reliabilities range from 0.67 to 0.89 for the separate subscores. Test-retest reliabilities over a 3- or 4-week interval are in the 0.80s and 0.90s. Validity data consist primarily of correlations with other inventories and with ratings of various academic groups. Norms for the scales are based on 7,283 college freshmen from 37 institutions. At its present stage of development, the OPI should be used primarily for research.

Personality Research Form (PRF), Third Edition
Research Psychologists Press
Grades: 6–16 and adults
Testing time: Untimed (approximately 35–70 minutes, depending on form)
Last *MMY* review: 10th

There are six forms of the PRF. Forms A and B are alternate forms that yield 15 scores for individuals 16 years old and older (30–45 minutes). Forms AA and BB are alternate forms that yield 22 scores for college students (40–70 minutes). Form E yields 22 scores for Grades 6–16 and adults (40–70 minutes) and is available in French and Spanish. Form G is for use in business and industry and yields 20 scores (40–70 minutes). Scales correspond to needs from Murray's theory of personality. Scores are expressed as T scores. Norms are available by gender for college students and normal adults. Additional norms are given for juvenile offenders. The inventory has superior technical sophistication, and reviewers consider it a promising inventory, although they note the lack of clinical interpretive data.

Sixteen Personality Factor (16PF) Questionnaire
Institute for Personality and Ability Testing
Ages: 6 and over (depending on form)
Testing time: Untimed (approximately 45–60 minutes)
Last *MMY* review: 9th

Construction of the 16PF was based on extensive factor analytic studies and research. There are forms for children 6–8, 8–12, and 12–18 and people 16 and over. The inventory yields 16 scores on primary factors as well as scores on four second-order factors. Split-half reliabilities for individual scales from a single form tend to be low, but pooling scores from alternate forms yields scores of adequate reliability. Norms are provided for each level of the instrument and are based on up to 15,000 cases. See Chapter 13 for further discussion.

Study of Values (or AVL Study of Values), Third Edition
Riverside Publishing Company
Grades: 10–16 and adults
Testing time: Untimed (approximately 20 minutes)
Last *MMY* review: 7th

The Study of Values, originally published in 1931, was designed to measure Spranger's six "value types": theoretical, economic, aesthetic, social, political, and religious. The second edition, published in 1951, redefined the social value type and added more discriminating items. The third edition, published in 1960, differs from the second only in providing more normative data. The median reliability coefficients for the different subscales are 0.82 (split-half) and 0.88 (test-retest with a 1-month interval). Validity data presented in the manual consist primarily of demonstrations of value patterns of various educational and occupational groups that differ in predicted ways. Norms are provided for college groups and for occupational groups that usually require some college education. Most material is quite dated.

Survey of Personal Values (SPV)
Science Research Associates, Inc.
Grades: 9–16 and adults

Testing time: Untimed (approximately 15 minutes)
Last *MMY* review: 10th

The SPV yields six scores: practical mindedness, achievement, variety, decisiveness, orderliness, and goal orientation. The instrument consists of 30 triads of statements, the respondent must select the statement from each triad that is most important and the statement that is least important to him or her. Raw scores are converted into percentile ranks. Norms are available for ninth-grade vocational students by gender (over 1,000 males and over 1,000 females), high school students by gender (over 1,300 males and over 1,300 females), vocational junior college students by gender (2,300 males and 587 females), college students by gender (984 males and 1,080 females), workers in routine jobs (1,461), and workers in managerial jobs (1,089). Alpha reliability coefficients ranged from 0.77 to 0.87. Retest reliabilities were 0.74–0.92 (one week) and 0.38–0.74 (one year). Validity evidence is accumulating, but the instrument is still best used for research.

Tennessee Self-Concept Scale (TSCS)
Western Psychological Services
Ages: 12 and over
Testing time: Untimed (approximately 20 minutes)
Last *MMY* review; 8th

The TSCS is a self-administering instrument consisting of 100 statements with five response options ranging from "completely false" to "completely true." Two forms, the counseling form and the clinical and research form, are available, but the two forms contain the same items and differ only in the method of scoring. The counseling form yields 14 scores, and the clinical and research form yields 29 scores. Items were constructed to appraise the following aspects of the self: identity, self-satisfaction, behavior, physical self, social self, moral-ethical self, personal self, family self. In addition, three derived scores are provided: total positive score, reflecting overall level of self-esteem; variability score, reflecting amount of consistency among areas of the self; and distribution score, reflecting a tendency to use extreme response ratings. Scoring by hand is tedious, but computer scoring is available. The manual for the test is incomplete and lacks essential information. At its present stage of development, this test is most suitable for research.

NAME INDEX

SUBJECT INDEX